William J. Walsh, Archbishop of Dublin, 1841-1921

William J. Walsh, Archbishop of Dublin, 1841-1921

NO UNCERTAIN VOICE

Thomas J. Morrissey SJ
with a foreword by Emmet Larkin

FOUR COURTS PRESS

1004636

Set in 10.5 on 12.5 point Ehrhardt for
FOUR COURTS PRESS LTD
Fumbally Lane, Dublin 8, Ireland
e-mail: info@four-courts-press.ie
http://www.four-courts-press.ie
and in North America
FOUR COURTS PRESS
c/o ISBS, 5804 N.E. Hassalo Street, Portland, OR 97213.

A catalogue record for this title
is available from the British Library.

ISBN 1-85182-587-8

Printed in Great Britain
by MPG Books, Bodmin, Cornwall

FOREWORD

The office of archbishop of Dublin was graced by a remarkable group of men in the nineteenth century. John Thomas Troy (1786-1823), Daniel Murray (1823-52), Paul Cullen (1852-78), and William J. Walsh (1885-1921) were all exceptional churchmen, and Walsh, the subject of this very able biography by Thomas Morrissey, was the culmination of that long-sustained tradition of excellence. All four archbishops were not only endowed with very superior mental gifts, natural and acquired, but they were also blessed with those character traits that are required for leadership. They were all, therefore, very intelligent, well-trained, learned, and articulate, and they were also all men of courage, determination and judgment with a large capacity for work and a considerable talent for administration. When it is also realized that this impressive array of abilities was allowed an unusual scope in the exceptional longevity they all enjoyed in office, the opportunities in fulfiling their potential for leadership in the Irish Church become self-evident. The four archbishops, in fact, averaged some thirty-two years in office, which not only permitted them to achieve a great deal in terms of the goals they set for themselves, but also to reinforce cumulatively over time each other's work. The great difficulty, however, in taking the measure of the archbishops of Dublin in the nineteenth century has been that, up until now, none of them has been the subject of a modern biography worthy of their historical significance.

Father Morrissey, therefore, has placed everyone interested in modern Irish history deeply in his debt with this pioneering biography. Indeed, he has set a very high standard for all those who shall undertake the daunting task of researching and writing the lives of Archbishop Walsh's predecessors. What Walsh's final ranking will be among the great archbishops of Dublin, of course, must remain an open question until all the evidence is systematically considered. What Father Morrissey has certainly made clear, however, is that, in any comparison that may yet be made, Archbishop Walsh will not be found wanting either in terms of his gifts or achievements. In regard to his gifts, the most striking thing about Walsh was his extraordinary intelligence, which was as swift as it was strong. He had received his training in the disciplines of canon law and theology, and the basic keenness and penetration of the mind of the lawyer was informed by all the subtleties and distinctions that are the hallmark of the theologian. He delighted in dialectic, and he was as skilled a rhetorician as he was a polemicist.

As Father Morrissey makes amply clear, however, this very powerful forensic machine was also wonderfully attractive. The qualities that made Walsh's mind so attractive certainly included his versatility, range, and comprehensiveness, but more important than any of these was its extraordinary openness. There was perhaps not another prelate in the Irish Church in the nineteenth century, except Archbishop Murray, who was so unprejudiced. Walsh's legal training, of course, made him very partial to the maxim *audi alteram partem*, but it was really his judicial temperament that was the source of his marked propensity towards fairness and justice. Walsh's governing passion was a quest for a basic equality that was rooted in the concept of justice. This quest was the underlying motivating force of his long life, and it informed all his works and achievements.

Walsh's achievements in Church and State, over a period of some fifty years, were as manifold as they were impressive, and there was scarcely an important area in Irish life in which he did not have a serious impact. He was perhaps the most publicly visible ecclesiastic in the Irish Church in the nineteenth century, except possibly for John MacHale, the archbishop of Tuam. Like MacHale, Walsh's medium was the public press rather than the pulpit. His *métier*, moreover, was the pre-concerted 'interview', or 'letter to the editor', rather than the sermon or the homily. He ranged widely in the press, and politics, economics, education, social questions, language, music, canon law, and theology were all areas of his expertise and therefore ready grist for his intellectual mill. There was, moreover, nothing superficial about either his knowledge or his learning, and he appeared to have it all at his fingertips.

Walsh's most important achievement was the essential part he played in the consolidation of the modern Irish political system between 1885 and 1891. The consolidated system of leader, party, and bishops as a body not only endured the collapse of the Irish Parliamentary Party, the Anglo-Irish War, and the Civil War, but survived to guarantee the Irish people a stable and representative democracy in the twentieth century. Walsh's second most important achievement was the significant contribution he made to the effecting of a social revolution that was a consequence of the transfer of the ownership of the land of Ireland from the landlord to the tenant farmer class. The crucial turning-point in the great debate on the resolution of the Land Question was the pointing out by Walsh that Gladstone's Land Act of 1881 had created a system of dual ownership in land, and the only solution to the anomaly in the last analysis was the creation of a peasant proprietary. The cumulative effect of the Irish Land Acts between 1885 and 1910 was a monumental tribute both to his analytical mind and his remarkable tenacity.

Walsh's other important achievements must be treated here in the form of an epic catalogue because they were so many and so varied: in economic theory, whether it was a consideration of Henry George and the single tax or bimetallism; or education in all its various levels, primary, intermediate, and university; or social questions involving the arbitration of labour disputes and the making of the Irish welfare state more real; or the revival of the Irish language and culture; or the encouragement and promotion of music, which was a life-long passion. Such achievements, when taken in their entirety, were simply astounding, especially if it is understood at the same time he had to administer the most populous and complex diocese in the Irish Church. When all is said and done, however, in taking the measure of William J. Walsh, his true greatness is to be found not merely in his accomplishments, which were formidable, but rather in his determined quest for equality in all his achievements, without which, he understood, there was no dignity, or justice, or real freedom for the Irish people.

Emmet Larkin
The University of Chicago
March 17, 2000

CONTENTS

PART FOUR
A MORAL FORCE – FOR JUSTICE, EQUALITY,
INDEPENDENCE, 1913-21

PREFACE

Few are familiar now with the name and career of William J. Walsh, archbishop of Dublin, yet in his lifetime he was so long and vividly associated with the struggle for educational, social, and political equality for the majority population that his death seemed to mark the passing of an institution rather than a man. For more than thirty years he was the leading voice of the Irish hierarchy, and his wide interests and penetrating intelligence found expression in many books and in an almost unending flow of letters to newspapers on topics as varied as theology, canon law, social justice, human rights, land ownership and responsibility, education, politics, music, bimetallism, the environment, and arbitration. His standing and influence was such, indeed, that at his death the lord mayor of Dublin, Laurence O'Neill, felt moved to the hyperbolic observation that he was "the greatest archbishop of Dublin since St Laurence O'Toole"! The remarkable fact that his coffin was draped in a tricolour, while "the troubles" still raged, speaks more emphatically than words of how he was viewed by the nationalist majority.

But why another biography? The answer is that P.J. Walsh's biography, which had the benefit of being written by the archbishop's secretary, was published as long ago as 1928, and a great deal of new material has come to hand since then. P.J. Walsh, moreover, had little to say about the archbishop in the years after 1912, partly, perhaps, because he was too close to the period to see it in perspective, but also, undoubtedly, because the active participants in those troubled years were very much alive. Biographies of the participants of the period have appeared in more recent years, the diaries and comments of Michael Curran, the archbishop's long-time secretary, have become available, and more archival material is accessible than when P.J. Walsh was writing. Hence, although the 1928 work remains a valuable source, it is now possible to provide a more complete biography, which depicts the subject more fully, in his failings as well as in his gifts and achievements, and thereby makes possible, some eighty years after William Walsh's death, a more accurate assessment of the man and the bishop in the context of his times.

A book of this size, researched over many years, is in debt to many people. I should like to acknowledge particularly the advice and enthusiasm of Professor Emmet Larkin of the University of Chicago, who focused my attention on this subject and has contributed the Foreword. I also greatly appreciate the research conducted into Archbishop Walsh's antecedents by Sister Pius O'Farrell, Cork. The work would not have proceeded without the support of the present and previous Jesuit provincials, and the support of the rector and members of my Jesuit community, and I particularly wish to express my thanks to Fathers Paul Brassil and Peter Hannon for guiding my path through various computer hazards. In terms of places of research, I am indebted to Archbishop Desmond Connell of Dublin, Archbishop Sean Brady, Armagh, Bishop Dermot Murray, Limerick, for permission to avail of their diocesan archives, and to Father Fergus O'Donoghue for making available the resources of the Irish Jesuit archives and those of the Miltown Park library, and Father Brendan Woods, librarian, for his unflagging encouragement and support. I am grateful also for the assistance and courtesy received from Most Rev Charles Burns of the Vatican Library, Ms Helen Langley, Mr Colin Harris, and Mr Michael Webb of the Bodleian Library, Oxford, Monsignor Michael Clifton, archivist of the diocese of Southwark, Monsignor John Fleming, rector of the Irish College Rome, Ms C. Austin, dept. of manuscripts, British Library London, Father Michael Wall, diocesan secretary, Limerick, Mr Jerome Aan der Wiel, Glenstal Abbey School, who kindly made available to me the fruits of his research in the O'Riordan Papers, Irish College Rome, and Dr Aidan J. O'Reilly, Maynooth College, who allowed me consult his thesis on the Sir Anthony MacDonnell Papers in the Bodleian. Finally, in these areas of research assistance, I am particularly indebted to the constant interest, knowledgeable support and unfailing courtesy of David Sheehy of the Dublin Diocesan Archives. To my own readers of the manuscript, Professor Emmet Larkin and Dr Fergus O'Donoghue, I am, once again, deeply grateful for the gift of their professional expertise and time. Any flaws that remain are my own.

It would not be possible to publish a serious academic work of this size, and of necessarily limited circulation, without financial assistance. For their generous response in this regard, I gratefully acknowledge the special interest and munificent financial support of Archbishop Desmond Connell, the generous financial assistance of the trustees of the Maynooth Scholastic Trust, and of St Patrick's College Maynooth, and also the support and generous financial assistance of the Senate of the National University. As regards the publication itself, the standards of the Four Courts Press remain as high as ever, and once again I am happy to be indebted to Michael Adams and his highly competent staff.

LIST OF ILLUSTRATIONS

The illustrations appear between pages 180 and 181.

PART ONE

The years of preparation, 1841-85

I

From birth to ordination, 1841-66

On 30 January 1841, Ralph and Mary Walsh, of 11 Essex Quay, Dublin, were overjoyed at the birth of their first and only child. They christened him, William, and, like many parents, had great hopes for their boy. Ralph enrolled him on 6 October 1842, at the age of a year and nine months, in the book of the Repeal Association,[1] the organisation established by the 'Liberator', Daniel O'Connell. A friend and devoted follower of O'Connell, he proudly presented his young son to him at the age of five years. One of William's earliest memories was of being patted on the head by the great man, and of conversations on political matters between him and his father. The latter did not live to see his son attain positions of authority. He bequeathed to him, however, a strong pride in nationality and a spirit of independence. It is fair to assume also that accounts of the Liberator's exploits and values were frequently related in the Walsh household in William's presence, and that he would have learned of O'Connell's courage in challenging the establishment, of his emphasis on equality and human dignity even if it meant loss of support for his party as in his championing of the rights of the American negroes, of his use of Law in the cause of justice. Such actions and values found an echo in William's career. Law was to become his life-long interest, and a desire for equality and fair play was so ingrained that, as he grew in awareness of his own ability, he almost seemed compelled to speak out.

Ralph Walsh is said to have been born at Tarbert, Co. Kerry, to have trained as a watchmaker at Tralee, and subsequently to have worked for some years in Waterford.[2] Efforts to trace his links with Tarbert, however, have not been successful. In Dublin he opened up business as watchmaker and jeweller at Essex Quay in the early 1840s. He moved from there to 19 Parliament Street in 1853.[3] His wife Mary Pierce is reputed to have come from Galway. There are also indications of family ties with Knockkelly. In an undated, incomplete, and unsigned letter to Archbishop Walsh a woman announced that she was "the youngest daughter of Richard Creane, late of Knockelly, where your Grace knew and played with me as a tiny child".[4] She mentions a visit to Tipperary "during the summer", and names some families there in such a way as to suggest that they were known to the archbishop.[5] It is likely, therefore, that William Walsh as a boy spent some summers with relations of his family in Knockkelly. It is not possible to say more than that.

Ralph Walsh was much more than a successful watchmaker and jeweller with some distinguished friends. His personality, ability and political standing were

such as to lead in 1844 to his becoming honorary secretary to the committee
formed by O'Connell to oppose a bill, then being introduced in the House of
Commons by Sir Robert Peel, for the establishment of a board which would
have exclusive control of "Charitable Donations and Bequests" in Ireland. The
bill was viewed by O'Connell, and by Archbishop John MacHale and many
other prelates, as part of an overall plan of Peel to wean "wealthy and intelligent
Catholics" from the cause of repeal by a form of endowment for the church. A
third of the bishops, however, including Archbishop Daniel Murray of Dublin
and Archbishop William Crolly of Armagh, were prepared to support the measure, confident that agreement could be obtained in respect of objections to it.[6]
The measure occasioned serious division among Catholics. Ralph Walsh partic-
ipated in several parish meetings where resolutions were passed against the
Charitable Bequests Act. Finally, he was secretary at a large function representative of all the parish meetings, which was held "at the Royal Exchange, on
Monday evening, 20 January 1845", and which adopted an address directed to
"The Most Reverend and Right Reverend the Catholic Archbishops and Bishops
of Ireland" opposing the legislation.[7] The bill, however, was passed. Walsh was
the focus of extensive correspondence relating to the measure, and this passed
on to his son, who later availed of it to make a detailed study of the issue. The
result, ironically, was a booklet justifying and supporting Archbishop Murray's
position.

Ralph Walsh was involved in a variety of activities. He was known to be a
member of the Society for Promoting Irish Trade, and of the Association of
"The Volunteers of 1782 Revived", and he was a member of the general committee of the "Precursor Society – to Procure from the Imperial Parliament
Justice for Ireland".[8] His independent spirit also led him down unaccustomed
paths for a Catholic layman of the time. There is extant an episcopal letter to
him, dated 15 September 1859, thanking him for his views on the jubilee fast,
but disagreeing with him.[9] He was active in a number of religious and charitable works and societies in his parish of SS. Michael and John. Among these was
the Malachean Orphan Society, called after St Malachy, 12th-century archbishop
and primate of all Ireland. The *Catholic Register* for 1838 noted that the president in that year was Ralph Walsh. His son, as archbishop, was to show a special concern for orphaned children. One of his early memories was being
brought by his parents to the old Queen's Theatre to attend a performance in
aid of the Orphan Society.[10]

Music and singing were an integral part of such public performances, and it
is likely that William's life long enjoyment of music commenced even before he
went to school at the age of about eight years. The school was a rather select
private establishment for Catholic middle-class children, run by a Mr Fitzpatrick
in Peter Street. Training in music and singing was part of the school programme. William was an eager pupil. While most other boys were engaged in
outdoor games and physical activity, he tended to devote his spare time to learn-

ing and playing the piano and violin. In his next school – St Laurence O'Toole's seminary, in Harcourt Street, where he was a boarder for some years – he was to combine with music another life long interest, foreign languages, by participating in "Italian cantatas and operettas".[11] His early feel for music, and a meticulous temperament, drew him on to acquire a sound knowledge of the theory of music and harmony, and in time he could read and sing with ease almost any piece of music placed before him. As a student at Maynooth he was to be called frequently to play the organ, and in later life playing the piano was a favoured way of relaxing. He was to develop, too, a great familiarity with the scores of operas. Amongst these, Wagner's *Ring* was most favoured. Frequently, during his years as archbishop, as will appear, he made his holidays in Germany fit in with the performance of *The Ring* at Bayreuth, and the scores were carefully scanned before each performance.[12] A fruit of his love of music was a short book, the *Grammar of Gregorian Chant*, which he was assured had been described by "an excellent musician", Sir Patrick Keenan, as "wonderfully good".[13]

Apart from his father, the other major influence on young Walsh appears to have been a priest in the parish church of SS. Michael and John where he served mass. He was C.P. Meehan, who was deeply interested in Irish history, the author of the well known *The Fate and Fortunes of the Earls of Tyrone and Tyrconnell* and of other works, and a regular contributor to the Young Ireland newspaper, the *Nation*. He was a friend of the poet James Clarence Mangan and of Thomas Davis and other prominent members of the Young Ireland movement. Meehan was an able but choleric man, who took a liking to young Walsh, lent him books, directed his early reading, and had him read his proof sheets, copy extracts, and other similar services. In this way William's interest in Irish history and archaeology was stimulated, and, although he had little appreciation of poetry, he was enthused by Mangan's poems and Davis' patriotic verse. His first literary efforts, while he was an ecclesiastical student, were to be in the *Nation*, at Meehan's suggestion.[14] Also perhaps due to Meehan's influence, was his participation in a youths' Young Ireland club. His involvement was such that he was credited with persuading his companions to march in military fashion up to the walls of Dublin Castle.[15] If the story is accurate, it represents one of the first indications of that power of persuasive argument and assertive presence which helped make him a commanding figure as bishop for more than thirty years. His mother, it appears, determined to be firm with her only child, put a check on his military ardour as soon as she heard of the occurrence.[16]

At St Laurence O'Toole's boarding academy in Harcourt Street William's progress as a student was reflected in the results. In the printed booklet of the school conveying the report of the Annual Academic Exercise and Distribution of Premiums, July 1855, based on pupils' "answering throughout the year, as well as the annual examination", he is recorded as obtaining first place in Italian and Science – Algebra and Geometry; sharing first place in Latin and German;

and sharing second place in Religious Instruction, Greek, French, Ancient History, and Elocution. He obtained a certificate, or honours distinction, in Geography.[17] English Language and Literature are not mentioned as subjects. "English History" and "Outlines of History" are mentioned, but he does not appear to have taken them.

His academic prowess brought him to the notice of Paul Cullen, the archbishop of Dublin. At the prize-giving, his Grace presented him with Manzoni's celebrated novel *I Promessi Sposi* as the prize for first place in Italian, recommended that he read the book during the summer holidays, and intimated that he would be happy to see him again to discuss the book with him in Italian. William seems to have taken up the offer, and their acquaintance ripened into a form of friendship. Over the next twenty years the archbishop took a keen interest in his progress, and William kept him informed of his work, and of problems experienced in his life. It was a fortunate and profitable relationship for a young man destined to enter the priesthood.

On 7 April 1856, aged sixteen years, William Joseph Walsh registered as a student at the Catholic University of Ireland and took up residence in the collegiate house of St Laurence.[18] The university had been opened two years previously under the rectorship of John Henry Newman. After an auspicious start, the institution was to lose momentum and virtually disappear. Among the reasons was the absence of unanimity between Newman and the Irish bishops, led by Cullen, as to the aims of the university, combined with insufficient funding and the government's refusal to recognise its degrees. William attended for three years, following lectures in Science, and in the faculty of Philosophy and Letters – taking lectures in Logic, Italian, French, and German Literature, Greek and Latin Language, and in Irish Archaeology. He addressed himself with industry to this wide field, and again did well. In the area of Science he demonstrated noteworthy proficiency in Euclid, Algebra, Plane Trigonometry and Conic Section, with the result that the University Calendar for 1856 records that the junior mathematical exhibition, valued £25 and tenable for two years, was awarded to him. In July 1858, when he had attained the grade of "Scholar", he left the university to take the step he had long contemplated.

TO MAYNOOTH

He had been brought up in a devoutly Catholic home, and he developed, as has been seen, into an able, ambitious, hard-working youth, who was also recognised as devout, upright in character, and with a sensitivity that shied away from coarseness in language, behaviour, or literature.[19] His choice of career was approved by James Quinn, the head of his collegiate house, who assured Archbishop Cullen that the young man showed all the marks of a genuine vocation to the priesthood. Cullen contemplated sending his young *protégé* to Rome for his ecclesiastical studies, but on it being represented that he was an only child and that the long absence would be very difficult for his parents, the arch-bishop agreed to his studying in Ireland. He was sent to commence his ecclesi-astical course at St Patrick's College, Maynooth, in the autumn of 1858.

Two years later when his mother wrote to John O'Hanlon, the strongly nationalist prefect of the Dunboyne Institute at Maynooth, to ask if her son might spend a few days of the Christmas vacation at home, O'Hanlon, who pre-sumably was a friend of the family, replied that he would have pleasure in seek-ing the permission for her, and was happy to inform her "that William contin-ues to give satisfaction to his superiors in every respect".[20] William's academic career, in fact, was notably successful. He gave evidence not only of great intel-lectual ability, but of exceptional powers of concentration, allied to nervous energy, driving ambition, and physical endurance. His energy and enthusiasm, indeed, brought him into every aspect of the intellectual and social life of the college, apart from outdoor games and athletics. It was a mark of his enthusiasm and desire to be relevant that he took up the study of the Irish language shortly after his arrival in Maynooth; and it was a mark of his thoroughness and deter-mination that he carried off the annual prize for the best original article in the language, even though he was competing against native speakers and advanced students.[21]

In 1863 he was ordained deacon, and the following year he completed the fourth year of his theological course, but could not be admitted to the priesthood since he had not yet reached the canonical age of twenty-five years. He moved across to the Dunboyne Institute within the college to pursue a course of higher theological studies. There he spent two years, devoting special attention to the study of Canon Law and Hebrew. It was not an entirely untroubled time, to judge by the presence of his signature in a document complaining to the official Visitors to the college that funds assigned for their benefit as Dunboyne students were being otherwise disposed of by the college authorities.[22] He was ordained on 22 May 1866, the year Archbishop Cullen was appointed the first Irish car-dinal.

A fellow student of those years described William as he was then. He was, he observed, of below medium height, with a strong, well-knit body, and was, although not athletic, active and agile in movement. As he walked he leaned for-ward, which conveyed something of his alertness and energy, and there was, even then, a suggestion of a stoop. He had a large head, with thick black hair, a wide forehead, bushy eyebrows over lively grey-blue eyes, a straight, slightly short nose, good teeth, and a firm rounded chin. His voice was a strong bari-tone, his enunciation clear, with just a faint suggestion of a lisp. His features were not mobile, and his facial expression, as a result, was not always a reliable index to his thoughts and feelings. In lighter moments, nevertheless, a raised eyebrow conveyed a quizzical look. In congenial company he was bright, a good talker and a good listener. He was quick to appreciate humour, and exhibited a sense of the ludicrous and an impish playfulness. In terms of temperament he tended to be sanguine. Impetuous on occasion, he struggled, usually successfully, to keep a quick temper under control.[23] Although he radiated self-confidence and liked to be centre stage, there remained something of the reserve, shyness, and individuality of the only child which left him ill at ease in larger gatherings. With his fellow students he was never hail-fellow-well-met, but was highly respected, on easy terms with most, but with few close friends. These last tended to be friends for life, yet the extant correspondence between them was usually of the formal "Dear Father" variety. One correspondent, however, was sufficiently familiar to address him as "Don Guillielmo".[24]

Rounding off this largely impressionistic portrait, it may be helpful to bring together his interests and intellectual proclivities. Music, as noted, was a source of never failing attraction, but his interest in and appreciation of the pictorial arts seem to have been quite limited. His first biographer remarked that "he was stirred much more by intellectual argument than by appeal to imagination", and, as a consequence, was enthused by mathematical conundrums, legal arguments, and government blue books, rather than by great imaginative writing or poetry. His was an orderly and methodical mind, and he was blessed besides with a rare capacity for rapidly acquiring a grasp of abstruse and difficult subject matter, and with a retentive memory which stored an almost encyclopaediac range of knowledge. His special areas of interest were, in summary, music, languages, the positive sciences, and law. He was to become, in fact, an expert in the field of Canon Law and a theologian of repute.[25]

II

From professor to president, 1867-80

During his time at the Dunboyne Institute, Walsh was said to have excelled his able colleagues in Theology, Canon Law, Ecclesiastical History, and Hebrew, and he gained the annual prize for a theological essay, on the subject of "The Infallibility of the Roman Pontiff". Because of his success and assured eloquence he was chosen from time to time to lecture in the theological faculty of the college in the absence of Professor Henry Neville. He did so well that when Neville resigned his chair in 1867, Walsh was viewed as the probable replacement.[1] His most immediate concern in the early months of the year, however, was the death of his father. Ralph Walsh died at his residence, Claughton Villa, Booterstown, Co. Dublin, on 17 April 1867, and was buried in Glasnevin cemetery, Dublin, early on Good Friday morning, 19 April.[2] It is likely that William was deeply saddened by his father's death, and concerned for his mother, though no correspondence remains reflecting such feelings. In the public arena he would have been expected to present the resigned mask of manly acceptance, and, as frequently in his life, he presumably found relief by immersion in work.

By summer it was clear that his succession to Professor Neville's chair was far from certain. There was at least one other serious contender. He indulged in some skilful, even disingenuous manoeuvring in support of his case. There was an attempt to solve the dilemma by suggesting that Walsh take up the post of senior dean, and that the current holder of that office, a Father James O'Kane, the other main contender for the professorship, be appointed professor. Walsh disqualified himself from deanship on the grounds of weakness of sight, and managed to gain support for the chair in theology from the opposing camps of Cardinal Cullen and Archbishop MacHale. On 11 August 1867, John O'Hanlon, a devoted follower of MacHale, assured Walsh that he had "a most formidable competitor" in the person of the Revd James O'Kane, who was hopeful of the trustees' support on the grounds of his long service of the college and of "the merits of a recently published work". Walsh's flimsy excuse of weakness of sight could be countered, O'Hanlon continued, by O'Kane saying, with some reason, that he could not continue as dean because of his increasing lameness. O'Hanlon promised, however, that he would impress on the minds of such trustees as he could not fail to influence "that the appointment of Mr O'Kane to the professorship would necessarily deprive" Dr Walsh "of all chance of a place in the college". He concluded with the reminder: "Dr MacHale's promise to support you is a matter of great importance."[3]

In the event, the decision was made by the trustees of the college without concursus or public examination – an unusual procedure at the time. On 23 October 1867, William J. Walsh was appointed to the chair of Moral and Dogmatic Theology. He was twenty-seven years of age. He joined a faculty which had in the field of dogmatic and moral theology two professors of high reputation, Patrick Murray, and George Crolly. Both men had written celebrated books – Murray on *De Ecclesia* (Concerning the Church), and Crolly a three-volume abstruse work *De Justitia et Jure. De Injuria et Restitutione* (Concerning Justice and Law, and Injury and Restitution). The fourth member of the theological faculty was Gerald Molloy, who had published books entitled *Geology and Revelation* and *Gleanings in Science* and was much in demand in Dublin and parts of Britain for his public lectures on science and religion. A man of much charm, he also had a facility for expounding opaque subjects in clear, simple language. He was to be among the small circle of William Walsh's close friends.

When Walsh was appointed the practice was for each professor to lecture in both dogmatic and moral theology, devoting to each subject a prescribed part of each year. He commenced by lecturing on the fundamental principles of morals in the tract *De Actibus Humanis* (On Human Acts). He was to publish a book on this subject in 1880, which was well received by such critics as Fr Lehmkuhl, the well-known Jesuit moral theologian, and by Cardinals Manning and Newman, and was presented by Archbishop McCabe of Dublin to Pope Leo XIII.[4] Walsh's assured personality, clarity of exposition, strong clear voice, and enthusiasm for his subject, earned the respect of his students. He prepared his lectures with great care, and the numerous references to authorities and the many quotations gave evidence of wide reading. Not surprisingly, the motto inscribed in a number of his notebooks was the advice in *Ecclesiastes* 9:10 – "*Quodcunque facere potest manus tua, instanter operare*" (Whatever your hand finds to do, do it with your might). Initially, he used to write out a scheme or plan of each lecture and then make lithographed copies for each student. Soon he began to enlarge these outlines and had printed notes done – the pages containing the day's work frequently arriving by the morning train from the printers in Dublin. The "notes" meant to help students often proved too exacting for weaker students, as Walsh's penchant for exhaustiveness resulted in minuteness and attention to detail. His facility for clear, ordered exposition, however, was acknowledged by all. Outside the lecture hall he was approachable, and sympathetic to those who consulted him, but he was reputed to have a marked predilection for the very able students, and to be dismissive of the "stupid".[5] In 1874 he obtained the degree of Doctor of Divinity from the University of Propaganda Fide, Rome.

An indication of his good relations with the general body of students during his years as professor was that he was a favourite confessor, and many in later years paid tribute to his kindness, and to his fatherly interest in helping them cope with doubts and difficulties, and in fostering their growth in spirituality and maturity.[6] Away from the classroom he also promoted the study and proper rendering of ecclesiastical music, and subsequently, in 1885, when president, he produced his *Grammar of Gregorian Chant*, mentioned earlier, for the use of the students. As well as an exposition of the principles of ecclesiastical chant, it contained a collection of liturgical chants for use at high mass, vespers, compline, and for special occasions. Later again, when archbishop of Dublin, he prepared an edition of the *Requiem Chant* for the use of the priests of the diocese. At a more prosaic level, he was not only called on to play the organ from time to time, he acted as the college organist in the academic year 1878-9.[7]

A further extra-curricular activity was the cultivation of writing skills. He contributed to theological reviews, especially to the *Irish Ecclesiastical Record*, which had been founded by Archbishop Cullen in 1864. Walsh became the expert adviser on the theological questions submitted to the editor for discussion and solution. A number of the questions posed anonymously in the *Ecclesiastical Record* were written by him, but usually he preferred to put his name to his contributions, for he was conscious of his knowledge and of his power of exposition, and he had a showman's desire and capacity for attracting public attention to what he said. A flair for journalism began to emerge. He revelled in controversial discussions, sometimes prolonging them unduly. In controversy he was a formidable opponent. He sought the last word, and could be at times scathing and heavy-handed. The *Ecclesiastical Record* ceased publication in 1876. He was to revive it in 1880.[8]

By the 1870s, he was sufficiently well known and respected to receive a vote in the terna (the chosen three names) submitted to Rome for the vacant see of Cashel;[9] and in December 1875, he was consulted for information and advice on Canon Michael Warren, who was a candidate for the see of Ferns.[10] That year, however, had been marked by a further personal loss. His mother, who lived at 6 Royal Terrace, West Kingstown, Co. Dublin, died on 17 April 1875, aged seventy-two years. It was the end of home for him. Her will, made six days earlier, doubtless in consultation with him, left all her property, "real and personal", to her "dear sister, Elizabeth Pierce". William was to act as the sole executor.[11]

All the foregoing took place against a background of tension and dissatisfaction at the college. A major change had been heralded for Maynooth with the Irish Church Act of 1869, which, from 1871, left the college disestablished and disendowed. As a result, the annual subsidy of £26,000, which rendered faculty, staff and students, comparatively well off, was removed. Moreover, the trustees, and the official Visitors, who previously included influential laymen, were now composed entirely of bishops; and this led to a more restrictive government not only economically but also in respect of the relative independence and self-government the college had enjoyed for seventy-five years. The main figure behind the change was Cardinal Cullen, who worked through two of the official Visitors, the Vincentian prelates, Laurence Gillooly of Elphin, and James Lynch, coadjutor bishop of Kildare and Leighlin; and these, in turn, influenced the trustees.

Gillooly, because of his assertive, often tactless manoeuvres, became very unpopular with the academic staff and students. Another focus of criticism was the vice-president, Daniel McCarthy, who, on 15 April 1872, had informed Cullen that a searching visitation of the college was long overdue, and who was personally very much associated with stricter discipline.[12] In a series of letters to Gillooly he had revealed his definite programme – "We need no change, and we never needed any, except active, unceasing and general supervision." To that end, a new students' rule was approved that year, 1871, and the obligations of the deans to enforce it were spelled out in minute detail.[13] A range of restrictions were soon applied also to academic staff. It has been remarked, indeed, that the trustees meetings in the 1870s, as evidenced by their minutes, conveyed "almost an obsession with securing minute exactness and uniformity in teaching and examining".[14]

As might be expected in a boarding institution, the reaction, when it came, came from the students, and, again predictably, the issue on which they eventually revolted was food. The trouble started with complaints, in December 1875, about soup and tea. The following days were tense and disorderly. The disorders continued. Five students were rusticated for the rest of the academic year. The annual retreat at Christmas Eve helped to calm the situation, but, although the protracted disturbances were over, serious outbreaks of indiscipline were to continue for some time.[15] A past student, who had experienced Maynooth under the earlier dispensation as well as in the years in question, added to the unease with series of unsigned articles in the *Whitehall Review*, September 1880, which complained of "tyrannical" episcopal government and "the domineering spirit with which we were ruled".[16]

For the staff, too, as suggested above, the 1870s were not happy years. McCarthy, as well as Gillooly, bishop of Elphin, was one of the cardinal's key instruments of change. The cardinal, however, had other sources of information; among them, Walsh. The latter kept in contact because of his accustomed links with Cullen, but also, no doubt, with career prospects in mind. This did not deter him, nevertheless, from criticising to Cullen, from time to time, the policies and actions of Gillooly. Thus, on 11 October 1874, he pointed out that the Visitors at their visitation had caused annoyance among the staff by asking students their views as to whether moral and dogmatic theology should be taught separately, and also by asking students for their views of their superiors' conduct of college affairs.[17] The following year, again on 11 October, he drew attention to the discontent among the professors at not being consulted more fully by the Visitors during their visitation.[18] And on 17 June 1876 he protested against Visitors asking students how one of their superiors had carried out his duties. Such procedure, he declared, was "most demoralising and the natural result has been a disorganised condition of the college this year, such as no one here ever remembers to have experienced before". The Visitors' conduct had buoyed up the students during the recent disturbances, persuading them that the bishops were critical of their superiors and that they could appeal to them. Hence, Walsh asserted, "a spirit critical of ecclesiastical authority was being fostered in the college".[19]

His criticism of the bishop of Elphin reflected an unease with the latter's general approach as Visitor, and he was determined not to be intimidated by him. This, perhaps, influenced his reaction when he received a letter from Gillooly informing him that the Board of Trustees, at their October meeting, had appointed him to the office of librarian. It was a laborious post at a salary of £20 a year, "if claimed". It had formerly been attached to the prefectship of the Dunboyne establishment; but when the Dunboyne was disestablished in 1871, in the interests of economy, the office remained unfilled for a time. Walsh replied on 20 October 1876. He appreciated the mark of confidence, but, he added firmly: "It would be absolutely impossible for me to undertake a work so responsible and laborious, as in addition to the classes of which I have charge in my own department, a great deal of my spare time, and a substantial portion of my free days – and even Sundays – is occupied with the charge of singing classes and the choir management in the Junior House." He then went on to explain that the matter was also one of some sensitivity in that the two senior professors of theology were upset about being passed over by the trustees in favour of their junior colleague, and, in the interests of community harmony, this was a factor in his declining the offer.[20] Gillooly was not so easily put off. He pressed Cullen to urge Walsh to accept the office. This the cardinal appears to have done, because Walsh accepted the appointment of librarian, and continued to fill that position, with the help of two assistants at a salary of £10 a year each, until the Dunboyne was finally reestablished in June 1879.[21]

Part of the problem with respect to student indiscipline and staff frustration was the president of the college, the benign, scholarly, Charles William Russell, who shied away from confrontation and allowed wide latitude to his vice-president. In the face of personal experience of student disrespect and defiance, Walsh, on 13 January 1877, determined to engage the full attention of the president and the college's administrative council. In a letter addressed to them jointly, which was also signed by Thomas J. Carr, professor of moral theology, he protested against "insubordination on the part of the second year's divines", the second class of theology. He had felt, he wrote, "that the spirit of insubordination and disorder which was last year manifested to such an alarming extent in the college, had been suppressed". But evidently the spirit still prevailed. The students, "as a demonstration of disrespect", did not turn up at the examinations centre. The reason? One professor had changed the method of correcting the students' Latin pronunciations. "This has constituted, in the opinion of the students of the second year's class of theology", Walsh declared, "a sufficient cause" for the above mentioned "unprecedented display of insubordination". "So determined an attempt to overawe a professor in discharge of his duty", Walsh added, "has never, we believe, before occurred in the college.

We, therefore, feel bound at once to place this ... statement of the case in the hands of the superiors."[22]

It is not clear what effect, if any, the letter had. The president, indeed, was shortly to be removed from all active participation in college affairs. On 16 May 1877, he was thrown from his horse in Maynooth village, and from then until his death on 26 February 1880, he was an invalid, and the task of acting president was carried by his vice-president, McCarthy, who also had a heavy teaching load. The fact that McCarthy continued his lectures in Scripture after his appointment as vice-president reflected the trustees preoccupation with economy. That preoccupation, together with changes due to promotion to the episcopacy, or other vicissitudes, rendered the teaching power of the college greatly weakened during the 1870s and early 1880s. There was an atmosphere of "making do". Thus, when Gerald Molloy left in March 1874, to take a position in the Catholic University, Walsh had to carry his classes as well as his own. When James Tully, professor of Irish, died in October 1876, his classes were entrusted to a student. In 1877 George Crolly, professor of Theology, ceased teaching because of poor health (he died the following year), the president had his accident, and it was generally expected that McCarthy would become bishop of Kerry in succession to David Moriarty, who died on 1 October 1877.

Not surprisingly, the teaching situation had added to the student unrest. The cumulative picture at the end of 1877 gave grounds for serious disquiet. Gillooly assured Cardinal Cullen on 28 January 1878, that it would "be difficult to maintain order in the absence of the president, on the eve of the vice-president's departure", and "with new deans, and with junior professors over senior classes".[23] In these circumstances, William Walsh, for all his assurance and readiness for responsibility, hesitated when approached about the post of vice-president, for which he was deemed the obvious candidate. That he was so viewed probably went back to the year 1875, which was a watershed for him in many ways.

On 17 April 1875, Walshe's mother died.[24] His life thereafter focused almost exclusively on his work, and that work expanded considerably when he became involved in a much publicised court case, which required careful preparation and which greatly enhanced his reputation, self-assurance, and self-importance. This was the case of *O'Keeffe v. McDonald*, which was tried in Wicklow town in July 1875, and which, as the culmination of a long dispute, evoked interest in Britain as well as Ireland.

Much has been written about the protracted and complicated story.[25] Here it is considered only so far as it concerns Walsh's participation. The main protagonists at this stage were Robert O'Keeffe, parish priest of Callan in the diocese of Ossory, and the vicar-general of the diocese, Edward McDonald. The charge was of libel (written defamation) and slander (spoken defamation). O'Keeffe claimed that McDonald's words in a letter to him on 10 October 1870 – "I, vested with requisite authority, suspend you from your office" – were libellous, and also the words written three days later – "I repeat the sentence of your sus-pension". The innuendo was "that the plaintiff had been guilty of such conduct as would render him liable to be suspended from the office of parish priest". McDonald's defence was a plea of "justification". O'Keeffe, in fact, had defied his bishop, Edward Walsh, for many years and had sued him in 1870. Walsh settled out of court for £500. Subsequently, O'Keeffe sued Cardinal Cullen for damages of £10,000 for libel. That case dragged on until February 1875, and greatly worried Cullen, who went to Rome to discuss the problem personally with the pope. He was given full papal authority to deal with the dispute. O'Keeffe had been suspended for his defiance and for undertaking a civil court action. He ignored the suspension. The parish was placed under interdict. A majority of parishioners, nevertheless, supported him; and the diocese was divided. Ecclesiastical authority was being openly challenged. The charge against McDonald was the latest and final stage of a prolonged and disagreeable contest.

In the course of the trial, Walsh was called as one of the expert witnesses to explain to the court the laws, ordinances, and discipline of the Catholic Church relative to the case. His exposition, as might be expected, was clear; and in the face of cross-examination by O'Keeffe, who sought "to show his ignorance of canon law", Walsh displayed a wealth of knowledge which he applied cogently and relentlessly to the case. The jury found against O'Keeffe, asserting that the statement – "Fr O'Keeffe has been suspended" – was true, and therefore legally justified.[26] The judge, Baron Dowse, a Protestant, paid a special tribute to Walsh.

> With reference to the evidence of Dr Walsh, I must say that I have never heard evidence given more clearly and distinctly in a court of justice. He appeared to me to be eminently master of his subject ... If Maynooth in former days was distinguished for great scholars ... and if Dr Walsh is a specimen of those of the present day, all I can say is the glory of the present will not be overshadowed by that of the past.[27]

Walsh's performance placed him very much in the forefront as a canonist and theologian.

The lustre carried over to another major occasion some weeks later, namely the second plenary synod of the Irish church convoked since the Reformation. The first had been held at Thurles in 1850, presided over by Archbishop Cullen. Now as cardinal he summoned and presided over the second synod, which lasted from 30 August to 20 September and was held at Maynooth. Walsh was present as theological adviser to the new bishop of Ossory, the cardinal's nephew, Patrick Francis Moran. Walsh was also appointed one of the secretaries of the synod. He attended all the sessions and general congregations, and had a significant role in drafting the statutes. One chapter was written entirely by him. There had been disagreement among the bishops as to how the statutes relating

to the vicar-general and vicar-forane should be drawn up. The cardinal consulted Walsh that evening. He set about working at once, and by four o'clock
next morning had completed the whole chapter and had prepared lithographed
copies for each bishop. When the draft was formally submitted to their lordships
later that morning it met with unanimous approval.

Molloy and Walsh were entrusted with the task of keeping a record of the
proceedings of the synod, and of compiling an accurate summary of the discussions on various topics. This, too, was completed satisfactorily. Walsh's over all
performance at the synod enhanced the reputation he had acquired as a theologian and canonist, and which had so recently received public recognition at the
O'Keeffe trial. Many Irish bishops thereafter engaged him as their theological
adviser, and from this time he was frequently engaged in correspondence on
questions of morality and law.[28] All this made it almost inevitable that when the
position of vice-president of Maynooth became vacant in 1878, on the appointment of McCarthy as bishop of Kerry, he was considered to be the obvious successor, not least because he was known to be acceptable to the cardinal.

The appointment of a successor to the late David Moriarty, bishop of Kerry,
was delayed due to the illness and death of Pope Pius IX and the election and
coronation of his successor, Leo XIII. On 6 May, the first congregation of the
cardinals of Propaganda recommended McCarthy to the new pope for the see of
Kerry. Next day Cullen relayed the news "confidentially" to Walsh, who then
informed McCarthy, at the same time swearing him to secrecy.[29] McCarthy, to
judge by his subsequent actions, may not have relished this way of learning
about his elevation. Cullen, meanwhile, having made Walsh indirectly aware of
an impending vacancy in the vice-presidency, set about carefully arranging for
his appointment to the position. On 18 May he remarked in a letter to his auxiliary bishop, Edward McCabe, that as McCarthy would be leaving Maynooth,
"it will be necessary to fill his place – it will not be easy to do so". "It would be
well", he added as a seemingly tentative suggestion, "to enquire and see who the
candidate will be. Would our friend Dr Walsh like to leave his theology for the
office?" "Probably the duties of president", he continued, "will still devolve on
the vice-rector – as Dr Russell is not well restored."[30] Later in May, shortly
before he left Rome, Cullen wrote to his nephew, the bishop of Ossory, asking
him to find out whether Walsh would accept the vice-presidency.

On 3 June Moran informed Walsh that he and others were of the opinion
that he, Walsh, was the person for the post of vice-president. He wished to learn
if Walsh would "give any opposition to such an appointment". There would be
many new professors coming in, Moran added, and, the president being infirm,
the college would "go to the bad" if there were not a vice-president who would
take a deep interest in the students. It was to be presumed that the president
would not continue in his post "for more than a few months" and that "of
course the vice-president will take his place". "I need hardly say", he concluded,
"that the views I have expressed harmonise entirely with those of His

Eminence."[31] Cullen, indeed, was otherwise providing further indications of his interest. On the way home from Rome he stopped over at the Irish College, Paris, where he canvassed the archbishop of Cashel, Thomas William Croke, and the bishop of Ross, William Fitzgerald, in favour of Walsh. "I have spoken to Dr Croke", he wrote to McCabe from Paris on 8 June, "about Dr Walsh and he is altogether for him. I suppose he will meet no opposition. Dr Croke and Dr Fitzgerald of Ross are here." On the same day he informed Gillooly that he had been thinking about Maynooth and how difficult it would be to fill so many vacancies. "It appears to me", he continued, "that Dr Walsh would make an excellent vice-rector or, should Dr Russell resign, an excellent president. He has his heart in the welfare of the college and on that account he is likely to succeed." He supposed that Walsh, if promoted, would have to give up the class of theology, but might teach scripture which had only two classes per week. Knowing Gillooly's desire for professors from outside to raise standards at Maynooth, he explained that there was no prospect of a professor of theology from Rome, adding predictably that if the Jesuits made a learned man available "the bigots will get up an outcry against us".

Walsh, however, decided not to accept. He was conscious of the college's many serious problems, and, as has been indicated, he did not approve of the methods of Gillooly and his fellow Visitors.[32] He informed Moran of his decision, and he, in turn, informed the cardinal. On 13 June, however, Moran wrote to Cullen that Walsh had changed his mind. He had received a letter from him, Moran stated, "in which he says he had a long conversation with Dr Gillooly and as a consequence has relaxed his opposition to the appointment as vice-president". Moran believed that the bishops would "be unanimous in his appointment".[33] It is believed that Walsh sought and received certain assurances from Gillooly, but what they were is not clear.[34] They did not prevent Gillooly, however, from suggesting other candidates for the vice-presidency. McCabe explained to the cardinal on 18 June that he had learned that among the contenders which Gillooly had suggested was Dr Denis Gargan, professor of ecclesiastical history at Maynooth, "a very excellent man" but not one to ensure effective government. He added candidly that although Dr Gillooly had done much in the college, he feared that he was "disposed to act with a high and strong hand" which might "do mischief in the end". He was "very unpopular with the bishops".[35] Strong words from the mild mannered McCabe; and the bishops reluctance to approach Cullen directly, and McCabe's slowness in speaking up, says much about Cullen's style of government and their awe of him.

When the bishops convened for the meeting of the Maynooth Board on 25 June, only two candidates were presented as candidates, Walsh and Gargan. That the latter was presented at all, when it had to be known that Walsh was the cardinal's candidate, was, perhaps, a sign of the resentment among some concerned with the college at Cullen's controlling policy. Before proceeding to a ballot, the bishops decided that whoever was appointed was to continue teaching in the department of which he was a professor, and would receive a salary of £300 a year for both offices. Walsh was then appointed on these conditions as vice-president.[36]

VICE-PRESIDENT AND ACTING PRESIDENT

Walsh was not able to commence immediately because McCarthy delayed his resignation of the post. "Dr Walsh is placed in a very awkward position", Archbishop Croke wrote to Cullen on 26 July, "by this meaningless vacillation on Dr McCarthy's part; and it is now really appearing to me that the bishop-elect positively means to hold his post in the college as long as possible". McCarthy finally decided to accept the mitre, but right up to his consecration, on 25 August, he ignored requests to resign the vice-presidency. An exasperated Walsh exercised as much pressure as he could muster. Gillooly informed McCarthy the day before his consecration that he had written to the Visitors of St Patrick's College, Maynooth, "on the demand of Dr Walsh", stating to them that Walsh "cannot make himself responsible for the administration of the college during the coming year, if he is not authorised to assist officially in making the arrangements for the year".[37] He begged him to send his resignation "by return of post – or better, by telegram".[38] He gave Tuesday, 27 August, as the latest date for the reception of the reply. When there was no word by 26 August, Gillooly informed Cullen that the bishop of Limerick, George Butler, had informed him that he and Croke were on their way to Killarney and would urge McCarthy to resign at once.[39] In the end, McCarthy gave way. He resigned; and his resignation was made retroactive so that Walsh was officially listed as having assumed the office of vice-president on 27 June 1878.

Within a short time, Walsh found himself facing a range of problems as vice-president and, in effect, acting president. The college's finances were in an unsatisfactory state, and the trustees were exasperated at the imprecise reports and secretive demeanour of the long-standing bursar, Thomas Farrelly. An episcopal finance committee was put in place on 16 October 1878, and one of Walsh's contributions was to produce a detailed report for the committee, and, after them, for the trustees, which analysed frankly the problems and solutions.[40]

Soon after the establishment of the finance committee, a part of the college was destroyed by fire. The fire was first noticed about eight-thirty on the morning of 1 November 1878, at a point adjoining the senior oratory and the reading room, and not far from the college library. Walsh at once despatched three telegrams – one to the Dublin fire brigade requesting their assistance, another to the lord mayor of Dublin asking his permission for the fire brigade to leave the city, and the third to the railway authorities at the Broadstone terminus asking them to have in readiness a special train to convey the brigade to Maynooth. Pending the arrival of the train, professors, students and servants worked to stay the progress of the flames. Walsh, with a band of students, concentrated on saving the library. Thousands of volumes were hurled through the window. When the fire brigade arrived about 11.00 a.m. they first endeavoured to save the library by severing the connection between it and the oratory and reading room. This they accomplished, and after some hours the fire was checked; but the building where it started was destroyed. Fortunately, the damage, amounting to thousands of pounds, was covered by insurance, which also proved adequate to allow for the rebinding and rebacking of numerous damaged volumes.

After the fire, Walsh had had prepared a large meal of beef and mutton for the firemen, whom he assured that, although it was Friday, they were dispensed from the ecclesiastical law of abstinence from meat. Questioned about his liberal dispensation, he remarked that he was just applying the accepted principle of *epikeia*, namely, making the reasonable assumption that the legislator did not intend the law to apply in such exceptional circumstances. Three days later, on 4 November, the trustees, at a special meeting, expressed to Walsh their appreciation of his prompt and resourceful action, and also passed a resolution thanking all who assisted in saving the college.

Another event of a dramatic, but less traumatic, nature, occurred early in 1879, only a few months after the fire. On Monday, 24 February, about 3.00 p.m., a deer, chased by the Ward Hunt, entered the college grounds, closely pursued by staghounds and a solitary rider, who turned out to be the Empress Elizabeth ("Sissi") of Austria. By the time the main body of the hunt arrived, the stag had been saved from the dogs, the empress had dismounted, and Dr Walsh was present to invite her – perhaps in German – to partake of some refreshment in the college. Anxious not to catch a chill after her exertions, she asked if she might have a wrap or shawl for her shoulders. The vice-president gallantly took off the light academic gown worn over his soutane, which she donned. When leaving, Walsh invited her to come again. To his surprise, presumably, but also to general gratification, the empress returned the following Sunday and attended mass in the junior chapel, where the celebrant, at Walsh's thoughtful invitation, was Patrick Murray, senior theologian and "now a kind of father of the house".[41] The empress then made an inspection of the library and other buildings. In memory of her visit, she sent to Walsh a magnificent gold ring which he treasured all his life, invited him to visit the Austrian imperial court, and sent to the college an equestrian statue of solid silver representing St George's conflict with the dragon. She presumed, it appears, that George was also Ireland's patron saint. The following year she visited once again, and this time presented a set of gold vestments, embroidered with shamrocks worked in green silk, and her name and the date – "Elizabeth 1880". She was then in her early forties, and celebrated for her beauty. Sadly, great tragedy lay ahead: her only son, Crown Prince Rudolf, was to commit suicide in 1889, and she was herself to be assassinated by an Italian anarchist nine years later.

Apart from such indelible events, Walsh's years as vice-president were marked by a number of other significant, if less memorable occurrences. In

October 1879, there appeared in the *Dublin Review* an article entitled "Theology, Past and Present, at Maynooth" by Dr Henry Neville, the former professor of theology at the college, in which he claimed that for nearly fifty years, due to the influence of the French professors who taught in Maynooth in the early years of the century, Gallicanism had flourished there in dogma and moral doctrine, and because of this the Irish clergy became "Gallicans to the core". The doctrine of Gallicanism, it may be noted, had its roots in royalist France and consisted mainly in denying that the papacy had any authority from God extending to temporal and civil affairs, asserting the supremacy of general councils of the church over the pope, and implicitly denying papal infallibility in questions of faith and morals. Gallicanism in morals, as outlined by Neville, referred to a harsh, intolerant rigorism.

The article was seen as an attack on the reputation of Maynooth, and the ailing president, Dr Russell, was particularly upset and suggested to Walsh that he should answer it. An inconclusive interchange of letters between Neville and Walsh followed in the *Tablet*, before Walsh eventually dealt fully with the issues in an article entitled "The Alleged Gallicanism of Maynooth and the Irish Clergy" in the *Dublin Review* of 1880. In it he drew a distinction, mentioned to him by Dr Russell, between Gallicanism in dogma and rigorism in morals. He freely admitted that a rigorist morality was taught at Maynooth but on principles very different from Gallicanism. The rigorism, indeed, came not from French professors but from Roman textbooks and influences prevailing in Rome at the time. As to Gallicanism in dogma, Walsh analysed the college's tradition and showed that there had never been a full blown Gallican theology in Maynooth, and such tendencies as there were had gradually moved towards the position of the papacy defined at the first Vatican Council.[42]

A further noteworthy contribution of a literary nature was also made that year. He revived the *Irish Ecclesiastical Record*. In 1879 he wrote to each of the Irish and English bishops soliciting their approval and support. The new archbishop of Dublin, Edward McCabe, warmly approved, as did, from England, Cardinal Henry Edward Manning, and bishops J.C. Hedley and Herbert Vaughan. McCabe requested Walsh to act as editor. He declined, recommending instead Dr Thomas Carr, who was appointed. The first number of the resuscitated periodical was published in January 1880. Thereafter, it continued to be issued from Maynooth, and its editor was appointed by the archbishop of Dublin. Walsh was to contribute numerous articles to it.

Other areas demanding his attention included raising funds for the building of an imposing college chapel, which dragged on for years; and care of the health and reasonable convenience of the students. In respect of convenience, the students had asked for some years to be allowed study in their rooms, which had been heated in the 1870s, rather than in the large heated study halls. The administrative council approved, but the trustees refused. One of Walsh's first acts as vice-president was to repeat the request. This time, after discussion, the trustees agreed to give it a year's trial on the understanding that the students supplied candle-light "at their expense"![43]

A more pressing situation was presented by the need to care for the students' health. A large gaunt infirmary always had a number of young men afflicted by tuberculosis, and in 1880 steps had to be taken to preserve the college from an epidemic of typhus in Maynooth village. The college had its own surgeon and consultant physician, and the local doctor catered for ordinary needs. A problem arose in 1880, however, when the consultant, Robert S.D. Lyons, was elected a Liberal MP for Dublin city. On a particularly urgent case, when the local doctor needed to consult him, he was in Westminister. Walsh found himself wondering about the medical conventions regarding consulting another physician. Later, Lyons was requested to resign, and when he refused his employment was terminated by the trustees, in September 1882.[44]

Walsh was not slow to prompt decisions or to make them. In 1880 he arranged for a dentist to come to the college on fixed days, instead of attending only when sufficient patients had built up.[45] The decisiveness was evident also in dealing with problems of discipline, so far as one can judge from limited extant instances; but it appears to have been tinctured, at least in serious cases, by a desire to protect the culprit's reputation, and prevent public embarrassment for him, so far as was possible. Examples of this occurred most noticeably during his tenure as president: as when he took the painful decision to hold back from ordination some young men who had been approved by their bishop, Patrick F. Moran of Ossory;[46] and when he persuaded a student priest, who had been drunk in public on his way home for vacation, not to return to college rather than be formally sent down.[47]

A MAJOR CONTRIBUTION TO CATHOLIC INTERMEDIATE EDUCATION

The most striking manifestations and best chronicled instances of his energy, persuasiveness, and leadership, during his time as vice-president, related to events outside the college – in the area of intermediate, or secondary, education.

The provision of adequate intermediate education for the majority population had been under discussion for many years. The requirements of Catholic schools were not just to secure endowmental equality with the Protestant schools, but to obtain means of motivating themselves and raising the low academic standards in many of their establishments. To Sir Patrick Keenan, assistant commissioner for education, William Delany, rector of the Jesuit college at Tullabeg, in the midlands, and Jules Leman, of the Holy Ghost Congregation, at Blackrock College, Dublin (often called the "French College" because the Holy Ghost priests at that stage were mainly French), the answer to the problem appeared to be to provide a system of competitive public examinations, which would carry money prizes on the basis of results. This, it was claimed, would make available a form of indirect subsidy and would also encourage the schools to lift their standards. Direct subsidy in any form was not acceptable to the House of Commons.

The proposal was attractive to the chief secretary, Sir Michael Hicks-Beach, and to Randolph Churchill, who had arrived in Ireland in 1876 as secretary to his father, the new viceroy, the duke of Marlborough. Churchill persuaded the government to avail of the surplus funds of the disestablished Irish state church to provide the indirect subsidy. The resulting education bill of 1878 was drafted by Edward Gibson, the attorney-general, and Gerald Fitzgibbon, the solicitor-general, but Sir Patrick Keenan, and William Delany – who was on friendly terms with both Churchill and Marlborough – made a considerable contribution to the eventual shape of the bill.[48]

In the aftermath of the act, a board of commissioners was appointed to draw up a common curriculum and to administer the measure. They sought the advice of the headmasters. The Protestant schools were represented by a head-masters' association. The Catholics as yet had no point of unity. The Protestant headmasters invited Delany to join their association – on the strength presum-ably of the success of his school in London University examinations. He declined, and wrote to his friend, Walsh, on 27 September 1878, of the need for an association of Catholic headmasters if the new scheme was not "to be shaped from the very start so as to suit the Protestant schools".[49] He wrote on similar lines to Gillooly. Walsh took up the challenge, and he, Delany, and Fr Edouard Reffé, headmaster of Blackrock, became the triumvirate which established the Catholic Headmasters' Association. Three men with confidence in their own ability, and who in the case of Delany headed a school which, as mentioned, had won distinctions in the London University examinations, while Reffé's Blackrock was the outstanding school linked to the Catholic University. They did not share the widespread lack of self-esteem among Catholics that their schools had no chance of competing successfully against the well-endowed Protestant colleges.

Walsh wrote to the bishops who had preparatory seminaries, or other sec-ondary schools, in their diocese, asking if they would be willing to send repre-sentatives to a conference of Catholic headmasters that he proposed to summon for the purpose of taking common counsel on the implementation of the act. Many of the bishops supported his proposal. Some, however, were less than enthusiastic. Amongst these, not surprisingly, perhaps, was Gillooly. He favoured the idea of a common cause amongst Catholic schools but wished to put off a decision until the meeting of the bishops at Maynooth. This, Delany pointed out in a letter to Walsh, was leaving matters much too late, given the pressing need to prepare the schools for the examinations in the following June. A more surprising critic was Walsh's supporter for the vice-presidency, Patrick Moran of Ossory. He wrote to his uncle, Cardinal Cullen, to express his fear that the conference would prove a failure, and his conviction that it was "simple folly for a number of good priests, who know nothing whatever about the work-ing of the act, to meet together to frame rules and to send instructions which will only make our schools a laughing stock to those who are closely watching us".[50] He expressed similar misgivings to Walsh.

Moran was referring to a longer letter sent by Walsh on 27 September 1878, to the bishops and the heads of schools, in which he argued for an organisation of Catholic schools and an immediate conference of heads or representatives of the schools. The objects to be aimed at in such a conference, he declared, were the interchange of ideas as regards methods of teaching, the best school books to use, and "the special training required in preparing students for examinations" conducted in the anticipated system to be adopted by the examiners. To indicate the need for haste, he quoted from Delany's letter to him, without mentioning Delany's name. Finally, he assured the bishops that he did not envisage the conference, or the standing committee, having "any controlling power"![51] To counter the objections of Gillooly and Moran, Walsh went to see the cardinal, and, as he informed Bartholomew Woodlock, bishop of Ardagh and Clonmacnoise, on 30 September, obtained "his Eminence's formal sanction".[52]

On 8 October 1878, forty-four Catholic headmasters, representing nearly all the chief Catholic boys' schools, met at Maynooth. The Catholic Headmasters' Association came into being. Dr Walsh was appointed its first president, and William Delany its first secretary. At that first meeting a list of school books was drawn up, and the draft of a programme for submission to the board of commissioners was approved. It had been put together on the basis of the Oxford local programme. The Protestant and Catholic headmasters' associations reached substantial agreement on it. The commissioners, in consequence, sanctioned its publication over Christmas to enable pupils commence their preparation for the examinations scheduled for the coming June.

The outcome of the examinations was awaited with much anxiety. In the event, there was little cause for worry about the results. The pattern for the immediate future was indicated in the first year. Blackrock came first, Tullabeg second, in the total of exhibitions and prizes won; and a little known Jesuit school, the College of the Sacred Heart, at the Crescent, Limerick, produced the student who headed the list of successful candidates, Charles F. Doyle, who later became a prominent judge.[53] Walsh was delighted to be the first to announce the good news by telegram to the rector of the college.[54]

The principals of the first two colleges, Reffé of Blackrock and Delany of Tullabeg, became the natural leaders of the Catholic Headmasters' Association under the strong chairmanship of Walsh. Delany remained secretary of its standing committee until the end of 1881, when he was succeeded by Reffé.[55] The latter became a close friend of Walsh, who developed strong links of affection with Blackrock. Delany remained a friend and admirer of Walsh all his life, though later events would suggest that the friendship was more on his side than on Walsh's.

TOWARDS THE PRESIDENCY, AND DIFFERENCES WITH
ARCHBISHOP McCABE

Within Maynooth, meantime, discontent continued to simmer among the staff and the general body of students despite Walsh's efforts. There were changes in the professorial staff, unfilled vacancies, and the need for considerable filling-in, which involved Walsh and some Dunboyne students teaching additional courses. At the same time, the student body claimed that too much was being demanded of them in work and discipline. On top of all this, where Walsh was concerned, his great support, Cardinal Cullen, died in 1878, and was succeeded by a man for whom he did not have the same regard or respect. Edward McCabe was a mild, sometimes impetuous, peace loving and forgiving man, who did not approve of priests being involved in politics, or of words and actions in defiance of the law. Walsh, on the other hand, with his strong nationalist background, would have agreed with Patrick F. Moran of Ossory who was to explain to the Sacred Congregation of Propaganda in 1882, that for a priest to be involved in politics in Ireland was to some degree inevitable.[56] Walsh, in fact, appears to have become somewhat estranged from the archbishop during his years as vice-president. This is suggested by his behaviour when the position of president became vacant following the death of Dr Russell on 26 February 1880.

Walsh, knowing the many problems of the college, and the need for a reorganisation of the Dunboyne Institute, and the reaction there would be to that, was hesitant once more about undertaking a major position of authority. Others expected him to become president, but he felt that something more than his appointment was required. At the time of the trustees meeting on 22 June 1880, he twice set out to call on his archbishop, but, uncharacteristically, his courage failed him each time, and he ended up slipping a note under his door. In it he stated that in "the extraordinary condition of affairs ... now grown almost inveterate" he felt that a solution on the lines adopted in 1812 was called for, namely, that a bishop should take over for a while. He had discussed this with John MacEvilly, coadjutor archbishop of Tuam, and Bartholomew Woodlock, bishop of Ardagh, and he would be happy to see either of them as president. He suggested his colleague, Thomas Carr, as vice-president. His letter had little effect. He himself was appointed president that very day by the trustees, and his friend, Carr, vice-president.[57]

As noted earlier, Walsh had received certain assurances from Gillooly before going forward for the vice-presidency. In office, the assurances seem not to have made much difference to either man. On 14 September 1879, Gillooly complained to Archbishop McCabe that Walsh was going behind his back;[58] and during his presidency, Walsh was to make a similar complaint against Gillooly![59] The latter's intrusion in the life of the college was not as prominent as previously, yet it remained an irritant. Even towards the end of his time as president, Walsh found himself at cross-purposes with the Visitors. On the death of the theology professor, Patrick Murray, he hoped to reorganise the college, especially the Dunboyne Institute, and he requested the Visitors not to appoint a successor until the reorganisation had taken place; but to no effect, for, as he remarked dourly to Cardinal McCabe, on 21 March 1884, "of course, Dr Gillooly had his way".[60]

The mention of Murray evokes a perennial problem faced by college presidents. Murray retired in 1883 and was succeeded by John Healy; the latter was succeeded the following year by Patrick O'Donnell; and he, in turn, was succeeded just four years later, 1888, by Walter McDonald. The rapid turnover was mainly the result of elevations to the episcopacy. Of the twelve appointed professors of theology between Walsh's appointment as vice-president in 1878 and the centenary year 1895, eleven were appointed bishops. This was not good for theology or discipline at Maynooth. Walsh and the Dunboyne students continued to fill in during his time as president. The problem was further exacerbated in June 1883 when Thomas Carr was appointed bishop of Galway, leaving two vacancies – a chair of theology, and the vice-presidency.[61]

Despite the deficiencies, Bishop Moran, on 30 April 1882, had replied to "a list of questions about Maynooth", sent to him by Tobias Kirby, rector of the Irish College in Rome, that the theology course in general was sound and serious, though he was critical of other courses, especially philosophy and Latin, and the pastoral training provided. He also remarked on the need for a spiritual director for the students; and observed that the trustees scarcely helped the overall situation, in that at every meeting they kept chopping and changing things.[62] Kirby, himself, however, responding to a query from the Cardinal Prefect of Propaganda two years later, 28 August 1884, remarked that the Maynooth courses were thin and restricted, and that nearly all the professors had been prepared simply by passing through these courses. He also considered the students' spiritual formation to be unsatisfactory, observing that the goodness of Irish priests came from their family background rather than from the college's formation.[63] On discipline, he remarked, as had Moran, on the problems created by student numbers, over 500 in the year 1881-2.[64] An extant "outline plan" in Walsh's papers indicates an effort on his part to overcome the problem of numbers, at least among the first-year theology students. The plan envisaged dividing the students of first-year theology into four groups and providing tutorial assistance for each group.[65]

As well as the diverse problems presented by the foregoing, there remained the on-going difficulty of financing the construction and furnishing of the college chapel. The overdraft in 1882 stood at more than £12,000. The trustees, in some alarm, passed resolutions about fund collecting in Ireland, America and Australia; but without much effect, it would seem, in that in the summer of 1884 Walsh was instructed to sell as much stock as would meet the debt. In October he presented the final account. The overall cost was £30,575, and after various collections there was a bank overdraft of £12,734, to eliminate which securities had been sold. Walsh was given the task of collecting further funds to complete the chapel, but little had been done before his appointment the following summer as archbishop of Dublin.[66]

On Walsh's years at Maynooth as professor and president, a past student and later a colleague, Professor Walter McDonald, was to comment in his frank *Reminiscences of a Maynooth Professor*. As a student under Walsh, he found him "a hard worker and a successful professor". When he came on the staff in 1881, McDonald used walk with Walsh around the grounds after breakfast and dinner. "Apart from these walks", he observed, Walsh "took little or no recreation or exercise, but read or wrote in his rooms all day, except when he went to Dublin." "He was interested in the working of the Intermediate Education Act", McDonald continued, "gave no small share of his attention to the Royal University", and "was interested in the land question". On Walsh as president, McDonald was almost clinical in his comments. "He was eminently constitutional, never pressing his own views unduly at the councils, though their decisions were very different, at times, from what he would have done if unembarrassed by their advice." "He was fair, too," Mc Donald added, "and always showed a sense of justice, public justice especially, which in his case, was the more easy, as, with the possible exception of Dr Browne, he had no friends. He did not, indeed, seem given to friendship – to have much heart."

Despite this, McDonald acknowledged: "I regard his administration, on the whole, as successful – more so than any I have known." He was of the opinion, moreover, that Walsh would have been "a happier, more efficient, and even more famous man, if he had remained at his books, as professor of theology". He could have done outstanding work "in the way of reforming the canon law".[67]

Apart from the mainly internal college matters which have been considered, Walsh as president, as previously when vice-president, achieved considerable notice in the public arena because of external involvements. These as McDonald indicated, were in connection with university education and the land question. Both involved the issues of justice and equality for the majority population, and both were of major significance for his future career. They merit particular attention.

III

First involvement in Land and University questions

In the generation following the great famine, the population of a predominantly rural Ireland had declined considerably. The number of small tenant farmers, however, had greatly increased, as, relative to the total population, had the number of clergy, and of members of religious congregations. Many of the latter were actively engaged in providing primary and intermediate education, and in working among the poorer population in the cities, and some of them, assisted by the expanding railway system, conducted popular missions througout the country. These last were occasions of much fervour and more regular religious practice. The number of religious confraternities and sodalities increased markedly in urban and rural areas.[1] In short, more than any time previously, an extensive spiritual transformation took place. Catholicism entered, as it were, into the bloodstream of the people, and Ireland was viewed as the provider of missionaries for the Irish diaspora across the world.

In this climate, clergy and religious were highly regarded, and many of them, especially in rural areas and poorer urban districts, identified with the needs and injustices of the people they served. This led, not infrequently, to criticism of an unheeding government, and to a dilemma when their people, especially on the land, felt driven to violence: they could not support violence, yet they did not wish to lose the confidence of their people as had happened to much of the church in mainland Europe. The problem became particularly acute for bishops and clergy when the grounds which occasioned violence were taken up in a wider political movement.

In the year prior to Walsh's appointment as vice-president, and in his first years in that position, that is, from 1877 to 1879, the country experienced three successive harvest failures which, along with the collapse of world agricultural prices because of competition from North America, radicalised both the agricultural labourers and the more influential class of tenant farmers. "The former were faced with the poor house, the latter with eviction", and both with emigration, if they could afford it, as the only other alternative.[2] The resultant agrarian unrest and militancy was marshalled, at least in part, by members of the Irish Republican Brotherhood, and was harnessed to the political movement for Home Rule by Charles Stewart Parnell, who thereby brought about a powerful political consensus.

Walsh was to show himself keenly aware of the Church's need to keep in tune with the political consensus, just as the political leaders were conscious of their movement's need of avoiding church disapproval. Walsh, Archbishop Croke, some other bishops, and numerous clergy, responded to the development by upholding the people's rights, especially in the areas of land and education, and, in terms of the overall consensus, by supporting constitutional Home Rule. The strain came when the government and landed classes repeatedly turned a deaf ears to calls for relief and justice, and violence spread, and Rome, influenced by British government representatives and propaganda, was in danger of condemning the violence one-sidedly and thereby appearing to oppose also the people's political aspirations, a consequence fraught with danger for the Catholic Church in Ireland. This was to be the *mise en scène*, as far as Walsh was concerned, for the twenty years or so which followed his first public venture into the complexities of the land question. This occurred in June 1880, shortly after his appointment as president, when the college's trustees deputed him to appear before the Bessborough Commission to give evidence on their behalf regarding a farm from which the college had been evicted by the duke of Leinster.

The Bessborough Commission and the Land Act

The commission, of which Lord Bessborough was chairman, had been appointed in 1880 by Gladstone's ministry. Its task was to inquire into the Irish land system and to take evidence regarding the conditions of tenure of land in Ireland. The investigation took place during the height of the Land League agitation, and its findings influenced subsequent legislation. Walsh in giving evidence displayed an intimate knowledge of the Irish land question.

The college's dispute with the duke of Leinster was related to the provisions of an earlier Gladstonian land act in 1870. That sought to relieve the plight of the vast majority of Irish tenant-farmers, who were yearly tenants-at-will. They did not have a lease. Their rent was fixed arbitrarily by the landlord. If the tenant improved his holding by his own unaided efforts his rent could be raised, and, without giving cause or providing compensation, the landlord could turn him out of the holding. The act of 1870 sought to remedy this situation by requiring the landlord to pay compensation for both improvements made and for disturbance, and this, it was hoped, would extinguish "wanton eviction" and "unjust augmentation of rent".[3] Unfortunately, there were so many provisos and restrictions relating to compensation, that lawyers were able to draft leases and other agreements which evaded the provisions of the act. This is what appears to have taken place in the Maynooth case.

The college possessed two holdings under the duke of Leinster: one in perpetuity, on which the college was built; the other a farm, the Laraghbryan farm, which was held from year to year. In 1867, the third duke, who always had friendly relations with the college, re-arranged the boundaries of his property. This expanded slightly the Laraghbryan farm, and the duke raised the rent from £295.2 to £300. The college's trustees understood the new rent to be "the rent for the future", and they expended a considerable amount of money in improving their holding. Then, in 1877, the next duke, through his agent, proposed raising the rent from £300 a year to over £400. The trustees objected. Following a report from his valuator, the duke increased his demand to £470. Eventually, under constraint, the trustees agreed to pay £400, but then the duke imposed conditions which the tenants found unacceptable. The most objectionable of these was a clause by which the tenants were to agree to contract themselves out of the benefits of the Land Act of 1870, with respect to claims for compensation. The trustees refused to accept the conditions. To sign such a lease would place them in an indefensible position in the country; their action could be used to put pressure on defenceless tenants to sign similar instruments. The duke declared that his conditions, termed the "Leinster lease", applied to all the tenants on his estate, that they had been approved legally, and he could not make an exception in the case of the trustees. They were given notice to quit, and were evicted from the farm. They claimed and received some compensation, but not for disturbance.

The case of the Laraghbryan farm and the "Leinster lease" was brought up before the Bessborough Commission. Walsh in his evidence ranged over various aspects of tenant conditions in Ireland. On the question of the inappropriateness of state interference with "freedom of contract between landlord and tenant", he pointed out that such freedom of contract did not exist, as the tenant was not really free. He did not have freedom of bargaining. Because of the land hunger in Ireland, and their need to survive, tenants were prepared to promise exorbitant rents and then found themselves at the mercy of extortionate landlords. The state, for its part, permitted the landlords to act callously, not requiring them to meet their responsibilities as owners. Vast areas of land, moreover, were in the hands of a few, often absentee landlords. Effectively, they were monopolists; monopolists, indeed, whose ancestors had acquired the land by power and conquest. The state, in Walsh's view, had an obligation to intervene for the public good to ensure that landlords dealt fairly with their tenants. He illustrated his arguments by examples, some of them relating to the duke of Leinster's estate.

Walsh's view on "freedom of contract" was re-echoed in the commission's report. "Freedom of contract in the case of the majority of Irish tenants, large and small," it declared, "does not really exist."[4] The commission also observed that "Irish tenants were justly entitled to proprietary rights on the grounds of outlay on improvements embodied in and inseparable from the soil", and that the act of 1870 "had completely failed to protect tenants' property in their improvements". The commission recommended, inter alia, fixity of tenure at arbitrated rents, and increased facilities for the purchase of their farms by tenants.[5]

In the course of his presentation, Walsh, almost inevitably, expressed criticism of the "Leinster lease", and he pointed, moreover, to the favourable taxation position of Irish landlords compared to their English counterparts. The duke's agent, a Mr Hammond, attempted to rebut his argument concerning the "Leinster lease", only to meet with a response which greatly pleased some of the hierarchy.[6] The bishop of Meath, Thomas Nulty, a strong supporter of the Land League, informed Walsh on 10 April 1881, that he had read with much pleasure his reply to Hammond – "as it simply stamped him out". The tenant farmers of Ireland were in Walsh's debt, he claimed, "for the masterly manner" in which he "unmasked the duke, who is now universally held to be the worst landlord in Ireland".[7] Congratulations also came from the benign Bishop George Butler of Limerick.

Despite the "unmasking" of the duke, Walsh's relations with his distinguished neighbour remained cordial. On 28 December 1880, he had written, somewhat disingenuously, to Leinster to "assure him that it was only out of a sense of public duty that he had undertaken the painful task of appearing as a witness before the commission".[8] The duke, appreciating, it seems, the attempt to preserve friendly relations, replied next day that he quite understood his position with regard to the commission and fully reciprocated "the kindly feeling" he had expressed.[9] It was the duke's custom to bring certain distinguished visitors staying with him to visit the college. This practice continued. Hence, in a letter of 1 November 1883, he informed Walsh that G.O. Trevelyan, the chief secretary of Ireland, wished to see the college, adding, "I shall be much obliged if you will allow me to take him to the library etc. between 11 and 12 tomorrow".[10] For Walsh, becoming acquainted with Trevelyan was another opportunity to meet with a person of influence, which he then followed up by initiating a correspondence.

The report of the commission was presented in March 1881, and on 7 April Gladstone introduced a new land bill which contained a number of the commission's recommendations. The new bill was a most complex measure. It was so long and complicated that it was commonly said that only three men in the House of Commons had mastered it, namely, Gladstone, Hugh Law, the Irish attorney-general, and T.M. Healy, the member for Wexford. Walsh was also to become known as an authority on the bill. When it was presented, it was eagerly read in Ireland, but was found to be confusing. On 12 April, Walsh's admirer, George Butler, the bishop of Limerick, urged him to try his hand "at the exposition of the land bill". "Since the Apocalypse was written", he declared, "nothing so abstruse has appeared ... To make it intelligible to your fellowmen would be at once a great boon and a great achievement."[11] Walsh set about the task with his customary single-mindedness and energy, and in a short time produced a pamphlet, of about 150 pages, entitled *A Plain Exposition of the Irish Land Bill*, by "A Layman". He dedicated it to Butler, but published it anonymously because, as he admitted in one of the later editions, he "was not without misgiving as to the opinion which might be formed of the work as a whole", and did not wish the position of president of Maynooth to be compromised by a failure[12] – not to mention his own reputation!

In the event, the work was much praised. In a couple of weeks it ran through two editions. "Without flattery", observed Bishop Butler, "I never met a commentary on anything so absolutely lucid and satisfactory."[13] The authorship was soon known – presumably revealed by Walsh once success was ensured – and the author was praised and congratulated by prominent acquaintances such as H.C.E. Childers at the War Office, who had presented a copy to Gladstone, and Sir Charles Russell. Walsh even sent a copy to the duke of Leinster, who politely acknowledged it on 28 April.[14]

When the bill was before parliament, Walsh, through Childers, was kept in touch with the cabinet, and is said to have "had a share in shaping some of the main provisions of the Land Bill".[15] His advice and comments were not just those of an academic with a sense of justice but little practical experience. First hand information came to him from rural areas suffering hardship, and these increased his understanding and gave authority to his comments. One such contributor was the Land League bishop, Patrick Duggan of Clonfert, who wrote to him from Loughrea on 2 August 1881, reminding him that across the country one third of the population were "in a state of semi-starvation, whilst millions of acres lie half cultivated". The "axioms now publicly annoounced from platforms", Duggan added, "– 'The Land for the People'; 'Back to the Land'; 'God gave the Land for all his creatures' etc. – will not be shot down easily." It would be well, therefore, for Walsh, at the head of the future clergy of Ireland, to examine "the root from which the conflict has arisen". Such knowledge would be of great importance in dealing with his students.[16]

The measure received the royal assent in August 1881. Among the Bessborough findings it reflected were: legalising the right of yearly tenants to sell their tenancies at the best available price; providing for the establishment of a land court to which tenants, or landlords and tenants acting in common, but not the landlord alone, should have access for the fixing of a fair rent. A limited fixity of tenure was secured to the tenant in that the judicial rent was fixed for fifteen years, and during that time the tenant could not be evicted except for a breach of contract or non-payment of rent. Nothing was laid down as to what constituted a "fair rent", but what was known as "the Healy clause", after its author, provided that "no rent shall be allowed or payable in respect of improvements made by the tenant or his predecessors".[17]

With the publication of the act, there were suggestions to Walsh from Childers, Sir Charles Russell and others, that he should bring out a clear exposition of the actual act as distinct from that on the bill. He responded with a pamphlet, published on 12 September 1881, over his own name, and simply entitled *A Plain Exposition of the Irish Land Act of 1881*. It met with high praise from members of the bench and bar in England and Ireland. Among these were John O'Hagan, shortly to be the land judge administering the act, Thomas, Lord O'Hagan, lord chancellor of Ireland, and Edward Gibson, KC, the former Conservative attorney-general for Ireland, who in parliament had been a strong critic of the bill. Walsh had advised Gibson on canon law during the O'Keeffe trial, and they remained on friendly terms. Gibson was to be three times lord chancellor of Ireland. He would become Baron Ashbourne in 1885, and be associated with the Ashbourne Act of that year which facilitated the sale of holdings to tenants. In that and subsequent land purchase acts, Walsh was to be consulted by him.

2. THE UNIVERSITY QUESTION AND UNIVERSITY COLLEGE, DUBLIN

Walsh's participation in the University Question at this time was, in contrast, far from winning acclaim. The main sources for his involvement in the university issue during his time as president of Maynooth are his papers in the Dublin Diocesan Archives, and the detailed papers of Fr William Delany in the Irish Jesuit Archives. The necessary backdrop to the story was provided by the establishment of the Queen's University Colleges and the founding of the Catholic University of Ireland.

The Catholic University had been set up by the Irish bishops in 1854 because of their dissatisfaction with the undenominational education provided by the colleges of Queen's University (at Belfast, Cork and Galway), established in 1845, and their own lack of control in such institutions. These colleges were endowed by the government, and survived despite episcopal disapproval. The Catholic University, as noted earlier, was not endowed, its qualifications were not recognised by the government, and hence it did not effectively meet the needs of Irish Catholics. Some private Catholic colleges, such as Carlow College and William Delany's Tullabeg, put forward their students for the London University examinations. The success of Delany's students, against competition from Britain and Ireland, established his reputation as an educationist, and confirmed him in his belief of what Catholic students could achieve if properly motivated. The government, meanwhile, was hampered in all educational concessions to the Catholics by the strong political opposition of non-conformists in Britain. The only practical way of proceeding seemed to be on the lines of undenominational, or mixed, education.

Gladstone, however, aimed to solve the problem on a grander scale. In 1873 he had introduced a university bill which sought to find a solution by opening Dublin University, as distinct from Trinity College, in order to comprise within it Trinity College, the Catholic University, the Queen's Colleges of Belfast and Cork, and any other colleges which fulfilled certain conditions set forth in the bill as entitling a college to university status. The bill was rejected by a majority of three in the second reading, and led to the ousting of the Liberals from office.[18] Walsh was very taken by Gladstone's plan, and it remained the basis of his ideal solution right up to the foundation of the National University in 1908.

The next attempt to provide a solution came under Disraeli's Conservative government in August 1879, when, looking to the principle followed in the Intermediate Education Act, it was decided to provide an indirect form of subsidy at University level. The Royal University of Ireland was established: a purely examining body, which, however, enabled Catholic colleges to compete for recognised degrees, and which had a senate empowered to draw up a scheme of exhibitions, prizes and scholarships, and to allocate fellowships, as a form of indirect endowment. As a result of the Act, the Queen's University was abolished, but its constituent colleges continued to receive direct government endowment, as well as competing for the exhibitions and other forms of indirect endowment. This anomaly was offensive to Catholic educationists, and with Walsh it became a burning issue. Apart from the inequality involved, any concession to the Queen's Colleges, he informed Woodlock, the bishop of Ardagh, was "a concession to institutions formally condemned by the Holy See". He was opposed to their receiving any fellowships, and feared that the "liberal Catholics" on the senate would be easily persuaded to give way.[19] Delany, who reasoned with him to little effect, pointed out to Reffé in March that if Walsh and some of the bishops continued to oppose any concession to the Queen's Colleges they were leaving themselves wide open to attack. They could make their case on only two grounds: one, that the Queen's Colleges were endowed already – but then so was Maynooth, and it could be excluded on that ground; or that the Queen's Colleges were not doing good educational work – but that would lead to a query about the Catholic colleges and to "a disgraceful exposure".[20]

Meantime, the all important questions were: how would the government arrange the membership of the senate, and how would the fellowships be allocated? Archbishop McCabe made it clear that he would not consent to any scheme "which did not secure for Catholics at least half of all the appointments".[21] Eventually, in October 1881, the government announced that of the twenty-six proposed fellowships the "Catholics should have half the fellowships and examinationships and other appointments". Thus, the bishops, despite the worries of some of them about the "liberal Catholics" on the senate, had reason to be satisfied with the senate's arrangements. Not only were there thirteen Catholic fellowships, each carrying £400, whose holders were to be official examiners of the Royal University, but the senate had also decreed the previous February that "every fellow should hold his fellowship on the condition that, if required by the senate, he should teach students of the university in some educational institution approved by the senate".[22]

On 11 January 1882, the bishops, at their general meeting, decided to divide the Catholic fellowships between Maynooth, the Catholic University, and St Malachy's College, Belfast. They envisaged Maynooth as part of the Royal University. Walsh, for his part, had worked hard through the previous year to secure a majority of the Catholic fellowships for Maynooth, vying with Henry Neville, rector of the Catholic University, who wanted all the fellowships for the University. In his report to the bishops, in preparation for their visitation of the college on 14 April 1882, Walsh assured their lordships that with the concentration of the fellows at Maynooth they would have no need to fear about "the future position of Catholics in the Royal University".[23] Many bishops, however, were opposed to linking Maynooth with the Royal University. Only McCabe, who became cardinal on 30 March 1882, Woodlock of Ardagh, and McCarthy of Cloyne, were positively in favour. In June, the trustees of Maynooth, and a majority of bishops, rejected the link with the Royal University. McCabe was appalled. He asked Giovanni Simeoni, the cardinal prefect of the Propaganda, to write to the bishops to reconsider their decision. Simeoni wrote, but the bishops at their meeting in October reaffirmed their decision by a larger margin. The Maynooth staff also indicated reluctance to participate in the Royal University courses.

In October 1882, the bishops decided to hand over the Catholic University, now reduced to a handful of students, to Cardinal McCabe.[24] The latter, on the advice of Bishop Woodlock, supported by Henry Neville, decreed that, henceforth, the Catholic University would be but a moral body with some six constitutional colleges, of which one, University College, St Stephen's Green, was to occupy the buildings of the Catholic University. Moreover, as Neville recorded in a memorandum for the bishops in October 1882, the episcopal education committee, chaired by the cardinal, decided on 2 October "that all the fellowships allotted to Catholics at present should be centralised in the Catholic University College, St Stephen's Green".[25] As a result, the bishops now had concentrated in one institution an indirect endowment of thirteen Catholic fellows, paid by the senate, who would teach its students and serve at the same time as their examiners. The scene had changed considerably. Neville was convinced that the change would attract students to University College. Yet a year later, in face of the lack of progress and the financial costs involved, the bishops voted, on the proposal of Archbishop Thomas Croke of Cashel, that the college be handed over to the Jesuits with William Delany as president. On a division, the Jesuits received 24 votes to 4 for Blackrock College.[26]

On 26 October 1883, Delany, on behalf of the Society of Jesus, signed an agreement with the episcopal trustees of the Catholic University,[27] whereby the Jesuits were to take over, at an annual rent, 84 and 85 St Stephen's Green and the upper storeys of 86. The existing staff of fellows and other professors, although weak in teaching power, was to be retained. What appealed to Delany, however, was the concentration of all the Catholic fellowships at Univeristy College, with the one exception of St Malachy's College, Belfast. This he saw as a means of surpassing all the Queen's Colleges and proving, through the success of his students, that the Catholic case for a recognised university was overwhelming. Within the consolidation Delany also believed that if he could obtain a sufficient number of highly qualified Jesuits for the fellowships, men from Britain and Europe if needs be, who would be appointed truly on merit, their stipends would not go to them individually but to the college and become a much needed resource for an inadequately financed and equipped institution. Walsh, strongly supported Delany's case to the bishops. Delany's and Walsh's friendship was to come under serious strain the following year, however, when a dispute arose concerning the allocation of all the Catholic fellows to University College.

The fellowship controversy

In Delany's view the allocation of the fellowships was the key consideration in the Jesuits' decision to take over the college, and was central to their agreement with the bishops. He understood that Walsh shared his view. He was taken aback, therefore, to receive an invitation from Dr Walsh on 23 January 1884, to attend a meeting to discuss a request to the senate by Blackrock College to be recognised "as a college in which fellows of the Royal University may be autho-rised to lecture", and also to have Fr Reffé of Blackrock appointed a fellow.[28]

Walsh had been appointed to the senate the previous year, on the recom-mendation of Cardinal McCabe. As senator, his abiding sense of equality and fair play became disturbed by the fellowship issue. Although he had supported Delany's case to the bishops, and had himself previously pressed for the con-centration of the Catholic fellowships in Maynooth, he now became convinced that this was unfair. He became critical, therefore, of the monopoly at University College and began to emphasise the need for fair play towards the other Catholic colleges. He focused, however, on one college, Blackrock. It had stood by the Catholic University to the end, and had proven itself academically by outstand-ing results in the intermediate examinations and in the first Royal University examinations. Its case for recognition as a college where fellows might be autho-rised to lecture was, as he understood it, unassailable. He seemed to think that Delany would be of the same mind, and if not, that he might be persuaded. After all, when Delany was recently in charge of a short-lived Jesuit college in Temple Street he had argued for a fellowship for it, and for Blackrock.

Delany, although embarrassed at the prospect of the meeting, agreed to attend, but that there might be no misunderstanding he sent on his views in writing beforehand. The choice of Fr Reffé, the head of another college, as a fellow, he believed, would be invidious, but if Reffé were suitably qualified and both Walsh and the cardinal supported him, he, Delany, would not oppose him; Reffé as a fellow, however, would have to lecture at Stephen's Green, just as Fr Tom Finlay, though stationed at Temple Street, had to do when he was made a fellow of the Royal University. But, Delany continued, it was one thing to approve of an individual fellow, it was quite another to approve of the French College as a place for fellowships. Such a decision would lead to a dispersal of the fellows. Once one exception was made there was no reason why other suc-cessful Catholic colleges might not apply and expect the same reward. The result would be rivalry for fellows, the dissipation of the Catholic teaching power, and the purpose of the concentration of the fellowships in one college would be abandoned, and the conditions of the Jesuit tenure of the college would be altered. Having forwarded his views, he attended what must have been a very tense meeting, though no account survives.

The day after the meeting, Walsh put forward, at the preliminary session of the standing committee of the senate, a proposal supporting Blackrock as a place where the fellows of the university might be authorised to lecture. He found himself unsupported. He then determined to propose Reffé for a fellowship in classics at the next meeting of the standing committee on 30 January. Delany, meanwhile, had put forward a highly qualified English Jesuit classicist, Gerard Manley Hopkins, for the position. On 29 January, Walsh persuaded the episcopal education committee, including his old opponent, Gillooly, to support Fr Reffé's candidature, and to ask to have Hopkins's name withdrawn. Bishop Butler, a supporter of Delany's plans, was unable to attend the meeting, and the chairman, Cardinal McCabe, although he did not approve of the committee's decision, let it go forward as unanimous. Walsh spent that evening at Blackrock preparing the case for the senate. Delany also spent the evening out, unaware of any impending crisis, since the cardinal had informed Lord Emly, the vice-chancellor of the university, that he would be supporting Hopkins. On his return home, he was surprised to learn that the cardinal wished Hopkins' name withdrawn. Delany decided that it was too late to communicate with Stonyhurst College, England, and, besides, having reason to know of the cardinal's yielding disposition, he suspected that Walsh had stage-managed the committee's decision, and that it did not express the overall view of the hierarchy.[29]

Prior to the meeting of the standing committee of the senate on 30 January, the lay Catholic senators pointed out to the cardinal that his candidate was not sufficiently qualified in the classical languages, and that his selection, besides, would undermine the building up of one great central Catholic institution. They urged him not to propose Reffé. McCabe replied that as the representative of the committee of Catholic bishops he had to persevere with his proposal, even though his personal preference was otherwise. In the subsequent election, Hopkins was elected by twenty-three votes to three. Afterwards, to Sir Thomas Redington, under-secretary at Dublin Castle, who expressed his regret at having voted against his eminence's candidate, the cardinal replied, "I am just as glad things turned out as they did."[30] Before the session ended, Dr Woodlock gave notice that at the next meeting he would move for the recognition of the French College as a college where fellows of the university might teach. This, presumably, was Walsh's plan in the event of Reffé's canditature being defeated, just as it was his advocacy that induced the episcopal committee to decide that the cardinal should resign from the senate if his proposal in support of Reffé was not carried.[31] The next day, McCabe resigned from the senate. After some days, however, following a special request from Lord Spencer, the lord lieutenant, McCabe withdrew his resignation, much to Walsh's disgust.

In the succeeding weeks, Delany was under considerable pressure. Gillooly wrote a strong letter to the Jesuit provincial, Thomas Browne, deploring his "opposition to the *coetus episcoporum*, represented by the episcopal committee" in not withdrawing Hopkins' name and thereby bringing about the resignation of the cardinal.[32] Support for Delany, however, came from George Butler, bishop of Limerick, who, on 14 February, expressed his delight at Hopkins election; and by a letter from Dr Croke on 19 February who observed that the powers of the episcopal education committee were limited "to matters of comparatively inconsiderable interest", and that it was not competent "for Dr Woodlock to speak before the senate at the next meeting, in the name of the bishops of Ireland, seeking approval for the French College." With his characteristic ability of stripping away non-essentials, he added:

> Let the French College or the Stephen's Green College be *the* university college, sustained and fostered *as such*; but let us not have two competing establishments in or near Dublin at least, both certain to lack vigour, because both lacking funds.[33]

In the months before the next standing committee of the senate, scheduled for 29 May, Walsh and Delany maintained amicable relations. Walsh, in addition to his other activities, was engaged, by means of letters in the *Freeman's Journal* and questions in parliament, in attacks on the Queen's Colleges. Through the Irish party he pressed for a royal commission to inquire into the colleges. On 7 April, after a commission was announced, he wrote from London to Delany stating that he had hopes of the Queen's Colleges being handed over to Catholics. Delany could not see the government sanctioning such a solution, and even if it did the result would be utter confusion as there were not sufficient trained Catholic teachers for the existing colleges, let alone finding additional staff for the Queen's Colleges. Shortly after this, his easy relationship with his Maynooth friend received an unexpected jolt. He was preparing material for a senate meeting, and as had been his custom, sent a draft copy to Walsh for his perusal. To his surprise he received what seemed an excessively strong reaction to the wording of one sentence. He had written: "As it is contemplated, I believe, to assign to this college three of the fellows who are to be appointed." Walsh replied curtly that such a statement should not be made without the cardinal's approval. To do so was to "simply invite the Protestants and the lay members of the senate, not merely to differ from the cardinal, but to ignore him". Surprised at the interpretation, and even more at the reaction, Delany altered his words to read: "In the event of it being determined to assign ..." Walsh declared himself happy with this version as it did not prejudge the case. On reflection, Delany thought his friend's previous reply "the first letter that showed any trace of wounded feeling".[34] It seems possible, however, that it mainly reflected Walsh's precise legal mind at work.

At the senate's standing committee meeting on 29 May a surprise was sprung. Woodlock's proposal seeking approval for the French College was joined to a proposal in favour of Fr Reffé for a fellowship, in modern languages instead of classics. Delany later regarded this as a tactic inspired by Walsh to obtain full recognition for Blackrock. James Kavanagh, president of Carlow College, responded with notice of a counter proposal. Should Bishop Woodlock's proposal in favour of Blackrock be adopted, he intended to propose that Carlow College be approved by the senate "as a college wherein the fellows of the Royal University may lecture".[35] In face of this complication, there was no seconder for Woodlock's proposal. That evening Walsh resigned from the senate. Later he would claim that he did so disspassionately, but there seems little doubt that he was angry and frustrated. Next day, at the senate meeting, Woodlock announced that he was withdrawing his motion for the present. The Abbé Polin, an examiner at the college, the only remaining candidate, was appointed to modern languages. Although a highly qualified Jesuit was available, Delany did not put his name forward. Cardinal McCabe was offended that Walsh had resigned without first consulting him. He invited John Healy, professor at Maynooth, to allow himself be proposed for the vacant place. On Healy questioning the propriety of this, he being a member of Walsh's staff, he was informed that he was to be appointed coadjutor to the bishop of Clonfert. Healy, having consulted Walsh, accepted the appointment to the senate.[36] An independent, forceful personality, Healy was to prove a staunch supporter of the Stephen's Green College.

Following this challenge, all subsequent Catholic fellowships went to University College as a matter of course, except for the special concession to St Malachy's College, Belfast. Walsh did not come well out of the fellowship dispute. His biographer, and former secretary, Patrick J. Walsh, seems to have been reflecting Walsh's own perspective when he represented the dispute as one between Dr Walsh, as champion of Catholic nationalism and fair play, and the Whigs, lay and ecclesiastical, on the senate. In fact, there was no justification for applying the term "Whig" to the policy of concentrating the fellowships at Stephen's Green. It was the policy which the bishops as a body had initiated, and had insisted on while University College was directly under their control. Walsh's alternative policy of dividing the fellowships was never subsequently approved by any of the bishops. It was one of the two important matters regarding university policy – the other being the nature of the final solution to the university question – on which Walsh held a view differing from the majority of the episcopate. On this occasion he had persuaded the episcopal education committee to endorse his views; but Croke, whom he greatly admired, and whom no one could term a "Whig", had considered that they had exceeded their powers; and neither he, nor James Kavanagh, of Carlow College, Bishop George Butler, nor the cardinal, concurred with his stand.

Kavanagh wrote to Walsh, following his resignation, regretting his departure and assuring him that he agreed with him on every aspect of Irish education except the issue of one central college. He could not see the wisdom of raising up a rival college to Stephen's Green before it was six months in existence. "Stephen's Green", he continued, "is a national college and the bishops are but the trustees of the nation for the present." They had confided that trust to the

Jesuits, but they had done so in such a way "that at any moment they can resume their authority if the interests of Catholic education require that they should do so." Blackrock, on the other hand, though it had been very successful, was a private college over which the bishops had no authority,[37] and, besides, he added in a further fragment of a letter on the same subject, "the Blackrock people are French" and as such were "unfit to conduct the great National College of Ireland" which he hoped one day to see on Stephen's Green.[38]

The disagreement with his admirer and adviser, Bishop Butler, might have been expected to carry much weight with Walsh. "It greatly surprises me", Butler declared, "that you should be an advocate of fritting away the teaching power of the Catholic fellows, by dividing it between several schools. It looks like a 'change of front' on your part. I was always under the impression that you were in favour of the policy of concentration – so as to create, in Dublin, a great centre of Catholic thought and feeling, and educational work, which by its eminent success in connection with the Royal University, should of necessity, and in the not very distant future, force recognition and endowments at the hand of the government". Like Kavanagh, he stressed that Stephen's Green was the bishops' college, that the Jesuits could be removed if not satisfactory or if the government was prepared to subsidise a Catholic college but not one run by Jesuits. There were, he explained, three possibilities considered by the bishops with respect to the college, "but in all of them the concentration of the fellows at Stephen's Green was a central factor", and "if the Jesuits took it up they were to have all the fellows".

He then took Walsh to task for some of his public utterances following his resignation, particularly his comparing the monopoly at University College with the unfair monopoly enjoyed by the Queen's Colleges, and his decrying of Lord Emly's suitability as senator. Surely, he declared, there was not a trace of similitude between the monopoly of the fellows at Stephen's Green and the monopoly of state endowments. enjoyed by the Queen's Colleges. For nearly forty years the bishops had asked for an endowment for the Catholic University College at Stephen's Green. "Suppose", he asked, "they had granted our petition and endowed the Stephen's Green school with £50,000 a year, would you think this a monopoly as offensive as the Queen's Colleges, because Blackrock was not also endowed?" Butler concluded with a quiet defence of his Limerick friend. "I am puzzled", he chided, "by your reference to Lord Emly in connection with neglect of duty as a senator or committee man. I think you will find on inquiry that he has been constant in his attendance at senate and committee meetings."[39] Walsh remained unmoved by the arguments of Croke, Kavanagh, and Butler.

An interlude

In the meantime, he and Delany exchanged letters. The latter, although greatly relieved at the result of the senate meetings, deeply regretted having to oppose Walsh. He wrote to him to express his concern at the announcement in the

Freeman's Journal of his resignation from the senate. Walsh replied on 31 May that he had personally written the account in the newspaper "so as to shut out the possibility of any effort being made by Lord Spencer" to persuade him to do "what the cardinal was unfortunately induced to do after his resignation". It had been a source of great pain to him as a senate member to take a course at variance with what Delany regarded as the interests of University College. Hence, he found it a relief to be rid of the responsibility imposed on him by the senate. He had not acted precipitately. Though he had not posted his letter of resignation until after the senate meeting, he had in fact written it the night previous, having, he explained, a distrust of his own judgement "on any matter when formed under anything like excitement, or without the fullest consideration".[40] "The night previous", as the case was being prepared at Blackrock, was unlikely to have been free from "anything like excitement".

Walsh's letter to Delany seemed to signal the end of the fellowship dispute, but his "relief" at being off the senate was to prove short lived. Ironically, he resented not being officially requested, as McCabe had been, to reconsider his resignation; and the memory of the senate defeat continued to rankle to the point of virtually blinding him for many years to any side of the question but his own. The senate became a *bête noire*.

Even as he and Delany exchanged letters, however, they were occupied preparing for the royal commission of inquiry into the Queen's Colleges. Both presented very cogent evidence to the commission in the month of June. Despite their contributions, the findings of the commission were inconclusive. The majority report minimised the defects alleged by Walsh.

Meantime, to Delany's delight, the publication of the Royal University examination results showed University College achieving considerable success in its very first year – winning more distinctions in classics and modern languages than the three Queen's Colleges taken together, and in science excelling Cork and Galway. It was an auspicious start. Within a short while, however, Delany's sense of exultation was disturbed when he learned from a friend and co-educationalist, Thomas Higgins, that in a letter to him Walsh had announced that "the disorganised condition of affairs" had forced upon him "the very painful necessity of withdrawing from the senate of the Royal University", and that he had determined "to have nothing more to do with any organisation for Catholic educational interests" until he saw "some prospect of justice being done in the matter of university education to those who had successfully fought our battles in the critical time, and who had now been left out in the cold by the unnatural alliance of certain Catholic members of the senate of the Royal University with those who, to say the least, are not friends of Irish Catholic interests".[41]

The public phase of the fellowship controversy

Walsh's sense of injustice and grievance led him in the last weeks of November and the first week of December 1884, to turn the fellowship dispute into a public controversy. The unseemly quarrel was waged mainly in the pages of the *Tablet*, the Belfast *Morning News*, and the *Freeman's Journal*.

The president of Maynooth fired the first shots with a letter to the *Tablet*. The *Morning News* then drew attention to his remarks, and there followed a series of letters and articles attacking or supporting the special position of University College. Walsh, himself, argued with eloquence and vigour, but, as the controversy developed his vigour was not matched by his usual clarity of exposition. Briefly, he conveyed his public disapproval of the Royal University and his opposition to the fellowship scheme, as such, because it created the illusion that Catholics enjoyed an endowment. University College, he believed, could manage without fellowships. Blackrock had shown that a college could do brilliantly without such aids. But given that there were fellowships, it was unfair for University College to have a monopoly of them; and it was doubly unfair – a strong point – to have the fellows who taught at Stephen's Green also setting the questions and being the examiners of the Royal University examinations. Rather than all the fellowships being concentrated in University College, some should be granted to Blackrock in recompense for its splendid contribution to Irish education. To grant it a fellowship would lessen to some degree, at least, the unfairness of the examination system.

Walsh's denunciation of monopoly struck a chord in other Catholic colleges which felt unfairly treated at having no such boon of indirect subsidy. The Belfast *Morning News* eagerly stirred the discontent. On 22 November it made reference to Walsh's letter in the *Tablet* and went on to state that educationalists were concerned at the scandalous waste of teaching power at Stephen's Green, and commented on the unfair proportion of teachers to students there compared to Belfast and other colleges. Bishop Butler wrote to Delany asking how he would answer the charges. Delany replied at length, adding that he had contemplated a public answer but hated the prospect of a newspaper squabble between priests, and feared "that Dr Walsh's propensity to newspaper writing" might lead him to begin a controversy no matter how mildly the opposition case was put. On 24 November Butler expressed his satisfaction with the answer, but added – "the attack on the Royal University Senate for giving you all the Catholic fellows should be answered by some Catholic members of the senate ", and they should show "that the Jesuits undertook to work at Stephen's Green school under an express arrangement with the bishops that all the Catholic fellows should teach at Stephen's Green". It was strange, he continued, "that Dr Walsh should close his eyes to the fact that this inviolable principle for whose sake he has resigned his place on the senate, has been wholly overlooked by the cardinal, the bishops of Ardagh and Clonfert, and Dr Neville".[42]

For the president of Maynooth, however, ' inviolable principle' had become charged with strong feeling, and on 29 November he published contributions in the *Tablet* and the *Freeman's Journal* which hammered away at the injustice perpetrated by the senate in allocating all the Catholic fellows to University College,

and queried the college's right to have them. Delany met with two of his sena-
torial friends, Kavanagh of Carlow College and the highly regarded Dublin
physician, Sir Francis Cruise, both of whom decided to come publicly to the
defence of the senate and of University College.

Kavanagh took Walsh to task on the issue of University College's monopoly.
Walsh replied at considerable length on 1 December. His persistence at this
stage was occasioning some episcopal unease. "The attacks of Dr Walsh on the
university school, Stephen's Green, are becoming simply intolerable", Dr Butler
wrote the Jesuit provincial on the same day; and he added that he had "pointed
out to Dr Walsh some months ago that if there was anything wrong in giving
the Catholic fellows to Stephen's Green, it was the *fault of the bishops*, and that
to attack the arrangement was to attack the bishops", but Dr Walsh had "either
forgotten or disregarded" his reminder.[43] That to attack the decision of the
senate and the Jesuits at University College was, in effect, to attack the bishops,
was something that nobody had yet ventured to say in public. Sir Francis Cruise
finally said it, and much more, in a scathing polemic which appeared in the
Freeman on 2 December 1884, and so upset the president of Maynooth as to virtually terminate the public controversy.

Cruise ranged over the history of the Royal University, the bishops' attitude
to it, the fellowships, the desire of the college and bishops for a central college
for Catholic students, the handing over of such a college with the fellowships to
the Jesuits, their opening of the institution in November 1883 and the remarkable results already in a year, which gave hope "that after thirty years of darkness and confusion" there was "good prospect of brighter days and of a better
order of things". Having thus set the scene, he turned a sarcastic eye on Walsh's
behaviour. From the moment Walsh was appointed senator, in April 1883, just
before the transfer of the college to the Jesuits, he had "set himself to work with
all his well-known vigour and ability to accomplish, if he possibly could, the
subdivision of the fellowships allotted to the Stephen's Green College". Cruise
did not pretend to judge his motives, but he could not suppose "that he was
ignorant that this subdivision of teaching and financial power, if obtained, would
speedily paralyse and ultimately destroy the youthful college". He noted that
Walsh in his contributions had held back "the undisguised fact that his real contention was for the formal recognition of Blackrock College, which would have
enabled all the fellows to fulfil their statutory obligations of teaching there in
place of the Stephen's Green College". The senate at its meeting in May had
differed from Walsh, and now "the Rev. ex-senator" endeavours "to organise an
attack from without to accomplish what he so signally failed in doing while on
the senate".

Speaking than as a Catholic senator, Cruise regretted Walsh's charging the
senate with a policy "essentially based on unfairness and injustice". "Surely", he
declared,

in these days of enlightenment, men may differ without taxing each other with base motives, and the fact that the senate was not prepared to accept his *ipse dixit* cannot justify even so accomplished and distinguished a churchman as the president of Maynooth College in this accusation against a body of gentlemen whose time and energy, as well as his, may be worth something – and who may be presumed to have, as well as himself, some conscience, some education, some interest in the great question of Catholic higher education, and some little knowledge of university affairs.

Passing on, he observed that it was a puzzle to a layman like himself how Walsh could claim that his withdrawal from the senate was on a point of principle seeing that the cardinal and several other prominent churchmen found no problem staying on the senate. Regarding Walsh's emphasis on "the supposed iniquity of 'monopoly'" he did not need to dwell as Dr Kavanagh had let in "so much light upon this fallacy", but he did wish to ask one question: "Is not Maynooth a monopoly, and a very big one?" What reply would its president make if anyone declared that its professors and funds should be divided "amongst the provincial colleges througout Ireland engaged in training young men for the priesthood?"

The "iniquitous policy of the senate", Cruise summed up, was simply "to support the bishops' college – University College, Stephen's Green – in order that it may be what Catholics want, an efficient training college for undergraduates, under perfect religious discipline". What Walsh wanted, on the other hand, was to divide the fellowships throughout Ireland.

He yielded to no one, Cruise concluded, in his admiration for the work of Blackrock and its splendid staff, but "as the bishops of Ireland did not select it to represent them at their college, Stephen's Green", he, as a Catholic senator, felt that he had no option but to give his best support to the University College, Stephen's Green.[44]

Faced with this potent mixture of hard facts, relentless logic, and sustained reproof, Walsh apparently was deeply stung, though he did not immediately grasp its implications. Instead, he slipped immediately into a rejoinder: making a detailed response the following day to demonstrate that Cruise had given both an inaccurate presentation of the facts and an inaccurate exposition of his motives. Two days later, however, it seems to have come home to him, perhaps from the comments of others, that what Cruise was actually saying was that he was acting out of pique in continuing publicly to support Blackrock and that in reality he was opposed to the Jesuits and to the policy of the Irish bishops.

On 5 December, he wrote a private, rather disjointed letter to Delany. He was clearly in a state of some distress, and the humiliation he experienced in writing was not conducive to easy relations between them in the future. "I really fear", he wrote, "that if I do not write to you to ask you not to be led away by all the terribly false things that Dr Cruise has written about me in reference to your college, even you may be carried away by the current into the belief that I am in reality one of the deadliest opponents of your great work." He then continued, to Delany's astonishment:

> I can quite *understand* the view taken by some and, I dare say, not unnaturally by yourself and many of your Fathers, that the appointment of anyone but a Jesuit, as fellow of the university, even with the obligation of teaching as a fellow in Stephen's Green, involves as a necessary consequence the paralysis and destruction of the college. Preposterous as the notion seems to me, I can make allowances for the influences, as I believe of prejudice etc. which led to its being adopted by those who hold it.

What he most objected to, however, was that "a man like Dr Cruise" had publicly charged him with opposition to the bishops. He hoped Delany at least would believe that he would not be party to any line of action that would damage the success of the Stephen's Green College. Delany knew how much he had done to remove obstacles to the transfer of the college to the Jesuits, but there was one critical moment which even Delany did not know about where his intervention had been necessary to secure the college for him. He had written a further reply to "Dr Cruise's shocking misrepresentation", demonstrating that he had been from the beginning an advocate of the transfer of the Stephen's Green College. He felt it a great humiliation to have to write this in public about what he hoped would have been taken for granted, "but the bold assertion of a respectable Catholic like Dr Cruise" made it impossible for him "to remain silent under his misrepresentation". "I really would prefer", he concluded, "that when next writing to me you would make no reference to all that I have written now. I only want you to know my real position. And may I ask you to show this letter to the provincial? I would not venture to write so freely to him."[45]

As he finished the letter, Delany, not surprisingly, remained confused as to where Walsh really stood. He seemed to want two conflicting things, the continuing success of University College, and the dispersal of the fellows on which it depended for successful continuance. The one thing that did seem clear, from both his actions and his words, was that he sought above all recognition for Blackrock College. He had resigned from the senate not over the election of an individual fellow, but because recognition of the college was rejected.[46]

Delany replied that evening. It had never occurred to him to doubt, he wrote, either Walsh's "personal friendship" or his "sincere interest" in University College, and he had borne witness "on all occasions" to Walsh's staunch and strong advocacy of the Jesuits coming to Stephen's Green. He differed with him, he continued, only on the question of one approved college for Catholics, but he recognised his "right to hold and maintain strenuously" his "different judgement". With regard to the fellowships in themselves, Delany sought to make his own position clear. "I do not at all hold as you seem to imply that it was absolutely essential that Jesuits should be appointed to every fellowship." It never occurred to him. for example, "to press Fr O'Carroll's candidature against Abbé Polin's."[47] As to Fr Reffé's case, Delany added, he had personally assured Reffé that he would put no obstacle in his way, but that it was "quite useless to raise the question of 'approval', which the senators had very strong views about". "In the appointment of the fellows to the one approved college", he believed it was due "to the self-respect of the Catholic senators as well as to the interests of Catholic education that the rule of selection ought to be simply – in all cases – give it to the best man, the man who seems plainly the best qualified for the post, no matter where he comes from; and far from asking a vote for a Jesuit against a more competent man, I should think it a calamity to have him elected." He assured Walsh, in conclusion, that he considered the case for one central college to be so strong that if it were a choice between having the Jesuits at Stephen's Green or "keeping it a central place", he would prefer "that the Jesuits be removed".[48]

In Walsh's public letter in response to Cruise's "shocking misrepresentation", to which he referred in his letter to Delany, and which was written on 5 December 1884, Walsh declared that he was writing again, on the advice of friends, to defend himself against Cruise's chargess. He then stated that it was quite false to suggest that he had been opposed to the transfer to the Jesuits of the Stephen's Green College. On the contrary, he had been one of its strongest advocates and viewed it as "the most practically useful step" taken by the bishops in the cause of Catholic university education. As to his action in the senate, far from being opposed to the bishops he was supported by Cardinal McCabe and Bishop Woodlock; and as to his alleged aim to obtain recognition of Blackrock College, the proposal was Dr Woodlock's and it was withdrawn. He had used the cardinal's and Woodlock's names without their permission, but he was sure they would support his doing so in the cause of the president of Maynooth College. He concluded his rather evasive and deflated letter with the mortifying, and uncharacteristic, request that Cruise would now "have the propriety to let the matter drop".

Cruise closed the public disputation two days later. He was brief, but scarcely merciful. He noted that Walsh had not consulted the two prelates before writing. This was to be regretted, as was his omission to consult them before resigning, as any layman would have done. Since Walsh had appealed to him to let the matter drop, he, as a Catholic layman, would gladly do so. Walsh had written many letters to English as well as Irish newspapers. He had written only one, and that in defence of the senate of which Dr Walsh had been a member and of which "many of the highest dignitaries of the country are members". He observed that Dr Walsh wanted him to desist even though he had not withdrawn his charges. He (Cruise) was doing so out of respect, while, at the same time, restating his belief in the accuracy of the picture he had drawn of Walsh's policy and its effect on the bishops' college. "I deeply regret", he concluded, "the grave imprudence which originated such a controversy and conducted it so strangely".[49] An unexpected footnote to all the publicity and emotional ferment was provided a few days later when Delany called on Cardinal McCabe. The latter informed him that he had told Dr Walsh that his letter of resignation "was most uncalled for and inopportune", and he expressed the view that it had been a mistake to put forward Fr Reffé's name.[50]

From the mid-years of the nineteenth century to the second-half of the twentieth century respect for the cloth in Ireland largely sheltered Catholic clergy from public criticism by lay Catholics. A letter such as Cruise's was rare; all the more in that as a lay man he claimed to speak in defence of "the bishops' college" against a prominent priest. For Walsh, who courted public attention and valued the approval of significant people, the sense of public humiliation was immense. Never again would he experience the like. There would be criticism and abuse following the Parnell split, but then he could feel justified in proclaiming the Church's teaching and in the support of fellow bishops. Not surprisingly, therefore, although usually a large-minded man, not prone to indulge grievances, his humiliation in the fellowship controversy continued to rankle. He appears to have dealt with the hurt he experienced by blotting out the memory of his own failings in the case, and transferring all the blame to the senate of the university. Thereafter, his attitude to the Royal University and the senate was dismissive or openly hostile, and he continued to find opportunities of proclaiming the injustice suffered by the French College. University College, as the institution favoured by the senate, experienced, inevitably, some of his disapproval. He had "closed his eyes", as Bishop Butler suggested, to the consequences of his actions in the fellowship business. Something similar had happened with respect to the Queen's Colleges. It was to recur on at least two other occasions: an *idée fixe* would be asserted in defiance of all arguments to the contrary, and the prestige of his office as archbishop of Dublin, to which he was to be appointed in 1885, would add special weight to his advocacy. William Delany, interestingly, remained devoted to his Maynooth friend, retaining a great admiration for his intellectual ability and quickness, but with a gradually growing question-mark about his judgement on university matters which was to stiffen his own resolve in later years when they came once more into disagreement.

Death of Cardinal McCabe

Walsh's uncharacteristic withdrawal from controversy on the advice of friends suggests some very strong pressure was put on him, including the inevitable reminder that future promotion would be jeopardised by continuing a controversy where he seemed to be challenging the episcopacy and exacerbating his already strained relations with the cardinal.

Walsh's attitude to McCabe was influenced by the latter's political views, and particularly by his denunciation in 1881 of the Ladies Land League for its involvement in the agrarian struggle. Archbishop Croke had been so incensed by the denunciation that he publicly criticised and ridiculed Archbishop McCabe in the *Freeman's Journal* of 17 March 1881. Croke's frequent private criticism of McCabe's "execrable politics" contributed, in the view of P.J. Walsh, "to fostering a prejudice in the mind of Dr Walsh".[51] The strained relations between Walsh and the cardinal was sufficiently widely known for George Errington, member of parliament for Longford, to make use of it to discredit Walsh at Rome. He alleged that after Croke's public difference with Archbishop McCabe over the Ladies Land League, Croke was cheered by the Maynooth students at the annual prize-giving, and that when McCabe protested about this to Walsh he was snubbed.[52] Following his defeat at the senate, Walsh withdrew from the "University Consultation Council", a body of Catholic educators whom the cardinal had invited to assist him, declining to give any further advice. Sadly, his estrangement from Cardinal McCabe lasted up to the latter's death,[53] which occurred quite unexpectedly on Wednesday, 11 February 1885.

In an appreciation of the dead prelate, Sir George Fottrell spoke of his absence of ambition and his great courage,[54] and significantly, Earl Spencer, the lord lieutenant, commented: "He not only stoutly supported the cause of law and order in the face of popular opposition, but he was also most friendly and moderate in all his views".[55] The comments were deliberately pointed, because it was well known that the late cardinal's views and stance on certain socio-political issues had resulted in disagreement with some of his fellow bishops, as has been seen, and with some prominent ecclesiastics such as Walsh, whose very prominence and ability led to his being widely mentioned as successor as soon as news of the death became known.

Walsh's succession to Dublin was certain to be strongly opposed by the British government. He was seen as too disputatious and nationalist, too close to Archbishop Croke. Already, indeed, the government had indicated its preferred candidate when, in 1883, through its unofficial representatives in Rome, George Errington, and Bernard Smith, OSB, abbot of San Calisto, Rome, it sought to have Canon Nicholas Donnelly appointed coadjutor to Cardinal McCabe with right of succession.[56] Errington, a member of an old Catholic family, and a Home Rule member of parliament, expressed his views on Walsh to the British foreign secretary, George Leveson-Gower, Earl Granville, on 12 February, the day after Cardinal McCabe's death. He feared the appointment of Walsh as archbishop, he declared, because he was "a violent and dangerous man", who would be vigorously supported by Croke and his friends. He asked to be allowed to urge on the pope as strongly as possible that the government had "a right to expect that as important a post as the see of Dublin should be occupied by a man of loyal and moderate views".[57] He had in mind, of course, Nicholas Donnelly, who, in 1883, had been made not coadjutor bishop but auxiliary bishop to Cardinal McCabe.

Rome was not unsympathetic to such views just then. It viewed Parnell and the Irish party with much suspicion, and was not convinced by a recent change of emphasis from agrarian agitation to political constitutionalism. It had been taken aback, moreover, by the Irish bishops, at their October meeting, 1884, entrusting to the Irish parliamentary party, without consultation with the Roman authorities, the task of urging the government to meet "the unsatisfied claims of Catholic Ireland in all branches of the education question".[58] Besides, there was the lure of British government support for Rome in its quarrel with the Portuguese government regarding ecclesiastical jurisdiction in Goa, the Portuguese protectorate in India, and also the attractive possibility of diplomatic relations with Britain, which would give a welcome diplomatic standing to the then much beleaguered papacy.

IV

From president to archbishop

On the death of a bishop jurisdiction passes to the cathedral chapter who, within
a short time, pass it to an elected vicar-capitular. When the chapter, consisting
of twenty canons, met on Friday, 13 February, just two days after the cardinal's
death, there was anxious speculation about who would be selected. How the
canons voted was likely to be an indication of how the more conservative Dublin
clergy would vote a month later, when the clergy of the diocese met to choose
the customary three names to be sent to Rome. The canons' vote gave Walsh a
substantial majority. He received twelve votes, and his nearest rival, Dr
Donnelly, only four. The latter, moreover, seems to have been strongly criticised
by members of the chapter.[1] Robert Browne, vice-president of Maynooth, sent
a telegram to Archbishop Croke with the news. Croke, in an exalted state at the
unexpected result, wrote immediately to Walsh: "Nothing ever reached me that
pleased me more than that which I have just got from Browne by telegram.
Thank God." He concluded: "All day I was brooding over the Dublin affair; but
was quite sure that the old fogies would go in for Donnelly. The tables are
turned completely. I'll say no more now."[2] Walsh replied briefly next day,
expressing his thanks and remarking, "awkward as the proceeding is for me, it
has one good side to it at all events. The 'Pale' is out of fashion."[3]

The lord lieutenant, Spencer, agreed with this last statement, but with very
different feelings. He found it most disturbing, he informed Granville on 19
February, that canons, appointed by Cardinals Cullen and McCabe, and therefore unlikely to be radical in their politics, should exhibit by their vote a basic
change in political outlook. And he observed that currently there was a reluctance among the clergy generally to be seen as supportive of public expressions
of loyalty.[4] If Walsh became archbishop this mood would spread and deepen,
hence it was imperative to prevent his appointment. Already for some years
Spencer had been one of Errington's strongest supporters. Errington had been
busy for more than four years exercising influence at the Vatican against such as
Archbishop Croke and Parnell. At the beginning of 1885 the Irish parliamentary
party thought it advisable to send Michael Davitt to Rome to counteract his
activities. Davitt was well received, and eventually had an audience with the
pope to whom, presumably, he expressed what he informed W.J. Stead of the
Pall Mall Gazette he would say to his Holiness if granted an interview: that
although "Ireland is today the great propagandist of the Catholic Church", and
"Irish emigrants have taken the seeds of the faith into England, Scotland, Wales,
America, Canada, South Africa, Australia", yet "this missionary work has never

been recognised at the centre of the Christian world", and "Ireland's enemies" had more than once been on the point of poisoning his Holiness against "the most devoted of Catholic nations" simply because he had never commanded his "faithful Irish people" to send "an accredited representative to reside at Rome" to advise from time to time "regarding Irish political or social movements, and their real bearing on religion and morals."[5]

Davitt was a strong advocate of Walsh's appointment to Dublin. His visit helped to weaken Errington's influence at Rome. Walsh, however, remained personally undecided about accepting the position if appointed. As previously when faced with new appointments – to vice-president and president of Maynooth— he hesitated and procrastinated. On 14 February 1885, he informed Dr Donnelly that he was "simply stunned" by the previous day's election result and was only "beginning to realise the position in which" he had "been placed".[6] Three days later following the funeral of Cardinal McCabe, he disconcerted Croke by stating that while he realised the importance of securing the appointment of an able churchman who would also be independent of the party of the Pale, he did not wish to have his own name put forward. Croke sought to dissuade him by describing his misgivings as "scruples", and he continued to exercise his considerable influence to have him commended by the Dublin clergy, and to plead his cause in Rome.

On 28 February, however, Walsh informed Croke that he was convinced that "by far the most useful position" he "could occupy for the service of the Irish church would be that of a representative in Rome". He was satisfied as to his fitness for such a position. He asked Croke to "think over this", and then proceeded to reveal his inner anguish and doubt about the position of archbishop.

> Speaking as I would speak to no one else, I am so thoroughly satisfied as to my unfitness for the place in Dublin I have not had two hours unbroken sleep since the election to the v. cap'ship. I twice went to Dublin fully determined to lithograph a letter to the p.p's and canons which would infallibly save me from getting even one vote on Tuesday week.[7]

Croke's reply has not survived. It was perhaps "burned when read" as Croke had requested.[8]

It is evident that Walsh's hesitation did not arise from any blindness about his own abilities. He could not but be aware of the qualities which persuaded many prelates and priests of his suitability for the see of Dublin. Prelates sought his advice as a theologian and canonist. He had demonstated administrative ability at Maynooth. He was familiar with and influential in educational affairs; and he was a fluent writer and formidable apologist in the Church's interests. A number of bishops would probably have echoed the words of John MacEvilly, archbishop of Tuam, when approached by Tobias Kirby, rector of the Irish College, Rome, in 1883 for his recommendation as to the auxiliary bishop of

Dublin. He did not know the Dublin diocesan clergy well, MacEvilly observed, but if pressed he would point to Walsh of Maynooth – "for learning, zeal, industry, indefatigable vigilance, he has no equal".[9] His words underscored the high reputation Walsh enjoyed outside his own diocese, and why his appointment to Dublin was to become a national issue.

But Walsh had no desire to be a bishop. His preference was for academic work, and his experience was almost entirely in that field and in administration. He had little inclination for a bishop's pastoral duties, and he disliked and dreaded preaching. As a preacher he had almost no capacity to convey fervour or other deep feeling, or to evoke such in his listeners. The pomp and circumstance of episcopal functions, moreover, held no attraction for his shy disposition, and his highly-strung, and impatient temperament; and the constant encroachment on time and attention which the position of archbishop required was not welcome to one who cherished the world of books, study and writing.

This did not mean that he was lacking ambition, as has been seen. He coveted distinction and being highly regarded, but he hoped to achieve this in the world of learning, or, more accurately, in an ambience where he would not be constricted by heavy pastoral obligations, but would be in a position to use his learning and specialised knowledge to influence ecclesiastical policy, and thereby Irish social and political affairs. To achieve this ambition in Rome itself, as the accredited representative of the Irish Catholic Church, was, evidently, the pinnacle of his desires.[10] Nevertheless, there was an aspect to the Dublin appointment which made him loath to withdraw his name. It was what he called in his letter of 28 February, "the political side of the case". He did not wish to leave the field to Donnelly because of the latter's conservative political leanings. The predicament oppressed him. "I feel that no one", he moaned, "was ever placed in such an awkward plight."

Croke, meanwhile, as indicated above, had been making the case in Rome for Walsh as archbishop. On 19 February 1885, he wrote to Dr Kirby at the Irish College, whose support was of major importance, pointing out that Walsh would have "the vast majority of the Dublin clergy" voting for him and that he was "a young, active, zealous, earnest, and wonderfully gifted man". He added, no doubt to Kirby's wry astonishment, that "in politics" Walsh was, he thought, "neutral".[11]

As the date of the clergy's vote on the *terna* (the three names to be sent to Rome) drew near, Walsh was the recipient of advice, support, and attack. The attack came from unionist newspapers and the government; the advice and support primarily from Croke. At the end of February, or the beginning of March, Croke forwarded a letter received from Michael Davitt, which advised that the Dublin clergy should be organised in favour of a candidate of sound nationalist principles. To this Walsh replied informatively that there was "no organising power, or next to none, in Dublin", and that in any event he did not "like the idea of wire-pulling in such a matter".[12] The following day, 4 March, he wrote again to his friend in Cashel. His confusion about his own preferences was growing. If he did receive the support of the Dublin clergy and was then passed over, it would be "such a public mark of disapproval from the Holy See that it would make it practically impossible" for him to maintain his position at Maynooth.[13]

To Errington at this stage, Walsh's cause appeared ominously strong, and Donnelly's quite weak.[14] In a letter to Cardinal Dominico Jacobini, secretary of Propaganda, as a consequence, he was at pains to emphasise how seriously the British government would view the appointment as archbishop of one who was "in accord with a political party hostile to the actual regime in Ireland", and, as if in passing, he remarked that it was a pity that Moran, archbishop of Sydney, was no longer in Ireland, as he alone among the Irish bishops was "fortified with the true Roman traditions" and in recent years had "displayed a rare prudence and firmness that would be very valuable to us at this moment in Ireland." He asked Jacobini to bring his obserations to the attention of his holiness.[15] It was a shrewd attempt to bring Moran into the reckoning to block Walsh's appointment, for nationalist support in Rome was likely to be split as Kirby could be expected to throw his considerable influence behind Moran, an old friend and protégé.

On 10 March, Walsh received 46 votes, of the 63 cast, compared to 12 for his nearest rival, Donnelly. The *Freeman's Journal*, commenting on the result, noted that Walsh had received more votes from the Dublin diocesan clergy than any episcopal candidate since the process was prescribed in Ireland in 1829. Walter M. Lee, dean of the cathedral chapter and a vicar-general of the late cardinal, explained to Kirby on 16 March: "The large majority in favour of Dr Walsh is to be ascribed to a conviction on the part of the clergy that this diocese, especially at the present time, requires a bishop of exceptional ability joined to a life of exemplary virtue; such is the opinion formed of Dr Walsh in and out of this diocese."[16]

Walsh's success was the signal for libellous attacks on him in the Dublin *Evening Mail* accusing him of being a dangerous revolutionary and the instigator of the 'no-rent manifesto', and, in a similar vein, Lord Granville, in April, solicited Lord Spencer to come up with definite anti-Walsh information which could be used by Errington in Rome. The lord lieutenant could only gather innuendos: Walsh was too much in league with politicians who had worked against "the firm administration of just laws". He had little respect for the crown. There was "a very strong feeling among lay Roman Catholics" against his appointment. "I cannot find more facts than these for you", Spencer concluded.

Frustration at rumours and innuendos, and at not being in a position to respond, added to Walsh's inner uncertainty. On 31 March 1885, he had informed Croke that every day made him "more and more anxious that the whole affair should be dealt with as soon as possible" and that some solution be found "that will make it unnecessary for me to be disturbed from where I am".[17]

Still, political issues continued to keep him in two minds. "Every fresh step that is being taken" made it more difficult for him, he informed Fr Michael Murphy, vice-president of Carlow College, shortly after the election result. "You cannot possibly realise", he explained with reference to the clergy, "the want of knowledge of the state of the country that exists in many minds".[18]

The increasing pressure on Walsh to resign himself to accepting the archbishopric was indicated by a letter of 31 March from "An Irish Catholic Nationalist", which reminded him that his nomination had been acclaimed by all points of view – by the "notorious" *Irish World*, New York, by the *Irish Times*, the *Nation*, *Tablet*, and *United Ireland*.[19] Meanwhile, Kirby had come out in support of Walsh; and on 26 March Errington had informed Granville that the pope had taken the appointment to Dublin from Propaganda and reserved it to himself.[20] As a result of this decision, and on the advice of Cardinal Manning, Leo XIII decided to summon some of the Irish bishops to Rome for consultation.[21]

On their way to Rome, Archbishops Croke and Mac Evilly, and five bishops, broke their journey in London and stayed with Cardinal Manning. They sought his support for the appointment to Dublin, and information about the purpose of their visit to Rome. Manning, however, had a concern of his own which he wished to explore. He was much opposed to the establishment of a parliament in Dublin, as he believed it would lead to separation, as he had informed the pope on 17 February, and this was not in the interest of either Irish Catholics or the Church in the empire. "Ireland", he emphasised, "is not a colony like Canada, but an integral and vital part of our country, as is often said, of the mother country."[22] On 12 April, immediately after his interview with the bishops, Manning was able to report that he was "greatly comforted" to find "Monsignor Croke's complete agreement" with his "humble opinions". Croke had informed him, he stated, that he, and all the Irish bishops, were unanimous "that the union between England and Ireland ought to be inviolably maintained". But, Manning continued, more ambiguously, "the exclusion of a parliament" did not mean the exclusion of "the system of administration or domestic (local) government that is called 'Home Rule';" and he was certain that Ireland would "shortly receive from the Imperial Parliament the same freedom and control over the internal administration that Scotland and England possess".[23]

As the Irish bishops' conception of Home Rule was so modest, and as Manning was easily convinced of Walsh's suitability for Dublin, the London meeting was deemed satisfactory by both sides. It marked the beginning of an informal, effective alliance between Manning and the Irish bishops. By virtue of this understanding, which continued until the cardinal's death early in 1892, Manning acquired some very real political influence through the Irish party at Westminister, while the Irish bishops gained the cardinal's much-needed support at Rome.

Manning went to work on Walsh's behalf later in the month. He met with Sir Charles Dilke, president of the Local Government Board, an old friend, and, on 26 April put his proposals to him in writing. He requested that the government should "in no way either officiously through Errington or any other, attempt to influence the election", and went on to single out Walsh as the outstanding candidate, "who would unite the whole episcopate". As to efforts "to represent Dr Walsh as a nationalist", the cardinal remarked disingenuously, "he is no more so than I am, and whether that is excessive or obstructive you will judge".²⁴ Dilke was given permission to use the letter as he saw fit. When he brought the cardinal's estimate of Walsh to Earl Spencer's notice, the latter commented dryly: "I wish it may be so. Responsibility does wonders." But in a minute to Joseph Chamberlain, MP, the lord lieutenant was blunt: "H.E. the Cardinal is wrong in his estimate of Dr Walsh."²⁵

Rumours in Dublin that Moran was being recalled from Sydney to become archbishop of Dublin, led Walsh to write to Croke in Rome. The latter had no information, but was depressed and angry, announcing that the bishops had been brought to Rome "for a lecture on politics from the pope"²⁶ He himself had not helped matters by having had "a rather bitter controversy" with Monsignor Machi who had complained to the pope.²⁷

As the days passed and there was no papal decision, Croke returned to Ireland. Next day, 7 June, he wrote to Manning that the people could not be persuaded that the pope had not entered into some sort of agreement with the government by which he would obtain "certain privileges for Catholic minorities in England, Malta, and elsewhere", in return for setting aside "the popular candidate for Dublin", and appointing instead Dr Moran who was "detested", or some other "equally cold and colourless ecclesiastic". He earnestly warned Manning that if it turned out that English influence was so strong in the Vatican "as to cause His Holiness to discredit one of the foremost ecclesiastics of the day", simply because he happened not to be '*persona grata*' to the government", he really feared "that the Irish people at home and abroad" would "cease to believe in the impartial(ity) or to respect the person and office of the present pontiff". This, he assured the cardinal, was his "solemn and sober judgement", and he hoped that Manning, as the "most influential ecclesiastic within the realm", would convey it "to the proper quarter" and "thus prevent, if it be not too late, one of the greatest church disasters that have occurred within our time."²⁸ Five days later Manning responded to this rather apocalyptic letter with the assurance that "no adverse, or other decision, has been yet come to", that he would leave nothing undone that he could do, and that he had already written fully about Dublin, pointing out: "1. The supreme danger of even *seeming* to be swayed from here (England). 2. The *united* wish of the bishops. 3. The *worthiness* of the man."²⁹

Before he received that reply from Manning, Croke had heard from Kirby and from Walsh that Moran had actually been summoned to Rome from Sydney. The fact seemed conclusive. "There will be bad work, and I shall never raise hand or voice to prevent or allay the trouble ...", he informed Walsh on 13

June.[30] Meanwhile, on 9 June, Walsh had written to Manning in a mixture of confusion and relief. The office of president could not be held by one "on whose career an adverse judgement had been passed by the Holy See", yet he personally rejoiced at the propspect of getting back to theological work. "But", he added, "I cannot shut my eyes to the prospect of all that may happen besides."[31]

What "may happen besides" happened eventually, and unexpectedly, on 23 June, when Leo XIII informed Cardinal Simeoni, prefect of Propaganda, that he had appointed William J. Walsh archbishop of Dublin, and directed him to inform Walsh at once. The news was telegraphed to Walsh that day by Kirby. The appointment was published the following day, 24 June 1885.

There were expressions of relief and joy in many parts of Ireland which continued for some days. On 30 June Croke expressed his relief in a letter to Kirby, and on the same day the dean of the Dublin cathedral chapter, Walter M. Lee, assured Kirby, in language similar to that used by Croke, that "the providence of God" had brought them through "perhaps the greatest danger the church in Ireland ever encountered: the exclusion of Dr Walsh would have shaken the fabric to its foundations and the result would have been worse than the infliction of the penal laws."[32] High-flown language was also used to convey the sense of exultation. On 7 July, Archbishop MacEvilly informed Manning "that there *never was* a more popular man in Ireland than our Holy Father", and that "nothing was ever witnessed here" like the ovations given the bishops on their return to Ireland. "It proves", he declared in conclusion, "that there is still a great union between clergy and people. The appointment to Dublin will be a firm bond to keep all together."[33] The public welcome represented as testimony to the "great union between clergy and people" was rather a product of national feeling, the celebration of a triumph over British opposition and a belief that Walsh was anything but the neutral figure which Manning and Croke had depicted. Errington, partly recognising this, pronounced the appointment "most unfortunate on the state and the church". "The misfortune is", he declared, "that his (Walsh's) nomination throws the whole Irish church, and the hundreds of good quiet priests who are now painfully resisting the agitation, into the arms of the nationalists."[34]

On 28 June, Walsh informed Croke that the pope had requested that he be consecrated in Rome. Croke urged him to respond positively, and, lest he be short of money, enclosed a cheque for £500. "I would wish you to be open-handed in Rome", he observed, "and the cheque would enable you to be so. Nothing takes so well in the Eternal City; and word spreads like wild fire."[35] Much moved, Walsh described this as "the truest act of friendship I have ever known" and remarked that the money was welcome as he did not have "a private source of income" and his "balance at the bank" was "not worth talking of."[36] On 7 July, on the eve of his departure for his consecration in Rome, he returned Croke's cheque with thanks. There were now sufficient funds in hand. Then he went on to raise doubts once more about accepting the archbishopric.

Before accepting the archbishopric, he planned to put before the pope his suitability as an Irish representaitve in Rome rather than as an archbishop.[37] Croke
responded to Walsh's letter in his usual down-to-earth manner. "Do not be
coquetting at all with the Dublin See", he admonished. "Fit or not fit, you must
go ahead now ... I now tell you *deliberately* that Dr Moran was called home to
be appointed to Dublin, and that he would have been appointed had we not
spoken out so plainly as we did."[38] This letter seems to have brought an end to
Walsh's temporising.

At this point, as a means towards a better appreciation of Walsh, it is worth
pausing to review his appointment from his perspective, and also to note once
again how, as in the university dispute, there was a certain ambivalence, involving an element of unreality, so that he appeared to be functioning in apparently
contradictory ways. With respect to Univeristy College he had claimed to be
wholeheartedly in its support, while pursuing a line which many thought undermined the college. In respect to the archbishopric something similar seems to
have happened. He left himself in the race, encouraged support, while yet saying
privately, even after his selection by the pope, that he did not wish to be archbishop but wished to be the bishops' accredited representative in Rome. He
wrote in those terms to Croke as late as 7 July, as has been seen, and also to
Dilke.[39] In other letters to Croke, however, he seemed to accept his consecration
as archbishop as a fact. To Bishop Donnelly on 24 June, the day after hearing
of his appointment, he spoke of already experiencing "the feeling of difference
... between looking up at things and looking down at them."[40] Again, a few days
before he wrote to Croke and Dilke expressing his reservations about accepting
the archbishopric, he had conveyed his thanks to the Revd Mother of the
Convent of St Alphonsus, Clonliffe West, Dublin, for her congratulations, and
had added unreservedly:

> I am placed indeed in a position of heavy responsibility and this in most
> critical times. And it is the very difficulty of the crisis in all its circum-
> stances that makes it, I fear, impossible for me to decline the position.[41]

Walsh's blowing hot and cold on his appointment as archbishop reflected, no
doubt, his struggle with conflicting motives: his personal preference as opposed
to a sense of responsibility "in most critical times". But it seems fair to assume
from all the evidence that there was a further factor drawing him towards acceptance, namely, the prestige, power, and influence that went with the position.
To a man who enjoyed public notice and prominence the declarations of support and praise from bishops, clergy, and people, in the face of opposition from
an unpopular government, could hardly fail to be intoxicating; and all the more
so when his name and cause "was discussed in the columns of newspapers not
merely in the British Isles but also in Canada, Australia, India, even at Shanghai,
and of course in the United States."[42] Finally, and personally persuasive, was the

linking of the power and influence with what he termed "the political side of the case", in order that, unlike Cardinal McCabe, he could be a prominent, assertive voice in support of Catholic and nationalist rights, particularly in such areas as education, land tenure, and Home Rule.

ASSERTING HIS POSITION

The government was very conscious of the importance of the Catholic archbishop of Dublin to the cause of peace and good order. The strength of Spencer's opposition to Walsh's appointment emphasised this. Aware of his privileged position, Walsh called on the new Conservative lord lieutenant, Henry Howard Molyneux, earl of Carnarvon, on 8 July, just prior to setting out for Rome. He was not unmindful that his overture would be well received at the Vatican.

Writing of the meeting to Kirby from London, *en route* to Rome, on 10 July, Walsh detailed how he and Molloy had been graciously received by Carnarvon and how the latter had invited him "to speak freely with him, not merely on the education question, but also on the state of the country generally". Walsh thanked him, and availed of the opportunity. The two most urgent matters, he explained, were "an inquiry into some of the judicial proceedings of the last four years, and a good measure to enable the tenants to *purchase* their lands". As to the first, he singled out the convictions in the Maamtrasna trial, as a result of which three men were hanged and five sentenced to penal servitude for life for the brutal murder at Maamtrasna, Co. Mayo, of three children and their parents on 8 August 1882. "I am satisfied", Walsh observed, "that one poor man who was hanged, and three others undergoing penal servitude for life, are as innocent as his Excellency or myself." Walsh also reported to Kirby that "on the education question his Excellency is *with* us to a surprising extent"; and he added, "I dare say there will be an outrage about my going to the vice-regal lodge", but, he concluded, "to my surprise" the Irish members of parliament "all seemed glad to hear that I had called on his Excellency, and established friendly relations with him".[43]

Carnarvon was impressed with Walsh, and set about following his advice. He spoke with the lord chancellor, Edward Gibson, Lord Ashbourne, an old acquaintance of Walsh from the days of the O'Keeffe case, about his meeting with the archbishop-elect, and the following day emphasised in writing "how strongly", with reference to the Land Purchase Act, the archbishop "had dwelt upon 1. the payment of a very *moderate* annual payment, 2. the consequent extension of time over which these annual payments may be spread with regard to a purchase bill."[44] The successful Ashbourne Land Purchase Act, which became law on 11 August 1885, was an important step in meeting both requirements.

On the Maamtrasna issue too, Carnarvon demonstrated his good will, and the importance he attached to the advice of the new prelate. He discussed the matter with members of the Irish party, and on 17 July the issue was debated in the House of Commons. Walsh, shortly after his arrival in Rome, read in the *Freeman's Journal* of the debate in the House on Maamtrasna and on the land purchase bill, and, much gratified, wrote to Carnarvon on 21 July to express his appreciation of his efforts "at this critical time". "At last", he observed, "we begin to see some prospect of a restoration of feeling among our Irish people of respect for the law, and for the maintenance of order in Ireland. Your Excellency's personal action has, I believe, contributed more than any other influence to the bringing about of this better state of things." Walsh trusted that he was "not taking too great a liberty in saying this". But, he continued artfully, "I have promised your Excellency to use the privilege of my office in speaking very plainly to you as her Majesty's representative in Ireland".[45] Carnarvon in reply conveyed his appreciation of Walsh's "frank and kindly expressions", and added: "I hail your Grace's recognition of my desire to meet the constitutional desires of all good and loyal Irishmen."[46] Before long, however, even before Walsh returned from Rome, the viceroy was to experience further "frank" but less than "kindly" expressions from the new assertive archbishop.

PAPAL INTERVIEW AND CONSECRATION AS ARCHBISHOP

Walsh arrived in Rome on Sunday, 19 July, and was received by Cardinal Simeoni, to whom he had forwarded the written statement asking the pope to excuse him from accepting the archbishopric. On the following Wednesday, 22 July, he had audience with Leo XIII. "It lasted three-quarters of an hour", Walsh reported to Croke the next day. "Nothing could be more satisfactory, whether as to substance or as to tone." "I was quite prepared," he explained, "for a sort of a homily on the necessity of observing moderation etc., there was nothing of the kind, nothing even approaching it." The pope spoke most freely about the opposition to his appointment, the stories about his "most extreme politics etc., but he said that he had satisfied himself it was *tutto esagerato, tutto falso*". With respect to his (Walsh's) letter to the pope, Walsh observed, "he told me that Simeoni had come to him with a letter of mine but when he heard it was to raise difficulties about accepting the appointment, he (the pope) said he had refused to listen to it". "This", he said, "is a *'cosa risoluta'*." "He knew", Walsh added, "I had not looked for the position (of archbishop) and he put me under obedience to go on without hesitation", and the pope reminded him that to refuse work from lawful authority was not the spirit of the Church.

His Holiness spoke of many other things: of Errington, of Dr Moran coming from Sydney, of appointing a recognised Irish representative at Rome – concerning which the pope was favourable and approved Walsh's offer to bring the matter before a synod of the Irish church. But where the choice of Walsh as archbishop was concerned, "he told me repeatedly", Walsh emphasised, "that it was the strong recommendation of the Irish bishops" who had been summoned to Rome "that had most weight with him in my appointment – their confidence in me, and the prospect of their being more united if I were in Dublin than if anyone else were there. 'They were', the pope said, 'unanimous – we may call it unanimous'." Finally, Leo XIII instructed him to take a good rest after his consecration, but, Walsh commented ruefully, "his idea of resting is staying in Rome for the month of August!"[47]

Subsequently, Moran was to add in a letter to a friend, Bernard Fitzpatrick, that the pope infomed him that he had planned to transfer him from Sydney to Dublin and send Walsh to Sydney, but that he changed his mind because of the strong feeling among Irish Catholics in favour of Walsh and because he had found out for himself the lying nature of the anti-Walsh conspiracy.[48]

The change of plan, which meant that Moran, instead of becoming archbishop of Dublin would be appointed a cardinal and consecrate the new archbishop, seemed to have quietly amused Leo XIII. For, as Walsh informed Nicholas Donnelly from Rome on 24 July: "The pope seems to attach some extraordinary importance to my being consecrated by Sydney, for he is talking of it to everyone who has an audience."[49] William Walsh was consecrated on Sunday, 2 August 1885, in the church of St Agatha dei Goti. Cardinal Patrick F. Moran was the consecrating prelate, and the assistant bishops were Tobias Kirby, rector of the Irish College, and James Donnelly, bishop of Clogher. On the following Thursday, Walsh set out for Ireland by easy stages.

FIRST EXPRESSIONS OF PRELATICAL DISPLEASURE

On his homeward journey he learned of the passing of the Educational Endowments Bill on 14 August. The act provided for a commission of five "to regulate the various endowments that had been made to Irish educational institutions".[50] Clearly, in the contemporary ethos, the religious composition of the commission was a key factor. Walsh was displeased and disappointed with the representation afforded to Catholics. He and Molloy had impressed on Carnarvon the importance of having the bill passed in that session of parliament, and they had hoped that the lord lieutenant's good will would be reflected in the composition of the commission. The bill had been passed on the last day of the session, but the representation on the commission did not meet Catholic expectations. As structured, the commission had two commissioners (each of whom could veto decisions made by the commission as a whole) and three assistant commissioners. The commissioners were Lord Justice Gerald Fitzgibbon, a member of the Church of Ireland, and the lord chancellor, John Naish, who was distrusted by Walsh as a 'liberal Catholic'. Of the assistant commissioners, two were Protestants, Professor Dougherty (Presbyterian) and Anthony Traill (Church of Ireland), and the third was to be a Catholic.

The bishops at their July meeting "had passed a most reasonable resolution", Walsh reminded Kirby from Paris on 24 August. They had asked "that in all such cases Catholics should be represented in proportion to our numbers". "Now on this new commission", he complained, "they have actually put us in a minority!" He felt sure that Carnarvon had not been listened to by his colleagues. It illustrated "how hopeless" it was to proceed satisfactorily "while purely Irish questions of this sort" were "dealt with, in utter disregard of Irish wishes, by an English legislature and administration".⁵¹ The following day Carnarvon, who presumably thought that as much as could be expected from an English legislature had been obtained, wrote Walsh seeking his recommendation for the third assistant commissioner. "It is a matter in which", he explained, "I specially desire to make a wise choice, and one that will generally commend itself to public approval, and I know that in requesting your aid I cannot go to a better authority."⁵² Walsh's reply took him aback.

On 30 August the new archbishop replied from Meanieres-en-Bray, Normandy, where he was spending a few days of quiet retreat near the shrine of his predecessor, St Laurence O'Toole. He availed of his position to express displeasure as if on behalf of the entire Irish Catholic church, before finally providing an indirect response to the viceroy's request. "I fear", he proclaimed, "that in the circumstances I cannot be of much help in the very important matter about which you have been good enough to write." "The constitution of the commission, as regards the provision to be made for the protection of the interests of our Catholic schools, is so decidedly unsatisfactory that I cannot but regard as hopeless the prospect of its proceedings commanding the confidence of the country". Consequently, Walsh continued, he would be putting himself in a "wrong position" if he put forward someone as requested, and thereby implied that the act made "even fairly satisfactory provision for the protection of the interests of the Catholics of Ireland". He then proceeded to virtually lecture the viceroy on the complexities of Catholic interests in education, and at the end, without making a direct recommendation, suggested that Dr Molloy, if he accepted the position, would probably be acceptable to the different Catholic interests because of "his neutral position as rector of our Catholic University organization."⁵³

It was Carnarvon's first experience of Walsh's capacity for unexpected, and seemingly mercurial reactions. Thereafter, he proceeded more cautiously. He replied on 4 September, the day Walsh was due home. It was a brief, gently diplomatic response. He thanked the archbishop for his letter. "I understand the difficulty in which you feel yourself placed", he assured him, "and thank you for the suggestion which you informally make me." "I shall hope", he added, "to act upon it." He concluded: "Personally, of all with whom I have become acquainted, none could be more agreeable to me than Dr Molloy."⁵⁴ The soft answer left Walsh with a desire to make amends. The opportunity came on 12 September, when he had a free moment from engagements. Knowing Lady Carnarvon's wish to visit the Mater Misericordia Hospital, he invited the viceroy and his wife to the hospital, offering to act personally as their host and guide.⁵⁵ But before that there was the memorable and remarkable homecoming.

THE HOMECOMING

Archbishop Walsh arrived at Kingstown harbour (Dun Laoghaire) on Friday afternoon, 4 September 1885, to an enthusiastic reception. Crowds lined the pier to greet the mail-boat, and before he came ashore he was presented with two addresses of welcome. From the harbour he travelled by train to Westland Row station, Dublin, where again he received an ovation and was met by the lord mayor and city corporation in their robes of office. He was presented with an address which extended to him a civic welcome, expressed pleasure at his appointment, and the hope that peace and unity would mark the onward progress of the country towards the restoration of a native legislature. Walsh took particular note of this expressed hope and declared significantly in his reply, that it was his deep conviction that for the many grievances of the island there was "but one effectual course – the restoration to Ireland of that right of which we were deprived now nigh a century ago", and he rejoiced with them "that the flag which fell from the dying hand of O'Connell had once more been boldly uplifted".

Conscious, however, that there were Catholics in the archdiocese who would differ from this point of view, and that he was archbishop of all Catholics, Walsh earnestly insisted: "In every scene and sphere of duty I shall, with God's help, know no difference between those whose views in public affairs are most thoroughly in sympathy with mine, and those from whose honest opinions I am most widely divergent".[56]

Following his induction into his see at the Pro-Cathedral, Marlborough Street, on Monday, 7 September, Walsh and the members of the corporation moved to Holy Cross College, Clonliffe, where there was the presentation of an address from the clergy and laity of the archdiocese. Among those who contributed to the words of welcome, was William Delany, of University College, who spoke of his Grace's "marvellous" intellectual powers, and "largeness of heart", and predicted that he would be "a centre of unity". "He was", Delany declared interestingly, "a man largely tolerant to those who differed from him, and even though he could not join them he would go with them in unity of action."[57] In the official address, reference was made to the many evils to be remedied, and, once more, to the need for "a thorough reconstruction of the system" under which Ireland was governed. Walsh concluded his reply by thanking all present, and asking their prayers that he "might not betray the trust reposed" in him by the pope, and might not be swayed to the right or to the left "by the fear of human censure or by the foolish and unprofitable desire of human praise."[58]

Up to the end of September the new archbishop received addresses and made speeches almost daily. In a number of the speeches he mentioned special interests, or features which he wished to have associated with his period as bishop. On 14 September, again at Clonliffe College, which had been founded by Cardinal Cullen, he spoke of Cullen to the students with much feeling, and suggested that all bishops, priests and students, might find "a noble model for imitation" in the cardinal's "steadfast devotion to duty, untiring energy in the work of the pastoral office, and unfailing care for the poor and afflicted". Another characteristic quality of his celebrated predecessor which he emphasised "was the kindly and affectionate interest he always took in the progress ... of every ecclesiastical student who came within his inspiring influence."[59]

In the areas singled out as "a model for imitation", Walsh showed an active interest almost immediately. Devotion to duty and untiring energy in work were almost second nature to him, but he manifested a deep concern for the poor and disadvantaged from the beginning of his episcopacy. Approached by the orphanage committee of Our Lady of Mount Carmel, who sought to provide a large house for Catholic children rescued from proselytisers, he provided financial and moral support. The committee, in their address to him, denounced the proselytisers, as distinct from other Protestants, as part of a society founded during the great famine whose members were "mission agents who degrade religion" by bribing "the homeless, the sick, and the dying". Such practices, it was pointed out, were frequent in Dublin: the agents calling importuningly on the houses of the poor without hindrance from the law. Referring to such behaviour on 21 September, Walsh spoke so trenchantly as to lead some Protestant papers to accuse him of inciting to a breach of the peace. If the law was powerless to protect the poor "in their humble homes from the visits of those insidious emissaries of sin", he observed, "it would seem to me anything but strange, if they had long since taken the matter into their own hands to protect themselves."[60] The following year, June 1886, the house sought by the orphanage committee was opened, and named Sacred Heart Home, Drumcondra. The same year, Walsh purchased premises in Abbey Street to provide accommodation for Catholic working boys – newsboys, orphans, and other neglected children living a precarious existence on the streets of Dublin, including also country lads apprenticed to traders in the city.[61]

Other occasions during these weeks when he revealed personal aims or attitudes were – in the course of an address to the people of his mensal parish, and during his response to an address from the Dr Cahill Memorial Committee.[62] In the former, he acknowledged that the success of his ministry must "chiefly depend on the union of the clergy ... with one another and with me their bishop", and on the union which would bind the members of the faithful "with us their pastors and spiritual fathers." On the occasion of his response to the Cahill Committee, he observed that "in Ireland the line between religion and politics is a line by no means easy to draw", adding "I have never known that feat to be accomplished with success."[63]

By 23 September even Walsh's energy was evaporating. On that date he complained to Kirby: "I am worked nearly to death receiving addresses; but I try to turn them to some practical account by making my reply an exposition of some important question – such as education and the like."[64] On education he was on familiar ground and had much to say. At different venues from 9

September, when he was at St Vincent's College, Castleknock, to 29 September at St Patrick's Teacher Training College, Drumcondra, he gave expression to years of study on the needs and grievances in primary, intermediate, and third level education in Ireland. The one common denominator, in the comprehensive exposition, was a demand for at least equality of treatment for the majority population. In his presentations he arraigned the past policy of various governments, but on 1 October, at Blackrock College, he turned his attention to the current administration – subjecting the Educational Endowments Act to public criticism, and speaking as if he were the voice of the entire episcopate. He was to become such on most issues.

The Endowments Act touched a deep chord. Although Catholics held "the vast majority of the successful schools in the country", they were to be, in respect of the five commissioners, "in a minority of two". "Is this equality? Is this fair play?" he queried: questions which, as noted, reflected a driving force within him, and which underlined what was to be a predominating preoccupation of his episcopate. Four days later, the Catholic bishops at their general meeting, pressed by Walsh, called on the government to give Catholics their due representation on the Endowments Commission, and recommended that if no action was taken the Catholic commissioners should resign at once.[65] Reconciliation with the government was effected only after some time and with difficulty. The new archbishop had made his presence felt. It was clear that he would not be taken for granted, and that he was likely to be no uncertain voice with respect to the rights and needs of his people.

PART TWO

The politics of a churchman, 1885-91

V

The leading episcopal voice on Land and Home Rule, 1885-7

IMPATIENT TO ACHIEVE

Walsh's assurance and assertiveness had, as noticed already, an impatient and intemperate side which occasioned difficulties for himself and for others and which he had to learn to curb. One of the first to remind him of this after his consecration as bishop was a fellow prelate, one of the few who had anything comparable to Walsh's intellectual powers, John Healy, coadjutor bishop of Clonfert. There was little love lost between them. Sending belated congratulations to the new archbishop, Healy made a pointed reference to his speech at Clonliffe, in the course of which he had assured his audience that he would respect difference of opinion. Healy expressed the hope "that you will extend the same toleration to those of your brethren in the episcopate, who in some things may differ from you ..."[1] Healy, however, did not confine his criticism within the episcopal body. Little over a month later, on 28 October, Lord Carnarvon noted after a long conversation with him:

> Evident suspicion of and friction with Dr Walsh – who is driving the bishops, as well as the Irish parliamentary party, much farther and faster than they like. The bishop complained, *inter alia*, of Dr W's opposition to the R. University and the grounds on which it rested – and he hinted that Archbishop Croke was of the same mind in this respect.[2]

Croke's opposition to his protégé and friend, Walsh, on university matters had surfaced previously on the fellowship issue, now it came to the fore during the bishops' general meeting of 6 October. The occasion was a resolution criticising the Jesuits for seeking a state endowment for University College. The story has been told in some detail elsewhere.[3] Here, a brief outline serves to further illustrate the complex personality of the new archbishop of Dublin.

The issue arose because of the financial needs of University College. Although owned by the bishops, it received no financial assistance from them. William Delany, learning that there was a possibility of a grant-in-aid from the government, discussed the matter with Walsh and, believing he had the latter's approval, made out his case and sent copies to the lord lieutenant and to members of the Irish party, which acted in the House of Commons on behalf of the bishops with respect to educational matters. In a parliamentary debate on 25 July

1885, the proposal for a grant-in-aid was put forward by Justin McCarthy in the absence of Parnell. It was narrowly defeated. Two months later, on 25 September, Delany was shocked to learn from Bishop Butler that his motives and actions were being misconstrued and that there was a motion before the bishops' October meeting querying the action of the Jesuit Fathers in seeking a public endowment for University College. At Butler's request, Delany drew up a statement of the facts relating to his grant-in-aid proposal and sent copies to Butler and Croke on 4 October. Butler replied next day that he had "never read a stronger case, or one better put". Also on 4 October Delany called to Archbishop Walsh's residence, handed in a copy of his report, and requested a brief interview before the bishops' meeting. Walsh evidently felt under attack. To Delany's astonishment, the only reply he received was a curt letter on the morning of the meeting acknowledging his "extraordinary document" and stating that, in view of the statements in it regarding himself, he must "in self-defence" say "that for the present it is better that any communication between us on this question should be in writing". Walsh also remarked that he felt it necessary, "on a question of such importance as this", that he should be in a position to produce, should the occasion arise, "unquestionable evidence" of the precise nature of any views expressed by him.[4]

Mystified and upset, Delany contacted Croke, who was in Dublin for the meeting. The archbishop promised "to do all that lay in his power to have fair play done". At the meeting, the resolution was vigorously opposed by Croke who, in Delany's words, "declined to be a party to any action of the kind, deprecated strongly the bishops placing themselves in seeming antagonism to the Jesuits, and stopped the whole transaction".[5]

Walsh was fortunate in having Croke's friendship. He knew that the older man understood him and was on his side. A further counsellor and guide was Cardinal Manning, who also made allowances and was supportive. This appeared, among other instances, with respect to Walsh's belligerent criticism at Blackrock on 1 October of the Educational Endowments Act,[6] and his subsequent persuasion of the bishops to call on the Catholic commissioners to resign.[7] Some time later, Carnarvon recorded a meeting with Cardinal Manning in the course of which they "discussed Archbishop Walsh" and the cardinal "spoke of him as an eager, impulsive man, who was not quite as prudent in his utterances as he could be". "I told him", Carnarvon then added, "what had passed in the Educational Endowments Commission with regard to Molloy, and I could see he was much distressed."[8]

A historic year for Walsh ended with a supportive letter from Manning. In response to a communication from Walsh suggesting that Irish interests were being subordinated "to the interests of the English Catholic body in the question of education", he assured him that they were "on the same lines". "You may rely on me", Manning promised, to refuse "to subordinate the Irish movement to any English question", and he continued with a blend of humanity and spirituality that could not but appeal to the much younger churchman. "I know that I labour under the *peccatum originale*" (the original sin of being English), "but ... let us lay aside all mistrust, for if you and I are of one mind we may better serve Ireland and the Church than if we were doubtful of each other". As to the newspapers, including the *Tablet*, about which Walsh had complained, Manning too "read with indignation" the language of most of them. "And I know how I stand alone", he declared, "in my judgement about Ireland among the old Catholic families. It was so in O'Connell's time; it will be so till this generation is passed away. But if this divides, it weakens us, and if we should be weakened the faith and souls will suffer with you and us". Finally, he remarked with respect to the *Tablet*, "let me ask you always to let me know what you find unfit in it. I will always, as I have always, do my best to correct it."[9] The promise was welcome. Herbert Vaughan, the bishop of Salford, who was responsible for the *Tablet*, had not been particularly responsive to a letter from Walsh.

The care and sensitivity manifested by the elderly and most influential of English-speaking prelates, was not just a mark of kindly interest in a young colleague; it was also a recognition of Walsh's capacity for leadership and immense good, and perhaps great harm, and that, therefore, he was someone deserving, and needing, special guidance and support. Even as Croke was a support to Walsh, the astute and influential cardinal was a support to both.

Despite the experiences of Carnarvon and Delany, and the reminder from Healy, Archbishop Walsh was generally considered a temperate and gracious man, and an attentive listener. In the popular perception, moreover, his assertive running-start as archbishop was greatly appreciated. Before long, indeed, his intellectual prowess, powers of administration, concentrated work, and decisive leadership, were to evoke general respect, and to raise episcopal authority and morale. The bishops' dependence on the Irish party to represent them in parliament with respect to educational issues, and other matters of interest to them, became less marked as Walsh's influence increased. His ability, assurance, and outspokenness made the hierarchy a force on the popular issues of land purchase and Home Rule, and in the quest for educational equality. In these he became the leading episcopal spokesman, and carried the great majority of the bishops with him except in relation to certain aspects of university education. The dissenting minority tended to include Bishops John Healy, of Clonfert, later archbishop of Tuam, to a lesser extent Andrew Higgins, of Kerry, and T.A. O'Callaghan, of Cork, and strongly, before long, Edward Thomas O'Dwyer of Limerick. In the public mind, however, Walsh and Croke, but especially Walsh, who was so often in the news, were identified as the upholders of two of the people's cherished heritages – their nationhood and their religion.

The year of Walsh's consecration opened with Parnell's '*Ne plus ultra*' speech at Cork, 21 January 1885: "No man has the right to fix the boundary to the march of a nation". In July the government introduced Lord Ashbourne's Irish Land Purchase Bill in the House of Commons; and, sensing that the time was right, Parnell sent the draft of a Home Rule constitution for Ireland to Gladstone on 30 October. When the latter declined to make an explicit declaration on Home Rule, Parnell, on 21 November, issued a manifesto calling on the Irish in Great Britain to vote against the Liberal party in the forthcoming general election. In the election, which ran from 23 November to 19 December, the Irish parliamentary party achieved a resounding victory, capturing 85 of the 103 Irish seats as well as an English seat in Liverpool. It gave them the balance of power between the 335 Liberals and the 249 Conservatives.

COMBINING POLITICAL INVOLVEMENT AND DIOCESAN DUTIES

Walsh involved himself in political elections immediately after his return to Dublin. He supported the candidacy of Edmund Dwyer Gray, MP, owner of the *Freeman's Journal*, for a Dublin constituency, despite Parnell's disapproval. Gray was elected, and became more than ever a supporter and promoter of Walsh in his newspaper. It was an exhilarating time for the new archbishop. His energy appeared endless. He seemed to be everywhere at once. "I have just come from a heavy day's work at Bray", he informed Kirby on 29 November 1885. There was meeting after meeting, address after address, all on one day. "So," he exclaimed, "Your Grace sees that I am incorrigible!" "At any rate, I cannot see our good people disappointed." "Is it not a grand thing", he asked, "to see them thus crowding around me in the very midst of their election excitement?" "Whether I am here long or short," he continued, "I do not like to lose any opportunity of keeping our good hold of them."[10]

The result of the election made a great difference. Having the balance of power "is a great advantage", Bishop James Browne of Ferns wrote to Kirby on 15 December 1885. He trusted it would mean an end to dissension among Catholics and bring some measure of Home Rule.[11] Another, less sophisticated but enthusiastic correspondent of Kirby's, Maurice Mooney, parish priest of Cahir, Co. Tipperary, exulted that same day: "Since the appointment of the archbishop of Dublin, our poor Ireland scarcely knows herself. She is full of life and hope and gratitude. There is no doubt now of Home Rule."[12]

On 17 December 1885, Gladstone's conversion to Home Rule was announced. It now seemed that a form of Irish self-government was likely sooner rather than later. The bishops, at Walsh and Croke's prompting, were to secure their political position by announcing their approval of Home Rule the following February. Prior to this the hierarchy had established the right of the clergy to a major say in the selection of parliamentary candidates, and had conceded that Parnell's movement was essentially 'constitutional' rather than 'revolutionary' in its methods. A new arrangement had effectively come into being. In place of the former conventions between church and government, the arrangement now was that the nationalist representatives would work to defend and enlarge the Catholic Church's interests in education, while the bishops would approve the party's efforts to achieve Irish self-government along 'constitutional' lines. The arrangement was unwelcome to the Conservatives, but relatively acceptable to the majority of Liberals who had declared for Home Rule.

The imminent expectation of Home Rule, together with the relations between tenants and landlords, occupied much of Walsh's time and attention in the closing months of 1885 and during 1886. There were also numerous letters to Kirby to keep him informed, and to explain happenings from the point of view of the bishops and the Irish party for the benefit of the pope and his advisers. Many public letters, moreover, were written by the archbishop to newspapers, and there were letters to prominent politicians, as well as numerous meetings and discussions.

With all, he still found time for diocesan business – correspondence with priests, regular meetings with the canons of the diocese, canon law issues, attention to priests with problems, and no end of addresses to and involvements with parish confraternities and organisations, especially those concerned with the poor and marginalised, not to mention the large number of confirmations to be performed across the diocese. In that first year there were also structural developments needing attention, such as laying the foundation stone for a new primary school at Rathmines, and for the Hospice for the Dying at Harold's Cross, decorating the Pro-Cathedral, opening the Sacred Heart Home for children rescued from proselytisers, the completion of the purchase of a Working Boys' Club, and of a church extension at Greystones. In addition, there were the requirements of attendance at various civic and organisational functions, the need to meet with teacher organisations, and to look to the special needs and demands of the numerous primary schools in the diocese. He increased his work load by availing of his visits to educational establishments to speak at length on primary and university education, and on school endowments.[13] His Roman correspondence for 1886 shows him, moreover, dealing with many marriage cases: relating to dispensations for mixed marriages, dispensations from the impediment of affinity and from consanguinity.[14]

His range of interests, and the volume of work he generated, required new personnel and new structures. He appointed a new secretary, William Murphy, and chaplain, Denis Pettit. Both resided at Archbishop's House, 4 Rutland Square. He added a new layer to the "diocesan dignitaries and officers": in addition to the usual advisory and administrative body of vicars-general, he introduced five vicars-forane, all canons of the diocese with special care for different outlying areas such as Balbriggan, Maynooth, Wicklow, Narraghmore, and Ballymore-Eustace. The vicars-general, as previously, were to attend the archiepiscopal vicariate, 47 Westland Row, for the transaction of business on "Monday, Wednesday, and Friday each week (holidays of obligation and the vigil of holidays excepted)"; but it was further announced that the archbishop's "hours at home" were "from 11.00 a.m. to 2.00 p.m., on all weekdays except

Saturdays", and "to prevent disappointment", his Grace suggested that those who wished to see him communicate "beforehand".[15]

Something of the charged atmosphere emanating from Walsh in those years was conveyed by Wilfrid Scawen Blunt, an English supporter of Home Rule, in his *The Land War in Ireland*.[16] On 24 March 1886, he noted in his diary: "My first visit today was to Archbishop Walsh, for whom I had a letter from Cardinal Manning, and who gave me an interview of an hour or more. The archbishop is a young fellow of 42, a very unmistakable Irishman, short, plain-featured, quick witted, alert, and without pretension." "His dignity sits loosely on him", Blunt observed, "and the gravity of his position seems a burden. He jumps up while speaking and runs about, calls to his chaplain or servant, and has a telephone which he works himself. His house in Rutland Place is a good one, bequeathed to the see by Cardinal Cullen" (the donor was in fact McCabe).

On Walsh's views, Blunt was informative. Walsh spoke "of the difficulty English people had of getting correct information about Ireland; of the lies of the *Times* and the other English papers, as when it was said he had called Trinity College a 'nest of vipers'." On the land question, he thought landlordism "doomed." "The church", he added, "could not altogether prevent outrages, but could do a good deal; they were only bad now in Kerry and Galway, and he thought it was very much the fault of the priests there; they had let things go, and he had several times meant to suggest to the National League that they should suppress the Kerry and Galway branches; he had begged the League to stop the outrages, that is to say, to use their influence in that direction."

Concluding his account of the interview, Blunt reported that Walsh spoke warmly of Cardinal Manning, who, he said, had always been a friend of the Irish. On other points, Walsh observed that Ireland was conservative except on the land question, and "that Protestantism ran no danger of persecution, but that Irish Protestants thought they were being persecuted if they could not have all things their own way". Walsh believed that under Home Rule the outrages would cease "because public opinion would be against them"; and that now the government was looked upon as the public enemy.

Blunt's references to the land question and to Home Rule indicated the issues that were making Walsh a national figure. The popular belief that Home Rule in some form was imminent had been enhanced by the close relationship between the bishops and Parnell's nationalist parliamentary party, and by the fact, as Lord Carnarvon had reported to Lord Salisbury on 7 December 1885, that the Catholic clergy, despite the reluctance of the hierarchy, had "been drawn more and more under the influence of the National League" (successor to the Land League) "and into the ranks of the nationalist party."[17]

Walsh gave new purpose and vigour to clerical involvement in the political process. As early as 20 September 1885, he proclaimed at Enniskerry, with respect to the proceedings of the Wicklow convention in preparation for the forthcoming election, that the priests had "the inalienable and indisputable right" to guide their people where the interests of Catholicity as well as the interests of Irish nationality were involved.[18] And five days later he emphasised to Canon Dillon, parish priest of Wicklow town, the importance of having a strong representation of the clergy at the Wicklow convention to assist in the selection of appropriate candidates. As this was the first convention to be held in Ireland in preparation for the coming elections, it was important that it "serve as a model" for all the others that were to follow.[19]

At the end of December 1885, Walsh reported to Kirby in regard to the general election, "we have had, thank God, a glorious victory" in both this city and county.[20] Carnarvon, not surprisingly, spoke of the archbishop as being the person who had done most to consolidate the clerical-nationalist alliance;[21] while Randolph Churchill judged him "a very ambitious man", adding – "he will never permanently submit to the ascendancy of Parnell".[22]

Earlier in December, Carnarvon had forwarded to Salisbury a report which presented an account of the condition of the country, and of the ways available to the government to meet the country's needs. "Agrarian crime and outrage have been and continue low", he observed, although the National League had acquired "a remarkable organisation and force". This last was partly due, he thought, to the influence of the Catholic clergy. He also noted that links existed between secret societies in America and in Ireland and that funds were coming from America; and that despite there being something of a truce just then, landlords and tenants were hopelessly alienated so that the way forward required either "large concessions" or "repression". In general, there were three "burning questions", the land, education, and local self-government. The "self-government", however, meant not just "the establishment of county or district boards, but some elective body" with "all the outward form and semblance of a parliament". The three questions would have to be faced before long, he warned, but of them the land was most important. In the event of the Conservative party not wishing to face the issues, the alternatives were to do nothing or bring in something like a large scheme of higher education, though it was now too late for such a scheme "mainly through the efforts of one man". The archbishop of Dublin had made an alliance with Parnell and had publicly declared against such a proposal and had "within the last few weeks, strange to say, apparently won over a majority of the bishops".[23]

Walsh, indeed, by January 1886, was considered by R. Barry O'Brien one of "the five most influential men in Ireland", the others being, Parnell, Michael Davitt, T.M. Healy, and Archbishop Croke.[24] To Walsh, Home Rule seemed sufficiently within reach to render lesser measures unacceptable. Home Rule, in effect, had taken on a panaceacal significance, even for the more discriminating of nationalists. When the Conservatives were succeeded in office, in February 1886, by the Liberals under Gladstone, a Home Rule bill and a Land Purchase bill were expected. On 16 February, an important letter written by Gladstone to Lord de Vesci was published. In it, he announced that with regard to "the wants and wishes of the Irish people" the three issues demanding the attention of the government were, in his view, self-government, the settlement of the land question, and social order. The first two of these were intertwined. Hence, he viewed a Home Rule bill and a Land Purchase bill as "separated only for convenience" and being, "in fact, one indissoluble scheme". He added that he was open to suggestions from any quarter which would help him satisfy "the wants and wishes of the Irish people".[25]

The following day, Walsh was deputed by the bishops, perhaps at his prompting, to convey their views to Gladstone on the three issues. His letter, written on 17 February 1886, was written with care, clarity, and an economy not frequent in his correspondence. It was acknowledged with appreciation by the prime minister,[26] and was to be the first of a number of letters between the two. Those which have survived from 1886 to 1890, include Walsh forwarding, sometimes at Gladstone's request, newspaper copies of his "interviews" or public letters,[27] or writing at some length his opinions on the land question,[28] and most especially on Home Rule. He also conveyed to Gladstone, on occasion, some of the views expressed by the bishops as a body on Irish political or social issues,[29] and, at least once, forwarded for his perusal some letters sent him from influential friends or correspondents, such as Cardinal Manning and the Congregationalist minister and Liberal-Unionist from Birmingham, Robert W. Dale, treating of aspects of Home Rule.[30] He also wrote at length in support of denominational education and argued for a change of attitude among Liberals,[31] and during Gladstone's time in opposition he furnished him more than once with comment critical of the Tory administration in Ireland.[32] Also, as will appear in a later chapter, Walsh corresponded with Gladstone with regard to his celebrated library at his residence, Hawarden, Chester, and visited the house to view the library. Gladstone was absent at the time, but subsequently he and Mrs Gladstone invited the archbishop to revisit and stay at Whitsuntide when they would be both at home. Regretfully, it was too busy a time of year for him to accept the invitation.[33]

Walsh cultivated his contacts with Gladstone, and the latter, for his part, valued the correspondence both as a source of information and as a means of contact with a highly influential body in Ireland. On 1 June 1887, he emphasised the value he placed on their role in furthering Home Rule. He hoped "to deal with Ireland as an *integer*", and respectfully recommended that Walsh and his colleagues, who counted "as important factors in the promotion of definitive Irish opinion, should communicate much together" so that he might be able to say to himself, "this, no less or more, is what Ireland wants and accepts".[34]

Walsh's letter of 17 February 1886, to Gladstone, had established him as the voice of the hierarchy, especially on political and social issues. The letter illustrated the power of his advocacy, and indicated why he had so soon become the dominant figure in the hierarchy. He took the three matters emphasised in Gladstone's letter to Lord de Vesci, self-government, the settlement of the land question, and social order, and wrote at some length under each heading. Briefly, "a large and representative body of Irish Catholic bishops" were represented as stating (1) on "the most reliable information", that self-government or Home Rule alone could satisfy "the 'wants', the 'wishes', as well as the legitimate aspirations of the Irish people", that (2) as regards 'the settlement of the land question', a final solution was imperatively required, and the most effective measure would be the purchase by the Government "of the landlord interest in the soil, and the reletting of the latter to tenant farmers, at a figure very considerably below the present judicial rents", and that (3) as regards 'social order', particularly with respect to public outrages and "what is called personal intimidation", these would no longer exist once the land question was settled, because every disturbance of social order that had occurred for years had arisen "from the sense of wrong entertained by a large majority of the occupiers of the soil, owing to the remorseless exaction of needy or extravagant landlords". Facing the immediate problems presented by evictions and poverty, Walsh concluded with an appeal that, "pending the final settlement of the land question" which was now near at hand, "the power of eviction be suspended in Ireland", and that in "the most impoverished districts, some provision, in the shape of remunerative labour, be made, out of the public purse, to support the starving poor … and help them on to better times."[35]

Gladstone's Irish Government Bill, introduced on 8 April 1886, envisaged a legislative body in Ireland, with some twenty-five matters reserved to Britain. Ireland's representation in the British House of Commons was to cease when the Irish legislative body came into existence, though there was a right of attendance for a certain quota of Irish members on occasions when the interests of Ireland required their presence. The lord lieutenant was vested with the power of veto on all legislation from the Irish body. Ireland, moreover, was to contribute to the imperial exchequer an annual sum equivalent to one-fifteenth of the total imperial expenditure. The issues of Irish representation in the imperial parliament and the rate of Ireland's contribution to imperial expenditure became contentious matters for Walsh and other supporters of Home Rule.

With respect to the financial provisions of the bill, Walsh maintained that Ireland's contribution to the imperial expenditure should not exceed one-twenty-fifth or one-twenty-sixth. As to Irish representation in the imperial parliament, he favoured its continuance for the present, suggesting that the representation be proportionate to the Irish contribution to imperial expenditure. He was undoubtedly influenced with respect to representation by Manning's strong belief that the losing of the Irish Catholic members from the imperial parliament would be "a Catholic and world-wide danger". The clause including Irish members was amended, and Walsh hailed the decision in a letter to the cardinal on 14 April 1886.[36]

The Home Rule bill was defeated on 8 June by a majority of eighty votes. A decisive factor in the defeat was the decision of a number of Liberal members,

including Lord Hartington, and Joseph Chamberlain, to vote against the measure; and a further factor was the aggressive hostility of the Conservatives who,
irresponsibly, inflamed Unionist feeling in Ulster. Churchill, visiting Belfast on
22 February, declared that the government's bill purported to "hand over the
loyalists of Ireland" to "the domination of ... a foreign and alien assembly" in
Dublin, and later, in a letter to a fellow member of parliament, used the sedi-
tiously jingoist phrase, "Ulster will fight, and Ulster will be right". Salisbury,
who praised Churchill's speeches, was himself guilty, in the eyes of the vast
majority of the Irish population, of the unpardonable insensitive comment, that
if a "great store of imperial treasure" were to be expended in Ireland, "instead
of buying out landlords it would be far more usefully employed in providing for
the emigration of a million Irishmen."[37] Some members of the English Catholic
laity, such as the duke of Norfolk, played a part by conveying the impression
that Rome was opposed to, rather than in favour of, the proposed plan of Irish
government.[38]

The Land bill was introduced on 16 April. It proposed a major system of
purchase. Means were to be set in place whereby landowners could sell their
property to a specified state authority at twenty years purchase, to be sold subsequently to small purchasers. The bill was furiously attacked in Britain as
taxing the labouring and rate-paying classes of England and Scotland for the
benefit of Irish landlords and Irish farmers. The landlords themselves showed
little enthusiasm for the measure. The landlords seem quite blind just now,
Walsh had complained to Manning on 26 March, adding presciently: "I have no
doubt that if some reasonable settlement be not made this time, the people will
take the land question into their own hands and solve it by a general refusal to
pay rent."[39]

Following the failure of his two bills, Gladstone dissolved parliament on 26
June 1886, hoping that the electorate would give him the backing which had
been refused in parliament. In the resulting election, the Irish party led by
Parnell held their seats, but Gladstone's party was defeated. On 20 July 1886,
the Conservatives, under Salisbury, again formed the government. With their
return to power, landlords in many areas were emboldened to evict. Faced with
the suffering and hardships which ensued, Parnell, in August, put forward a
proposal seeking relief for evicted tenants. It was rejected. Subsequently, he
drafted a Tenants' Relief bill, but this, too, was rejected.

VIEWS ON THE LAND, AND NATIONALISATION AND HENRY GEORGE

Walsh, meantime, responded to the situation by contributing two articles to the
Freeman's Journal in the form of "interviews" on the state of Ireland. They dealt
with Home Rule and the Land Question and were aimed at the Irish in the
United States as well as at home. He intended them to be a salutary force at the
convention of the American League, an auxiliary organisation of the National

League, which was meeting in Chicago in mid-August and was in danger of recommending an extreme violent policy in Ireland. The "interviews", which had the approval of Manning and of Michael Davitt, were published on 11 and 16 August.

The outlook in Ireland, Walsh explained, "is in one way as gloomy as gloomy can be". From this opening, however, he moved immediately to a less gloomy aspect, namely, the inevitability of Home Rule. "It must come", he commented. "Mr Gladstone's bill, with the conflict that has arisen out of it, has made it impossible for the English Liberal party to go back." He took it that the future lay with the Liberal party, though he would not be surprised if Home Rule came through the Tories. But come it would, "and that very soon". When he spoke of "a gloomy outlook", he explained, he was thinking of the land question. "What fools our Irish landlords have proved themselves to be!" The land struggle was nothing more nor less than a commercial struggle. It was a struggle "between the landlords, as a class, who insist upon obtaining extravagantly exorbitant rents for the land, and the tenants, as a class, who are unwilling, and indeed unable, to pay more than the land is really worth."

In his second article, on 16 August, he expanded on the argument. There was a difference, he maintained, between the accepted asking price for land and its *real value*. Thus, in a case in his own experience, the landlord refused to sell for less than twenty years purchase price – or twenty times the annual rent paid by the tenant – but when the yearly value, or worth, was examined, it came to the equivalent of fifteen years purchase, which was the amount offered by the tenants. This was because in selling the land the landlord was no longer liable for his part of the poor rate nor of the county cess, which liabilities were now transferred to the purchasing tenant; also the landlord was freed from the payment of an agent to collect the rents, from law charges, and all other charges incidental to land ownership. "The Ashbourne Act", Walsh pointed out, made "no provision for the price to be paid for the land. That matter was left entirely to the joint discretion of the landlord and the tenant."[40] The landlords in most cases did not feel free, or were unwilling, to make an arrangement based on the worth or real value of the land. They "hold out very often against reasonable offers, chiefly as a matter of class feeling." They "are unwilling", Walsh charged, "to bear the odium of their brother landlords, which they would certainly incur by selling their land at what would be regarded as an unduly small number of years purchase." The tenants, for their part, he further pointed out, were likely to be accused of 'communism' if they sought to have their rents adjusted to their needs in a bad year. Such a charge levelled at Irish tenants by "political partisans", Walsh commented, was, in the words of Frederick Lucas, as "a tin kettle ... tied to the tail of any unfortunate animal whom it was desirable to hunt to death."[41]

In another part of the "interview" Walsh left himself open to just such a charge of 'communism'. He subsequently explained to Cardinal Manning, on 28

December 1886, that he had "felt convinced" since he read "Henry George's *Progress and Poverty* several years ago", "that the nationalisation of the land will infallibly be a point of practical politics before long."[42] In the "interview" of 16 August that conviction first appeared in public. He thought "the nationalisation of the land" as "the only system fully consonant with the principles of justice", but he was careful to add that he supported nationalisation in Michael Davitt's sense as differing from Henry George's. That is to say, he explained, "I hold that the nationalisation of the land, whenever it be effected in this country, must be effected on the basis of fair compensation to the owners or actual holders of the land." To think of solving the land question any other way was "a chimera". His "interview", as telegraphed to the United States and Canada by T.P. Gill, MP, created, as might be expected, "a profound sensation".[43]

Walsh's regard for the works of Henry George, whom he described as "a writer of singular definiteness and clearness", brought him, early in 1887, a peripheral involvement in a burning church issue in the United States At the end of 1886, the archbishop of New York, Michael Corrigan, censured a celebrated, social-reforming priest of his diocese, Edward McGlynn, for certain published views concerning George's teaching on the private ownership of land. Michael Davitt, then in North America, strongly defended McGlynn, as did many others; and his supporters urged Davitt, on his return to Ireland in November 1887, to see Manning and Walsh with a view to enlisting their aid to ensure an impartial hearing of McGlynn's case by the Holy See. Walsh and Manning had already been in communication on the subject for nearly a year, and Walsh, in fact, had received a letter from Corrigan early in January. On 7 January 1887, he enclosed Corrigan's letter in his own communication to Manning. "I cannot at all agree with what the archbishop says about H. George's use of language", Walsh observed, and he added trenchantly that the mistake made by the archbishop in his pastoral was in ascribing to George the denial of all right to property. "I do not think it possible", Walsh continued, "that anyone who had read *Progress and Poverty* could have made such a mistake" or failed to see "the irrelevancy of the arguments on which his Grace relies".[44]

McGlynn, who openly defied his archbishop and refused to go to Rome, was accused of being a socialist, and was excommunicated. At the end of five years, an apostolic representative to the United States, Archbishop Satolli, had McGlynn's teaching examined, found nothing reprehensible in it, freed him from ecclesiastical censures and restored to him the full exercise of his functions as a priest.[45]

THE LAND QUESTION AND THE PLAN OF CAMPAIGN

Returning to the Irish scene, Walsh, as has been made clear, was optimistic about the advent of a form of Home Rule, but gloomy about the land question. His dark forebodings regarding the latter were fulfilled before the end of 1886.

In the autumn of 1885 the worst effects of a dismal harvest had been diluted by the prospect of a Parnellite victory in the general election of late November and early December. A year later, however, there was an even more dismal harvest, prices for crops and livestock were still very low, credit was being restricted, and the landlords, making no allowances, were pressing for their rents; and, in addition, the political excitement had evaporated with the defeat of the Home Rule and Land Purchase bills and the replacement of the Liberals by the Conservatives, who were seen as a landlord party. As the parliament had refused to sanction any remedy or relief, and turned down Parnell's Tenants' Relief bill, and as the tenants half-yearly rents were due in November, it was evident by October that, with the prospects of eviction and starvation before them, many tenants might vent their anger and helplessness in agrarian crime.

Parnell refused to deal with the situation, and three of his lieutenants decided to take the initiative. John Dillon, William O'Brien, and Timothy Harrington, secretary of the Irish National League, devised what became known as the Plan of Campaign, which was published in October 1886, in O'Brien's paper, *United Ireland*. It was a scheme whereby the various tenants in a landlord's estate were to bargain collectively. Where a landlord refused to lower his demands, the combined tenants were to offer him reduced rents. If he declined to accept these, the tenants were to pay him no rents at all, and the money they were prepared to pay him became an 'estate fund' for the maintenance and protection of the tenants likely to be evicted for their action. In the case of someone bidding for the land where an eviction occurred, he was to be boycotted, that is placed in a 'moral coventry' and, in Parnell's words on another occasion, shunned by his neighbours "as if he were a leper of old".

The Plan of Campaign was avidly taken up among a section of the farmers of the south and west, and the organised movement seized the imagination of the country. It cost the government much trouble and expense, even though it was confined during the years of its effective operation, 1886-90, to 116 estates. On sixty of these the campaign led to peaceful settlements, on a further twenty-four terms were agreed after a clash, on fifteen estates the tenants returned on the landlords' terms, and on eighteen no agreement had been reached by 1891.[46] Not surprisingly, the Plan of Campaign was condemned by the *Times* and by the Tory press generally "as a criminal conspiracy to repudiate legal contracts; as a system of robbery organised by disaffected tenants against loyal landlords".[47] The plight of the tenants was such, however, that many of the clergy were moved to side with the tenants' organisations.

Archbishop Walsh had been away on a well earned holiday in the weeks before the launch of the Plan. He had left for the continent on 9 September and returned in the second week of October. On his return, he found himself inundated with a variety of diocesan demands on his time and attention. Also that month there was published *Addresses and Letters of Most Rev. Dr Walsh* from the date of his Grace's appointment: an indication of the range of his spoken and written words and, perhaps, of the interest taken in them. On a lighter note, he found time to attend the presentation of "The Merchant of Venice" at Belvedere College, together with the lord mayor, T.D. Sullivan, MP, John Redmond, MP, and other dignitaries. With reference, however, to what was meant to be a public diversion, namely, the visit to Dublin of the celebrated giant ocean liner, *The Great Eastern*, the archbishop played an unexpectedly active role. Reflecting the widespread contemporary concern about the evils of intemperance, he was one of a number of people who appeared before a police court to oppose the granting of a licence to sell wine and spirits aboard the ship during public visits. The licence was refused, and there occurred what the press described as "a notable incident" during Walsh's examination before the police court, namely, "his Grace's refusal to be sworn on the Protestant Testament offered to him, which, he said, he believed was not the correct version."[48]

In the midst of so many demands, Walsh still managed to keep an eye on the mounting rural crisis. He viewed with apprehension the emergence of the Plan of Campaign, and privately conveyed to Harrington his doubts whether the Plan could be morally justified, but he made no public pronouncement. Under pressure to speak, he reflected at length before eventually doing so on 2 December 1886, in the form of an 'interview' in the *Pall Mall Gazette*.

He had been "startled" and "grieved" at first by the Plan of Campaign, he confessed, "but", he added, "when I looked into the matter carefully, as of course it was my duty to do, my anxiety was relieved." "The great difficulty" with the Plan of Campaign, he explained, was that it left it "practically to the judgement of the tenants", that is to one of the parties to the contract of tenancy, "to fix the terms on which that contract is to continue in force." That seems at first sight, he added, "a formidable difficulty", but, as against that, the other party to the contract, the landlord, also "only one of the contracting parties", had been fixing the contracts on his own for a long time. He then went on to point out, with forceful clarity, that ever since the Land Acts of 1870 and 1881 "the system of land tenure in Ireland is a system of *dual ownership*". "The tenant now is recognised by law as having his ownership as well." This fact was recognised "even by the present Tory government", he observed, "who have proclaimed their intention of getting rid of dual ownership – of buying out the landlords." Hence, "a tenant forcibly ejected from possession is ejected from possession of the landlord's property, no doubt, but he is ejected also from the possession of *that which is his own*." "The maintenance of social order", Walsh continued, required that "rent-fixing" be "dealt with by some authority independent of both". The tenants and their friends had made every effort to achieve this, but they failed through the influence of the landlord class. The government, for its part, had not moved. They had permitted landlords evict, while the tenants took the stand "that they will not give up at the landlord's bidding that which the law has fully recognised as being their own property".[49]

Although Walsh made it quite clear that he strongly denounced crimes and outrages, and had done so effectively on number of occasions in his own diocese, his 'interview' caused a sensation. It was reproduced in the leading newspapers of England and Ireland, and roused to fury the *Times*, the *Morning Post*, and most of the organs of unionist opinion. The *Tablet*, however, which Walsh frequently found unsympathetic, put the position very clearly just two days after the 'interview'. It commented on "the frankness and directness" with which his Grace of Dublin had answered the questions put to him, and had "little doubt but that this 'interview' will long be famous in the history of journalism". The paper continued:

> The archbishop's bold and unequivocal defence of the action of the tenants in the present crisis is well calculated to cause a sensation in this country; but for all that, if any man can see his way to accept his Grace's facts, he must not hesitate at the conclusion. What we have got to do first is to rid our minds of all notions of the tenures of England. The state has recognised a dual property in the soil of Ireland. Recent legislation has made the word 'owner' in relation to Irish land a word of equivocal meaning. The fields of Ireland belong neither to the landlord nor the tenant, but to both. The tenant is lord of the land he tills, subject to the payment of a certain money tribute known as 'fair rent'.

The *Tablet* noted that such legal rents had been fixed, but that it was now asserted that rents fixed two years ago were no longer 'fair', but "unjust and impossible", in the presence of "the heavy, unforeseen, and permanent fall of prices all over Ireland"; and this raised the question – was the landlord "taking advantage of the seasons to make profit out of his neighbour's extremity" and, by resorting to eviction, invading the property of another and possessing himself also "of the tenant's lawful share of the ownership of the farm?" "The facts", the *Tablet* observed, "are the only things which can possibly be in issue". If the fall of prices was as asserted, then the tenants were "entitled to a readjustment".

The legislature, by declining to intervene, the article concluded, had "practically decided against the tenants' claim and in favour of the landlords", and, as a result, the leaders of the National League had accepted the tremendous responsibility of advising the tenants "to disregard the decision of the legislature and treat it as ill-informed, and to act on their own judgement and knowledge."[50]

Walsh's sympathetic depiction of the Plan of Campaign was supported strongly by Croke, one of whose priests, indeed, Arthur Ryan of Thurles, went so far as to proclaim in the Christmas issue of the *Tablet* that the Campaign constituted a "high and unassailable morality – a holy war in the cause of the poor and oppressed, a struggle for hearths and homes".[51] Most other bishops were sympathetic to the tenants, though not so prominently, and all, like Walsh and Croke, opposed crime and violence. Two prelates, however, came out with trenchant criticism of the Plan of Campaign, namely, Edward Thomas O'Dwyer of Limerick, and John Healy of Clonfert. O'Dwyer, who had been consecrated bishop in June 1886, publicly denounced the Plan, and its method of 'boycott', to be a weapon of warfare opposed to the divine laws of justice and charity, and condemned it in his diocese. Healy, although he had allegedly one of the worst of landlords, Hubert George de Burgh Canning, the earl of Clanricarde, in his own area of jurisdiction, and had great sympathy for the tenants, also took a similar line. It required considerable courage on his part, and for a time his life was in danger. But, he not only spoke out against the Plan of Campaign in the troubled district about Portumna, he also complained to the Prefect of Propaganda about it.

"Matters of great moment to our Church and of gravest peril to the State", he informed Cardinal Simeoni on 6 December 1886, "are taking place daily in Ireland." He outlined how the Plan of Campaign was employed against the proprietors, and how the government, on the other hand, was "prepared *vi et armis* to enforce the rights of the landlords", so that "a quasi-civil war seems impending." Moreover, what was still worse, he commented, the archbishop of Dublin "on the 1st of December, in a quasi-public interview with the editor of a daily paper called the *Pall Mall Gazette* formally declared that those tenants are not to blame for acting in this manner, for although at first sight it would seem that a contract may not be determined by one of the contracting parties, nevertheless, for reasons that I cannot understand, it ought not be so in Ireland". This view, Healy continued, was now published in all the newspapers, not only as the teaching of Dublin, but as the teaching of all the bishops of Ireland; "for none of them has spoken against this view, or rather, none of them has dared to speak". A war was accordingly coming – a war for every reason to be deplored. He added trenchantly: "That nefarious system, the boycott – a social excommunication which disregards all justice and charity – almost everywhere obtains, especially in the south and west, and terrifies everybody, even the bishops themselves and the priests, who hardly venture to absent themselves from the meetings of the National League. This system we see daily in operation with our own eyes."[52]

Healy may have been driven to take his courageous stand in his own jurisdictional area, and to write the foregoing letter, by what Bishop Thomas Carr, of Galway, termed "his stern adherence to Catholic principles",[53] but his reading of Walsh's 'interview', and the touch of exaggeration in his account, were not likely to further his case in Rome; that case, however, was far from depending on his report. The government had directed considerable attention to enlisting the aid of Rome against the agitation, not hesitating to discuss an exchange of diplomatic representatives as a lure to Leo XIII, who was ambitious to reinvigorate diplomatic relations with all of the great European powers.

On 12 December 1886, indeed, Walsh reported to Kirby that English Catholic noblemen were making speeches and boasting that by the establishment of diplomatic relations with the Holy See "they will destroy the constitutional Home Rule movement". The London *Saturday Review* had stated, moreover, "that a deputation of English Roman Catholics, including a representative of the Irish hierarchy", had "waited on the prime minister in this connection". The Irish bishops refused to believe the report. But, Walsh declared, "the alarming information I must ask you to convey to the pope is that a bishop was present this time – Healy. He is openly partial to the landlords, but this impudence and imprudence with a coercionist prime minister is incredible." "Read this letter to the pope", he concluded. "Destroy it when read."[54]

EDUCATIONAL CHALLENGES, HOPES AND DISAPPOINTMENTS

False reports, charges, and misrepresentations in the British press, including the *Tablet*, and Reuters agency, and speeches by English members of parliament and members of the House of Lords, a number of them Catholic, placed Walsh and Croke under intense pressure. Walsh, nevertheless, still found the time and energy to deal with the pressures of educational issues, and, through Kirby, to keep Rome informed of developments.

The pressure came from a new episcopal voice on university education, the recently appointed bishop of Limerick, the very able, but temperamental, Edward Thomas O'Dwyer. Friendly with Walsh for many years,[55] he was not content to leave educational affairs passively to his friend as did the majority of the hierarchy. "It would be highly deplorable", he told Walsh on 18 October 1886, to postpone the question of a university settlement much longer. If Parnell and his Grace agreed on a a university bill, it would be passed "and Home Rule need not be touched one way or another".[56] He followed up his letter with a public pronouncement favouring negotiations with the government on the university question. Walsh wrote to congratulate him on his public letter, and then outlined his basic attitude towards the government on the university question, an attitude tacitly accepted by most of the bishops:

> We must keep hammering away at the grievance and insisting on it being dealt with. If we *propose* anything definite, they will simply fall back on a criticism of details. Just now it will be easy to force them to take the initiative in proposing. Then we can criticise from our side with a much better chance of good results.[57]

O'Dwyer's dissatisfaction with Walsh's policy and the general nature of his letter was shared by John Healy, who was a senator of the Royal University. Healy not only praised O'Dwyer's public letter and expressed agreement with it, he also observed that there was a vacancy on the senate of the university "for a cleric", in the place of the late Cardinal McCabe, which might be offered to him if he were interested and which would offer an opportunity to influence the educational question.[58]

In successive letters to Walsh, on 2, 3, and 24 November, O'Dwyer continued to press the case for active negotiations. The matter was of concern to millions of Catholics. It was time, he insisted, for the bishops as a body to make their views felt. And reiterating a view which he knew was unwelcome to Walsh, he declared "that a more disastrous policy to religion was never manifested than to postpone the question to an Irish parliament". O'Dwyer had little confidence in Parnell.[59] Walsh's reply on 6 November disclosed that he was acting closely with Parnell, and that the latter, at his suggestion, had appointed a committee to confer with the bishops on the education question.[60]

O'Dwyer, however, remained unimpressed. On 24 November he informed Walsh that he had accepted from the lord lieutenant, Lord Londonderry, an offer of nomination to the senate of the Royal University. He viewed the appointment, he said, as putting him in a position which might make him "more useful in working for a settlement". He had made it clear to Lord Londonderry that he did not see the Royal University, or any conceivable development of it, as a settlement of the just claims of the Catholics of Ireland, which it would be his duty as a bishop to urge.[61]

Walsh, who, as has been seen, studiously ignored the senate except when it was opportune to denigrate it, was greatly annoyed. When the royal warrant announcing the appointment was issued on 8 December,[62] Walsh pressed O'Dwyer to withdraw.[63] O'Dwyer came under pressure also from some of the other bishops. Michael Logue of Raphoe, on 13 December, urged him to withdraw his acceptance on the grounds that the bishops were opposed to appointments "made without any regard to their wishes".[64] Logue subsequently pointed to the unhappy 'historical' relations between the bishops, the government, and the Catholic lay members of the university senate, and made the egregious claim that, after Walsh's resignation from the senate, "Dr Healy was appointed without any reference to the opinion of the bishops".[65] There seemed to be no awareness that Healy was appointed at the express wish of Cardinal McCabe, who resented Walsh's resigning without consulting him! Walsh's version of the story had apparently became the official one among many of the bishops.[66]

O'Dwyer was impressed at first, and, following a meeting of the episcopal standing committee in December, agreed to withdraw. But consultation with Healy and Lord Emly, who would have had a very different version of past events, led to his delaying his announcement. On 3 January 1887, the *Freeman's Journal* did it for him. The archbishop's hand was suspected. On 8 January his Grace wrote to O'Dwyer that "arrangements were being considered for filling up the vacancy". Feeling that he was being brushed aside, O'Dwyer replied bluntly the same day:

To prevent any further misunderstanding, I wish to say explicitly that notwithstanding the announcement in the *Freeman*, I have not resigned, and as things have gone, it is less likely than ever that I shall.[67]

The following day he assured the editor of the *Freeman's Journal* that his paper's announcement was "utterly untrue".[68] The pressure on him to resign however, did not cease.

The emphasis on negotiations led Walsh to open discussions with the chief secretary of Ireland, Sir Michael Hicks-Beach in December 1886. He informed Kirby on 19 December that he was hopeful of the outcome.[69] On 22 January 1887, he returned to the O'Dwyer case. He informed Kirby that the episcopal standing committee had called on the bishop of Limerick to resign, but he had not done so. "If this government", Walsh declared, "can pick and choose such people, out of harmony with the others, the influence of the bishops in education will be gone. The case must be referred to the Holy See."[70]

Kirby wrote to O'Dwyer recommending his resignation, but to little effect. "I agree", O'Dwyer acknowledged on 9 March 1887, "that a bishop chosen by the bishops is infinitely preferable; the government will accept him; I will gladly resign in his favour, but only when he is appointed." "Walsh is the obvious man", he continued, "but he has left the university senate on some side issue, and so there is a deadlock. Dr Walsh has attempted to dictate to me: I will not resign until a full bishops' meeting." O'Dwyer's tendency was to bristle at dictation from any source, and he was aware that the episcopal standing committee was largely under Walsh's control, and that its views were not necessarily those of the bishops as a body. He then added more pointedly that in the pressure being brought to bear on him he saw "the spirit of resistance to civil authority" which had been growing in Ireland, and which might weaken religion in the country. "The priests", he concluded in a prophetic vein, were being "accepted as useful political agents, and they" would "be applauded and flattered while the political leaders find them useful. In the meantime, our position is being undermined."[71] O'Dwyer retained his position on the senate, and became, with Healy, a key supporter of University College in its policy of persuading the government, by outstanding academic achievements, of the need of a university for the majority population.

On the wider issue of negotiations with the chief secretary, Walsh by 28 February 1887, felt able to assure Kirby that the government "were prepared to give a Catholic college within the Royal University, with endowments equal to TCD", as "a satisfactory *modus vivendi*" rather than a final settlement.[72] Three weeks later he had to report that matters were delayed due to the chief secretary being incapacitated by blindness,[73] and by 30 May 1887, he had become very pessimistic. "A month ago", he explained to Kirby, "we were miles ahead of any previous advance in the education problem; now it is hopeless."[74]

IMPACT OF THE LAND STRUGGLE IN IRELAND AND ROME

Meantime, in the more immediate political arena, Walsh, supported by Cardinal Manning, continued to respond to a barrage of falsehoods, insinuations, and misrepresentations. The onslaught strained Croke's patience to breaking point. He still tended to equate moderation, on the part of priests and bishops, with pusillanimity, and believed that when "the people are starving ... we must not play the policeman for England."[75]

In the *Freeman's Journal*, 17 February 1887, he gave vent to his anger. "On principle", he questioned the paying of taxes to a government that paid its forces to enforce and protect the "outrageous exactions" of landlords. "Our money goes", he fumed, "to fee and feed a gang of needy and voracious lawyers; to purchase bludgeons for policemen, ... and generally for the support of a foreign garrison, or native slaves, who hate and despise everything Irish and every genuine Irishman."[76]

The tone, and text of his letter caused a furore in England. It was construed as "a deliberate incitement to revolutionary action", and the English Catholic colony at Rome called on the Holy See to issue a public rebuke to the archbishop. The Holy See did not respond, but, as Kirby explained to Walsh on 2 March 1887, "the impression produced" by the letter was exceedingly bitter, "as such things, coming from an archbishop, embarrass and compromise in some way the Catholic hierarchy and the Holy See itself."[77] Croke, in the event, felt constrained to request Manning on 5 March to use his "kindly offices" for him in Rome, as he had done "on similar occasions in the past."[78] Manning did so; and also wrote to the Home Secretary, Sir Richard Cross, to avert any attempt to arrest the archbishop.[79]

Walsh also appealed to Rome, but through the agency of Tobias Kirby, who, as a former classmate of Leo XIII, was, with Manning, the main bulwark in the Holy See against the wave of complaints and misrepresentations. "It would be very easy", Walsh protested, "for Dr Croke, for myself, and for the body of bishops who wish to serve our people, to stand aside, as two or three have done, and leave the people in the hands of the secret organisations that are so ready to spring up if they only get the chance." "The government think", he continued, "they can succeed in crushing our people by coercion. They will simply succeed, if they try it, in throwing our unfortunate country into a storm of revolution."[80]

Leo XIII, however, was becoming concerned about the moral implications of the agrarian agitation, and the active support of a number of priests for it, two of whom, Canon Donal Keller and Mathew Ryan, had been imprisoned, as well as the defence of the Plan of Campaign by the majority of the bishops, and especially by Archbishops Walsh and Croke. Inevitably, too, the rashness of the latter's letter on taxation raised questions about sound judgement. Walsh, unwisely, had refused to write directly to Rome about Irish conditions unless requested by Propaganda to do so. He depended on his letters to Kirby, and his less frequent communications with Manning, to counter the effects of hostile criticism. Reminders from Kirby on the need for him to write directly to Propaganda fell on deaf ears. By June 1887, however, he had come to see the need. "You should write to Propaganda often during these times," Kirby counselled on 17 June. "They receive 'whole files' of accusations against us." Some days earlier, on 9 June, Kirby's vice-rector, Michael Verdon, had emphasised the same need and warned that in the past four months he had seen a great change in the opinions at Propaganda about Irish matters. "The English party", he declared, had been "making desperate efforts of late to get some condemnation from the authorities. The worst of it is that they have the field almost entirely to themselves here in Rome."[81]

On 18 June Kirby alerted Walsh that the pope was "considering the entire Irish question", and that the re-establishment of diplomatic relations between the English government and Rome seemed "most likely". On that day, in fact, a special representative of Leo XIII arrived in London for Queen Victoria's jubilee, bearing a special jubilee gift. Two days later Kirby reported that the pope was following a carefully balanced, two-pronged course of action. "Two ecclesiastics", he declared, "are going to Ireland from Rome. It is as yet a secret. One, Archbishop Persico, and the other, Signor Gualdi." The latter had informed him, Kirby explained, that "the motive of their being sent" was that the Holy Father wished to assure the Irish prelates that his envoy to the queen had nothing to do with Irish ecclesiastical matters, and that he was sending his own envoys to Ireland so that the bishops woud be able to make known to them and enable them to see with their own eyes "the true state of the country and the religious feeling of the people, and the consequent falsehood of the calumnious reports continually spread against our country".[82]

The news of two representatives being sent from Rome filled Walsh with concern and misgivings. The fact that the envoys were being sent without any of the bishops receiving even the courtesy of a direct communication from the Holy See, evoked the spectre of a papal condemnation which would alienate the people from the church. On 27 June, he informed Kirby that the announcement of the intended mission had caused much ferment of mind among the people. "I have the gravest fears about it".[83]

Meanwhile, on 25 June, Manning sought to assuage his fears by telling him that Persico and Gualdi were "intimately known" to him. Both men, the cardinal reported, spoke English well. Gualdi had been a priest in England for fifteen years. Persico, a Capuchin, had been a bishop in British India, and Manning had known him for thirty-six years. "He knows the English-speaking world", he observed, "and I am much mistaken if his heart is not with the poor." "It all now depended, "upon his relations and contacts in Ireland." "Let him be kept in Ireland", the cardinal advised, "till he has seen with his own eyes the Glenbeighs and the Bodykes", referring to two particularly cruel eviction sites in Counties Kerry and Clare respectively. Finally, he assured Walsh, "the selection of these two implies impartiality and a desire to know the truth."[84]

Walsh replied promptly. Persico, despite the reports of anarchy, would find himself "among the most peaceful people in the world." In confirmation of this last, he announced that Propaganda had been impressed by a paper he had recently sent them "giving the statements of the Irish judges in their charges at the last assizes, as to the presence or absence of crime in the country."[85] Nevertheless, despite this attempt to see the bright side, Walsh added glumly, "I find, however, that there is an uneasy feeling in reference to Monsignor Persico's visit."[86] Manning, for his part, also manifested some unease in replying to Walsh on 27 June. He expressed relief that Walsh had written to Propaganda and that his report was well received, for, he admitted, he had been "full of fear about Propaganda and Rome" because they were "so easily misled; and, inculpably, so unable to understand the state of Ireland".[87]

On 4 July Walsh requested Kirby to inform Cardinal Rampolla that the jubilee Peter's Pence collection had proved very successful, but only because of his, Walsh's, intervention. Without his special efforts, it would have been "disastrous"; for the people feared "that English influence has once more prevailed", and that the pope in sending Monsignor Persico was implying that the Irish bishops were not to be trusted.[88] In this climate, Persico was faced with the formidable initial task of allaying the fears and suspicions of churchmen, nationalist politicians, and many of the Catholic population.

VI

The complexities of the Persico mission

Monsignor Ignatius Persico, papal envoy to Ireland, arrived in Dublin on 7 July 1887, accompanied by Enrico Gualdi, as secretary. As the date of his coming had not been publicly announced, his arrival went relatively unnoticed. The *Freeman's Journal*, however, greeted his arrival with the information that Monsignor Persico was "a middle-aged, grey-haired man, distinguished but homely looking" who "appears more Irish than Italian". A Capuchin, he had been chaplain to British troops in India, and was then promoted as coadjutor bishop of Bombay. The *Freeman's* account further noted that subsequently he was made bishop of Savannah in the United States of America, resigned from that position in 1873 because of poor health, and was sent on diplomatic missions to Canada, Malabar, and Malta. He became a consulting prelate to Propaganda, and currently was titular archbishop of Damietta. He had visited Ireland during Cardinal Cullen's episcopacy, and now came as "Commissary Apostolic to inquire into and report on the condition of Ireland". "Fr Gualdi", the *Freeman* added, "is a small man of Italian appearance. He speaks the English language well." He had served as a priest in Manning's diocese for eleven years.

On the evening of his arrival, or perhaps the next day, Persico appeared on the balcony of the archbishop's house in Rutland Square to greet a welcoming crowd and band. The archbishop stood with him, wearing his soutane and a small cape, red biretta and pectoral cross. The papal envoy was "clothed in the brown Capuchin habit, his rank being denoted by little more than his ring, gold cross, and purple rabbi". They blessed the multitude, and Persico shouted "God save Ireland".[1] The cry "God save Ireland", associated with the unofficial national anthem, "A Nation Once Again" by T.D. Sullivan, reflected the empathy of the new envoy. Despite the assumptions and latent hostility of nationalists, Persico, on his own testimony to Cardinal Manning on 12 February 1888, had "from his early youth become acquainted with the sad history of Ireland". "That history made so deep an impression upon me", he declared, "that even then I became convinced of the fact that Ireland had been the most tried and persecuted nation on the face of the earth; while England, the most cruel and cold-blooded towards poor Ireland."[2]

The day following his arrival, the papal envoy reported to Mariano Cardinal Rampolla, secretary of state, that he had been warmly greeted by Archbishop Walsh, who had read Rampolla's letter with great respect, welcomed the purpose of the mission, and had insisted on his staying at the archbishop's house, 4 Rutland Square, rather than at the Gresham Hotel as he had planned.[3] On the same day, Walsh, in mischievously gleeful mood, wrote to Manning that it had been "most industriously circulated that Monsignor Persico was to stay with his religious brethren, not with the bishops", but, he added, "it will rather disturb the minds of certain friends of ours to find that I am to have the honour of his staying with me while he is in Dublin". Walsh determined to avail of the opportunity to put before the papal representative "in fullest detail, an exposition of the present state of Ireland under the following heads:

1. The *political* movement; not *revolutionary*, but thoroughly constitutional in its aim and in its means ...
2. The *land* movement; not communistic etc etc., but a just and reasonable demand, to save people from eviction so long as they pay a really *fair* rent.
3. Comparative freedom of Ireland from crime...
4. All that is satisfactory in the preceding, "the result of the guidance of the movement by the bishops and priests." This was to be contrasted with a past time "when Fenianism was the only line of action in Ireland designated as nationalism".4

Manning, replying on 10 July, approved the heads drawn up by his colleague in Dublin, but drew attention to the charge that the bishops had not spoken out strongly enough against outrages and atrocities, and asked if it were true that moonlighters had abused wives and daughters. He also added the hope that Persico would "go and see the next eviction with his own eyes", and that he would keep in mind that "as late as 1776", "by English law a man for forging a shilling was hanged, a woman was burnt. A theft of 5s. in a shop was capital-hanging. All these executions were *legal*. But they all cried to heaven." "I hope", Manning concluded, "Monsignor Persico will master this distinction well."5

Replying on 12 July, Walsh pointed out that the complaints about outrages applied mainly to Kerry and Clare, where the bishops were ineffective and where there seemed "to be no energy and no care for anything". Such outrages did not occur in Cashel or Dublin. He had had one mild case of a priest making "a rude personal reference to the family of a prominent Catholic gentleman". "Next morning ", Walsh declared, "the priest in question had a letter from me putting an absolute restriction on him against taking any further part in political affairs."6 "As regards the Kerry moonlighters", he continued, "instead of trying to defend them, I should try to collect all possible evidence against them. They have no claim upon us for protection or sympathy of any kind."7

Almost as soon as he arrived, Persico began to receive callers, including, as he reported to the secretary of state on 11 July, many upper-class Catholics, giving their views on the Irish situation, and many written submissions on the state of the country.8 This continued during his stay in Dublin. The callers included not just Irish people. Wilfrid Scawen Blunt, the colourful traveller, member of parliament, landlord and author, in his *The Land War in Ireland*, published in 1912, described a visit to 4 Rutland Square on 19 July 1887.

At half-past ten we went to Rutland Square, saw the archbishop, and then had a long audience with the papal envoys. Monsignore Persico is a worthy old Capuchin, a diplomatist of the silent, sleepy school, with an enormous nose. Gualdi, *est petit, mais il est tout nerf* (is small but all sinew). I should judge from his physiognomy that he was a Jesuit, but am not sure of it. He seems the cleverer one of the two.

"They begged me to speak and tell them all I knew," Blunt continued, "and I improved the occasion to the best of my ability, treating the land question especially, which they said was a special difficulty. 'How', Monsignore Persico asked, 'should people behave when the law was bad until it was repealed?' I said I was not casuist enough to answer that. But in England we agitated for repeal. In Ireland they were obliged to combine against the law, because they could not make the English people hear. There was no means of forcing attention except by breaking the law. Formerly the Irish had resorted to crime, moral crime – this was bad – now they sought to replace these violent remedies by combinations, to resist the civil law, which should not break the moral law. There was a higher law which all peoples must obey, the right to live; and the English law as it stood was exterminating them. What made most impression on them", Blunt concluded, "seemed to be that I was an English gentleman and a landlord. This they said was 'good testimony'. O'Hagan and Gavan Duffy came in as we went out."[9]

Persico's physical features seemed to attract comment. James Healy, the celebrated parish priest of Little Bray, alleged that a carman said to him that the papal envoy had "an eye like a coortin [courting] hawk". To which Healy is said to have replied: "Never having seen one in that interesting condition, I cannot say."[10]

Blunt, and the friend who accompanied him, returned to the archbishop's house for lunch. He remarked:

> Dr Walsh looks more than a year older than when I saw him last year, and the grey of his hair improves him. But he is still far too brisk for his dignity as a prelate according to received ideas. I like him all the better for it. A straightforward, plain man without pretension, very eager in his duties and an enthusiast in his politics.

"We talked quite unrestrainedly before the papal envoys of all that was going on", Blunt added, "and when I said we were going tomorrow to lunch with Davitt, the archbishop exclaimed, 'Well, you must make haste, for he will be arrested before the end of the week'."

Davitt had been visiting Coolgreaney, Co. Clare, Blunt explained, "inciting Captain Hamilton's tenants to resist eviction, and there had been some striking and wounding", and this clearly came within the Crimes Act which her Majesty was due to sign shortly. "The lunch at the archbishop's", Blunt concluded, "was a very frugal meal, mutton chops and cheese." He and his companion, however, rounded off the day on an idyllic note. They "went on to a National League meeting in Sackville Street, and finished the day with a walk in the Phoenix Park and a sound sleep on the grass, where the British garrison was playing cricket."[11]

The Crimes Act, mentioned by Blunt, was to take a very heavy toll on Walsh and Croke, and on the Irish clergy generally. Introduced under the new chief secretary, Arthur Balfour, it led on 19 August to the "proclaiming" of the National League as a dangerous association, and gave the government extensive powers of arrest and coercion. Some twenty-four Irish members of parliament and six priests were to be arrested before the close of the year. Balfour sought to undermine the clerical-nationalist alliance by bringing as much pressure as was legally possible to bear on priests and politicians, and by encouraging condemnation from Rome of the Plan of Campaign. Walsh, Croke, and the clergy generally, feared that they would not be able to contain the violence of the people in the face of the chief secretary's provocatively repressive policy and his blatant support of the landlords, and that, as a result, the constitutional agitation would slip back into Fenian hands. Their efforts to preserve the clerical-nationalist alliance, moreover, continued to be undermined from within by prelates such as Healy and O'Dwyer, and from without by the duke of Norfolk and a number of English Catholics.[12] In this developing scenario, the impressions received by Persico, and his eventual report, were seen to be of major significance.

"Monsignor Persico", Walsh informed Manning in his letter of 12 July, "sees everyone who comes to call on him. Consequently, I have as yet had but little opportunity of talking with him, and only indeed on the education question as yet."[13] The absence of "opportunity of talking with him" was partly Walsh's own fault. He was determined to show off his diocese to the papal envoy. "This morning", he explained to Kirby on 10 July, "Monsignor Persico at my suggestion said the 8 o'clock mass in the Capuchin fathers' church in Church Street. After breakfast I drove him round to visit six or seven of our city churches – including the cathedral – that he might see the people in the ordinary way hearing mass. I need not say how edified he is at all he has seen. As yet, of course, he has seen only two or three of our institutions, but what he has thus seen has filled him with wonder."[14]

Walsh's diary shows him accompanying the envoys on visits to the Dominican sisters' convent and college at Sion Hill, Blackrock, on 12 July, and the following day to the Sacred Heart Sisters' convent and school at Mount Anville, where they were entertained by the pupils. It is also clear from the *Freeman's Journal* that visits were made to the Loreto convent, Rathfarnham, to the college of the Holy Ghost Fathers at Blackrock, to the Jesuit-run Belvedere College, to the Presentation convent, George's Hill, the Mater Hospital run by the Irish Sisters of Mercy, and the Franciscan church, Merchants' Quay. The diary also indicates visits to other parish churches, and to St Patrick's College, Maynooth.[15]

Meantime, coincidental with Persico's arrival, a new land bill was introduced in the House of Commons. It was immediately assailed from all sides as unsatisfactory. Walsh joined in the general attack a few days after the bill was introduced. He contributed two long letters to the *Freeman*, on 16 and 19 July, in which he produced a range of statistical information dealing with means of revising the judicial rents in the event of amendments to the bill; and he also argued that as a general settlement of the land question seemed imminent all evictions should be suspended. This last was not heeded, but the general swell of opposition, and the inability of many tenants to pay the prevailing and suggested judicial rents, obliged the government to revise the rents to be set by the courts.[16] On 19 July, Walsh also wrote to contradict a comment in the *Evening Mail* on his letter in the *Freeman's Journal*. His letters introduced Persico to his proclivity for writing to newspapers.

Five days later, Persico informed Rampolla that although there seemed to be overall approval of his mission, the nationalist politicians and press were attempting to present it in a negative light to the ordinary people. He praised, however, the hospitality of Walsh, and, knowing how awkward it must have been for the archbishop, expressed his appreciation of Walsh accompanying him on a visit to the viceroy and signing his name with him in the visitors' book.[17]

Despite this praise, Persico was not at ease staying with Walsh. He recognised that the latter was quietly endeavouring to control and manage the mission. Walsh's insistence on the papal envoys staying with him, and his efforts to ensure that they saw every positive manifestation of Catholicism in Dublin, were attempts at control. He also set about winning the confidence of Monsignor Gualdi with a view to obtaining inside information concerning the mission. It was an approach that was to backfire. Behind the diplomatic facade, it occasioned resentment on Persico's part and led eventually to tension and barely concealed dislike between Walsh and himself. Already, on 18 July, he expressed concern at Gualdi's friendly relations with some Irish bishops and clergy, and at the way he was putting pressure on him (Persico) to conclude their work as soon as possible.[18] Some weeks later, having left Dublin, he complained to Rampolla from Galway that Gualdi, "during our stay in Dublin, ... spent time with the archbishop and I greatly fear that he did not keep the precepts of discretion, thereby revealing to that prelate what was better not disclosed". "The archbishop is eminently alert", he explained, "and he questions with such fine tact that I am sure that Gualdi is not able to hold him at bay." Moreover, because of Gualdi's acquaintance with many Irish bishops and clergy from his time on the staff at Propaganda, his impartiality, in Persico's view, was in question, and, unhappily, he had a tendency to proclaim his own views on the Irish situation.[19]

Gualdi, as it later turned out, was seriously ill, and this probably played a part in his desire to conclude the mission. He felt sufficiently unwell during

August to request a return to Italy. From Cork on 14 September, Persico informed the secretary of state that Gualdi had received permission from Propaganda to return home on grounds of ill-health, but wished to stay on in Ireland until the mission was completed and the report written. At the same time, he was pressing for the completion of the mission, and this, together with his intimacy with the archbishop of Dublin, and the likelihood of indiscretions and communications to his Grace, made it necessary that he be recalled.[20] At the end of the month, from Kilkenny, the papal envoy mentioned again that his secretary had not been "discreet and cautious enough" in his contacts with Dr Walsh, who knew how to win him over. It was imperative that he return to Rome without delay. Persico hoped to replace him with a Capuchin friar as secretary, and when he returned to Dublin he intended staying at the Capuchin friary in Church Street. "In this way", he observed firmly, "I will receive my letters directly, and not any longer through the archbishop of Dublin."[21]

Persico's personality and astute diplomacy tended to disarm suspicion and hostility in those he met. "He has", George Errington informed Gladstone, "the Italian gift of making the people whom he sees on both sides believe that he is firmly convinced that their views are the right ones: a useful gift I suppose for a commissioner in search of information."[22] In every diocese he was well received, and his visitation provided him with an insight into the general state of the country, and into the character of the people, priests and bishops, and how Walsh was viewed by bishops and priests outside his diocese.

For a man with his diplomatic gifts and experience, however, Persico made what some considered a serious blunder on his first excursion out of the Dublin area. He left on 26 July on a private visit to Lord Emly at his estate at Tervoe outside Limerick, never thinking, it seems, of the effect on Archbishop Croke of the papal envoy visiting a see in his ecclesiastical province without first calling on him, or even acquainting him of the visit. "Great indignation loudly expressed here, and generally felt in the south," Croke wrote to Walsh on 4 August, "at Monsignor Persico's extraordinary manoeuvre in passing me by here, and going to meet Lord Emly and his gang."[23] The very insensitivity displayed by such an experienced diplomat, raises a question about motivation. It would appear that the papal envoy was deliberately asserting his independence and impartiality and making it clear that he was not, as some were saying, "entirely in the hands of Dr Walsh" and of those in the archbishop's camp.[24] The fact that he insisted that his was a private visit, and that it was conducted discreetly, further suggests the likelihood of a carefully weighed decision rather than a diplomatic blunder. The press noted that "the distinguished party" of Persico, Gualdi, and an Italian servant, "made the journey almost unnoticed", occupying "a carriage to themselves". Persico, besides, appears to have had a previous acquaintance with Emly. The same report observed that at Limerick station his lordship "was immediately recognised by Monsignor Persico". They proceeded to Emly's country seat at Tervoe, about five miles from the city.

Subsequently, Emly was careful to make it clear to a newspaper representative that the visit was "purely a private one and altogether unconnected with Monsignor Persico's mission in Ireland".[25]

At Tervoe the envoy was likely to have met his lordship's close friends, Sir Stephen de Vere and Edwin Wyndham-Quin, earl of Dunraven, both, like Emly, resident and improving landlords, and converts to Catholicism. Also likely to be present during his visit there was a frequent visitor, Edward Thomas O'Dwyer, bishop of Limerick, whom, indeed, Persico had met at a gathering in Dublin the night before he left for Limerick. At that gathering, Colonel Alfred Turner, a special commissioner of the Royal Irish Constabulary, took care to inform the papal commissary "about the priests in Kerry and Clare", while O'Dwyer told the company "that the parts of Limerick near Clare were made a perfect hell through boycotting and intimidation".[26] The stay at Tervoe, in the circumstances, was likely to provide Persico with a different view from what was readily available in Dr Walsh's company.

Persico appears not to have mentioned to Colonel Turner his plans to visit Lord Emly, leaving him with the impression that he was going on visitation to Limerick, and thence to Kerry and Clare.[27] It was clearly an indirection. As papal envoy the expected and appropriate protocol was to commence with the diocese of Armagh, the seat of the primate of all Ireland. He and Gualdi moved from Limerick to Armagh, arriving there on 30 July. They stayed, not with the primate, but at the Charlemont Arms hotel. That day, Persico wrote to Cardinal Rampolla that they had been warmly received by the ailing archbishop, Daniel McGettigan, and his coadjutor bishop, Michael Logue.[28] After some days, they moved to the other dioceses in the ecclesiastical province of Armagh, and Persico wrote to Rome from both Sligo and Belfast. He was particularly pleased at the welcome he received from the clergy and people of Belfast, "the bastion of Orangism", where everything was "tranquil and orderly", and everywhere he was shown "great respect".[29]

After the northern dioceses, the envoys travelled to the archdiocese of Tuam. Again they received a respectful and warm welcome. Persico remarked, however, on the danger of a Fenian resurgence because of the harsh coercive measures applied by the government. On 27 August Archbishop Croke received a note telling him that the papal commissary would arrive in Thurles on Monday, 29 August, at 8.30 p.m.[30] Persico stayed three days with Croke. On 2 September, the latter, mollified and more hopeful, confided to Walsh: "The envoy has come and gone. He is a nice man and, I think, friendly in a high degree. So, indeed, is Gualdi. We received him warmly, and of course respectfully here." "We made no displays, following your example, either in demonstration or address. We parted last evening on the best of terms."[31] A lighter comment on the affectionate parting, as the two men kissed good-bye Italian style at Cashel railway station, was the overheard remark of a bystander' – "'Twould be hard to say which is the greatest skamer!"[32]

Persico and Gualdi moved on to the other dioceses in the ecclesiastical province. Persico wrote to Rome from Limerick and Cork. In Cork, although there was the usual enthusiastic welcome, he observed that some nationalist agitators were endeavouring to undermine his efforts by spreading stories that the mission was the result of English pressure on the Vatican.[33]

Walsh, meanwhile, in face of such nationalist fears and criticism, was trying to keep the clerical-nationalist alliance intact, In September he chaired a public lecture by William O'Brien in Leinster Hall on "The Lost Opportunities of the Irish Gentry", which was attended by a "great gathering of Irish and English members of parliament", and at which he was "greeted with prolonged applause".[34] The lecture was related to an initiative of his at the end of August calling for a round-table conference between tenants and landlords. Many of the latter had shown little enthusiasm. Walsh continued working for the conference, both as a means towards settlement, and with an eye to Roman approval. Needless to say, unionist critics, and the under-secretary of Ireland, Major General Sir Redvers Butler, interpreted his effort as solely designed to impress Persico.[35] The rather more neutral Professor Samuel H. Butcher, of Edinburgh University, commented on 13 September, following a meeting with the papal envoy, that Walsh's proposal was clearly meant to impress Persico, and had succeeded. Persico told him that he wrote to Walsh to commend him for it.[36]

Persico, by the end of September, was moving back towards Dublin. Writing to Manning on 4 October, Walsh reported that Persico was at Wexford in the diocese of Ferns, and that on his return to Dublin he would stay with the Capuchins. He intended to remain for ten days or a fortnight during which Walsh expected they would have "many talks over the whole situation".[37] One of the reasons Persico gave for staying with his Capuchin brethren at Church Street was to have a secretary available to him, as Gualdi had at last returned to Italy for reasons of health. The latter was to die within a number of weeks. On 15 October, Persico wrote from Dublin to Cardinal Rampolla informing him of his visitations in the archdioceses of Cashel and Dublin, and of the few visitations still outstanding. For the present he planned to spend some time in Dublin to facilitate those who still wished to see him. All should be completed, however, within three weeks. He had sought to avoid public notice, but his movements and statements were noted and were daily reported in the press. He awaited decisions, he concluded, as to when he should return to Rome, and whether or not he should visit Cardinal Manning when passing through England.[38]

The press and various functions awaited him almost as soon as he arrived back in the city. He had been impressed, he assured the newspapers, by "the devotion and attachment of the Irish people to the Holy Father", and although he had been affected by the poverty in the west of Ireland, he did not find matters particularly bad elsewhere. "His mission was now concluded," he remarked, but he was not sure how long he would stay in Dublin. As the lord mayor and the corporation planned to present him with an address, he would, of course, stay for that, and arrange with his Grace a date for the presentation.

The archbishop, concealing any embarrassment at Persico's decision not to stay at his house, called on him shortly after his arrival, and, after mass, they spent the rest of that day visiting charitable institutions. On other days, the envoy visited Glencree reformatory in the Dublin foothills, Maynooth, where he met a number of assembled prelates, Arklow, Co. Wicklow, and Blackrock College.[39] Persico also managed to complete such diocesan visitations as remained outstanding, before he wrote once more to Rampolla on 2 November. He was still, he reported, receiving callers and written submissions. The Irish people were caught, indeed, between two fires: on the one hand, they were frustrated by the repressive policy of the government; and, on the other hand, they were being egged on to violence by the political agitators. He was convinced that their religion alone exercised a salutary influence on the Catholic population, and that they would respond if their clergy led them along the path of moderation and justice. He believed that he had now collected sufficient material on the state of the country to begin writing his report, but he could not do so in Dublin where he had not a free moment from morning to evening.[40]

He stayed on for more than two weeks, some days of which were spent in bed because of a deterioration in his health. Around 15 November, he preached at the pro-cathedral to mark the feast of St Laurence O'Toole, patron of the diocese; and afterwards at Clonliffe met a distinguished company assembled by the archbishop. The awaited presentation by the lord mayor took place shortly afterwards, and Persico took the opportunity to express his gratitude to the people of Dublin, and also to extend praise to Walsh for his hospitality and kindness. Almost immediately, he left Dublin for the last time, travelling southward to the Capuchin monastery at Rochestown, Co. Cork. Some press reports on his departure from Dublin carried the comment: "We are requested to add that his Excellency's medical advisers have enjoined absolute rest and retirement, so that during his stay at Rochestown he cannot receive any visitors".[41]

Walsh, meantime, was experiencing persistent pressure. The air was thick with rumour and misrepresentation from both the nationalists and unionists. Much was made of Gualdi's return to Rome, and of Persico's staying with the Capuchins rather than with Walsh as hitherto.

Persico, for his part, had begun to write his report at his "quiet location" in Rochestown. But on 18 November it became evident that Rochestown was not proof against outside intrusion. He conveyed his distress to Rampolla at the continuing meddling in Irish affairs of certain English Catholics, and, in particular, at comments in the *Tablet*.[42] He had to admit, however, that unrest was on the increase throughout the country and that it was being deliberately promoted by agitators within the popular political party. Many of the clergy, unfortunately, were supportive of the unrest, and the majority of the bishops were remaining silent. He intended to enlarge on this in his report, he declared, and to suggest what action was to be taken to curb clerical collusion with the politicians. All that being said, he still wished to impress on his Eminence that "the English press reporting on Irish affairs was greatly exaggerated and with many falsehoods".[43] His concern also focused on the activities of certain individuals, namely the duke of Norfolk and Captain John Ross of Bladensburg. The latter, he believed, was a British agent. He had pestered him from his arrival in Dublin, and greatly tried his patience. In Rome, Ross was likely "to move heaven and earth to get the pope to see the need for the condemnation of the agitation in Ireland".[44]

These endeavours to present both sides of the situation indicated the path Persico was to follow in his lengthy and important report. The first part of the report was completed by 24 November. This gave a bleak account of the Irish situation in terms of agrarian violence and priestly involvement. He requested Rampolla, however, to reserve judgement until he received the entire report.[45] Bleakness was a feature of his correspondence at this time. The previous day he had heard from Walsh that Gualdi had died. "I must confess", Persico replied, "that, though half prepared for it, the news has terribly affected me. He was indeed a good priest and an able official, and the Propaganda has lost one of its best officers." His own health was "more or less the same", and there was no need, he added, for Walsh to write "a memorandum on Home Rule or on the Land Question, a memorandum on the Education Bill will be sufficient".[46] On 5 December Persico had to report another death, that of Archbishop McGettigan of Armagh. Writing to Rome, he noted that the immediate successor was the coadjutor prelate, Michael Logue. The succession, he thought, might prove advantageous, as the new archbishop would be in a position to assume Armagh's rightful place as chairman of the bishops' meetings, a role which had been taken over by the archbishop of Dublin.[47] On the very day that Persico wrote of McGettigan's death, Walsh embarked on a leisurely journey to Rome to celebrate Leo XIII's jubilee. This was to be interpreted in the *Pall Mall Gazette* eleven days later as a *summons* to Rome by the pope.[48]

On 10 December, Persico completed his report on the civil and religious state of Ireland, and was ready to add an appendix which would comment on the bishops and their respective dioceses. Finally, on 14 December, he registered the completion of the task. He had sent on the entire report and appendix.[49]

PERSICO'S REPORT AND HIS TRIBULATIONS

The full manuscript, not often consulted, is a long and impressive document.[50] It comes all told to some 123 pages (*c*.A4 size), of which 96 deal with Ireland's civil and religious condition, and the remaining 27 pages are given as an Appendix in which are outlined the number of churches and educational institutions, the number of religious and clergy, in each diocese, with comments on the zeal of the clergy, their involvement in agrarian or political affairs, and on the character, zeal, allegiance, and effectiveness of the bishops. As a document the report throws much light on the thinking and feeling of Irish Catholics, bishops, priests, and people, and is also of interest as the attempt of a well-disposed foreigner to grasp the history of the majority population and to relate the agitation and violence of the National League and the Plan of Campaign to that history. It is an indication of Persico's empathy for a people emerging from centuries of oppression, that he observed that English Catholics should keep in mind when they start criticising Irish bishops, priests, and people for their links with agitation, that they themselves owe their religious freedom to the agitation of Daniel O'Connell and Irish Catholics.

In presenting the prevailing situation, he commenced from a critical, governmental perspective. There were two key, inter-related issues: Home Rule and the Land Question. Home Rule was sought by four-fifths of the population as a virtual El Dorado. The opposing fifth included almost all the landlords, who thereby were brought into opposition to their tenants on two counts. Nearly all the clergy desired Home Rule. Those who did not tended to be viewed as traitors. Again, nearly all the clergy favoured the rights of tenant farmers, and many of them supported the activities of the National League, even though that organisation exercised "terrorism on the poor population", who feared to go against it, subverted public order, and was responsible for "the serious evil" of the Plan of Campaign and boycotting. The League's meetings were held in church halls, or outside the church, after mass on Sundays. Priests sometimes acted as secretaries to the League, and young clergy had been openly violent and crude in their language against landlords and government, without any correction from parish priests or bishops. The English government, therefore, might seem to have strong grounds for criticism of the Irish clergy and people.[51]

Justice required, however, the report pointed out, that the views of the other side be appreciated, the views of a conquered nation which had experienced "six hundred years of injustice and persecutions unexampled in the history of peoples", and whose children had passed on the memory of the past to their children so that "the deeds of centuries are the happenings of today", and everything coming from England is viewed with suspicion.[52] In this situation, secret societies took root and were fuelled by money from emigrants, especially in North America, and by the absence of good will on the part of Britain. Justice was still denied the Irish in such areas as land, education, and gross taxation;[53] and it had to be kept in mind "that whatever Ireland has got from England has been through agitation and menaces".[54] The attitude of the clergy and bishops had to be viewed against that background. Persecution had made people and clergy a compact family, and a common cause in politics and religion had proved important in preserving Catholicism. Today, perhaps, the fear of being abandoned by the people, or that the people would throw themselves into the arms of professional agitators, or secret societies, had led the clergy to yield too much to popular demand, but it must be remembered, Persico insisted, that the clergy were influenced personally by the widespread "mania for national independence" and by the agrarian struggle, for they themselves were part of the popular class, especially the farmers, and had experienced the history of the suffering of the people in their own family.[55]

This, of course, did not excuse the clergy from asserting the principles of the gospel. The bishops were at fault, he emphasised, "in tolerating things manifestly opposed to justice and to Christian charity, in allowing priests take part in the activities of the National League – especially in support of the Plan of Campaign and boycotting", and in failing to prevent young priests participating in public meetings and exciting the public to acts undermining the authority of the law. The Irish people remained Catholic at heart, but they needed leadership from the clergy and unity among the bishops. The latter, Persico continued in words reminiscent of O'Dwyer, had made the mistake of putting themselves "in the hands of the political party, without considering that the politicians have different ideas to the bishops and should not inspire blind trust and confidence". In effect, he warned, "the politicians have acquired such power in the country as to exclude the influence and power of the clergy, and to put at risk the trust of the Irish people in their clergy and church".[56]

What was to be done? Little had been achieved by past letters from Propaganda, by the exhortations of his Holiness, or by resolutions passed by the bishops.[57] Persico's presence had resulted in some progress at first, even to "persuading the archbishop of Dublin to make an act of homage to the viceroy" in company with him, and to make friendly overtures to other authorities. But then "the lightening exploded in a clear sky, and suddenly everything changed. The publication of the Coercion Act threw the country into an indescribable state of agitation and indignation, and people became so enraged that they would not suffer any reasoning."[58]

The application of the Act with its indiscriminate arrests, evoked condemnation from all the bishops. The archbishop of Dublin, in a public letter, attacked the Act, demonstrated its weakness constitutionally, and concluded by saying that he could not speak of the law with the respect he would wish to have. The archbishop of Cashel, Persico noted, went much further – calling for "a solemn contract to make war *au outerance* against the actual government and its ignoble legions".[59] Other bishops, such as Thomas Nulty of Meath, and Patrick Duggan of Clonfert, had shown themselves strong on agrarian and nationalist issues,[60] but the real "standard-bearers of the episcopal body", he continued, were Dublin and Cashel, and if they were won over it would be easy to gain the adhesion of the others.[61] This, Persico cautioned, would require much care and prudence, but it was the way forward. The bishops, if united and strong, would be able to recall the people to their christian duties.

Hence, his own "humble recommendation" was that

> there should be no condemnation, ... no edict or manifesto, either to the
> clergy or to the people of Ireland, about the abuses and troubles which

exist. Any publication of this kind could have the most deplorable consequences, and increase rather than diminish active agitation.

This, he added, was "also the opinion of the most sensitive and impartial per-
sonages of the country". What was required, therefore, was to "act directly on
the bishops, and through them" the "carrying out of the remedies" would prove
"not only possible but easy".[62]

As to the means of achieving this goal, he suggested "that the four archbishops be called to Rome, together with one or two bishops from each province",
that meetings be held there on the issues agitating the country and involving the
clergy, and that practical conclusions be reached. Among the issues should be
the clergy's participation in the National League, especially in the Plan of
Campaign and boycotting, whether it was expedient for clergy, and especially
younger clergy, to take part in public meetings; whether meetings should be permitted in church halls after mass on Sundays; and whether clergy ought publish
letters against the laws, especially when these were not opposed to religion?
"The necessary decisions being taken," Persico concluded, "the bishops should
be obliged by a sacred agreement to carry them out", and be further required to
hold a synod to enunciate, and give effect to the decisions made.[63]

The succession of Michael Logue to Armagh, Persico observed, would facilitate the foregoing development, as he was "moderate and prudent, and although
a nationalist", was "of devout conscience and most attached to the ecclesiastical
discipline".[64] As he had indicated previously to Rampolla, he viewed Logue as a
check against Walsh's dominance; and in his report he again expressed concern
at the extent of Walsh's political involvement, and his doubts about his judgement. He had compromised himself by his many publications and speeches in
"open support of the National League, and, what is worse, of the Plan of
Campaign". His interview in a public journal in defence of the Plan of Campaign
"became like the pillar of fire for the Irish, but especially for the clergy", who
used "such an authoritative exposition" by "a prelate become, so to say, the idol
of the people" to justify their disposition, without considering the manifest injustices which were involved and the bad example given the people. "Too late",
Persico continued, "the archbishop of Dublin became aware of the terrible consequences of the statement made by him, and of the great misuse that was made
of it, but he has not had the courage to withdraw it or, at least, to hold back, and
I fear further that he will not do so publicly." It seemed likely, however, that
little by little he would cease to be a promoter of the Plan of Campaign.[65]

THE APPENDIX

Persico's appendix to his report is in many ways the most informative part of it.
It presents a brief pen-picture of each diocese with a frank assessment of the
clergy and bishops. His frankness highlights aspects of Walsh, and of others, not

usually mentioned. Clearly, he wrote of persons and situations as he experienced them, and he could be very sharp in his comments. Thus, of Bartholomew Woodlock of Ardagh, he wrote that he was "a man of good heart, but of weak, vacillating character, who has not got the respect of his clergy, nor is he a good administrator ... He lets things drift into a state of confusion."[66] This frank comment, however, seems almost adulatory in comparison to his estimation of Andrew Higgins, bishop of Kerry, as "a cold and indecisive man" who "holds people in suspense". "He is not popular either with the bishops, or the clergy, or the people, and he is not accepted by the conservatives, and is not loved by the nationalists. The diocese suffers immensely."[67] On the other hand, his observations on Edward Thomas O'Dwyer of Limerick would have seemed benignly credulous to Archbishops Walsh and Croke. The bishop of Limerick, Persico remarked, had governed the diocese for only eighteen months, but he was "a man of tender conscience and of right principles, alien to politics and animated by zeal" and represents "a true type of bishop". He was young, and needed experience, prudence, and discretion, but these qualities would come easy to him "because he is docile and open to reason". "He should be one of the bishops to be called to Rome as one of the province of Cashel".[68] Persico's portrait of Croke was more immediately recognisable. Thomas William Croke, in his view, followed the dictates of his heart rather than his head, was of "impetuous character", often committed acts of imprudence, and did not know "how to hold himself within the limits of moderation". "Loved by the people", he never failed to defend their rights by letters and manifestos, but he was excessive in doing so. "He could do great good as archbishop", Persico judged, but his "mania about political issues destroys all his good works".[69]

The archbishop of Dublin, as might be expected, appears in a number of places in the appendix. Some of them are in relation to other bishops. Hence, speaking of John MacEvilly, archbishop of Tuam, Persico observed that he lacked the courage to go against the current, and in episcopal meetings he seconded "all the proposals of the archbishop of Dublin without ever saying a word". Francis McCormack, of Achonry, is represented as "opportunistic" and going with the current. "He follows the theories of the archbishop of Dublin, and shows no sign of disapproval of the violent actions of the clergy."[70] Of the archbishop of Armagh, those features were accentuated which differentiated him from Walsh. Hence, of Logue it is stated that he "professes himself to be a nationalist and for Home Rule, but he is moderate and has not got the mania for publishing letters and manifestos on political questions. A man of tender conscience, who loves ecclesiastical discipline, he is humble and without human respect." "The Holy See can count on him," Persico added, "and so it would be opportune that he be called to Rome" to promote understanding of "the need to introduce new ecclesiastical life in Ireland".[71]

The papal envoy's most telling and revealing comments about Walsh necessarily appear in that part of the appendix treating of the archdiocese of Dublin. He reported:

The archdiocese is amply provided with priests, regulars, teaching religious, monks and sisters, churches, hospitals, and pious places. It is a marvel how, in just fifty years, religion was able to make such progress. The number of male religious and sisters is something that surpasses all description; and the great number of brothers and sisters dedicated to teaching and works of mercy. Dublin presents religion in all its prestige and greatness. In a few years the number of churches has quadrupled and all are sumptuously and beautifully built.

In all this, tribute was due to the charity and generosity of Catholics, and to the great zeal and industry of the last two archbishops, Cardinals Cullen and McCabe.[72]

The present archbishop, Persico continued, was Monsignor William Walsh who had governed the diocese for the last two years. He had never exercised pastoral ministry, "having been always professor in the seminary of Maynooth, and president of the said seminary when he was nominated. He possesses eminent qualities of knowledge, quickness, and energy. An excellent worker, and facile writer, he can sustain great fatigue and difficult enterprises, but he lacks the pastoral spirit and that dignity that is proper to his high ecclesiastical status."

"One sees him every day in the public press", Persico declared, "with either letters or manifestos, always on political and literary affairs but almost never on religious matters. He is a declared nationalist and for Home Rule. Tightly bound to Parnell and his companions, he has espoused the cause of the National League and the defence of the Plan of Campaign. Very popular with all the nationalists in Ireland, he has imposed himself on the bishops and the greater part of the clergy. Some bishops admire him, many bishops criticise him and consider him more secular than episcopal, but none have the courage to resist him in the meetings or episcopal conferences. The archbishop is conscious of the popular support, and the bishops fear to confront the idol of the people."[73]

ON THE HEELS OF THE REPORT

As mentioned, the entire report was sent to Rome on 14 December. But Persico's preoccupation with the role of Archbishop Walsh was manifested in two letters sent in close succession on the heels of the report. Fearful, perhaps, that his references to building up Logue as a counter to Walsh might lead to a cool reception for the latter in Rome, he emphasised to Rampolla on 15 December that Walsh "may be said to be the leader of the Irish clergy in the present movement"; and reminded him that he was "so very alert, and so able and astute in affairs" that "immediately, if one is to achieve something for Ireland, one must make him leader, in other words it will be necessary to win him over ... Hence, he should be received and dealt with in a cordial manner, and be shown that one has confidence in him."[74] Three days later, he reported that Walsh had left for Rome for the papal jubilee, and then, having said that he would say no more about him, that he had already said enough in his *Relatio and Appendix*, Persico could not resist referring again to his "exceptional astuteness". He was "able to perceive the sentiments of others" and hence it was necessary "to show him confidence", otherwise he would "think himself badly judged" and would "put up a guard against whatever proposals" were offerred. On the other hand, if he were "treated with courtesy and gentleness", he would "be open to discussion and reason. Winning him, it "would "be easy to win others."

Tuam, Elphin, Galway, and Cork, will be in Rome, Persico concluded. They "are weak and wont have the strength to resist the archbishop of Dublin. If you accept my proposal, it will be necessary to call to Rome the archbishop of Armagh", and the others mentioned.[75]

PERSICO ATTACKED AND DEPRESSED

No sooner had Persico completed his report than he found himself misrepresented in the press. The *United Ireland*, edited by William O'Brien, printed, on 15 December 1887, a rumour current in London that the government had secured the support of the papal envoy and some of the Irish bishops for the policy of coercion, and that in return there would be granted a richly endowed Catholic University in Ireland, and an exchange of ambassadors would be approved between Britain and the Vatican. The *Pall Mall Gazette* enlarged on the canard the following day, adding that "Archbishop Walsh had been suddenly *summoned* to Rome by the pope".[76] The *Freeman's Journal* republished the stories. Persico felt deeply upset, but considered that in his official capacity he could not make a public reply. He expressed his views, however, to Manning on 21 December, and again the following day.

On 21 and 22 December he assured the cardinal that there no truth in any of these reports, and he also wrote twice to Walsh to deny the rumours.[77] On 6 January 1888, he wrote to Manning agreeing that the opening of diplomatic relations between the Vatican and London would be unwise and stating that he had made such views known to the Holy See. He concurred that "the true nunciature for England and Ireland" was the episcopate. "If the bishops did not know the state of the country they were not fit to be bishops."[78]

Meanwhile, Walsh's leisurely journey brought him to Florence on 27 December, and to his destination two days later. He found Rome alive with rumours, including one that Gualdi's return to Rome had been at Persico's insistence, and that the disgrace felt by Gualdi led to his death shortly afterwards. Unisely, he wrote to Persico about it, enclosing a piece from the *Irish Times* carrying the report of Gualdi's recall. Persico replied on 12 January 1888, that Gualdi had written more than once, "and towards the end *most urgently*, to be allowed to return to Italy". "The idea of his having been recalled", Persico continued somewhat disingenuously, "is the offspring either of malice or ignorance", and "all that is said about his recall, disgrace etc is nothing but calumny and falsehood".[79] Walsh, however, had received sufficient circumstantial evidence in Rome to leave him unconvinced by Persico's disavowal. Informing Manning of this on 22 January, he added, more significantly than he realised: "the pope now thinks he can settle the Irish question. I am to play some important part in the transaction. The details are reserved for some conference or conferences to which I am to be called after 1st February. All this may mean something particular."[80] His stay in Rome was to be much longer than he anticipated.

About mid-January, Persico arranged to leave Ireland to spend a month or more in the more salubrious climate at Teignmouth, Devon. He went for "the benefit of his health", and planned to return to Dublin.[81] From Devon on 12 February, the papal envoy sent a long letter to Manning, in the course of which he expressed strong feelings of friendship for Ireland, and also confided his "impression about the archbishop of Dublin". "He has most eminent qualities", he observed, "and can do an immensity of good, not only in his own diocese, but for the whole of Ireland. I would like to see him a little more spiritual and more attached to his *pastoral* duties. I am in hopes that he will do so in time, for he is young, and has only been a professor all his life. To your Eminence also I must *confide* that this is the opinion of many bishops in Ireland." Persico's own relations with the bishops had been "of a most friendly character", he assured Manning, and so it had been with the archbishop of Dublin, who had written to him constantly "except for the last month". "On his arrival in Rome", Persico remarked, "he heard (as he himself wrote to me) many things about me. Among others, that I had caused Fr Gualdi's recall and similar things, and from the tenor of his letter I could see that he had doubts about me." Persico assured the cardinal that he saw the letters Gualdi wrote to Propaganda and that Gualdi "obtained leave to return in *consequence of his own request*".[82]

That Manning was upset by the envoy's criticism of Walsh, and that he had come to Dublin's defence, was indicated by a further somewhat misleading communication from Persico to him on 29 February 1888. He begged to assure his Eminence that he agreed with him as to "the character and aptitude" of the archbishop of Dublin, but that it must also be taken into consideration "his being taken from college life and other circumstances". He was of the cardinal's opinion, too, "that it would be a great disaster if the confidence of his Holiness in him should be shaken", and he had "shown the necessity of *hearing and acting in concert with him about everything*". And writing to cardinals Simeoni and Rampolla, he concluded, "I have insisted on their showing and placing in him great confidence."[83]

In fact, as has been seen, Persico's letters to Rome were far more critical of Walsh than he had indicated to Manning; and the criticism increased rather than diminished in the new year and the new location. On 6 February he warned

Rampolla that the archbishop of Dublin had so implicated himself with politics and politicians that he could only extricate himself with the help of authoritative pressure; and, meantime, the majority of the bishops, "out of fear, or from good will, follow him blindly. Woe to the bishop who does not think like the archbishop of Dublin!" The new archbishop of Armagh had sought to assert himself, but already had to yield in certain areas to Dublin. Persico still hoped, nevertheless, that Logue would be independent and courageous and assert the position "of the true primate of Ireland". The archbishop of Dublin, however, drew his power from the support of politicians and public esteem. Hence, Persico concluded glumly, "it would be a real miracle if this archbishop retraced his steps and rose above politicians and popularity. He is disgracefully vain and secular". "I say 'secular'", he added, "purely in the sense of being more occupied with politics than with religion."[84]

In his subsequent letters to the secretary of state, he continued, in a depressed mood, to present a dismal picture of Ireland, its bishops and priests, and especially its influential archbishop of Dublin. On 21 February he commented that the Irish bishops did not desire the continuation of his mission, and that he had suffered much personally at the hands of journalists. The difficulty of his position might be seen from the fact that the most esteemed newspapers, which had published and were "publishing letters and comments against the mission or papal intervention", were "under the direct influence of the archbishop of Dublin".[85]

At this stage, he had abandoned, in effect, any attempt at objectivity where Walsh was concerned. The latter's implied criticism of him with respect to Gualdi, when, in fact, the problems with Gualdi had arisen because of Walsh's manipulation of him, was akin to a last straw. With regard to the papal mission being attacked by "most esteemed newspapers" (the papers of the *Freeman's Journal* group) "under the influence of the archbishop of Dublin", this was a misreading of the situation. The *Freeman* had come essentially under Parnell's control. Walsh managed to apply some constraint on the paper while he was in Ireland, but once he left the country that constraint was weakened, as, indeed, was the clerical side of the clerical-nationalist alliance; and, on the other hand, the combined pressure on the clergy to promote law and order, from Rome and the government, gave rise in the press generally, and on the part of John Dillon in particular, to accusations of Rome bargaining with Britain, and supporting the pacification of Ireland in return for formal diplomatic relations. Persico, to his pain and disgust, found himself represented as playing a key role in this allegedly treacherous process.[86]

On 15 March he forwarded a confused jeremiad to Rome, which probably exasperated the secretary of state. It reflected his ill-health and his physical separation from the Irish scene. He had modified his official report to the point of now favouring a papal condemnation and showing little faith in the bishops. It was a letter likely to confirm decisions already embraced by the Holy See.

"Things have reached such a state", he commented, "that only a miracle can change them. The evil lies in the fact that the politicians and agitators have acquired absolute power over the people, while the clergy believes, or deludes itself, that it has power when, in fact, they have in great part, if not entirely, lost it." "The clergy to hold the people", Persico continued, "have followed them instead of guiding them"; and the bishops, "do all they can to gloss over, or defend, their action".

Persico then moved to an analysis which pointed in only one direction. The bishops deeply desired that his Holiness not condemn the involvement of the clergy in the national movement, especially with regard to the Plan of Campaign and boycotting. "And yet", he continued, "this Plan of Campaign and boycotting are the two issues which obscure their case. Everyone would have sympathy for Ireland, except that the means used are such that the cause of Ireland loses prestige and the sympathy of good people." The bishops did not condemn the means, because the archbishop of Dublin had "declared them lawful". And the archbishop, for his part, defended them "because they have been adopted by the politicians!"

Going further in his searching but faulty analysis, Persico maintained "that the bishops, by making a supreme effort to disengage themselves from the politicians, could largely reacquire their influence over the people and guide instead of following them." But he saw little prospect of this happening. Nevertheless, he reminded Rampolla that "the only means of probable success was that of calling to Rome the four archbishops along with other bishops, and there compel them to a serious discussion of diverse points" and to the admission of the need for remedies. "All this, corroborated by the authoritative and resolute voice of the Holy Father, would ", he felt, work "the desired miracle, that is, the conversion of the bishops."

As if all this was not sufficiently confusing for the secretary of state, Persico turned once more from this prospect of success, previously in his report, to a depressing account in which he confessed that he did "not have the minimum confidence in a good outcome" and repeated the now familiar theme:

> The archbishop of Dublin is the most compromised (of the bishops) because the most tied to the politicians, and the bishops do not have the courage to oppose the archbishop. I had trusted that in Rome the archbishop would have modified his ideas, but I notice there is no change.

Finally, he repeated yet again "that the politicians, and with them the bishops, do not want the intervention of the pope, but rather do everything to divert him from intervention".[87] In an attached note, he observed sadly, "the bishops, with some exceptions, are cool to me and entirely changed ..."[88]

In Rome, meanwhile, Walsh had become aware that a papal condemnation of the Plan of Campaign and boycotting was likely. He was under the erroneous impression that this was largely due to Persico's report. The pope, irrespective of wider diplomatic considerations, had been drawn towards a moral statement involving a condemnation, rather than the summoning of Irish bishops to Rome and the establishment of a synod of the bishops to bring about a resolution such as Persico had recommended. The factors promoting this course of action appear to have been: the divisions among the Irish bishops; the fact that most of them, and especially the two leaders, Archbishops Walsh and Croke, were strongly nationalist in sympathy and had close links with politicians who supported the Plan of Campaign and boycotting; the strong lobby of influential English Catholics and of the British government for condemnation on moral grounds; and increasingly the letters from Persico expressing disillusionment with the Irish bishops and, at least implicitly, favouring direct intervention. In the circumstances, the safest and most generally productive procedure seemed to be to present the Irish bishops and people with a *fait accompli*, and to neutralise any strong reaction amongst them by detaining their rallying point, Archbishop Walsh, in Rome.

VII

Papal condemnation of the Plan:
its manner and effect, 1888

In the aftermath of the clandestine papal decision, Walsh, with Thomas A. O'Callaghan, bishop of Cork, was invited to a private audience on 12 February 1888, which was also attended by Cardinal Rampolla. The pope requested them "to explain fully the Irish question". They ranged over a wide area, including the Plan of Campaign and the policy of boycotting. "He seemed really impressed with all we said", Walsh wrote to Croke later that day, "and then, he said, now you must set to work and give me a whole *relatio* on the whole of this land question that we may see how we stand, and what can be done."[1]

Walsh set about the task straightway. He retired to the Augustinian convent at Genazzano, where he worked intensively for seven weeks.[2] He decided to write "a *historical* statement, giving all the prominent incidents, including the various bills and acts of parliament, for the last 30 or 40 years".[3] In a letter to Manning at this time he illustrated from a historical perspective the dilemma of Irish Catholics between legal right and moral obligation, which remained such a puzzle for Roman authorities. "The Holy See, judging from the outward peaceableness of the country, could hardly realise", he observed, "that the seventeenth century had not passed away, that the people were still struggling for their religion and their land, and that the permanency of the one depended to no little extent on the possession of the latter. A conscientious regard for the letter of English law in the eighteenth century would have left their fathers without the Faith, as it seemed likely to leave them now without an acre."[4] Walsh's labours at Genazzano resulted in a volume of sixteen chapters, and an introduction, in all 329 pages.[5]

Even as Walsh was seeing his *relatio* through the press, Leo XIII approved a decree of the Holy Office of the Inquisition condemning such aspects of the Plan of Campaign and of the practice of boycotting as had been submitted to it for examination. His Holiness, on 18 April, approved the reply of the Holy Office, and the decree was published on 20 April 1888. The published document gave the reply of the Holy Office, the pope's approval, and a letter from Cardinal Monaco giving the reasons for the Holy Office's responses to the issues it considered. The document was sent to the Irish bishops, and the reasons provided by Cardinal Monaco soon became the focus of interest.

Among the main judgements and reasons for them were: "A rent fixed by mutual consent cannot, without violation of contract, be reduced at the arbitrary will of the tenant alone." This was all the more the case as courts had been established for the settling of such disputes and these made allowances "for fail-ure of crops or disasters which may have occurred, and catered for the reduc-tion of "excessive rents" and for bringing them "within the limits of equity". Again, it was not lawful "that rent should be extorted from tenants and deposited with unknown persons, no account being taken of the landlord". Finally, it was "altogether foreign to natural justice and Christian charity that a new form of persecution and proscription should ruthlessly be put in force against persons who are satisfied with and are agreed to pay the rent agreed on with their landlord: or against persons who in the exercise of their right take vacant farms". Each bishop was exhorted to "prudently but effectively admon-ish the clergy and people in reference to this matter, and exhort them to observe Christian charity, and not to overstep the bounds of justice while seeking relief from the evils which afflict them".[6]

Walsh first received news of the decree in a report in the *Times* of 19 April 1888, and only received an official letter, accompanied by the decree of the Congregation of the Holy Office, on 23 April. The initial reaction had to be one of shock, followed, one suspects, by feelings of anger at having been manipu-lated. Realising before long, however, the need to prepare people at home for the news, he telegraphed Croke and some other fellow bishops, and the *Freeman's Journal*, on 26 April. The substance of his telegram may be gathered from the *Freeman's* editorial reaction the next day. "The Irish people will receive the decree of the pope, or of the Propaganda, with respect the most profound." "They will await the propounding of it by the prelates whom they love and trust as ever heretofore with anxiety but with courage."[7] It was clear to Croke that the said prelates were in danger of losing such influence as they had in the political and agrarian scene to their more militant lay colleagues. He moved immediately to arrange a meeting with the most influential of the lay leaders involved in the agitation, John Dillon. On 2 May he wrote to Walsh with reference to Dillon that they had agreed with the condemnation of the 'Plan' and 'boycotting' where they were attended with the conditions mentioned "as a basis for the decree". In fact they were not so attended and the decree did not apply.[8]

Dillon openly proclaimed this at a meeting of tenants at Herbertstown, Co. Limerick, on 29 April. The decree did not apply, he explained, because there was no freedom of contract, the land courts were landlord run and, therefore, not impartial, and the Plan, furthermore, was not operated "by force and intim-idation".[9] That same Sunday evening, Walsh received a telegram indicating the line being taken by Dillon. Writing to Croke, he confessed that he was not sure what way to proceed. "The thing which the decree practically announces that it condemns does not exist". Rome had misunderstood the method of rent-fixing in Ireland. He wondered whether the bishops might represent this to the Holy See, but, he confessed, "all this has been explained already, as clearly at all events as I could explain it". With uncharacteristic indecision, he wondered "ought anything to be done?"[10]

Despite this apparent confusion and indecision, Walsh, in another letter that same day, to his auxiliary, Dr Nicholas Donnelly, manifested a surprisingly detached demeanour. "I am afraid a bad mistake has been made", he remarked. The decree, "if published *without the reasons* might, and probably would have carried weight with the politicians. But the reasons added take away all chance of its carrying any." "It is lucky for me I am not at home," he concluded.[11] A little over a week later, on 8 May, he clarified, in passing, why the decree on its own might have carried weight with the politicians. "No one seems to have a good word to say for 'boycotting'. There would be very little said for 'the Plan' either, if the cardinal (Monaco) had not revealed the reasons. These are now, of course, thrown overboard here."[12]

Despite this relatively detached attitude of Walsh, it was freely suggested in the newspapers following the publication of the decree, that he had tendered his resignation as archbishop, and it was mooted in Rome that his resignation would be accepted and that he would be made a cardinal in the curia. On 6 May, Manning wrote to him in a spirit of concern, and to stiffen his resolve. He was happy to have received a letter from him, he said, as the papers had been "full of folly". "It is strange", he commented "that you were not consulted, and that no one verified the reasons alleged for the decisions as to rents." He agreed with Walsh that a condemnation of boycotting could hardly be objected to, but the Plan of Campaign itself was "a true reflex of the Irish situation, 'legal right and moral wrong'." Finally, sensitive to what Walsh had endured, he advised that he not allow pain, or any other factor, lead him to leave his "post of duty, difficulty and danger". God had chosen him to fill it, and to stand there till he died.[13]

Meantime, the efforts of the unionist and British press to present the decree as a denunciation of the nationalist movement, together with the anger of the supporters of the Plan of Campaign at what was seen as interference by Rome in Irish political affairs at the behest of the British government, created a climate of disruption in Ireland and a situation susceptible of bitter divisions amongst Catholics. Conscious of this, and of a forthcoming meeting of the National League to discuss the decree, Walsh wrote to the secretary of the League, Timothy Harrington, MP, on 5 May. He suggested that the League at its forth-coming meeting should take care not to play into unionist hands, should avoid criticising the decree, and should keep in mind that the Holy See was concerned with faith and morals and had a right to pronounce on the Plan of Campaign in that context. Two days later he published a long letter in the *Freeman* in which he made the point even more emphatically that "the decision of the Holy See is a decision on a question, not of politics, but of morals".[14]

On 17 May a meeting of the Catholic members of the Irish parliamentary party, summoned by the lord mayor of Dublin, Thomas Sexton, MP, passed a number of resolutions critical of the decree and its "unfounded allegations of fact", and concluded with the statement that while "as Catholics the Irish rep-resentatives acknowledged unreservedly the spiritual jurisdiction of the Holy

See, they could recognise no right in the Holy See to interfere in their political affairs".¹⁵ It was a theme going back to O'Connell, and for those seeking Home Rule it was essential that the movement be seen as politically independent of Rome, otherwise it would be quite unacceptable to both the British government and Irish Protestants. The feeling of hostility to papal interference in political matters, however, was too intense to be satisfied with resolutions. Members of the parliamentary party, led in vehemence by John Dillon, conducted a campaign of public criticism across the country. The demonstrations lasted for almost three weeks; their effects much longer. "The feeling throughout the country was most intense", Bishop O'Callaghan of Cork reported to Dr Kirby at the Irish College on 2 June. Women threw the likeness of His Holiness out of the house, and the excitement extended even to the children. On 6 June, Croke informed Kirby that "the stability of Irish faith" had been "severely tested". "The pope is cursed in every mood and tense from Donegal to Baltimore; and wherein his picture was found in private houses, it has been either displaced simply or torn to bits." He added that "the archbishop of San Francisco" told him it was "worse still in the United States".¹⁶

It was Walsh's role from a distance, and Croke's at home, to provide the ballast and leadership to keep the eruption from causing lasting divisions between clergy and people, and to help to restore relative harmony and an end to meetings of criticism. Both men emphasised again and again that the pope was a friend of Ireland, had no desire to interfere in political matters, yet had a right and a duty to speak out on moral issues such as he had done in respect of the Plan of Campaign and boycotting. Their record on nationalist issues ensured them a hearing.

Their case and that of the church, however, was greatly helped by the known sympathies of Cardinal Manning. His empathy for the Irish tenants and his sense of Irish history were appreciated by Irish nationalist politicians. When the Irish party sent Wilfrid Blunt to him, on 11 May 1888, to see where he stood, the cardinal availed of the opportunity to affirm his sympathies and to calm angry feeling. He gave Blunt a letter for the Catholic members of the Irish parliamentary party, urging them to wait before they enunciated any "irrevocable matter" at their Mansion House meeting, and giving as his belief "that Monsignor Persico has had no part in this late event". Speaking of "the decree of Leo XIII", Manning's view was that it "was absolutely true, just, and useful. But in the abstract." "The condition of Ireland is abnormal", he explained.

> The decree contemplates facts which do not exist. The political condition
> of the world is not contained in the deposit [of faith]. Pontiffs have no
> infallibility in the world of facts, except only dogmatic. The Plan of
> Campaign is not a dogmatic fact, and it is one thing to declare that all
> legal agreements are binding, and another to say that all agreements in
> Ireland are legal.¹⁷

Not without reason did Manning, in defence of Walsh, inform the pope that "he, Cardinal Manning, would long ago have merited much more to be chastised had he been archbishop of Dublin instead of Westminister".[18]

But to return to Rome. On 23 May the *Freeman's Journal* announced that Dr Walsh had a most gracious farewell audience with Pope Leo XIII. The *Times* correspondent, in a well informed report, dated 27 May, announced that Walsh had left Rome the previous night, and that in his final audience the pope assured him that he had not any wish to be involved in political matters, but that he desired the decree "to be obeyed by all good Catholics". "In high ecclesiastical circles", the correspondent noted, "it is felt that the bishops have committed a serious error in neglecting to publish it (the decree) before the politicians had taken it up, and this is said to be the feeling of Archbishop Walsh himself.[19] Just before leaving Rome, Walsh wrote to Archbishop Logue informing him that the decree was "to be communicated at once to the clergy for their guidance" and also "that the reasons stated in Cardinal Monaco La Valeta's letter are in no way to be taken as limiting the sense of the decree."[20]

This last closed a discussion on reasons, hence the only road left open was a diversionary one. Walsh used it as effectively as possible. Thus, in an important telegram sent to a meeting of the municipal representatives to consider, and – if approved – to adopt the resolution of the members of the parliamentary party, Walsh focussed on just one point. His telegram was read to the meeting on Thursday, 24 May, by the lord mayor, Thomas Sexton. It assured those present that apprehensions of political interference by the Holy See in Irish affairs were "absolutely groundless", that "the cause of Ireland" had "nothing to fear from Leo XIII".[21] The telegram seems to have contributed towards calming excited feelings and creating more positive dispositions.

Had the council members, however, been privy to letters from Walsh to Bishop Donnelly from Rome on 15 and 17 May, and from Freiburg Baden, on his way home three weeks later, their feelings would have been roused rather than quietened. Politics had a great deal to do with what happened here, he observed on 15 May,[22] and two days later, "the pope now finds he has practically no one whom he can trust".[23] From Freiburg Baden he felt free to elaborate. "The corruption that surrounds the pope", he confided, "is something frightful to contemplate. Confidential communication with him, except by word of mouth, is now practically impossible, that is, in any matter in which the subject matter of the communication is worth money." And he reflected: "If our good people only knew one tenth of what I can state as to the way in which the recent proceeding was managed, the last chance of bringing them back to their old feelings about the pope would have disappeared." "I must, of course," he concluded significantly, "try to put matters in the best light I can. But I don't see how very much can be done, consistently with the truth."[24]

Well before that letter, however, the Irish bishops, on 30 May, met at Clonliffe College, Dublin, to "try to put matters in the best light" they could.

They followed the sanitised mode used by Walsh in his telegram to the municipal council. They confined themselves to four statements, which announced in summary that the recent decree "was intended to affect the domain of morals alone, and in no way to interfere with politics, as such, in the country"; the pope had "a deep and paternal interest" in the welfare of Ireland; hence, there should not be "any hasty or irreverent language with reference to the Supreme Pontiff or any of the Sacred Congregations"; and finally, while they wished to express their "deep and lasting gratitude to the leaders of the national movement" for the signal services they had rendered religion and country, they deemed it their duty to remind them, and their flocks, that the Roman Pontiff had "an inalienable and divine right to speak with authority on all questions appertaining to faith and morals".[25]

Significantly, the majority of their lordships decided against publishing a covering letter on the decree from Cardinal Rampolla, as they judged portions of it likely to give offence and to reopen the controversy.[26] The mass demonstrations were called off soon afterwards, and the peace held despite a provocative address on 11 June by the bishop of Limerick. Walsh, on his way home and with Roman prelates in mind, observed: "The meetings in Ireland seem to be at an end. In one way they were unfortunate. But, in another, they may possibly prove to have been useful."[27]

Exhausted from the work, disappointment, and stress experienced at Rome, he decided, as has been mentioned, to make his homeward journey in easy stages. It was the second week in June before he reached London. He had a long meeting with Cardinal Manning, and then gave two interviews, on 21 June, one to the *Star*, a London evening paper, the other to the correspondent of the *Freeman's Journal*. The interview for the *Star* was geared to an English audience, and dealt with the rights of property, and the alleged mockery that was being made of those rights by the attitude of the tenants towards contracts. Walsh pointed out that there were conflicting rights, and drew attention to the plight of the tenants. Once again he quoted to effect the report of the Bessborough Commission of 1881 which stated that "freedom of contract in the case of the majority of Irish tenants, large or small, does not really exist". He ended with a strong appeal for the staying of evictions for the coming year, pending a general settlement of the land question. The interview with the *Freeman* was pointedly aimed at an Irish audience on the eve of his return home. Having reiterated the pope's right to speak out on moral issues in the political arena, as much as in the medical and social arenas, he emphasised that his Holiness had been greatly pained at the suggestions that he was unfriendly to Ireland and Irish nationalism.[28]

Moving to a more emotive plain, he attacked the British newspapers for misleading people as to Rome's purpose and intentions, and singled out the *Tablet* as a particular distorter of truth, almost as if with diabolical intention "to drive our people into schism". Turning to parliament, he hoped "some substantial act of justice", or "at least something effective", would be done in the present session "for the protection of our poor people".[29]

The interview merited an editorial in the *Freeman* which indicated how highly he was still regarded in nationalist eyes, in spite of the tensions of recent months. "The thoughts and language of the archbishop", the editorial commented, "are in every way worthy of a great prelate and a great Irishman." He had made it "transparently clear" that steadfast fidelity to the national aspirations of the country were "wholly consistent" with inalienable attachment to the Holy See. His Grace himself was "a practical example of it".

He arrived back quietly in Dublin on 22 June, and was met by a small welcoming party that included Archbishop Croke. He was in time for the bishops' meeting at Maynooth. There he heard, in some detail, of the hundreds of tenants turned out on the roadside with their families because they could not pay rack-rents, some of them in his own diocese.[30] Responding to the needs of their stricken people, the bishops called for impartial courts, and issued a warning "that unless parliament at once apply some effective measure for the protection of Irish tenants from oppressive exactions and from arbitrary evictions, consequences the most disastrous, no less to public order than to the safety of the people, will almost inevitably ensue."[31] At meetings such as this, it was borne in on Walsh how removed he had been from the Irish scene. He had tried to keep in touch by means of newspapers and correspondence, but now he realised how circumspect the reporting had been, how deep was the sense of betrayal, and how intense the feeling was still against the papacy. In this situation, the relative detachment he enjoyed at a distance almost deserted him, and within a fortnight of his return he gave vent, in an unusually frank and revealing letter, to his anger and frustration at the way in which the decree was issued, implicitly at his own treatment, and how authority was used for diplomatic and political ends. The letter was written to Tobias Kirby on 3 July.

"The strong feeling of indignation which the *circumstances* of the former decree so naturally gave rise to", he announced, "is very far indeed from having as yet subsided". "We had no idea in Rome", he assured Kirby, "of the feeling that existed here." "The testimony from all parts of the country is unanimous," he continued. "During the present pontificate, at all events, the old feeling of confidence can never be restored." The people had submitted to the explanation given by the bishops as to the authority of the Holy See in moral questions, "but" Walsh pointed out, "they are now shrewd enough to know that the *exercise* of that authority is a matter of discretion: they cannot see why it should have been exercised against them, and in no way against the landlords whose treatment of them is at least equally characterised by injustice and want of charity". "The extended visits of the Duke of Norfolk", he noted, "the communication of private information to papers like the *Daily Chronicle*; the well-known fact that the decree was issued upon one sided information, although a sort of sham was gone through of seeking information from me and others – all this has

made it simply impossible to remove the impression that the *exercise* of authority was largely influenced by political and diplomatic considerations." "The bishops", Walsh insisted

> could not remove *this* impression if they tried. But the fact is that they
> have no thought of trying to do anything of the kind. If any sort of
> respect for ecclesiastical authority is to be saved out of the general wreck,
> we must abstain from asking the people to believe what they know very
> well we do not believe ourselves.

"As I have often remarked to your Grace", he added, "the people of Ireland,
Catholic as they are, might easily enough be brought into the same state of mind
that now so manifestly prevails throughout the peoples of Italy, France, and
other so called 'Catholic countries'." "The same influence is at work", he
warned in conclusion, "which had wrought such mischief there. We must be
careful how we incur any share of the responsibility."[32]

Carefulness, indeed, had to be exercised straightway in respect of a letter
addressed to the bishops of Ireland by Leo XIII, and forwarded by Cardinal
Rampolla. The letter was likely to rekindle feelings of anger. It assumed that the
protests against the decree were still going on, and criticised such behaviour. It
asserted somewhat disingenuously that considerable care had been taken to
gather information before issuing the papal rescript, even to having a report
from a special envoy (Persico). The pope required the bishops to present the
letter to the Irish people, and to ensure that there was no doubt as to the force
of the decree. Let the people confine themselves to lawful means.

On 9 July Walsh wrote to the *Freeman* to try, as he informed Kirby, "to put
a good face on the pope's letter".[33] Four days later, he sent a careful covering
letter to each parish priest in his diocese to be read before the papal document
was presented. He followed the general lines used already with some success:
focusing on the Holy Father's genuine interest in Ireland, but adding that the
pope's letter was evidently written before the public meetings ceased, and then
emphasising the need to turn from the past and to look forward to achieving
even-handed justice for all. Similar dialectical skills, side-stepping bordering on
casuistry, were employed when faced three days later by the Dublin municipal
council in full robes bearing an address "of Welcome Home". They called on
him at Clonliffe College.[34]

His politic response, which appeared to face up honestly to all the problems
that had been raised, rounded off this time of serious challenge for the Irish
church. "Men's minds were strangely troubled", he acknowledged. "It seemed
almost to be the opinion of some that all the ancient moorings of our Irish
Catholicity had been disturbed." "It is only since my return to Ireland", he confessed, "that I have been able to realise the painful intensity of the crisis through
which our people had, thank God, safely passed." Referring to the council's

endorsement on 24 May of the resolutions of the Irish parliamentary party, he ventured to state that in his opinion the resolutions had been "grievously misrepresented and misunderstood". The formal assertion of the Irish Catholic members of parliament on "the right of Irish Catholics, and of the people of Ireland, to manage their own political affairs, and to do so free of all external control", had been represented, Walsh suggested, "as if it put forward, on the part of the Irish people, a claim that in politics the end justifies the means ... utterly regardless of whether the means in question were or were not in accordance with the law of God". "No such preposterous doctrine", he declared, "was ever laid down by anyone who could establish the faintest shadow of a claim to speak for the Irish people (Applause)." Again, the resolution seemed "to contemplate a possible or probable danger of some political interference of the Holy See in the affairs of Ireland". "There is no such danger," he stated categorically. "On this matter I can give you an authoritative assurance."[35] Regarding the alleged *reasons* given for the decree, and the references to statements of fact, these were not "a portion of the decree of the Holy Office". "The Irish members in correcting those statements", Walsh pronounced guilefully, because, in their own words, 'of the responsibility inseparable from their public trust as the constitutionally elected representatives of the Irish People', "were not only within their rights, but they acted in fulfilment of a public duty (hear, hear)."[36]

By such adroit tightrope walking, Walsh and the body of bishops preserved the tenuous unity of lay and clerical nationalists, and kept in check the forces of violence. They were clear that they had a strict obligation to speak up for their suffering people, and that it was important not to be at cross purposes with the elected representatives who fought the tenants' cause and were also identified with the popular panacea of Home Rule. Disunity was the great enemy. They were conscious that had they attempted to enforce the decree with full and prompt literalness, they would have been seen as supporters of government policy and would have wrecked the clerical-nationalist alliance, and with it the Irish church's power and influence with the Irish people. Moreover, there was the consideration that by and large Catholic tenants were being evicted by Protestant landlords, which contributed to the stark estimation conveyed by Walsh to Cardinal Manning during 1888, "that the seventeenth century had not passed away, that the people were still struggling for their religion and their land, and that the permanency of the one depended to no little extent on the possession of the latter"![37]

All this, in Walsh's and Croke's experience, was something not easily appreciated in Rome, where clear cut problems and decisions were desired, and where the dice were weighted on the side of property, order, and peace. Persico, nevertheless, had perceptively recognised the reality that the real power over the people had passed to the politicians, that the Irish hierarchy, led by Walsh, had so closely allied itself to them that, as a necessary result, the bishops were seriously hampered in acting with honesty and freedom when faced with moral issues arising from the nationalist struggle. Their role as spiritual leaders had been compromised.

This, too, and more intensely, was the view of Lord Emly, and of Sir George Errington, Captain John Ross of Bladensburg, and others. Ross, indeed, sent a report critical of Walsh to Rome at the end of July, collected information against Croke, and forwarded complaints of the dioceses where the decree was not published.[38] Walsh, regardless of past, present, and even prospective criticism, continued to advertise his links with national issues and the national party. On 20 August he made it known to the *Freeman* that he had contributed £50 in support of Parnell and "in vindication of the constitutional character of the national movement of which he is the accepted and trusted leader"; and in September he visited John Dillon, following his unconditional release from Dundalk gaol, where he had been imprisoned for his activities in connection with the Plan of Campaign. That month, responding to the complaints he had received, Rampolla, on the insistence of the pope, it seems, informed the Irish bishops that his Holiness was grieved at their response, and that of the Irish people, to his recent letter. Walsh, in his reply, stated that the Irish bishops would send their responses after their October meeting.[39]

In October and November the secretary of state again wrote strong letters virtually telling the Irish bishops that they were wanting in loyalty, and failing in their duty. The episcopal reaction was far from apology. A prepared reply was undertaken. It should contain, Croke suggested to Walsh on 22 November, "a protest against the utterly unprecedented and apparently unconstitutional interference of Cardinal Rampolla, Secretary of State, in the affairs of the Irish church."[40] A week later, he complained calculatingly to Cardinal Simeoni, prefect of Propaganda, that the Irish church "hitherto confided to the guidance of the Propaganda" had now "apparently fallen into the hands of his Holiness's secretary of state, a diplomatic official, but only partially acquainted with, if not wholly ignorant of, the Irish 'situation' in its various bearings, and naturally more conversant with diplomatic manoeuvres than with the feelings and requirements of a national church". "The bishops generally", Croke continued, playing on the rivalry between the two cardinals, "had felt in a safe and friendly keeping when dealt with by the authorities of the Propaganda" and were not happy at being withdrawn from their "immediate control". With blunt frankness he then got to the nub of the grievance. "Permit me to add", he wrote,

> that so long as the authorities in Rome believe, or affect to believe, that they know more about the actual state of what is called the 'Irish Question' in all its complicated and varying phases than the Irish bishops do, there will be a strong current of revolt against Roman views, and Roman interference in this country.[41]

On 7 December Walsh forwarded to Kirby the bishops' firm, but circumspect, response. It had been signed by all except O'Dwyer and Healy. Walsh sent with it a covering letter in which he informed Kirby: "I wrote to Cardinal Rampolla a few days ago protesting against the sending of letters, such as his late letter to all the bishops. I simply demand as an act of justice to my priests that any charges made against them be submitted to me for examination, and until the facts of the case are ascertained no further defamatory letters be written about our Irish church." "I am satisfied", he observed, "the pope does not know to what political use his name and authority are being turned. Cut off as he is from free communication with the church, this is not to be wondered at." He instructed Kirby that, having read his main letter, he should "give it to Cardinal Rampolla for His Holiness".[42]

The intermingling of political nationalism and religion in Croke's militant letter, and in the more circumspect response of Walsh and the episcopal body, confirmed what Persico had explained to Rampolla four months earlier, that the fate of the papal rescript lay with the politicians and the Irish people, and not with the bishops.[43] What he had not appreciated, however, was that while the bishops' power was effectively limited, they managed, by not going against the Irish party and people, to preserve their place in the governing consensus of the future. By the close of 1888, the bishops were seen as responsible for all aspects of the education question, they had the right to be consulted on the suitability of parliamentary candidates in their respective dioceses, and their priests had the right to be represented in convention at the selection of parliamentary candidates, as well as act as officers in the local branches of the National League. Hence, what has been termed the *de facto* Irish state retained a strong confessional Catholic ethos, without being a Catholic confessional state or, of course, a clerical one.[44]

Persico's judgement in the final months of his visitation was equivocal and uncertain, as has been seen. Following the publication of the decree, he expressed his approval of the condemnation of the Plan of Campaign in yet another confused letter to the secretary of state. "Confused" in that he hailed the condemnation as likely to bring enormous advantages to the Holy See and the pontifical commission, but in the same breath announced that for him to return to Ireland now "would be to walk into a barrage of insults" directed not only against himself but against the pope as well![45] Anxious to stand well with Cardinal Manning, and conscious of the accusations that his Report had led to the papal decree, he wrote twice to Manning to assure him that he had written his Report "with a most friendly feeling towards Ireland" and "had been most impartial" in every respect. How he wished that everything he had said had been carefully studied in Rome![46]

That summer, 1888, Persico was recalled to Rome. Subsequently he was appointed general secretary of the congregation of the Oriental Rite, and in 1893 he was created cardinal and became prefect of the sacred congregation of

Indulgences. In 1895, while in that post, Walsh visited him. He died a short time later.[47] Walsh, presumably, was aware of Persico's letters to Manning denying that his Report was in anyway responsible for the papal rescript. He was most unlikely to have been aware, however, of the papal envoy's comments about him to Rome as a vain, 'secular', ambitious man, of great ability, but deemed by many bishops not sufficiently spiritual and pastoral and too given to seeking publicity. More important, he was presented as excessively nationalistic, tied to politicians, and of unreliable judgement – a formidable litany of factors which had to weigh heavily against William Walsh ever becoming a cardinal as his two predecessors had in the see of Dublin. Persico, moreover, in keeping with his report and letters, was likely to have personally vetoed Walsh as cardinal and supported Logue.

Considerations of ecclesiastical preferment were far from Walsh's mind, however, as 1888 passed into 1889. His diary and papers for 1889 point to key moments and developments in both his life and his country. He is a witness in the *Times* forgeries case, plays an important part in clearing Parnell's name, and then finds himself faced with the consequences of Parnell's affair with Mrs O'Shea. Such major issues require separate consideration.

VIII

Pigott. The Parnell split and sequel

> ... Respect! Mr Dedalus said. Is it for Billy
> the lip or for that tub of guts up in
> Armagh? Respect! ... The priests and the
> priests' pawns broke Parnell's heart and
> hounded him into his grave.
>
> James Joyce, *Portrait of the Artist as a
> Young Man*

These bitter words of disagreement which shattered the harmony of a Christmas dinner, convey vividly something of the intense feelings generated by the train of events from the Pigott forgeries and vindication of Parnell to the crisis precipitated by the O'Shea scandal and the splitting of the Irish parliamentary party. The story has been told in considerable detail in a number of works; and in the past thirty years Walsh's role has been presented carefully and fairly by reputable historians. Much, therefore, can be taken as read, and what follows, apart from a necessary outline of the historical context, is concerned with those aspects of Walsh's role which throw light on his character and motives, his judgement, beliefs, and feelings.

PIGOTT, ARCHBISHOP WALSH AND PARNELL

Richard Pigott was known to Walsh as the proprietor of the *Irishman*, a successful newspaper of strong nationalist sympathies. Not content with the revenue from the paper, Pigott supplemented his income by blackmail. By 1879, when the Land League was founded, "the circulation of the *Irishman* had gone down almost to zero", according to Michael Davitt, "and Pigott's character and reputation had followed suit".[1] Pigott wrote to Walsh on 6 February 1885, with a different explanation. The Land League, he stated, had boycotted his paper and brought him to the verge of bankruptcy. Now he was virtually a pauper, his wife was ill, he had children to care for, and he owed £100.[2] Walsh sent him "a kind letter and cheque". Pigott in response mentioned that he had a "grievance" against the Parnellites, who had put him "out of business" because he "would not blindly do their bidding".[3] Subsequently, he had an opportunity to give vent to his "grievance" when he met with the journalist Edward Caulfield Houston, secretary of the Irish Loyal and Patriotic Union, a society established to defeat the Home Rule movement by showing that its leaders were intimately associated with crime and lawlessness and unfit to be entrusted with the responsibility of government.

Pigott, anonymously produced a pamphlet for the ILPU entitled *Parnellism Unmasked*, and was commissioned by Houston to search for documentary evidence connecting the Parnellite movement with the crime prevalent in the country. Pigott claimed to have uncovered a source in Paris who had incriminating documents connecting Parnell and his associates with murderers and a policy of assassination. Houston agreed to purchase the documents from the unknown source through Pigott. Subsequently, Houston sold the letters to the *Times*, which used them to publish a series on "Parnellism and Crime" commencing on 7 March 1887.[4] Some weeks later, on 18 April, there appeared what purported to be a letter written by Parnell in May 1882 in which it was clearly suggested that the Irish party's protestations of horror at the assassination on 6 May 1882, of Lord Frederick Cavendish and the under secretary, Thomas Henry Burke, were feigned, and that Burke, in particular, "got no more than his deserts".

Parnell denounced the letter as a forgery, but received little credence. Eventually, on 6 July 1888, he called for the appointment of a select committee of the House of Commons to examine the matter. The House agreed, but widened the investigation. A commission of three judges, established by act of parliament, was instructed to inquire not merely into the letters but into ten years of Irish history, conducting what its president, Sir James Hannen, termed "a great inquisition" into the whole Irish movement – political leaders, the Land League, the National League, and all the pronouncements of the nationalist papers. The sittings commenced on 22 October 1888. The last public sitting took place 128 sessions and thirteen months later, on 22 November 1889.

Pigott, meanwhile, seemed to have experienced twinges of conscience. On 4 March 1887, three days before the publication of the first of the *Times* articles on "Parnellism and Crime", he wrote the first of a number of letters to Walsh. It set the tone of the others. He was aware he said of "certain proceedings that are in preparation with the object of destroying the influence of the parnellite party in parliament". The proceedings consisted in "the publication of certain statements purporting to prove the complicity of Mr Parnell himself and some of his supporters with murders and outrages in Ireland". He added: "Your Grace may be assured that I speak with full knowledge, and am in a position to prove, beyond all doubt and question, the truth of what I say." And he was able, he claimed, "to point out how the designs may be successfully combated and finally defeated". In a postscript he remarked that he would not raise the matter with Walsh if he considered "the parties really guilty of the things charged against them". He trusted that the archbishop would regard his letter "as private and confidential, except in so far as it may be used or referred to in furtherance of the motive with which it is sent".[5] Walsh replied cautiously on 9 March:

It is well that all such "evidence" as you have heard of, should be brought out into the light of day. No honest cause has anything to fear from the publication of falsehood.

It was unnecessary to add, he concluded, "that I shall respect your wishes as conveyed to me in your marking your letters 'private'."[6] In the further exchange of letters, Walsh observed that he had assumed from Pigott's letters that he had some knowledge which he could communicate, either as to the author of some fraud or as to the means employed to procure 'evidence' of a fraudulent character. Anything short of this, in his opinion was absolutely useless.[7] Pigott was not prepared to go any further.

On 20 February 1889, Pigott appeared as a witness at the Parnell Commission. In the course of his evidence he made reference to his correspondence with Archbishop Walsh. When this was reported in the press, Walsh, it seems, felt free to send the correspondence to Sir Charles Russell, senior counsel for the defence. The latter's production of the letters in court caused a sensation. His skilful use of them shattered the unfortunate Pigott, who protested that "it was a correspondence under the seal of the confessional".[8] He made a formal admission in the presence of witnesses on 23 February 1889, in which he stated that "the circumstances connected with the obtaining of the letters, as I gave in evidence, are not true. No one save myself was connected with the transaction. I told Mr Houston that I had discovered the letters in Paris, but I grieve to have to confess that I simply fabricated them."[9] Some days later, as he was about to be arrested in Madrid, he took his own life.[10] With this, the central part of the *Times's* case had collapsed, but Russell, nevertheless, decided to put forward the rebutting arguments.

Parnell was the first witness. He began his evidence on 30 April, and concluded on 8 May 1889. Walsh, who had gone to London "to discuss some semi-legal aspects of the case with Sir Charles Russell", found "that all the lawyers" were anxious that he should be "the first witness after Parnell". Explaining this in a letter to Bishop Donnelly, from the Grand Hotel, London, on 4 May, Walsh added, "it is clear that the *Times* people have been totally misled on all the important points by some information on which they foolishly relied". He concluded with the observation that "the contrast between the bearing of the judges here and the sort of thing that takes place in political trials at home is, to my mind, the most instructive incident of the case".[11]

Walsh was called as witness on 8 and 9 May. He was examined mainly on the working of the National League, and on boycotting and "exclusive dealing". The various newspaper accounts of his performance were complimentary. W.T. Stead in the *Pall Mall Gazette* observed that he made "a splendid witness", adding: "He is extraordinarily clear and precise in his statements, and the skill with which he sees and checkmates the drift of a question calculated for an ambiguous answer is highly amusing."[12] Another paper, however, observed that "the archbishop of Dublin, Dr Walsh – whose intellectual features have been familiar to all connected with the commission from the regularity of his attendance during the past fortnight – seemed somewhat flurried in his unaccustomed character as witness. At first he fidgeted with a pencil-case, or turned over his papers in an aimless manner. He soon became more at ease, however, and answered the questions put to him in a clear, intelligent, and decided manner".[13]

Walsh's preserving of Pigott's letters was fortunate for the vindication of Parnell. He was also of assistance to the nationalist party during these months in another unusual way. As the Parnell Commission was proceeding, Joseph Soames, the *Times* solicitor, sent agents to various British, Irish, and American cities to hunt up witnesses and information. The agents communicated with him by coded messages. Frequently the messages fell into the hands of Parnell's supporters, who were easily able to decipher most of the codes. One cipher message from Colorado, however, gave the readers of the cryptic cables much trouble. It followed no scientific or systematic plan known to them. "Fortunately", in Michael Davitt's words, "a distinguished Irishman, a learned embodiment of all the sciences, arrived in London at this time, and the puzzle from the Colorado Springs was submitted to him in the despairing hope that, as he was an authority on almost everything, he might unravel its hidden story. He succeeded after a whole night's labour."[14] The "learned embodiment of all the sciences" was Walsh.

Following the Pigott disclosure, Parnell was on a pedestal. He was followed by a cheering London crowd down the Strand; and in the House of Commons on 1 March was given a remarkable standing ovation by Gladstone and almost the entire opposition. On 18 December he stayed at Gladstone's residence, Hawarden, where Gladstone found him "one of the very best people to deal with that I have ever known".[15] Parnell, for his part, expressed, publicly and privately, his extreme satisfaction with the visit, praised Gladstone in glowing terms, and called upon the English people to help in winning "the great battle I trust we are on the eve of entering upon".[16] The great achievement of Parnell's life seemed closer than ever. Yet that very month the tocsin sounded.

THE O'SHEA DIVORCE CASE

For many years it had been known to many in political life that Parnell was conducting an adulterous relationship with Captain William O'Shea's wife, Katharine, and some were aware that O'Shea had turned a blind eye to the affair. Then, in December 1889, O'Shea filed a divorce suit. Interviewed by the *Freeman's Journal*, on 30 December 1889, with reference to a report in the *Evening News and Post* that O'Shea was filing for divorce against his wife, Katharine, sister of "distinguished soldier, Sir Evelyn Wood", Parnell calmly stated "that he had received reliable information that Captain O'Shea had been incited for some time past to take these proceedings by Mr Edward Caulfield

Houston, the hirer of Pigott, and he believes O'Shea had been induced to take these proceedings by Houston in the interests of the *Times*, in order to try to diminish the damages likely to be given in the forthcoming libel action ... That journal having failed to assassinate his character by means of the forged letters, now attempts the same end by other means".[17]

There were some grounds for Parnell's accusation. O'Shea was friendly with Houston, and had been a *Times* witness. Among the tangled factors in the captain's decision in December 1889, was the support and advice of Houston and Joseph Chamberlain, in conjunction, it would seem, with the expedient fact that Katharine's wealthy aunt had just died. While she lived, it was feared that the scandal of a divorce would prejudice the disposition of her considerable wealth.[18] In the event, the *Freeman* took Parnell's response as an indication of innocence, assuming that he would be vindicated as he had been against the seemingly unassailable evidence in the *Times* case.[19] Parnell followed the same line of implied innocence in an interview with Michael Davitt and in letters to members of the parliamentary party such as William O'Brien and T.P. Gill. Davitt was much impressed with his interview with Parnell.[20] Parnell bade him, Davitt reported, to "say to friends who might be anxious on the matter that he would emerge from the whole trouble without a stain on his name or reputation."[21] Davitt immediately informed the Radical MP, and former chief secretary for Ireland, John Morley, and also Archbishop Walsh. Months later he wrote that both men were delighted and relieved. He told them, and other of his friends, that he had never known Parnell to lie to him, and that until the charge was proved, he would believe implicitly in his innocence.[22]

Subsequently, Davitt construed Parnell's words as based on the belief that O'Shea would be induced to withdraw his case from the courts, and that in this way Parnell's assurances of innocence would be negatively confirmed.[23]

Matters remained in the hopeful condition conveyed by Davitt nine months previously until the trial in November 1890. On 15 and 17 November the petition for divorce was heard before a London jury. It was not defended. Neither Mrs O'Shea nor Parnell appeared in court. "The details", Davitt recalled, "filled the press of Great Britain, Ireland, and America for two days", and "the facts disclosed in evidence ... added nothing but discredit to Parnell's name".[24] The bishops and nationalist supporters were stunned, but the *Freeman* called for unity behind Parnell. Most sought to defer decision. "Disgraceful revelations in the O'Shea case", Walsh wrote to Kirby on 21 November. "They are bound to be disastrous. But we must wait a few days more before forming a final judgement."[25] In the absence of any comment from Parnell on the court decision, he hoped against hope that the Chief might still be exonerated. The last thing Walsh wanted was to be seen as interfering in politics and damaging the prospect of Home Rule. He had, in fact, been taught a sharp lesson the previous June.

In June he had publicly criticised the Irish party in the *Freeman's Journal*, and his comments had been taken up by other papers. He complained of the

absence of many members of the party, including Parnell, during the previous
week when, on three occasions, the ministry had survived by only a narrow
margin. His concluding words caused much resentment "among the rank and
file of the Irish parliamentary party". "For my part", he wrote, "I feel bound to
lose not a moment in stating that if a satisfactory explanation be not forthcoming for what occurred, I do not care who the absentees may be, I shall find it
hard to place any further trust in the action of the present Irish parliamentary
party." It was Walsh's first open expression of disillusionment with the parliamentary party, and it represented, perhaps, a shrewd attempt to preserve his
hegemony amongst the bishops, many of whom were uneasy and critical of the
increasingly independent line being pursued by the party.[26] In the event, the
nationalist press rallied in support of the party members, while some unionist
papers latched on to Walsh's criticism and concluding words, asking if there
were "two uncrowned kings in Ireland – Mr Parnell and Archbishop Walsh?"
and if "the Irish priesthood" would "interfere with the Dublin legislature as they
do now with the nationalist party?"[27]

The party's intolerance of episcopal criticism became quite marked during
the remainder of the summer. The bishop of Limerick's denunciation of the
Plan of Campaign in his diocese was treated with defiance by John Dillon, and
William O'Brien's attacks on his lordship in the *United Ireland* upset many bishops who had little sympathy with O'Dwyer's views. Walsh became so cautious,
and anxious to preserve his nationalist image, that, when appealed to by both
sides in the Limerick dispute, he announced in the *Freeman* on 27 August 1890,
that he did not wish to be drawn into the controversy, "with which, in any of
its aspects – political, personal, or otherwise controversial – I have nothing whatever to do". He was writing this, he said, because he would be away for some
weeks and not in a position to speak for himself.[28] He then went on his holidays.
His action did not pass without comment. One unionist paper invoked Cain's
question, "Am I my brother's keeper?" and remarked that "the archbishop's
sudden skip from Ireland at this time, and his firm resolution not to say which
side of the dispute had his blessing, strikes us as being not only undignified but
pusillanimous in the extreme".[29]

Following the divorce case, therefore, Walsh was determined that the odium
of condemning Parnell would not fall on himself or the body of bishops. He
emphasised that the issue was a political one, and the responsibility lay with the
members of the Irish party who had to keep in mind the overall good of the
country. He discussed the situation with individuals of the Irish parliamentary
party while assiduously avoiding any sign of dictation. He was conscious of the
different factors counselling delay. Reaction in America had to be carefully considered. Anything that alienated American friends might lead to a drying-up of
the flow of money to the Evicted Tenants' Fund, and a weakening of the
national movement. Moreover, the absence of John Dillon and William O'Brien
in the United States gave further cause for pause. One of Walsh's immediate

worries was that the pope might make a pronouncement. It was vital to keep Rome informed and contained. On this last even O'Dwyer agreed. "Rome should make no move" except "confidentially through individual bishops", he informed Kirby some weeks later. "Men are so excited that any suggestion of interference would cause great resentment."[30]

Inevitably, however, once the divorce was granted, Walsh and Croke came under intense pressure to speak out. Among those prompting action were Cardinal Manning, Michael Davitt, W.T. Stead, and such Irish bishops as Laurence Gillooly and Francis Mac Cormack of Elphin and Galway respectively, and James Donnelly of Clogher and Bartholomew Woodlock of Ardagh and Clonmacnoise. On 19 November, Manning wrote twice. he was sure, he announced magisterially, "of the judgement and feeling of Rome".[31] Two days later he wrote to Gladstone: "Mr Parnell cannot be upheld as leader. No political expediency can outweigh the moral sense. I trust the Irish people will on reflection see this". He added: "Mr Stead tells me today that Archbishop Croke is for Parnell's retirement. If Archbishop Walsh agrees I think it will be done. But it rests more with you than with any man."[32]

Meanwhile, on 20 November, Davitt, in the *Labour World* severely censured the Irish bishops and priests for not speaking out. "It has been left to the Nonconformists in England", he pointed out, "to speak out in plain language about this crime of Mr Parnell's." "It might not be too late", however, "something may be said by Archbishop Croke or Archbishop Walsh before next Monday."[33] On Monday the annual election of the leader of the party was to take place. The same day, 20 November, Davitt wrote directly to Walsh asking why Parnell could not "retire for this session", and adding that "if he appears next Tuesday at the opening of parliament as the *newly-elected* leader of the Irish people, good-bye for this generation to Home Rule and God help Ireland". The following day Walsh replied succinctly and carefully. "A particular course is publicly urged on the country with the greatest vehemence," he observed. Those who differed from this view were left with the choice of "effacing themselves" or "causing a split". Perhaps he ought to be glad, Walsh concluded, that the whole affair had been so managed as to leave him and the episcopal body "no voice in the consideration of it in principle or in detail".[34]

On 24 November Gladstone wrote his celebrated letter that announced that despite Mr Parnell's "splendid and unrivalled services to Ireland" his "continuance at the present moment in the leadership would be productive of consequences disastrous in the highest degree to the cause of Ireland", and would render Gladstone's own "retention of the leadership of the Liberal party, based as it has been mainly upon the prosecution of the Irish cause, almost a nullity". The letter was entrusted to Morley for Parnell, and Justin McCarthy, deputy leader of the party, was asked to convey the message to Parnell by word of mouth before the Irish parliamentary meeting on Tuesday, 25 November. It proved impossible to contact Parnell in the days before the meeting. The members re-elected Parnell with acclamation; and he, in his acceptance speech, again induced mystification by saying that he could not speak about the divorce at present, and he asked his followers to keep their lips sealed about it "until the time came when he could speak freely on the topic".

After the meeting, Morley met Parnell, delivered his letter, and urged him to retire for a time. He remained obdurate. Morley reported all this to a greatly surprised Gladstone. It was decided to publish the letter. With the publication of the letter, the Irish party, and the Irish people, were faced with a choice between Parnell and Home Rule. The English press cried out for Parnell's removal. In response, Parnell was to adroitly point out that an English prime minister was dictating to the Irish people on their choice of leader, and that their choice was between their own chosen and tried leader and a mess of pottage in the form of a flawed Home Rule bill. It was a move that was to label those who opposed him as lackeys of England and virtual traitors to Ireland, and this was to render the eventual split in the Irish party a fissure of unparalled depth and bitterness.

Prior to the fateful meeting of 25 November at which Parnell was confirmed as leader, Walsh had met Joseph Kenny, a close friend of Parnell, and strongly urged on him that Parnell should retire, and on 24 November he wrote Kenny a private letter to show to Parnell. Kenny did not do so prior to the parliamentary party meeting. When Gladstone's letter was published, there was concern among the members. A number of them requested a special meeting of the party for 26 November. William Martin Murphy, who was the member of parliament for St Patrick's division, Dublin City, and who was of one mind with Walsh, sent a telegram to him on the morning of the 26th: "Parnell determined to hold on, and no one here strong enough to avert catastrophe."[35] He asked the archbishop to wire him. Walsh immediately replied by letter: "Dr Kenny knows my views by private letter. It is unchangeable." But he then went on circumspectly: "Manifestly, members hold no mandate from the country to wreck the national movement. Take time. There never was a case more clearly requiring calm and full deliberation."[36] That evening Murphy sent a long letter, in the course of which he recounted that there was a majority in favour of Parnell retiring, but that despite "the most passionate appeals" Parnell set his teeth and refused to stir "unless the party voted him out of leadership".[37]

Once the party had raised the issue internally, Walsh and Croke felt free to speak publicly. It was known that the party was to meet again on Monday, 1 December. Walsh made it clear that the Episcopal Standing Committee was meeting on 3 December. "This", he informed Manning, "will exercise a strong influence on Monday's proceedings, and in a form no politician can object to."[38] To reinforce the "strong influence" he made the first public episcopal statement, in the *Irish Catholic*, on 29 November. Again, it was the essence of caution. He announced that he was not speaking for the body of bishops, who had not yet met, but wished to point out that the decision come to at the meeting of the parliamentary party on Monday "may be one that will put upon the bishops of

Ireland collectively, as well as individually, a very grave duty" as to how far they might "place in the Irish parliamentary party that confidence" which, as a body, they "felt justified in placing in it in the past". He concluded, however, by offering a loophole. Recalling the Pigott case, he was "unable as yet to feel absolutely convinced" that he was "even now in a position to form a final judgement in the case."[39]

On 29 November, as Walsh's statement was appearing in the *Irish Catholic*, Parnell issued a defiant manifesto which proved decisive for many. He gave a very hostile interpretation of his meeting with Gladstone at Hawarden, concerning which he had been previously eulogistic; asserted the independence of the Irish party from any British party, and demanded from Gladstone an assurance that Home Rule would give the Irish parliament control of the police force and power to deal with the land question, if this had not already been settled by the imperial parliament. There was not a word about the divorce issue. Encouraged, perhaps, by the support for him up to then in the nationalist press, he appealed over the heads of the party members to the Irish people. "It was a masterpiece", in Randolph Churchill's view, lifting the issue "to the large ground of a great political question".[40] It caused consternation, however, among party members, heralding as it seemed to do the end of an alliance with the Liberal party and an end to Home Rule. This effect was underlined by Gladstone's refusal to respond on the grounds that he could only deal through the Irish parliamentary party with a leader authorised by the party to approach him. But Parnell "had renounced this party" and exercised "a right of appeal to the Irish nation".[41] Cardinal Manning was moved instantly to urge the Irish bishops to speak out. "This is the supreme moment to convince Rome that you do not put politics before faith and morals."[42]

Walsh now felt he was in a better position to speak out. He telegraphed Murphy on 30 November. "Strong telegram from Croke of Cashel to vice-chairman [Justin McCarthy] urging Parnell's retirement. See it at once, see also detailed interview of mine *Central News* tomorrow's papers. Standing Committee of bishops meets on Wednesday to consider our position if present leader is retained. We have been slow to act trusting that party will act manfully. Our considerate silence and reserve are being dishonestly misrepresented. Cashel's telegram goes to *Freeman* for publication tomorrow. This will make further misrepresentation in any quarter impossible. It will also go through *Central News*. I write."[43]

In the interview with the representative of the *Central News*, Walsh stated that he had hoped for a public protestation of his innocence from Parnell, such as he had made when he was first "arraigned before the bar of public opinion" by the publication of the Pigott forgeries. Instead he had published a manifesto that made it clear "there was no longer any reason for reserve". He then went on to pay a striking tribute to Parnell, which was subsequently commented on with appreciation in the *Freeman's Journal*.

Whatever happens, Mr Parnell's unrivalled services to the cause of
Ireland during the past ten or twelve years never can be forgotten. He has
done for his country what no leader before him has ever been able to do.
He found our people politically dead. He put life and hope into them. He
took them out of the hands of unsafe guides. He brought back to them
their lost trust in peaceful, lawful, constitutional methods. He built up for
them a parliamentary party that could at any critical moment be counted,
if called upon, to act as one man. He had kept that party together for
years with its unity unbroken.

"Until a week ago", Walsh noted, "the unity of that party seemed to all appear-
ances unbreakable. Now all is changed in that party of which he is the centre of
unity. His position, so long as he maintains it, is one that makes maintenance of
unity impossible. It can result only in disruption and disaster." Asked about
Parnell's assurance to Davitt, he remarked that if Parnell could not pledge his
word as a gentleman that his honour was still unstained, his colleagues might
rest assured "that the party that takes him or retains him as its leader can no
longer count upon the support, the co-operation, the confidence, of the bishops
of Ireland". He then added carefully, "In speaking as I have spoken, I confine
myself all but exclusively to the moral aspect of the case. If Mr Parnell can set
himself right as to that, I raise no question as to the possible political results of
yesterday's manifesto. That is a political matter, and I leave it to be dealt with
by those who are the accredited representatives of the Irish people." Thus the
bishops' stance on the moral issue was made clear; and the political independence of the elected representatives was emphasised, although their responsibility with respect to a moral issue was strongly indicated.[44]

Walsh at this point, whatever his hopes, could have had but little doubt
regarding Parnell's "unstained honour". He pressed Healy and Murphy to rally
the opposition. "Mr Parnell", he observed, "is bound, like the rest of you, by
the pledge to abide in parliamentary matters by the voice of the party."[45]

On 3 December, as the meeting of the Irish party continued unresolved, the
standing committee of the bishops held their scheduled meeting in Dublin.
From the meeting, a telegram, signed by Walsh as chairman, was sent to Justin
McCarthy.

Important you and members should know bishops issue unqualified pronouncement. Mr Parnell unfit for leadership, first of all on moral
grounds, social and personal discredit as a result of divorce court proceedings, also in view of inevitable disruption, with defeat at elections,
wreck of Home Rule hopes, and sacrifice of tenants' interests.[46]

A fuller statement for the press was also issued on the same lines as the
telegram. Before the publication, the standing committee (of four archbishops,

four bishops representing the ecclesiastical provinces, and two episcopal secretaries) sought the adhesion of the remaining bishops and received the approval
of most of them. Three declined to sign the statement, though they did not disagree with the committee's stand. These were O'Dwyer of Limerick, John
Coffey of Kerry, and John Healy, coadjutor bishop of Clonfert.

The day following the standing committee's meeting, Walsh reported
somberly:

> The meeting was a full one. The Committee consists of ten; *all* were pre-
> sent, except the primate, who is in Rome. We are in every respect
> absolutely unanimous. Popular feeling runs very high just now in Dublin
> and Cork. We are sure to have many noisy manifestations. *It may be of
> use to some of us to find ourselves, for once, on a really unpopular side!* It is
> plain that Parnell can do great mischief. I see no prospect of our escap-
> ing a disruption of the party and the consequent wreck of everything that
> was of promise.[47]

Two days later, 6 December, the series of long meetings in committee room 15
of the House of Commons came to an end. Murphy chronicled the final developments in two telegrams and a letter to Walsh. The letter informed him:
"Turned out just as forecast in my earlier letter – 45 withdrew ... Elected Justin
McCarthy chairman, and adjourned 'till Monday. Parnell will 'cut up' very
badly, I feel sure. Will hold on to the funds and otherwise endeavour to destroy
the Irish cause to revenge his defeat ..."[48]

THE SPLIT

On 6 December also, Bishop O'Callaghan wrote from Cork to Kirby at Rome –
"State of the country indescribable. Even good pious people carried away by
fury"; and O'Dwyer commented from Limerick: "Fierce controversy over
Parnell's leadership, strange as it may seem in a Catholic country. I feel the
reason is that for several years our moral sense has been dulled into putting
expediency before principle."[49] The fury and anger was to grow more and more
as Parnell and his supporters opposed the majority of the party in a series of bit-
terly contested by-elections.

The first of these by-elections took place at Kilkenny. It was fiercely fought.
Parnell had the advantage of having the support of the main nationalist paper,
the *Freeman's Journal*.

Faced with clerical opposition and influence, the Parnellites became openly
anti-clerical in their speeches. Violence found expression: Davitt was struck with
a stick, while Parnell, after a fierce verbal onslaught on Davitt, had mud, stones,
and slack lime thrown at him, and appears to have been hit in the eye by the
lime.

While all this was going on, Walsh remained outwardly calm. He avoided hurtful language, and hoped he might be able to meet with Parnell and that somehow some form of satisfactory solution might be found. On 17 December he wrote to Dr E.J. Byrne, editor of the *Freeman*, intimating that if Parnell cared to make a confidential statement to him, he, Walsh, would be happy to hear it.[50] Parnell seems to have intimated that he would be prepared to communicate confidentially with him, but, in the end, appears to have felt that he could not respond without endangering his future marriage to Katharine. The decree *nisi* in relation to divorce proceedings required that six months must pass before the divorce became absolute, and it might be endangered if during that period any hint of O'Shea's connivance in the relations of his wife with Parnell had been made public. Parnell had set his heart on the divorce so that he could marry Katharine. Moved by Walsh's letter, however, he replied in a tone very different from that which had come to dominate exchanges in recent weeks. "I highly appreciate", he wrote somewhat ambiguously, "the feeling which induced your Grace to accept the suggestion that I should speak to you fully and confidentially upon a certain subject." He had explained to Byrne, he said, that while "most anxious" to do anything in his power, it was not possible for him to speak freely "at present" even to the archbishop. "I do not however wish your Grace to suppose that this reticence need be permanent as after a brief period I hope to be in a position to speak confidentially." "I will always remember," he concluded, "the kindness which has induced your Grace to consent to receiving any confidential communication from me upon this subject."[51]

On 22 December the Kilkenny election took place and the Parnellites were defeated. Parnell was now depicted by his opponents as desiring to confine the clergy to the sacristy, seeking, in Manning's view, a form of lay state, a new 'Tudorism', which would deprive the priests of their due influence in Irish life and leave the laity in command.[52] Reports to Kirby, such as that from O'Callaghan of Cork, gave ample grounds for such fears and depictions. "In Cork the mob is for Parnell," the bishop reported, "and priests are hooted in the streets. The country and country towns have taken the opposite side." It was "extraordinary", he thought, "that even pious men and women are for Parnell". He concluded ominously: "A shot was fired at Dr Healy of Clonfert. I myself was attacked, but fortunately the assailant slipped and fell."[53] Christmas, 1890, witnessed little peace and good will.

In the new year, the nationalist majority were determined to produce their own newspaper to counter the propaganda of the *Freeman*. On 2 January, a group led by Healy and William M. Murphy called on Archbishop Walsh "in reference to the new paper".[54] Some days later Croke writing Walsh commented: "The paper is now the great question. The country is literally clamouring for it, and cannot understand why it is not forthcoming, being quite ignorant of the difficulties in the way".[55] Parnell, and his lieutenant, Timothy Harrington, meanwhile, sought to discredit episcopal influence. On 10 January at Limerick,

Parnell charged: "The bishops say it is all a question of morality. I say it is not a question of morality. If it had been a question of morality these estimable men would have interfered at once ... But they waited for a whole fortnight before they expressed their opinion." They waited until Gladstone and other English people expressed their views. No, the question was one of politics.

He was partly right, as suggested earlier. It was not *just* 'a question of morality'.[56] There was concern for the depletion of the Evicted Tenants' Fund, and preserving American financial support – and this was a particularly strong consideration with Croke, who was one of the trustees in charge of dispensing such funds. Moreover, as has been emphasised, both Walsh and Croke were determined that political action, political responsibility, should be taken first by the Irish party, so that the hierarchy would not be seen to be publicly telling politicians what to do, while yet at a one-to-one level spelling out to politicians the moral implications of the Parnell scandal. At the end of the day, there was a power struggle involved, as the bishops sought to preserve their leadership role among the Irish people.

To the implication that they only acted after Gladstone expressed his opinion, Walsh responded in a public letter on 12 January that he personally, "previous even to Mr Parnell's re-election to the chairmanship of the parliamentary party", had expressed himself very plainly on the subject of leadership in a letter to Dr Kenny, "one of Mr Parnell's most devoted supporters". "In that letter", Walsh declared, "in the plainest terms I stated my conviction the Mr Parnell's duty was clear, that he was called upon, by a manly act of self-sacrifice, to add one more to the many claims that he had established upon the gratitude of out country." He regretted, Walsh concluded mildly, that his letter had not been shown to Mr Parnell, as he felt sure, that if it were shown him, he would not have used the argument that "the present controversy as to his leadership is not a question of morality".[57]

Meanwhile, negotiations were underway which envisaged a compromise involving a temporary retirement by Parnell and many concessions to him. These negotiations, known as the Boulogne negotiations, centred around the optimistic figure of William O'Brien. In danger of arrest for his involvement in land agitation, he conducted the business from Boulogne. From his arrival there on Christmas Day, 1890, to 8 February 1891, hopes of a solution flared and receded, until eventually they faded away. Walsh had been made acquainted of the secret negotiations by a letter from O'Brien on 2 January 1891, asking the archbishop to trust him and Dillon in what they were doing.

On 26 January 1891, in a letter to Dillon, Walsh observed that he would never have accused Parnell of an untruth until the manifesto. Now there was a policy of "daring open lying". Evidently convinced that Dillon and O'Brien, having been abroad for many months, were out of touch with feeling in the country, he warned: "You do not know the man you are dealing with. You could not possibly know him." After these seemingly presumptuous comments to men who had been Parnell's intimate colleagues for many years, Walsh explained:

> You should be on the spot here, in close contact with all that is going on, to be able to realise to any extent how deplorable has been his fall. He has, however, at the same time developed a tactical skill that seems almost superhuman.

It was "almost universally feared", he continued, "that he may succeed in drawing you both into an acceptance of some arrangement which will put him in a position to take the field at the general election". After this firm, and to Dillon probably quite unwelcome frankness, Walsh pointed out that "no matter what arrangement the party may come to, the opposition to him will go on"; and he concluded uncompromisingly: "The only way to save the elections, and to save the cause, is *to get rid of him at once*. Whether he is willing to go or not, should not make a particle of difference in the case."[58]

At this point Walsh was "far from well", as Bishop Donnelly noted in a letter to O'Dwyer. "He caught a cold a week ago, and he is not quite rid of it yet; moreover, the state of public affairs must necessarily worry him a good deal. All settlement or patching up is hopeless."[59] The strain under which Walsh laboured was reflected in a rather testy letter to Kirby on 28 January, responding, it seems, to criticism from Rome.

> It would be well if you would tell any persons who presume to offer you advice about Irish affairs in detail to keep to matters on which they are capable of forming an opinion. Above all, let them look at home. We mean to strain every nerve to keep our people from the fate that has come on the Catholics of Rome and Italy.[60]

On 28 January also, the Liberal shadow cabinet, to facilitate Parnell's resignation, gave the assurances he sought, namely that Home Rule would grant the Irish parliament control of the police force and power to deal with the land question. The Boulogne negotiations entered on their final phase with confident expectation. On 6 February, Dillon wrote Walsh that "a definite conclusion" was to be expected in a few days. But on 10 February both Healy and O'Brien wrote him that six weeks of painstaking negotiations were all in vain.[61] On 11 February, a letter from Walsh to Kirby chronicled the end of all accommodation with Parnell. "Inform the pope", he announced, "that according to information confidentially received today the negotiations have broken down ... Hope was slender from the beginning, but every effort had to be made to get him to retire peacefully. Gladstone, at great personal risk, went as far as he could to guarantee Home Rule. Parnell rejected his assurances." The only consolation was that "everything possible was done to save the country from the turmoil which is now almost certainly before it. There can be no doubt of the final result. But in the meantime there is much to be traversed."[62]

With the breakdown of negotiations, Parnell faced the challenge to his authority with burning energy and an indomitable pride. He drove his delicate constitution through a cold and wet winter, and into the by-elections of Sligo in March, and Carlow in June, at which, despite the support of the *Freeman's Journal*, he still faced a storm of vituperation, and violent clashes took place between his supporters and those of his opponents. Clerical influence throughout the country was crucial in rallying opposition, though it was not quite the uniform phalanx sometimes represented. Logue reported to Kirby on 21 February that there were rumours that in Dublin some of the regular clergy were "serving Parnellites",[63] and Walsh confirmed this the following day when he acknowledged to Kirby that "one or two communities of Friars in Dublin are strongly pro-Parnell".[64] In Sligo a great many of the priests were active Parnellites, and one of the local bishops, Hugh Conway of Killala, was lukewarm. In the election there, the winning margin was only 768 votes between the anti-Parnellite, Bernard Collery, with 3261 votes, and Valentine Dillon, the Parnellite, with 2493. "The whole affair has given our men an awful shake", T.M. Healy wrote Walsh on 4 April, "and has enormously encouraged Parnell."[65]

During that month, however, the majority party's new newspaper, the *National Press*, began to make its presence felt. The circulation of the *Freeman* declined precipitously.[66] At the beginning of July, the Catholic bishops assembled at Maynooth formally approved a resolution proposed by Walsh, and seconded by Croke, that Parnell "by his public misconduct" had disqualified himself from the leadership of the Irish people. "We feel bound on this occasion", they concluded, "to call on our people to repudiate his leadership".[67]

Parnell and Katharine O'Shea were married on 25 June. It was the moment for which he had longed and sacrificed so much. The honeymoon, however, lasted but one day. Soon his febrile energy was directed once more to elections, the last one he was to fight, the Carlow by-election. His marriage had different effects on his followers. Some left his ranks, others hailed the marriage ceremony as setting everything right. Walsh denounced this view in a public letter on 5 August 1891, which emphasised "that adultery is a grievous and shameful sin" and that its guilt was "deepened and blackened when sinners, instead of turning from their evil way, deliberately enter into a public compact to continue their sinful career".[68] He asserted that the view he propounded was also the Protestant position. On 8 August, the *Rock*, "the well-known organ of English Protestantism", agreed, stating: "We are fully in accord with Archbishop Walsh in the conviction that Mr Parnell's marriage with Mrs O'Shea, so far from wiping out the stain of the previous adultery, deepens it." Reporting these comments in the *National Press* of 9 August, Walsh contrasted "the manly, honest action of the English newspaper" with the "insidious attack upon the Catholic Church" being pursued by the *Evening Telegraph*, "under the responsibility of its Catholic directors!" Pointedly, he wondered how long the directors of its sister day paper, the *Freeman*, could keep their eyes closed to the "evil work" being done under their sanction. "That work, it is useful to remember, is paid for largely out of the pockets of Catholic shareholders who are true to their religion in practice as in faith." The *Freeman* bowed to an amalgam of falling sales, shareholders' uneasiness, and episcopal pressure, in August 1891, and withdrew support from Parnell. It was a sure sign that Parnell's cause was lost, even though he fought on, founding his own newspaper, the *Irish Independent*.

DISSENTING BISHOPS

Amid all the excitement, vituperation, and anger, two episcopal friends exchanged critical comments regarding the controversy, and especially with respect to Archbishops Walsh and Croke. The friends were Nicholas Donnelly, auxiliary to Dublin, and Edward Thomas O'Dwyer of Limerick.

The pope wished Dr Walsh to come to Rome "to open the provisional church of St Patrick" on St Patrick's day, Donnelly informed O'Dwyer on 9 February 1891, and two weeks later announced with regret that Walsh was not going to Rome. It would have been a rest for him, which he badly needed, he observed, and it would have removed him "from the temptation of *cacoethes scribendi* (the bad habit of writing) that seems to have come upon him with preternatural force". Donnelly enclosed copies of the *Evening Mail* and the *Daily Express* which contained two letters of the archbishop and editorial leaders on both.[69]

O'Dwyer in reply deplored Walsh exposing himself to affronts from "those Protestant papers, who hated him more intensely than Parnell", and then went on to observe that he could not see how "Healy & Co." differed in principle from "Parnell & Co.". It bordered on a farce "to have bishops and priests joining one gang to denounce and damn the other".[70] On 9 March, O'Dwyer declared that a letter of Walsh in the press that day displayed poor theology, and then proceeded to challenge the expressed view of the body of bishops. "It is no sin to support Parnell", O'Dwyer asserted,

> if a man repudiate sympathy with his offence, and all sympathies with him as an offender, and in merely political grounds supports him as the ablest political leader, he may be held in my opinion as mistaken, and has certainly loose views of decency, … (but) he acts within his rights … And finally there is nothing wrong in Cork re-electing him, but he must not be put on a pinnacle. But if a man think that on a pinnacle is the place where Parnell will be most useful, like Nelson on the quarter-deck, why may he not vote for him!

The case was one, he added, in which "the Church" was "entirely outside her jurisdiction".[71]

By 20 March, however, O'Dwyer confessed that he was so upset by the *Freeman* that his earlier "sneaking partiality for Parnell" was being changed by "the open attacks upon the bishops of that wretched paper". It was now, he announced on 1 April, becoming "a stand up fight between the Church and Parnell", and at this stage all had to stand by the ship, however they might "deplore the management that have brought things to that pass".[72]

That O'Dwyer was not the only episcopal voice deploring the management, was conveyed to Donnelly on 26 June in a letter from Bishop John Coffey of Kerry. The latter refused to approve a directive from the bishops' standing committee because it could be construed as favouring "Tim Healy and the Sullivan gang". He went on to scathingly enquire why there was this "strong denunciation of the sixth commandment" while not a word was spoken, except by one or two brave people, against the shedding of blood by assassins, the violation of women, and the maiming of animals. If there was to be any episcopal pronouncement, he declared, it should find fault with people on both sides.[73]

O'Dwyer, not surprisingly, viewed Coffey's letter as "written with common sense", and added his lack of confidence in Dillon to Coffey's in Healy and the Sullivans. Indeed, between Parnell and Dillon, he told Donnelly on 30 June, he thought Parnell "a less evil". "There is little danger to public morals", he averred, "from Parnell's peculiar sin. The evil is in the indecency rather than the danger of contagion, but Dillon's leadership is a practical and immediate danger to the faith and religious spirit of the people, and their loyalty to Rome".[74]

O'Dwyer's final letters in the context of the Parnell crisis followed the Carlow election in July. He assumed that Walsh was in "great elation" with the result, though he believed that his troubles were far from over with the defeat of Parnell.[75] Then, on 17 July, he bemoaned to Donnelly the absence in Dublin of a leader of the calibre of Cardinal Cullen, "who went straight and was a churchman first of all". As it is, he observed, referring to Walsh, "we have been led by a ... political gadfly into our present wretched position, and I see no sign that our body, as a body, has learned anything. They are plotting away for Dillon's leadership as hotly as if nothing happened."[76]

Walsh, certainly, seemed to feel the struggle was over in the weeks after Carlow, but he was far from elated. Hence, on 14 August he wrote rather aggressively to Kirby that he might silence criticism amongst his "good friends" by asking "if they knew of any other nation which at the call of the bishops cut off its profligate leader at the cost of wrecking its national hopes".[77] On 9 September he felt free to take a month's holiday, mainly in France and Germany.[78]

DEATH. LIBEL. AFTERMATH.

Charles Stewart Parnell died unexpectedly at Brighton on 6 October 1891. Most people learned of the death from the evening papers on 7 October. His body was returned to Ireland on 11 October, and was buried in Glasnevin cemetery as vast crowds thronged the streets of Dublin in a spirit of deep respect and regret. Archbishop Walsh was in England when the news broke. He returned to Dublin on 9 October. Within a few days he found himself the focus of some most unpleasant and libellous publicity.

There was published in an American newspaper, 8 October, a message "By cable to the *Advertiser*" stating: "London, Oct. 7 – The *Dublin Catholic*, an official organ of the Catholic hierarchy, will print tomorrow a leader by Archbishop Walsh which will create a sensation and meet with expressions of dissent. The prelate follows Parnell into the grave with the denunciations of the church." The main part of the text of the alleged leader read:

> Mr Parnell's death is one of those events which remind the world of God. So far as known, Mr Parnell died unrepented of the offence against his God and his country. He died plotting fresh discord, while the champion or tool of faction, steeped in traitorism to the very lips. By the grave now open, charity can scarcely find a place. Such tears as are shed must be for the memory of what he had once been. ... To Catholics the close of Mr Parnell's career is one of terrible significance. Death has come in the home of sin, his last glimpse of the world unhallowed by the consolations of religion, his memory linked forever with her whose presence seems to forbid all thought of repentance ... He has passed into eternity without a sign of sorrow for the insult offered to morality, for his offence against the law resting at the base of society, for his revolt against his native land and against the anointed prelates and ministers of God's church.[79]

These sentiments, so shocking in a Christian minister, and, in fact, so unlike in style and attitude to anything written by Walsh, appeared in the *Chicago Herald* on 8 October, and was then taken up by other papers in the United States and England.

The *Herald*, in its comment, deplored "the spirit of vindictiveness" in the words, the amazing "personal hate" reflected "in tone and temper".[80] The *United Press* quoted a Catholic nationalist as saying that there was "something very strange in the representative on earth of the never failing mercy of God declaring that 'by the grave now open, charity can scarcely find a place'."[81] The English *Times* carried an editorial on 10 October relating to the matter. If the purpose behind the attribution to Walsh was to evoke criticism of the Irish bishops and to undermine in America support for the followers of McCarthy, Dillon and company, the attempt was successful in the short term. Walsh received a personal indication of the distaste and anger aroused in America from a letter which accompanied a news clipping of his alleged words. It was sent on 8 October, and the clipping may have been his first acquaintance with the article.

The letter, from a P. Kelly, New York, distilled venom, terming Walsh "a loath-some reptile" and "a crawling maggot", to use only its less offensive expletives.

Walsh, remarkably, appears not to have heard of the article in the *Herald* for many days after his return to Ireland on 9 October. Doubtless there was a back log of diocesan work to catch up on, and if he did hear of the articles and comments, perhaps he thought it best in the current climate to ignore them. After some time, however, he sought legal advice as to how he might counter the charges at their source, in an American newspaper. Eventually, he contacted an American lawyer, John Dillon's older brother, William Dillon of Castle Rock, Douglas, Colorado. Walsh wrote to him on 28 October 1891, and set the record straight. There was not "one particle of truth", he declared, in the *Herald's* story. The sole foundation for it seems to have been an article in "a strongly denunciatory spirit" which was published in the *Irish Catholic*, but he had nothing to do with that paper or its articles. He, in fact, had been in England at the time of Parnell's death, and never heard of the article until some days after he returned home.[82]

Walsh also denied authorship to newspapers nearer home. It turned out that "the article" in the *Irish Catholic* was an editorial.[83] Walsh, according to his secretary and first biographer, received many apologies.[84] The American lawyer assured Walsh that he would communicate at once with some eminent lawyers in Chicago, who were friends of his.[85] The next extant reference to the case was not until 15 March 1892, when Dillon replied to an enquiry from Walsh's Dublin solicitor. He was surprised, he stated, to receive his letter, as he had been informed that the *Herald* claimed it had made ample apology, and from this he had presumed that the case had been settled.[86] Nothing other than apologies appear to have been obtained.

A RETROSPECTIVE VIEW

Examining the Parnell crisis in retrospect, it seems clear that two issues combined to bring Parnell down: the issue of immorality, and the issue created by his manifesto – the spurning of Gladstone and the prospects of Home Rule. To counter the opposition created by these factors, Parnell manoeuvred with great skill to shift blame from himself to others, and so perfidious Albion was once again made the villain of the piece, with Catholic churchmen as its willing dupes. Many of the latter over-reacted and, as Bishop O'Dwyer indicated, demonised Parnell, seeing themselves as saving the faith of the people but also, in the process, reasserting their hold on the same people, a hold which had been loosened during the hegemony of Parnell. The bishops' and priests' links with the anti-Parnellites, and the vituperation of the *National Press*, further intensified the anti-clerical reaction among sections of the Parnellites; and there were also individuals from other religious traditions, with their own distorted views of Catholic churchmen, to stir the pot, then and later. Among the later eloquent promoters of the Parnell myth were not only the youthful Joyce, but also the more established W.B. Yeats, who glorified the Chief and endowed posterity with his own partial view:

> The Bishops and the Party
> That tragic story made,
> A husband who had sold his wife
> And after that betrayed;
> ...
> And Parnell loved his country
> And Parnell loved his lass.[87]

Walsh, in practical terms, had found himself in an impossible situation once the scandal was confirmed. His strong nationalist sympathies led him to hope against hope that Parnell would prove to be innocent. He strongly wished him to continue as leader, but once the scandal was confirmed he understood that he could not be any longer a supporter of a national party led by Parnell, and, moreover, that he could not remain silent. To do so would be interpreted as approval, and this conflicted essentially with his obligations as bishop, and, besides, would have been strongly opposed by Cardinal Manning and the authorities in Rome. He deferred opposition, nevertheless, and entered into discussions with the members of the national party who believed that Parnell had to go. He did so with a view to the condemnation coming primarily from the party, rather than from the official church. In the bitter protracted conflict, therefore, he avoided precipitous action in the political sphere and so conducted affairs as not to ruffle the sensibilities of Rome or of most of his fellow-bishops.

The price, however, that he, the bishops and priests, and the majority of the party, had to pay for destroying Parnellite power on the parliamentary level and containing it in the country was "the consolidation of a sizable, hard-core, anti-clerical minority, which would continue to exist whether it could find adequate expression in parliament or not".[88]

IMMEDIATE AFTERMATH

In the months following the intense and bitter struggle culminating in the death of Parnell, there was deep division and a disillusionment with politics. Walsh moved between a mild euphoria and a weariness with political matters. On 4 November he assured Leo XIII that Parnellism was overcome, thanks "to the unwavering firmness of the bishops, and, I should add, also of the priests, with scarcely an exception". He followed that over-statement with the comment that in the aftermath of Parnell's death "there has, not unnaturally, been, in many quarters, a sort of revival of sympathy and kindly feeling, inspired by the recollection of his unquestionable political capacity and of the services he rendered to

Ireland before his unhappy fall". "But", he affirmed, "this is little more than a matter of personal feeling".[89]

Croke felt quite spent and let down. He wrote to Walsh on 8 November with respect to a fund for the anti-Parnellite body. "We cannot support the new fund. It is a sectional thing. Our subscriptions were always given for a national purpose, and to a national fund. Dillon is not the country; Healy is not the country. So, of course, *we* should have nothing to say to either of them." "As for me generally", he continued, "'the shutters are up' never to come down. I am done with Irish affairs in *church and state*. I have played my last card. Going on for 74 years of age, I should have something else to think of besides Irish politics. Charity begins at home."[90]

Walsh refused to get involved in disputes between nationalists in an election contest between Redmond and Davitt, and urged a truce and peace over Christmas, but the local clergy intervened in support of Davitt. Redmond won. Walsh's energy and desire to fix matters, however, led him to print a letter addressed to the lord mayor of Dublin outlining a scheme for unity among the contending parties. Croke praised the copy Walsh sent him on 27 December, but advised that "the one and only wise course just now is to let the row go on, and look out in time for the survival of the fittest". He concluded, however, with – "Go ahead, all the same".[91]

Walsh went ahead, irrespective of numerous other concerns. Such was his capacity for disciplined work, that one has to remind oneself that in the midst of all the tensions and negotiations relating to Parnell, he remained first and foremost the episcopal administrator of the country's most populated diocese, with all the responsibilities and cares, spiritual and social, which that involved. His care of the poor, indeed, and his active concern in the cause of Dublin's workers was to help overcome much of the residue of Parnellite hostility to be expected in the city's working class. In addition in these years he was actively involved in pressing the cause of the teacher training colleges, and the national schools, and writing numerous letters on the impending Education Bill, as well as being involved successfully in a public debate with a Mr T.W. Russell who had "spoken and written much against the recognition in Irish schools of the religion of the Irish majority".[92] He was also engaged in protracted negotiations on the future of the *Freeman's Journal*.

THE DEATH AND LOSS OF CARDINAL MANNING

This first period of Walsh's episcopacy came to an end early in the new year with the death of his friend, supporter and mentor, Cardinal Henry Edward Manning. A report from the Archbishop's House, Westminister, on 14 January, announced that at eight o'clock that morning the cardinal had "expired calmly without any agony". Messages of sympathy came from across the world. In England the labour unions, equally with the diplomatic corps, mourned his loss.

Irish newspapers recalled his breadth of vision, interest in and generosity towards Ireland. The Dublin municipal council passed a resolution of regret, and observed that the cardinal was "a friend of the poor and a champion of justice to all men"; and the standing committee of the bishops sent their heart-felt sympathy. Walsh, Brownrigg of Ossory, and O'Callaghan of Cork, went to London for the funeral.[93]

As if to mark further the end of an era, a letter from Kirby to Walsh, five days later, reported the death of Cardinal Simeoni, prefect of Propaganda Fide.[94] Kirby was happy to report, however, on 27 January, that Simeoni's successor was "the pious and learned Pole, Cardinal Ledochowski", a great friend of Cardinal Cullen.[95] The news from Westminister was far less happy. The old friendly relationship was over. The cardinal's successor was an 'Old English Catholic', William Vaughan, who resented "Walsh's attitude to his beloved periodical the *Tablet*, and also his friendship with Manning",[96] and this was to play a part in one of the great disappointments of Walsh's life, namely his being passed over for elevation to the cardinalate. He was aware that his political sympathies and involvements had made him enemies at London and Rome, but he was also aware that in ability and powers of leadership he surpassed all his fellow bishops.

He had it "on good authority", O'Dwyer informed Donnelly on 29 Novemiber, that the pope at his next consistory intended to appoint an Irish cardinal, and that the merits of Walsh and Logue "were being weighed", but that Logue was likely to be appointed.[97] His information was reliable. Walsh's opponents in Rome included Persico, in the important position of secretary at Propaganda, while from England Lord Salisbury, the prime minister, publicly charged Walsh with defying the pope's authority,[98] and Archbishop Vaughan, as a result, found further grounds for expressing his opposition. On 18 December, Walsh wrote graciously to Logue:

> I hope I am among the very first to congratulate your Grace on the signal honour conferred upon you by the Holy See. I do not know whether any official news has yet reached you. But I had a telegram today from a friend in Rome which leaves no uncertainty about your promotion to the cardinalate. I sincerely trust this may be the means of strengthening your Grace's hands in the management of your somewhat unruly team!"[99]

A letter from Patrick O'Donnell, bishop of Raphoe, in the ecclesiastical province of Armagh, summed up the views of a great many of the clergy and the laity across the country. He wrote to Walsh from Letterkenny, on 3 January 1893:

> In this part of the world, while there is general gladness at the elevation of the primate to the cardinalate, there is general regret that the red hat for your Grace has been kept back. I believe these two currents of feeling

are not confined to any one part of Ireland ... With some reason you will be considered to have suffered from the enemies of Ireland's cause.

Being "clothed in scarlet", he went on, would have been the prize for keeping quiet, but "no one who knows your Grace would for a moment dream that anything could turn you from taking the part you have been taking in every holy cause and in the affairs of our poor country."[100]

At this stage, towards the close of the tumultuous first fifteen years of his prelacy, it is almost a relief to turn for a while from strict chronology to critically consider William Walsh from a more thematic point of view: as bishop, as a human being, and in terms of his distinctive roles as an arbitrator and as an educationalist.

PART THREE

The bishop. The man. The arbitrator.
The educationalist, 1885-1912

Each mortal thing does one thing and the same:
Deals out that being indoors each one dwells;
...
Crying *What I do is me* ...

The Poems of Gerald Manley Hopkins,
ed. W. H. Gardiner & N.H. MacKenzie, London 1970,
Poem 157, p. 90 (italics added)

IX

The bishop in retrospect, 1885-1900

1. ADMINISTRATOR. MAN OF SPECIAL INTERESTS

Apart from five months spent in Rome in 1888, and the two months there in 1891, William Walsh was seldom absent from Dublin for longer than his annual five weeks holidays. These were taken in the autumn, and included visits to France, Belgium, Austria and Germany, Italy and Spain. They were usually planned to coincide with opera festivals and concerts.

Administration and temperament

In administering the diocese he relied very much on his diocesan council. The council met on Tuesdays, and sometimes more frequently. Even minor ecclesiastical appointments were made in council. He always presided at these meetings. It was sometimes remarked that he relied too much on the advice of his counsellors, but such reliance was deliberate on his part. He was not a pastoral bishop, as Persico remarked, at least not in the sense of a man who went about among people and whose door was always open to them. As was noted during his student days, he was not a "hail-fellow-well-met", he had not the common touch. His upbringing as an only child, who had no interest in team games, meant that, to a large extent, he became accustomed to being on his own and to pursuing his own intersts and amusements. The world of books and music became particularly fulfilling for him. Accordingly, he realised that as a bishop his personal temperament and studious habits would tend to keep him at a distance, and hence, as his secretary Patrick J. Walsh observed, "he felt that in estimating the character and appraising the merits of his priests he ought generally to rely on the judgement of his official advisers, whose knowledge of the clergy was more intimate and likely to be more accurate than his own".[1]

Walsh's aloofness, which also made possible the volume of work he accomplished, became a byword in the diocese. It was commonly remarked by clergy and laity that it was easier to gain audience of the pope than of Dr Walsh. This feature of distance became marked within a year of his being made archbishop, and seems to have been calculated to discourage people from dropping in casually at Rutland Square, seeking alms, or favours for relations or friends, or with a complaint of some sort. To this end, as has been seen, he placed a notice in the *Irish Catholic Directory* for 1886 advising visitors to write in advance for appointment, and advertising restricted hours 'at home'.[2] This is said to have reduced by half the visitors to the residence. Visitors seeking favours were further deterred by a notification that his Grace had made it a rule not to make any intercession on behalf of seekers for office or positions of trust. This stance, partly to preserve his independence, he was not always able, or willing, to maintain. Applicants for educational positions wrote to him throughout his career, and the unsuccessful amongs them retained, not infrequently, a sense of grievance.[3]

In a further effort to escape intrusion and facilitate work, Walsh leased, in March 1886, a substantial house in its own grounds, "Thorncliffe", in the fashionable suburb of Rathgar. This provided a haven, especially at weekends. Before long, however, he decided to pursue Cardinal Cullen's intention of building a permanent archbishop's residence on land adjoining Clonliffe College, in the less fashionable northern suburb of Drumcondra. The house at Drumcondra became a preoccupation. He was determined that it would meet all his requirements. It featured prominently in his thoughts from September 1888 to October 1890 when he moved into it.

Building and moving house

William Hague Jr, a leading Catholic architect, was appointed to plan the edifice. Walsh was clear that he wished the building to contain a hall for the conferences of the episcopal standing committee, a large library, an attractive oratory, and bedrooms and offices, and the whole illuminated by electric light.[4] The eventual construction was a substantial, detached, two storey over basement residence, set in its own grounds. The upper storeys were largely in red brick, which gave rise to the contemporary sobriquet, ' the brick palace'.[5]

The work of construction did not pass without problems. In November 1889, a deputation from the plasterers' union demanded of the contractor, William Connolly & Son, that "none other than regular plasterers" be employed "in the erection of the new palace at Clonliffe". The assurance was given, and potential trouble averted. More problems, however, arose in February 1890, when an unfounded charge was made at a Dublin Trades Council meeting that the "ornamental plaster casts" for the archbishop's house were ordered from London when they could have been obtained in Dublin.[6]

Where Walsh was concerned, certain features occupied his special attention. One was that the house be lit throughout by electric light.[7] Another feature reflecting his special interests, this time in astronomy, was the installation of a telescope on the roof of the new building. In keeping with his usual attention to detail, he had the celebrated designers of telescopes, the Dublin brothers, Thomas and Howard Grubb, assemble a three-inch achromatic instrument. Walsh's main preoccupation, however, was the building of a library. He had a voluminous collection of books, and with his varied interests was likely to accumulate many more. How best accommodate them was the problem. He had still not resolved this as late as March 1890, when an article appeared in the *Nineteenth Century* magazine on the arrangement and shelving of books in large private libraries. The author was William Ewart Gladstone. Walsh wrote to him, and in May accepted an invitation from the former prime minister to visit him at Hawarden, North Wales, and inspect his newly-built library holding some thirty thousand volumes. On his return to Dublin, Walsh wrote to Gladstone to say that he would follow his plan of projecting bookcases "to a large extent". In the event, he confined the installation of the bookcases to one end of the room and made the library fulfill the dual purpose of accomodating his books in projecting bookcases and providing space for holding the meetings of the episcopal standing committee.[8] This last, emphasised further his dominant role in that committee. It was here that the meeting was held whence the telegram was sent on 3 December to the Irish parliamentary party in London declaring "Mr Parnell unfit for leadership ..."

In the autumn of 1890, as the house neared completion, Walsh took his usual continental holiday. On this particular trip, he and his secretary visited Belgium, France, Germany, Austria, Italy and Switzerland. In Germany, they followed by boat and train the course of the Rhine from Cologne to Mainz, taking in Johannes Schilling's impressive monument to German feats of arms in the Franco-Prussian war. From Mainz, they headed east to Ratisbon (Regensburg), where they saw the Danube in full flood. On the homeward stretch of the journey, they climbed the Eiffel Tower in Paris, then a novel tourist attraction open to the public barely a year. While the archbishop was abroad, his friend, Thomas McGrath, professor of science and philosophy at Clonliffe College, wrote enthusiastically that he recently saw the house lit up by electric light for the first time and "the transformation wrought in the appearance of the largest rooms was almost magical".[9]

On 7 October, shortly after Walsh's return to Dublin, his brief diary entry – "4.30. New house", heralded his moving to his new home. A month later he expressed his satisfaction with his new residence in a letter to Tobias Kirby at the Irish College, Rome:

> I am now in a grand new home, where I have, for the first time since I left Maynooth, the advantage and comfort of a library. This facilitates my work enormously.[10]

Contacting the parishes and the clergy

The practice in the diocese was that there was an episcopal visitation, and the administration of confirmation, in every parish at least once every three years, and in some of the more populous parishes every year. Walsh generally managed to confer the sacrament personally in each country parish, and frequently in the other parishes of the diocese. It was his custom on these occasions to examine the children in their catechism, and to address them in homely, simple language. The extent of the demands on him at such times is suggested by a newspaper report in June 1893, concerning confirmations at Athy, Co. Kildare, for over 400 children, after which he "visited the new convent schools ... erected at a cost of over £3,000". "In the evening three local bands escorted his Grace to the railway station upon his departure."[11]

Except on these occasions, he scarcely ever preached. It will be recalled that one of the reasons he raised against being appointed bishop was his inability to preach. On the few occasions on which he preached formally from the pulpit, he was embarrassingly ill at ease and nervous. On the other hand, when it came to carefully prepared addresses on special occasions, such as the formal opening of churches and schools, the laying of foundation-stones, or appealing for funds for works of religion or charity, he seemed to have little difficulty. Indeed, he appeared to welcome such opportunities; and as these were usually reported at some length in the Dublin and national papers, they were occasions for expressing his views, and the means whereby those views were brought to the notice of the mass of the Irish people. The people of his diocese rallied to him, especially when he appealed to their charity, with the result that he was able to contribute, month after month, thousands of pounds to Catholic charities. He took to heart Archbishop Croke's advice given him early in his episcopal career: "Give constantly, give lavishly, munificently. Promise even when you have nothing in hand. You have the confidence of the country, and Dublin and Ireland will never see you short."[12] The diocesan archives indicate how he availed of that "confidence". Records survive of considerable sums contributed by him towards the building, enlargement, and furnishing of churches, schools, hospitals and other charitable institutions. Between 1885 and 1916 some 24 to 30 new churches were erected in the diocese, mostly in rural and suburban areas, and most of them after the turn of the century.[13] Many other churches had extensions added to them. With respect to primary schools there is reference to approximately seventy new schools, and over forty extensions.[14]

The overall size of the diocese has to be kept in mind. According to the census of 1891, Dublin city had a population of 384,000 Catholics out of an overall population of 493,690. In addition, there was the considerable Catholic population in country areas. The diocese had 64 parishes in 1895: 14 in the city and 50 in rural and town areas. To be serviced also, with chaplains and/or masses, were eight workhouses, four prisons, two asylums, ten institutions of military or police personnel, and a range of charitable institutions – 8 hospitals, 2 institutions for the blind, 2 for the deaf, 2 houses for the aged, one house for widows, and 4 Magdalene homes or places of refuge for women who had been sexually abused or been obliged to practise prostitution. The main educational needs of the large Catholic population were met by national schools and private schools providing primary education. Fourteen colleges were engaged in intermediate education, some of them also in third level education. In addition, there was one "ragged school", two industrial schools, and one reformatory. Many of these varied educational establishments were run by religious congregations, of which there were 27 of priests, and three of religious brothers. The religious sisters had some 80 convents in the diocese.

Finally, a grouping of special interest for Dr Walsh were the refuges: for homeless boys – the Sacred Heart Home, and the Catholic Boys Home; a night refuge for unemployed and homeless men; and fourteen orphanages.[15] The Poor Law authorities, during the 1880s and 1890s, found it hard to cope with the numbers of homeless and unemployed men. Improvements in transport, and developments in the retail trade, which allowed cheap mass-produced goods to penetrate all corners of Ireland, led to more and more skilled workers and artisans appearing in the jail registers on vagrancy charges. One Poor Law inspector in 1886 attributed the rise in the numbers seeking temporary overnight accommodation to the destitution of artisans in particular.[16] In the 1890s the annual total admission of night lodgers to work-houses in Ireland for the first week of every month was 27,261 men, and 7,057 women.[17] On the streets of Dublin a considerable number of the homeless were young boys, undisciplined, with little or no schooling or training, and harshly treated by the law. For them, the archbishop had a deep and special concern.

At the close of Walsh's life it used to be said that few bishops had conferred the sacrament of Holy Orders more frequently than he, or ordained a greater number of priests. Apart from the general diocesan ordinations on the days prescribed by the liturgy, he usually presided at the annual ordinations at Maynooth. This could be very demanding. Thus, to take the example of ordinations in June 1893: on Sunday, 18 June, 68 students received the tonsure; on Monday, 19 June, 80 received the minor order of lectorship and 73 the order of acolyte; on Wednesday, 49 were ordained sub-deacons: on Saturday, 36 were conferred with the order of deacon; and on Sunday, 25 June, he ordained 31 as priests.[18] Some years the numbers were greater. In 1899, 83 received the diaconate, and 82 were ordained to the priesthood.[19] In addition to Maynooth ordinations, he conferred orders each year at the Jesuit theological college at Miltown Park, Dublin, and, whenever possible, at All Hallows College for missionary priests. He invariably conducted religious ceremonies with dignity, precision, and endless endurance. The only occasion when he admitted near exhaustion was when, in his seventies, he consecrated over a hundred altar stones, which required numerous incensations and the recitation of various prayers and formulae, and ended with the celebration of mass. The ceremony began at 7.00 a.m. and lasted until 1.00 p.m., and he was on his feet for most of that time![20]

In the harmonious running of a diocese, the bishop's relations with his priests is of major importance. When visiting parishes for confirmation, or other occasions, Walsh made it a point to meet the local clergy. He was sensitive generally in his dealings with them, whether in speaking or writing to curates, or in suggesting to an aged parish priest that he should consider retiring, or to another that he would be better suited to another parish.[21]

The archives for each year have one or more files relating to the diocesan clergy. These, to take 1893, a not unusual year, for example, contain such mat-

ters as: conflicts between parish priests and curates; the needs of schools; problems about wills; arranging for confirmations and retreats; parish appointments
and the appointment of military chaplains; marriage problems; problems created
by a difficult curate involved in a boycott of parishioners on political grounds,
and without reference to his parish priest; the need to reprimand curates mentioned in the *Freeman's Journal* as immersed in political affairs and hindering the
unity of the parliamentary party. In some years there were complaints against
priests on the grounds of neglect of their duties because of alcoholic indulgence.
In 1893 the occasion of scandal was a charge of "depravity" against a priest said
to have been in bed with a woman. The archbishop had an investigation carried
out, and the evidence seemed doubtful. He summoned the curate to him, and
removed him from active service. The curate's parish priest wrote to say he had
never heard any criticism of the man. The possibility of false charges was always
present, as instances of sexual immorality were known to evoke a quick response
from bishops. In 1894, an accused priest claimed to have been dealt with
peremptorily and unfairly. Because of alleged imprudent behaviour with women
in the Baldoyle district, he was moved to Newtown-Mount-Kennedy, Co.
Wicklow, and, he claimed, he was given no chance of defending himself. He
denied that anything untoward had happened and stated that he was prepared
to meet anyone making such charges.[22]

As a rule, Walsh tried to be fair, and to err on the side of leniency. He
could, however, as suggested above, take a firm and definite stand. To one
priest, who again and again seemed to have set at nought "diocesan authority",
Walsh wrote on 7 November 1893. "I regret to have to say that the time has
passed when we can allow our action" (his and the vicar general's) "to be stayed
by anything short of actual compliance with what you have been authoritatively
directed to do. It is exceedingly unpleasant to me to find myself compelled, as
you have compelled me, to write in such terms to any priest in the diocese. I
have now, for the second time, to name a date for your compliance with the
diocesan statute. I have hereby to require you to send to me the paper, setting
forth the settlement of account, signed by both you and Fr Dunne before next
Monday."[23]

To another priest, whom he had not had occasion to correct previously, he
wrote the previous day in a caring, yet firm way. He was "sorry to find" that
the priest in question was "unable to discharge the chaplaincy of the convent
with that regularity which is essential". "I trust you will be able to assure me",
the archbishop continued, "that the cause of the irregularity was temporary and
that I may count on the convent mass being said regularly in future."[24]

The mention of chaplaincy duties in a convent points to Walsh's care of
nuns or religious sisters. They were dependent on the clergy for mass and the
sacraments, and often they were taken for granted and at times treated cavalierly.
The considerable extant correspondence between the convents and the archbishop suggests that he was accessible and kind to those in difficulty.[25] It also

reveals him involved in a whole range of activities on their behalf., with respect, for example, to their schools and the qualifications of the sisters who were teachers, the payment of teachers, examination papers, new foundations, and so on, at primary and secondary education levels; or with regard to hospitals, or the work of the Little Sisters of the Assumption nursing the sick poor.[26]

In his relations with the religious congregations of men he was correct and careful, though at times he could prove unduly sensitive, high-handed and intransigent, especially with respect to educational issues. Something of this has been seen with respect to the Jesuits and higher education. The Carmelites, as will appear, were to experience these aspects in relation to primary education.

Some of Walsh's special interests flowed over into his work as bishop and made an impact on the diocese and, at times, on the entire Irish church. Among these special interests may be mentioned: music; religious education; social issues relating to the deprived, the underdog, and the sick; and an issue which combined national and religious history, namely, the cause of the Irish martyrs.

Music

The archbishop's well known interest in music and pride in nationality led to his being invited to become a patron and financial supporter of the first Irish musical festival, known as the Feis Ceol. On 27 May 1896, the committee of the festival invited him to a public meeting at the Mansion House on 15 June, where a report on the progress to date would be read and at which his Grace was requested to speak in support of the festival and its aim, "to promote the practice of choral and instrumental music amongst the people".[27] Two years later his interest and financial assistance made him a foundation member of an enterprise led by Signor M. Esposito to develop a permanent orchestra in the city. Esposito, who was a major figure in the Royal Irish Academy of Music and in Dublin musical life, established a strong piano school in Dublin, and Walsh, as a pianist, became both a supporter and a friend. When the Italian commenced a series of Sunday orchestral concerts, they were frowned on as irreverent until it became evident that at 4.00 p.m. each Sunday, as the concerts were about to begin, his Grace was present. So, too, when Esposito introduced a Christmas-day orchestral concert.

In liturgical music, as might be expected, Walsh's influence was most marked. As noted earlier, he promoted the fitting rendering of ecclesiastical chant, and to that end edited a handbook for the clergy. His interest in church music prompted Edward Martyn, of Tellyra in the west of Ireland, a landowner and active patron of music and theatre, to found the Palestrina Choir at the Pro-Cathedral, and to place in trust a substantial sum towards its endowment.[28] Another musical group which greatly interested the archbishop was the Society of St Cecilia. He regularly attended their concerts and promoted performances by financing prizes. In July 1895, his liturgical and musical standing, and his long friendship with

Archbishop Croke, made it appropriate that he personally sing the high mass at his friend's magnificent episcopal silver jubilee, graced by a great array of bishops and clergy, and by the corporations of Limerick and Clonmel.[29]

Religious education

Much as he was concerned for the development of music in the schools, he was even more concerned about the quality of religious education being provided.

Shortly after his appointment as archbishop, Walsh modified the system of religious inspection and examination in the schools, appointing two priests to visit periodically and hold in each school an examination in christian doctrine. They presented annually to the archbishop a detailed report on the examinations. He also planned to bring out a revised catechism. After some years examining children at confirmation, he became convinced that the catechisms in use were unsatisfactory. The works in question were the *Butler Catechism,* going back to 1775, when Dr James Butler was archbishop of Cashel, and a modified version, 1882, known as the *Maynooth Catechism.* He established a committee of priests, secular and regular, with a view to securing a satisfactory revision. The catechisms were defective, in his view, in omitting matters relating to the practice or observance of religion, and the carrying out of ordinary Catholic duty. Among serious omissions, he noted "the virtue of temperance".

The committee, after four years work, produced in 1895 a draft of a largely new catechism. Copies were sent to each priest in the diocese, and to a number of bishops, for comment. In the meantime, arrangements were being made for the holding of a plenary synod of the Irish Catholic church, where the question of a uniform catechism for all the dioceses was expected to be discussed. In the light of this, work on the Dublin catechism was suspended. At the eventual synod of 1900, the question of the catechism was not dealt with, and, as Pope Pius X was said to be contemplating a catechism for general use throughout the church, Walsh abandoned the idea of publishing his catechism.[30]

Assisting the poor and sick

When it came to social issues Dublin's problems seemed endless. Walsh realised that what he could hope to achieve was very limited. He set out to alleviate distress as concretely as possible by giving financial assistance, motivating others to help, and acting on the boards of hospitals.

The Society of St Vincent de Paul presented a very practical way of providing aid. Walsh spoke publicly in support of the work of the Society from time to time, and in 1912 he was to provide funds for the establishment of a much needed Vincent de Paul night-shelter. It was the first free night accommodation for Catholic homeless men. Nightly accommodation, and a frugal meal, was provided for fifty men. Reports on the first year of operation revealed that some 34,736 men (about 100 a night) had to be refused permission so great was the demand.[31]

Newspaper reports during Walsh's long episcopacy provide many instances of his concern for the less well off. In the early 1890s he subscribed to, and wrote in support of the "Fresh Air Association", an organisation founded to bring poorer children to the country or seaside for some time in the summer, or for single days when there were larger numbers to be catered for. Some 1,700 children were given single-day holidays in 1891. Thereafter, numbers declined because of shortage of funds.[32] Concern for poorer children led to his first foundation, as has been seen. The Sacred Heart Home, Drumcondra, was to claim on 22 January 1911, that since its foundation twenty-five years previously "1,500 children had been rescued from proselytism and maintained until they were able to earn a living for themselves. They were then apprenticed to trades or placed in situations."[33]

The archbishop, at times, also subscribed to alleviate distress outside Ireland. The *Daily Chronicle*, on 1 November 1893, quoted with approval his donation and letter of support for the women and children who were suffering because of a deadlock in the Welsh mining industry. Unheralded, however, was his request seeking financial assistance, and his intercession with the Cemeteries Association, in respect of the funeral of the dying founder of the Irish Republican Brotherhood, James Stephens. It was a delicate decision for Walsh, but he was encouraged to help, apart from considerations of compassion and charity, by hearing "Canon Flanagan speaking well of the old man", who, Walsh understood, was "now observant of the duties of religion".[34]

The archbishop's concern for people's health was linked to the work of hospitals. He was chairman of the governing body of the National Maternity Hospital, Hollis Street, and, in addition to praising its work, he availed of opportunities to praise the work of St Vincent's Hospital and the Mater Hospital and to urge financial support for them. He was also a governor of what was then called the Royal Hospital for Incurables. In 1890, moreover, he presided at the thirty-second annual meeting of the friends and supporters of the Adelaide Hospital and gave the address. It was a carefully balanced, ecumenical presentation in a hospital with a Protestant tradition. He drew attention to two things: the fact that a debt of £2, 000 had been reduced by half, and that the institution had lived down "the misrepresentation and misapprehension of its enemies". "Every Protestant effort", he observed, "which had for its object the temporal advantages of those who came within its reach had had to pass through a cross-fire of criticism. Were an institution established by Protestants to which those of every denomination could gain access, then they had been accused of having in view the unworthy object of winning over those of other religions; and when such an institution has been confined solely to Protestants, they had been accused of sectarianism. To both these charges they had been subjected, but now," he asserted, "by a continuance of well-doing they had lived them down, and it was now admitted that all they had been doing the last thirty-two years had been to follow the apostolic injunction that it was right to do good to all

men, especially to those who were of the household of the faith (applause). The
work of the hospital was now recognised as a holy one."[35]

Walsh's alertness to public health needs encouraged him to co-operate whenever he could with the public health authority. An instance of this was his promotion of vaccination against smallpox. On 7 January 1895, Albert Speedy,
physician and surgeon, wrote Walsh expressing concern at the spread of a smallpox epidemic, especially among the poor. He asked the archbishop to have his
priests speak in favour of vaccination. Many of the poorer people came from the
country and had not been vaccinated. Walsh had himself re-vaccinated, and sent
a circular letter to all the parishes recommending that all over ten years of age
be vaccinated. The public health committee passed a vote of thanks to him, on
the recommendation of the medical officer, Charles A. Cameron.[36]

Temperance

One of the omissions in the catechisms which Walsh criticised was "the virtue
of temperance" He was very conscious of the damage to families caused by
excessive drinking, and how the country's image was tarnished by such indulgence, which not infrequently led to violence and drunkenness at fairs, wed-
dings, funerals, and during elections; but, at the same time, he did not wish to
associate himself with the puritanical attitude that condemned alcohol as bad;
and he was only too well aware that publicans in Ireland were frequently shop-
keepers as well as sellers of drink, that they were important sources of credit to
farmers, and were major contributors to both the Irish party and to church collections. One vitriolic commentator spoke, indeed, of the alliance between
"whiskey and holy water" as vital to the Home Rule party.[37]

Walsh endeavoured to solve the dilemma by promoting total abstinence for
adolescents, while, in the case of adults, encouraging total abstainers and moderate drinkers to work together in the cause of temperance. His total abstinence
focus was centred on Confirmation ceremonies, at each of which he concluded
by administering a pledge against intoxicating drink to the children until they
reached the age of twenty-one.[38] Where adults were concerned, his advocacy of
an association of moderate drinkers and total abstainers evoked strong criticism
from the *Catholic Times* of Liverpool,[39] and from Fr Walter O'Brien, founder of
the Fr Mathew Union, a total abstinence society for priests.[40]

In 1890 the archbishop inaugurated a national temperance movement to mark
the centenary of Fr Mathew's birth,[41] and two years later welcomed Fr James
Cullen's *Catechism on Temperance and Total Abstinence*, which sold 60,000 copies
within a year,[42] and was the harbinger of the most successful of Irish temperance
movements, the Pioneer Total Abstinence Association. Walsh, like the other
bishops, was careful to avoid any condemnation of intoxicating liquor as such,
or of publicans, but in January 1893, nevertheless, he drew attention to the
"gigantic network of temptation" presented by the excessive number of public
houses in Ireland. He noted that a bill prepared by Mr Gladstone's government

in 1871 had envisaged 7,000 public houses as adequate to meet the requirements of Ireland's population. In fact, there were 17, 000, or sufficient for a population of eleven and a half millions! Noting also the marked increase in prosecutions for drunkenness, he recommended a limiting of the hours in which public houses might open.[43]

During the 1890s, although both sections of the Home Rule party remained closely identified with the drink trade, the idea of "Ireland sober, Ireland free" was coming very much to the fore in the revitalised nationalism appearing in the Gaelic Athletic Association and the Gaelic League.[44] This facilitated the call for temperance, and in 1905 the bishops felt empowered to launch a national crusade against intemperance. Walsh, again, was very much to the fore. He entrusted to the Capuchins the leadership of the crusade, and its inauguration was marked by a huge demonstration in O'Connell street.[45] Significantly, the cause of temperance was now being taken up by worker leaders as well as by nationalists.

The cause of the Irish martyrs

In addition to the wide range of social issues which occupied his Grace at different levels, there was the area of special interest which had a historical and devotional dimension for the entire country, namely, the cause of the Irish martyrs. Work had been conducted in England for some time on the British Catholic martyrs. The "cause", as it was called, required the preparation of the *prima facie* (first impression) case for the beatification of Irish priests, religious, and laity, who were thought to have laid down their lives for their belief in the Catholic religion between 1537 and 1710. Much of the groundwork was done by Patrick F. Moran, later cardinal archbishop of Sydney. It is not clear how early in his episcopate Walsh undertook the task. Certainly, it had commenced by 1891. In that year, in a letter without any further date, Fr Denis Murphy, SJ, wrote from Miltown Park to inform the archbishop that he had written to Dr Donnelly, as his Grace had advised, "asking him to come on Thursday at 6.00 to make a beginning in the case of our martyrs". He added that he expected every moment from Rome the document "containing the official declaration of O'Herley's [*sic*] and O'Brien's death for the faith".[46] The assistance had been sought of the English Jesuits who had the experience of working on the cause of the British Jesuit martyrs. On 8 July 1891, John Morris, SJ, wrote to Walsh that he was sending "the 2 vols. of the process of the English martyrs, which contain the evidence re-arranged by the Roman lawyers".[47]

On 20 February of the following year, Murphy made it clear in a printed circular headed "private and confidential", that his Grace had established a tribunal to carry forward the process, and had made him postulator of the cause. His first duty was to present to the tribunal the required evidence. As a first step, he invited witnesses to come forward to establish by evidence that there was a traditional belief that the men and women put to death were "martyrs for the

Catholic faith and for the special authority of the vicar of Christ". The church's tradition required that the fame or public repute of martyrdom be established by oral testimony, and that the "witnesses" giving the testimony "might speak to public repute", "local or general traditions", as well as to information acquired by books.[48]

In June 1896, following the death of Denis Murphy, the archbishop petitioned the Jesuit provincial for a replacement to continue the work. He suggested Edmund Hogan, professor of Irish History and Language at University College, with whom he corresponded from time to time.[49] Hogan, in fact, came to work with him on the cause of the martyrs, as did Fr John McErlean, Jesuit archivist and Irish language scholar, but it was another Jesuit, John Conmee, who assumed Murphy's mantle as vice-postulator of the cause.

At this point it is well to view the martyrs' cause as a whole during the course of the archbishop's life. His contribution was of major significance. The key figures, apart from Walsh, were the postulators and vice-postulators. The postulators resided in Rome and were, Monsignor William H. Murphy, rector of the Irish College, Rome, until his death in 1905, and then his successors as rector, Monsignor Michael O'Riordan, and Monsignor John Hagan. John Conmee was vice-postulator from 1903 until his death in 1910, when he was succeeded by the Dominican, Fr M.H. MacInerney, who contributed two important articles in *Studies*, June and December 1921, entitled, "Archbishop Walsh and the Irish Martyrs".

The Irish bishops, in 1902, formally entrusted care of the cause to Walsh. The work rate and range intensified almost immediately. Lay scholars as well as those from religious orders, and bishops such as Drs Healy, Moran, and O'Doherty of Derry, were at different times involved in the process. In January 1903, an informative and perceptive letter came from the English Jesuit historian and author, John Hungerford Pollen. Walsh had written to him about the cause of the Irish martyrs. In the course of his letter he conveyed his pleasant memories of Pollen's father. Pollen was gratified, and ventured some serious historical advice based on his own work on the English martyrs and on his experiences at Rome.

Pollen's historical advice

"Looking at your list of names", he wrote, "I would (if I may make bold to do so) suggest that *no names should be Latinised*, but that form should be taken at once which will be most useful in popular devotions. We have steadily done this, and with good results." Moving on to historical accuracy and scholarship, he observed:

> I fancy that your Lordship need not fear any serious attack from the *Promotor Fidei* at Rome. *Entre Nous* the opposite is rather to be dreaded. They will delay a long time, and then perhaps pass the weakest causes ...

I am therefore tempted to beg you Lordship to be just a *little* severe in arranging your catalogue. The ages in front of us will probably be more cynical, or critical, or at all events less simple than ours, and we must endeavour to do what will be helpful to them. For the attacks of the open enemies of our Faith, we need not fear so much, but the harm that may come from want of adequate sensible criticism of ancient evidence – may be serious.

This, no doubt, his Lordship knew better than he, "but", Pollen continued:

I have had a good deal of experience of Rome, and I know some of the dangers there. They are excellent at canon law, but execrable at history. Do not leave historical problems to be solved by them. It is only too easy to get favourable verdicts by trading on their want of general information. But the advance of the martyrs' cause will suffer, unless the first steps are taken with great deliberation, unless the foundation stones are laid perfectly square, and of a faultless material.

In bringing his letter to a close, he apologised for letting his pen "run off like this *apropos of nothing* but a few *ineptiae*, of which" he "was an irritated witness, when in Rome". "Still", he concluded, "I will let this letter go, in the chance of it serving to remind you to moderate the zeal of some over fervent *cultores martyrum*. Their cause is a noble one, and your Lordship will find that in promoting it you will have given an impetus to the study of church history – to an extent which will surprise and delight you."[50]

Towards completion

Following the completion of lengthy research preparations, the first session of the judicial proceeding, known as the Information Process, was held at Archbishop's House on 18 February 1904. The examination of witnesses was held two or three times a week, each session lasting about three hours, at most of which the archbishop presided. The examinations continued until 23 December 1904. Walsh observed to Edmund Hogan that if "the case were pushed on with phenominal activity" they might live to take part in the 'apostolic process'.[51] Sadly, "phenomenal activity" could not work miracles with the 292 names which were considered worthy of inclusion. The weighty volumes were brought to Rome by Fr Conmee. It was not until 1915 that the Sacred Congregation of Rites gave approval to the introduction of the names, and then not of the 292 but of 259. Dr Walsh was then appointed judge-delegate of the Holy See to institute and direct the apostolic process in the Dublin diocesan court. With the assistance of the bishops and of religious orders, some 20 to 30 competent scholars were assembled as "witnesses", and, after additional preparatory evidence had been gathered, the first session of the apostolic process was held on 5 June 1917. From then until the day before Archbishop Walsh left for hospital for the last time, sessions were held three times a week and he presided over almost all of them. The evidence for candidates, now reduced to 107, and its translation – running to some 9, 000 folio pages – was transmitted to the Holy See. The first fruits of it all, and of intensive later labours, had to wait until 1995, when seventeen named persons, of the 107, were declared beatified. The cause, however, and its vast monument of historical work, remains a memorial to the motivation and dedication of Archbishop William Walsh.[52]

Some observations and Monsignor Persico

In the light of all the foregoing, the observations of Monsignor Persico that "he lacks the pastoral spirit" and "many bishops consider him more secular than episcopal",[53] seem quite wide of the mark. True, he devoted a vast amount of time and correspondence during his first years as archbishop to non-diocesan matters, but then he did not view the secular as necessarily separate from the episcopal or the pastoral, and like Manning he resolutely opposed any effort to confine bishops and priests to the sacristy. He believed they had a role to play in 'secular' areas such as education, health, social justice, and the moral standards of professional and public life. The point of the criticism, however, maybe that he was 'secular' because of his involvement and partisanship in politics. But to proceed from there to "he lacks the pastoral spirit" is quite excessive. Walsh was not a bishop who rubbed shoulders in the market place, but his care for the poor, for standards amongst his priests, for social justice, for the building of churches and schools, and the careful provision of church services, show a man with strong pastoral concerns, even if he remained personally aloof. Moreover, in more indirect yet influential ways, he was also pastoral in favouring woman-suffrage and the admission of women to the universities and professions; in encouraging Sunday amusements provided they did not clash with the times of public devotion; in abhorring religious rancour, promoting mutual respect between the Christian churches, and seeking no Catholic ascendancy. Even his 'secular' involvement served the pastoral function of keeping the official Catholic church in touch with the majority of the people at a time of great division and change.[54]

Another remark of Persico, however, seems nearer the mark. In a letter to Manning on 17 February 1888, he ventured the comment, "I would like to see him a little more spiritual".[55] Walsh's faith, despite his learning and sophistication, remained the simple faith of the unsophisticated Irish Catholic, and the piety he had been schooled in from childhood remained with him to the end. It was a largely hidden piety. Even at home his devotions were largely private. At mass in his oratory he normally had only his valet in attendance, who served the mass. The divine office he used to say in the privacy of his bedroom. The rosary and the litany of the Blessed Virgin were favoured devotions, again said privately or with a few friends.[56]

Walsh's privacy projected little in the way of spiritual fervour to his people, and his extant letters and papers are devoid of any unction and make little mention of personal prayer. One experiences no sense of the man of God envisaged by the exemplar post-tridentine archbishop, St Charles Borromeo: "There is nothing quite so necessary to all churchmen as mental prayer, prayer that paves the way for every act we do, that accompanies it, and follows it up".[57] In this, Walsh reflected what has been seen, more than fifty years after him, as a basic weakness in the Irish Catholic church, its neglect of "religious experience and prayer – the mystical dimension". "Perhaps", it has been suggested, because 'the faith of the simple people' was seen as strong, "the main emphasis was towards strengthening the institutional church; marginal effort was put into strengthening the intellectual basis of the church's pastoral presence, and the prayer, religious experience, mystical element was given the lowest priority rating".[58] Such spiritual deficiency as Walsh may have had was probably shared by most of the hierarchy, and certainly did not prevent his acknowledged ascendancy amongst his fellow prelates. No consideration of him as bishop would be complete without considering this aspect.

Walsh's friend and confidant, the priest historian, Myles V. Ronan, observed that "his personality was of the dominant type", and that he was "a man who could lead and unite others", not only by his strength of will and intellect, but by his powers of persuasion. Few were prepared to enter into controversy with him. Ronan conveyed something of his ascendancy in a graphic illustration, which, if overdrawn, still suggests his undoubted influence.

> Often at a meeting of the hierarchy in Maynooth the bishops would discuss matters and come to no conclusion. Then Cardinal Logue would say: "My Lords, I think you have discussed long enough. But what has his Grace of Dublin to say?" The archbishop then would put his case. He spoke as one having authority. He spoke as if he were expounding a thesis to students. When he had finished, the cardinal would say: "Well, my Lords, you have heard what his Grace of Dublin has said. Has anyone anything else to say?" The discussion was over. "Well, now", the cardinal would say, turning to the archbishop, "will your Grace put in writing what you propose?" This was done in perfect style, and delivered to the secretaries of the meeting.

"This is just an indication", Ronan continued, "of the universal respect of the Irish bishops for his Grace's opinion in ecclesiastical and secular matters. They looked to him for guidance in difficult and critical affairs."[59]

As has been seen in the story so far, there were bishops who took an independent stand, such as Croke on university education, and Healy and O'Dwyer, who resented having matters expounded to them and stood out against him on a number of issues, but even then they felt obliged to listen to his advice "in difficult and critical affairs".

2. APOLOGETICS, AUTOCRATIC INTERLUDES, AND ILL-HEALTH

When the *Catholic Times* criticised Walsh's support for an organisation embracing moderate drinkers and total abstainers, it received an angry response. Walsh accused the paper of innaccurately reporting Irish ecclesiastical affairs, and subsequently at a public meeting declared: "No Irish Catholic newspaper would criticise an English Catholic bishop, so why should any English paper do the reverse. The *Catholic Times* is a bit too independent and the Bishop of Liverpool has little control over it."[60] To which the *Times*, not unreasonably, expressed itself "amazed" at the vehemence of his Grace's reaction. Dr Walsh was sensitive to criticism. Not infrequently, however, his response was justified and restrained, as in a complaint to the congress of the National Teachers' Organisation, on 27 March 1894, over "a calumnious letter" printed in the *Irish Teachers' Journal* which stated "that the national school teachers of Ireland would not be safe appointing to the office of secretary of their organisation any teacher of a school in the diocese of Dublin". His Grace had done much for primary education, and had been a good friend to the Irish National Teachers' Organisation. The president, Mr D.A. Simmons, apologised on behalf of the body, the writer of the "calumnious letter" apologised, and congress appointed to the position of central secretary, Mr J. Coffey, a member of the Dublin diocese![61]

Walsh's predilection for writing to the newspapers, and his combative style, left him vulnerable and, as indicated earlier, was a cause of embarrassment to some of his fellow bishops. His defence, at least in part, was the need to challenge the anti-Catholicism of the British and unionist press. This last aspect was highlighted by a much publicised occurrence on 20 October 1892. On that date there appeared in the *Evening Herald* a letter signed by Teresa M. Boyle, of 77 Lower Leeson Street, Dublin, which stated that when her three daughters attended the school of the Sacred Heart Sisters in Leeson Street on "Ivy Day" (commemorating Parnell' death) wearing sprays of ivy, these were pulled from their buttonholes by Sr. Mary Agnes, who trampled the ivy underfoot and slapped and scolded the children for wearing "Kitty O'Shea's emblem" in the convent of the Sacred Heart. The writer claimed that she wrote to the archbishop, who did not reply for a fortnight and then supported the nuns "in their Healyite bullying". She no longer had her children at that school.

Another press cutting in the Dublin diocesan archives asked with respect to the foregoing: "Is there any trick too mean for the factionist journals?" The writer went on to describe the Leeson Street allegations as "an all round calumny so absurd that it is not worth denial". "A reference to the Directory", the writer observed, "reveals no such name at the address" given by the woman. "His Grace's name is dragged into the controversy on the strength of an alleged statement of the hypothetical correspondent." When this writer checked at the school he found that no children of the name of Boyle had attended the school for years, that no such incident ever took place, and that there was no 'Sr. Mary

Agnes' in the convent. Moreover, no complaint was sent to the archbishop! Following the exposure, the *Evening Herald* apologised to the nuns, but not directly to the archbishop, even though the story was taken up in the *Freeman's Journal*, the *National Press*, *Evening Telegraph*, and *Cork Herald*.

Walsh was usually fairly guarded in his public correspondence. In his private letters, however, he was more open to testiness, and prone at times to write himself into an embarrassing situation by impatience and over-reaction. This occurred both with individuals and with organisations. An unfortunate instance was his response to Josephine, Countess Plunkett, on 30 July 1895. It was at a time when he was over-wrought due to poor health, intensive work, and vitriolic attacks from the Parnellite *Independent* newspapers because of his association with Dillon's party. The countess wrote to him on 28 July to say that she, her husband, Count George Noble Plunkett, and family, intended spending a holiday at a convent in Brittany, that the nuns requested "a letter from one's archbishop", and, hence, she asked if he would be so kind as to send her a letter which she could show to the reverend mother. Walsh's reply to her simple request took her aback. "I trust it has not come to this", he wrote pettishly, "that the dignity of Count of the Holy Roman Empire is not sufficient warrant of a hearty welcome for all of you in a convent in Brittany." But however that might be, he found it "quite impossible" to write such a letter. "The shocking publications, directly calculated to bring the priesthood of Ireland into contempt," he explained, "are, as we are now informed on excellent authority, largely sustained by Count Plunkett". If the statement that had been publicly made on the subject was not true, it was "the duty of Count Plunkett to contradict it". As he had not contradicted it, Walsh continued, "I have, therefore, to regard him as disgracing the dignity conferred upon him by our Holy Father, and I am consequently unable to write any letter of introduction in his favour."

On 2 August 1895, he received a dignified, and quiet devastating reply. "As your Grace says", the countess responded, "the title of Count of the Roman States (not Count of the Holy Roman Empire which is no longer conferred) ... is sufficient recommendation to the nuns in France." "With regard to your Grace's reasons for refusing to give so simple a document", she continued, "I am performing but an act of duty in trying to remove what I know to be an erroneous impression in your Grace's mind." She then went on:

> I do not know whether the 'excellent authority' your Grace refers to is a false report in the *Freeman* and *Telegraph* ... My husband has *not* largely supported the *Independent* papers, nor is he a director, as stated in the *Evening Telegraph* and *Freeman*; he has not one hundredth part of the influence with, or interest in, the *Independent* papers that your Grace has in the *Freeman* company; yet is he to hold your Grace responsible for the shocking articles and reports that have been published in the *Freeman* columns and in its libel actions within the past three years?

"I may remind your Grace", she added, "that my husband's life was put in imminent danger in Tyrone owing to a libellous article in the *Freeman*." He, for his part, had observed with pain the articles and letters in the press "calculated to bring the priesthood of Ireland into contempt". He, in fact, had done all that he could "to prevent irreverent references to the clergy", and when ecclesiastics attacked him he did not reply. As to the question of the count correcting false comments, the countess commented pointedly: "The life of any man, public or private, who would go about denying and denouncing any public announcement (the exaggerations of friend or enemy) of which he did not approve, would be a busy one indeed. As well might we expect your Grace to reply to such a public statement as appeared the other day, 'Count Plunkett Denounced by the Church'! or assume by your silence that your Grace was responsible for Father Murphy's letter." (A letter, she declared, "founded on misstatements" and personally hostile to the count.) She concluded by pointing out that her husband by "his temperate way" of putting the issue of Home Rule won support from nationalists previously opposed to him, and that he had never "made a personal attack on any public man".[62]

Embarrassed, presumably, by his intemperate *faux pas*, the archbishop appears to have made overtures of amendment. His diary mentions an appointment with Countess Plunkett at twelve noon on 18 August 1895.[63] The count later became a staunch supporter of Walsh on national boards,[64] and they exchanged letters on easy terms.[65] With the countess, too, he worked closely in later years. Except rarely, the archbishop, it should be said, was gracious and sensitive towards women. There was a quality in him which they, for their part, found hard to resist: what a friend of over sixty years spoke of as social charm overcoming a natural bashfulness, an innate moral refinement, and a constitutional repugnance to any word or action that was coarse or unseemly.[66]

Overtaxing physical resources

The early months of 1896 were characterised by over-work, tiredness, testiness, and a breakdown in health. "I am nearly stranded from overwork", he informed Bishop O'Dwyer on 27 January, and he continued:

> On Saturday I had to spend 5 hours at the National Education Office at work with a committee, and today after a meeting of over two hours with a committee of priests here on religious instruction business, I had to spend two and a half hours at the Education Office with a committee on the reconstruction of our training colleges. And so on from day to day. Now I find that the laymen have utterly failed to do *anything re* the university declaration.[67]

Two days later, he again reported to O'Dwyer regarding the university declaration: "I had to take the thing into my own hands in the end to get anything done."[68]

He continued to drive himself very hard during February. On 20 February, in a further letter to O'Dwyer, with whom close relations had been temporarily restored, he wrote at length on primary education. He apologised for the confusion of his letter, adding: "I am dead tired, having come in from confirming 690 little girls in Marlborough Street."[69] Four days later, he reported on a successful meeting of the National Education Board at which unanimous agreement was reached on staffing in schools. At the meeting he "got good help from the two Protestant members of the committee – both *Presbyterians*."[70]

The endless pressure led at the beginning of May to what Walsh himself termed "an unexpected collapse" and to a "precipitate flight" to the baths near Cleves, in Germany. It had been brought on by "overwork", he admitted. He wrote of this to Dr Donnelly, who, in turn, relayed the contents of the letter to Bishop O'Dwyer, and added that his Grace's decline had been so marked that "some of the medical men (though in confidence)" were "whispering cancer amongst themselves". Donnelly hoped "they may be mistaken", and then complained:

> I do think it unreasonable that the bishops at their meetings are so ready to throw upon his willing shoulders much of the burthens that they should more justly share amongst themselves.[71]

Disagreements with members of religious bodies

Under the mounting strain during these months it was to be expected that Walsh would prove testy and would over-react from time to time, and not just with members of the laity but also with members of religious orders. A noteworthy example of this last was his reaction to a man who was generally popular and highly esteemed but whom, for some unexplained reason, he viewed with suspicion and dislike. The Jesuit, Tom Finlay, rivalled his Grace in his range of abilities and interests. In his career he was, in turn, professor of classics, philosophy, and economics, and seems to have excelled in each. He was the author of a novel, of numerous educational texts, the member of many boards and commissions, a commissioner of intermediate education, a co-founder of the Irish Cooperative Movement, and founder and first editor of the movement's magazine, the *Irish Homestead*, and then editor of the *New Ireland Review* (1894-1911), which was replaced by *Studies* in 1912. Finlay was also a popular lecturer and retreat director, and a much sought after preacher for special occasions in many dioceses. Not surprisingly, his successor as professor of economics, George O'Brien, was to observe in *Studies*, in March 1940, that "to write about him is like writing about a number of persons rather than a single man".

The occasion of the archbishop's reaction was the appearance in the *New Ireland Review*, 1896, of two articles on university education which expressed strong criticism of a Catholic college in the University of Dublin as a solution to the university question. It was described as "a specious and tempting scheme

... an agency to imperil the faith among Catholic students".⁷² The articles were by William Magennis, a member of the staff of University College Dublin, but because Finlay was the editor, and Magennis professed in a Jesuit college, his Grace thought he saw an ulterior Jesuit purpose at work. He published a strongly worded reply. In a letter to Cardinal Logue on 2 March 1896, he perceived the articles as an instance of the difficulty presented by having "religious bodies in the management of our affairs". The *New Ireland Review*, he explained, "is run by Fr Finlay, and is being made use of altogether in the interests of schemes in which that body is interested. There undoubtedly have been informal negotiations going on with a view to the settlement of the university question by simply endowing the Stephen's Green establishment, removed, of course, to a more suitable site, leaving the bishops simply on the shelf. I think the danger is now averted for the present."⁷³ The reference was to Delany's effort to obtain a government grant towards University College, in the absence of any financial assistance from the bishops and given the loss being sustained by the Jesuits in running the bishops' college. Delany had discussed his plan with Archbishop Walsh and believed he had his approval. He conveyed forcefully and clearly to Cardinal Logue his sense of frustration and grievance.⁷⁴ As regards the articles in the *New Ireland Review*, Magennis, the author, who also wrote to Logue, seems to have acted out of his own personal concern for Catholic students in the non-Catholic setting of Dublin University.⁷⁵

That the archbishop's words reflected an attitude towards "religious bodies in the management of our affairs", and more particularly towards any implied criticism from one of them of views or positions held by him in the field of education, and not just an instance of suspicion of 'Jesuit intrigue', was brought home to a priest of the Carmelite order, and his provincial, in 1898. In the *Daily Nation* of 19 December 1898, Walsh read a report of a sermon by Fr Aloysius Coghlan, ODC, which he found offensive. His reaction was influenced by the nature of the paper – a conservative English Catholic organ, with a daily Irish edition, which considered him far too liberal. Coghlan, in the course of his sermon in support of St Brigid's schools of the Holy Faith, declared that "the true principles of Catholic primary education" were carried out to the letter by the nuns, unlike the national primary schools where "education was not carried out on Catholic principles. It was secular, it was anti-Catholic, it was Protestant, for it came from a source of Protestantism in England". These schools were not anti-Catholic in practice, and this "was due to the ever-vigilant guardianship of the bishops and priests of Ireland". "The schools of the nuns of the Holy Faith", however, "were Catholic not only in practice, but in principle. They would have nothing to do with government endowments, and sooner than accept them they would rather depend on the public for support."

Walsh chose to see Coghlan's words as "wild and most reprehensible", and asked for an "equally public assurance that he said nothing of the kind". He sent the cutting from the paper to the Carmelite provincial, Fr Jerome O'Connell, pointing out that "the extract as published is simply the following up of a very scandalous publication in that newspaper practically arraigning me before the world as participating in the administration of an 'aggressively secularist' system of education in our schools, and as acquiescing, if not participating, in an attempt to render that system 'more aggressively secularist'." But bad as that was, it could not compare with what was preached in the Carmelite church yesterday. For, Walsh declared, it was stated "that the system of which the bishop of the diocese is known to be an active administrator is an 'anti-Catholic' one, and that it is only by what is described as the vigilant guardianship of the bishops and priests of Ireland that I, with my colleagues, the other commissioners of national education, are kept from having anti-Catholic doctrine taught in the schools – a gross and utterly groundless calumny against every member of the Board of National Education."

The provincial replied expressing regret, and spoke to Coghlan, who then wrote to the archbishop. The latter was far from mollified. He wrote to the provincial on 22 December 1898, that he had a letter from Fr Coghlan which did not deny "those shockingly untrue things that are ascribed to him". Walsh went on: "You have by this time all the facts of the case before you: a series of extraordinary statements, necessarily most injurious to the bishop of the diocese, and to all the members of the National Education Board, Catholic as well as Protestant, publicly reported as statements made in your church by a member of your community; no repudiation of the statements by the Father in question; no withdrawal of them; no expression of regret for having, through ignorance or otherwise, uttered such calumnies. The matter of course cannot rest there. I am sure you will see what the exigencies of the case demand."

Responding on Christmas Day, 1898, to this unseasonable epistle, Fr O'Connell announced that it was "a cause of great bewilderment" to him. In the subsequent interchange of letters, the provincial argued that what Coghlan said about the national schools was not nearly as trenchant as what had been stated in a letter from Propaganda to the bishops in 1841, or what had been had stated by the national synod at Maynooth, xvi, 282. Walsh accused the provincial of championing Fr Coghlan's "wild assertions", and issued a suspension against Coghlan. This meant that diocesan faculties (such as to hear confessions, and say public masses) were withdrawn from him, and he was desired to reside outside the diocese. "This", according to a note in the Carmelite archives, "was a big blow to Fr Coghlan, who was then transferred to Loughrea, Co. Galway. By all accounts, several requests were afterwards made to the archbishop for the restoration of faculties, but he always refused."[76]

Even the religious congregation closest to his Grace, the Holy Ghost Fathers, did not escape an expression of the archbishop's temperamental disfavour. No place was there greater rejoicing at Dr Walsh's elevation than in the Holy Ghost congregation. On his homeward journey after his consecration, he stayed, at the invitation of Fr Francis Liberman, at Mesnieres Castle, Normandy, a college of the congregation, where he was greeted with fireworks, a volley of artillery, a myriad of coloured lanterns, and a range of academic presentations in his honour.[77] Yet some ten weeks later, on 18 November 1885, the occasion of the silver jubilee of Blackrock College, at which Archbishop Croke was to preach and Archbishop Walsh was to preside at the pontifical high mass, the latter sent virtually a last-minute telegram saying he would not be attending.

Writing subsequently of the jubilee celebrations, Fr Reffé observed that "his Grace had been offended by the superior's declining to attend the opening ceremony at the Catholic University, 27 October". The superior, Fr Peter Huyvetys, was a retiring man who disliked public occasions, and presumably did not attach great importance to his attendance at the annual opening ceremony of the Catholic University, even though Blackrock was a major college of the institution. As a censure the archbishop's telegram was effective. "It cast a gloom over the whole feast", Reffé concluded, "and nearly cost Fr Superior's life. He was so completely upset by the occurrence that he was unable to do anything that day. I had to preside at the banquet at 5.00 p.m. at a moment's notice."[78]

The All Hallows saga

An instance of Walsh's assertiveness against a corporate religious organisation which backfired badly on the prelate, was in relation to a body of secular priests living in community in the archdiocese, at All Hallows College. The archbishop became embroiled in Rome and suffered something of a humiliation.

All Hallows had been founded in 1842 by a Fr John Hand to supply priests for English-speaking missions. The community of men conducting the college were secular priests drawn from different dioceses. The founder had established a rule for them based on that of the Congregation of Saint Sulpice in Paris. By the 1880s, they had become a community of hard-working individuals, who, yet, in many instances, did not follow the rule, and who accorded the superior of the community little or no authority. The superior, at that stage, was William Fortune. Conscious of the departure from the original vision of the founder, Fortune felt that the only prospect was to have the college run by priests from a religious congregation. He looked to Saint Sulpice and planned to introduce members of the Sulpician congregation to All Hallows as soon as the senior directors left, died, or were promoted.[79]

In 1885 his proposals for the reform of the college and the entrusting of it to the Sulpician Fathers, or some other religious congregation, were put forward in Rome. In December 1886, the cardinal prefect, Giovanni Simeoni, ordered a visitation of All Hallows to be conducted by the archbishop of Dublin and by Bartholomew Woodlock, the bishop of Ardagh, and subsequently approved the proposal in favour of the Sulpicians. In March 1887, the entrusting of the college to the Sulpicians was announced. Negotiations about their arrival, however, dragged on; and then, in 1890 John Mac Devitt, a prominent senior director of the college, who had studied at Rome and had influential friends there, and two members of staff, Frs William Dowd and Brian Kelly, protested that the introduction of an outside religious congregation was contrary to the aims of the founder, and they presented themselves as defending the "sacred trust" of John Hand. They also protested that the community of the college had not been consulted; and it was evident that they strongly opposed All Hallows, meaning themselves and their work, being brought under the jurisdiction of the local ordinary, the archbishop of Dublin.

The protesting priests, in fact, made this last very clear by bypassing Walsh and directing their protest to Archbishop Logue. Within the college, besides, they made life intolerable for Dr Fortune, and sent an insulting letter to Bishop Woodlock. The latter complained to Walsh, who determined to have the rebellious priests dismissed.

MacDevitt appealed to Rome. Fortune offered to resign. Walsh refused to accept his resignation, since to do so, he informed Simeoni, "would have been a fatal blow to ecclesiastical discipline".[80] Walsh, in the unusual situation, and with many other issues weighing on him, acted less than consistently. He sought a juridical solution – the right to judge the case by virtue of his jurisdiction as ordinary of the diocese; at the same time – being constrained by the three priests being from outside dioceses – he called on the cardinal prefect, in a number of letters, to remove them from the college.[81] MacDevitt, meanwhile, went to Rome and seems to have made a favourable impression on Simeoni. The latter wrote to Walsh urging reconciliation, and stating that MacDevitt would write a letter of apology.[82] Walsh however, considered that "the course prescribed would be disastrous".[83] MacDevitt formally appealed to Rome. A rescript was issued on 23 July 1890. The archbishop was told to postpone the introduction of the Saint Sulpice congregation. MacDevitt and the other two were to write a letter of apology and submission to Dr Walsh, but might remain at the college. The rector had not been consulted and was placed in an impossible situation. Walsh was angry.

On 14 October 1890, he decided to go beyond the congregation and make his case directly to the pope. He requested that the 1890 decision be cancelled and the case returned to his jurisdiction. There was no reply. He applied once more to the congregation. His complaint necessarily involved criticism of Simeoni. In Rome for the blessing of the church of St Patrick on St Patrick's day, he stayed on into May to deal with the All Hallows business. The case was eventually heard on 13 July 1891. On 19 July, Leo XIII signed a rescript which totally rejected Walsh's plea. First, it decreed that all the bishops of Ireland in meeting were to decide whether All Hallows was to be committed to the care of a religious community, and if so, which one. Then, directly referring to Walsh, the rescript stated: "The archbishop of Dublin shall be informed that the S. Congregation cannot accede to his petition either for the annulment of the decree of 1890, or for the case to be remitted to his own cura: firstly, because it is the right of every Catholic to have recourse to the Holy See; secondly, because the S. Congregation took the case in hand; and thirdly, because it also took it in hand at the repeated request of the same archbishop. "[84]

The Irish bishops at their October meeting decided to entrust the college to the Vincentian Fathers, who would have "the appointment of professors etc. subject to the approval of the Sacred Congregation". The College being in the diocese of Dublin all the rights of the ordinary were to be respected. Donnelly writing of the decision to O'Dwyer on 16 December 1891, added:

> The archbishop considers that Propaganda is beaten having to revoke its former decree. I don't quite see it in that light, for Mac Devitt and confreres can continue in residence and give much trouble, whilst his jurisdiction is limited to the mere rights of the ordinary of the diocese.[85]

Kevin Condon, the historian of All Hallows, judged, however, that there were no winners in the eighteen month conflict. Walsh was successfully defied by the recalcitrant priests, he lost his appeal to Rome, and in trying to pressurise Propaganda to revoke a decree and in challenging the Cardinal Prefect he further weakened his standing and support at Rome, and enfeebled the case for his elevation to the cardinalate. MacDevitt and his supporters lost out in the college. Control passed to the Irish Vincentians. Their provincial superior, Thomas Morrissey, not Dr Walsh, was entrusted with the task of reaching a settlement with the dissident priests. He did so considerately and generously, and they left All Hallows. The new situation moved smoothly forward under the new administration, as Dr Fortune happily acknowledged in a letter to Bishop Woodlock on 20 October 1892. "Everything is going on very smoothly and pleasantly. Nothing could surpass the kindness of the new directors to the old hands."[86]

These "autocratic interludes" are presented with view to a complete portrayal of Archbishop William Walsh. But it must be remembered that they were "interludes". Walsh had in his diocese a great many male religious congregations. There were Augustinians, Carmelites – calced and discalced, Capuchins, Dominicans, Franciscans, Holy Ghost Fathers, Jesuits, Marists, Oblates of Mary Immaculate, Passionists, Redemptorists, and Vincentians, not to mention at least five different congregations of religious Brothers; and practically all seem to have had good relations with him, and where relations were strained it was usually with individual members rather than an entire congregation. Again, with respect to autocratic, insensitive letters to different people, these too must be viewed in context: the context of a very busy life, a life where he was often pulled hither and thither, and where his nerves were run thin by pressure and fatigue. In this context he received, read, and wrote his letters. It was his invariable custom, according to his secretary, to open and read each letter that came to him. A great many of them demanded a response, and he tried to be prompt in answering. What this involved may be conjectured from the consideration that although he regularly sorted the correspondence he received, destroying most of what was of mere passing interest, there still remained in the archives at his death some 40,000 letters dealing exclusively with ecclesiastical matters.[87]

It is appropriate, therefore, to endeavour to present in the next chapter what one of his close friends called "the true man".[88] This can only be done by viewing the pattern of his life over an extended period, from 1885 to 1912: a pattern in which concentrated work intermeshes with diocesan and public events and with increasing bouts of ill-health, and nevertheless those human features are present which endeared him to his friends. Such a presentation involves some inevitable overlapping, references to matters already mentioned or yet to be treated.

X

"The true man": the pattern of a life, 1885-1912

When Walsh's friend, Myles Ronan, spoke of "the true man" he had mainly in mind the off-duty, human side of the archbishop that was experienced on continental holidays or at dinners with a small circle of friends. Instances of this kind, as will appear, are illuminating, but they are not the only insights into the human aspect of William Walsh. The motivations in his daily life, the pressures and frustrations he experienced, and their effect on him, were also part of the inner person. Such features, in turn, were part of a pattern of life which was largely driven by a relentless work ethic and seemingly endless energy, which brought him into contact with all sorts of people and organisations, and which exacted a price on his body and nervous system. The man behind the mask of outward reserve, therefore, is glimpsed first of all in the very pattern of his life. In a real sense he mirrored Hopkins' words, "What I do is me."

Much of this chapter is devoted to a consideration of the variegated pattern of that life, and particularly its recurring graph, after 1894, of pressure and intense activity followed by illness followed by bouts of physical exercise and recuperative continental holidays, and how he acted or coped at each stage.

Walsh's capacity for work astonished his friend and close colleague, Archbishop Croke. "I don't know at all how you can get up such steam every day, and on every variety of subject," Croke wrote to him on 4 May 1894.[1] By then, however, Walsh's physique and nervous system were showing the first signs of wear and tear. The onset was heralded by a painful experience in the dentist's chair. The forceps broke in the process of extracting four teeth. He was laid up for some days,[2] and was unable to accompany a pilgrimage to Rome.[3] The following year he endured a serious attack of erysipelas – a disease, said to be "characterised by diffuse inflammation of the skin ... attended with fever", and also to be "highly infectious" and usually accompanied by "considerable pain".[4] Although his physician, Dr Hayes, remarked that the attack left no trace in his constitution,[5] it was to reappear in later years.

Despite these physical setbacks, and the psychological pressure exerted by the hostile criticism in the parnellite press, Walsh could not resist new challenges in the area of education. Early in 1895, as mentioned previously, he was invited by the lord lieutenant to join the Board of National Education. Having consulted the bishops individually, he accepted. By July, however, he was once again "in the hands of good surgeon Hayes and of his dentist",[6] and on 20 August he informed the Jesuit historian, Edmund Hogan, "I am only just recovering from a rather severe bronchial attack, and I am ordered to go away at once".[7] Despite the attack, he did not go to bed. His diary for August, indeed, reveals him, between 13 and 19 August, conducting visitations in Athy, Co. Kildare, then nearer home with the Redemptoristine Sisters, and later at Aughrim Street and Cabra, and, also meeting a number of people, including Hague his architect. Little wonder that Bishop Brownrigg ventured to reprimand him mildly on 24 August 1895:

> I greatly fear your Grace sometimes borders on the reckless where your health is concerned, and you really ought to take a lesson from the numerous fatalities that have occurred in our own ranks of late.

He urged him to stay in a warm climate 'till every vestige of his bronchitis passed and he was ready to face the winter.[8]

During 1896, Walsh added to his workload the role of arbitrator in labour disputes, and he also became actively involved in the development of Irish technical education. Once more his constitution gave way. On 11 May 1896, he wrote from near Cleves, in Germany, to Bishop Donnelly that he had decided to take the baths there for a few weeks following "an unexpected collapse". "I had a curious swelling of the face", he explained, "which was said to be an indication of failure from overwork, and so Dr Hayes ordered me off peremptorily as soon as I was able to go out." He now felt "wonderfully invigorated".[9] It was the deterioration of his health at this time that, unknown to him, gave rise to the rumours of cancer to which Donnelly referred in the letter to O'Dwyer quoted in the previous chapter. In the same letter he further explained: "I consulted (Dr) Cruise and he says there is no foundation for the 'cancer' scare". Walsh's ailment arose from overwork. According to Cruise, Donnelly observed in conclusion, the archbishop "leads a very unhealthy life, and unless he makes some change he will shorten his days considerably".[10]

Walsh's secretary, P.J. Walsh, indicated in passing what was meant by a very "unhealthy life". The archbishop passed a great part of his day and evening in his study, writing or reading. He never sat on an easy chair, save when ill, and his extensive reading was always done pen in hand. It has been noted that his was an analytic mind, and that, although he read widely in English literature, he was "more interested in literary problems than in literary form".[11] His other secretary, Michael Curran, added that Walsh's own writing was devoid of images. "He wrote like a legal draftsman."[12] The impression, therefore, is of one who read for a purpose, hence the pen in hand, and not for pleasure. His regime, in short, was one which stretched an active brain in a sedentary body.

Convinced that he had to take exercise, Walsh, characteristically, did so abundantly. Together with his friend Dr Molloy, he had been among the first to take up cycling, riding "a bone-shaker round the grounds of Maynooth college".[13] By 1896 the bicycle had taken on its more familiar aspect, and he determined to avail of it to enhance his holidays on the continent. Part of the attraction of the exercise, besides, was the novelty, and the challenge to more conservative clergy. "He used to tell, with a gleeful twinkle in his eye," according to his secretary, P.J. Walsh, "of the discomfiture of a venerated colleague in the hierarchy, who, in the early days of cycling, had resolved, after much anxious thought, to issue a mandate forbidding his priests to cycle. Before coming to a final decision, however, the bishop decided to consult his metropolitan, who advised him to talk the matter over with his vicar-general. As the prelate approached the vicar's house with this object, he saw on the road an athletic figure in shirt-sleeves wobbling from side to side, and mounted on a bicycle. It was the vicar, taking his first lessons. The bishop chatted – about the weather; and nothing more was heard of the mandate."[14] The point of the story was that Walsh was the metropolitan, who, as part of the cycling fraternity, knew that the vicar-general was an enthusiast and learning to ride.

Despite his apparent insouciance regarding the views of fellow clergy on the propriety of riding a bicycle, he was interested in the views of distinguished episcopal colleagues. Thus, on 26 September 1896, after "cycling across France", he wrote under the letter-head "Gasthof zur Marienburg" to Fr Jules Botrel, rector of Blackrock College, requesting that he obtain for him a copy of "a circular of the archbishop of Paris to his clergy ... recommending the cycle as a useful adjunct to the ministry!"[15]

His diary for that holiday, in the autumn of 1896, shows him, characteristically, taking his exercise to extremes. On 4 September he noted that he and his companions cycled from Dieppe to Rouen. On each subsequent day he entered the distances travelled. On 9 September they covered 50 kilometres; on the 10th they cycled 33 kilometres and "got pedal mended". On 12 September, the entry read: "Train to Caen. Pedal renewed. Rode Caen to Liseux, 49 kls." And so on until 3 October; sometimes covering remarkable distances for the bicycles and roads of the time. He observed that on 19 September they cycled 100 kilometres, "Rheims to Sedan", whilst his longest recorded journey appears to have been from Coblenz to Heidesheim and back, on 1 October, "160 kls or 100 miles".[16] His renewed energy and exhilaration were reflected in a letter to Bishop Donnelly, again from "Gasthof zur Marienburg", on 27 September 1896.

> It is high time for me to report myself. We have had an exceedingly interesting tour, beginning with a good round in Normandy, continuing with a ride across France from Caen to the Meuse, where we entered Belgium at Givet, and now winding up with the Moselle and Rhine districts. Fifty or even sixty miles a day in now quite an ordinary matter of course![17]

It is not recorded how his companions, which always included one of his secretaries, felt about the journeys. He was said to be a considerate companion, but it was he who planned the routes, with meticulous care each day. These led at times to "out-of-the-way places, unspoiled and almost unknown to the ordinary traveller", which held some historical interest for him. Many of these were recorded, for he was a proficient photographer. There was "scarcely a monument or church of historical importance in Italy or Germany", according to his friend and companion, Myles Ronan, "that he had not photographed" with professional competence.[18]

The bicycle united Walsh to the companions of his travels, and to some others whom he met in his work and who enjoyed cycling. Prominent among these was Joseph McGrath, later Sir Joseph, registrar of the Royal University and subsequently of the National University. On 14 September 1900, Walsh wrote to him from Charing Cross Hotel saying that he and Fr Healy were going cycling in France. He had had an "exceptionally heavy" amount of work at the recent synod and decided "to get away for a few weeks". "I have no fixed plan as to route", he added. "Possibly we shall work our way across 'the continent of Europe' as Dr Molloy calls it."[19] The easy relationship between them is evident in their correspondence. On 1 June 1905, McGrath received a brief note: "Can you come over to dine at six tomorrow, for a consultation on an important point about the purchase of a new bicycle? (No one else is coming.)"[20] That September, from near Frankfort, Walsh gave McGrath an account of his journey to date. He had cut down on distances travelled each day to a maximum of forty miles. "The free wheel is an unqualified success", he observed. "What has most surprised me is its evidently greater safety over greasy roads. But I can tell you all this when I get back." Finally, responding to a letter from McGrath, he remarked in mild raillery:

> I am glad to hear of your pleasant experience of golf. It is wonderful what an extraordinary fascination the game has for those who have taken it up – a thing quite unaccountable to the ignorant outsider.[21]

Three years later his Grace was still cycling. Then he recounted to McGrath how they followed the route travelled by Queen Maria Antoinette in her flight to Varennes and her return journey as prisoner. After Varennes they planned to go "by Verdun to Metz, then by Luxemburg and Treves to the old route down the Mozelle to Coblenz and the Rhine to Cologne". Their "usual day's work" was from 20 to 25 miles, with photographs en route. He concluded semi-humourously:

> If you hear of any nervous rider intending to take the road from Honfleur to Trouville, *warn him against it*. That ride was really a fearful experience. ... It is bad at the sides. It is both windy and switchbackly. These things I did not notice when I rode it some years ago. But now it is simply infested with motor-cars coming and going, and frequently at a reckless pace.[22]

McGrath's jovial reply said much for their relaxed relationship. "We have gone on the tour and one of the conclusions we have come to is that there is no need for flying machines. Dieppe, St Anne D'Auray, Metz, Cologne! *That* pretty well boxes the compass!"[23]

Three years later Walsh's youthful enthusiasm for new experiences in travel was turning towards the motor-car. The day before the international Gordon-Bennet motor race in Co. Kildare, in 1903, as the magazine *Autocar* proudly recalled on 23 April 1921, he accepted a seat in a Mercedes which reached 60 m.p.h. as it covered forty-seven miles of the course in an hour! Not surprisingly, therefore, by 1910 the archbishop and his companions in their journeys abroad were travelling largely by rail and motor-car. Having conducted business in Rome in record time, they made their way home in leisurely fashion. "I feel thoroughly restored by the pleasant trip," Walsh wrote McGrath from Sienna on 11 April. "I had undoubtedly been completely run down but I was not two days away when I felt as well as ever. Keep yourself free for dinner usual hour on Thursday, the 28th." He asked if it would be a good idea to invite "C. Doyle".[24] McGrath's response on 16 April expressed their unfettered manner of communication while preserving the formalities of respect – their letters opening "Dear Mr McGrath", or "My dear Lord Archbishop". "Your letter, which came yesterday, gave great satisfaction. 'Richard is' (evidently) 'himself again'. (Martin Harvey is doing Richard III here this week, and so you will pardon the quotation!) I will keep myself free for Thursday 28th, and I think your idea of having Charles Doyle an admirable one."[25]

Finally it was a testimony to the humanity of the "reserved" archbishop, that McGrath wished him to be the first to know of the decision of his only son, Fergal, to join the Jesuits in October 1913. He and his wife, he confided, were naturally disappointed, but yet pleased and consoled. He asked his Grace's prayers that the boy might persevere. The latter had wished to join last year, but he had prevailed on him to defer it for a year.[26] Walsh, writing from Angers, six days later, 16 September 1913, remarked that the news came as a surprise, and then added thoughtfully: "No doubt it is a trial to Lady McGrath and to you. But it is a matter for congratulation also." He trusted, too, that Fergal would persevere. Sir Joseph had done all he could in that respect "by keeping him back for a time until he had considered the matter well".[27]

The fellowship of cycling and the long holidays enabled Walsh, as has been seen, to relax, be himself, and get away from the daily pressures of work and the importunity of others. But it was only for a relatively short time, and then he was back once more to the intensity of work and to undertaking more commitments than even his rugged constitution could bear. Thus he commenced 1897 with participation in two further commissions, the Model Schools Commission, and the Commission on Manual and Practical Instruction in National Schools. On 1 March he had to ask Dr Donnelly to stand in for him at Francis Street church. "I was absolutely done up this morning", he confessed, "and had to stay in bed.

I am now ordered to take in my sails generally as regards work." "No doubt work always agreed with me", he continued, adding with a temporary insight, "but I see that an unending strain, rushing from one occupation with barely time to catch up another, won't do."[28] Yet a fortnight later he went to Birmingham as a member of the commission on technical education, and from 14 March to 12 April he was away, much of the time following a heavy schedule of visitations and work with the commission. As a result, he informed Donnelly on 19 March 1897: "I thought it the simplest plan to put back the Westland Row Confirmations to some early day after Easter. This avoids all complication. Our work here has been incessant."[29] During May there was a further visit to England with the "commission visiting schools"; and his multiple activities continued through subsequent months with little indication of physical weakness. His diary, indeed, noted on 12 July, "cycle Maynooth and back", and on the 17th "cycle to Ratoath", Co. Meath.[30] On 24 August he was off once more to the continent.

On Walsh's return on 7 October, he moved to Maynooth for the concursus and visitation, which took place from 9 to 13 October. He then caught up with diocesan business, and on 17 October met a dockers' deputation.[31] Two days later he set off again with the commissioners of Manual and Practical Instruction, this time to visit schools in Scotland. They spent a week there,[32] and then it was back once more to diocesan concerns, and his variety of other works, for the remainder of the year. It was that year, too, in which he published his book on *The Irish University Question*!

Walsh's health during 1898 appears to have been good despite a number of new pressures, but the following year he received an unspecified injury in London which, he informed Bishop Donnelly on 19 May, he supposed he had made serious "by not treating it in time". Dr Hayes insisted "on all sorts of precautions",[33] fearful, perhaps, of a recurrence of erysipelas which sometimes arose from infected wounds.[34] On 31 May Walsh was still laid up. He asked Donnelly to take some Confirmations for him. By 10 June he was back at work, but his doctor intervened to insist that he take a rest.[35] On 7 August, earlier than usual, he embarked on his continental holiday. He returned home on 5 October, in time for the episcopal meeting at Maynooth. The sign that he was currently back to full health, and perhaps overdoing it once more, was his diary entry for 8 October, "rode to Maynooth", and for the next day, "rode to Dublin".[36]

From the references to Walsh's health between 1895 and 1899 it is evident that by temperament he tended to push himself to extremes both in work and in physical relaxation. The number of activities, indeed, in which he was engaged in these years is virtually impossible to recount. They included, as indicated, active membership on commissions for national education, intermediate education, manual and technical education, and on the management boards of hospitals; active support for Dublin's poor, for the provision and maintenance of refuges for young people at risk, and of night shelters; outspoken involvement in aspects of university education, of health and social needs; working for unity among the

nationalist parties, for arbitration, and as arbitrator, in labour-management disputes, and in relation to the *Freeman's Journal*; endless correspondence, much of
it public, the writing of articles and of a book; leadership and frequent meetings
on the cause of the Irish martyrs, deliberations and meetings on a new catechism,
on liturgy and music; all these in addition to regular diocesan meetings and consultations, to the planning, building, and blessing of churches and schools, to ministering to the needs of priests, teachers, and the wider Catholic population. The
pressure of all these and more, "the unending strain", as he acknowledged, "of
rushing from one occupation with barely time to catch up another",[37] gave rise on
occasion to the outbreaks of impatience and the instances of poor judgement
which have been mentioned, and to a breakdown in health; and work pressure and
deteriorating health also led to the passing on of many chores to the patient and
gentlemanly, Bishop Donnelly. During these years, Walsh changed the dates of
Confirmation on a number of occasions, and on at least one occasion postponed
the sacrament for a year. At other times, he requested Donnelly to fulfil these and
other tasks in his place.[38] In the spring of 1897, Donnelly wryly remarked to
O'Dwyer, "I have had the honour of doing all the Confirmations."[39]

A similar pattern of work and relapse continued into the new century, but as
he got older the illnesses tended to persist longer and his strong recuperative
powers to take longer.

Early in January 1900, "a touch of influenza"[40] kept him laid up until the end
of February. Episcopal colleagues advised him to retire from the educational
commissions and to take more rest.[41] Months later, Walsh sent notice of his
retirement from the commissionerships of intermediate education and national
education to the viceroy, Lord Cadogan, on the grounds that he could only hold
these posts "at the cost of neglecting important duties" of his "ecclesiastical
office". He yielded, however, to Cadogan's plea that he stay on because an
Intermediate Education Act had just been passed, and the primary system was
"to be reorganised and recast" in a direction "in accordance with your Grace's
views".[42] In January 1901, there was influenza again,[43] and in June he testily
resigned publicly from the National Education Board over a disagreement about
a minute of a previous meeting.[44] His action moved the mild Cadogan to regret
"that your Grace should have thought it necessary to depart from the usual procedures in such cases, and that your resignation should in the first instance have
been published through the medium of an interview with a newspaper correspondent".[45] Cardinal Logue ventured to question the wisdom of resigning –
"You should have had a better chance of fighting them from within, as the Castle
people are past masters in hushing things up".[46] Walsh as usual found relief from
exhaustion and nervous strain in a continental holiday, returning early in October
with renewed energy and, as ever, plunging almost straightway into work.

The renewed zest and energy carried him without serious illness for the next
four years, despite intense university discussions in 1902, and in 1903 the
burden of a court case brought against him by a zealous, but unbusiness-like

priest, J.E. O'Malley, who claimed he was owed £4000 by the archbishop. O'Malley lost the case, but there were public hearings before a jury which were fully reported in the press. The year 1906, however, brought illness on top of other upsets. He was visited regularly by his physician and friend, Dr M.J. Cox, from 8 February until the end of March. During the year, in addition, well-known acquaintances died, Michael Davitt on 2 June and the O'Conor Don on 30 June. But the cruellest blow was the sudden demise in Scotland, on 5 October, of his close, long-time friend, Monsignor Gerald Molloy, vice-chancellor of the Royal University. Walsh was on the continent and could not reach Dublin in time for the obsequies.[47]

The following year passed without he being confined to bed, though he was visited by Dr Cox on six occasions during February and March. That year, 1907, he established friendly relations with the new viceroy, Lord Aberdeen, and his wife, who involved herself in many works of mercy and was president of the Women's National Health Association of Ireland. His friendship with them, however, did not entice him to give any support to the International Exhibition of 1907, which instead of being a showcase for Irish industrial work would rather result, he believed, "in the opening of new markets for England and other eastern manufacturers".[48] Walsh's view was close to that of Arthur Griffith, whose Sinn Fein philosophy advocated self-reliance and the active support of home industries.[49] The subsequent years, 1908 and 1909, were filled with significant happenings as regards the university question and the assertiveness of the Irish language movement. Walsh's health remained sound, though he was probably quite tired by the autumn of 1909. He took an extended holiday from 17 August to 9 October, and at the end of October finally resigned, after seventeen years, from the Intermediate Board of Education,[50] strategically ascribing his resignation to the current "vehement ad malevolent criticism of the board" by the essential Irish language supporters, "which made it unsuitable for someone in his office to remain a member".[51] The next year a British political crisis made the Liberal government dependent on the Irish nationalist vote. Home Rule seemed imminent. A further occasion of celebration was Walsh's silver jubilee as archbishop. He almost missed the celebration. A specialist, Dr Joseph Redmond, had to be summoned in August 1910, to treat a severe swelling in his foot as the result of a sting. The ailment took many days to clear up, draining further the energy being absorbed already by the taxing work of the commission of the new National University and the demands of the Irish language lobby. He planned, in consequence, a long continental holiday at the end of August. Cardinal Logue wrote to him in his supportive way on 23 August:

> I am very glad your Grace is going to take a prolonged vacation. You stand in black need of it after your long and hard work. I don't know anyone else who could have got through what you have gone through without a breakdown.[52]

Walsh did not get away in August. Writing to Logue shortly after his return on 9 December, he acknowledged: "I was greatly run down when I went away. The university and other work kept me here until the end of September, but the two months away did me a world of good." He had six weeks in Spain. "I had never been there before", he remarked, "and of course enjoyed it very much." Despite the reports he had heard about Spain, he found the hotel accommodation, railway arrangements, and punctuality, very satisfactory.[53]

The year 1911 was marked by industrial strife, a royal visit, and "the university and other work". The real pressure on Walsh, as the very actively involved chancellor of the new university, was the time and concentrated attention required in preparing the statutes of the university. Eventually, the statutory commission completed its work on 31 July 1911, but the pressure involved was such as to bring on finally "a nervous breakdown".[54] The archbishop's cure was to head for the continent, and to escape from mental fatigue by plunging himself into the world of emotional, flamboyant opera. Indeed, to enjoy more fully Czech opera he set about learning the language, and word that "the chancellor of the National University and archbishop of Dublin had set about learning Czech" was said to have "sent a thrill all over that beautiful country". It was "accepted as a compliment and honour" and "all the papers" were said to have taken it "as a recognition of their nationhood".[55]

The following year brought no let up in pressure, with the by now almost inevitable decline in health. Within weeks of his homecoming, Walsh was involved in a prolonged public controversy with reference to the decree *Quantavis Diligentia* issued in October 1911, by Pope Pius X. The decree dealt with summoning Catholic clergy before civil tribunals. The decree was interpreted by the Dublin Protestant press as "a new papal aggression", preventing Catholic magistrates and policeman discharging their sworn duty. Walsh, on 30 December 1911, pointed out that it was evident from canon law and the history of ecclesiastical jurisprudence that the decree did not apply to Ireland. His views were ridiculed in the *Daily Express*, the *Times*, and what Cardinal Logue termed "the Orange newspapers".[56] Walsh responded with a definitive pamphlet, March 1912, in which he pointed out that misunderstandings had arisen because matters were measured in terms of civil rather than canon law.[57] Logue, complimenting him, remarked that the work showed "a knowledge not only of canon but of civil law" which would open the eyes of his critics.[58] The controversy, nevertheless, continued for some time. It was a drain on time and energy on top of other responsibilities, and it was added to by public comment and protest over the removal of Fr Michael O'Hickey from the chair of Irish in Maynooth because of words abusive of the hierarchy with respect to their attitude towards the Irish language, and because of his subsequent recalcitrance. Besides, there was the university business, which apart from the pressures from the essential Irish lobby, also involved at this stage discussions regarding a suitable location for the offices of the National University, and discussions and correspondence

1 Archbishop William J. Walsh in 1885

2 On tour in Italy

3 'Leaders of the Irish Nation'

4 Archbishop Walsh in 1910

5 William Croke, archbishop of Cashel

6 Peter E. Amigo, bishop of Southwark

7 William Delany, SJ, president of UCD

8 Cardinal Ignatius Persico, apostolic commissary

9 Archbishop Walsh with Queen Mary and
Dr. Daniel Mannix during the royal visit to Maynooth in 1911

10 Archbishop Walsh with a 'boneshaker' bicycle

11 Archbishop Walsh in 1920

12 The funeral of Archbishop Walsh, 14 April 1921.
Note the tricolour-draped coffin.
Photograph from the NLI Keogh Collection, KE222,
courtesy of the National Library of Ireland.

concerning lectures in theology at University College. At Maynooth, there was the question of appointing an editor for the *Irish Ecclesiastical Record*, and the appointment of a president of the college following the appointment of Daniel Mannix as coadjutor archbishop of Melbourne.

These and other matters filled his days. Hence, when John Redmond wrote on 7 March seeking his support as Home Rule loomed, Walsh did not reply until 20 March. He regretted he was unable to write earlier, he said, but he had been very hard pressed "working against time" the previous fortnight. He also felt no urgency about replying. To Redmond's letter, and the Irish party leader's offer to call on him, he responded rather bluntly: "I can only say that it is now some years since I made up my mind to have nothing more to do with Irish politics, and that nothing in the world could induce me to change my mind in the matter."[59]

The beleaguered prelate continued to work "against time". Among the items which encroached unexpectedly on his time and energy was one recorded in one word, in his diary of 11 April 1912: "11.00 (Titanic)". But there were also items of a farcical nature. Hopefully, he was sufficiently relaxed to smile at one such item, a petition from a lady in Kingstown (Dun Laoghaire), dated 2 February. That he preserved it, suggests that he cherished it! It informed him:

> You would be doing a great charity and prevent much evil if you got Canon Murphy, P.P. of Kingstown, to get a pants painted up to the waist on the Roman soldier in the 5th Station of the Cross. It is absurd and shocking as it is.[60]

In May there occurred the archbishop's most prolonged decline in health. On 30 and 31 May, Dr Cox was mentioned as attending him, and he continued to call frequently right through into August. Walsh was not bed-ridden for the most part. On 2 June he was able to carry out the ordinations at Clonliffe College, and seventeen days later the minor orders at Maynooth, yet he was so obviously unwell that serious reports of his condition circulated amongst the bishops during June. The bishop of Limerick, as a result, was moved to write an unexpectedly warm and moving letter to him.

> What prompts me to write is a feeling that the estrangement ... which for some time past has arisen between us, ought not to continue as we both are advancing into the sere and yellow leaf. Our friendship reaches back to our boyhood, and continued unbroken for many years after we became bishops, and I should be glad that it was renewed and remained as strong as ever until the end."[61]

Amongst lay friends, the archbishop's deterioration was remarked. Christopher Palles wrote to the archbishop's secretary on 5 August that he was glad to learn that his Grace was "somewhat better" and was about to go to the continent. "For some time I have been seriously concerned about his health", Palles continued, "and feared a nervous breakdown. The amount of mental strain he subjects himself too [*sic*] is to my mind far too great." He added: "I was grieved when in the early part of the year I learned that, in addition to all his other duties, he was undertaking the analysis of ... two important marriage cases." He trusted that "on his return" the archbishop would "reduce his work very considerably".[62] This last was urged by all concerned about him. To a close friend, Fr John Healy, parish priest of Dalkey, Walsh had written of some of the symptoms of his illness, which included a tremor in his hands, and a "sensational" and alarming experience in saying mass. Healy urged exercise, and a "real holiday", taking "the rest cure". On this last he added realistically:

> Hitherto, this could have no meaning for you. No more than it could for anyone over-flowing with energy and real vigour. But there *is* such a thing. For my part, I have no doubt of what I hear, that an occasional day off will well repay. But I am afraid this is a thing your Grace will not understand, having had little practice in it.[63]

What was this illness of Walsh? A clue was provided a fortnight later in a letter from one of his Grace's secretarial staff and cycling colleagues, another John Healy, who was on a Mediterranean cruise and wrote from Jerusalem on 24 October. Trusting that the archbishop was returned, and rested in body and mind, he added: "I am sure there is as much need for rest of mind as there is for exercise of body. Neurasthenia, I understand, is the great complaint of the age. Ours is a cargo of neurastheniacs!"[64] William Walsh suffered from neurasthenia, a medical condition no longer mentioned in modern medicine. *Black's Medical Dictionary* (1906), in the 1928 edition, when the term was still in use, described it as a "condition of nervous exhaustion in which although the patient suffers from no definite disease, he become incapable of sustained exertion". It was frequently associated with "overstrain through intellectual efforts or worry". With respect to the many and varied symptoms "the most prominent and constant symptom is that of weakness and weariness on exertion. The person may feel fresh enough in the early part of the day, but after very slight effort he becomes exhausted and trembles." Walsh was likely to have driven himself when exhausted and to have accentuated the trembling. Among other symptoms. of which there was some indication in accounts of Walsh's behaviour, it is noted that "the temper changes ... the sufferer becoming as a rule intensely irritable and emotional", and again, "the neurasthenic becomes worried by the smallest incidents and a prey to groundless fears and to anxiety", and there is "shakiness in making an effort". Other features, of a more corporeal nature, not expressly recorded in Walsh's case but which may have added to his distress, were sleeplessness, loss of appetite, stomach and bowel disorders, and even palpitations.

What was the recommended cure? Among the recommended treatments, the following were applied in Walsh's case: "a complete holiday, with the cessation of all business and intellectual work", and the leaving of home "for a new environment". It was also recommended that there should be "regular massage, by an attendant, which takes the place of exercise" and "is unaccompanied by any discharge of nervous energy". All this, of course, to be assisted by attempts "to stimulate appetite by tonics, fresh air etc."[65] Clearly, where a cure was concerned, neurasthenia, as Fr Healy implied, was a wealthy person's ailment.

Dr Cox recommended a programme somewhat as above: prescribing massage treatment and a foreign holiday, both of which were available at the celebrated health resort at Marienbad in Austria. He invited Walsh to accompany him and his family thither on 24 July 1912. Also taking the waters there at that time were the members of the Irish party, John Dillon and T.P. O'Connor, whom Walsh was careful to avoid. David Lloyd George, M.P., the future prime minister, had just departed. Dr Cox and family departed after some days. Walsh stayed on, and his improvement by mid-August was such that his secretary, P.J. Walsh, who remained at home and kept him up to date by post, observed in reply to him on 22 August:

> Your handwriting in signing cheques is perfect. There is no trace of a shake – a great contrast to your condition before leaving. You ought to take a real holiday when you finish in Marienbad.[66]

By 3 September Walsh felt sufficiently self-confident to take that advice. He left Marienbad for the opera festival at Munich, and went from there to Augsburg, Ulm, Stuttgart, Heidelberg, Manheim, in all of which he attended opera as the occasion offered. By 29 September he was at Cologne for Wagner's *Valkerie* and two days later at Essen for *Carmen*. Eventually he travelled from Aachen to Louvain on 6 October and reached London three days later. There on 10 October he visited the Coliseum once more to see Sarah Bernhardt, and on the following day the Hippodrome for an opera of Leoncavalla. At 6.00 p.m. on 13 October he arrived back in Dublin feeling quite well, and was met by an anxious, larger than usual reception party of Frs McGrath, Pettit, Dunne, and Dwyer.[67]

By now Walsh seemed to have acknowledged that he could no longer act as if he was fifty-two rather than seventy-two years. On his return to Dublin he endeavoured to pace himself. His diary indicates he was engaged in meetings relating to plans for the university, and concerning the National Museum, and the National Library; and attending a special function at the Mansion House to mark the opening of the first night shelter for homeless men in Dublin. It was run by the Society of St Vincent de Paul, but funded by himself.[68] In December, there were the elections to the senate of the university. His many meetings were spaced, with a day or more between some of them. On 15 November, Cardinal Logue reminded him that he "must take things easier and not work himself to death as heretofore",[69] but three weeks later he acknowledged – "everybody tells me that you have come back from vacation completely restored".[70]

Despite his extraordinary recuperative powers, Walsh knew his own history sufficiently well by now to realise that under the pressure of work and circumstances he could have a recurrence of illness in the next year or so; that health and energy could no longer be presumed. He could not have envisaged, however, the degree of pressure that was to come within a short time as the city was riven with industrial strife, and the country north and south was gripped with militancy as rival volunteer forces formed, nor could he have expected that the entire known world was to change as Europe lapsed into war and opportunities for visiting the continent disappeared for good. Yet, apart from the impact of such events on his work and health, he, with his experience of Europe and its main languages, and his feeling for radical responses in social and political situations, was psychologically more prepared than most people for sweeping change. Through it all he had the inner resources, the outlets for relaxation, and the reservoir of compassion towards others, which combined to prevent his strong intellectual preoccupations having a dehumanising effect on him.

OUTLETS OF RELAXATION

In the midst of his compulsion to work and not lose time, the archbishop, explored outlets of relaxation other than cycling. He played billiards from time to time, though he was an indifferent player; and late in life he took up bridge, became an authority on the principles of the game, but on the rare occasions on which he played a rubber he found himself "outdistanced by more practised if less intellectual habitués".[71] Far more important to him, however, was the opportunity for relaxation provided by his Steinway grand piano, "on which, sometimes for hours, he would play Mendelssohn, Chopin etc. In later years he had a pianola fitted on to the piano, by which he continued to enjoy his favourite composers. Bach, Beethoven, Grieg, Mozart, Saint Saens, Sullivan, Wagner, were in his repertoire."[72] In the world of music, also, one of his great escapes from pressure was, as noted, concerts and especially opera. Linked also with leisure moments, as his secretary, P.J. Walsh, recalled, was the sorting and "arranging in albums with his own hand a most interesting collection of some thousands of photographs taken by himself when travelling in various parts of Europe".[73]

Throughout his life as bishop, Walsh found enjoyable relaxation in playing dinner host to friends and others likely to be interesting and congenial. Among these last was the celebrated talker, Dr Mahaffy, provost of Trinity College, who, for his part, praised the archbishop's skill as a conversationalist. Walsh, many of his friends agreed, "talked much better than he wrote". His mind was well-stocked with literary allusions and quotations, and his almost encyclopaedic knowledge and retentive memory enabled him to take part in discussions on almost all topics likely to arise. In addition, he was said to be an attentive and appreciative listener, tolerant of the views of others, and able to put at ease the youngest and most inexperienced in the company.[74] Despite his sober, analytical style of writing, "he always retained", in his secretary's words, "a boyish *joie de vivre*, and even in old age he laughed so heartily that tears would run down his cheeks".[75]

The close and very well disposed friend, already mentioned, Myles V. Ronan, spoke of him as a "genial" and "delightful companion", who "at his own table was a charming host". "It was then", he continued, "one could see the true man, an able raconteur, with humour sparkling in his keen eyes ... a man of extraordinary knowledge ... It was always a delightful treat to be seated at table with him." The same friend and uncritical admirer added that it was "in holiday time" that the archbishop "showed himself the real friend and companion, unselfish, taking extraordinary pains to make everything pleasant, arranging his journeys to fit in with this musical treat or that". He would sit up late at night reading everything concerning the following day's itinerary, hence, "sight-seeing with such a companion was a real pleasure and a liberal education".[76] Yet despite this eulogy, Ronan conceded that "few gave him the credit of having a heart. They thought of him as a colossal intellect, cold and logical". But, he insisted, "those who knew him intimately knew that he had a warm heart".[77]

THE COMPASSIONATE MAN

The "warm heart" was experienced in a special way by many who were ill, bereaved, or in poverty. The compassionate side to William Walsh certainly outweighed the expressions of pettiness or rancour in his life. The instances of care for others greatly exceeded, as might be expected, those which have been chronicled. Among the latter were words of sympathy to the bereaved and acts of kindness to the very ill. To the widow of Professor Fitzgerald, a former colleague on the National Board, he sent not just words of sympathy but his own warm and glowing memories of her late husband.[78] Lord Cadogan expressed his appreciation of his Grace's words of sympathy on the death of his brother;[79] and Henrietta Mac Donnell, wife of the under secretary, Sir Anthony Mac Donnell, sent word from London concerning her husband's operation because, as she said, "you were so extremely kind during my husband's long illness".[80] In a similar spirit of helpfulness he went to considerable trouble in response to a request, on 31 January 1903, from Professor Anthony Traill, provost of Trinity College, for his assistance with respect to the "exclusion of a Protestant orphan from an exhibition which he obtained by examination".[81] Walsh frequently showed himself ready to rectify a wrong, and not infrequently this occurred where primary teachers were concerned. One such notable intervention was acknowledged in a letter, dated 3 January 1903, from a Jerome Lehane, thanking him "for the prompt withdrawal of the three months notice of dismissal served on me by Father O'Neill".[82] The main beneficiaries of his care and concern, however, were the sick and the poor of Dublin, especially the children.

His work for the sick was manifested on hospital boards and in financial appeals and contributions, but also at times by personal encouragement. Lord Aberdeen wrote gratefully to him on 6 December 1907, for his "cordial and sympathetic manner" towards Lady Aberdeen in respect of the exhibition she had organised to heighten understanding of tuberculosis, its causes, steps to avoid it, and how to treat it. She returned home "very cheered and gratified" by his Grace's attendance the previous day.[83] Walsh's work for the poor was also not just in terms of buildings and funding but in personal contact. This was especially so with regard to children. It took place in hostels and hospitals, but also on the streets of Dublin, for cycling was not the archbishop's only physical exercise, he also enjoyed walking.

His small, well-knit frame, and brisk walk, with his silk hat tilted backwards on his large head, was a familiar sight in the poorer areas on the north side of the city. Frequently he returned home through lower or middle Gardiner Street, then teeming with a juvenile population, amongst whom the boys had been trained by their teachers and encouraged by their parents to doff their caps, or touch their forelocks, to the priest and say, "God bless you, Father!", while the little girls bowed or curtsied. The children recognised him, and he regularly stopped to chat with them. He was amused and moved by them. On the mantelpiece of his study for twenty years he had the photograph of an ebullient young boy, Jim Treacy. He was a fair, curly-headed, bare-footed lad who "read" an address to his Grace on the occasion of a visit to the schools in Dorset street. At the time compulsory school attendance was being discussed. When the archbishop entered, Jim stepped forward and, getting on a chair, began to read with great aplomb an address which he had rehearsed beforehand, following the text with his eye, line by line, from left to right. His statement was a demand for educational equality but without being "compulsed". When he had finished he solemnly handed the address to his Grace, who found, what he had already suspected, that Jim had been holding the address upside down. The bright youngster was unable to read.[84] Walsh cherished some of the sayings of his young acquaintances and used regale his friends with them. Indeed, an unexpected recreation of his was to attend polo matches at the Phoenix Park, at which, instead of taking a seat in the stand, he preferred to remain by the rail to hear the remarks of the young urchins, seated on the grass, on the merits of the play and the players.[85]

Among the works which he held in highest regard was the Catholic Working Boys' Home and the Sacred Heart Home for Homeless Boys. Having a strong belief in the efficacy of children's prayers, he visited the Sacred Heart Home before he left for hospital for the last time and asked the children to offer their

Holy Communion for him. In the same trust he requested his valet, William Kelly, the night before his operation, that his three children offer their Holy Communion for him the following morning. "On hearing that they had already intended to do so unsolicited, the archbishop broke down – the only occasion", in his secretary's experience, "on which his emotion overcame him." "Behind a mask of outward reserve," the same witness explained, "Dr Walsh concealed great bashfulness, a kindly heart, and solid piety."[86]

In this chapter's endeavour to present aspects of the humanity of William Walsh against the pattern of a life of work and pressure, mention has been made of the pressures occasioned by the university question and by the essential Irish controversy. In many ways, his participation in the solution to the university problem was the high point of his episcopacy. But before treating of that role, there is another important but less well-known role which merits special consideration, namely, his work as mediator and arbitrator in labour disputes and occasions of commercial and even political disagreement. In the 1890s he pioneered in Dublin a new constructive approach to conflict in the workplace, an approach characterised by respect for both parties and by an endeavour to reach a fair and just solution acceptable to both.

XI

Arbitrator in social, commercial, and political disputes

William Walsh's Dublin now seems as remote as Dickens' London. The city proper lay between two canals, and from the close of the nineteenth century until his death it was marked by "lurching trams, distinctive electric light standards, and rows of small houses with a horse of Hanover or an Infant of Prague statue over the fanlight of their hall-doors". It was, by and large, "an orderly and ordered world, the world of the pound sterling and the rule of law". In that world, Dublin was still governed by distinctions of class, religion, and politics.[1] And yet considerable change was taking place in social and church affairs.

The *Echo*, an English journal, providing a pen-portrait of Archbishop Walsh on 8 August 1890, commenced by noting "the change" that had "come over the spirit of the Catholic Church during the pontificate of Leo XIII", and explained that "a leading idea of his pontificate is the effecting of a social transformation by espousing the cause of labour; and hence we have the unique spectacle of the heads of the Catholic Church in England, Ireland, and the United States, not to speak of countries on the continent, coming to the side of workmen".[2]

The success of Cardinal Manning as arbitrator in the great London dock strike, 1889-'90, undoubtedly influenced Walsh. "We have been under the despotism of capital", the cardinal wrote to him on 1 March 1890. "The union of labourers is their only shelter, and the capitalists have now wisely formed a union of their own. This is altogether legitimate, and it has rendered the intervention of a third party necessary to peace and fair play on both sides."[3] But, as the *Echo* acknowledged, Walsh's public interest in social matters was chronicled as early as the Bessborough Commission, when he was in Maynooth; and he had later "developed the arbitration idea, and warmly advocated its adoption in disputes between landlord and tenant". "A striking example of the wisdom of his persistence in the cause", the paper continued, "was the agreement between Captain Vandeleur and his tenants in the County of Clare". Highly pleased with that outcome, Walsh wrote to the *Freeman* on 10 April 1889, praising Vandeleur and the tenantry of the Kilrush district, Co. Clare, for seeking an independent arbitrator to help solve their problems.[4]

But despite this, a month later Walsh acknowledged in the *Times* that he had almost abandoned all hope of his proposal of arbitration being adopted generally "by the landlords and their advisers". The chief secretary, Balfour, he noted, had stated in the House of Commons that there was no need for arbitration, that the tribunals of the Land Commission sufficed. The tribunals, Walsh asserted, did not suffice. They were not empowered, as they were in Scotland, to cater

188

for the pressing problems arising from the accumulation of arrears of rent.⁵ As a consequence, *Punch* magazine on 25 May carried a full page depiction of a benign Archbishop Walsh holding an olive branch, inscribed 'Arbitration', standing between a belligerent landlord with an eviction notice, backed by an armed soldier, and a mournful, bedraggled, seated tenant; and underneath there was a quotation from Walsh's letter, followed by a long doggerel which referred to his honest effort in the cause of peace, spoke of him as standing "with friendly mien, and olive-branch in hand, a messenger of peace", and asked:

> Is it not time
> That stern constraint and fiercely furtive crime,
> So long relentlessly opposed should cease
> To have the field between them.⁶

Seizing the opportunity, Walsh contributed an article in the *Contemporary Review* in June, which gave an account of his endeavours during the previous two years to promote peace in Ireland by round-table conference and arbitration. His proposal had been met in certain quarters, he declared, by "an ungracious, not to say unfriendly spirit".⁷ There was an unexpectedly friendly response from the *Daily Chronicle*, which described his article as "an important contribution to the history of the Irish question" and, approving his proposal of arbitration, declared that it had "the merit of being the only remedy for the agrarian deadlock which can be termed an alternative to the policy of wholesale eviction and emigration of which Englishmen are not enamoured". The paper added:

> Dr Johnson once said that "to hinder insurrection by drawing away the people, and to govern peaceably by having no subjects, is an expedient that argues no great profundity in politics". It is because we are of the same way of thinking that we wish success to the principle of arbitration which Archbishop Walsh so ably advocates.⁸

Before the year was out, Walsh had the opportunity of applying the principle to labour disputes in the city of Dublin, and this was to lead in 1890 to his active promotion of a scheme for the establishment of a Board of Conciliation, which was to be thoroughly representative, for the purpose of hearing and settling disputes between capital and labour. This, in turn, induced Dublin corporation to forward "an appeal to all the leading traders in the Irish metropolis with a view to adopting the project".⁹ Walsh's reputation in the field subsequently resulted in his being contacted by J.C. Hedley, bishop of Newport, for information and advice "in the midst of a most disastrous strike or lock out in the coal trade in South Wales".¹⁰ The summer of 1889, however, marked the break-through in the practical application of Walsh's arbitration proposals.

THE BRICKLAYERS STRIKE

On 27 June, at their summer meeting, the bishops endorsed the proposals, and the opportunity of applying them came with the bricklayers' strike in Dublin. During July and August the bricklayers struck "for an advance of wages and a reduction of one hour's work". The impact on the building industry was severe, and the side-effects were manifold. On 21 August, Walsh wrote to the *Freeman's Journal* recommending arbitration, and referring the bricklayers to "the constitution of the new tenants' defence organisation, so wisely projected by Mr Parnell", in which "a fundamental article had been inserted to the effect that *the help of the organisation will be given to those tenants only who are willing to submit their cases to arbitration*". He suggested that employers and bricklayers agree "to an arbitration on the basis of the following proposals: 1. The Dublin bricklayers to be paid at the English rate of wages, and on the terms as to hours etc. that are usual in England. 2. The English scale of work, as regards the average number of bricks laid each day, to be adjusted here."

The trades council executive body, with W.J. Leahy, president, in the chair, strongly recommended to the bricklayers "the eminently patriotic and timely suggestion of his Grace ... in today's *Freeman*". The result of the recommendation was that arbitrators were agreed: Alderman J.M. Meade, representing the builders, Mr J.P. Cox for the bricklayers, with his Grace as chairman. They came up with a provisional settlement which ended the strike, and a recommendation that a permanent council be established representing "the various interests connected with the Dublin 'trades', which by acting as a court of arbitration would obviate recourse to such extreme measures as a strike or lock-out". Some time later permanent proposals were put forward.[11]

Walsh's involvement in a further initiative benefiting workers was indicated by one of the final entries in his diary for that year. The entry for the dates 29 and 30 December read simply, "Labourers". What it signified was suggested by the newspaper reports for those dates. There was a public meeting, under the auspices of the National Labourers' Dwellings and Sanitary Association, for the purpose of considering the housing of the working classes and the available provision of open spaces and recreational grounds. Letters of support were received from Archbishop Walsh and Cardinal Manning. At the meeting, William Martin Murphy, a prominent employer as well as a member of parliament, who acted as arbitrator at times with Walsh, moved the adoption of the report.[12] Murphy, together with Michael Davitt, worked with the archbishop in helping to settle the next major strike, that of the Dublin United Builder Labourers' Trade Union.

BUILDER LABOURERS' STRIKE

The strike was called by the secretary of the union, Mr W. Jones, on 18 March 1890, to take effect the following day, Wednesday. The union's grievance was that the master builders had refused to meet the man's demand of 4 pence per hour. The strike was expected to affect "nearly two thousand labourers"[13] The background was filled in by an important letter from the archbishop to the editor of the *Freeman* on 20 March. He pointed out that on 12 March Mr Jones declared that the men were quite willing to submit their claims to arbitration, and had suggested that he (the archbishop) act as chairman. The following day, Mr Wardrop, honorary secretary of the Master Builders' Association, wrote to Jones accepting his proposal, and both he and Jones wrote to Walsh inviting him to arbitrate. On Tuesday, 18 March, Walsh presided at his house "at a conference between five representatives of the Builders' Association and five representatives of the Labourers' Association". The conference broke up, Walsh explained, when one of the labourers' representatives asserted that they were "2, 000 strong" and that if they did not get what they sought "they would all be out on strike next morning". He wrote this letter, Walsh continued, to counter rumours that the employers were opposed to arbitration, and had only agreed to it after the men had resorted to strike, and that the men, therefore, could not be expected to proceed any further with the builders' representatives. In his view, the person behind the rumours was seeking to cause upset. He felt sure that he knew who the person was, and he hoped that the rumours would be countered by Mr Jones and others.[14]

That day there was a mass open-air meeting of the men on strike, at which a resolution was adopted to refer the issue to arbitrators. Writing to the *Freeman* on 21 March Walsh announced that he was proud of the result of the meeting and was now very hopeful of a quick settlement. He then outlined his aims and procedures.

> To the two contending parties I have said from the beginning, as I said in similar circumstances in the case of the bricklayers' strike, that, strong as my sympathies may and must be with the working man, I cannot take upon myself in such a case the office of an advocate merely of their interests. Both sides have honoured me with their confidence.

"The men on strike", he continued, "have now manfully declared in favour of a reference of the matter in dispute to the arbitration of three impartial gentlemen, acting with me as president of their tribunal. I have no hesitation in publicly appealing to the employers to accept this practical proposal. They will, I am sure, as a matter of course, accept it."

He added that because people's livelihood and trade were suffering a quick settlement was essential, and hence he was availing of this letter to invite the president and secretary of the Builders Association, and of the Labourers' Association to meet at his house "at one o'clock tomorrow (Saturday)". "I am at their disposal", he promised, "for any help I can give them in the settlement of the dispute." The first matter to be considered was the selection of the arbitrators, and, that being achieved, he believed the dispute would soon be settled.

One of the results of a successful outcome would be, he hoped, "the establishment ... of a permanent committee of conciliation between the working men and their employers".

That day, 21 March, the representatives of both sides met the archbishop. Next day, Saturday, Walsh had a further letter in the *Freeman*, and its recommendations were brought to the attention of a mass meeting of the workers at the Phoenix Park on Sunday, 23 March. It suggested that as arbitration had been agreed, and as it would take time to choose the arbitrators, the workers, meanwhile, should return to work on Monday, 24 March. The meeting agreed. Putting the motion to the meeting, the chairman, Adolphus Shields, "expressed his opinion that his Grace deserved all the thanks they could possibly give him (cheers). He had done a great deal of good for the working men of Dublin. He had helped the bricklayers through their difficulty, and he was now helping the labourers out of theirs (cheers)."[15]

On 28 March, the arbitrators in the dispute met at 4 Rutland Square. "The arbitrators appointed were – on the part of the Builders Association, Alderman Sir George Moyers, LLD, DL, JP; and on the part of the Labourers' Association, Mr Michael Davitt. Alderman Meade, president of the Builders Association, and Mr William Jones, secretary of the Labourers' Association, were present as assessors. His Grace, the archbishop, presided as chairman and umpire."[16]

In the account in the *Freeman's Journal* of 29 March, the claims were noted: "1. That the system of payment of wages by the hour be adopted. 2. That the rate of wages be four and a half pence per hour." The award was presented as follows: "1. We do not, for the present, see our way to recommending the introduction of the system of payment of wages by the hour". It would cause "a general dislocation of trade arrangements ... so long as the men employed in the building trade generally are paid by the day or the week." 2. "As regard the rate of wages". The arbitrators had no difficulty in agreeing that the wages ought to be increased. The increase awarded was substantial, and as it was something for which contractors had not budgeted in contracts already entered into, it was recommended that a period of three months at least should be allowed elapse before the full increase was given. So the arbitrators fixed on 1 July as a not unreasonable date. In detail, the award decreed that wages were to be immediately increased to 2s. 9d. per day or 16 shillings and six pence per week; while from 1 July the rates were to be: "summer wages, for the 8 months from 1 March to 31 October, 18s. per week. Winter wages, for the 4 months from 1 November to end of February, 16s. per week".[17]

That night there was a crowded meeting at St Patrick's Temperance Hall, Lwr. Clanbrassil Street, to hear the verdict. The *Freeman* of 29 March chronicled the occasion. "When Mr Michael Davitt, Mr William Murphy, MP, and Mr Charles Dawson, appeared on the platform, they were received with loud cheering. On the motion of Mr Jones, secretary of the labourers' union, seconded by Mr Clinton, president of the union, Mr William Murphy, MP, took the chair. The chairman, who was received with cheering, called on Michael Davitt, as the representative of the men at the arbitration, to announce the decision that had been agreed. Davitt then gave a long explanation of the decision, and the award was carried without dissent. Having advised that the increase not be spent on alcoholic drink, Davitt stated: "He had done the best he could for them, aided by their very intelligent secretary, Mr Jones ... It would give him greater pleasure to be able to announce better terms, but he thought that everything considered they had come out of this dispute with a considerable victory. If they owed anything to him (Mr Davitt), or anything to Mr Jones, they owed fifty times as much to his Grace, the archbishop of Dublin (applause). Mr Davitt then left the meeting."

The chairman, William M. Murphy, declared once more how honoured he was to have been asked to preside. "There was no member of their own body", he said, "who had a deeper sympathy with the poorly paid working man than he had." Finally, Jones, seconded by Maurice Canty, a prominent figure in the Labourers' Association, proposed a vote of thanks to Archbishop Walsh, Davitt, Murphy, and others "for the sympathy they had shown us during the dispute between us and our employers, also for the kind assistance they have given us in bringing about a friendly settlement of the same".[18]

IN SUPPORT OF ARBITRATION COUNCILS

The settlement provoked an editorial comment in the *Freeman* the same day in terms of the importance of the precedent. "It holds out", the editorial observed, "an example to other great cities of the Empire" on the value of arbitration "as a means of averting strike, or, where it may have occurred, of instantly bringing it to an end". The great influence of Archbishop Walsh, it observed, had been exerted in favour of this excellent plan for many years.[19] The previous week the paper had run articles dealing with a new law on the establishment of arbitration and conciliation courts throughout Germany, and on French arbitration courts. In an editorial the hope was expressed that "as his Grace the Archbishop has frequently urged most strongly, the present interest in the status of labour in this country will not be allowed to vanish without something being done, even in a voluntary and non-legislative way, to establish some system of workable arbitration courts". "And towards such an end," the writer concluded, "the articles which we publish today should help."[20] Walsh was careful to preserve the articles.

On 26 March, Walsh, on the occasion of a lecture at the Workingmen's Club, 10 Wellington Quay, on "The Revival and Development of Irish Industries", sent a letter to the press apologising for his absence and appealing to all concerned to take cognisance of the great importance to the trade of Dublin of "the establishment of a board or council representative of both employers and employed, and, to some extent, representative of the general public of the city".[21] Despite this, and the support of the *Freeman's Journal*, and the appeal of Dublin corporation to the traders of the city, mentioned earlier, the board, or council, or court, remained unestablished for another fifty-six years.

THE GREAT SOUTHERN AND WESTERN RAILWAY STRIKE

The most striking example of Walsh's readiness and determination in the role of arbitrator was in connection with a dispute which had repercussions far beyond Dublin, that involving the workers and management of the Great Southern and Western Railway. With confidence based on previous successes, Walsh wrote to the *Freeman* on 27 April 1890, stating that he knew nothing about the merits of the issues in dispute, but he regretted that the men had gone out without giving sufficient notice of their intention to do so. The men had struck, it would appear, because the directors of the company had refused to meet their representatives and listen to their case. Walsh went on to point out that in the past twelve months he had gained "some little experience in the matter of trade disputes in Dublin", and the experience had taught him that the most likely means of gaining a settlement was to have a conference between representatives of both sides to the dispute. "Why", he asked, "should not such a conference be held in this case at an early hour tomorrow?" If the men had any difficulty about asking for such a conference, he was taking on himself the responsibility of asking for them. The conference, he added, should "include a representative of each of the various classes of men on strike". He invited the directors to the conference, and asked them, meantime, to postpone a legal action they were taking against the signal men.[22]

Next morning Walsh drove to Kingsbridge railway station and met with Mr Colhoun, the traffic manager, and the chairman, Mr J.C. Colville. Then he drove to 90 James's Street to meet the strike committee presided over by a Mr Foreman. Later, Colhoun, Foreman, and a Mr Kelly, secretary of the Kingsbridge branch of the Railway Workers' Union, visited Archbishop's House for preliminary discussions. Subsequently, according to a report in the *Freeman*, his Grace arrived at Kingsbridge terminus at four o'clock "and had a consultation with the directors, which lasted till six o'clock. On its termination", the paper continued, "our representative was informed by his Grace that the negotiations had completely failed. He had done what he could, but the directors had been 'wholly unreasonable' while the men had behaved admirably, doing what they could to bring about a settlement. His Grace then drove to 90 James's Street, where he informed the strike committee of what he had done and of the result. Mr Davitt remained in the company of the men during the afternoon."[23] Walsh had experienced first hand, for the first time, the unyielding, domineering aspect of contemporary management.

Meantime, side effects of the strike were plain to see. The newspapers told of trains being kept running by the clerks doing the porters' jobs, assisted by passengers, and a few army reserve men. On 28 April disruption to the Kilkenny races received coverage. As far as the men on strike were concerned, their anger and sense of grievance was deepened by the directors summoning six signal men to answer charges in the police court of leaving their posts and impeding the passage of trains.[24]

On 28 April also, Walsh gave an explanation in the *Freeman* of why negotiations had broken down. He was clearly irate with the directors. The latter had required that the men apologise, he reported, and state that their conduct was 'inexcusable'. The men had given a promise "never again to enter upon a strike without giving a full month's notice", but this was not acceptable to the directors.[25] They insisted on 'inexcusable'. As Walsh put it in a letter to the *Evening Telegraph* the following day, "no other adjective in the English language would be accepted".[26] "In the interests of the men", he had explained in his letter in the *Freeman*, "I feel bound to say that I am as yet unable to see any grounds on which I could represent to them the duty of making any such humiliating confession. I do not think anything of the kind was looked for in the settlement of the great dock strikes in London or Liverpool. I certainly know that nothing of the kind was thought of in the case either of the bricklayers' strike or of the building labourers' strike in our city. I should be surprised to hear that anything of the kind was thought of by the directors of the Dublin, Wicklow and Wexford railway in the settlement of the recent strike upon their line."[27] He also intensified the pressure on the directors in his conclusion in the *Evening Telegraph*. "The directors", he pronounced, "with their favourite adjective – to say nothing of their ill-timed prosecution – must now bear the responsibility of the inconvenience to the travelling public, of the stoppage of trade, and of the loss to the shareholders which continuance of this unhappy strike cannot but involve."[28]

Walsh had been scheduled to go to England. He deferred his visit, following a telegram from Cork, in order to be available to bring about a settlement.[29] In a detailed interview for the *Freeman* he again came out strongly against the intransigence of the directors, and suggested that meetings of the shareholders, and those generally affected by the continuance of the strike, "was now perhaps the most effective remedy".[30] This, indeed, was to prove the way forward. The key figures in the resolution appear to have been the Cork harbour commissioners. Facing heavy losses, they passed a resolution recording their view "that the directors of the G.S. & W.R. should be held responsible for the consequences if they do not, as is their first and most pressing duty, come to such terms with their employees as will enable the traffic to be immediately reopened on the line, and for doing which his Grace, Archbishop Walsh, has offered a favourable opportunity".[31] Looking to Cork, Walsh, on Wednesday, 30 April, sent a telegram to the mayor of Cork saying that he had telegraphed Kingsbridge that if the directors did not insist on the word 'inexcusable', and were prepared to accept another satisfactory form of expression, he could induce the men to adopt it, and might be able to effect a settlement. "As yet", he concluded, "I have received no reply, so I have telegraphed again. Wire what Cork will do – Archbishop."

Before the mayor could reply, he received another message. "Directors have communicated with me in an amicable spirit. Cork need take no action now. Everything looks hopeful." The mayor replied expressing gratification at the news contained in the telegram. "Cork, and the whole country", he observed, "will bear in lasting remembrance your Grace's zealous and unselfish labours in this most vital crisis."[32]

Events piled on each other within a short space. Complications seem to have crowded out the directors new 'amicable spirit'. An official of the company expressed to the *Telegraph* the directors annoyance that the GSWR was being used as a test case for English reforms so that the battle of English employees was being fought on Irish ground. A reply from the directors to the archbishop, with terms of settlement, was sent to the *Daily* and *Evening Mail* on 30 April. The following day, negotiations went on most of the day. The directors were unyielding. Walsh feared that the strike would spread to other Irish railway companies, and was greatly annoyed when the directors dispersed without any agreement being realised.[33]

On 1 May he wrote strongly in the *Freeman* on the intransigence of the directors, and revealed the humiliating way he had been treated. "A situation of the utmost delicacy had arisen in the railway strike", he announced. "I have been forced at last to recognise the impossibility of conducting a successful mediation between two bodies of men, one of which indeed was always accessible to personal interview, the other being always inaccessible. I have willingly waited, without a word of complaint, in one of the offices at Kingsbridge for hour after hour on several days this week, whilst the board of directors, in a seclusion equal to that of a cabinet council, sat in their boardroom rejecting proposal after proposal which, with a perseverance amounting, I fear, to pertinacity, I continued to submit to the judgement of their exalted authority." "I have now exhausted", Walsh declared, "every possible means of bringing about a satisfactory agreement by means of a mediation conducted under conditions of such difficulty. So far as the resources of mediation are concerned, the dead-lock on our greatest line of railway seems bound to go on forever."

He added: "The men have really been struggling for a thing that ... is not worth struggling for – the privilege of an interview with the directors." If the men were to strike at all, it should not have been for something like that which might bring them nothing, but in a demand "for *arbitration and nothing short of it*". He had asked the men to consider the matter tomorrow. His advice to them was: "They struck without sufficient notice. They struck for a thing that is not worth striking for." They could now put things right and earn the gratitude of the country, and demonstrate their disdain for the obstinacy of the directors, by going back to work, but not abandoning their organisation, and placing "their whole case into the hands of two staunch friends of theirs – Mr Harford, the chief official of their organisation, who is now in Ireland, and myself."34

Next day, he addressed the men (to cheers) in the Pillar Room of the Rotunda building. A ballot was held. The response was almost unanimous in leaving matters in the archbishop's hands, and agreeing to return to work. The directors, in turn, agreed to deal with grievances within a fortnight, and that there would be no discrimination against the signal men. Walsh and Harford asked Professor J.A. Galbraith, of Trinity College Dublin, to join them as an arbitrator.

In their subsequent report, the arbitrators singled out the issues which existed between the workers and the directors. These were three: 1. The directors' insistence that the men were to blame in striking without sufficient notice – which the men concede, and that the signal men make a further public acknowledgement that their action was "inexcusable". 2. The demand of the men that the directors "recognise" their organisation. 3. The men's further demand that the directors consent to receive a deputation from the men on strike to lay before them their grievances – (these grievances "the directors have already in general terms undertaken to take into consideration 'as speedily as possible, not exceeding a fortnight'").

Commenting on these issues, the arbitrators observed: 1. That the directors no longer pressed for 'inexcusable'; 2. that the organisation did not depend on the recognition of the directors, who, besides, had no objection to the men being members of the organisation (despite rumours to the contrary); 3. their only objection was to the organisation being the "medium of communication" between the employees and the directors, and communications being made to them on "the letter paper of the organisation". They as directors wished to communicate directly with their own workers. The arbitrators thought there was no substantial obstacle to agreement in such an objection. Large numbers of employees, they pointed out, were members of the organisation. There was nothing to prevent one of them, who was also secretary of the organisation, communicating with the directors "on behalf of fellow-employees", who were also members of the organisation. As to whether "the particular kind of paper" was a sufficient matter for which the directors were prepared to dislocate the trade of the country, the arbitrators would not offer an opinion, but it would not be worthy of the men so to act.35

In making their announcement the three arbitrators – "William J. Walsh, Archbishop of Dublin, Joseph A. Galbraith, SF, TCD, and Edward Harford, General Secretary of the Amalgamated Society of Railway Servants etc." – named 12.00 a.m. the following day for return to work. On Saturday, 3 May, the *Evening Telegraph* announced:

Today at noon the fifteen hundred porters, guards, and signal men of the Great Southern Railway, who have been on strike for eight days, were to present themselves for re-employment. By Monday traffic over the line will again be in full operation.

The directors paid the fine imposed on the signal men, and took back two others who had been dismissed in Cork. On the settlement, the paper commented: "These are terms of truce, not terms of settlement. It must be observed that the men have not capitulated. They have not surrendered to the mercy and will of the directors." As Mr Foreman, the workers' leader, stated, they had made "a sacrifice, not a surrender".[36] The following day, 4 May, Walsh availed of the settlement to make a further plea in the *Freeman's Journal* for a Board of Conciliation for Dublin. He referred to his previous letter of 21 February, which the paper printed again. The municipal corporation of Dublin formally welcomed the suggestion.[37]

Letters and telegrams of congratulation were received by the archbishop from "civic dignitaries and representative bodies all over the country" on the "successful outcome" of his labours;[38] but the most practical and prestigious vote of thanks came from Cork. On Friday, 15 May, Cork Corporation, at a special meeting, agreed "to confer the freedom of the city on his Grace the Most Rev. Dr Walsh, Archbishop of Dublin, in consideration of his services in connection with the settlement of the strike in the Great Southern and Western Railway".[39]

FROM RERUM NOVARUM TO DECLINING POPULARITY

One year later, it was announced in the *Freeman* that Pope Leo XIII's encyclical letter on Labour was about to be issued, and that it was expected to be the "most important" document of his pontificate. "To his Eminence Cardinal Manning and the Archbishop of Dublin", the paper added, "was entrusted the making of the English version, which will be published early next week."[40] On 5 June 1891, Walsh sent a letter to all the churches on the Labour Encyclical, as it was being called. In his letter, he encouraged, along the lines of *Rerum Novarum*, the formation of societies of working men and of employers, and in conclusion suggested that all aim at earning the praise bestowed by the pope on those who "have taken up the cause of the working men, and have striven – to make both families and individuals better off; to infuse the spirit of justice into the mutual relations of employer and employed; and to keep before the eyes of both classes the precepts of duty and the laws of the Gospel ... that Gospel which, by inculcating self-restraint, keeps man within the bounds of moderation, and tends to establish harmony among the divergent interests and various classes which compose the state."[41]

In these years, Archbishop Walsh was riding the crest of a wave in public esteem. The *Echo's* pen-portrait of him in August 1890, observed:

Archbishop Walsh is a good man of business, masters with rapidity the details of complicated matters, is clear and orderly in his exposition, and unflinching in maintaining what he believes to be the correct course.

All these qualities were in evidence in his arbitration between employers and employees. The *Echo* went on to remark that Walsh was "not only popular with the mass of his countrymen", to whom he had "devoted his great talents," but also enjoyed the respect of those who honourably differed from him "in religion and politics".[42]

Within a couple of years, however, his popularity suffered a serious decline among the working-class populations of Dublin and Cork, who were vehement supporters of Parnell, and for the same reason among sections of the middle class – as instanced in James Joyce's *Portrait of the Artist* ... His two closest collaborators in the work of arbitration, Michael Davitt, and William Martin Murphy, who also challenged Parnell, were also to lose popular favour, Murphy to the extent that he lost his parliamentary seat.

ARBITRATION AND CONTROL OF THE 'FREEMAN'S JOURNAL'

After Parnell's death, Walsh, with more good will than prudence, took steps to preserve unity in the main body of the Irish parliamentary party, and in the process became estranged from Murphy. Sadly and ironically, the estrangement occurred because of an arbitration! The occasion was Walsh's involvement in an effort to resolve the rivalry between the successful *National Press* and the virtually bankrupt, but long established *Freeman's Journal*, by bringing about an amalgamation. There was no point, he argued, in having two national daily newspapers supporting the one political party. Unwittingly, he was being used by Dillon, who was engaged in a power struggle with Healy and Murphy and sought to have the *National Press* absorbed in a *Freeman's Journal* managed by a new board. The shareholders of the *National Press*, including the two figures who had done so much to make it successful, William Martin Murphy and T.M. Healy, did not approve. Eventually, the shareholders agreed to dissolve the *National Press*, provided they held a third of the shares after the amalgamation and were represented on the new board by Healy, Murphy, and a Dublin businessman, Joseph Mooney. This was agreed. Archbishop Croke, however, warned his Dublin colleague that John Dillon and William O'Brien were unlikely to be happy with this arrangement.[43] So it proved. The resultant quarrel, with its convoluted mixture of argument, attributions of unworthy motives, envy, power-hunger, and self-interest, is abundantly illustrated in the Dublin diocesan archives.

John Dillon, assisted by Thomas Sexton, set out to gain control of the *Freeman* board. In January 1893, after Healy and Murphy had left a board meeting, Dillon had Sexton nominated and elected as chairman of the board.[44] Complaints, charges, and counter-charges came to Walsh from both sides. Dillon informed him on 17 January that the members of the board wished him to act as arbitrator and were prepared to offer their resignation in order to give him a free hand. All were pledged to accept and carry through whatever he decided.[45] Walsh, on 24 January 1893, allowed himself be persuaded by Dillon and Sexton. He agreed to complete the report within a month. As he worked, he again was subject to pressure and advice from both sides. It was known that he favoured a board of businessmen, and the not unfounded report circulated that he planned to invite a Dublin businessman, Alderman Michael Kernan, a Parnellite, on to the board, and that the latter, in turn, planned to bring in other "commercial men" and parnellites, as board directors.[46] Dillon, meanwhile, had drafted Kernan onto the current board of the *Freeman* despite the opposition of the *National Press* representatives.

Walsh completed his report on 20 February, well within the month, but then suggested that it not be presented until the board meeting on 6 March at which he would discuss the carrying out of his recommendations. On the very day of the board meeting, he received letters from Messrs Murphy, Healy, and Mooney, stating that they could not regard his decisions as binding on them. The meeting was unpleasant. The fact that the report was presented later than promised, and that a parnellite had been put on the board, were among the excuses presented by Healy and Murphy for their non-acceptance of the report. Walsh felt betrayed and was incensed. When Murphy called to the archbishop's residence later that day, therefore, and left a letter explaining his action, he received a dismissive response:

> Your letter of today needs no detailed reply. All I feel called upon to say for the present is that whilst the newspapers controlled by the board remain under the present management the less they venture to say about 'pledge-breaking' the better.[47]

The following day Walsh wrote to Sexton stating that the manner in which he had been treated by a certain section of the *Freeman's* board called for a formal protest on Sexton's part. 'I protest most strongly", he declared, "against the proceeding which I cannot but regard as a distinct breach of faith."[48] Nearly six weeks later his wounded *amour propre* found an even more emphatic expression in a letter to Dillon. "I am really sick of the whole wretched affair", he exclaimed, "you are dealing with people who will not keep faith. It was plain to everyone concerned that they broke faith with me."[49] Dillon took advantge of the wounded feelings by representing to the archbishop that it was "essential" that no partisan of Murphy be left on the board, because if there was a man left to back him he would never cease to give trouble, and with "his extraordinary gift for intrigue" might succeed in gaining ascendancy.[50]

From 7 to 28 March the controversy over the board occupied page after page in the *Freeman's Journal*. The whole country became aware of it. The process began on 7 March with Healy, Murphy, and Mooney writing to the *Freeman* to place before "the shareholders and the public" their recent dispute with the other members of the board, arising from Mr Dillon's cooption to the board of Alderman Kernan, who had previously been removed from the board by the proprietor, Mr E.D. Gray, in order to change from the parnellite policy of the paper. In justice "to the men who founded the *National Press*" they could not sanction the appointment of a parnellite to the board. Walsh, seeing this as special pleading, responded strongly that the board itself had accepted Kernan. Murphy and Healy replied on 9 March, asserting that Kernan had been forced on the board in an unacceptable manner. The next day, Walsh publicly appealed to the other directors not to enter into the controversy in the national interest, and then poured oil on the fire by praising the patriotism of Dillon and Sexton, and speaking of the "shockingly wanton", "grossly calumnious", and "wholly devoid of truth" statements of Murphy and Mooney. This, not surprisingly, led to a response from Murphy and Mooney, to which Walsh replied in turn. On 25 March, Murphy and Mooney put aside any inhibitions they may have had in their public controversy with the archbishop, and, noting that Walsh had avoided his previous intemperate charges in his recent letters to the press, they presented the whole of their correspondence with him, demonstrating that they had given previous notice of their action of 6 March and indicating that Walsh had not been entirely forthright in his presentation of the facts of the situation. On 27 March, Walsh entered "a public protest against the charge of untruthfulness" and set out to prove it unfounded. Next day by "unanimous agreement" the differences between the board's directors were said to have been settled; and a letter to the *Freeman* from Murphy and Mooney assured Walsh that nothing was further from their thoughts than to make the charge against him of which he accused them! The "agreement", however, was short-lived.

Meantime, Walsh's episcopal colleagues were far from happy with his policy and performance. The normally supportive Dr Brownrigg firmly warned him on 20 March that he was "far and near suspected in this matter of a desire to rehabilitate the metropolis politically at the expense of the country generally."[51] He added that Healy believed that the bringing of parnellites on to the board was a plan to kill off the *Independent* newspaper and bring parnellites on side, while they retained their parnellism. But the opposition was not only from the country. In Dublin, many of the clergy had unpleasant memories of their treatment at the hands of the parnellite *Freeman* and did not wish to see a revival of parnellite power in the paper.[52]

On Easter Sunday, 1893, Brownrigg expressed relief at the resolution of the *Freeman* dispute. "The confidence of the people in the Irish party", he judged, "has received a very rude shock from this whole business, and it will take a long time to restore it."[53] The truce, as indicated, lasted but a short time. By the end of April the differences surfaced once more, and again Walsh was drawn into the conflict.

Walsh, then, in his role as arbitrator between the representatives of the *National Press* and those of the *Freeman's Journal* had promoted rather than dissolved divisions within the Irish party. Under the adroit influence of Dillon, he facilitated the latter's gaining control of the *Freeman* while becoming estranged from Healy for a number of years and permanently from Murphy. The latter, for his part, was destined to become an unrelenting enemy of Dillon and of the Irish party. Meanwhile, throughout the remainder of the 1890s the country endured the bitter bickering of those who had been former colleagues.

POLITICAL DISSENSIONS AND MEDIATING FOR UNITY, 1895-1900

There was now a three-fold division in the once formidable Irish parliamentary party: the Parnellites under John Redmond, with the *Irish Independent* as their organ; the major rump, associated with Dillon and O'Brien, and supported by the *Freeman's Journal*; and the smaller vocal grouping associated with Healy and Murphy, which published the *Daily Nation* and drew support from among many of the Catholic clergy. In this factious political climate, the prospect of Home Rule evaporated, and many turned from politics to areas where more positive and uplifting opportunities offered, to the ideals and heroes of a romanticised Celtic past, to the Irish language revival, to the cultivation of gaelic sporting activities, and to seeking in their racial past a new sense of identity and pride.

Walsh, for his part, despite his close association with the Dillonite faction and his unwillingness to talk to the Healyites, still sought to be an arbitrator in the cause of unity, and viewed himself as having almost a mission in this respect. In February 1895, he wrote to the *Freeman* urging political unity. This evoked hostile criticism from the *Herald* and the *Independent*, both the parnellite papers. Having, however, some reason to think Redmond might be open to reasonable discussion, Walsh on 20 February contacted Timothy Harrington, lord mayor of Dublin, suggesting that he might approach Redmond. "I have for a long time past been convinced", Walsh observed, "that if ever this ruinous dissension is to be put an end to (and if it is not, we may as well give up all hope of Home Rule for the next ten years at all events) *your Lordship and I can do more than any other could to bring about the good result.*" He added, by way of explanation, "in any support I have given to the main body, I have been influenced *altogether* by the fact that, to my mind, they represent the great principle of Parnell's policy — that the Irish Home Rule representatives should form a solidly-united body, bound by the parliamentary pledge".[54] On 24 February 1895, he lamented to Dillon that there was "little sign of any move in the right direction" and that he was "rapidly coming to Dr Croke's conclusion, that the sooner he and I 'put up the shutters', so far as Irish politics are concerned, the better". "I, at all events", he concluded, "am now in a position to retire with a good grace, and with a fairly good record, especially after my late apparently fruitless appeal."[55]

Dillon responded on 1 March 1895, urging him not to withdraw from Irish politics, and assuring him that "there never was a time when your help was more needed, or when you could exercise a more beneficial influence";[56] but even before he received Dillon's letter, Walsh had changed his mind. Towards the end of February 1895, he met with John Redmond at the Mansion House, the lord mayor's residence, [57] and on 3 March informed Dillon that he had some hopes for political unity.[58]

He continued to remain, however, quite ambivalent in mind and behaviour. He refused to place any reliance on Healy and Murphy because of their "disgraceful public breach of faith",[59] and, despite his recent talks with Redmond, when it came to a by-election in East Wicklow, he proved quite intransigent. Redmond had informed him on 8 July 1895, that a W. Corbett had announced his candidature for the East Wicklow election. He continued: "Knowing your view that the only issue before the country is a purely political one, I venture to ask you to permit such of your priests as may desire to do so, to support W. Corbett on the platform. In the case of one of your priests, namely Father Hurley, I know he would gladly avail of your permission."[60] Walsh replied on 12 July. The normal line of approach in these matters, he pointed out, was for the priests themselves to approach their bishop. The priest whom Redmond mentioned had written to him on the same subject in the late election and he had been "unable to comply with his request". The reasons given then still applied. But, Walsh went on, "quite apart from all this, I cannot see how any priest can support the candidature of any one at your side in the present unhappy division without compromising himself to some extent in the deplorable line in journalism taken by the newspapers under the control of yourself and your colleagues". "No priest", he declared dogmatically, "identified in any degree with the views advocated by those papers could be considered worthy of a place in the sacred ministry."[61]

Redmond's response on 14 July was a model of dignified protest. He regretted very much the decision reached by his Grace. On that, he remarked, he could say no more, but, he continued:

> I trust your Grace will forgive me if I respectfully protest against your Grace's statement that "no priest identified in any degree with the views advocated by these papers (viz. the *Independent* etc.) could be considered worthy of a place in the sacred ministry". This is a very sweeping statement. Your Grace does not specify the "views" you condemn. Are they political "views" or what? For my part I entirely disclaim the advocacy of any "views" which would be unworthy of the support of the clergy of any church, and I am glad to know that several amongst the most devoted of your own priests are heartily in sympathy with my views.

"I am sure", Redmond concluded, "your Grace will not complain of my writing thus strongly in a matter upon which I feel very keenly."[62]

Walsh at this period seems to have been very near breaking point. In July there also occurred the exchange of letters with Countess Plunkett in which, as has been seen, he again behaved in an intolerant, somewhat unbalanced manner. In December 1895, moreover, he was to over-react and had then to retract in an exchange of letters with the Clarke family of Kilmacanogue, Co. Wicklow, who had complained of the offensive remarks of the local curate on the occasion of their mother's funeral.[63]

He was very conscious that many of his episcopal colleagues were critical of his efforts to bring about unity in the political sphere. Moreover, he personally experienced bouts of frustration and a desire of withdrawal from the whole political scene, and, as usual, he was trying to do too much at the one time. Writing to Cardinal Logue on 26 January 1895, regarding some unspecified function, he observed that "Thursday, or any day in the coming week" would be out of the question for him "as every day of the week is full of engagements with all sorts of people and places that could be no more interfered with than the timetable of the London and North Western Railway."[64] And on 23 February, in the week in which his appeal in the *Freeman* for political unity met with a strongly dismissive response, he confessed, uncharacteristically, "I have had an awful week of it".[65]

The following year, however, tensions eased, owing to the unexpected intervention of Bishop O'Dwyer. He had written to T.M. Healy to enlist his co-operation on the university issue, and through this medium to build bridges between him and Walsh. On 24 October 1896, Healy agreed to give any assistance he could on the university question, although he archly pleaded inadequacy on the matter having left school at thirteen. He would respond cordially, he said, "to any proposition made by his Grace the Abp. of Dublin, for whom I have the highest respect and admiration, and in case he honours me with an interview I shall speak my mind frankly to him as I trust I have always done." Turning to the issue on which he had offended the archbishop, and to which O'Dwyer had evidently referred, Healy continued:

> With regard to the personal matter to which your Lordship so kindly alludes, I have no difficulty whatever about it. If his Grace is good enough to pass over his feeling as to what occurred, I shall be very glad to show I intended no slight upon one whom I always so highly esteemed.[66]

O'Dwyer informed Walsh of Healy's readiness to be of service that same day,[67] and thereafter the archbishop and Healy worked in harmony, the latter exerting all his charm to keep on the right side of his Grace. It facilitated the movement towards political unity. By the end of the year, Walsh was suggesting to the lord mayor a political unity based on accepting "all the three principles of contention: Mr Dillon's shibboleth of 'majority rule'; Mr Healy's ' independence of the constituencies in selection of members of parliament, and extra-parliamentary control of national funds'; and Mr Redmond's ' independence of all English political parties'."[68] On 29 January he wrote on unity in the *Evening Telegraph*, in which he stated that "if the question of the chairmanship of the parliamentary party could only be handed over to the decision of a small representative committee, the composition of which had been approved for the purpose by Messrs Dillon, Healy and Redmond, our parliamentary forces could be reunited within a month". A letter from William O'Malley, a member of the Irish parliamentary party, accepted Walsh's suggestion, and declared that though he was a member of 'the majority party' he was of the opinion that Mr Redmond "would make the best chairman of a united party".[69]

Harrington was hopeful about unity as the year 1897 commenced, though he noted "that the newspapers on both sides are resolutely opposed to any reunion".[70] On 28 February a branch of the Irish National League, Hanley, Staffordshire, sent an approved resolution hailing "the prospect of the settlement" of the long dispute, and stating that Archbishop Walsh and Mr T. Harrington were "entitled to our sincerest gratitude for the patriotic way in which they have initiated and developed that spirit of reconciliation which we believe to be the safest augury for the knitting together of the Irish people".[71]

The expectations were again premature. Still the impetus had been provided, and it had become evident that the country was not prepared to put up much longer with the ceaseless bickering. The new mood was indicated in the Cashel branch of the Dillonite Irish National Federation on 24 April 1898. The chairman, the Revd Dean Kinane, made a vigorous declaration, subsequently adopted as a resolution, that all Irishmen wanted unity, but that "the union of Christendom is but child's play compared with the union of Dillonites, Healyites, Redmondites. For union I propose that Messrs Dillon and O'Brien, Messrs Healy and Knox, Messrs Redmond and Harrington, be called upon to retire for a certain time from public life."[72] Such reactions focused the minds of politicians, as did the centenary commemorations of the 1798 rebellion with their reminders of both unity and division. All sections of society were levied to raise a national monument to Wolfe Tone and the United Irishmen, and Walsh availed of the occasion of the laying of the foundation stone to express to the organising committee on 12 August 1898, the hope "that the spirit of unity that has thus been evoked may not be allowed to pass away with next Monday's ceremonial"; and invoking the aspiration for Home Rule, he recalled the words of Tone – "the misfortune of Ireland is that we have no national government".[73]

With the further impetus generated by such events, the choice of an agreed chairman became imperative. Attention centred more and more on Redmond. Reading the signs, Healy moved closer to him in 1899, and Dillon was forced into negotiation lest he be excluded from all influence in a reunited party. At joint meetings of the parties in late January and early February 1900, the details of reunion were worked out, and on 6 February 1900, John Redmond was unanimously elected chairman of the reunited Irish parliamentary party.

Walsh's role in the preliminaries to the reunion is not clear. The diocesan archives provide little evidence of such activity. There is evidence, however, that Walsh's advisory and mediating role continued to be valued by the leaders of the different factions in the Irish parliamentary party just prior to Redmond's election, and in subsequent months. On 3 February, three days before the election, Harrington called on him,[74] and on 22 November 1900, sent him a frank and striking letter.

"I have been long tempted to write to your Grace", Harrington began, "to implore your intervention in this fresh quarrel with which we are threatened in the Irish party. I feel certain that a little influence exercised with O'Brien and Dillon would set matters right. The fault in the present instance lies wholly with O'Brien who wants Healy's scalp, and unfortunately Redmond is too weak and too attached to the chair to make a protest." In the re-united party, Harrington continued, Healy had acted "with the utmost loyalty". For the past year the business of the party and its meetings were carried on with the utmost cordiality. There was neither friction, nor divergence of opinion. But, he explained,

> O'Brien, notwithstanding his public utterances in reference to unity, opposed by every means in his power the re-union of the parliamentary sections. Now, he and Dillon want to go back on the quarrel they had with Healy in past years and put him on trial for acts committed against a party that no longer exists.

In concluding, Harrington – who had inveighed against clerical interference in the Parnell affair – appealed for a protest from the hierarchy and clergy against O'Brien's "pretension", as he believed such a protest would end the pretension. Finally, he appealed to Walsh's unique standing. "I think also", he declared, "that a word from your Grace to the belligerents themselves would settle it. Healy, I feel certain, would agree to any suggestion you make, and I don't think O'Brien could refuse."[75]

There is no indication, one way or the other, that Walsh intervened. There is extant, however, an interchange of letters with Redmond, including a public letter dated 22 December. In this, Walsh praised Redmond's intervention in bringing about a compromise candidate for a vacant Monaghan seat, and thereby "saved the country from the calamity ... of an angry political conflict in Christmas week". He wished Redmond "every success", congratulated him on the manner in which he had so far grappled with difficulties "with exemplary success", and then announced that the time had come when he should resume his "old practice, now in abeyance for many years, of subscribing to the Irish parliamentary party". He enclosed "a cheque for £10".[76]

ENTERING ON THE NEW CENTURY

The archbishop, therefore, entered on the new century with the hoped-for political unity accomplished, and with his own standing particularly high with leaders of all the main political groupings. He was very conscious, however, how
fragile the current unity was. In the meantime, another newspaper imbroglio was
unfolding that was to have a major influence on the party's future. As the different political groupings drew closer in 1898 and 1899, the readership of the
Independent newspaper declined, and by 1900 the paper was bankrupt. The
Freeman bid for it, but Redmond, not wishing perhaps to give Dillon too much
power by having the *Freeman* acquire it, suggested to Healy that Murphy step
in "and offer to reconstruct the company or buy it".77 Murphy agreed, invested
large sums in the modernisation of *Independent* newspapers, and produced an
efficient, highly popular and influential product, which, when he was slighted by
the party leaders, he turned against them with devastating effect. But that was
very much in the future in 1900. As the new century commenced, peace and
unity appeared to have been achieved on the political front.

ARBITRATION BETWEEN EMPLOYERS AND EMPLOYED RENEWED

Among workers, also, the alienation brought about by the Parnell split seemed
to be largely a thing of the past. Walsh had assisted the process as early as 1896
by condemning publicly "the pernicious system of buying foreign made goods
in preference to home made goods". His words were received with acclaim by
the Dublin Trades Council on 16 March 1896. Three months later, in response
to an appeal for assistance from the builders' labourers, who, with their wives
and children, were "suffering very acutely" owing to a dispute in the building
trade,78 Walsh sent a gentle, sympathetic letter and enclosed £10. "I am personally aware", he announced, "of the distress that has made itself felt in many
quarters of the city as a result of the present calamitous deadlock in the building trades. I know nothing of the merits of the dispute, but one thing is plain –
whoever may be right, and whoever may be wrong, the unfortunate labourers
have to suffer." "Is there any possibility of the strike being brought to an end?",
he asked; and he offered to act as arbitrator again "for the establishment of
industrial peace". He had to add, however, that he would not be available for
three or four days as his hands were "so full of diocesan work of various kinds
in town and country" that he did "not have a moment to spare" just then.79

On 11 June, the Irish Industrial League, acting on behalf of the city labourers, invited him to act on a committee scheduled to meet at the Mansion House
"for the formation of a board of arbitration".80 On 12 June, Michael Ennis, of
the Brick and Stone Layers' trade union, stated that, in response to his Grace's
communication, his union was prepared to meet representatives of the Builders'
Association in friendly conference.81 In subsequent days, Walsh exchanged letters with the Master Builders' Association and the Irish Industrial League; and

again, on 24 June and 11 July, with the Builders' Association, until eventually, on 22 August, after further communication with both sides, Joseph Meade of the Builders' Association wrote to thank him for his "great kindness, courtesy and invaluable assistance in bringing to a settlement the dispute between us and the Brick and Stonelayers' Society".[82]

The following year, Walsh continued the process. In July 1897 he gave financial assistance and public support to the Dublin Cork-Cutting Trade;[83] and when approached by the Tenants' Defence Committee of the artisans' dwellings in the Coombe area, because of an increase in their rents, his intervention brought a deferment of the increase. Support was sought also by William Partridge, on 8 December 1897, when he appealed for financial aid for the "locked-out engineers", who, he claimed, were being assailed, as members of the Amalgamated Society of Engineers, by the Masters' Federation.[84] In 1898 it was the turn of the congress of the Irish National Teachers' Organisation to express formally their appreciation of his work and assistance.[85]

On 27 June 1899, Walsh explained the basic principle which guided his approach as arbitrator. He was responding to a request from the Printers' Societies that he assist in the settlement of their dispute. It had always been a pleasure to him, he declared, to intervene for the settlement of differences between employers and employed in Dublin. But he had always felt that the success which hitherto had followed his interventions "on occasions of serious dislocations of trade in this city and diocese", had in great measure been the result of a principle on which he had "invariably acted", namely, never intervene "except at the request either of some disinterested person, or of representatives of both parties to the dispute".[86] He did not know if such was achievable in the current situation, but if not, and if they considered that there was "anything to be gained by a conversation on the subject", he would be happy to meet them "on Friday next at any time between 11 and 1 o'clock". He added, – with the empathy and courtesy which seemed to mark his relations with representatives of striking or unemployed workers – "that is the only time within this week which it would be possible for me to see you. I am sorry to have to feel that the hour which I know would otherwise be a very inconvenient one for members of your trade is at present, unfortunately, as likely as any other to suit your convenience."[87]

Walsh carried his work as arbitrator into the new century. There is reference to his services being requested in 1905 when another Bricklayers/Master Builders dispute broke out,[88] and again in a disagreement between an architectural and quantity survey firm and Clongowes Wood College, Co. Kildare.[89] In 1905, also, his assistance was sought by M.J. O'Lehane of the Drapers' Assistants' Union in relation to the long hours of work being demanded of his members.[90] The following year heralded the beginnings of a welcome, major change in workers' prospects and attitudes. In the past, the widespread incidence of distress, and its seeming irreversibility, had induced a sense of helplessness and apathy, especially among the general or unskilled workers. Two factors combined to effect the change. First, the Trades Disputes Act of 1906, which rendered trades union officials immune from liability for damages when they were judged to act "in contemplation or furtherance of a trade dispute", and which prohibited actions of tort against trade unions; and second, the arrival in Dublin in 1908 of James Larkin, whose powerful personality and fiery rhetoric gave hope and dignity to the unskilled labourers.

Walsh, with his deep desire for equality and just treatment, welcomed the new prospects for workers and their families. In this, as the *Echo* journal noted at the commencemnt of this chapter, he was very much in accord with the teaching of Leo XIII's great social encyclical, *Rerum Novarum*, concerning the translation of which Walsh and Manning, indeed, had corresponded. Both men shared the encyclical's insistence that a chief duty of rulers was "to provide equally for every section of the community by acting with unshakeable impartiality towards all", and the papal document might have almost had Walsh's abiding conviction in mind when it insisted that "No one may outrage with impunity that human dignity which God himself treats with *great reverence* ... Man himself can never renounce his right to be treated according to his nature or to surrender himself to any form of slavery of spirit".[91]

Walsh, as has been seen, viewed arbitration as the best way to achieve the industrial and commercial harmony sought by the encyclical, and to secure just wages and conditions for working people, but he was very conscious that arbitration could only function if it were accepted by both parties to a dispute. Sadly, the deep-rooted confrontational tradition of industrial relations in Britain was to delay acceptance of a system of arbitration there long after it was established in many other countries. Walsh's advocacy and example, however, may be considered part of the long process which eventually led to the establishment of an Irish Labour Court and a variety of other arbitration bodies.

XII

The University Question: reaching a solution, 1897-1912, and consolidation. An era of formative beginnings

AN INFLUENTIAL NATIONAL FIGURE

William Walsh's influence in the field of education, including university education, rested not just on his knowledge and interest, but on his eminence as a national figure. By his fifty-ninth birthday in January 1900, he had regained most of the popular standing he enjoyed prior to the Parnell split; so much so that, no doubt much to his embarrassment, he was hailed in a popular illustrated magazine, towards the close of that year, as 'the Pope of Ireland', and as being 'better informed than most men on most questions'.[1] He was undoubtedly the best known, most widely respected Irish Catholic of the time.

Knowing the weight attached to his words, Walsh strayed at times into unexpected areas. Thus, in his Lenten pastoral letter, 1901, he drew attention to the display of objectionable hoardings across the city, which, he suggested, were likely to have a "demoralising tendency";[2] and later that year he wrote to the Inns Quay branch of the United Irish League to publicly support their criticism of the abuse of the principal thoroughfare of the city on Sunday and other evenings "by soldiers and their female companions".[3] Three years later, in a pastoral letter, published in the *Times* of 18 January 1904, he denounced the Catholic Association, which had been set up to counter discrimination against Catholics in business and in the work place, as having become over-zealous and detrimental to Catholic traders, employers, and benevolent societies. The Association was disbanded the following June.[4] This strong pronouncement served also as a conciliatory gesture to the Conservative administration with a view to the solution of the university question, and with an eye to Home Rule. It made clear that giving Catholics equality did not involve discrimination against Protestants. Walsh, indeed, was at particular pains to preserve good relations with Protestant churches. This was illustrated rather strikingly on the occasion of the levee at Dublin Castle in July 1903 in honour of the visit to Ireland of the new monarch, Edward VII.

Walsh's presence at Dublin Castle levees was eagerly sought because of his office. He usually made excuses for not attending. The first exception was the levee in honour of Edward VII, because the latter, on his arrival in Ireland, made "sympathetic reference" to the death of Pope Leo XIII. At the levee, Walsh unwittingly preceded the Church of Ireland archbishop of Armagh and primate. Afterwards he wrote a letter to explain how the mistake happened, adding that he ventured to assume "that even in the absence of this explanation, your Grace would not suppose that I could be guilty of any discourtesy towards you". He went on to express his respect for his Grace's office and for himself personally. Much moved, the primate assured him that he would never have supposed he meant any discourtesy, as he was "incapable of littleness". He cherished Walsh's letter as coming "from the hands of one who has something more than the dignity of a great churchman, or the intellectual power which often makes even an opponent exclaim ..." It touched him, he concluded, "to feel how clearly it breathes throughout the refined courtesy of a Christian gentlemen".[5]

As has been seen, however, the "refined courtesy" of a large-minded "Christian gentleman" gave way at times to acts of impatience, harsh remarks, and even pettiness. Both aspects of Walsh's personality were reflected in respect of the two great settlements of the early years of the new century, the settlement of the land and university questions. The archbishop, in short, was a complex personality, subject like many people to unexpected aberrations, and not readily categorised. Earlier in the year in which he exhibited such "refined courtesy", he had held out against the much praised Land Conference's attempt to settle the old dispute between landlords and tenants, stubbornly seeking to tie down financial arrangements deliberately left vague, and publicly accusing the members of the Irish party of blindfolding and misinforming "the tenant farmers of Ireland". Reading what he had written, a bemused John Dillon entered in his memorandum book, on 12 February 1903: "This day in *Freeman* vitriolic letter from Dr Walsh – He is a strange man."[6]

TOWARDS THE SOLUTION OF THE UNIVERSITY QUESTION

The "strange man" brought to the final years of the university question the eminence of his position, reinforced by his national reputation, powerful intellect, and adroit, manipulative political skills.

Walsh, as has been observed, had no time for the Royal University as a means towards solution. His preference was the model proposed by Gladstone. It envisaged the expansion of the University of Dublin into one national university having affiliated colleges, which included Trinity College, the Queen's Colleges, and the Catholic University. It had been opposed by supporters of Trinity and the Queen's Colleges, and by the Catholic bishops because the scheme did not contain an endowment for a Catholic institution. Walsh hoped for a solution that provided for such an endowment. It would not achieve across the country the full equality in education which was the *leit-motif* of his advocacy of the question over many years, but it would mark an important forward step and would deprive Trinity College of its monopoly. His career demonstrates how pertinacious he could be, at times almost to arrogance, in his assertion of the rights of Catholics to justice and equality, and that they not be at a disadvantage compared to their Protestant fellow-citizens. His intense desire for equality, respect, and fair play, as he perceived them, and his abhorrence of injustice and condescension, provide the likely clues to his at times bewildering and seemingly contradictory behaviour.

In the final months of 1897, under a Conservative government, the Catholic claim for university education received sympathetic mention in parliament, and in Dublin the question was agitated. At a lecture by Charles Dawson on "Irish Catholics and University Education" on 24 November 1897, a letter was read from Archbishop Walsh. Apologising for his inability to attend, he encouraged all present to continue to force the question "upon the attention of the government" and to press "with vigour for a speedy settlement of it". "We have also to make it plain to all concerned", he continued, "that this is not a case for half-measures, and that nothing can be regarded as a settlement of this long-unsettled question which does not give to the Catholics of Ireland what our Protestant fellow-countrymen have so long had in Trinity College –

> A place of higher education, free of everything to which they could object on any religious ground, and enjoying every advantage at present enjoyed by Trinity College, whether in respect of endowment, or in respect of university status ... The granting of all we ask for need deprive Trinity College of nothing except, of course, the monopoly which it has too long enjoyed, as the only university college, adequately endowed and worthy of the name, in Ireland. It is against this monopoly, maintained by the state, in this Catholic country, in favour of a Protestant institution, that we protest.[7]

As in the case of the fellowships, the removal of a monopoly remained a pressing concern.

In October 1898, R.B. Haldane, though a Liberal, crossed over to Ireland to examine, with the approval of Prime Minister Balfour, how far the latter's plans for a university bill would find acceptance. He received assurances from Cardinal Logue and Archbishop Walsh, and from the heads of the Presbyterian assembly. Balfour, as a result, outlined a scheme, in January 1899, which would provide Ireland with three teaching universities: the long established University of Dublin, and two new universities – one for Catholics in Dublin, and one in Belfast for Protestants. To overcome prejudice, he pointed out in his celebrated 'Letter to a Manchester Constituent', January 1899, that the new arrangement would provide two Protestant universities to one Catholic university, "which, as there are nearly three Roman Catholics ... to one Protestant seems not unfair to the Protestants"!

His proposals, nevertheless, met such an outcry in England against "endowment of papacy" and "priest domination" that the cabinet declined to press ahead with them; and Haldane informed Walsh on 7 February 1899, that the old spirit of intolerance was abroad, and that Balfour's attempt had failed at least for the time.[8]

Meantime, the Irish bishops as a body showed little enterprise. Walsh continued to speak of extending the University of Dublin, but otherwise discouraged any positive episcopal policy. Cardinal Logue spoke of equality but insisted that it was the government's task to come up with proposals and the bishops' role to comment on them.[9] O'Dwyer, who wanted an independent Catholic university – *de facto* if not *de jure* – deplored the apathy. "As to our university question", he observed to Donnelly on 9 May 1899, "I have almost come to despair. All we bishops have no definite policy. We do not even agree as to an aim".[10]

The Conservative party won the general election in the autumn of 1900, and the university question became a live issue once more. A number of schemes were proposed by individuals in Dublin,[11] but the first decisive move came in February 1901, when, following further complaints about the inequality of the examining system in the Royal University, the senate of the university, on the prompting of O'Dwyer, made "an attempt on its own life".[12] It declared it desirable "that a royal commission should be issued to inquire into the working of the university as an examining and teaching body in relation to the educational needs of the country at large, and to report as to the means by which university education in Ireland might receive a greater extension and be more efficiently conducted than at present."[13]

The viceroy, Lord Cadogan, wrote to Walsh on 25 February asking his views on the senate's decision.[14] The archbishop replied straightway, along the lines expected by O'Dwyer and Healy. He appreciated the importance of what had been done, he informed the viceroy, "all the more so as the crisis had been developed out of the very point upon which I revolted and left the senate, after a very short experience of the so-called 'university' system that it chose to maintain. To do it justice, it did not have very much option. But it had some".[15] In the same vein, he wrote several weeks later to a Franciscan friend in England, a Fr David, saying that the scandal because of which he resigned had become so obvious that "to ward off a more ignominious form of exposure, the senate itself a few weeks ago unanimously passed a resolution asking for a royal commission of inquiry into the working of the system and into the condition of university education in Ireland generally". The government had granted the request, he continued, but "with an express reservation that Trinity College" was "not to be touched by the inquiry!" He did not believe that the government was willing to do anything "but establish some sort of hybrid thing" that might turn out to be "a source of serious danger to Catholic interest". He concluded tantalisingly, "I have my own view of the whole case, but I keep it to myself."[16]

On 28 June the names of the members of the royal commission were announced. The commission took its title from its chairman, Lord Robertson. The task of the commission was set out as follows:

> To inquire into the present condition of the higher, general and techni-
> cal education available in Ireland outside Trinity College, Dublin, and to
> report as to what reforms, if any, are desirable in order to render that
> education adequate to the needs of the Irish people.[17]

The commission spent from September 1901 to June 1902 in hearing some 147
witnesses, whose evidence was published in three instalments.

Already on 17 November 1900, Walsh had announced in the *Freeman's
Journal* that he had never concealed his personal preference for a settlement on
the basis – "1. Of one national university for Ireland, a university, of course, so
constructed as to provide the maximum of possible freedom for all its colleges.
Failing that, a settlement on the basis 2. Of the establishment of a second college in the University of Dublin ..." Both these solutions, Walsh emphasised,
had been considered by the hierarchy and deemed satisfactory, though, of
course, the establishment of "a separate university for Catholics" was preferred.
He made it clear, however, that he was opposed to proposals for an endowed
college within "the so-called Royal 'University'."[18] His hostility to the Royal and
its senate made him reluctant to accept any solution coming through the senate's
efforts, and this, given the Robertson commission's apparent exclusion of Trinity
College, and the virtual unattainability of a separate Catholic university, left him
uninterested in the commission. His disinterest rendered the majority of the
bishops leaderless, and without stimulus.

O'Dwyer, who was to be a witness at the commission, was appalled at their
lordships' casual attitude to something so important as a royal commission. He
pressed for agreement among the bishops so that there might be "some common
understanding among the Catholic witnesses at the commission". Logue proposed a meeting of the standing committee at which resolutions were passed
covering "pretty well the whole case" O'Dwyer had to make. He was able as a
result "to give authoritative information" to Fr Delany, and to lay witnesses,
Nixon and Ross. Walsh was one of those who approved the line to be followed,
but O'Dwyer was not convinced. "I hope your man won't upset the cart", he
observed to Bishop Donnelly. "One can never know."[19]

O'Dwyer and William Delany worked closely together. Both favoured the
type of university solution proposed by Balfour and Haldane: a university without religious tests, but controlled *de facto* by Catholics, even as Dublin
University had no tests but was *de facto* controlled by Protestant Episcopalians.
They did not want a Catholic college in the University of Dublin. They had
little respect for the quality of that university's qualifications, and believed that
in the current state of Catholic self-confidence and the small number of suitably
qualified Catholic lecturers, the ambience of the university was certain to remain
strongly Protestant, and the Catholics would be absorbed and undermined in
their Catholicism and their Irishness.[20]

Both men proved the outstanding witnesses before the commission. Both
were annoyed that, despite the terms of reference, the chairman permitted an

influential group of lay Catholics, which included Chief Baron Palles, the O'Conor Don, and N.J. Synnott, to argue for a Catholic college in a reorganised University of Dublin. In this Walsh and Palles worked closely together. It has been suggested that Walsh was out-manoeuvred "rather treacherously" by O'Dwyer and Healy in that they had worked with the senate of the Royal University to bring about the Robertson Commission,[21] but, "treacherously" apart, once the commission got underway the outmanoeuvring lay very much with Walsh. He declined to be a witness himself, but through Palles and others managed to ensure that the commission would not come up with an agreed recommendation that would leave the University of Dublin untouched. Catholic opinion was clearly divided. The commission's report, when it appeared on 23 February 1903, reflected the division. It was clear to the commissioners that most Catholics favoured a separate university for Catholics, and that this would establish equality, and would be likely to have "a liberalising influence", but there was an "intrinsic objection" to giving the right to confer degrees "to an institution intended for one religious denomination and largely controlled by ecclesiastics". The "consolidated opinion" of the time, according to one of the most influential commissioners, Professor H. Butcher, fellow of Trinity College Cambridge, and University College Oxford, considered such control as the bishops sought to be unacceptable, and where Catholics were concerned required a system of education which was expressly undenominational.[22] The commission's suggested alternative was a reorganisation of the Royal as a teaching university, having the Queen's colleges and a new college for Catholics as its constituent institutions. This was attractive to a number of Catholics, but, as Lord Robertson added, in a rider which doubtless had Archbishop Walsh in mind, it would not satisfy "those who determine Roman Catholic opinion".[23] The report was received with considerable disappointment. Activity on the university question was virtually suspended for some months.

New prospects with Sir Anthony MacDonnell

The university question came alive again with the arrival in Dublin as undersecretary of Sir Anthony MacDonnell, an Irish Catholic, who had proved an outstanding administrator in India. He had been enticed to Ireland by the chief secretary, George Wyndham, with the prospect of achieving major reforms in land, education, and self-government.[24]

MacDonnell arrived in Dublin on 9 November 1902. Little more than a week later, he wrote to his wife: "My interview with the archbishop passed off very satisfactorily and we had a most amenable conversation for half an hour."[25] Three days later, in a six-page document, partially typed with many hand-written amendments, he sketched his solution to the university question in terms of a Catholic college in the University of Dublin, built in the grounds of Trinity College. He entitled his sketch: "Heads of a Scheme to Establish a new University in Dublin, 21 November 1902".[26] From further letters to his wife, it is clear that he again met the archbishop on three occasions – on 4 January, 17 January and 16 February 1903;[27] that is, prior to the appearance of the report from the Robertson Commission! Clearly, then, Walsh had reason, privately, to hope for a different solution to that proposed by the commission.

At their June meeting, however, the hierarchy unanimously adopted a resolution favouring the enactment of the Robertson recommendation. They did not publish their decision, perhaps at Walsh's behest lest it hinder the adoption of a Dublin University plan. The Castle authorities, that is primarily MacDonnell, were informed in confidence of the bishops' decision.[28] When in September MacDonnell informed Redmond of the bishops' unanimous agreement in June, the party leader was "very much mystified" and "astonished" as he had been led to believe by Archbishop Walsh that the hierarchy were solidly in favour of the idea of a Catholic college in the University of Dublin![29] The following month, when MacDonnell was actively pursuing his scheme, Walsh wrote to Redmond to explain his position. As regards the Robertson recommendation, he had refused "to have anything whatever to do with the working out of the scheme", because "from first to last my position has been, and is, and must continue to be, that *equality*, nothing short of it, and nothing in excess of it, should be the measure of our requirement".[30]

The summer of 1902 had been of much moment for Walsh. Cardinal Vaughan had died on 19 June, and a month later Pope Leo XIII. On 21 July the new king, Edward VII, arrived at Kingstown and won widespread approval by his words of sympathy and appreciation regarding the late pontiff. The royal visit to Maynooth, as a result, took on an added significance. The king and queen were received by the archbishops of Dublin and Tuam, and as Cardinal Logue was absent in Rome for the election of a new pope, Walsh performed the key role as host.[31]

Meantime, following the success of his land bill, Wyndham felt ready for the next great challenge. In a letter to prime minister Balfour on 17 September he announced – "The moment is propitious for settling the Catholic Higher Education question."[32] His under secretary was already working actively for a "University of Dublin" solution. He negotiated quietly with the Presbyterians, with Trinity College, and the archbishop of Dublin. He envisaged the University of Dublin having three constituent colleges – Trinity College Dublin, Queen's College Belfast, and a new Roman Catholic College in Dublin. In the scheme, the position of Galway, Cork and Maynooth was downgraded. Fearing opposition from within the episcopacy concerning the downgrading, MacDonnell sought clarification from Walsh, who informed him that the bishops had left negotiations to the committee composed of the four archbishops and that "everyone will (and *must*) stand by whatever *we four* do". Significantly, he added, regarding Maynooth, that he and Archbishop Healy of Tuam could make out "a *modus vivendi*", and MacDonnell might take it "that whatever *we two* say will be said by the four".³³ As the year drew to a close, a private conference took place between Wyndham and MacDonnell on the one side and Walsh and Healy on the other. "The main principles of the project were approved by the episcopal representatives and a memorandum, to be submitted confidentially to the episcopal body, was prepared" by MacDonnell.³⁴ Not the least tribute to Walsh's powers of persuasion was the support coming from his long-time opponent, Healy. Support for the scheme from the Presbyterians, meantime, had begun to waver, and Trinity was not well disposed.

Walsh, determined as ever to push the case forward by every means possible, sent a letter on 8 December to a meeting of Catholic graduates and undergraduates of various universities, which was being held at the Mansion House to form a new association "to organise and voice the claims of the Catholic body for equality in university education ... without, however, declaring in favour of any specific form of settlement". In his letter to them his Grace fully approved of their attitude;and then urged them, in words which to those who knew his views seemed to point to one particular solution, to

> make it publicly and widely known that equality is at once the high-water mark and the low-water mark of your claim, that you will be satisfied with nothing less than equality and that you ask for nothing more.³⁵

At the end of December, MacDonnell drafted a long eloquent letter to put added pressure on Trinity to accept the scheme.³⁶ It appeared over the name of the highly-respected Co. Limerick landlord, Lord Dunraven, in the *Freeman's Journal*, 4 January 1904. The letter proposed the establishment of three well-equipped, autonomous and residential colleges within the University of Dublin – Trinity College, Queen's College Belfast, and a new King's College, Dublin, acceptable to Catholics. This development, which, he claimed, was contemplated by the original founders of Dublin University, would result in "the highest attainable measure of academic efficiency with perfect equality of treatment for all sections of the community". "Trinity College", Dunraven continued, "has a splendid record ... but it never has been, is not and cannot pretend to be, a national institution." It represented "a section of the nation only". "Its walls", were "saturated with racial distinctions, its atmosphere redolent of religious ascendancy". It was unrealistic to expect Catholics to be easy in a community "mainly Protestant and largely of a different race". He did not think that Protestants would feel easy in their own minds sending their young men to a college which for centuries had represented the dominant Catholic minority. He appealed to Trinity to co-operate for the good of the nation. This solution was of national importance, he went on, because "a university based on the report of the Royal Commission would from the beginning bear in its bosom the seeds of failure". It would lead in less than a generation to "the creation of a Presbyterian university in Belfast and of a Catholic university in Dublin", thereby "intensifying and perpetuating the lamentable animosities of the past, now happily beginning to abate and disappear". He protested against such an outcome, and urged his alternative plan. In this plan "three strings of one instrument would vibrate in harmony"; whereas "three separate instruments would sound a discordant note".[37]

It is to be presumed that MacDonnell discussed the letter beforehand with Archbishop Walsh. It resonated with much of his Grace's thinking, even to the musical imagery, and one can visualise it featuring as part of his persuasive reasoning with his episcopal colleagues. The attitude of the latter was crucial. The *Freeman's Journal* of 5 January 1904, wondered whether the proposed plan would be seen as providing sufficient safeguard to faith and morals in the new college. The *Belfast Newsletter*, on the same day, was critical of the 'Dunraven proposal', and predicted, besides, that it would be "scornfully rejected by the hierarchy". A public meeting was arranged for Limerick on 13 January where it was feared Dr O'Dwyer would come out publicly against the scheme. Trusting to his own powers of persuasion, Walsh secured a general meeting of the bishops for the day before the Limerick meeting.[38] Next morning, when Wyndham and MacDonnell came as arranged to meet the archbishop, he was able "to intimate confidentially" to them that the bishops, while not expressing any preference for Lord Dunraven's scheme, considered "that a satisfactory settlement of the university question can be arrived at on the lines indicated in his lordship's letter". "But, if from the attitude of Trinity College or any other cause, the government" were "not prepared to give legislative effect" to the Dunraven proposals, they then called upon them "to adopt the alternative scheme ... recommended in the report of the Royal Commission".[39]

O'Dwyer did not attend the bishops' meeting. At the Limerick meeting he was restrained and, in the course of his speech conceded that he believed "that through a college in Dublin University our claims can be substantially satisfied". But he reminded his listeners that until the views of Trinity College were known "discussion of the Dunraven scheme must remain hypothetical".[40] By the end of January it was clear that Trinity was opposed to the plan, as were the unionists in the north led by Lord Londonderry. Although the lord mayor held a large meeting at the Mansion house on 29 January, which was addressed by O'Conor Don and Archbishop Walsh, in support of the plan,[41] Balfour, with his unstable government, did not relish trying to introduce legislation in its support. When this was made clear, intense annoyance was expressed by the Irish party, and annoyance and disappointment was experienced by Walsh, who had been assured by MacDonnell that the Irish government would try to introduce a bill in the coming session.

With the collapse of the Dublin University scheme, Walsh turned a more friendly face towards University College. In March 1904, he surprised a large attendance at University College by stating that he had always been grateful to the Jesuit Fathers "for the great work that has been done in this place", and that as a bishop he could not err by excess in any statement he could make "of the magnitude of the service that has been rendered to the cause of Catholic higher education in Ireland by the brilliantly successful work done by the Jesuit Fathers and the staff of this University College". He trusted that when the measure of justice at length came, there would be nothing in it to stand in the way of the Jesuit Fathers continuing "those great services as teachers" which they had rendered to the cause of higher education.[42]

In the hiatus, the mounting tendency towards self-help found expression. With the approval of the bishops, a broadly-based committee was established to administer a system of "Catholic scholarships" for men students to University College, and for women students to Loreto College, St Stephen's Green, and to the Dominican College, Eccles Street. The women colleges, it should be noted, owed a great deal to Walsh. The Royal University was the first Irish university to offer degrees to women students. The latter, however, did not have a college at which to attend lectures. Application to University College in 1882 was unsuccessful. William Delany was preoccupied with the considerable problems presented by his new venture. Four years later, when Alexandra College, a school for Protestant girls, opened a university department, Archbishop Walsh approached the Dominican Sisters at Eccles Street to open a university department for Catholic students. He gave moral and financial support to the new venture, and chaired the college council which directed the course of studies to be undertaken there.[43] His interest in higher education for women was also manifested in his support of the further university department for Catholic women opened by the Loreto Sisters in 1893. William Delany, who also served on the college council, made lecturers and professors available from University College to give classes to women students in accommodation provided by the Royal University at Earlsfort Terrace; and at a later date enabled women students attend lectures in the Aula Maxima of the college. The students from the two Catholic women's university departments performed very successfully in the Royal University examinations,[44] and, hence, scholarships to them were attractive propositions.

The chief workers and leading spirits of the committee to administer the system of scholarships were Walsh as chairman, William Delany as secretary, and Fr Andrew Murphy of the Catholic Headmasters' Association. The idea was taken up eagerly by a number of committees.[45] Similar self-help thinking led to Professor Tom Finlay proposing in May 1905, that instead of waiting for England to do something about university education, the Catholic University should be revived, now that degrees could be obtained without sacrifice of principle. Some temporary structures were added to University College as part of his initiative. In the *New Ireland Review* he set forth in detail an overall scheme of self-help which met with an enthusiastic response.[46] The county councils and other bodies responded generously to the scholarship proposals, but the challenge to further lay generosity was not made. A general election intervened with the possibility of a new government initiative.

The response to the scholarship and autonomous university proposals reflected the creativity and atmosphere of new beginnings that was in evidence on many sides at this time. The Abbey Theatre opened in Dublin in December 1904, Eoin Mac Neill gave his first lectures on early Irish history at University College, and the Revd Patrick Dineen's *Focloir Gaelige agus Bearla* appeared. In the political arena, a variety of developments were also taking place. Wyndham resigned in March 1905, the Ulster Unionist Council was formed, and Bulmer Hobson, in Belfast, inaugurated the first Dungannon Clubs – heralding the revival of the Irish Republican Brotherhood. On 14 November, John Redmond and T.P. O'Connor secured a promise of Home Rule from the leader of the Liberal party, Sir Henry Campbell-Bannerman. A fortnight later, Arthur Griffith, at the annual convention of his National Council, originally formed in 1903 to protest at the royal visit, proposed a policy known as sinn fein (we ourselves). As the year drew to a close, Campbell-Bannerman, on 8 December 1905, became prime minister, and on 14 December, James Bryce, a Belfast Presbyterian of ability and energy, author of noted historical works – *The Holy Roman Empire* and *The American Commonwealth*, was appointed chief secretary of Ireland. MacDonnell remained as under secretary. The prospect looked bright again for a forward movement in university affairs, and this was heightened by a "Liberal landslide" in the British general election in January 1906.

All this was accompanied by an intense and expanding interest in things Irish – in the Gaelic language, and in Irish music and history. In such a climate, Trinity College's opposition to university education for the nation seemed quite contrary, and Walsh determined to make this very clear. Already in 1904 he had expressed to John Redmond his doubts about "the efficacy of parliamentary action" in "getting redress of our grievances in Ireland",[47] and in repeating similar views to Sir Christopher Nixon clearly indicated that he was seeking alternative ways of putting forward what he termed "the Catholic and national claims of the people of Ireland."[48] One way he saw of doing this was to bring intense public pressure to bear on Trinity College.

In July 1905 he embarked on a concentrated campaign of criticism against Trinity College, that "last stronghold" of ascendancy, which he continued well into the following year. In his assault he availed of some severe strictures which the medical council had passed on the method of conducting examinations there, and on the quality of the degrees.[49] On 23 January 1906, the episcopal standing committee called on the Irish party to bring to the attention of the government "the anomalous position of Trinity College". "We have had quite enough commissions", the bishops stated. "No further enquiry is needed to establish the fact that Trinity College holds for a small minority of the population the funds that constitute the Irish national endowment for higher education."[50] The standing committee's suggestion was well-timed. The reforming instincts of the Liberal party were already expressed in plans to deprive the denominational primary schools of England of their privileged position, and hence the party might be presumed to be disposed towards a levelling-down of Trinity's endowments. Redmond forwarded a copy of the bishops' letter to Bryce with a plea for the government's immediate consideration of the university question.[51] P.A. Barnett of the Board of Education in London, who visited Ireland in January and February 1906 to assess the state of Irish education, reported to Bryce, "Wherever I turned I found myself face to face with the University Question."[52]

The second MacDonnell campaign

MacDonnell felt the time was right for a new effort. The bishops, especially Walsh, were receptive to his ideas, Bryce was amenable, and the Presbyterians could be persuaded. Trinity was the one major obstacle. Carrying forward Walsh's campaign, he determined to put further pressure on the college. On 8 March, he made an appointment with Dr Traill, provost of Trinity College. They had a long discussion on university reform in Ireland, and the likelihood of parliamentary questions about Trinity's method of government and its finances. Traill, although he claimed "that Trinity by internal reforms could supply all reasonable facilities" for Catholics, accepted MacDonnell's proposal that an enquiry be conducted into the college.[53]

Despite the bishops' expressed reluctance for another commission, Bryce and Mac Donnell chose that option. The decision to do so was announced in March 1906. The members of the commission were appointed on 1 June under Sir Edward Fry, lord justice of appeal, as chairman. The commission was required: "to inquire into and report upon the place which Trinity College and the University of Dublin now hold as organs of higher education in Ireland, and the steps proper to be taken to increase their usefulness to the country".[54]

In view of the coming inquiry, the provost and some six senior fellows of Trinity College drew up a scheme suggesting certain changes within the college but opposing a Catholic college in Dublin University. Subsequently a number of Catholic laymen circulated a statement proposing certain changes in Trinity as a basis for dealing with the university question. Not happy with the statement, Walsh, in an interview in the *Freeman's Journal* on 31 July 1906, sought to clarify the bishops' position. They were willing to accept:

> A new college as Catholic as Trinity College is Protestant in a reconstructed Royal University, as recommended by the late Royal Commission, or a similar college in the University of Dublin, as proposed by Mr Wyndham and Lord Dunraven.

They would co-operate in every way in their power to make either a success.[55] On 4 August, he published a statement of the episcopal standing committee which further explained that a scheme of mixed education in Trinity College was not acceptable for Catholics, but the bishops were willing to accept any of three solutions, the two above mentioned, and "a university for Catholics".⁵⁶

MacDonnell and Bryce went ahead with plans for an enlargement of Dublin University, quite independently of the commission's deliberations. On 14 August, Bryce wrote to MacDonnell, "Your draft bill for a reformed University of Dublin, including a new college, agrees in all essentials with that I sent you two days ago."⁵⁷ Four days later, Mac Donnell reported to him that Walsh "agreed that the nomination of a bishop *qua* bishop to the visiting board or to the senate would not be practicable: and said that he should be quite satisfied with a promise that a bishop should be nominated to the board of visitors". "The archbishop's views", Mac Donnell added, "were as I could have expected from my dealings with him in 1903-4, quite liberal and on the lines of our drafts."⁵⁸

That Walsh's views did not reflect those of many of the clergy, nor of many of the bishops became evident during September. One of his closest friends, Gerald Molloy, vice-chancellor of the Royal University, published a long letter in the *Independent* on 15 September 1906, in which, while acknowledging the statement of the standing committee in July, he made clear his own distaste for the incorporation of a Catholic college in the University of Dublin, and expressed his preference, in the absence of an independent university for Catholics, for the plan outlined by the Robertson commission. The bishops at their October meeting resolved not to offer evidence before the Fry commission beyond what had been stated by the standing committee in July.⁵⁹ Walsh, feeling that his prior presentation of episcopal unity might be somewhat discredited, provided MacDonnell, on 28 October, with a letter to be submitted to the commission in which he reiterated the bishops' previous concessions on the matter of religious tests and with regard to ecclesiastical representation on the governing body of a Catholic college. He stated, besides, that the bishops had agreed on a settlement on the lines of Dunraven's scheme when they were consulted by Wyndham, and he emphasised the provision in that scheme that the governing body of the new college would be "selected *exclusively* on academic grounds".⁶⁰

Further embarrassment came shortly afterwards at the hands of a some other eminent educationalists. It had come to be widely believed during the autumn of 1906 that MacDonnell and Bryce sought a federal National University, through the agency of the University of Dublin. In the view, however, of Bertram Windle, president of Queen's College Cork, a federal university was the worst "of all abominable ideas". The colleges brought into it would be of different standings in age, equipment and income. Their interests would be vastly different. Cork would "fight it to the death" he assured Delany of University College Dublin on 14 October. He suggested that Delany and the presidents of the Queen's Colleges send a joint statement to the commission to the effect that a federal solution would be the worst possible solution. Bishop O'Dwyer agreed with him, Windle concluded.⁶¹

Delany was of a similar mind, but from an even more pragmatic point of view. He had assured Chief Baron Palles, at the time of Wyndham's plan, that he would not oppose a Catholic college within the University of Dublin, if it were an autonomous college equal to Trinity. But he felt very differently about a federal university. One might expect, he commented to Archbishop Healy, that a college within the University of Dublin would enjoy a half-share with its neighbour, "but when, along with Trinity we have the three Queen's Colleges, what chance will Catholics have of half?" The federal solution was in the interests neither of education nor of the Catholic population. On 23 October 1906, he proposed, Dr Healy seconded, and the other senators of the Royal University passed unanimously the resolution: "That in the judgement of the senate of the Royal University, it would be disastrous to the interests of education in Ireland to concentrate the control of higher education in one university."[62]

The embarrassment for Walsh was not in the resolution as such, but in the follow up to it which occurred in giving evidence before the commission. Delany appeared before that body on 12 November, very conscious that, as the only Catholic witness, he would have to present the best case for Catholic education as he viewed it. The thirty-two columns of his evidence in the First Report of the Fry Commission testify to his range and abundance of facts. He underlined a favourite theme. The solution of the university question must not be something "forced upon people against their will". It was in answer to direct questions, however, that a stir was caused. Asked bluntly by the chairman whether he thought the scheme whereby the University of Dublin would embrace the main university colleges was the worst solution possible, he answered, "the worst I can imagine".[63] Asked further, about the resolution of the senate of the Royal University against "concentrating the control of higher education in one university" and how this related to the bishops' views, he answered:

> The Archbishop of Tuam, who seconded my motion, said that he might tell the senate that he represented in those views the views of substantially the whole of the episcopate of Ireland with just one possible doubtful exception.[64]

Next day, 13 November, Walsh felt it necessary to grant an interview to the *Freeman's Journal* to deny rumours that he had changed his views on the acceptability of a second college within Dublin University. Pressed by the interviewer as to whether all or most of the other bishops were not opposed to that solution, Dr Walsh answered at length, providing a rear-guard action to preserve his claim of episcopal support for the Dublin University scheme. The reports in circulation of disunity among the episcopal body were untrue, he declared, and put in circulation by "wreckers". That did not mean that the solution within the University of Dublin "would be preferred by the bishops to any other". Of the three solutions mentioned in the bishops' statement, some would prefer one solution, some another. "I really do not know", he continued, "how many of us would regard the establishment of a new college of the University of Dublin as the best." But that was "not a practical matter just now". If he were the only one among the bishops who regarded it as the best solution, this would not affect "the really important fact" that it was "a solution which the bishops, with a united voice ... have assured the Royal Commission that they are prepared to accept." Walsh concluded his remarks with the reminder that of the three solutions which the standing committee had offered to accept, only the establishment of a new college within Dublin University was within the commission's terms of reference.[65] The critical issue of a federal university was neither raised nor addressed!

The Fry Commission issued its report on 12 January 1907. Its members, as expected, were divided. The chairman, and Professor Butcher and Sir Arthur Rucker, declared for the Robertson solution; Chief Baron Palles, Sir Thomas Raleigh, Dr Douglas Hyde, Dr Denis Coffey, and Professor Henry Jackson with reservations, favoured a federation of the five colleges under Dublin University; and Mr S.B. Kelleher of Trinity College expressed opposition to both.

Knowing that the Report was likely to present divided opinions, MacDonnell and Bryce had determined to press ahead with their own scheme, along the lines of the federal scheme put forward by Palles in the commission's report. The draft of a letter of MacDonnell to Walsh, dated 11 January,[66] indicated that he was in consultation with the archbishop with a view to forestalling difficulties with the hierarchy. Bryce had been appointed ambassador to Washington in late December 1906, but as his successor was not to be announced until well into January 1907, he was anxious to commit the government to a university bill before he left Ireland. He secured the approval of Augustine Birrell, the new chief secretary, to announce his scheme for an enlarged Dublin University to a deputation from the Presbyterian general assembly, and a separate deputation of Catholic laymen, who were to wait on him in Dublin on 25 January. On 23 January he explained to the prime minister, Campbell-Bannerman, that it was necessary to move quickly. Those who wished "to block our course" depended on inducing the Roman Catholic bishops "to withdraw from the consent they gave to the plan which approved itself to us". "This", therefore, "makes it all the more desirable that our view should be declared before the bishops are tempted to withdraw, so the policy I suggested to you of pinning the bishops at once becomes all the more necessary."[67]

Walsh's role at this stage seems to have been crucial. He was clearly the main adviser as to how to deal with his colleagues. On 27 January, Bryce informed the prime minister that it would be necessary to give careful attention to details and "possibly to resist some prelatical demands". He had been assured, however, "that they were so impatient to have something done that they will not let this chance slip".[68] In his address to the House of Commons, Bryce avoided details. He gave the general outline of the projected bill: the Royal University would be abolished, and Dublin University was to be enlarged to a National University which would include Trinity College, a new college in Dublin, and the colleges in Belfast and Cork. Colleges giving teaching of a university character, such as Galway, Magee (Derry), and Maynooth, might be affiliated to the university by the governing body of the university. The scheme was acceptable, he alleged, to "the heads of the Roman Catholic Church in Ireland", and he understood that "the large majority of the Irish representatives" were also prepared to accept it. He personally believed, he declared, that it was the only scheme "politically possible under the conditions" and, he added, "I can hold out no hope that any other will be proposed by the present government."[69]

It was a skilful presentation. The assurances he had received regarding the bishops proved accurate. Archbishop Healy, on 24 January, having got word of the forthcoming plan, agreed with Delany that "the Palles scheme" was "the worst of all proposals" and he believed that the archbishop of Dublin was "at the bottom of the business". He, however, could not speak out until the bishops discussed the plan, but he encouraged Delany, Windle and Nixon to do so.[70] More strikingly, O'Dwyer remained passive. To Sir John Ross, who had complained to him of the bishops' indecision and their not giving a lead in support of the Robertson proposals, which would have "put an end to all this intrigue and would have secured public opinion",[71] O'Dwyer replied on 27 January 1907, that while he agreed with him "about the domination of a clique in the entire proceedings", "we have to ask ourselves: If we refuse it what chance is there in our lifetime of getting better, indeed of getting anything at all."[72] Cardinal Logue, in reply to Delany, also indicated a reluctance to comment until the hierarchy had a definite bill before them.[73] Even Healy limited his public protest to championing the cause of the Galway college.[74] John Redmond, addressing the directory of the United Irish League on 5 February, announced that the parliamentary party, while not committing themselves to any particular scheme, were prepared to give Bryce's pronouncement "favourable consideration".[75]

An exultant MacDonnell wrote to Walsh suggesting an immediate meeting of the hierarchy. Walsh's reply on 4 February brought him down to earth. It conveyed both the need to hasten slowly and his own capacity to read and virtually manipulate his episcopal colleagues to his purposes. Having pointed out the practical difficulty of calling such a meeting at such short notice, especially as the approach of Lent was a particularly busy time, he added that, apart from such obstacles, he would regard it as "most injudicious" to hold a meeting just then. He explained:

> There are points in the scheme, (for instance the inclusion of the three provincial colleges, the inter-collegiate arrangements in Dublin etc.), to which many would object, and it *is at least possible that the objectors might be in the majority*, and might insist on the publication of their objections. In a word, the whole thing, if it was to be dealt with now (when the

scheme as to details is more or less in a state of fluidity) would have to *be dealt with on the merits* ... Later on, things will have developed a little, and then the question to be considered will be quite a different one. It will be: *is there anything in this that cannot be put up with, or acceded to by way of concession. At that stage the upholders of the Robertson scheme will be practically powerless.*[76]

But, he warned, "they are by no means powerless now, and they would on many grounds wish to show their *comparative* dislike of *any* University of Dublin scheme".[77]

In the same letter, however, Walsh noted with satisfaction that Bryce's statement that the scheme accorded with the views of the bishops had "not evoked a whisper of questioning in any quarter, and is thus taken as having been tacitly assented to". Where he himself was concerned at the present time, although he was prevented, "by a useful provision of our domestic discipline", from publicly pronouncing in favour of the scheme before it should be formally accepted by the hierarchy, he was otherwise "quite free to act" and he was already taking steps to rally public opinion in favour of the plan.[78]

His rallying, combined with that of the government and of the Irish party, proved very effective. The Catholic Young Men's societies of Dublin, gathered at the Mansion House towards the end of February, approved the Bryce proposals, as did many representative bodies around the country. The senate of the Royal University withdrew its opposition in the interests of an early settlement, while emphasising the need for autonomy for each of the colleges in the new scheme. Even Windle, of Cork, despite his misgivings, wished the government's proposal God speed. The lay professors of University College, while requesting adequate endowment and "the fullest possible measure of autonomy", declared that the scheme merited their "strongest support".[79] The support became a mounting tide driven ever higher in response to the high level of opposition to Bryce's proposals presented by Trinity College and its influential supporters. At the end of January and the beginning of February, the Trinity College staff and the Ulster unionist council, and eleven of the thirteen Church of Ireland bishops declared their opposition to the government's scheme. A special defence committee proclaimed the college's links with the Protestant people of Ireland and their rights, and appealed to its graduates. Four thousand of the latter sent a memorial to Balfour. A deputation visited the universities of Britain, with the result that protests were issued from Oxford and Cambridge, the universities of London, Birmingham, Liverpool, Sheffield and Bristol, the Scottish universities and the University of Wales, and also from two hundred and thirty-five fellows of the Royal Society.[80] Conservative members of parliament, and many non-conformist members, also rallied to the cause. "Trinity College is making gigantic efforts to stir up opposition in England and is trying to influence all the newspapers", MacDonnell wrote to his wife on 13 February, and he added portentously, "it is an uphill struggle to attack any 'Garrison' interest in Ireland. I don't suppose that Balfour will look at the question otherwise than as a means of making party capital."[81]

Walsh, as might be expected, was unlikely to refrain from references to monopoly and exclusivity when there was a controversy choreographed by Trinity College. He was impelled, as it were, to public pronouncements. Its image of "non-sectarianism" was little more than a velleity, he declared on 26 February 1907. It remained, at the tax-payers expense, "a precious monopoly of the Protestant Episcopal church in Ireland".[82] Weeks later, after further public statements from Walsh, Professor Windle commented that "the Archbishop of Dublin by his tactics" had "aided and abetted" the supporters of Trinity College in their opposition to the government's plan. "To constantly attack a place with which you wanted to be connected and thus to embitter the feelings on both sides is not the way to accomplish your object."[83]

The Birrell approach and touch

The Trinity protest was one that the new chief secretary could not ignore. He had never been enamoured of Bryce's scheme. The fever of opposition it was generating in England, and between Protestants and Catholics in Ireland, made the scheme's long term hopes of uniting Catholics and Protestants by means of a common university seem unreal. MacDonnell, on 12 March, wrote to Bryce that he found Birrell "rather reticent", and he was upset that "the only important dissentients, Windle, Dr Hamilton and Dr Delany have asked Mr Birrell to see them ... and he has consented". MacDonnell was still hopeful that Bryce's scheme would be supported, but there had been "a serious difference of opinion" between Birrell and himself, and he felt that on the university question Birrell did not see eye to eye with Bryce.[84]

It is not clear what the "three dissentients" –Windle of Cork, Delany of University College Dublin, and Hamilton of Queen's College Belfast – said to Birrell, but to judge from an undated letter to Birrell from Delany it is likely that there was an emphasis on hard political realism. It would be advisable, Delany suggested, "to ascertain confidentially" whether a majority of the Catholic bishops really approved of the scheme. Then having outlined reasons against the scheme on educational grounds, he pointed out that Bryce's solution was similar to that of Gladstone, which, Delany alleged, had been wrecked by concerted Protestant opposition. The same situation would materialise again. Bryce's proposal would be made to seem destructive to Protestant interests on a large scale and would add substance to "the argument constantly pressed" that Home Rule, to which the government was dedicated, would mean "the sacrifice of the loyal Protestant minority to the hostile will of 'the rebellious papist majority'." On such a thorny issue, it seemed to him it was "a plain dictate of common sense, as well as of political prudence", to opt for a solution which would involve the least disturbance of existing institutions and vested interests and would be, at the same time, most in harmony with educational experience. Such a solution had been proposed by the Robertson Commission.[85]

Augustine Birrell may have been blessed with "literary sense and knowledge, sympathy, good-nature, humour and breadth of view", as Campbell-Bannerman informed the king at his appointment,[86] but he was also a pragmatist and did not relish trying to forward a bill not of his own making. In his memoirs, *Things Past Redress* (London 1936), he was to remark that he had seen two objections to Bryce's solution. 1."It involved laying violent hands on the only English institution that has ever taken root in Irish soil", and 2. he was convinced that such a proposal had no chance of being enacted.[87] He also sensed, it would seem, that his Under-Secretary's carefully nurtured consensus of all parties outside Trinity College was less than solid.[88] In a letter to Cambell-Bannerman, 24 May 1907, Birrell signalled his intention to take his "own line" and leave Sir Anthony "in the lurch".[89] The following day he made it clear to Redmond that he was not interested in a scheme including Trinity College. A bill interfering with it stood no chance of becoming law. He had plans of his own and intended to make them clear to "everybody in Ireland".[90] On 3 June 1907, the prime minister announced in the House of Commons the abandonment, for the present, of the Irish University Bill. A month later, in reply to a challenge from T.M. Healy, Birrell assured the House that he was firmly set on finding a solution to the Irish university question, and in Ireland during the autumn would "strive to discover one which would enable the vast majority of the Irish youth to obtain education in a university to which parents and priests could send them with perfect confidence that nothing would be taught them destructive of their religious beliefs".[91] It was the beginning of a campaign marked by diplomacy, flattery, charm, wit, disarming guile, and the achievement of the possible.

Birrell's successful plan and tactics

In the autumn of 1907, Birrell won over Redmond and Dillon to the general idea of two universities other than the University of Dublin. One of these would be centred in Dublin, the other in Belfast.[92] Trinity College was happy with the concept, provided it remained untouched. Birrell, mustering his considerable powers of urbane persuasiveness, approached Walsh to explain why he felt he could not interfere with the University of Dublin, and why the time was not opportune for just one national university. The archbishop, recognising that the Trinity campaign was lost, proved open to an alternative scheme.[93] On 31 December 1907, Birrell forwarded "Heads of Proposals for new Universities and Colleges", adding, with seeming ingenuousness, that "unhappily nobody in England *really* cares a straw about the university question in Ireland except a fanatic crowd who ... see papacy writ large over the whole subject." In his own constituency of Bristol he was thought "a visionary and a bit of a fool for taking so much trouble about so *sentimental*(!) a grievance".[94] Walsh responded on 6 January 1908. The scheme, he declared, was better than any other he could think of "excepting, of course, one that would give us equality with Trinity College Dublin *in point of university status*, e.g. a *second* college in the University of Dublin, or a scheme such as Mr Bryce's." But supposing, he admitted sardonically, that as regards academic status "we have to succumb to our fate as representatives of a conquered and subject race ... are we to have *equality* in anything in this scheme?" Would the Catholics get as much money "as the two great Protestant colleges and universities all get?"[95]

The chief secretary's plan envisaged Queen's College Belfast becoming Queen's University, and serving the northern, particularly the unionist, population; and the Queen's Colleges of Cork and Galway joining with a new Dublin College as the colleges of another university catering mainly for the majority population. He envisaged two senates, with each college having its own governing body as a mark of its autonomy. The members of the senate would be nominated initially, but elected thereafter for fixed terms.

The appointments to senates, governing bodies, and to the presidency of the different colleges, occasioned, as might be expected, much discussion, correspondence, and political intervention. One of the main talking points in Dublin, rumoured as touching the archbishop, was the exclusion from the senate and governing body of Professor Tom Finlay, SJ, whom Professor W.E.H. Lecky of Dublin University was to describe as "probably the most universally respected man in Ireland",[96] but who, as noted, was not considered such by Walsh.

Many appeals on the matter were addressed to Birrell. On 8 July 1808, Birrell informed Walsh that while he had "no personal desire" to see Finlay on the senate, "Butcher and Delany would like to see him there". He asked for his Grace's views. The archbishop's reply does not appear to have survived. Three weeks later, on 28 July, Edmund Talbot, MP, who had pressed Birrell on the matter, informed Delany that, according to Birrell, "high ecclesiastical authority is the chief opposition". Some days later, on 4 August, the day after the signing of the Bill, Birrell expressed his regret to Delany:

> This was a painful business, and perhaps I ought to have been more adamantine than I was; but I was frightened at the beginning of the controversy of the letters S.J. ... Then again, I had to conciliate certain high potentates, so that my path was perilous ...[97]

It is likely also that members of the Irish parliamentary party expressed opposition to Finlay's appointment, because of his criticism of the party and of Parnell, but it seems undeniable that Walsh could have ensured the appointment had he wished and, indeed, if Talbot's report of Birrell's words is accurate, namely, that "high ecclesiastical authority is the chief obstacle", Walsh was undoubtedly the most likely opponent of the appointment.

Turning again to the passage of the bill. It was introduced in the House of Commons on 31 March 1908. In the months it was under discussion, the country indicated little enthusiasm. The Presbyterian general assembly opposed it. Bishop Sheehan of Waterford and O'Dwyer opposed it, but only O'Dwyer among the Irish bishops spoke publicly against the measure. He attacked it in the *Irish Educational Review*, May 1908, for making no provision for religion. Its constitution was as applicable to a Mohammedan country, he observed, as to a Catholic one. It was not the kind of university that the English people were careful to give themselves. Birrell, appreciating the divisions in their ranks, avoided dealing with the body of bishops. All episcopal negotiations were conducted through Archbishop Walsh. This led at the bishops' general meeting on 23 April to expressions of annoyance that Walsh had negotiated so intensively with Birrell without keeping the episcopal body regularly informed. Criticism of different aspects of the bill was expressed at the meeting, but the bishops as a body did not make their criticisms public. During the month of June, Walsh persuaded the body of prelates to give guarded support to the bill as it stood.[98] The measure was signed into law on 1 August 1908. The effect was that "an examining university", the Royal, was replaced by two teaching universities, at Dublin and Belfast; and the former Queen's Colleges of Cork and Galway became University College Cork and Galway respectively, while University College Dublin retained its name. The three were the constituent colleges of the new university called the National University, which body was empowered to affiliate "such institutions as have a standard deemed satisfactory by the university", an arrangement which permitted the affiliation of Maynooth College, a key factor in ensuring episcopal support. To O'Dwyer's disgust, and the unease of many other bishops, "no test whatever of religious belief" was to be permitted for any appointment in either of the universities.

The bill received no hindrance from the opposition. It was a triumph of what was practically possible, but it mirrored future division as well as current disagreement. Birrell had solved the current problem by giving a separate university to the Protestants of the north of Ireland, and treating the institution for the Catholics of the rest of the country as the "national" university. Moreover, on the nominated senate for the Belfast-based university, containing thirty-five persons, there was to be only *one Catholic*, and on the senate for the "National" university, containing thirty-six persons, there were to be seven Protestants. In retrospect, Birrell's concluding words in introducing the bill make melancholy reading. Having affirmed that the new universities would not be denominational, would not "be marred by tests", he concluded:

> The most that could be said was that the government were planting one university on what may be called Protestant soil, although there were many Catholics in Ulster, and another on Catholic soil, although there were many Protestants in Dublin, Galway and Cork.[99]

On 12 July, just before the bill's third reading, Walsh could not resist firing a final shot before the closing of the university question. At a church function at Greystones, Co. Wicklow, he emphasised that the scheme as it stood had one drawback of a "terribly serious character", namely, the absence of a residential college in Dublin. It would stand in painful contrast to Trinity College with its residences for its students. For the saving of one or two hundred thousand pounds "what has been won by years of agitation was in danger of falling far short of what was anticipated".[100] Another major regret was to be voiced two years later, at the opening of the academic year of University College Dublin with a solemn high mass in Newman's Catholic University church. Then, recalling his own days at the college in Newman's time, Walsh deplored the glaring defect in the University Act that no allowance was made "for the provision or maintenance of any church or chapel or other place of religious worship". He contrasted that situation with Oxford and Cambridge where "no one would contemplate ... the introduction of a system which would remove religion from a place of honour in these venerable homes of learning".[101]

Establishing and consolidating

The National University Act was scheduled to come into effect on an appointed day within two years of its passing. To set up the new establishments, two bodies of commissioners were appointed, and to these bodies was entrusted the responsibility of drafting the statutes and appointing the staff of the universities and colleges. The Dublin commission consisted of ten members, named in the Act. Archbishop Walsh was one. The chairman was Chief Baron Christopher Palles. Walsh also accepted a place on the senate of the university. Its members unanimously elected him chancellor of the university on 18 December 1908. It was an acknowledgement not only of his great ability, but also of his prominent role over many years in the struggle for equality in Irish education. To Walsh, who had scorned the senate of the Royal University ever since his difference with its members and his resignation from it, there was a sense of justification and fulfilment in being elected chancellor of the senate of the new national institution. He was to honour the position by dedicated commitment, especially in the early years when his concentrated efforts helped to ensure a good beginning. He also brought to the office a personal dignity, and a lofty vision of the National University and of University College Dublin and of their role in the new emerging Ireland.

The Gaelic League and the demand for essential Irish

One of the major challenges facing him in his early years as chancellor came from a body with a narrower, highly focused vision, who brought to their cause an evangelical intensity, the Gaelic League. Walsh, as noted previously, had learned Irish as a student and had taken a keen interest in the language. For years he had been a staunch supporter of the Gaelic League in its work for Irish language and culture. His interest and support, however, did not blind him to the internal politics of the movement and to the manifestations of intolerance amongst its members.

The League's promotion of the Irish language received a boost in 1900 when the Intermediate Education Commission, of which Walsh was a member, agreed to Irish being given a prominent place in the curriculum for the Intermediate examinations. This success achieved through the powerful eloquence of Douglas Hyde, supported by John MacNeill of University College Dublin, and Professor Michael O'Hickey of Maynooth, gave a new status to the language and greater confidence to its promoters. They determined, therefore, that a knowledge of Irish should be a requirement for entry to the new National University. They were supported by the insistent voice of a nationally conscious Irish-Ireland, which identified national identity with the language (conveyed in the compact slogan, *gan teanga gan tir* – without the language one is without a country) and was intolerant of opposition.

The issue came to a head at the inaugural meeting of the Gaelic Society of University College on 27 November 1908, when Fr Delany, long a supporter of Irish historical studies and the Irish language, frankly stated, on being challenged, that he "would give Irish a privileged, a predominant place in the university, but he would stop there". Compulsory Irish would be harmful, in his view, to both the university and the country. It would restrict the international role which he, like Newman, envisaged for the university, and would also prevent the university being truly national, open to all Irish people whatever their tradition.[102] As much of the credit for the new university was attributed to him, his words were seen as an indication of how the senate of the university was likely to vote, and he was publicly assailed in the press and from public platforms. He found himself derided as "a West Briton", a derogatory term applied to those Irish who emulated English fashions and ways in hopes of social and political advancement and were not "truly Irish". He was, moreover, the recipient of intolerant letters from even senior and distinguished churchmen such as Canon Ryan, a parish priest and vicar general of the Cashel archdiocese.[103]

The issue divided both churchmen and laity. Many of the younger clergy favoured the League. Among the Jesuits, although Delany was then provincial, there were enthusiastic supporters of compulsory Irish, if not to the extremes of a Canon Ryan or of Professor O'Hickey of Maynooth. The latter, a long time friend of Walsh, became a *cause célèbre*. Given to extravagant language, he published a number of sharply worded letters in which he branded opponents of compulsory Irish, or "essential Irish" as it was being termed, as not genuinely Irish people. On 13 December, moreover, in a lecture to Maynooth students, he singled out Walsh as a friend of Irish Ireland compared to the other four Catholic churchmen in the senate of the National University. The lecture and his public letters were produced in a pamphlet entitled significantly *An Irish University, or Else*. Under the pseudonym "An Irish Priest", he also published a pamphlet entitled *The Irish Bishops and an Irish University* (Dublin 1909), which assailed the hierarchy in unmeasured language. At their June meeting, 1909, the bishops, as trustees of Maynooth, called on O'Hickey to withdraw certain of his remarks on pain of loss of his professorship. He refused, was removed from his post, and spent the remaining five years of his life in fruitless appeals to Rome.[104]

Walsh attempted to avoid an open conflict with the League, but shortly before his election as chancellor he had informed Hyde and MacNeill that he had doubts about the legitimacy of "the popular feeling" that was being roused. Originally he had been "unconvinced, but anxious to be convinced" on the language and university issue, but he had been alienated by "the shocking vulgar abuse in which a number of them (Gaelic Leaguers) seem to revel and the utterly irrelevant arguments they bring forward". He discerned, he declared, "a determined, and to judge by some of the language used, a vicious attempt to intimidate and terrorise".[105] As chancellor, on 7 December 1908, he turned down an invitation to a League function from Padraig O'Dalaigh, general secretary of the League. "The course now being pursued", he declared, made it impossible for him to associate himself "in anyway with the meetings or other proceedings of the League".[106]

To the bishops as a body, however, a key concern was that the essential Irish campaign, with its demand for Irish as a matriculation requirement, might tempt Catholics who did not know Irish, or wish to learn it, to go to Trinity College. In the middle of January 1909, as a result, the episcopal standing committee issued a statement declaring the question one for "fair argument" but making plain their own opposition to compulsory Irish for entry to the university.[107] The controversy continued unabated. For many enthusiasts it represented the old struggle of Ireland against England – with which the opponents of compulsion were now, somehow, identified. Branches of the Gaelic League mushroomed at home and overseas. Massive processions were organised to insist on essential Irish; and intense pressure was brought to bear on local government authorities, which were empowered to levy rates to provide scholarships in the new university. This proved decisive. A deputation from the general council of county councils appeared before the university senate to demand essential Irish. Eventually, the senate of the National University gave way, enacting on 23 June 1910, a requirement that, from 1913, Irish should be compulsory for matriculation.

Already on 15 April 1910, Walsh had written to Joseph McGrath, now registrar of the National University, that although what was being put in place was what was sought by the people agitating the question, what they really wanted was to have Irish made, *"through the university*, an obligatory subject in the intermediate schools in the country". He feared there might be disruption at convocation, and made suggestions, including entry by ticket only, to lessen the prospect.[108] He was correct as to what would be the next step by those advocating the essential Irish programme. The Gaelic League turned its focus to the development of Irish in the primary and intermediate schools. The secretary of the League wrote to Archbishop Walsh on 16 January 1912, proposing the establishment of an education commission or conference to reconstruct the national and intermediate boards of education, so as to ensure that Irish became an essential subject in their schools. He spoke bluntly: "Times have changed, as your Grace knows, and we no longer beg; we demand, and providence has given us our long waited-for opportunity."[109]

In the crusading atmosphere many lost sight of what was ultimately at stake. Those like Delany and John Dillon, who, in somewhat different contexts, openly pointed to the narrowing of the meaning of "National" and to its divisive implications, were shouted down, and those who protested, like Walsh, were ignored. As Home Rule approached, the country was being declared markedly Gaelic and Catholic, without reference to the considerable section of the population who were neither Catholic nor Gaelic-speaking yet proud of Ireland as their country, and who were expected to welcome, or acquiesce in, this new Ireland.

THE HEAVY DEMANDS OF THE EARLY YEARS

The agitation over the language issue added to the heavy burdens already being borne by the members of the Dublin commission preparing for the new university. The labour undertaken by the commissioners, and especially by Chief Baron Palles and the archbishop, was enormous. "The duties necessitated visits to Liverpool, Manchester, Leeds, and London, in order to take evidence on the matter of higher technological studies, with frequent consultations in Dublin and Belfast, between members of the joint committee" of the new universities.[110] Walsh gave up hours several days a week to the sittings of the Dublin commission; and frequently he had conferences at his house, sometimes 'till a late hour at night, with the secretary of the commission, Robert Donovan, or with the legal draftsmen. He revelled in the work, and his energy, endurance, and legal acumen often surprised, and sometimes exasperated, the draftsmen, D.F. Brown, KC, and James A. Murnaghan, BL, who was to become the archbishop's own legal adviser and friend.[111] The statutory commission brought its labours to an end on 31 July 1911. The work contributed to the breakdown Walsh experienced that autumn. Poor health was to interfere with his attendance at meetings in subsequent years, with the result that much of his work was done by correspondence.

On 8 June 1912, he wrote to McGrath stating that his attendance at meetings was doubtful for some time ahead. "First, I am in a crippled condition", he declared, and when that cleared up there would be a backlog of church work to be completed.[112] Six days later he sent recommendations on how to honour the two hundredth celebration of Trinity College's medical school. "Everything possible" should be done "to show civility on such an occasion" and this required presenting an address as well as sending a deputation. He was still, he added, "a prisoner but in no pain" except that he had "not been allowed to put anything but a slipper" on his left foot "for the last fortnight".[113] His correspondence as chancellor over the subsequent years was conducted with meticulous care, even to correcting the wording of McGrath's circular letters.[114] When required, McGrath called on him to discuss business.

Despite the illnesses and irregular attendance, Walsh does not seem to have considered resigning. He continued, by attendance, or by writing and instruction through his friend McGrath, to take an active interest in the working of the National University and its colleges until his death in 1921. He lived to see the university securely established. When UCD attained a student population of 1,300 in 1920, he rejoiced and, in keeping with his long preoccupation, he publicly congratulated the college on surpassing Trinity College in student numbers![115]

THE ARCHBISHOP AND THE YEARS OF CHANGE, 1897-1912

Looking back with 1912 as a watershed, the extent of the change was remarkable. Not only was Irish identity and pride rediscovered by means of Irish language, music, dance, and gaelic sporting activities, it was also fostered by interest in literature, archeology and history, and expressed in a political and social assertiveness such as Arthur Griffith's concept of Sinn Fein (ourselves alone) and the corresponding spirit of self-help manifested in the Irish agricultural cooperative movement. On the industrial and business front, as has been indicated, the trade union act of 1906, and the arrival in Ireland of James Larkin, radically changed the employer-worker scene.

In politics, the apparent failure of constitutional politics at the end of the nineteenth century, and the centenary commemoration of 1798, promoted the revival of the Irish Republican Brotherhood and an openness to achieving by force what Britain refused to concede to peaceful argument. The majority of the population, nevertheless, still supported the Irish parliamentary party, which attained the crest of its popularity in 1910, following Asquith's promise of 'self-government' for Ireland and the results of two general elections which gave Irish nationalists the balance of power in the House of Commons. By 1912, however, when the Home Rule Bill was passed, there were ominous signs of militant opposition from unionists, and dissatisfaction with the terms of the act on the part of a significant section of nationalists, a dissatisfaction daily fuelled by attacks on the Irish party by the *Independent* newspapers. The overall climate of a growing and articulate popular democracy, and of new assumptions reflected in a move away from inherited attitudes amongst the younger generation, fostered an outspoken, often savagely critical minority press, represented most powerfully by D.P. Moran's *Leader*, Arthur Griffith's *Sinn Fein*, and recently Jim Larkin's *Irish Worker*. In this dynamic atmosphere, which had seemed dull and stultifying to James Joyce, traditional figures of authority no longer carried the same weight or engaged ready attention.

Archbishop Walsh's national reputation rested on his central role as a highly publicised churchman, educationalist, arbitrator, and elder statesman. His silver jubilee as bishop, in 1910, was marked not only by numerous telegrams and letters of congratulations from clerical and lay friends and colleagues, but also by resolutions of congratulation from public bodies and such diverse organisations as the Dublin Trades Council and Labour League and the Dublin County Board of the Ancient Order of Hibernians! A hyperbolic profile by Francis Cruise O'Brien in the *Leader* of 14 May 1910, described him as a man "of vast works and tireless days" who had "no narrowness and no intolerance" and was the best liked of the Irish bishops by non-Catholics. O'Brien also observed acutely that "as a publicist he is voluminous ... he wants no point to be missed, no link in the chain of argument to be overlooked".

Despite the profile, by 1912 Walsh was no longer a central figure in primary and intermediate education, and the long university struggle was over. He had been one of the early promoters of the Irish language, but the language movement no longer looked to him for support. Indeed, as has been seen, he had censured some of its leaders for their domineering and intolerant ways. He had held aloof from the Irish party and politics since 1905, and his role of mediator in workers' disputes had been curtailed by ill health and by the palpable intransigence in industrial relations as Larkin, on the one hand, asserted workers' right to combine and engage in collective bargaining and the sympathetic strike, while the employers closed ranks, branded Larkin and his lieutenants as socialist anarchists, enemies of good order and religion, and eventually refused to recognise Larkin's Irish Transport and General Workers' Union.

Industrial strife was, in effect, the dominating factor in Dublin in the last two years of the period under consideration. In 1908 Walsh had met with Larkin across a conference table. The carters, carriers and draymen were the most vulnerable of general workers. Larkin led them in a strike for better pay and conditions. Walsh offered to mediate. He and Dr Peacocke, the Protestant archbishop, and the lord mayor, were the mediating team. After a few days the employers withdrew. The Irish under secretary, Sir James Dougherty, informed Walsh, on 11 December 1908, that he had heard that the employers had "definitely made up their minds to refuse to meet Larkin or to recognise him in any way. They are relying upon starving out the men, whose means are slender and precarious, and whose wives ... are urgent for their return."[116] As well as the obduracy of the employers, Walsh also experienced Larkin's failings as a negotiator. His secretary, Fr Michael Curran, was later to comment: "The Archbishop fully recognised the grievances of the carters but deplored that the champion of their cause was so impossible a representative at the conference table."[117]

In 1911 the industrial unrest became widespread. By September 1911, a railway strike crippled the country. The directors of the main railway network, the Great Southern and Western Railway, determined not to yield an inch. They were supported by the Dublin Chamber of Commerce, in which the vice-chairman, William Martin Murphy, was particularly prominent. By the beginning of October, when Walsh returned from an extended vacation, the workers, in Murphy's phrase, "were beaten to the ropes".[118] The employers were also winning the propaganda war, though Larkin was dispensing abuse in his own vitriolic way in his *Irish Worker*. Letters came to Walsh emphasising the threat of socialism. Many of the clergy clearly believed the scare stories in the newspapers. The workers and many of their leaders, nevertheless, still believed they had a friend and supporter in the archbishop. In effect, this was so, despite increasing ill health. In 1912, indeed, he was largely inactive, a much weakened man, taking care to nurse himself back to health.

As a regular reader of the *Irish Worker*, however, he kept himself informed on both sides of the industrial struggle. His experience of industrial and commercial life had left him with no illusions about justice being on the side of the employers, and, moreover, the prominence of William Martin Murphy in the Chamber of Commerce was not calculated to win his sympathy. Murphy's powerful newspapers were critical of Larkin and his union. Larkin, on platform and in his own paper, verbally abused, lampooned, and taunted Murphy. It was evident that a head-on clash between the two men was only a matter of time. Walsh could not foresee how extensive and deep-rooted that clash would become the following year.

PART FOUR

A moral force – for justice, equality, independence, 1913-21

It is the oppressor who defines the nature of the struggle, and the oppressed is often left no recourse but to use methods that mirror those of the oppressor.
Nelson Mandela, *A Long Walk to Freedom* (London 1995), p. 194

XIII

From relative quiet to a city in turmoil, 1913

The neurasthenia, or severe "burn-out", which afflicted Walsh in 1911 and 1912, resulted in his reducing his commitments in the early months of 1913. That, at least, is what one is led to conclude from the few engagements and entries in his diary. The most frequent entry, indeed, for February and March is "Dr Cox". The archbishop clearly was not well. It may not have been a recurrence of neurasthenia, however, but a persistent bout of the influenza to which he was prone at that time of year. But, if his activities and outings were restricted, his correspondence remained considerable. Some of it is of interest in terms of information, or as an insight into attitudes, conditions, and issues at the time.

Thus, on 10 January, he informed Dr Coffey, president of University College Dublin, that he had heard that "the 'sites' committee of the NUI were thinking of recommending to the senate the Earlsfort Terrace rink as a site for the new university". He considered the site, he declared, "an ideal one for the university building".[1]

His Lenten pastoral letter for 1913 devoted attention to a problem causing widespread concern, namely, the proliferation of "immoral literature". Laity and clergy had joined in protest and a vigilance committee was formed. Walsh, in his pastoral, praised the work of the committee. On 9 February some fifty young men gathered outside certain newsagents' shops carrying bannerettes with mottoes such as "Suppress Immoral Publications" and "Read the Archbishop's Words".[2] Some members were later prosecuted by the police. How successful the movement was in the medium term is not clear, but it had sufficient support to organise on 29 May a great public demonstration at which the lord mayor presided.[3]

At the end of January, interchanges of a different kind revealed the critical eye kept on the clergy by the supposedly submissive laity. Knowing Walsh's fascination with the development of the combustion engine and the performance of different makes of automobile, his close friend, Chief Baron Christopher Palles, informed him on 30 January 1913, that to mark his 72nd birthday some of his friends wished him to accept "the gift of the motor car" which they had recently asked him to inspect.[4] When word of the gift became known, Mr Boyle of the Coachmakers' Society, at a meeting of the Dublin Trades Council, called for a strong condemnation "of the action of the presentation committee in having the car built entirely outside Ireland, while the coachwork could be easily done in Dublin", and he urged that his Grace be recommended "to refuse an article that would be detrimental to the best interests of Ireland". Mr Milner, the president of the Coachmakers' Society, however, deferred seconding the resolution pending a reply from the archbishop to a letter he had sent to him. The protest was reported in the *Irish Times, Irish Independent* and *Evening Herald* on 11 February. The letter to which Mr Milner said he was awaiting a reply on 10 February was not sent until 16 February! Not for the first time Walsh had to take the Trades Council to task for inaccurate statements at its public meetings. He added, with a mildness which reflected, perhaps, his lack of energy: "I lose no opportunity of doing what I can to encourage the use of Irish made articles. But I cannot do what is impossible."[5]

The motor car, however, was destined to evoke further comment. As archbishop he was familiar with complaints regarding some of his priests, that they never visited the complainants' houses, and that they paid more attention to the rich than the poor.[6] In July 1913, he himself became the object of similar criticism. It came from Philip Francis Little, an eccentric but prophet-like member of a prominent Dublin family, who requested him to consider the feelings of those who witnessed the yawning gulf between "a Catholic prelate riding in so splendid a manner" and the intense poverty all round. "Except amongst the Arabs", he concluded, "I have seen no children so ill-clothed as in Dublin".[7]

POVERTY AND PROSELYTISM

The widespread poverty, and the suffering and degradation it brought, was, as has been seen, a matter that greatly engaged Walsh. For him as archbishop, as for many of his priests, it also evoked, almost inevitably, the problem of proselytism.

Proselytism had an unpleasant history in Ireland. It was associated with trading food for religious allegiance during times of famine. The presence of active proselytism was one of the reasons Walsh opened the Sacred Heart Home for boys at Drumcondra in 1886, some of whom had been "rescued from proselytising 'Birds Nests'", as some of those establishments were called. The increased activity of proselytising agencies in 1912-13 is reflected in page on page of reports in the Dublin diocesan archives. The clergy's efforts to counteract the agencies is apparent in lists of what had been done, and was being done, and in information gathered on the names and activities of proselytising institutions and schools. There were said to be some twenty-two establishments between Dublin and Kingstown (Dun Laoghaire), and for most of these the reports listed the names of the children and staff involved. Parents and children turned to these places, it was stated, because they could not get sufficient food elsewhere.[8] "A Report of the Saint Vincent de Paul Society on Proselytism", on 11 February 1914, told of "ragged day schools where hundreds of Catholic children received an indifferent general education, and were imbued with a spirit of hatred of the Catholic faith and teaching". The children were drawn from homes demoralised by poverty, or/and drunkenness, where the parents had fallen away from attending mass and the sacraments.[9] Preaching in aid of the Sacred Heart Home, Drumcondra, on 22 June 1913, the popular blind preacher, Fr Robert Kane, SJ, claimed that a foundling hospital "which existed in James's street for about one hundred and thirty years, made Protestants of 56,000 children", and that "the 'Birds Nests' in or about Dublin were able to buy or to kidnap about 1,000 children each year".[10]

Whatever about the accuracy of such figures, the aggressiveness of the Protestant campaign in Dublin is well chronicled. The extent of the evidence in the diocesan archives on the prevalence of proselytising amongst the poorer population in Dublin is necessary reading for an understanding of the intensity of clerical and lay Catholic feeling at the sending of impoverished children to England during the strike/ lock out later in the year.

Apart from occasional bursts of energy, Walsh showed little indication of sustained effort or interest during much of 1913. This was reflected even during his vacation. He went on an extended holiday early in August, but there is no entry in his diary until 17 September, when there is one word "Angers", and on the next day, "Nantes", then nothing until 28 September and the words, "Boulogne to Charing Cross". On the 30 September there was the first sign of animation with two entries: "Hamlet, cinematograph", and then at 8.00 p.m. "S. Bernhardt" at the Coliseum. He arrived home as usual on 2 October, and was met on arrival by his two secretaries, and his friends Frs. McGrath and Byrne. Next day he had but one recorded appointment, that with Shane Leslie regarding his biography of Cardinal Manning.

Soon, however, he became immersed in a range of diverse work, for Dublin was in a grave state of industrial dispute and distress. He had followed the development of the strike/lock out while on holiday, by means of letters and newspapers forwarded by his senior secretary, Fr Michael Curran. The newspapers included, at Walsh's request, Larkin's *Irish Worker*.

THE UNREST AND THE DISPUTE PRIOR TO THE ARCHBISHOP'S
RETURN, 2 OCTOBER

The year had been marked by disputes even before the archbishop went on vacation. Between January and mid-August there had been thirty strikes in the Dublin area. Larkin and his "one big union" brought Dublin port to a virtual standstill, and subsequently, in August, forced the County Dublin Farmers' Association to agree to an increase in wages for farm labourers. Larkin was at the height of his power. His weapons were his own burning oratory, striking personality and control over his followers, and his use of the sympathetic strike and refusal to handle "tainted goods" This last tactic was subsequently described by George Askwith, chairman of the Board of Trade in 1913, as, "A refusal on the part of men, who may have no complaint against their own conditions of employment, to continue work, because in the course of their work they came in contact with goods in some way connected with firms whose employees have been locked out or are on strike".[11]

Larkin, through his Transport and General Workers Union, had gained ascendancy over almost all unskilled labour in Dublin, with the exception of the Corporation labourers and the builders' labourers, who were organised in their own unions. Now, only two large groups of workers remained unorganised. One was in Arthur Guinness and Sons, where the wages and the conditions were the best in Dublin and there was no scope for a strike, and the other was in the Dublin United Tramway Company under the chairmanship of William Martin Murphy. There, pay was not a real problem, but conditions of work were demanding and there was some unrest. Larkin determined to organise the Tramway Company, and Murphy was equally determined to foil him. For Larkin by 1913 the Tramway Company had become a personal challenge. For some years, as previously indicated, he had waged a war of personal abuse against Murphy as "the tramway tyrant", a "blood-sucking vampire", a "capitalist sweater", and "industrial octopus", and Murphy's *Independent* and *Evening Herald*, in their turn, had been trenchant in their criticism of "Larkinism". Murphy, in fact, was not a bad employer, as has been seen earlier, but he would not be dictated to in running his business. If Larkin, indeed, had made enquiries, he would have learned that all his life Murphy had made a point of standing up to dictation or bullying,[12] and he had the financial resources and steely determination to ensure success.

Murphy took the initiative on 21 August to forestall expected attempts by Larkin to infiltrate and disrupt the *Irish Independent* and the Tramway Company. Learning that some of his workers were sympathetic to Larkin or had been won over by him, he dismissed half the workers in the despatch section of the *Independent*, and some two hundred in the parcel section of the Tramway Company. A few days later all motor men and conductors were required to sign a document stating that "should a strike of any sort of the employees of the company be called by Mr Larkin or the ITGWU, I promise to remain at my post and to be loyal to the company". In this way, he endeavoured to seal off the company, and threw down a challenge to Larkin who, he informed his tramway employees, would "meet his Waterloo" if he launched a strike. Larkin responded predictably, announcing that there would be a strike on the trams and that the workers were "going to win this struggle no matter what happens".[13]

This was on the eve of Horse Show Week, the social event of the summer season in Dublin. On 26 August, the archbishop's secretary, Michael Curran, wrote to him in Paris: "The great tramway strike broke out this morning ... and for over an hour there was a general dislocation", but by 12.15 "about half the trams were running on the chief lines in the city, and everybody seemed to think that Larkin had failed." "Altogether", Curran concluded, "I think Larkin is meeting his Waterloo at the hands of Murphy. The directors say they won't take back any man who goes on strike or who leaves his car through fear". He quoted Murphy as stating that "he would spend his last shilling in beating Larkin."[14]

Curran was strongly nationalist in outlook and thought Larkin's brand of socialist anarchy was destructive of the prospects of Home Rule, and like most of the Dublin clergy he came from a middle-class background that was fearful of socialism, as synonymous with red revolution, anti-religion, and anti-clericalism. His outlook coloured his reporting of events as Walsh realised, which was probably a further reason for his insistence on having Larkin's *Irish Worker* forwarded to him.

On 2 September, Curran informed Walsh, "the disorder here has grown very seriously. It is no longer a question of a tram-strike. It is simply the scum of our slums versus the police. Unfortunately, the mob have the sympathy of the working-classes and nobody helps the police." "It is really surprising", he added, "to see how much support Larkin commands among the artisans." Even the printers, and "respectable carpenters and bricklayers", were prepared to do almost anything for him. In the same letter he spoke of rumours that the employers were determined to put an end to the employment of Transport Union men. "Everything", he announced, "points to a general lock-out in shipping, coaling, building, milling, and other trades".[15] His prediction was fulfilled. By 22 September, some 25,000 workers were affected.

Curran's partiality appeared even with respect to the much publicised police behaviour in O'Connell Street on Sunday, 31 August, when Larkin appeared dramatically at the window of Murphy's Imperial Hotel and the police baton-charged the onlookers. He spoke in mitigation of this and other police baton charges. "The *Freeman* and the Corporation", he commented, "are making a great fracas about the baton charges on Sunday. I suppose the statements made are true as far as the number who were injured etc. But one thing I can state, that within *five* minutes of Larkin's appearance, not only did the terrible charge of police take place, but the 200 or 400 inoffensive citizens were picked up and so quickly conveyed to Jervis Street (hospital) or Alderman McWalter's surgery, that when I arrived at the GPO [General Post Office] exactly at 1.35 not a trace of the disturbance was to be seen. There were great numbers of police engaged in moving the people from the Pillar beyond the tramway offices, but no excitement." Whatever about the police charge in O'Connell Street, and it was, he emphasised, "in a proclaimed street, on a proclaimed occasion", the charges in Beresford Place, Earl Street, Talbot Street were against "the lowest scum of Dublin bent on paying off the police the accumulated grievances of many a visit to Mountjoy (prison). There were some others there for curiosity, but they have themselves to blame for mixing themselves up with such a rabble."[16]

Feelings ran very high from the time of the O'Connell Street charge, and were fed by the newspapers. The *Freeman*, as the rival daily newspaper to Murphy's more popular *Independent*, was sympathetic to the workers and expressed criticism of the police, Larkin's *Irish Worker* was vitriolic against employers and police, Arthur Griffith's *United Irishman* was critical of Larkin and his methods, and Murphy's papers, the *Independent*, *Evening Herald*, and *Irish Catholic*, placed their denunciatory emphasis on Larkin and his close followers as socialists, syndicalists, enemies of religion, and, according to the *Independent* on 1 September, as raising "the red flag of anarchy". The resultant hysteria was fuelled by the frequent outbreaks of violence and looting accompanying the strike. "In this place", Captain Vane de V.M. Vallance wrote from Dublin to his mother on 13 September 1913, "the danger is not from the strikers but from the thousands of looting roughs who eke out an existence here doing nothing and wait an opportunity of looting shops."[17] Walsh's friend, Fr J. Healy of Dalkey, reflected the fears of many when he wrote to Walsh on 4 September that he saw "our only hope of salvation in the policeman's baton, in the decision of the government to keep the peace at any cost. Larkin wants what he calls 'revolution'." Healy had, he declared, "boycotted the *Freeman*".[18] Few were as detached as Æ (George Russell), who in the *Irish Homestead*, the organ of the Irish Co-operative Movement, dismissed talk of a syndicalist or communist plot and insisted: "Larkin is not the cause of labour discontent. He is the product of it himself ... The labour movement in Ireland at the moment is nothing else than a passionate discontent with present condition of wages, housing and employment."[19]

The O'Connell Street baton charge had wider repercussions. It took place the day before the British Trades Union Congress in Manchester. The hostility that many felt towards Larkin and his undisciplined strike tactics was swept aside by revulsion at police indiscipline and the government's irresponsibility, and this added to the principle of the right to combination that was at stake because of the Irish employers' limitation of the workers' right to join a particular union. The *New Statesman* of 6 September reflected the change that had taken place. "One may detest Mr Larkin more than Marat ... but at the present crisis, no socialist, no trade unionist, no democrat, can hesitate for a moment in ranging himself on Mr Larkin's side ... If Larkin goes down, it will be a victory for the employers who claim to dictate to their workers to what organisation they shall or shall not belong."[20] With support from the British unions, the Dublin dispute was no longer likely to be the short-lived conflict that Murphy, and probably Larkin, had envisaged.

On 22 September, Curran observed that the employers were "very determined that no transport men, nor those who refuse to handle 'tainted goods' will remain. They welcome the skilled men going out. Otherwise these would subsidise Larkin's men".[21] Despite this hardline behaviour on the part of the employers, Curran reserved his criticism for the workers, and in his next letter, on 26 September, made such an unfeeling comment that it still jolts a reader almost a century later. "The general body of the workers", he wrote, "are not yet sufficiently restored to their senses. Though considerably tamed and depressed, they are not sufficiently starved." As if recognising his own excess, and the archbishop's more sympathetic view, Curran added later in the letter: "I fear I am wearying your Grace with the 'strike', and it is so hard to generalise and form a correct opinion from the innumerable and rather contradictory facts that come under one's notice."

Walsh, it can be assumed, responded to Curran from time to time. But none of these letters appear to have survived. From a letter of Curran to Walsh on Saturday, 27 September, it is evident that the archbishop had expressed views different from those of his secretary. Curran agreed on reflection that his Grace was correct in saying that Murphy made a mistake in locking-out the despatch hands in the *Independent* and the parcel men in the trams just because they were Larkin supporters and before they had refused to handle "tainted goods". In this way he gave "some excuse to Larkin to retaliate, and, more important still, enables him to appeal to a common defence of trade unionism". "The latter cry", he added, "is evidently telling in some quarters". He sought to defend Murphy, however, from Walsh's comment that it was relatively easy for Murphy to be obdurate as he was losing relatively little compared to other employers, especially the smaller employers.

The previous day, 26 September, the government intervened in the dispute. The Board of Trade was deputed to hold an official inquiry under the chairmanship of Sir George Askwith, who had much experience of industrial relations. Both parties to the dispute were required to attend and to present their case. The court of inquiry was to open on 29 September.

BACK IN DUBLIN

Walsh returned home on Thursday, 2 October, having had, as he informed Curran, a successful vacation in favourable weather.[22] On 5 October he signalled his return and his renewed energy by a letter in the newspapers supporting the inquiry and pointing out that nothing could be achieved by negotiations carried on in the streets or in the press. A private conference between both sides offered opportunities for reasonable discussion. He wished to convey that there were two sides to the discussion. Privately, he held that the employers were in the wrong in insisting that workers not be members of the Transport Union, that they should only have required an undertaking that the men would handle all goods. On the workers' side, he was aware from the time of the Carters' strike in 1908 that Larkin was an impossible negotiator. In many ways, Walsh's main concern was the plight of the children of the men out of work. Their condition was a topic of conversation when the lord mayor, Lorcan Sherlock, called on him on 7 October. Sherlock's wife, Marie, was in charge of the Mansion House Relief Fund for children impoverished by the lock-out. Walsh subscribed £100 to the relief fund, to the astonishment of a number of clergy who had been conditioned to seeing aid to the workers' side as prolonging the struggle.[23]

The Askwith inquiry, meantime, had achieved little. There were able speeches by T.M. Healy for the employers, and Larkin for the workers. But while the employers produced evidence to support their case, Larkin was allowed make an eloquent attack on employers and the economic system without substantiation and cross-examination. This deficiency in the conduct of the inquiry was seized on by the employers to justify their ignoring its recommendations. Walsh's professional sense was outraged by this aspect of the inquiry. He expressed this, as well as his overall sympathies, in a letter to Lord Aberdeen, who had written to ask if he would act as a mediator in the dispute.

"I don't think the Askwith inquiry has done good in any direction", he declared. "I am quite unable to understand how the case was not treated as one with all the evidence on one side, and *absolutely none* on the other. Why did not Sir G. Askwith say that this was so, when Mr Larkin failed to produce any evidence?" Larkin would have probably said, Walsh continued, that his speech was as good evidence as the unsworn statements on the other side, "but then any competent commissioner of inquiry would have told him that, whilst a statement (even though not made under oath) submitted to cross-examination made very good evidence, a statement carefully screened against cross-examination was not evidence of any kind, and was simply worthless". In the event, "an opportunity should have been given to the employers to rebut the statements made in the speech of the labour leader". It was "an insoluble riddle" to him, Walsh observed, "how any competent commissioner, to say nothing of one who is known to be an able lawyer (and, in addition, an expert in matters of trade and labour disputes) could have conducted an inquiry in such an extraordinary fashion".[24]

While Walsh considered the inquiry to have done no good "in any direction", it did distribute blame to both sides, and in its immediate outcome strengthened the workers' position. The latter were criticised for the use of the sympathetic strike, and the employers were condemned for requiring workers to sign documents which were "contrary to individual liberty and which no workman … could reasonably be expected to accept".[25] The setting up of a conciliation board was recommended.

The workers were prepared to accept the findings of the inquiry as a basis for discussions with the employers, but the latter's executive rejected the recommendations. They favoured trade unionism, they stated, but they could not deal with the Transport Union because of its turbulent and unreliable history, and because its general secretary had declared in a speech in London, "To hell with contracts". Hence, they could only recommend to their members to withdraw the ban on the Irish Transport Union when it was "reorganised on proper lines with new officials who have met with the approval of the British Joint Labour Board."[26] In short, as Askwith commented, their sole aim was the defeat of Larkin and Larkinism.[27]

Walsh, in his letter to Aberdeen, made it clear where his personal sympathies lay. "The labour leader", he believed, had "an exceedingly strong case". The position of the workers had been strengthened by their attitude to Askwith's report compared to that of the employers, and this could not fail "to bring them abundant help from England". "I must say", he added,

> that on the merits of the case generally, my sympathies are altogether with them, and I trust that the outcome of the present case will be a radical change for the better in the position of the unemployed in Dublin.

In conclusion, he referred to Aberdeen's request concerning mediation, the next logical step of the inquiry. "As to mediation, my position always has been that I am prepared to intervene when I have reason to think that my intervention will be welcomed, but not otherwise."[28] Given past experience, Murphy was unlikely to welcome any such intervention.

A CHILDREN'S HOLIDAY AND PROSELYTISM

The obduracy of the employers in the face of Askwith's recommendations greatly increased sympathy in Ireland and England for the workers and their dependants. And then an ill-judged, philanthropic plan to alleviate the suffering of children affected by the lock-out by sending them on holidays to England, proved seriously damaging to the workers' cause.

The plan originated in London, when Mrs Dora Montefiore, a social worker, and an American, Mrs Lucille Rand, met Larkin and discussed the plight of the locked-out families. Although with the best of intentions, Larkin's approval of the project exhibited a lack of awareness of, or casualness towards the intensity of religious feeling with respect to proselytism; and that proselytism would be seen to be involved seems evident given the charges in the *Independent* newspapers and the *Irish Catholic* that Larkin and his lieutenants were socialists, communists, anti-clericals, and anti-Catholic. The plan brought the archbishop urgently into the struggle. He could no longer stand aside.

On 21 October all the main newspapers carried a strongly-worded letter from him. "I have read with nothing short of consternation in some of our evening newspapers that a movement is on foot, and has already made some progress, to induce the wives of working men who are now unemployed, by reason of the present deplorable industrial deadlock in Dublin, to hand over their children to be cared for in England by persons of whom they, of course, can have no knowledge whatever." And turning to "the Dublin women now subjected to this cruel temptation", he put it to them as Catholics that they could "be no longer held worthy of the name of Catholic mothers if they so far forget that duty as to send away their children to be cared for in a strange land, without security of any kind that those to whom the poor children are to be handed over are Catholics, or, indeed, are persons of any faith at all".

He then availed of this "mischievous development" to appeal for a settlement of the industrial dispute. He had no difficulty, he declared, in saying in public, what he had been freely saying in private, that he thought "the employers have been to some extent justified in hesitating to enter into an agreement for the removal of the present deadlock until some guarantee was forthcoming that any agreement now entered upon would be faithfully kept. For my part", he added, "I should like to see guarantees given at both sides." He then referred with approval to an interview given by "one of the leading representatives of the interests of labour, Mr Gosling, "during which he stated that "if the parties would come together, ample guarantees would be forthcoming to ensure the carrying out of agreements" and "the support of English trade unionism and public sympathy" would ensure this. He ventured to ask, then, Walsh concluded, "in the face of this explicit statement", why "the parties should not come together, and see whether something cannot be done to put an end to a conflict that is plainly disastrous to the interests of both?"

A reply from a Mr McGloughlin, claiming to speak for the employers, dampened any hopes Walsh may have had of a positive response to his appeal. McGloughlin wished to express the "strong feeling" that members of the Employers' Association had "that any suggestion that is not quite practicable coming from your Grace, only tends to lengthen the struggle; as men who are disposed to go back to their work hang on to any suggestion of the kind coming from your Grace, in the hope that it will induce an immediate settlement". As his Grace could hardly have read their full reply to Sir George Askwith, he enclosed a copy of the reply, and drew Walsh's attention to the conditions, A and B, "on which they will only recognise the Transport Union". And he concluded implacably: "Our personal opinion also is that the employers will not enter into any negotiations with a union that will contain Mr Larkin and some of his lieutenants as its principal officers."[29]

Where the children were concerned, however, Walsh received a more positive response. The *Freeman* reported on the very day that Walsh's letter appeared that "the great majority of the mothers refused to allow their children to be taken to a strange land, or anywhere where their care would not be under their own personal supervision by frequent visits and daily visits if necessary". Mrs Montefiore was also quoted in the same issue as saying that the plan was just an act of worker solidarity and that there were many precedents for it. It had been done during the dockers' strike in London, and also in America and on the Continent. The condition of children in Dublin, she commented, was deplorable. "Looking from my hotel window", she explained, "I saw three little nippers about four or five years of age – you know how they are dressed, or undressed – turning over the garbage, putting bits of coal and stuff they found into a sack and 'wolfing' any bite of bread and meat that they got mixed up in the refuse. That is an incredible state of things. It is a disgrace to any civilised country."

Dora Montefiore wrote to the archbishop on the day his letter appeared on the papers. She sought to bring to his notice some "facts about the scheme" which might otherwise be presented to him "in garbled form". "We have had now over 350 offers of working class homes", she explained carefully, "for Dublin boys and girls between the ages of 4 and 14. Most of the parents applying send a reference, or belong to some union or another, which union in many cases is collecting money for defraying the travelling and other expenses of the children." "Many of the applicants", she continued, "state that they are Catholics, and many are Irish. A Plymouth working class organisation wrote asking us to send 40 children and 5 mothers to look after them. In most cases, where the children are to be housed in large centres, they will be able to attend a Catholic school; and we shall write to the parish priest, giving him the addresses of the children, so that they may call upon them in their homes." If any further details were required, she would be happy to call on his Grace during her stay in Dublin.[30]

The good will was evident, even though legal proceedings at a later date were to reveal "that some of the children were removed to Liverpool without the consent of their parents".[31] The unfortunate aspect is that had the scheme been well thought out, the archbishop consulted, prior to all announcements, much hurt, frenzy and bitterness would have been avoided. By 21 October, the harm had been done. Walsh replied the next day. He was polite but unyielding. "You are evidently unaware", he wrote, of a fund in Dublin, "organised by our Lady Mayoress, for the providing of food for the poor children" who were "deprived of their ordinary means of support" by the present deadlock in the city. "The obvious and natural way to help these innocent victims", he pointed out, was "to contribute to that fund instead of spending money wastefully, as well as in a manner distasteful to the great mass of the poor mothers of Dublin, in paying the cost of deporting their children to England." "For my part", he continued very definitely, "I can give neither countenance nor support to any scheme of deportation. If the motive which has inspired the scheme is a purely philanthropic one, – and I dare say you have been made aware of some sinister rumours to the contrary that are afloat in Dublin – let whatever means are available be directed to a generous support of the fund to which I have referred." Provision was being made for the further extension of this good work, he concluded. The need would be met, and those engaged in meeting it, would, he felt sure, "be helped, as those engaged in the work of providing food for the children have already been helped, by the subscription of benevolent sympathisers in England".[32]

Among the many letters received by Walsh on the deportation issue, were a number from England. The day after his public letter appeared, a Mr F. McCormick of the Liverpool Victoria Legal Friendly Society expressed surprise at the arguments he advanced regarding the children being sent to England, and assured him that the Irish in England would never allow the faith of the children be tampered with, if any trades union interfered "with the religious beliefs of the children sent over it would be the beginning of the end of trades unions in this country".³³ On the same date, a Patrick L. O'Brien wrote from London in a sharply critical vein, that instead of endangering the faith and morals of the children in a strange land, his Grace should "direct some of the huge, rich convents" in his diocese "to offer the hospitality of their immense houses to these poor waifs, instead of conserving them for the benefit of the pampered children of the rich"; for "the Catholic Church", he added, "is the church of the poor" and his Grace's "cathedrals and these prosperous convents and institutions" were "built and sustained by the hard earned pennies of the lowly".³⁴ Another correspondent, Angela Connolly, who had held "the banner of Catholicism aloft for the best part of thirty-two years", berated him for not organising his clergy at home to feed the children and not getting into communication with the Catholic clergy in the main centres in England to which the children were mainly sent. He had failed as the shepherd of his flock in not being "particularly tender to the little ones" as Christ had been.³⁵

In fairness to Walsh, he and the administrator of the Pro-Cathedral, Fr James Flavin, whom he had requested to represent him on the whole issue of the children, established contact with Catholic clergy and organisations in Britain, especially in Liverpool, as soon as the problem arose. On 23 October, Flavin received reports from Canon Pennington, and the Revd James O'Connell, hon. secretary and assistant hon. secretary, respectively, of the Liverpool Catholic Children's Aid Committee. Pennington described how he had met the boat that morning. "The Liverpool police, who had been communicated with by the Dublin police, were in attendance. There were eighteen children – all Catholics – in the charge of a Miss Neal and two other young women, also Catholics." "The police, at my request", he continued, "satisfied themselves that Miss Neal had the consent of the parents of the children for their removal from Dublin, consequently we could not detain them. The names and addresses from which the children came were taken and I am to be supplied with the names and addresses of the persons with whom the children are placed, and I have an undertaking from those who arranged for the children to come here that their religion will not be interfered with. As soon as they are placed I will communicate with the priest of the district and ask him to visit them." He added that if any of the parents revoked their consent and furnished him with "a properly attested statement" to that effect, he would do his best to obtain custody of the children.³⁶

Of less hopeful import, however, was a letter from Canon Spring Rice, Cathedral House, Southwark, London, who reported that there appeared a paragraph in the *Times* that same day, 23 October, from a man "named Evans" asking for clothing etc for the Dublin poor. The address he gave, Rice knew to be "very near an institution which" had "practically robbed three generations of poor Irish children of their faith". His suspicions were aroused, and on calling to the house they were confirmed. He was "met with a storm of abuse" and refused any information.³⁷

A letter to Fr Flavin from Liverpool, from Fr James O'Connell, followed the lines of Pennington's letter, except that he noted that Pennington remarked to him that "the only disagreeable person was a girl of 19 who came from Dublin with the children. She was impertinent and gave vent to her feelings in regard to the way that they were treated in Dublin".[38] This, presumably, referred mainly to the unseemly scenes that took place as the children were departing from Dublin. Some of the clergy, and of the laity, went to lengths which the *Daily Herald* of 21 October described as "scandalous". It was alleged that "they even used violence against Mrs Rand".[39] Hysteria was whipped up by the *Independent* newspapers. The *Irish Catholic* was so frenzied, in an editorial on 27 September, as to link together "satanism and socialism".

The blend, in the event, of proselytism, 'socialism', and England was a potent mixture to stir the fears and zeal of even the most dispassionate Catholic clergy, as well as many Catholic laity. It provided scope for people with a grudge against Larkin, on the one hand, and the Catholic Church on the other; and it also presented a platform for the right wing fervour of the middle-class Ancient Order of Hibernians, who were intensely disliked by the worker movement and termed by Seamus Hughes in the *Irish Worker* the "Ancient Order of Hypocrites".[40]

The *Independent* of 23 October, and the *Freeman's Journal* two days later, convey something of the feeling generated, and the hyperbolic reporting evoked by the association of proselytism with the English holiday scheme. Under a black banner heading, "EXPORTING DUBLIN CHILDREN", and many minor headings, the *Independent* commented:

> Not since the days when Cromwell forcibly deported Irish children to the Barbadoes has such a determined attempt been made to deprive Ireland of her little ones, as was made yesterday in Dublin. Thanks to the spirited action of the clergy, acting on the instruction of the Most Rev. Dr Walsh – and supported by the laity – the attempted deportation of children was completely foiled during the day, but 15 children were deported from the North Wall by the City of Dublin steamer last night.

The account went on to state that fifty children were brought to the Corporation baths in Tara Street by Mrs Montefiore and some companions "in order to be washed first and afterwards clothed with the English garments before being transferred to Westland Row railway station", and that "at the instance of some of the parents" the priests of St Andrew's parish, Westland Row, were apprised of what was taking place, and the Revd W. Landers and T. MacNevin went at once to the baths. The *Independent*'s account further claimed that "the parents of the children denied that they had given their consent to the deportation of their children", adding that "many of the strikers themselves do not relish this way of dealing with their children". In the subsequent confrontation, "a large number of the crowd assisted the parents in taking the children from the ladies".[41]

An incensed Larkin, in a speech at Liberty Hall, denounced the clergy who had prevented the departure of Mrs Montefiore's charges as "a disgrace to their cloth". They were fearful that the children's faith "would be interfered with", he declared, "but the religion which could not stand a fortnight's holiday in England had not very much bottom or very much support behind it. Of course, he knew that many of these clergy had shares in the Tramway Company". The *Independent* highlighted his speech and his boast "that fifteen boys and girls had been sent away". The archbishop's own determination was strengthened by a letter from the Countess Plunkett which told of a visit to Liberty Hall with one of the mothers of the children being sent to Liverpool, and how her request for the return of the children was met with a verbal attack on her and on the clergy. Mrs Montefiore and Larkin told her "to get out".[42]

The *Freeman*, which had been sympathetic to the workers' cause, joined in the criticism of the children's departure for England. Under the heading, on 25 October, "Priests to the Rescue. More Children Saved" it told how priests and laity had frustrated "an attempt to deport another batch of Catholic children to England" and how the priests involved had been cheered, and that among those cheering were "a number of persons ... wearing the badge of the Transport Workers' Union". The paper also told of thousands marching in procession from Dublin docks to O'Connell Street, many of them singing hymns, while some, as they passed Liberty Hall, shouted "Down with Socialism", "Souper Larkin", "Kidnapper Larkin", and were countered by groans and cheers for Larkin. There was little or no mention in the newspapers of the impact of all the anger and the pulling to-and-fro on the children themselves.

In the face of the intensity of the opposition, the constant vigil at the ports, and the uneasiness of many of the workers with the alleged deportation, the scheme petered out. Among the prominent sympathisers of the union who supported Walsh's position, much to Larkin's disappointment, was Maud Gonne,[43] a symbol of social commitment, and intense national feeling, a woman of rare beauty who evoked the love poems of W.B. Yeats. For some time she had involved herself in schemes for feeding Dublin's needy children in Dublin. The holiday issue left the Transport Union particularly vulnerable, and provided opportunities for the *Independent* and the *Irish Catholic* to assert the 'truth' and relevance of their warnings, while the disreputable editor of the *Toiler*, P.J. McIntyre, an old foe of Larkin, revelled in exposing at last "the game of the Larkinist Socialist Syndicalists ... attempting to undermine and destroy the Catholic faith of the rising generation".[44]

Labour writers like James J. (Seamus) Hughes sought to put the best face on what he termed 'the holiday scheme'. On 8 November 1913, in the *Irish Worker*, in an article entitled "The AOH 'The Childer' and the Faith", written under the pseudonym Shane O'Neill, he argued that "the holiday scheme was not a question of faith and morals, it was a business transaction concerned with grub and clothes". The clergy had every right to warn people about the danger to their faith while away from home, but they should first have taken the trouble to inform themselves of the facts of the case rather than hearkening to "the lying crying of proselytism" and involving themselves in "the ludicrous scenes which have given religion perhaps a permanent set-back". The main orchestrators, he believed, were what he called the "Ancient Order of Hypocrites", who hired cars to "rescue" Transport workers' children "from a well-arranged holiday", and had not made the slightest move to obtain information about the holiday from Liberty Hall, nor had they made any effort to help the hungry children previously for two whole months.[45]

Despite the assertive indignation, and the effort to turn the blame on others, the real question remained, not why the clergy and the AOH did not consult Liberty Hall, but rather why did not Liberty Hall check out such a potentially explosive issue with the archbishop before embarking on it? This mistake or oversight, indeed the unwisdom of the whole concept, was indirectly acknowledged by James Connolly, with his sense of Irish history and the role of proselytism in it.

In an article in *Forward*, on 1 November 1913, Connolly made his views clear. Their British friends had been horrified at "the vile aspersions cast upon their motives". "For ourselves", he asserted, "we anticipated it all, and have never been enthusiastic towards the scheme … We felt instinctively that the well-meant move of Mrs Montefiore and her colleagues would arouse in Ireland hostilities and suspicions they could not conceive of, and would not believe were we to attempt the task of making the matter clear." He wished to deny, however, "the foul and libellous accusations brought against the noble-minded ladies" in charge of the scheme; and he denounced particularly "one scoundrel in clerical garb" who was said to have stated that the children were being "brought to England by treachery, fraud and corruption for proselytising purposes". This was venomous and unfounded, and utterly at variance with the behaviour of the archbishop. Connolly then went on to pay a striking tribute.

> Mrs Montefiore had given his Grace, Archbishop Walsh, her assurance that wherever the children went, the local Roman Catholic clergy would be given their names and addresses, and requested to take charge of them, and see that they attended to their duties as Catholic children. His Grace felt that, despite that assurance, and without doubting it in the least, there would still be dangers. But not for one moment did he impugn the motives of the ladies in question. His instincts as a gentleman, and his own high sense of honour forbade it.

These qualities, however, were lacking in the cleric in question. He left him "to be dealt with by his Grace".

Then, availing of the plight of the children to entice the archbishop to mediate in the struggle, Connolly continued: "The utterances of his Grace the archbishop on the question at issue deserve and no doubt will receive, the earnest consideration of every thoughtful man and woman in Ireland. Nobody wants to send the children away – the Irish Transport and General Workers' Union least of all desires such a sacrifice. But neither do we wish the children to starve." "The master class", Connolly charged, "calmly and cold-bloodedly calculate upon using the sufferings of the children to weaken the resistance of the parents". The workers, Connolly asserted, were prepared to fight to the death rather than surrender again "to the hell of slavery out of which they are emerging". Hence, he suggested to his Grace, if he were as solicitous about the bodies of the children as he was about their souls, that his duty was plain – to "see to it that the force of public opinion, that the power of the press, that all the agencies" at his "command are brought to bear upon the inhuman monsters who control the means of employment in Dublin to make them realise their duties to the rest of the community". They had spurned all negotiation, whereas the workers were prepared to meet all employers or any individual employer. It was his Grace's duty to mediate, Connolly stated, and concluded emphatically:

> If the employers reject your offer of mediation and still declare their contempt for any public opinion they cannot rig in advance, then it is your manifest duty to organise public support for the workers to defeat their soulless employers.

"We have read your Grace's character in vain if you shrink from that test, or fail in that duty."[46]

To tell Archbishop Walsh what his "duty" and his "character" was, was not the way to persuade him to your side, however much he sympathised with your cause. Nevertheless, although his suggestions regarding mediation had been repulsed a number of times already by the employers,[47] he wrote to the press on 24 November in a further attempt to encourage both sides to come together. He drew attention to two recent statements which gave grounds for hope. Mr William Martin Murphy, in a public letter, had stated that there "were not five per cent of the men out of employment who might not safely return, before their places were filled up, without any sacrifice of principle or without any undertaking except to do the work they were paid for doing"; and Mr Connolly, "Mr Larkin's chief lieutenant", speaking at Liberty Hall recently, said

> He would never consent to abandon the sympathetic strike in industrial warfare, but he would agree to check its operation to the extent that it should not be used recklessly and indiscriminately.

Walsh questioned – "Why people should turn their attention away from such significant statements and fasten exclusively upon other statements, recklessly

made, which, if they were to be taken literally, would amount to so many declarations of implacable and never-ending war."[48]

Shortly after, a conference took place between the Dublin employers' representatives, the labour delegates from England, and the representatives of Liberty
Hall. Strong hopes of an arrangement were entertained. On 1 December, however, citizens of every class learned with deep disappointment that, despite an
all-night sitting, agreement was not reached. There was a coming together on all
questions, it seems, except on the issue of "complete reinstatement" of all the
men "now disemployed", and on this the talks broke down.

On the children's issue, Walsh intensified the efforts which were already in
train. Their needs had been further emphasised for him by the recent report by
Sir Charles Cameron "On the State of Public Health in the City of Dublin",
which drew attention to the city's high death rate and high rate of ill health
because of the condition of the slums. The impersonality of statistics, moreover,
was given flesh and blood by a vivid letter from Countess Plunkett describing
the condition of the mothers and children she encountered in organising a holiday for children at her castle in Sandymount.[49]

On 27 October the archbishop appealed in the *Freeman's Journal* for food and
clothing "for the children who are the helpless victims of the present lamentable
deadlock in the industries of Dublin". The St Vincent de Paul Society had offered
their services. He would be meeting with them on Monday, he announced, to
establish a committee to collect funds. His letter also requested the administrators
of the three parishes, with which he was more specifically connected, to attend the
meeting. It was his belief that the policy of moving children from their homes "as
a matter of temporary relief", whether in Ireland or in England, was "an eminently unsatisfactory and unsound one". If a family had their home broken up,
however, it was most praiseworthy to provide shelter for them. At present there
were rumours of evictions in the city. In the event of this taking place he had had
an offer from the Christian Brothers of a house to accommodate over eighty boys,
and he was sure something similar could be done for girls.

That day, Marie Sherlock, lady mayoress, suggested to him that his letter
might give the impression that nothing had been done up to this for the children of the city. In fairness to the women involved, their work should be noted.
The money they received from subscribers had been spread over twenty-six
schools, which provided meals for the children; the nuns of North William
Street, in addition, gave relief to nearly 100 families a day; and a considerable
number received direct relief from the Mansion House.[50] The following day,
Walsh made amends at the meeting of the Vincent de Paul Society, Upper
O'Connell Street.

In the course of a long impassioned address, he paid a tribute to the work of
the Mansion House fund, and went on to praise the amounts of quiet distribution of food and clothing to the children of the poor by the clergy and nuns of
Dublin. They did not seek advertisement but he felt it was time "to expose the

falsehood of the statements that, especially of late, have been put in circulation from public platforms, and that have been, I regret to have to say it, listened to in cowardly silence by men, the children of many of whom have been fed and clothed by the charity of those about whom these calumnies were uttered". In the schools of the three parishes alone – Marlborough Street, Westland Row, and City Quay, 1,280 breakfasts had been given daily to the poor children attending the schools. That number had risen in recent times to 2,450 daily. In ordinary times, 690 children at these schools had dinner each day; and as regards clothing, in one 400 children were clothed each year, in others up to 780. To spend money to send children on a "holiday", he continued, was a waste of money. What was needed was to get "all the help we can for the continuance and extension of the work that is already being done". The effort had to be made, he believed, through the schools. The parents must send their children to the schools to be looked after, not onto the streets to beg.

A committee was formed to collect across the country for the children of Dublin. Walsh made a contribution of £100, and arranged for a diocesan collection to be held throughout the archdiocese on Sunday, 2 November. To raise additional funds the committee was empowered to issue a public appeal, and to approach the committee of the national pilgrimage to Lourdes for a grant out of their surplus funds. Sixteen parish committees were established to organise meals. The central committee apportioned funds according to needs. The committee also entered into contracts with clothing firms and boot manufacturers for supply to the schools. Subsequently it was recorded that from November 1913 to the middle of February 1914, between 9,000 and 10, 000 children "were provided with a meal, or meals, every school-day out of the fund. In most parishes the meals were also given on Saturdays and in some on Sundays. From mid-February the numbers gradually diminished but in a few schools the work was still carried on to a small extent, as it had been for years.[51]

Towards the end of October 1913, while the "deportation scheme" was still prominent in newspapers, Stephen Gwynn wrote to Walsh in a state of gloom.

> I cannot describe to you how uneasy the present turn of events in Dublin makes me. These idiot women have developed a situation which gives victory to the employers in a demand that they shall dictate to the employed the form of organisation and the persons to run it. A victory of this sort means infinite trouble in future.

"Further", he declared, "that victory will inevitably be regarded by the radical section amongst the workers as won by 'clericalism'. It is the seed of a dangerous growth."[52] A somewhat similar fear was felt by Bishop Donnelly, to judge from a section of an undated letter of his to O'Dwyer, who, in his view, underestimated what was happening in Dublin. "The fight to the finish here in Dublin maybe all very well", Donnelly wrote, but there is much more at stake than the mere economic question. Larkin has got our entire working population in his hands and *out of our hands* & he is working hard to accentuate the separation of priests from people.

"His Grace is not apprehensive", Donnelly continued. "He says it was the same at the time of the Parnell row. I fear it is not quite so harmless. There was no socialism and anarchy preached then."[53]

Walsh had remained uninfluenced by Curran's views, and remained undisturbed by the fears of Donnelly and other moderate clergymen. The emergence of the people's religious allegiance, and of his own high standing, from the cauldron of the Parnell split, left him hopeful for the future. His instinct was right. Despite much criticism of individual clergy by the workers' leaders, the overall standing of the Church was preserved among many of them, and among the workers generally, by their regard for Walsh. This was evident in Connolly's letter quoted earlier, and was even more marked in two declarations by the Catholic convert, W.P. Partridge, who had made some of the most inflammatory speeches on the workers' side. In the report of a public meeting on 27 October, he was quoted as stating that although there had been little response to the appeal for funds before the children were sent to England, he was strongly opposed to proselytism and "the Archbishop of Dublin only did his duty in publishing his letter. His Grace subscribed £100 to the fund for the women and children (applause)". But", he questioned pointedly, "how many priests subscribed?"[54] More than three weeks later he sent a letter to a Fr Ryan which probably casts light on the attitude of a number of Transport Union men at a deeper level than their own rhetoric, or their depiction in newspapers. He was alleged to have described the priests offering opposition to the sending of the children as acting like "corner-boys". He was pained to learn that Fr Ryan had taken this as meant personally. He thought Fr Ryan knew him sufficiently to know that he "would not be guilty of using such language to the ministers of my religion". Lest others also had been misled, he was "sending a copy of this letter to his Grace, the Archbishop of Dublin". Then, asserting the right of freedom of speech, he added firmly: "Surely in this enlightened age a Catholic workman may from his more intimate knowledge, disagree with the priest on industrial questions without being held up as anti-cleric and regarded as an enemy of religion". Partridge concluded by describing his visit to the Dublin children in Liverpool. He "was delighted to find them in high spirits and much improved as a result of their changed conditions". They attended "school regularly", and, he emphasised, "they go to mass every Sunday, and the lady of the house assured me she would send them every day if the priest so desired"![55]

A number of Walsh's episcopal colleagues were less understanding and perceptive than he. Cardinal Logue, like many of the clergy, took his views from the newspapers, and had an Irish party perspective. He seemed unaware of the obstacles presented by the employers. "Judging by their speeches, the Larkinites and their abettors", he wrote on 6 November, "do not want a settlement. They are working not in the interests of the men, but using the unfortunate men for the purpose of propagating and establishing their socialist and syndicalist principles". As long as they were receiving support from England they would continue, he believed, but when the support ceased they would "leave the men to take the consequences".[56] Brownrigg of Ossory also presumed the workers were the main culprits, though he noted that much of the "bitterness and contumacity" had been imported into the struggle by the Dublin press, especially by "its adoption of the picture craze to fire the imagination of the mob". He sympathised very much, however, with Walsh's "troubles and sorrows". In accordance with the gospels, a bishop might expect such, he observed, and then added less than diplomatically, "in your case they have arrived only after nigh thirty years in the episcopacy, when your vigour and health to combat them is not what it was in years gone by". Not a particularly palatable truth to a man as independent and self-sufficient as Walsh. Brownrigg sweetened the remark, however, by praising his "generalship in the case of the children". He had foiled the attempt in a way that was appreciated by his own people in Dublin and that would "deepen the faith of the people throughout the whole of Ireland".[57]

FINAL EFFORTS AT NEGOTIATION, AND THE END OF THE STRUGGLE

On 27 October, even as the extensive opposition to the sending of the children to England was making Larkin's position less popular, he was arrested and given an excessive seven months sentence for incitement to riot. Connolly took over in his place, and there was rumour of Larkin stepping down or being replaced. In that context it seems no coincidence that at a public meeting on the evening of 27 October W.P. Partridge proclaimed defiantly: "I am prepared to rot in jail rather than this dispute should be settled without Jim Larkin. He is the leader, and he is not going to be cast aside at the dictation of any man or men."[58] Connolly, keen to make his own mark and to put pressure on the employers to negotiate, called out about one thousand men in the steamship companies and finally closed the port of Dublin. On 14 November he took an even graver step. He called on the workers to arm. The Irish Citizen Army came into being, though at this period it was little more than a vigilante force being knocked into shape by a Captain Jack White, who had won a DSO fighting against the Boers. Larkin was released on 13 November because of strong public pressure, and immediately urged a general strike throughout Britain in support of their Dublin comrades. Three days later, at a mass meeting in Manchester, he made a powerful appeal for intervention by the British unions. The impact was such that the British Trade Union Congress was divided, and decided to hold a special meeting of congress on 9 December to consider the matter.

Walsh, meanwhile, by letters and other means, had been pressing for initiatives towards a settlement. His diary for October shows him meeting, apart from the mayor, Professor Tom Kettle and the mediating Peace Committee, "W. Seddon (labour leader)" who called twice, and Sir William Nugent, a prominent business man. On 10 November he is mentioned as meeting Maud Gonne to discuss further with her the provision of meals for the children of the unemployed. Many years later, writing to a celebrated successor of Walsh, namely, John Charles McQuaid, concerning the seriousness then of poverty in Dublin, Maud Gonne commenced her letter by saying that she ventured to write to him

> Because in 1913 when there was great poverty in Dublin and I was an active members of the Women's' Committee supplying school meals to some 750 children and working to get the English School Meal Act extended to Ireland, his Grace, the Most Revd Dr Walsh sent for me and said he was anxious necessitous school children should be fed and that he would use his influence to get the Act extended, if, in deference to the objections of some school managers, the Act should be only *permissive* in Ireland, instead of obligatory as in England. Through the Archbishop's great influence the Act was extended ...[59]

The very next entry after mention of Maud Gonne's visit on 10 November, was of "Dr Cox" on 11 and 14 November. Despite such suggestions of a physical relapse, Walsh, a few days later, enquired of Sir James Dougherty, at the Chief Secretary's office, regarding a statement made by Augustine Birrell, on 14 November, to the effect that the Executive was using all its powers to have Sir George Askwith's report used as the basis for settlement. Dougherty replied on 25 November. Askwith, he said, did not think the time ripe for public action; and he went on to give an informed view of what was going on in the trades union movement. "Larkin is busy exciting animosities among the leading men, some of whom have turned upon him, and this attack", Dougherty believed, "should be allowed to develop". "A week hence", he continued, "the sky may be clearer and the psychological moment for momentum may arise." "Larkin and his friends will be better inclined to compromise" after "the meeting of the Trades Congress on the 9th when they hope (vainly, it is believed by those best qualified to judge) that they will carry the English trade unions with them into the sympathetic strike". "The employers, on the other hand," he added, "have been heartened by the signs of dissension between Larkin and the trade union leaders, and are not disposed to come to any terms short of absolute surrender."[60]

The British Board of Trade sought to break the impasse by bringing together in conferences representatives of the Parliamentary Committee of the Trade Union Congress, the Executive Committee of the Labour party, and the General Federation of Trades Unions. These came to Ireland, held conferences for three days and broke up in failure when the Employers' Executive refused the workers' demand for complete reinstatement. Following a resolution at the Trade Union Congress of 9 December, further representatives of the British Joint Labour Board and delegates from local trades bodies met again with the Employers' Executive, from 18-21 December, and again the talks broke down on the issue of reinstatement.

In all these negotiations Walsh had taken an active interest, and appears to have been consulted, to judge from Shane Leslie's efforts to comfort him on Christmas Day, 1913:

> The employers have refused to listen to unreason in Larkin, and to reason in the person of their metropolitan ... If the strike could have been settled by human agency your Grace would have settled it the other day. But it is not an "economical strike" but a class feud.[61]

The breakdown of the December negotiations heralded the end, in effect, for the workers. The first move back to work in a firm occurred on 27 December, with the concurrence of the Transport Union. By the end of January 1914, virtually all the men, who could get work, returned; and at a meeting at Glasgow on 30 January, Larkin admitted that he was beaten.[62] No matter how he presented the contest as a victory, or Connolly as a draw, to the hundreds of men who had to apply for assisted passage to England and Scotland, in the first months of 1914, there was no doubt as to the result; and the ITGWU itself was reduced to a critical financial position.

THE AFTERMATH

Significantly, no important gains were recorded at the Dublin municipal election in mid-January, for which ten prominent union leaders stood on a 'lock-out' ticket. Disillusionment with Liberty Hall leadership was widespread among the workforce. One wonders, indeed, to what extent there had been whole-hearted support for the sympathetic strike and its prolongation. One undated letter received by Walsh during the lock-out, not all of which is extant, assured him that "nearly all the employees want to get back to work", that they "were made to come out whether" they "liked it or not". "Nobody will call us together", the writer continued, "and every fellow is afraid to make a start – the union body-guard, I call it, would destroy our house and homes". All except 120 wanted to get back to work, and that group "never did a day's work except to terrorise the decent men".[63] Whatever weight one gives to such fragile evidence, that there was some degree of intimidation and pressure seems inevitable. That aside, the dissatisfaction with the union leadership in the aftermath of the struggle was evident, and among the leaders themselves there was criticism at the neglect of the normal trade union tools of compromise and conciliation.[64]

The dissatisfaction was shared by the archbishop. He had emphasised to Lord Aberdeen on 10 October that he hoped that the outcome of the struggle would be a radical change for the better for the unemployed in Dublin. The result was very different. He felt strongly about the way the strike had been conducted, and how it was ending for the workers, especially the unskilled, who were the main victims.

His attitude to the entire dispute and to the negatively confrontational world of current industrial relations was reflected in the joint Lenten pastoral of the bishops, which focused on the labour dispute, and appeared on 22 February 1914. His stamp is manifest in the compelling, strongly written document, and its central recommendation.

"Whoever shares responsibility for the failure in the past to set up Conciliation Boards in Dublin", the pastoral declared, "has much to answer for. Had any reasonable system of arbitration or conciliation been in working order, it is more than likely that the recent strikes and lock-outs, with all their degrading consequences, would not have taken place." With the contemporary tendency to view Home Rule with great expectations, the document continued:

> Had the healing influence of native rule been felt for even a few years, we cannot believe that the bitter privation, the enormous waste, the loss, the shame, the sin of this insensate conflict, would have been entailed on a city in which commerce and manufacture need to be fostered with tender care, instead of being recklessly endangered in a senseless war between workers and employers.

"The great lesson from this sad experience is the imperative need of well-formed Conciliation Boards, duly representative of both sides, to adjust differences as they arise." Both sides needed strong unions. Both needed "to develop a sound tone and tradition in industrial relations". Inevitably there would be "sharp divergences from time to time", "and then", the pastoral emphasised, "a fair jury should have a chance of bringing in its verdict before the protagonists on either side let loose the horrors of war. Nothing less is demanded by the interests of the parties themselves. Nothing less is fair to the public."[65]

Walsh's anger at Larkin's handling of events was scarcely veiled in the intense words:

> A paralysis of employment that was altogether avoidable has left us the humiliating memory that in a year of plenty many thousands of the toiling masses in the capital city of our country were left for months in idle dependence on rations and strike pay from England, and that large numbers of children had to be fed by charity away from their homes when not deported into strange fosterage across the channel.[66]

He was further incensed at Larkin's indulgence in personal recriminations in which members of the clergy were included. He expressed his disapproval indirectly but effectively. He had refused for many years to support any candidate in a municipal election, and had desisted from attributing 'socialist', 'communist' and so on, to any candidate.[67] When, however, the results of the municipal election were announced, he issued a public congratulation, in the *Evening Telegraph* of 16 January, to Lorcan Sherlock, who had campaigned vigorously in the Mountjoy ward of the city "against the insidious enemy of socialism".[68] Sherlock was, of course, lord mayor, 1912-13, (and was to be re-elected the two following years), and had been, together with his wife, actively involved in helping to feed and clothe the poor of the city during the lock-out. Walsh bluntly congratulated him "on the notable victory gained ... over a combination of influences which, in addition to the havoc" they had "wrought in the industrial life of Dublin", had "done no little harm in blunting, if not deadening, the moral and religious sense of not a few among the working population of our city".[69]

His letter caused upset to a number of Dublin workers. A response from Thomas O'Guinety, on his own behalf and that of "some working men", was probably indicative of the feelings of many. They thought it "terrible" that the archbishop should "lend his name to the doings of unscrupulous, petty politicians like Mr Sherlock". In eulogising him, his Grace was "condemning at least half of the population of the Mountjoy ward and upholding the system by which" they were "being crushed and degraded". If it had been left to them "to look to Mr Larkin for guidance", O'Guinety continued, it was not their fault. "No one raised a voice in our behalf previous to his coming. We are poor and weak and ignorant, and every interest is arrayed against us, but it is a just struggle we are engaged in, and the power of the church, the church of the poor as well as the rich, should not be thrown into the balance against us."[70]

A further occasion of disagreement with Larkin and his immediate followers arose in June 1914. Then the secretary of the Dublin United Trades Council, John Simmons, wrote asking the archbishop to receive a deputation with reference to a workers' union recently formed in Kingstown by Fr Flavin in opposition to an existing union affiliated to the Trades Council.[71] Walsh had his secretary contact Fr Patrick Flavin, who was a curate in Kingstown (Dun Laoghaire). Flavin presented a detailed report. The union in question, he declared, was one of unskilled labourers: coal workers – former members of the Transport Union who had refused to go on strike after a talk from Flavin, and left the union; municipal workers – who had left the Transport Union three and a half years ago; and builders' labourers – over 100 men affiliated to a central branch of their union in the city, who had got permission from central office to form their own branch. So over all there were more than 300 men "dissociated absolutely from all unions". They sent four representatives to him saying they wished to form a joint union "if he would stand in with them". He agreed, formulated the union's rules, which were approved, and the first general meeting was held successfully last week. The Trades Council was annoyed because he was in the union, had been "invited to come in". He had been attacked scurrilously the previous week in the *Irish Worker*, but he did not think the Trades Council would bring the matter to the archbishop. Flavin assured the secretary,

Michael Dwyer, that if he were withdrawn "the men will not go on without me, and the union will collapse, with the result that these poor men will be again at Larkin's mercy". The skilled workers, he concluded, "can work out their own destiny, but the poor, unskilled and frequently illiterate labourers require the advice and guidance of some priest", hence it would be a special pleasure for him to remain with them even though it would require "a whole lot of additional effort".[72]

Having received Flavin's reply, the archbishop gave a quietly resolute answer to the secretary of the Trades Council. He regretted that he could not accede to the request conveyed in his letter, and explained:

> A number of working men, in the exercise of their natural liberty, have chosen to leave a society with the working of which they were dissatisfied and to join a new one formed by them, or at their request, for that purpose. In all this, they are perfectly within their rights and I am not going to do anything that would hamper them in any way.

"If I were to receive a deputation, as you suggest, it would be taken to imply that I was prepared to do something of the sort."[73]

Despite such indications of differences with labour leaders, Walsh preserved his reputation as "the friend of the working man",[74] the supporter of the poor and oppressed. That reputation rested on a belief akin to that expressed by Shane Leslie in a letter to him on 7 November 1913.

> I cannot say how one's heart feels torn over this unhappy dispute. As a Catholic democrat and a Manningite, I believe that though most of our vaunted causes are wrong, yet that the poor are bound to have more justice in their's than the capitalists.[75]

Such belief had found expression in Walsh's comment to Aberdeen – "My sympathies are altogether with them", and in the varied manifestations of priority in his career where the oppressed and less well-off were concerned.

Meantime, while Dublin was enduring industrial unrest and Larkin and some of his followers were being put in gaol for relatively minor incitements to disorder, far more serious incitements were taking place in the north of Ireland without any response from the government. During 1914 the example set by Edward Carson in the north was to be followed in the south, with different consequences.

XIV

At the turn of the tide, 1914-15

The impetus to follow Carson's example came from an article by Professor Eoin MacNeill entitled "The North Began", which appeared in the Irish language publication *An Claidheamh Soluis* on 1 November 1913. He viewed the emergence of the defiant Ulster Volunteers as an assertion of autonomy against Britain which pointed the way to the rest of the country. The article evoked widespread interest, and was actively promoted by the Irish Republican Brotherhood (IRB). At an overflow meeting at the Rotunda rink on 25 November 1913, McNeill asserted that "they have rights who dare to maintain them" and called for the formation of a volunteer force.[1] Some 3,000 enrolled that evening. By May 1914 the number enrolled was to reach nearly 75,000.[2]

Carson's defiance had called for strong government action. Instead, the officers at the central army camp at the Curragh were given the option of resigning rather than "coerce" Ulster. They resigned. Their action was falsely termed a mutiny. "If you follow the documents", Curran, the archbishop's secretary, wrote in his unpublished statement on events from 1913 to 1921, which he presented to the Bureau of Irish Military History, "you will see there was no refusal on the part of [General Sir Hubert] Gough and other officers but that they accepted the alternative so indefensibly offered to them by the weak Asquith government."[3] The government signalled by its action that there would not be any coercion exercised against the Ulster Volunteers. On 24-25 April the latter successfully landed, unchallenged, a large consignment of guns at Larne. In response, active training became more focused among the Irish Volunteers; and a minority section under the aegis of the IRB secretly planned the purchase of guns in Germany.

Archbishop Walsh's health, meanwhile, had taken a further bad turn. Fr Curran, in his written statement to the Bureau of Military History, presented a serious picture:

> At the end of April 1914, the archbishop's health commenced to fail ... The state of his health largely incapacitated him for long periods from active work. In my diary I have noted that on the day of the Larne landing the archbishop was unable to go out of doors, and on the 28 April I have recorded that the first noticeable signs of failing health showed itself by a nervous shaking of his hands and that Dr Cox was called in.[4]

There are some discrepancies in his account. Walsh's own diary shows the doctor with him also early in the month, and as for "the first signs of failing health" shown "by a nervous shaking of his hands" this, as has been noted, had happened previously and had cleared up after a long holiday. Again, if Walsh was ill, as suggested, on 28 April, he was sufficiently well two days later to go on a motor journey of 95 miles – "Dublin, Trim, Navan, Drogheda, Gormanstown and home". Moreover, perhaps as a recuperative measure, he commenced the month of May with a car journey of some 101 miles through Wicklow; and for 5 May there is a diary entry of a journey to Bundoran, Co. Donegal, and from then until 16 May there were drives through the northern counties. The sea air at Bundoran had evidently been recommended by Dr Cox. On 13 May, Shane Leslie, having praised a change of air, remarked, "I do hope you have fully recruited at Bundoran. Ireland can hardly do without you at the turn of the tide."5 Walsh's diary, however, indicated that on his return he had visits from Dr Cox on 22 and 26 May, the 11 and 13 June, and 6, 16, and 18 July. Curran was accurate in his observation that the archbishop's health in 1914 "largely incapacitated him for long periods from active work". Walsh acknowledged this himself on 27 September 1914, when responding to Dom Patrick Nolan, OSB, of the Maredsous Benedictine monastery, who sought refuge in Ireland for that community following the invasion of Belgium. He commenced his letter with an uncharacteristic admission of weakness: "I have not been very well, and it is not every day I can apply myself to matters of serious importance, so I trust you will excuse my delay in writing."6

Being incapacitated, however, did not necessarily mean being confined to bed or that no work was done. For the first three months or so of 1914 business was conducted as usual, and there was a range of correspondence. The year commenced happily with joyful news from Australia, where Vincent O'Brien was on tour with the cathedral choir. "Australian audiences", O'Brien wrote, "are enthusiastic to the verge of hysterics." He added that the choir would have its first American concert on 4 February.7 Although Curran stated that Walsh experienced "a nervous shaking of the hands" on 28 April, he responded with a firm hand that day to a request from the lord mayor for advice and suggestions about a censor for cinema/ theatre, the appointment of which the corporation was contemplating. The office was not one, Walsh observed, "for which an ecclesiastic would be suited". He then explained: "Good cannot fail to result from the fact of having a censorship, with the knowledge that the proprietors of theatre will have that they are not at liberty to produce pictures that are likely to be objected to by reasonable, respectable people. I should hope that with this knowledge – at least after the censorship has been at work for a short time – there will be but little need for its direct intervention." As for Sunday opening, the archbishop had only one requirement, that the theatre would "not be allowed to be opened during the hours of public devotions in the churches".8

Despite his poor health in the summer months, he was coping once more with correspondence in his own hand by the end of September. This was evident in his informative letter to Dom Nolan, in which he apologised for his delay in responding. The Maredsous community was most welcome "to obtain a temporary refuge in this diocese", he assured Nolan, but he could not easily sanction a more permanent establishment. "There are 28 dioceses in Ireland", he explained. "There are 7 of these in which there is no religious house of men: in most of the others there are but very few, in some, indeed, only one or two: in Dublin there are, I think, 30 or close upon 30." But, he added, "coming to the practical question in hand, I cannot give you too strong an assurance that the securing of a temporary shelter in this diocese for the Maredsous community, during the continuance of the war, has my best encouragement and blessing".[9]

Among the many other letters dealt with were letters from Wilfrid Ward during November and December. These urged Walsh to express support for the allied side in the war which had commenced the previous August. To appreciate Walsh's stance it is necessary to return to the sequence of political events in Ireland earlier in the year, and to view them in the light of his national outlook.

In the months after the Larne gun-running in April the immediate focus of attention was the Home Rule bill. It was passed on 25 May. A month later, there was an amending bill allowing for the temporary exclusion of parts of Ulster. This gave rise to indignation and talk of betrayal throughout most of Ireland. On 14 March, for example, foreseeing the trend, James Connolly denounced "the depths of betrayal to which the so called nationalist politicians are willing to sink".[10] His strong views represented the sentiments of an increasing number of the population. Fearing the swing of power to the Volunteers, Redmond, on 9 June 1914, issued a public ultimatum demanding that twenty-five of his nominees be added to the governing provisional committee of the organisation. The extreme nationalist minority in the Volunteers yielded. They awaited guns which they had bought secretly in Hamburg with a view to an armed rising, and were determined to avoid a split before the arms arrived. Their arrival, they believed, would radically change the scene.

In July there were a series of significant occurrences in close succession. Efforts to solve the Ulster impasse failed at the Buckingham Palace conference, 21-24 July. Then on 26 July the long awaited arms for the Volunteers were landed at Howth, Co. Dublin. The Volunteers marched back to the city in high excitement, only to be stopped by the police and a military detachment. While their leaders parlayed with the police, individual Volunteers scattered with their weapons. Later, a contingent of Scottish Borderers, over-reacting to jeers and stoning from a hostile crowd at Bachelors Walk in the city, fired into the throng, killing three civilians and wounding many others. The resultant sense of outrage was fomented by exaggeratedly dramatic headlines in the *Irish Volunteer* publication of 1 August: "*Murder in the Streets of Dublin … Savage Soldiery … Women and Children Bayoneted … The Right to Arms is Ours and No Proclamation can Vitiate that Right*. The chain of events allowed the IRB to argue: "Arms were landed in the north unchallenged. In Dublin the British army fired on an unarmed crowd. Britain promised Home Rule, and has now reneged on the original promise and is prepared to dismember the country. You can't trust Britain. Nothing will be gained except by force of arms."[11] To stir emotions and anger, the drama of a public funeral was invoked.

Walsh, despite his poor health over the summer months, insisted on presiding at the requiem mass in University Church on 23 July for the vice-chancellor of the university and his long time colleague, who had deputised for him in his illnesses, Sir Christopher Nixon; and on responding actively to the special situation created by the Bachelor Walk shootings. The day before the funeral for those who were shot, he sent a letter to the press which deliberately sought to calm feelings. He also announced a contribution of £25 towards the Lord Mayor's Fund "to lighten, as far as may be, the blow that has fallen so heavily upon a number of our poor fellow-citizens from what would seem to have been the unprecedented action of a portion of the military force garrisoned in Dublin last Sunday evening."[12]

On 30 July he presided at the requiem mass for the victims in the pro-cathedral. The emotion of the occasion was captured vividly by an English correspondent.

> The bodies had been all night before the high altar in the Pro-cathedral. Watchers kept vigil through the darkness, and three tall candles burned on either side of the triple catafalque. A few simple flowers, such as the poor can afford, rested on the coffins ... At 11 o'clock this morning a solemn Requiem High Mass was celebrated in the presence of the Archbishop of Dublin, Dr Walsh ... Profound poverty was everywhere apparent, but so, too, was profound devotion.

This "gathering of the Catholic poor around the dead", the writer continued, ... "was a fitting prelude to the tremendous scene of a more crude and popular mourning later in the day."

The "more crude and popular mourning" later on, also greatly impressed the special correspondent. "Eight thousand men", he reported, more than half of them from the Irish Volunteers, walked in step in a remarkable funeral procession. "Six bands, over a hundred priests, and eighty carriages took part, and the procession took nearly an hour to pass the point" where he was standing.

The Dublin Corporation expressed its horror of the "savage crime", and requested "the dismissal of the permanent officials at Dublin Castle who were responsible ... for the calling out of the military", and an amendment was proposed "demanding the recall of Lord Aberdeen and the dismissal of Mr Birrell".[13]

The sense of public revulsion and anger were further inflamed by a statement from the British prime minister, Asquith, that he was sure that the military would be found blameless in the affair! Previous to the incident, the numbers of Volunteers had fallen considerably, perhaps because of absence of weapons, now recruits flocked to the movement. By September the force's strength was to rise to 180,000, and a steady flow of financial support from Irish-American organisations had commenced.[14] Within a few weeks, however, there was a serious split in the movement.

Three days after the Dublin funeral, Germany and France went to war. Britain was committed to supporting France. John Redmond pledged Irish support for the British war effort and offered the Volunteers as a force for the defence of Ireland. The following day, 4 August, the United Kingdom declared war on Germany. A month later the *Irish Volunteer* expressed the view of the more radical members of the Volunteer organisation, namely, that Ireland should not become involved in an international struggle until it acquired the status of a nation. Five days later, on 10 September, Eoin MacNeill warned that the danger to Ireland was not from Germany but from Britain. When the time came, he said, to put the Home Rule Act into operation, there would be "an English invasion of our rights and liberties".[15] As if in confirmation, Asquith, on 15 September, announced the postponement of the operation of Home Rule. To MacNeill and many others the postponement was but another instance of British duplicity towards Ireland. To Redmond it was welcome. In a time of war, he claimed, it was absurd to try to erect in Ireland a new government and a new parliament.[16] Believing in the allied cause, and that Ireland's participation in the war would prove Irish loyalty beyond any doubt, impress Tories, and build bridges with unionists, he threw himself with immense vigour into the recruiting campaign and, on 20 September, told a parade of Irish Volunteers at Woodenbridge, near his summer home in Co. Wicklow, that it would be a disgrace to their country if young Ireland shrank from the duty of displaying on the field of battle that gallantry and courage which had distinguished the Irish race all through its history.

The speech occasioned an immediate disavowal. At a special meeting of the original founders of the Volunteer movement, among them all the IRB representatives, the speech was repudiated and a statement to that effect, prepared by Eoin MacNeill, was signed by those present and issued to the press.[17]

Walsh was also among those who disagreed with Redmond's offer of Irish participation in the war. Curran, writing to John Hagan, the strongly nationalist vice-rector of the Irish College Rome, on 30 September 1914, conveyed his own vehement disagreement and that of Walsh.

> I can't tell you how disgusted I am too at the way things are going here. If Redmond said we should turn Protestant this morning there are people who would say we should. The very people who denounced the idea of Volunteers serving abroad, were upholding it a week later ... I need not say how disgusted my chief is re. this particular phase although he is mildly anti-German.[18]

It was left to the Volunteer companies around the country to determine their course of action. The vast majority followed Redmond. The split was formalised by their becoming the National Volunteers. The more radical minority formed their own organisation, in October 1914, and retained the name, Irish Volunteers.

A month earlier, a committee of the American Clan na nGael secretly informed the German ambassador in the United States that it was their intention to organise an armed revolt in Ireland, and asked for military assistance. This decision was communicated to the supreme council of the IRB who agreed that a rebellion should take place before the war ended.[19] The Irish Volunteer force available to carry out such a revolt was very small. The "Intelligence Notes" in police reports, in December 1914, reveal a total of 2,282 Irish Volunteers in all of Ulster; 2,448 in Leinster; in Connacht, 1,965; and 3,276 in Munster; giving an overall total of 9,971.[20] Volunteer commitment, however, seems to have been strong, and some at least were clear about what they wanted. One such, Seamus Hughes, pointed out persuasively in the *Irish Volunteer* on 3 October, in an article entitled "Imperialism versus Nationalism", that everywhere German imperialism was denounced for its attitude to small nations, but what, he asked, of British imperialism and Ireland? As for "poor little Belgium", those now leading the chorus were the same as those who six years previously threatened "little Belgium" because of "alleged rubber atrocities in the Congo."[21]

Against this background, and his own strong sense of nationality, Walsh was not likely to approach a world conflict expressing strong support for the British empire against another European empire. His secretary, Michael Curran, who often discussed political issues with the archbishop, has left his own impression of Walsh's outlook in these years. Curran's account, presented in the unpublished statement already mentioned, seems over simplified in places, and suffers at times, it would appear, from a retrospective view of history from a republican stand point, yet it remains valuable as the observations of one close to the archbishop. Beginning rather obviously with the comment that "the archbishop had lost faith in the Irish party long before the Larne gun-running and the formation of the Ulster Volunteers", Curran maintained rather sweepingly that Walsh "had thoroughly realised that constitutional methods to achieve reform were utterly useless. They had failed in the first place through the subservience of the Irish party to the English Liberals, aggravated by place hunting for their supporters. But the final blow came from the downright treasonable speeches and activities of the highest placed and more aristocratic members of the Tory governing classes of England and their unqualified support of the Ulster Volunteers." He added soberly, "Between the politicians at home and the new rebels in England and Ulster, it was plain there was no longer any prospect that the influence of men in the archbishop's position would carry the slightest weight. If they intervened in any way, their position was misunderstood and misrepresented."

With respect to the original Irish Volunteers, Walsh "disapproved at first", then "fluctuated from time to time" but "never believed that the movement would succeed in its objects. Characteristically, he always feared that some wild, irresponsible element would force matters to extremes and ruin the entire national cause. He became more and more pessimistic, as much in respect of the helplessness for the time being of Irish effort, as of the strength of the anti-Irish campaign in England." In Curran's view, Walsh respected Eoin MacNeill as a scholar, but had no belief in him "as a political and much less as a revolutionary leader ... He was disposed to smile at the scholar turned revolutionary". Redmond's manoeuvre to seize control the Volunteers, he "regarded ... as dishonest and typical of the party's unconstitutional and underhand practices".[22] The archbishop, Curran noted, subscribed to Arthur Griffith's *United Irishman*, which emphasised "Ourselves Alone – Sinn Fein" and which criticised the subservience of the Irish party.[23] All in all, his Grace was not predisposed to respond favourably to Wilfrid Ward's request to him on 24 November 1914.

He had been asked, Ward announced, "to write a pamphlet for circulation in some of the neutral countries – Spain, Italy and America – setting forth the inevitableness of the war and our efforts for peace". He enclosed a statement for the signature of representative Catholics which stated "that the war was forced on us by engagements which we could not violate without dishonour". It had been signed already by Cardinal Bourne of Westminister and several other English and Scotch bishops. Archbishop Healy of Tuam, too, had agreed to sign it, and Ward asked if his Grace also would see his way to signing it. He sent a similar type of letter again on 7 December.[24] At that stage Walsh replied. Curran noted on 15 December that the archbishops refused to sign the declaration "chiefly because it contained a number of sweeping statements, of which he had no knowledge as to whether they were true or untrue. For instance, the statement that England had done all it could to avoid war was discounted by the resignation of [John] Morley etc.".[25]

Ward made a further appeal, in the course of which he asserted that "a large proportion of the Irish hierarchy is signing" (in fact only three signed, all, in Curran's words, 'faithful followers of the Irish party'). He added that Morley was opposed to all war, not just the present one; and, sending his Grace a copy of the government's "White Paper", asked him to reconsider his decision. Ward concluded with the declaration that Britain was "bound in honour to take up arms in defence of a small state to which our word was so repeatedly pledged" and that, in consequence, the war in which it was engaged was "a just one".[26]

Walsh remained unimpressed, and took further steps of a neutral nature in the final months of 1914. According to Curran, he "peremptorily refused a request of the military to allow recruiting posters to be placed on the railings of the Catholic churches in Dublin and, as the recruiting became more active, he caused it to be known that this procedure met with his strong disapproval". Moreover, as Curran recalled, "he went so far as to discountenance war hospital and Red Cross collections. He believed that these activities should be financed by the government and that the appeals were being used for recruiting purposes".[27]

The new year opened more pleasantly for the archbishop. Abbot Columba Marmion of Maredsous, a former priest of the Dublin diocese, called on him on 5 January 1915; and on 13 and 15 January he was dealing with congenial topics – plans for a cathedral, and a correspondence recalling memorable musical occasions.[28] A few days later, however, Dr Cox was called in again. From 19 to 28 January the doctor visited regularly and Walsh seems to have been largely confined to the house. On 22 he noted in his diary: "Cold down to chest, not down for dinner". His recovery was marked by a motor drive on Saturday, 30 January, and the recovery continued throughout February. During March, Cardinal Logue wrote in his caring way: "I am very glad your Grace is all right again; but you need to be more cautious than heretofore. You cannot expect to be able, henceforward, to go through the hard grind to which you were accustomed to subject yourself in the past."[29]

Despite Cardinal Logue's advice about being "more cautious" in the volume of work he undertook, Walsh was once more "exceptionally busy with diocesan work" during February and March so that he fell behind with his correspondence.[30] Once again, his busy schedule was impinged on by recruiting considerations. Curran noted in his diary for 31 March that Fr Mooney, parish priest at Ringsend and chaplain to the Beggars' Bush barracks, "received a very curt letter this morning from Lieutenant-Colonel Owens, officer commanding the 3rd Royal Regiment at Beggars' Bush, intimating the intention of the military authorities to hold a military parade on Easter Sunday, with a religious service in the Cathedral, and asking for him to arrange an hour with the cathedral authorities. This was announced also in the newspapers of Thursday". Learning of the letter, "the Archbishop at once scribbled out the draft of an equally curt reply for Fr Mooney to sign:

> I have, of course, no authority to interfere in arrangements for services in the Pro-Cathedral. The matter has been brought to the notice of his Grace, the Archbishop, who directs me to express his surprise that the military authorities, without having even applied for permission to make use of that church, announce their "intention" of holding a parade service there, and I am to add that no such service can be held.

"On the following day", Curran continued, "Captain Butler, son of Sir William Butler" who was "a great friend and former class-fellow of the Archbishop, called on the Archbishop to express regret, on behalf of the military authorities, for the previous day's letter, and to say they were going into it. The Archbishop was very firm in his attitude and repeated his opinion of their action."[31]

A week later, Butler reversed roles – complaining strongly of "the aloofness of the clergy" towards "Irish soldiery in the present time of war". At mass there was scarcely any reference to the war. "The parish priest of Ringsend is never seen within the barrack precincts, his curate very rarely", yet "these Irish soldiers, your Grace, are not outcasts, pariahs, men of no account. They are heroes, next-to-martyrs, men worthy of all esteem and honour. They are fighting among other things for the liberty of the Catholic Church in Ireland. Also they are giving their lives to prevent young priests having to go to fight, as fight they have to do in continental armies". He hoped his Grace would read what he wrote in the filial spirit in which it had been written. He remembered that "long ago he had the happiness of being confirmed" by him.[32] Butler's patent concern for his men rendered his strong criticism palatable. On a more positive note, where Walsh was concerned, was a deeply appreciative letter three days later from Cardinal Mercier, the celebrated archbishop of Malines, expressing his thanks for the "signal liberality" of his Grace and his "venerable colleagues of the Irish episcopate", and assuring them that the memory of their "brotherly help will live on in Belgium".[33]

On 7 May, Walsh wrote cryptically in his diary "Lusitania down". In public he described the torpedoing of the Cunard liner, with the loss of nearly 12 hundred lives, as a "horrible massacre". To his intense annoyance, he found his words being used to promote recruiting. On 12 May, Curran noted that that evening the archbishop had received "a flaming, red and blue printed poster from the central council of the Organisation of Recruiting in Ireland saying that they had 'taken the liberty of producing it', that ... they submitted a copy for the Archbishop's approval ..."

The poster ran:

ARCHBISHOP OF DUBLIN
AND
The Sinking of the 'LUSITANIA'
Describing it
As
' That
HORRIBLE
MASSACRE.'
Germany says she will do it again.
Will YOU do YOUR Part to Prevent Her?
If so – Join an Irish Regiment
Offer Your Services ...

By return of post they received the archbishop's definite response that their council in producing the poster had "taken a very great liberty indeed", and that he reserved his right to take such action as he deemed fit if he found "the poster 'distributed' in the manner which" seemed "to be contemplated".[34] "On the following day the Archbishop received a letter from the Recruiting Council, saying that, in view of the terms of his Grace's letter, they would not produce the poster, and that they had destroyed what copies they had of it."[35]

Walsh became so opposed to recruiting in Ireland that he refused to have anything to do with anything related to it. "Thus, he refused to attend a meeting to provide comforts and entertainments for the soldiers, although asked to do so in a personal letter from Lord Aberdeen."[36] This attitude hardened even more after the formation of a new British cabinet on 19 May. The Liberal cabinet was superseded by a coalition one, which included eight unionists, among them Bonar Law as secretary of state for the Colonies, Sir Edward Carson, attorney-general, and F.E. Smith, outside the cabinet as solicitor-general. Thus the most reckless and vehement rebels against the British government had been rewarded with highly influential positions, and with them lay the future of Home Rule. It was a dismissal of Irish national aspirations. "It is impossible", Birrell later told the Royal Commission investigating the 1916 Rising, "to describe or over-estimate the effect of this in Ireland. The fact that Mr Redmond could, had he chosen to do so, have sat in the same Cabinet with Sir Edward Carson, has no mollifying influence. If Mr Redmond had consented, he would, on the instant, have ceased to be an Irish leader. This step seemed to make an end of Home Rule, and strengthened the Sinn Feiners enormously all over the country."[37] That his view was accurate was made evident by Bishop Michael Fogarty of Killaloe in words that conveyed the disquiet and sense of betrayal which swept the country: "Home Rule is dead and buried, and Ireland is without a national party ..." He further prophesied that there would ultimately be a bloody feud between the people and the soldiers.[38] "In Ireland, whenever constitutional and parliamentary procedure cease to be of absorbing influence", Birrell observed, "other men, other methods, other thoughts, before somewhat harshly snubbed, come rapidly to the surface, and secure attention, sympathy and support."[39] The numbers in the Irish Volunteers increased, and there was a determination within that force to resist disarmament; while outside as well as within there was opposition to conscription.

To increase the spirit of resistance, the leaders of the Irish Volunteers turned again to the tradition of a patriotic funeral. The old Fenian, Jeremiah O'Donovan Rossa, who had suffered intensely in English prisons, had died in America. A symbol of resistance to England, to bring his body home would have immense emotional impact, especially now when disillusionment was widespread and the government was provocatively arresting people who spoke out against recruitment. The secretaries of the O'Donovan Rossa funeral committee wrote to the archbishop on 16 July informing him that the remains would arrive in Dublin about 27 or 28 July, and that a deputation had been appointed to wait on his Grace to obtain permission "to have the remains deposited in St Kevin's chapel in the pro-cathedral from the date of its arrival until Sunday, August 1, on which date it is proposed to have the public funeral".[40]

Faced with such an awkward request, Walsh made several drafts of a reply before sending one which expressed his interest and desire to assist, if the obstacles were not insurmountable. "There could, of course, be no difficulty in complying with your request if what you wished to have done could be brought within the limits within which alone the use of St Kevin's chapel can be granted in connection with funerals." He then went on to outline the obstacles: the chapel's use for baptisms and marriages, the disturbance to confessions by the great crowds visiting the remains, and so on.[41] The secretaries, now signing themselves in English, E.J. Kickham and John R. Reynolds, made a masterly response. They thanked him "for the courtesy of so prompt a reply" and added:"It has given us very great pleasure – and we are certain that vast numbers of our fellow-countrymen near and far will feel very grateful – to receive this assurance from your Grace that if what we wish to have done can be brought within the limits circumscribing the use for funerals for which St Kevin's chapel can be granted there will be no difficulty in acceding to our request. We anticipate the thrill of gratitude and pride that will circle the world when it becomes known that the principal church in the capital of his land has been the penultimate resting place of O'Donovan Rossa."[42] Thus, cleverly impaled, the archbishop was relieved at the subsequent decision to have the body lie in state in Dublin City Hall, and was pleased that it be brought to the pro-cathedral for a solemn requiem mass.

After the mass, the vast cortege – in which the National Volunteers and the Irish Volunteers marched together for the first and final time – moved on to Glasnevin cemetery, where Patrick H. Pearse was the orator. Encouraged by the old Fenian, Tom Clarke, to "make it hot as hell, throw all discretion to the winds",[43] Pearse's address was to be one of the magic moments of oratory in Ireland's history. It added immeasurably to his eminence and influence. Standing erect at O'Donovan Rossa's grave side, in the uniform of a Volunteer, his hand resting on his sword-hilt, he delivered the melodious words of challenge which were to be recited by succeeding generations, especially the defiant conclusion.

> Life springs from death; and from the graves of patriot men and women spring nations. The Defenders of this Realm have worked well in secret and in the open. They think they have pacified Ireland ... They think they have provided against everything; but the fools, the fools, the fools! – they have left us our Fenian dead, and while Ireland holds these graves, Ireland unfree shall never be at peace.

The speech was followed by the firing of a volley over the grave. Pearse's funeral oration proved an immediate sensation. Even the *Freeman's Journal* published the full text.[44]

The speech's significance, however, ultimately owed more to later events. The majority of Pearse's contemporaries still seemed to trust that the best way

forward lay in winning the war and thereby securing Home Rule. Those, moreover, who had husbands or sons in the army or navy had little sympathy for
those who talked revolution, or criticised those who had gone to fight "a foreign
war". Curran himself admitted in his submission to the Military History Bureau
that then he did not take Pearse seriously. From his own contacts in nationalist
ranks he was fully convinced, and represented to the archbishop, "that Pearse,
who, we knew, was determined to force a rising at any cost, whether in the case
of disarmament or otherwise, had such a small body of followers that he would
not be able to carry out his intentions". "That", he added, "was the position as
it seemed to me, and to most interested observers."[45] He did not know that
Pearse had assumed a position of real importance in the IRB, nor did Augustine
Birrell, the chief secretary.

There was disagreement among the leadership of the Irish Volunteers as to
how the force available to them might be used. The majority of the central executive wished "to build up the Volunteers into a powerful organisation, and to
resort to guerrilla tactics if and when attacked". A minority, in strategic positions, openly supported this policy while secretly planning an insurrection. The
same minority acted in a similar fashion with the supreme council of the IRB,
by-passing the council in effect. Hence, the plans for the 1916 rising were to be
largely the work of a small group of IRB men, some of whom also held positions
in the Volunteer executive. Funds for the project came from the United States
and were channelled through two of the minority section of the IRB, Thomas
Clarke and Sean MacDermott.[46]

None of this, of course, was known to Archbishop Walsh, though he was
well informed on developments among the general body of Volunteers, thanks
to Curran, who was a close friend of Sean T. O'Ceallaigh and other members of
the movement. From mid-September, indeed, until well into 1916, Curran was
to be almost his Grace's sole source of outside information, as his activities were
greatly restricted by a protracted and new debilitating ailment. His political
interests were now focused on developments other than those which concerned
the Irish party and the parliament at Westminster. On the Irish party he had
become almost openly dismissive, as Denis Gwynn experienced when he wrote
to him concerning his new weekly paper, *New Ireland*. Walsh explained bluntly
why he would not be subscribing to the paper. Because of the working alliance
between the leaders of the Irish parliamentary party and the late government, he
had, for a considerable time, found it impossible to take any further interest in
Irish politics. He was so saddened and sickened by government appointment
after government appointment, "due to the active intervention of some of our
leading politicians", that he had long since given up reading articles or letters
touching upon the political situation in Ireland. He never could have thought
thirty years ago when he came to Dublin as archbishop, he concluded, that he
"should live to see the great bulk of the nationalists of Ireland so hopelessly
misled by palpable misrepresentation of the obvious facts" as he saw today.[47]

This letter is given by Curran without a date. Presumably it was written before September 1915, after which all but the most necessary correspondence seems to have been avoided.

The first sign of a long illness was heralded in Walsh's diary on 3 September by the brief entry "Dr Cox". It occurs again on 16 and 24 September, and from 26 September to the end of November, the doctor called almost every day. Curran explained in part the nature of the affliction. "On the 24 September 1915, I have recorded in my diary the beginning of a long and serious attack of eczema which affected the Archbishop for more than twelve months. His condition varied at times. At this particular time it became so serious that his legs and arms had to be bandaged."[48] There was some relief on 22 October and 4 November when he was brought on a motor drive. On 8 November there was the first reference to a skin specialist, Dr O'Brien. After that visit, Walsh seems to have been confined to bed, and Cox continued to call daily. On 15 November, Cardinal Logue was mentioned as calling. Three days later, however, one of Walsh's secretaries, Michael O'Dwyer, noted, "Face terribly swollen". On Tuesday 21 November, following a visit from Cox and O'Brien, O'Dwyer observed, "much recovered". O'Brien called once more before the end of the month. Cox called each day until the end of November and then was not mentioned until the end of December.

Walsh would seem, therefore, to have received a remission or partial recovery by the beginning of December, but the indications are that his movements remained restricted. Robert Browne, bishop of Cloyne, wrote to him on 19 December – "I was sorry to hear recently that your Grace is still confined to your room, but it is gratifying to learn that your ailment is in no way serious."[49] Three days after Christmas, Dr O'Brien was back with Cox. The latter came again on 29 and with O'Brien on 30 December, and on his own again on new year' eve. So 1915 ended in illness. The ailment was to continue through the greater part of the pivotal year, 1916. Walsh was now in his 75th year.

XV

The archbishop's household and 1916

The Easter Rising of 1916, its prelude and aftermath, has been explored in numerous books and countless articles, and commemorated in poetry and in song. As the event drew near, while it was going on, and in the immediate aftermath, it would not have been surprising if Archbishop Walsh, given his long record of pride in nationhood and the respect felt towards him as archbishop, played a prominent role as dissuader, adviser, intercessor. It is the kind of part he relished. He liked to be prominent, as has been seen, to contribute and have a say in most situations. The agony and tragedy for him was that he was physically almost entirely cut off from outside contact during nearly all of 1916. The disfiguring and weakening nature of the new ailment, a virulent form of eczema, tended to drive him in on himself, and at times he must have wondered if the malady would ever subside. For a sensitive, vain man, careful of his appearance, it was a disheartening and depressing experience. He was dependent almost entirely on his secretaries, and especially, as has been seen, on the well connected Curran, for information from the outside. One result of the ordeal was that it curbed to a large extent his tendency to rush into print.

This view of 1916 will be almost entirely from the perspective of the archbishop's household; and will be largely based on entries in Archbishop Walsh's diary, sometimes kept by one of the secretaries, on letters received and letters dictated by him, and especially on Curran's valuable recollections of Walsh's illness against the background of the rising.

THE PRELUDE

The diary entries for January indicate daily visits from Dr Cox and frequent visits from Dr O'Brien, the skin specialist. Occasionally visitors were permitted. Thus, Bishop Brownrigg and Canon Pettit are mentioned on 12 January, and Cardinal Logue on 18 January. On that date, Walsh's secretary noted – "Face swollen". Yet the following day he was described as "clearly improving". Over the next few days, Walsh saw his vicar general, and his close friends Fr Healy and Canon Dunne. On Tuesday, 25 January, Curran recorded – "Archbishop came down to study. First time since Nov. 8th", 1915.[1] On 31 January, nevertheless, he had a "bad night. Bilious". These few words merited a letter from Curran to Cardinal Logue on 3 February 1916, informing him that Archbishop Walsh desired him to mention "that although the attack from which he has been suffering so long had practically passed away, he was completely prostrated on

Tuesday by a most severe bilious attack. Dr Cox is not at all uneasy about it, but absolutely forbids him to attend to any business, or even to give a thought to it". "Fortunately, before the attack came on ", Curran added, "his Grace had made all arrangements with Browne and Nolan for the printing of the canonisation papers that have yet come to hand."[2]

Dr Cox, in fact, called twice a day from 1 to 5 February. On 8 February, Walsh was described as "much better", and though the doctor continued to call each day, the archbishop saw a limited number of people, but cancelled anything involving much effort such as the Catechism Committee on 17 February. He continued, however, with necessary correspondence on diocesan and university matters. Walsh's physical improvement continued into March, though he remained confined to the house. Then on 29 March, Curran recorded in his diary: "New phase in the Archbishop's illness. Visited by Dr Cox. Was not feeling well. In bed. Both arms discharging. Temperature high." Subsequently, he added in his statement for the Military History Bureau: "From this date the eczema became widespread and most depressing in its effects. He suffered from it very severely for most of the year, 1916."[3] The archbishop's diary indicates that on 29 March his leg was "bad" and Cox called. On 5 April, he was obliged to stay in bed. Thereafter, he was visited by Drs Cox and O'Brien together on several days. There was clearly a sense of crisis. April, indeed, was to be a month of manifold stress.

On 15 April Patrick J. Little of the *New Ireland* office passed on a document, said to be from the files of Dublin Castle, which revealed a plan, involving the use of military forces, to arrest all members of the Sinn Fein National Council and all executive members of the Volunteers, Irish and National. Whole areas of the city were to be sealed off, and certain premises were to "be isolated, and all communication to or from prevented.", and these included "premises known as Archbishop's House, Drumcondra; Mansion House, Dawson Street".[4] Little believed the plan was to provoke armed resistance from the Volunteers and cause bloodshed. Curran passed on the information to the archbishop. Eoin MacNeill, perhaps out of concern for Walsh's health, did not approach Archbishop's House, but on 18 April wrote to Bishop O'Donnell of Raphoe, known for his ability and nationalist sympathies, outlining the details of the plan, the likelihood of "wholesale arrests, comprising several hundred persons in Dublin and throughout the country", and mentioning that "the Archbishop of Dublin is to be held a prisoner in his house, and forbidden all access to his clergy and people."[5] The Castle denied that the document was genuine,[6] but anxiety continued in the Volunteer leadership that disarmament was planned.

On 21 April, Curran noted "a further complication" in the archbishop's health. "His condition was getting worse and worse". That same day, Good Friday, James MacNeill, brother of Eoin, called to Archbishop's House and said that two men had called on Eoin and left him very upset. James said the situation was critical, and he sought to find out if there was "any hope of obtaining an unofficial assurance ... that no disarmament was intended". Curran responded, "I shall see the Archbishop, who, however, could hardly do anything." James made it clear that he was not sent by Eoin, "who said he would not disturb the archbishop when sick". Curran explained the steps he then took to deal with what was clearly a critical situation, and, which, unknown to him, probably referred to the visit to Eoin MacNeill by Pearse and some others to inform him of their plans for a rebellion, made independently of him, and of the expected landing of German arms the following day in Kerry. It was vital in the circumstance to know if the government planned to move and when. Nobody was allowed to see the Archbishop, Curran explained. His Grace at that point "was swathed in bandages from head to foot ... His malady was at its climax." "I knew", he added, "that Dr Cox was a friend of the MacNeills, that he was also a privy councillor and had access to the Castle, that, if anybody could act as an intermediary, he could, and that, if he were fortified by a talk with the Archbishop, it might strengthen his hand. I suggested this to James MacNeill and he accepted it. I said I would tell the Archbishop everything he had told me and the suggestion I had made about Dr Cox and that the latter would doubtless speak to him on the matter in the morning. Of course, I intended to see Dr Cox beforehand and speak about it." Curran then added: "I told the Archbishop all about James MacNeill's visit. He listened carefully but said nothing that night. Next morning I had a conversation on the James MacNeill visit with Dr Cox on his arrival, telling him that the Archbishop would be prepared to discuss the matter with him. He did so, but the attitude the Archbishop took was that he would not interfere."[7]

During that week the Volunteers and the Citizen Army had been conducting exercises and field manoeuvres openly. The Citizen Army, in Curran's view, was particularly provocative, marching each night and carrying out a planned programme "such as the seizure of all the canal bridges around about the city. One night they actually surrounded the Castle. It was not to be expected that the Castle authorities would remain inactive". Many moderate people, he remarked, were alienated by these incidents, Curran himself among them, fearing "that extremists wished to precipitate events". "Naturally", he declared, "I reported these things to the Archbishop. He considered such actions as the height of folly."[8] There had been talk of the possibility of an uprising with the help of German weapons, but neither his Grace nor Curran had any idea that Roger Casement was to land with the arms on the Kerry coast the following day, Holy Saturday, and that this was to be the signal to turn the country-wide parades arranged for Easter Sunday into an occasion for revolution.

Curran, in his report of that time, commented that his diary for Holy Saturday mentions the early morning religious ceremonies, and then Dr Cox's visit and his finding the archbishop "dull and without appetite".[9] Also mentioned was a visit from a curate, Fr Joe McArdle of the pro-cathedral, who was "in some agitation". He came to report that a Volunteer officer had told him that "the Easter Sunday mobilisation meant a rising". At this stage there were already rumours in Dublin about the failure to land German arms, and Casement's arrest. Curran later explained in his report: "I did not tell the Archbishop about the priest's visit or his information. I told him about the Volunteer Easter manoeuvres, Casement and the rumours in town. He took it very calmly, like a man who saw the inevitable but who had no power to alter events, who felt that both British and Volunteers were more or less equally responsible for the situation of the moment. Physically, he could do nothing in the condition he was in."[10]

On Easter Sunday, Eoin MacNeill issued an order countermanding the Volunteer mobilisation parades for that day. Notice of the cancellation appeared in the *Sunday Independent*. "I felt greatly relieved", Curran commented, "that there was some breathing space". Copies of a letter from Eoin MacNeill authenticating the order of cancellation, were brought to Archbishop's House. Curran went at once to Walsh "and told him of the new development. Of course, he said that he could not do anything; and my recollection is", Curran added, "that he said it was too late now, as whatever had been done had brought matters to a head". He had no objection, however, to Curran going to the priests "of the nearer mobilisation districts" to deliver the letters to various Volunteer assembly points.[11]

THE RISING

In Walsh's diary for Easter Monday, 24 April, the entries are: "'Rising'; Cox came at 11.15; Count Plunkett at 12.15; 1.0 Jas. O'Connor." Curran's recollections, however, are far more circumstantial. He wrote: "Easter Monday, 1916, was a holiday, everybody taking a sleep. I have a note in my diary that Dr Cox called at a quarter-past eleven in the morning." At 11.30 Curran encountered, at the garage, Mr Quinn from Dublin Castle, There was still no news of a rising. Towards noon a page-boy came down to the garage, where Curran was talking to Quinn, to inform Curran that Count Plunkett had called and was waiting to see him. "At five minutes past twelve" he interviewed the count, who said he had come to see the archbishop. Curran "informed him that the Archbishop was ill in bed and that nobody was allowed to see him except the doctor". The Count said it would suffice if Curran passed on the message. It was a bizarre message, offering an insight into the contemporary culture of violence.

"Count Plunkett then told me", Curran related, "that there was going to be a rising, that he had been to see the Pope and that he had informed Benedict XV of the whole Irish situation and the intended insurrection." He told the pope that the rising would take place on Easter Sunday, that his Holiness "should not be shocked or alarmed" as the movement "was purely a national one for independence, the same as every nation has a right to". At the end of his interview with the pope, he asked "his blessing for the Volunteers", emphasising that "the leaders of the movement" wished "to act entirely with the goodwill, or approval – I forget which now – of the pope, and to give an assurance that they wished to act as Catholics. It was for that reason they came to inform his Holiness." The pope, not surprisingly, was "perturbed", "and asked could their object not be achieved in any other way, and counselled him to see the *archbishop*". Curran added, that he had a letter from Monsignor Hagan, of the Irish College Rome, confirming that the interview with the pope had taken place.[12]

While he was talking with Plunkett, the telephone rang. It was a call from a jeweller, a Mr Stokes, to say "that the GPO was seized by the Volunteers and the Castle was attacked, and he asked could the Archbishop stop it. I told him", Curran observed, "that was impossible, but that I would go down town." He added:

> I had to hasten up and *tell the Archbishop* all about Count Plunkett's report and the telephone news of the seizure of the GPO. He (Walsh) thought less of the poor Count than of Eoin Mac Neill. He looked on the Count as a simple soul and could not conceive a man like him being at the head of a revolution as it really was. Never in my life did I tell so much or [make] so grave a report in such a brief time.

Curran then told the archbishop that he would go down town. He did not say that he had had a message to meet Sean T. O'Ceallaigh at Rutland Square, nor that he planned to visit the GPO.[13]

He met O'Ceallaigh at 25 Parnell Square "as cool as you could imagine". He told of "what had happened the evening before and that Pearse had determined to go on with the rising". Curran was surprised to hear that the organisation had made Sean T. a "captain in the intelligence department". Previously he had assumed his views were similar to his own, now he was not sure. Curran cycled on to the GPO.

> There were several hundred people, perhaps over a thousand, between Abbey Street and Henry Street. I saw Mr Rock, one of the officials in the GPO, who described how the Volunteers had marched in and ejected the entire staff out to the street. I asked him to bring my bicycle over to the pro-cathedral presbytery. The first person I saw in the portico outside the GPO was James Connolly in uniform, with a huge colt revolver, shouting out orders. Volunteers were battering out window panes. When James Connolly saw me, he called out, "All priests may pass!", as the Volunteers were keeping the inquisitive on-lookers at some distance. The crowd then showed comparatively little excitement.

Curran went in, asked for Pearse, whom he found "flushed but calm and authoritative". He told Curran that there was nothing to be done, "we are going to see it out". "Some of the boys would like to go to confession," Pearse said, and asked him to send word over to the cathedral. Curran went to the pro-cathedral, told them the archbishop knew of the situation, and arranged for a priest to go to the GPO. At that point, as he recalled, "I telephoned Archbishop's House, reported all the information I had, saying I would remain on". He added, with no apparent sense of incongruity, "I took lunch at the Gresham Hotel"; less than 100 yards from the GPO![14]

About 1.00 p.m. he noted that a squadron of Lancers appeared from near the Rotunda rink, some 100 to 150 men. "Riding up upper O'Connell Street in single file, the first two who passed the Pillar (Nelson's Pillar) were shot in the throat. Either four or six were killed. I attended one, but he was dead. He had a medal." People called him to attend the fallen Lancer, thinking he was a Catholic because he was wearing a miraculous medal, "but", Curran added, "at that time hundreds of English Protestant soldiers wore Catholic medals as charms".[15]

Before 2.00 p.m. the crowds on the street had greatly increased in numbers, and looting had begun. "At first all the ringleaders were women; then the boys came along. Later, about 3.30 p. m., when the military were withdrawn from the Rotunda, young men arrived and the looting became systematic and general ", and all efforts to stop it proved in vain.[16] What impressed Curran "most unfavourably, was the frivolity and recklessness of the crowd, most of all of the women and children."[17] Because of this, he prevailed on Dr Walsh to issue a public letter urging people to stay off the street for their own safety.[18] The Dublin Metropolitan Police, Curran observed, were not fired on by the Volunteers. "Their fight was against the British".[19]

Each day during the week he recorded the condition of the archbishop and the course of the rising.

On Easter Tuesday, there was just sporadic firing. "Dr Cox and Dr O'Brien called at 2.30 p.m. – leaving at 3.20 p.m. As the Archbishop was disappointed and discouraged by the failure of the medical treatment, he asked me to arrange with Dr Cox to invite Dr O'Carroll to be called in for consultation. Dr Cox fell in with this suggestion."[20] On Wednesday, Curran noted: "The Archbishop removed today to the drawing-room. The doctors were unable to come. This was his first day out of the bedroom since April 1st." The brief entry in the Archbishop's diary provided a further item of information – "Firing Liberty Hall. Went into drawing-room." This referred to the shelling of Liberty Hall by gun-boat from the river.

"Minnie Ryan (later Mrs Richard Mulcahy) and Phyllis Ryan"(later Mrs Sean T. O'Ceallaigh), Curran observed, "called on the Archbishop at 2.00 p.m. to say that the military were firing on the Red Cross post at Clery's (department store), and asked Curran whether the Archbishop could take steps to dissuade the military from doing so". Curran could not offer any hope "as the military showed a strong disposition to ignore all requests from any quarter". "At 2.30 p.m.", he added, "I went home, 211 North Circular Rd., between Grangegorman and Cattle Market, by Iona Rd and Cabra Rd." On the way he met Seamus Hughes, who was appointed to the Volunteer force holding Jacob's factory at the other end of town and was perhaps visiting his wife and family at Iona Road. He commented: "Mr Hughes told me that the reason why Amiens Street station was not seized was because that duty was left to the Ulster Volunteers. They arrived in mufti and were to have been armed on arrival. By some mischance, the arms were not at hand and nothing could be done." Curran personally observed inept attempts by Volunteers to use explosives to blow up a bridge. This confirmed his earlier impression of lack of training and competence.[21]

A fire at Laurence's premises, Upper O'Connell Street, threatened the pro-cathedral. "The fire brigade", Curran recalled, "was ordered by the military not to go out." The administrator of the cathedral telephoned Archbishop's House to request the Archbishop to procure the intervention of the Viceregal Lodge. The archbishop permitted Curran to do so. "After consultation with General French, the Viceregal [representatives] agreed to do their best [to allow the fire brigade to save the pro-cathedral], but nothing was done about the matter."[22] In the event, the cathedral was saved by a change in the wind.[23]

On the Wednesday, Curran complained again about the number of people on the streets despite instructions to keep away. But on Thursday, 27 April, he commented: "Very few in O'Connell Street." There was continual sniping fire. Then, at Archbishop's House they had their first experience of fire. "Towards 11.0 a.m.", he wrote, "fierce rifle fire took place here (Drumcondra). We counted several bullets singing by the gate lodge and the house. Later on, one struck the house and several sang over it." The bullet that struck the house pierced "the east window of the billiard room, now the Archbishop's room," and "was deflected to the left against an open bookcase ... In consequence, we arranged for the Archbishop to sleep on the north side, and barricaded the windows with mattresses".[24] On Thursday also, Curran reported, "the city fires are extending and look most alarming at darkness. O'Connell Street is burned from Abbey St to Eden Quay". "A third, small centre of fire, is the Provincial Hotel opposite the Four Courts." "Martial law was proclaimed yesterday", he added. Nevertheless, people crowded the streets after 7.30 p.m.[25]

There was an air of inevitability about the entry for Friday, 28 April. "Whole districts are without provisions – milk, butter, bread or meat." "The military shot an incendiary shell into the GPO and set it ablaze. The sight at night was most impressive. Firing had almost ceased, and everything was deadly quiet and black except the fires in O'Connell Street and Linenhall Barracks. An occasional shot from a neighbouring sniper alone disturbed the quietness of a lovely, calm, starry night."[26]

About the next day, Saturday, 29 April, there was more life in Curran's narrative, but it remained calm overall and largely detached. At 4 o'clock the phone rang in the secretary's office, Archbishop's House, and a girl's voice said abruptly, and then rang off – "The Sinn Feiners have surrendered." "I at once informed the Archbishop", Curran declared, "and it was arranged that I would go down to the pro-cathedral for information and with instructions." He walked down by Mountjoy Square and North Great George's Street. Nobody seemed to know anything about a surrender. The Archbishop was worried about his priests. To discover what was the actual situation was one of Curran's tasks. A Fr John Sullivan was alleged [incorrectly] to have been killed. Curran walked on by Cathedral Street and, as he recalled vividly, "emerging into O'Connell Street I witnessed an indescribable sight. There was not a soul but myself in the whole street. The GPO was a mere shell. The left hand side (east) of Lower O'Connell Street was a smoking ruin. The right hand side was little better. Clery's was burnt out and the DBC [Dublin Bakery Co.] also was a shell. The smell of burning materials pervaded everywhere. Smoke hung low about. The dead Lancer's horse lay killed at the foot of Nelson's Pillar, as I had seen it on Monday …The silence was deadly …"[27] At the Parnell Monument he met Colonel Portal, a commanding officer, who informed him of the surrender, and showed him six copies of the order of surrender signed by Pearse.[28]

On Monday, 1 May, Fr John Flanagan, from the Pro-Cathedral, who had been marooned in the GPO, called on the archbishop "to give him all the news" from his special vantage point. Next day, the Capuchin, Fr Aloysius, who had been prominent in attending to the wounded and dying during the week, called on the Archbishop at 5.00 p.m.[29] and gave him an account of the last stages of the fighting at the Four Courts, Jacob's Factory, and the South Dublin Union. Field Marshal Sir John Maxwell, commander of the British forces, had informed Aloysius that he wished to meet the archbishop. Aloysius passed on the message to his Grace, who asked Curran to make arrangements for a meeting with Maxwell. That evening came news of the arrest of Eoin MacNeill.[30]

Wednesday, 3 May, was a day of special significance for the future. "Pearse, McDonagh and Clarke", Curran wrote, "were court martialled yesterday and shot this morning at 3.30 at Kilmainham. The remains were brought at once to Arbour Hill military prison and buried, uncoffined, in a trench, 60 feet long. Fr Francis Farrington read the burial service over them at 4 o'clock."[31]

He then reported:

> Sir John Maxwell called on the Archbishop with Lord Decies, his aide-de-camp, at 11.30 a.m. He spoke of the bravery of the Capuchins on the one hand and, on the other hand, of the number of priests whom he accused of participation in the rising. Maxwell wanted to deport them straightway, and was apparently under the impression that the Archbishop could do this himself. On learning the names of the priests concerned, the Archbishop pointed out that he had no jurisdiction in the matter, as no Dublin priests' names appeared on his list. He advised

Maxwell to consult their bishops and, noting the presence of 2 Limerick priests' names, *had a little malicious pleasure in anticipating the reply he would receive from Dr O'Dwyer.*[32]

O'Dwyer had already demonstrated small sympathy for the war effort. "Any fair-minded man ", he declared in a public letter, "will admit that it is England's war, not Ireland's".[33]

Finally on that eventful day, "at 7.00 p.m., Miss Gavan Duffy called to ask the archbishop to request that the bodies of Pearse and the others who were executed be given to their relatives. The archbishop said he believed the military would not do so, in order to prevent demonstrations. He did not say he had already been twice refused what he had asked of the military."[34]

THE LONG AFTERMATH

The succeeding days made melancholy reading. On 4 May, Curran recorded: "Wholesale arrests are being made ... A kind of mild reign of terror reigns. Everybody is afraid to express his views. Martial law is supreme, and people must be in their houses at 7.30 p.m. or they will be fired upon".[35] That day the first Irish papers reappeared. People waited up all night for the appearance of the *Independent* to learn what had happened and was happening. Its editorial on 4 May was headed "Criminal Madness", and went on: "No term of denunciation ... would be too strong to apply to those responsible for the insane and criminal rising of last week. Around us, in the centre of Ireland's capital, is a scene of ruin which is heart-rending to behold." These men, it continued, were "the willing dupes of Prussian intrigue". And having criticised Birrell's ineffective government, the violence and irresponsibility of Carson, the paper called for leniency for "the young fellows under 21 who were innocently caught up in the rising", but added – "the leaders who organised, and the prominently active spirits in this rising, deserve little consideration or compassion".

On 5 May, the archbishop's diary introduced a new medical specialist, Sir Joseph Redmond, who seems to have taken over the entire treatment of his Grace. Dr Cox's name does not feature after 2 May. Redmond called every three or four days during May; only once during June; not at all in July; twice in August; and once in September. Evidently he succeeded where others failed. Curran's account for that day, 5 May, noted the execution of Major John McBride. He added the information that three weeks later, on 27 June, at Annamoe, Co. Wicklow, where Dr Walsh was recuperating, Tim Healy told the archbishop that the colonel or officer at the head of the court martial informed him that McBride greatly impressed the officers. "He simply said, ' I knew nothing of the rising until Easter Monday. I am a man of action. I joined the Volunteers. I knew we could not hold out 3 days. We held out six. I know the forfeit is death. Good evening'."[36]

On 6 May all the newspapers paid tribute to the fearlessness of the Catholic priests in ministering to the wounded and dying, irrespective of the danger, in all the areas where the fighting raged.[37] The papers, moreover, highlighted the problems in the archbishop's parish, in the area of the Pro-Cathedral. Not only was there danger from fire on the nights of Thursday and Friday, there was the problem of dealing with refugees and their needs as they flocked to the vestry and cathedral seeking shelter "from burning buildings and shell and rifle fire". "Their terror was evident in their piteous appeals". Over forty were catered for in the vestry. "The fierceness of the fighting in and about Marlborough Street" was such "that no less than ten civilians were shot dead in the streets".[38]

Archbishop Walsh was annoyed that day, 6 May, to have the *Daily Mail* attribute to him a letter written by Archbishop Bernard, the Church of Ireland archbishop of Dublin. Walsh wrote to the *Freeman* and *Independent* to draw their attention to the error. It was an embarrassing attribution, for Bernard had demanded the continuation of martial law and stern measures, pronouncing that "this is not the time for amnesties and pardons: it is the time for punishment swift and stern". He reflected, in Curran's view, the talk of Dublin unionists.[39]

Walsh's own view on the rising later came in for disputed representation from the pen of the former law officer of the crown, a prominent Catholic, James O'Connor (later Sir James) in his *History of Ireland, 1798-1924*. At Fairyhouse races on Easter Monday, O'Connor heard of the rising. He hurried back to Dublin, and about six o'clock called at Archbishop's House. His Grace received him in a room adjoining his bedroom. During the brief interview, Walsh, according to O'Connor, expressed his "detestation" of the rising. This was strongly disputed by P.J. Walsh in his biography of the archbishop. He declared that he went into the Archbishop's room after O'Connor had left, and was given his Grace's version of what took place. O'Connor, according to Dr Walsh, was excited and panicky. He asked his Grace to write a letter calling on the insurgents to desist from their mad enterprise etc. The Archbishop declined to do so, and declared the suggestion preposterous. He characterised as absurd and foolish the proposal to ask men who had actually taken up arms to lay them down unconditionally. He spoke of the effrontery of O'Connor and the government in trying to make a cat's-paw of him; and he roundly denounced the incompetence of the government, which, with the ample resources of military and police at their disposal had allowed blood to be spilt. He spoke of the *folly* of the rising, which, he believed, could only end in defeat. Finally, he told Mr O'Connor that he and his government should resign, and that, if they did not, they ought to be superseded.[40] P.J. Walsh drew attention to a number of other inaccuracies in O'Connor's book.[41]

On 4 May Augustine Birrell resigned; "giving up the office", in the unkind and inaccurate judgement of the *Independent*, "which he had held but never administered". Each day from that date the paper recorded executions, until by 10 May it feared a backlash, and warned that the government "must not be so severe as to create a revulsion of feeling that would make martyrs of all or any of those who have been sentenced". It noted with approval Mr Redmond's plea for clemency in the House of Commons, and Asquith's answer that General Maxwell had been instructed to confine punishment to narrower limits. It was understood that there would be no more executions. But, despite this statement, James Connolly, too seriously ill to stand, was taken out on a stretcher, tied to a chair, and shot. The "revulsion of feeling" became widespread.

Walsh's health continued to improve during these days, and more and more petitions came to him. Curran, and the other secretaries, sought to protect him. On 10 May, the first of the public appeals following the destruction in Easter Week reached Archbishop's House, the Lord Mayor's Relief Fund. The archbishop contributed £100.⁴² By 13 May, Walsh felt sufficiently well to motor out "for the first time" and to view "the ruined streets. He came back very tired". On that day he signed a petition calling for a fair trial for Alderman Tom Kelly. With Walsh's returning strength, it became one of Curran's tasks over the next few weeks to rent a suitable country house for his Grace's convalescence, as ordered by the doctors.⁴³ On 15 May Curran observed:"Quite a number of people called these days at the Archbishop's – some about their private troubles arising out of the circumstances of the time, others to make known what they thought the ecclesiastical authorities should know." Presumably they were not received by Walsh, as the latter, probably with relief, responded that same day to an invitation to meet prime minister Asquith, then in Dublin and anxious to talk to him, that he was still an invalid and regretted that he could not call to the Viceregal Lodge the following day.⁴⁴

Next day, however, Tuesday, 23 May, the day Eoin Mac Neill was court martialled, Walsh felt sufficiently well to telegraph "a reply to the USA agreeing to act as chairman of the executive committee of Cardinal Farley's Irish Distress Fund (later known as the National Aid Fund)".⁴⁵ At this point in his statement, Curran made what he considered an important observation. The rising had been roundly condemned as traitorous, as a stab-in-the back in time of world war. "In view of the widespread hysteria among many classes in England and Ireland", Curran wrote, and their views on "the obligation of Irish bishops to denounce murders, sedition and rebellion", it was significant that Dr Walsh wrote only three letters in this period: on 24/25 April 1916, warning the people off the streets; on 24 May instructing that the public masses be held according to new time; and on 28 May regarding a site for a cathedral. "The silence of Archbishop Walsh, I think, is a fact of enormous importance that ought to be noted."⁴⁶ Months after the rising, on 22 November 1916, a letter came, in fact, from the Irish National Association of Sydney, which, after expressing pride in "the flaming torch of spiritual idealism" displayed in April, expressed gratitude to his Grace "for the attitude you have taken up on an occasion when it would have been so easy and so acceptable in many quarters to condemn noble men".⁴⁷

With respect to Walsh's significant "silence" concerning a revolution in his own diocese, a number of factors have to be kept in mind. He knew many of the revolutionaries. Their idealistic pronouncements and writings spoke of rebellion and blood sacrifice and were familiar to him. Many of them were religious men. The visit of Count Plunkett with his story of an audience with the pope confirmed both the imminence of rebellion and the outlook of the planners. Walsh considered a rising, especially without outside help, to be futile and wasteful, but not traitorous; and though he might condemn the actual insurrection privately, he was not prepared to do so publicly. Irish history had a record of turning defeated patriots into posthumous heroes. He could not but recall the division and bitterness caused in the past by ecclesiastical denunciations of the Fenians, and the virulence he himself experienced when he spoke out against Parnell. Moreover, he was conscious that in condemning he would be seen as siding with the government, and of being used by it. The pressure on him from the government and a large section of the Dublin populace to denounce the rising was forestalled, however, within days of the surrender, by the government's precipitous and unwise policy of executing day after day prominent Volunteers, many of whom could not be described as leaders of the rebellion. In the days after the first executions, he was released from denunciation of the rebel leaders not just by his illness, but also by the growing distaste for the government's response. Even William Martin Murphy, who had suffered extensive losses to property as a result of the rising, found when faced with Tories gloating over the executions and imprisonments that "every drop of Catholic blood in" his "veins surged up" and he began like others to pity the insurgents.[48]

Walsh was silent about the actual rebellion, and discreet about subsequent representations with respect to prisoners. One bishop, however, championed the cause of the rebels. Ironically it was Edward Thomas O'Dwyer of Limerick. General Maxwell, following his meeting with Walsh on 3 May, sent a gracious letter to the archbishop three days later. "I send for your private information", he wrote, "a copy of the letter I have sent to the bishops concerned, relative to our conversation and the valuable advice you so kindly gave me. I trust your health is improving and that with God's grace you will soon be restored to health."[49]

Maxwell's letter to Dr O'Dwyer was dated, 12 May. It requested him to remove two of his priests, Fr Tom Wall and Fr Michael Hayes "to such employment as will prevent them having intercourse with the people". Wall was accused of "preaching against conscription in his church at Drumcollogher", of "attending a lecture by P. H. Pearse", and of blessing the colours of the Irish Volunteers at Drumcollogher on 17 March 1916". Hayes was "said to have been active, with a certain E. Blythe, organising the Irish Volunteers"; he was accused of being president of two branches of the Volunteers, and of being present at a meeting when "a certain John McDermott delivered inflammatory and seditious speeches". Bishop O'Dwyer, jealous as always of his authority and irked at any sign of dictation, informed the commander-in-chief on 17 May that both men were "excellent priests, who held strong national views" but who, to his knowledge, had not "violated any law, civil or ecclesiastical". Then, going on the offensive, he referred to Maxwell's conduct after the rising as "wantonly cruel and oppressive". He had shot young men "in cold blood". "Personally", he declared, "I regard your action with horror, and I believe that it has outraged the conscience of the country"; and having further charged him with deporting "hundreds even thousands of poor fellows without trial", he concluded: "Altogether your regime has been one of the worst and blackest chapters in the history of the misgovernment of the country."[50] The letter became public and appeared as a benediction to the supporters of the rising. It made O'Dwyer the episcopal voice of nationalism.

The two Limerick priests, it may be noted, became prominent subsequently in work for the Gaelic League and for the national movement. Wall, indeed, was elected to the ard chomhairle of Sinn Fein in 1917. Both men, it is claimed, were destined in that year to help change the course of Irish history. They were delegated by Sinn Fein to go to Lewes prison in Britain, following the death of Willie Redmond, member of parliament for Clare, to ask Dr Richard Hayes, brother of Fr Michael, to be a candidate in the forthcoming election. "They did so, in Irish, with a prison warder standing by, uncomprehending. Dr Hayes wasn't interested in going forward. On their way out of the prison, the two priests, it is said, happened to meet Eamon de Valera, another of the Lewes prisoners, and they suggested to him that he agree to go forward for Clare"![51] That, however, is to move beyond the more immediate aftermath of the Easter rising.

A Royal Commission of Inquiry was set up after the insurrection. Lord Hardinge of Penshurst, who headed the three-man inquiry, sent an invitation to the archbishop to speak to the members of the commission. Walsh replied positively on 26 May 1916, that he doubted whether he could give any helpful evidence, but as Mr Justice Shearman was kindly prepared to see him "and to have a talk over the matter", he did not think it would be right to raise any difficulty. He then carefully explained his condition and situation. "I am at present an invalid, but recovering slowly from a rather prolonged illness, so much so that I was unable to call at the Vice Regal Lodge and see Mr Asquith when he was staying there." "I do not, however," he assured Hardinge, "anticipate any difficulty in that score in attending the commission now. If Mr Justice Shearman lets me know at what time would be most convenient for him to call, any day after to-day, and at *any hour*, I can arrange to be free at the time mentioned."[52]

Having thus arranged for the commissioners to call on him, rather than the reverse, Mr Justice Shearman and Sir Mackenzie Chalmers called to Archbishop's House on Saturday, 27 May. Curran recounted something of what passed between them. "In reply to their queries as to what he considered the cause of the rebellion, the Archbishop ascribed the chief cause of the rising to the breakdown of the constitutional movement. He mentioned various defects in the Home Rule bill and its plain misrepresentation by the Irish party. He particularly criticised the clause on 'concurrent legislation' [Clause 31 or 41. Despite any act the Irish parliament might pass, the English parliament could pass an act annulling it]. While no intelligent nationalist could be misled as to the meaning and effect of the clause, yet Irish members of parliament misrepresented the bill as 'the greatest charter of liberty'.⁵³

On 6 June, after a visit from his physician, Sir Joseph Redmond, during which he was weighed at 12 st, 5 lbs, Walsh set out for Annamoe, Co. Wicklow, where he remained recuperating until 5 September. Curran accompanied him, and only visited Dublin every third week. For that reason, as he remarked, there were few entries in his diary on the political situation during that period.⁵⁴ The archbishop's other secretary, however, P.J. Walsh, forwarded material from Dublin which included some items of political interest, and, during June and July, the newspapers and some of his Grace's invited guests, had also much to relate.

The long drawn-out executions led John Dillon to accuse the government of "letting loose a river of blood" and undoing the life work of the parliamentary party; and the government, as Bishop O'Dwyer indicated, had further inflamed public feeling by the extent of the arrests. They had taken into custody as many as 3,430 men and 79 women, of which 1,423 men and 73 women were released after investigation. One woman and 169 men were convicted by court martial, and the remainder of the prisoners, 1,836 men and 5 women, were sent to England and interned there. Almost all of these last were to be released by Christmas.⁵⁵ Even the most moderate people were alienated by the government's actions. It was "the greatest act of folly any government could have been guilty of", Cardinal Logue judged.⁵⁶

The prison camps became, in effect, schools for rebellion. At home the IRB, and others of strong nationalist convictions, formed organisations to collect money in Ireland and North America for the prisoners and their dependants, and for the dependants of the executed. These organisations, moreover, pressed for the release of the prisoners and fomented criticism of the government. The shift in public feeling was reflected during June in the large numbers who attended requiem masses for those killed in the rising, and for the executed leaders. The large numbers led General Maxwell to write to Walsh on 19 June. Respectfully, he sought his Grace's "good advice" and "assistance" because he feared that unless something was done there might be "disorder and bloodshed" because of the section of the public who were "taking advantage of Requiem Masses ... to make political demonstrations outside the churches and chapels in which these Masses were said". Yesterday 200 marched along the quays "waving Sinn Fein flags, booing at officers and soldiers". He did not know whether the archbishop could interfere in the matter, but perhaps the priests conducting the masses might be asked to advise their congregations to disperse quietly. "I am sure your Lordship will agree with me", Maxwell concluded, "that Dublin has had quite enough trouble without asking for more and it is to avoid the possibility of disorder that prompts me to make this appeal."[57]

Walsh did not reply until 26 June. The extant copy in his own writing reveals a trembling hand and uncertain lettering, quite unlike his usual firm and clear calligraphy. He explained he was out of Dublin convalescing on doctor's orders, and that day was his first chance to come to Dublin to consult his official advisers. "Steps have now been taken", he assured Maxwell, "to apply a remedy but they are necessarily informal. I trust they may prove effectual, but I'm not very hopeful of a completely satisfactory result". "The real difficulty", he warned, "is that there is *a very widespread feeling of discontent*, already sufficiently strong and, as far as I can ascertain, growing stronger every day. This makes it a serious question whether even action taken from purely human motives for the avoidance of bloodshed may not be misinterpreted, with the result that more harm than good may follow. But we must hope for the best."[58]

Meantime, on 17 June, Lorcan Sherlock, on behalf of the provisional executive of the Irish National Aid Association, asked Walsh to act as president of the Association.[59] He agreed, and appointed Fr Bowden, administrator of the pro-cathedral, to act as chairman of the executive committee of the National Aid Fund. The financial aid came mainly from the United States of America. On 8 July, the Irish Relief Fund Committee of the United States wrote to Walsh to say that two men had been designated by their executive committee, John A. Murphy of Buffalo, N.Y., and John Gill, N.Y. City, to go to Ireland "for the purpose of distributing the relief funds", and that as his Grace had "accepted the honorary chairmanship of the relief fund in Dublin" they asked his "good services in behalf of these gentleman".[60] Curran met both men on 27 July, and the next day "the Archbishop, who motored up specially from Annamoe, had a conference with Mr John Murphy lasting over an hour, and returned immediately to Annamoe". Walsh, Curran added, was impressed by Murphy, and, of importance for the future, he was given a clear picture of the American system.[61] As a result of that meeting, Curran further commented, Mrs Tom Clarke's fund for the Volunteers, aided mainly by Clan na nGael circles in the United States, was joined to the Irish National Aid body, to form "a unified organisation ... under the name of the Irish National Aid and Volunteers' Dependants Association".[62]

Ten days earlier, on 18 July, Walsh had made another motor journey, this time to Courtown Harbour to meet Mrs Alice Stopford Green, the historian, who had written to him in mid-July concerning Sir Roger Casement. The latter's trial had appeared to many Irish people an act of cynicism on the part of the government. An old Norman-French statute was appealed to in order to charge him with high-treason, and the prosecuting counsel was Sir. F.E. Smith, who three years earlier had refused to recognise the Home Rule Act and had declared himself ready to defy parliament by force of arms! "I surmise", Curran remarked of Walsh's meeting with Mrs Green, "that he could only express his sympathy and confess his inability to achieve anything useful. I was not with the Archbishop on that occasion, it was Monsignor Walsh."[63] The latter did not mention Casement in his biography of the archbishop. The controversy over the charges against him of homosexuality may have influenced the decision not to do so, or he may just have felt that as his Grace could achieve nothing it was not necessary to refer to Casement. Yet despite the uncertainty and embarrassment on the part of many, Walsh was concerned, and did achieve something, as Alice Green informed him in a sad letter from London on 22 July. She came there, she said, "on a sudden summons" to meet Casement. He told her that he had been informed the previous Thursday that he was to be executed on 3 August. "I was at the distance of a large room from him, and three warders between." He said, "I am very lonely". Moved, she wrote: "I have never seen a man ... more selfless, with such a passion of patriotism". She went on:

> I told him, though I would never in general speak of such a thing, that you had shown the generosity of coming to see me. He begged me to send you as a dying man "his love" and his gratitude. The sense that you thought of him cheered him.

Feeling in England was "madly hostile", she observed. Asquith had said "that Ireland does not care a farthing about Casement". She believed there was "a very deep feeling among the people, who are silenced by martial law, whose letters are *persistently refused* by the press, whose voice is unknown". There were ten days left. She supposed "an appeal from the Irish bishops would really decide the matter". "I believe", she said, "all of them would wait for *your* lead. I understand the peculiar difficulties in your way. But I do implore you to think if there is any possible way in which a dignified Irish appeal could be made". She concluded: "Believe me, your Grace, with all gratitude for your kindness, and all reverence for your leadership in the long Irish battle."[64] It is not clear what further steps, if any, Walsh took, apart from the important one of putting his name to an appeal against the execution. The cardinal and a number of the bishops also signed, perhaps on his prompting. On 28 July, Colonel Maurice Moore of the Volunteers wrote to thank Walsh for permitting his name "to appear on the Casement petition".[65]

A final poignant comment appeared under a later date in Curran's account for the Military History Bureau. On Sunday, 10 September 1916, George Gavan Duffy, solicitor for the late Sir Roger Casement, called at Archbishop's House with copies of his correspondence with Cardinal Bourne of Westminster "over his action in refusing faculties for the reconciliation of Casement to the church unless he signed a statement expressing regret for any scandals he caused by either his private or public life". "Sir Roger", Curran continued, "declined 'in all humility'(to use his own words) to subscribe to the test." He was reconciled to the church of his baptism on 2 August, the eve of his execution. "It was a distinct opinion among the officials of the Roman Curia", Curran added, that Cardinal Bourne had acted wrongly, and he could not but be aware of this, though his action was never condemned as such.[66]

Although he was supposed to be recuperating and avoiding stress, July was proving a demanding month for the archbishop. Apart from journeys to Courtown and a few other places, there were four visits to Dublin; and the reminders of national problems kept intruding in various forms. On 23 July, Curran, who had returned to Dublin, sent him a long letter on the prisoners at Frongoch prison camp and how they were unwelcoming to their chaplain, Fr J. Stafford, of the Dublin diocese, because he wore khaki;[67] and every day brought more news of opposition to partition and the policy of the Irish party. On 23 June Redmond and Dillon had managed to get majority support in Belfast for a temporary partition, but this was followed by opposition and criticism from public bodies, public platforms and press. Faced with criticism and misgivings from many sides, Redmond withdrew his assent to the Act on 24 July. Three days later the details of the government's scheme, and the discrepancies between it and Redmond's presentation of it became apparent. Before that appeared, however, the archbishop of Dublin had decided to break the political silence of a decade.

On 25 July he forwarded to the editor of the *Irish Independent* what that paper termed "a trenchant letter", and which it headed – "Ireland Being Led to Disaster. Will Nationalists Any Longer Be Fooled?" He had been convinced for years, he declared, that the Home Rule cause was being led on disastrous lines, but it was generally believed that the party could do no wrong, and with the passing of the Home Rule Act the people were assured that it could not be "displaced or modified" without their consent and that at the end of the war the old Irish parliament on College Green would be reopened. Who now believed any of these party cries, he asked. In a characteristic postscript he expressed amazement that the country had "so long allowed its attention to be distracted with all sorts of side issues regarding the Irish parliament" whilst a barrier was kept up "against all real consideration of the question whether the parliaments that is to come to us, is to be a parliament in any sense worthy of the name."[68]

In early August, he returned to the subject in a more pointed manner in response to a resolution sent him by the finance committee of the Dungannon Urban District Council. He hoped his views might "prove to be unduly pessimistic", he stated, but this was to hope against hope. To him it was "a shocking thing to find any Irish nationalists approving of negotiations being entered into on the basis of the exclusion of certain counties or cities". It was "doubly shocking" to find those responsible for what had been done "endeavouring to extricate themselves from the responsibility by throwing the blame on an alleged breach of faith by the prime minister". Whatever blame attached to Mr Asquith, he stood "clear at all events of such a charge as that". Mr Asquith made his position clear long since.[69]

The dramatic decline in the party's fortunes was signalled by a letter to Walsh on 14 August from Laurence Ginnell, MP, stating that prominent people in Dublin and London thought the time had come "for the foundation of a new political organisation", and asking him to receive a deputation. Walsh replied that he did not think that the time "was ripe for a new organisation until the country generally realised how discredited was the policy of the Irish party".[70] A further indication of the low ebb of party fortunes was provided by talk of a reconstruction of the *Freeman*, which like the party, of which it was the organ, was said to be "on its last legs"; and there was also renewed "talk of John Redmond resigning the leadership of the party, and that " he was "suffering from a nervous breakdown".[71] Perhaps the most significant blow struck at the Irish party in those uncertain days, however, was delivered by the bishop of Limerick. On 14 September, in a speech accepting the freedom of his native city, he declared that instead of "trusting the party, who trust the Liberals, and are now reduced to the statesmanship of Micawber – waiting for something to turn up", his alternative policy would be to say to the Irish members of parliament 'Come home, shake the dust of the English House of Commons off your feet, and throw yourselves on the Irish nation'. He feared this advice would not be in favour "with our present parliamentarians". "Sinn Fein is, in my judgement, the true principle." His words were greeted with loud and prolonged applause.[72] It was a vital vote of confidence for Sinn Fein. The first episcopal voice approving their political outlook.

On 5 September Walsh "returned to Dublin from convalescence in Wicklow";[73] and found himself, in his restored health, beset by a range of letters dealing with ecclesiastical and more secular matters. Of long-term significance on the ecclesiastical side was a letter from a Fr John Blowick asking his Grace's support for his petition to the bishops at their next meeting for the establishment of "an Irish secular vicariate in China, and, as a necessary support, the foundation of a college in Ireland to train good Irish priests to work in this vicariate". Thus was foreshadowed the "Maynooth Mission to China", or the Columban Fathers, who when they could no longer labour effectively in China, were to turn to other areas in spiritual and material need in Asia, Africa, and South America.[74] The bishops approved the petition at their meeting on 10 October.

Meanwhile, the government was becoming increasingly burthened and embarrassed by the Irish situation: the country was being treated as conquered territory under an army of occupation; the Irish parliamentary party, for its own credibility, was demanding the recall of General Maxwell, the cessation of martial law, political treatment for convicted insurgents, and the release of internees; and with the virtual cessation of voluntary enlistment since the rising, Carson was calling for the conscription of Irishmen. Something of the unstable political situation was reflected at the bishops' meeting on 10 October. The standing committee, according to Curran's account, presented a statement appealing for constitutional methods and displaying a strong Redmondite tendency. In the course of the resultant discussion, Walsh, who perhaps because of his illness may not have attended the standing committee meeting, secured "the insertion of a demand for amnesty" for political prisoners, objected to "the absence of any reference to conscription", an omission which "would be noted and misconstrued", and opposed the general drift of the document. As the document might also be construed as favouring partition, the northern bishops opposed it. Walsh then suggested that the document should be left to the northern bishops. In the end, because of general lack of agreement, the whole matter was dropped. The bishop of Limerick appears to have taken a prominent part in the discussion. Walsh, according to Curran, chuckled "at the growing evidence of Dr O'Dwyer's intransigence".[75]

In the House of Commons on 18 October, replying to Redmond's criticisms, Asquith conceded that bad blunders had been made. In America, moreover, sympathy for those in prison and their relatives continued to grow amongst Irish Americans. An earnest of this was the sending on 16 November 1916, of $18,000 to Archbishop Walsh for the Irish Relief Fund. The money was contributed by the Catholics of New York and forwarded by the Cardinal Archbishop of New York.[76] These and other factors added to the British government's own internal problems in the midst of a very serious war situation. On 6 December, Lloyd George succeeded Asquith as prime minister. Edward Carson, however, retained his position as first lord of the admiralty, and Bonar Law became chancellor of the exchequer and leader of the House of Commons. Henry Duke, another Conservative, remained chief secretary of Ireland. During the summer a number of prisoners had been released. On 21 December, in reply to questions from John Dillon, Duke declared that "the time had come when the risk of liberating the internees would be less than the risks which might follow detaining them longer". On the following day six hundred untried prisoners were set free from the Frongoch detention camp in Wales, and on 23 December others were released from Reading camp just too late to spend Christmas at home.[77]

That same day, Fr L.J. Stafford, the chaplain at Frongoch who had not been accepted initially because he wore khaki, wrote from an empty camp to his archbishop. He told how he had worked strenuously behind the scenes for the release of the prisoners, "making two journeys to Ireland, and one to London, where a fortnight ago I spent most of a morning with Mr Duke ... and finally came away with the assurance that the 'auspicious season was not far from us and ... *that Christmas was Christmas*'." Clearly a zealous man of action, Stafford concluded his letter with the news that he had "applied to the Western Command" and expected to get "some short leave, after which", as he said, "I go straight to France". "I am delighted", he said finally, "that you have completely recovered."[78]

Mention of Walsh's illness and recovery, provides scope to refer to his characteristic endeavour to make use of his time while confined for long periods to bed and his room. He had reflected on and researched over many years the celebrated case involving Daniel O'Connell, Archbishop Murray of Dublin, and the Board of Charitable Bequests. It was a case in which O'Connell and the archbishop were on opposite sides, and O'Connell had been declared the victor. Walsh's own father had supported O'Connell's side, and from his father he had received much of the relevant documentation. Studying the case now in great detail, Walsh came to the conclusion that Murray was right after all. He had his findings and the presentation of the case printed in pamphlet form, which, as usual, he sent to a wide range of people. He received a variety of responses. Some, like Cardinal O'Connell of New York, on 6 January 1917, just thanked him for his pamphlet – "O'Connell, Archbishop Murray, and the Board of Charitable Bequests". Others, like John Dillon, on 18 December, and Cardinal Logue at Christmas eve, 1916, made comment. Logue was struck by a key practical factor – "One thing which struck me particularly was the extraordinary amount of research your Grace had recourse to."[79]

Comments from recipients of the pamphlet continued to arrive during the early months of 1917. Monsignor Michael O'Riordan wrote from Rome on 7 January to express his appreciation of the work and to say that he had told the pope about it. He went on to report on what was being done in the cause of the Irish martyrs, and to observe that Archbishop Bourne's continuance in Rome had given rise to rumours that his delay was related "to the conditions of Casement's conversion", or/and "that he is moving on again towards a slice of Southwark". Indicatively, he added, "Dr Amigo (bishop of Southwark) is expected".[80]

Whatever about the interest to Walsh of these items of information, the significant matter at the end of a tumultuous year was that hundreds of prisoners came home largely changed men, with a renewed determination, organisation, and focus, and found to their surprise that the country too had changed, that hostile, condemnatory groups had given way to welcoming crowds, to bonfires and torch-light processions affirming support for their association with the rising, and singing "songs of freedom".

XVI

Renewed energy, and significant interventions, 1917-19

In the four years after 1916 leadership passed to younger men and the history of Ireland was changed. In these circumstances, the aged and ailing William Walsh might have been expected to have faded from the scene, but he was still the archbishop of Dublin, revered for his nationalist reputation as much as for his office, and he was still determined to make his presence felt. His health, moreover, greatly improved, especially during 1917 and 1918.

1. 1917, A YEAR OF CONFUSION AND HARDENING ATTITUDES

At the beginning of 1917, it looked as if Walsh faced another year of illness. On 18 January 1917, the eczema re-appeared. Sir Joseph Redmond and Dr O'Carroll were called. On 23 January, according to Walsh's diary, his "blood-pressure was 220 instead of 167", yet two days later he attended the senate meeting of the university for the first time since 1915, and before the end of the month he had chaired a catechism committee meeting, and met and supported P.J. Brady, a local member of parliament, who was planning a conference "to consider the question of the housing of the working classes in Dublin ... and what assistance the government should give ... after the war".[1] His diary noted a "bad bilious night" on 2 February, but thereafter there was no reference to ill-health for more than two months, and then only briefly.

Meanwhile, Sinn Fein had put forward Count Plunkett, father of Joseph Plunkett, one of the executed 1916 leaders, for a by-election in Roscommon. On 22 January, as part of his election programme, Plunkett appealed to the principles enunciated by President Woodrow Wilson of the United States, to which Britain had declared its adherence, namely, that government must be "by the consent of the governed" and that "the equality of nations upon which peace must be founded must be an equality of rights", irrespective of the size or strength of the nations.[2] In the contest, Plunkett received 3, 000 votes, easily defeating his Irish party opponent. The government replied by arresting 26 members of the Sinn Fein national organisation on 23 and 24 February, ten of whom were deported to England. This was followed up on 7 March by a disturbing speech by Lloyd George in the course of which he claimed that "those in the north-east" of Ireland were "as alien in blood, in religious faith, in traditions, in outlook from the rest of Ireland as the inhabitants of Fife or Aberdeen".[3] It was an argument for partition. Anger flared all over Ireland except the north-east. Fearful of a violent outbursts, the government staged military manoeuvres in the streets of Dublin and throughout the country.[4]

During April government fears increased as the first anniversary of Easter Week approached. In an indirect acknowledgement of Walsh's continuing influence, the attorney general, James O'Connor, requested an interview for the chief secretary, Henry Duke, and himself. The archbishop met them on 13 April.[5] What passed between them is not known. The authorities, however, took no chances over Easter. Public meetings were prohibited, and the police were on the streets in force. The protests of Sinn Fein and the public were dignified and restrained. Thousands expressed their sentiments by wearing armlets with a tri-colour ribbon on black, and republican flags were widely displayed. The 1916 republican proclamation was reprinted and posted on walls.[6] The result was a boost to morale, which contributed to the success of an assembly of delegates from Irish corporate bodies called by Count Plunkett, which met on 19 April. Over 70 public bodies were represented, and over 120 priests attended. The differences between those seeking a republican form of government, and the followers of Griffith seeking a less defined form of independence, was temporarily masked by the establishment of a national council committed to an independent Ireland without the exact form of government being decided.

Walsh himself, seemed to have a preference for the equality represented by a full dominion status, and, as might be expected, had studied the matter fully. In May he authoritatively corrected an article by Sir John Robert O'Connell with reference to Australia. "I have looked up the Commonwealth of Australia Constitution Act", O'Connell wrote him on 27 May, "and find that your Grace's reference is quite correct."[7] At the same time, according to Curran, he did not share the prejudice against the word and idea of a republic prevalent among some of the bishops and "among older and more conservative elements of the national movement". Curran recalled an occasion in 1918 when Walsh spoke "with amused raillery" of how some people associated republicanism "with the excesses of the French Revolution … forgetting all about the United States of America".[8]

In the weeks following Plunkett's assembly, public attention turned to a by-election which was pending in South Longford, a stronghold of the Irish party. The Sinn Fein national council had chosen a prisoner at Lewes prison, in Sussex, Joseph McGuinness, as its candidate. The Irish party claimed that the issue was between a sensible option for a self-governed country united to the British empire and the chimera of an independent republic. The issue of partition, however, was present, and the party was associated with it. The northern Catholic bishops rallied support against partition. Bishop McHugh of Derry wrote to Walsh on 1 May asking him to lend his name to an appeal to the country against partition, and informing him that some Protestant and Catholic bishops had already agreed to sign.[9] Walsh did so, and on the eve of the election, 8 May, a manifesto appeared signed by three archbishops (the exception, Dr

Healy, was gravely ill), 15 Catholic bishops, three Protestant bishops, and several chairmen of co. councils, which proclaimed that "to Irishmen of every creed and class and party, the very thought of our country partitioned and torn as a new Poland must be one of heart-rending sorrow".[10]

Not content with just signing the manifesto, Walsh, having noted a significant comment in the *Freeman's Journal*, decided to add a personal letter. That morning, as he later explained to Michael O'Riordan, rector of the Irish College, "it was editorially proclaimed" in the *Freeman's Journal* "that on the question of partition, the leaders had a free hand". "The amazing part of the business", Walsh added, "is that no one but myself seems to have noticed the 'cat out of the bag' article ... on the election morning".[11] Walsh's public letter, which he knew would influence the voting, was printed in the evening press on 8 May, and was circulated the following day in Longford. It pointed out that the Catholic and Protestant bishops had chosen to protest against partition because, unlike many people, they believed that partition was still a live issue and that anyone who thought it was not was "simply living in a fool's paradise". Characteristically, he added a telling postscript:

> P.S. I think it a duty to write this, although from information that has just reached me, I am fairly satisfied that *the mischief has already been done*, and that *the country is practically sold*.

The letter was printed in full by Sinn Fein under the large black caption "SOLD!" and sub-heading: "Archbishop Walsh and Redmond's Partition Policy" The italicised words in the postscript were highlighted and made larger and heavier than the rest of the text.[12] Joseph P. McGuinness won by 32 votes, defeating the strong Irish party candidate, Patrick McKenna. The party was enraged at the bishops' manifesto, and especially at Walsh and his postscript, and also at the open support given to Sinn Fein by the younger clergy.[13] They criticised and ridiculed Walsh "up and down through the country".[14]

Immediately after the election, various newspapers commented on the impact of his letter. One rather poignant comment in the light of later events, under the heading "The Postscript Prelate", observed that this "brilliant churchman and a great Irish patriot" would "in days to come probably be known as the man whose courage saved Ireland the mistake of partition".[15] The *Pall Mall Gazette* of 11 May remarked that his "whole-hearted support of the Sinn Fein candidate" was not a surprise to anyone who knew his Grace's past record, adding that it would be remembered also "that he took deeply to heart the stern suppression of the Irish rising of last year".

Lloyd George was not one to remain long without discovering an expedient to serve a political purpose. The strong Irish lobby in the United States was the great danger to the Anglo-American alliance. Already in February he presented Redmond with a number of alternatives, the most attractive of which was that the terms of a Home Rule settlement be discussed by a National Convention representative of the Irish people, wherein the Irish people could state what form of government they sought within the empire. If substantial agreement was reached the British parliament would give it effect. The prime minister urged Lord Carson to get the Ulster unionists to attend the Convention, but gave him a private guarantee that they would not be bound by any majority. Arthur Griffith in *Nationality* on 2 June warned against Lloyd George's scheme. "He summons a Convention", he wrote, "and guarantees that a small minority of people will not be bound by its decision, and thus, having secured its failure" aims to tell the world that when England left it to the Irish to settle the question they could not agree among themselves.[16] Sinn Fein, the Labour organisations, the Gaelic League, and the National League[17] refused to take part. Walsh saw little prospect for the venture, but, rather than have the bishops accused of undermining it, agreed to episcopal representatives participating in the Convention. Despite their efforts and the intense activity of William Martin Murphy, Horace Plunkett, Lord Dunraven, and many others, the members of the Convention, even apart from the Ulster delegates, failed to agree on a united report and the Convention, in Dunraven's words, "fizzled out in confusion".[18]

On 15 June, Bonar Law announced that in order to secure a favourable atmosphere for the deliberations of the Convention, the government had decided to release the remaining Irish prisoners in English jails. The government had in mind also another scheduled by-election, this time in Clare. Public protests demanding that the prisoners be treated as prisoners of war shared the headlines with news of the Clare election. The vacancy in East Clare had been created by the death of Major Willie Redmond, brother of the parliamentary leader, who had been killed at Messines in France on 7 June. On 15 June, Walsh met with the lord mayor, Laurence O'Neill, the high sheriff, D. Keogh, and James O'Connor, the attorney general, to discuss arrangements for the requiem mass for Major Redmond. Great crowds were expected for he was a popular figure. On 22 June, Walsh came from Knockdrin, Co. Meath, where he was on vacation, to preside at the mass.[19] Katherine Tynan, journalist and poet, who was covering the event for the *Birmingham Gazette* and had attended the mass, commented on the "very motley crowd in the privileged places, as well as in the seats of the lowly ... Everybody who is anybody in the life of Dublin is there." There were also some strange dramatic ironies.

> One was that Dr Walsh, the archbishop who wrote the letter of some weeks ago, presided at the throne and the absolution. Well, well, Willie Redmond was one of the fortunate persons whom all the world loves. Not even the bitterness of politics in contemporary Ireland has touched him.

"The requiem was almost a great demonstration – of love and respect", Tynan continued. "Call no man happy 'till he is dead."[20]

To thousands of a younger generation, however, Willie Redmond's death symbolised the end of an era, if it symbolised anything. Their hopes and enthusiasms were focused on an emerging Ireland that just then was seeking further expression in the Clare election, a venue itself full of symbolism. Clare was the 'banner county' which concluded the case for Catholic Emancipation by electing Daniel O'Connell to the House of Commons in 1828. Now as a further symbol, the last living signatory of the 1916 proclamation, Eamon de Valera, was the Sinn Fein candidate. Young people poured into Clare to walk and cycle its roads and boreens in his support. For the first time for a century, the special correspondent of the British *Daily News* remarked sweepingly, Ireland had a generation of young men. The ban on emigration during the war had left in the country "probably seventy thousand or eighty thousand young fellows" from whose "spirit and enterprise" was "derived the great impetus of the Sinn Fein movement".[21] Although faced with a strong Irish party candidate, Patrick Lynch, KC, de Valera more than doubled his opponent's votes – 5,010 against 2,035. There was extensive rejoicing throughout the country. De Valera openly encouraged the Volunteers to defy the law by wearing uniforms on public occasions, and he publicly reviewed hundreds of uniformed marching men.[22] In August another Sinn Fein candidate, William T. Cosgrave, won a by-election in Kilkenny. Shortly afterwards, many Sinn Fein supporters were arrested and charged with "speeches calculated to cause disaffection". Among them was Thomas Ashe, who had been sentenced to death, which was commuted to life imprisonment, in 1916. He was sentenced by court martial to one year's imprisonment with hard labour and placed among the common delinquents in Mountjoy jail, Dublin. In this tense climate, Archbishop Walsh sought to be a moderating influence in order to avoid a second armed confrontation.

Meanwhile, there was the ordinary work of the diocese and a host of correspondence on non-political matters. Among these last was a letter from the Lord Mayor, Laurence O'Neill, regretting that Walsh would not agree to have his portrait painted by Sir John Lavery, but expressing his pleasure at his Grace's gracious recognition "of the feeling by which the members of the corporation were activated", namely, to express "that respect and affection with which your Grace is held by all Irishmen and particularly by all the people of Dublin".[23] Inevitably, too, there were intimations of mortality amongst his near-contemporaries. In July the eighty-one year old Bishop Brownrigg broke his leg. Walsh, with his usual sensitivity towards the sick, wrote to say he would travel to visit him. Moved, Brownrigg replied on 25 July. "Your proposal to come to Kilkenny to save me a journey to Dublin, overwhelms me with gratitude for your kindness. Unless in great extremities I could not think of permitting your Grace to put yourself to such trouble. Happily I am in no such extremity and shall be well able for the journey." His plaster would be off in time for their meeting on 6 August. He concluded "with renewed acknowledgements of your many grateful acts of kindness to me".[24] The other intimation was of a more final nature, namely, the death of Bishop O'Dwyer. Walsh did not attend the funeral, but O'Dwyer's friend, Bishop Donnelly, did, and wrote from Limerick on 20 August of "the huge and impressive demonstration" attended by 300 priests and "fourteen bishops including the cardinal"[25]

At the end of August, Walsh returned to Dublin ready to undertake the visitation of parishes.[26] On 18 September he chaired a long meeting on the Irish martyrs. Meantime, in Mountjoy jail, Thomas Ashe and other Sinn Fein prisoners were pressing their claim to be treated as political prisoners, and when this was refused they went on hunger strike. Meetings were held throughout the country in support of the prisoners. On 25 September Ashe collapsed in the surgeon's chair while being forcibly fed. He was moved to hospital, where he died five hours later. Subsequently, wounds and bruises were identified on his face and throat.[27] Despite the views of the medical witnesses given at the inquest on 28 September, forcible feeding of the prisoners on hunger strike continued. The lord mayor called on Archbishop Walsh in respect of this on 29 September, and also in relation to arrangements for the funeral the following day.[28]

The funeral was to be an occasion of a massive demonstration. Ashe had been a popular figure in Gaelic Athletic, Gaelic League, and Irish music circles. Moreover, he was president of the supreme council of the IRB, and that body was determined that his death and funeral become the occasion of a concerted political protest. The funeral became, in fact, the largest since that of Parnell in 1891. The coffin was preceded by an advance guard of Volunteers, including delegates from Redmond's Volunteers, bearing rifles in defiance of the government's ban. They were followed by one hundred and twenty priests, and representatives of numerous national organisations. Thirty thousand people marched, and countless thousands lined the streets. Walsh took care to make his sympathies clear. He formally sent a letter to the lord mayor before the funeral:

> I feel it a duty to take part in the public protest that will find expression in the funeral. Kindly say to what place I should send my car, so that it can most conveniently find its place in the procession.

At the grave side three volleys were fired, and a relatively unknown young man, Michael Collins, spoke just two sentences: "Nothing additional remains to be said. The volley which we have just heard is the only speech which it is proper to make above the grave of a dead Fenian."[29] Collins was, in addition to being a member of the IRB and of the Volunteers, also secretary to the National Aid Organisation. This provided him with contacts throughout the country and in the United States, and gave him a central role in the distribution of funds. Walsh was later to comment to John Dillon that despite his name being used, he had no idea how the funds were being distributed![30]

In the aftermath of the Ashe funeral and the demonstration of militancy, there was evident tension between those supporters of Sinn Fein who were expressly republican and those who, like Arthur Griffith, had a more flexible vision of a future Irish state. A Sinn Fein convention was called at the Mansion House, where tensions were eased by Griffith standing aside to enable de Valera become president of the organisation, and by de Valera coming up with a formula on which all could agree, namely, that: "Sinn Fein aimed at securing the international recognition of Ireland as an independent Irish Republic. Having achieved that status, the Irish people may, by referendum, freely choose their own form of government." On 19 November, de Valera was also elected president of the Volunteers. Many of his public statements continued to be blatantly aggressive.

The talk of independence in Ireland and the presence there of large numbers of young men, at a time when Britain was in dangerous straits in a great war, gave rise to calls in the British press for conscription in Ireland. Lloyd George was accused of 'Birrellism', of being half-hearted and dilatory. The military establishment urged the government to introduce conscription.[31] Despite the accusations of 'Birrellism' levelled against Lloyd George, the government in Ireland was involved in incessant arrests and suppressions. This promoted the growth of the Sinn Fein movement, and the movement, in turn, offered even greater provocation. Cardinal Logue, on 25 November, had a letter read at all masses which was highly critical of Sinn Fein's militancy and political aspirations. The achievement of an Irish republic was, he stated, the "pursuit of a dream which no man in his sober senses can hope to see realised".[32] Logue's letter, in Curran's view, "represented the attitude of the majority, or two-thirds of the Irish bishops, and a large number of elderly clergy, before the general election of December 1918".[33]

William Walsh, significantly, was publicly reticent on political matters during these final months of 1917, though otherwise active. On 1 November he led a deputation to the Viceregal Lodge to present the case for parliamentary representation for the National University. On 14 November he wrote vigorously in the *Irish Independent* that he had always felt it a duty to press for equality of treatment between Catholics and Protestants as the only basis for a satisfactory settlement of the university question. There was one remaining obstacle to be removed, the "glaring inequality" that Trinity College was represented by two members in parliament while the Colleges of the National University, and Queen's University, Belfast, were unrepresented.[34] As might be expected with his renewed energy, he also pressed forward eagerly with the "apostolic process" for the canonisation of the Irish martyrs. He was very conscious that research work in different countries had been delayed by the war, and that other work had been held up by his ill-health. The Dublin tribunal, which he chaired, was to hold 195 sessions from 1917 to 1919, dealing with the period 1537-1603, and 107 sessions from 1918 to 1920, dealing with the years 1603-25. In all, some eighty to ninety people were involved in the process between judges, assistant promoters, notaries, translators, scribes, experts in palaeography, and researchers and witnesses.[35]

During the war Walsh corresponded with his priests serving as chaplains with the British forces. He supported them as best he could, and seems to have enjoyed their confidence.[36] Supporting chaplains involved in an overseas war, however, was one thing, giving support at home to any public ceremony relating to the war was quite another matter. He continued to refuse permission for any church service relating to the war on the grounds that it would be regarded by sections of the Dublin population as "a military demonstration", and was likely to lead to "unseemly demonstrations in the streets".[37] His reluctance to show any appearance of support for the war effort was to be intensified late in 1918 following the heavy loss of life at the torpedoing of the mail boat, the RMS *Leinster*. Deeply upset at the tragedy, he had a notice inserted in the *Freeman* and *Independent* on 15 October to make known to the clergy of the diocese his wish, that, as far as possible, all the masses celebrated the following day in the churches of the diocese should be offered for the "victims to the cruel outrage perpetrated ... by hostile arms in the Irish sea".[38] A few days later he contributed £100 to the "Leinster Disaster Fund".[39]

Some time later he learned privately that the mail boat had been used by the government as a troop ship. Consequently, when a naval officer approached him on 3 November, from the Admiralty Recruiting Office, stating that he had "the task of organising a national campaign at Dublin against the sinking of the Leinster" in the form "of an appeal for the same number of volunteers to come forward as there were victims sunk in the tragedy", and then asked his Grace for "a small cheque" to enable the campaign obtain sufficient advertising,[40] he received a devastating reply. Having regretted that it was not in his power to do what was asked, Walsh went on to ridicule the idea of a campaign to compensate the military and naval authorities for losses sustained in the tragedy. Such compensation as should be made ought to be largely made "by those who were guilty of the shocking crime of turning an ordinary passenger steamer into a troop ship without giving adequate notice to the travelling public of the imminent and fatal danger that awaited those who might embark". He regretted that the means adopted "to screen from public indignation the criminal action of the authorities, who" were "scarcely less guilty than the German organisers of the evil work done by the torpedoes", had been "but too successful". But the facts would become generally known "when the freedom of the press was restored".[41]

Walsh had no illusions about political affairs, especially in time of war. His experience of Irish history, as has been seen, had left him with a strong sense of British duplicity when British interests were involved, and even more than ever now he was determined not to be seen as a servant or dupe of government policies, especially in the light of so many imprisonments without charge and the many reports he received of the deprivation and torture of prisoners, particularly in Belfast jail.[42] Hence, as he had observed a tactical silence regarding the Easter rising, so, as 1917 merged into 1918, he remained silent regarding the mixed signals of violence and constitutional means being sent out by Sinn Fein. He cautiously waited to see how that movement would develop. Nationalists seemed to have little else available to them. The Irish parliamentary party appeared to have lost popular appeal, and its leader had become grievously ill towards the close of 1917. He died in the early spring of the following year.

Death of John Redmond

The muted response to the death of John Redmond was a striking indication of the change in popular feeling. Only a few years previously, he was the esteemed and popular leader of nationalist Ireland. The archbishop of Dublin sent no message of condolence, nor did he have a public requiem mass as was held for his brother, Willie Redmond. In Limerick, Dr Denis Hallinan, Bishop O'Dwyer's successor, also refused permission for a requiem.[43]

Truly, in Redmond's case, "the good was interred with his bones". His considerable achievements were forgotten. Not surprisingly, nevertheless, there was a feeling of resentment amongst many people at Walsh not expressing condolence and not having a public requiem. It was expressed in a brief, sharp letter from an M.E. Harrison on 11 March 1918.

> I am sorry and ashamed to think that the Catholic Archbishop of Dublin acted in such an unchristian like manner in connection with the death of Mr John Redmond – one of Ireland's Catholic and most brilliant sons.[44]

An extenuating factor with respect to the public requiem mass may have been, the excuse given regarding military funerals and services, namely, that "in the exceptionally excited state of public opinion" such a public action might occasion scenes of unseemly protest and confrontation. There seems no possible excuse for the absence of a message of condolence or some public statement.

On 12 March, John Dillon was unanimously elected chairman of the Irish parliamentary party by forty-five of the parliamentary members. The others were said to have been deliberately absent. Within days, however, Redmond and inter-party differences were put aside in the face of a national emergency.[45] It presented a challenge for which Walsh was particularly prepared in terms of temperament and historical reputation.

2. UNITY IN DEFIANCE, 1918

The challenge of conscription

The powerful German spring offensive of 1918 increased the demand in Britain for conscription in Ireland, so much so that on 9 April the standing committee of the Irish bishops felt it necessary to publish a strong resolution against conscription. "With all the responsibility that attaches to our office", they declared, "we feel bound to warn the government against acting upon a policy so disastrous to the public interest and to all order, public or private".[46] That night, Archbishop Walsh told Curran "of his astonishment at the ardour and almost revolutionary sentiment of some of the bishops who had spoken that day – but he also spoke of his anxiety over the hesitation and misgivings of Cardinal Logue. The cardinal was entirely nonplussed at the strong attitude of his usually ultra-prudent colleagues ... "[47] Walsh also informed Curran that a summons had been quietly issued for a general meeting of the bishops on Thursday, 18 April.[48]

The very day of the meeting of the bishops' standing committee, Lloyd George expressed the government's intention of passing without delay a measure for conscription in Ireland. The declaration of the bishops' standing committee became, in consequence, a moral rallying point for resistance.[49] Three days later, on 12 April, de Valera called to Archbishop's House. He met Curran, the archbishop, perhaps, not wishing to be seen meeting him before the bishops' meeting. De Valera informed Curran that Sinn Fein proposed to take strong action against conscription, and wished to ensure that their stance would not be weakened by the hierarchy. Curran took it on himself to inform him of the bishops' private meeting on 18 April. He did so, he later explained, because he knew of Walsh's fear of Logue's attitude and he wished to give Sinn Fein the opportunity of formulating a strong policy and presenting it at the bishops' meeting. He felt that the bishops would follow a strong lead given by laymen. Curran also informed the lord mayor, the Sinn Fein councillor Laurence O'Neill, who was due to host a public conference on conscription at the Mansion House.[50] The country was alive with meetings.

On Tuesday, 16 April, the third reading of the Conscription bill was passed. The Irish members of parliament withdrew from the House of Commons in protest.[51] That evening, and the following morning, newspapers carried a letter from the archbishop of Dublin. "Floods of vague declamation", he declared, were deluging the country and obscuring two key points: 1. "What political action are the people of this country to take in order to meet the crisis?"; 2. that the introduction of a Home Rule bill before the Conscription bill was passed into law, even "the most satisfactory Home Rule bill, would not in the present angry state of feeling in Ireland contribute in the slightest degree to the pacification of our country."[52] He emphasised "that the people, collectively and individually, need a definite lead as to what to do if conscription is enforced".[53] It was a clarion call. The *Daily Express* on 17 April followed its summary of the archbishop's letter with the observation: "It is not without interest to note that the Sinn Fein leader, Mr de Valera, had an interview recently with Dr Walsh. The interview lasted nearly two hours". On the evening of 17 April, the lord mayor, Laurence O'Neill, who, as has been seen, was on friendly terms with Walsh, called on him in preparation for the Mansion House Conference the following day. Significantly, "the Archbishop", according to Curran, "spoke of the bishops' meeting, of which the Lord Mayor did not reveal his knowledge, and it was arranged that the Lord Mayor would telephone towards lunch the next day for the reception of a delegation from the Conference. In order to conceal this pre-arrangement the Archbishop's name was to be kept secret."!54 Thus the stage was set, without Walsh consulting any other member of the hierarchy.

At nine o'clock next morning, Thursday, 18 April, the day of both the conference and the bishops' meeting, de Valera called to see the archbishop in case the latter had any questions for him, and to request that the bishops "would say nothing which would hinder those who were prepared to defend themselves with arms to the last".55 The archbishop, Curran stated, "considered it safer not to see him". Curran conveyed fully to his Grace "the tenor of de Valera's mission". At ten o'clock the Mansion House Conference commenced. It concluded with a defiant declaration asserting "Ireland's separate and distinct nationhood" and the principle "that the government of nations derive their just powers from the consent of the governed", and hence the absence of authority on the part of the British government "to impose compulsory service in Ireland against the expressed will of the Irish people". "The passing of the Conscription bill by the British House of Commons must", therefore, "be regarded as a declaration of war on the Irish nation."56 During the day a representative deputation was chosen to go to Maynooth to wait on the hierarchy. Those chosen were: de Valera, John Dillon, Tim Healy, William O'Brien of Labour and the Irish Transport and General Workers' Union, and the lord mayor, Laurence O'Neill.

The bishops, meanwhile, who were in a bellicose mood, which pleased Walsh and upset Cardinal Logue, agreed to the statement:

> An attempt is being made to enforce conscription upon Ireland against the will of the Irish nation and in defiance of the protests of its leaders.
>
> In view especially of the historic relations between the two countries from the very beginning up to the present moment, we consider that conscription forced in this way upon Ireland is an oppressive and inhuman law, which the Irish people have a right to resist by all means that are consonant with the law of God.

Following that strong statement they called for "strict adherence to the Divine law", and urged "fervent and persevering prayer", a "national novena in honour of Our Lady of Lourdes", and the recitation of the rosary in families every evening, with the intention of "bringing us safe through this crisis of unparalleled gravity".57

The deputation from the Mansion House received a warm welcome. As a result of their joint meeting, the bishops made a public pronouncement directing the clergy "to celebrate a public mass of intercession" the coming Sunday "in every church in Ireland to avert the scourge of conscription". They further directed "that an announcement be made at every public mass on Sunday next of a public meeting to be held for the purpose of administering a pledge "against compulsory military service in Ireland". Finally, the clergy were also required to announce at the Sunday mass "that at an early suitable date a collection will be held outside the church gates for the purpose of supplying means to resist the imposition of compulsory military service".[58] In addition to this strong endorsement by the hierarchy, Archbishop Walsh agreed to act with the lord mayor as trustee "to the anti-conscription fund". It was also agreed to hold a one-day general strike. The combination of politicians, trade unions, and a united hierarchy was both an unusual, and a very formidable alliance. The 18th of April was, as Curran exclaimed, "a day of dramatic effect".[59] Following it, "there was great relief and excitement across the country". Curran's friend, "Mr Quinn, Assistant Commissioner of Police," said to him "with great relief" the next day, "that ends conscription in Ireland".

Walsh was invigorated at being centre stage once more in public affairs. Curran further recalled:

> I remember vividly the elation of the Archbishop of Dublin that evening on his return. He related to me every incident of the day and took a certain amount of pleasure in picturing the discomfiture of the Cardinal, how he was led on from point to point before he realised it. He had first advocated "passive resistance" but the Archbishop of Dublin and others made short work of his passive resistance, for nobody could define what passive resistance meant, and passive resistance was the only panacea of the Cardinal. Standing on the steps of the front house after the meeting, awaiting the arrival of their cars, the Cardinal mournfully remarked to the Archbishop, "I think this is the worst day's business the Bishops ever did". On the Archbishop expressing dissent and saying that he thought everything went off very satisfactorily, the Cardinal could only repeat, "I fear this is the worst day's business the Bishops ever did".

With the advantage of hindsight, it is difficult not to sympathise with the cardinal faced with colleagues caught up in the pervading emotional righteousness that gripped the national community. The evening of the meeting, "the Conscription Bill was read for the third time in the House of Lords, and received the royal assent. Earlier in the day, Lord French and his staff arrived in Dublin, and there were many signs of military and naval activity".[60]

Each day brought new developments. At 8.15 p.m. on Friday, 19 April, de Valera and Tim Healy called on the archbishop to discuss what was being called the National Defence Fund, the legal aspects involved, "and to make arrangements by which the archbishop and the Lord Mayor would act as trustees with a third person to be named by the Mansion House Conference".[61] On the Sunday, Dr Walsh conducted ordinations at Clonliffe College at 8.30 a.m.,[62] while outside every public church where Catholics worshipped a million people signed the following pledge: "Denying the right of the British government to enforce compulsory service in this country, we pledge ourselves solemnly to one another to resist conscription by the most effective means at our disposal." There was no flag waving, no band, no rhetoric or mob hysteria, just an "unmistakable, deep, tense determination to fight conscription ..."[63] Two days later, Tuesday, 23 April, there followed the general cessation of work. "There were no trains, trams, cars, or papers. All shops without exception were closed. The opening of courts, banks or post offices, made no impression. There were no trains to Punchestown races and jarveys refused all bribes to go. In the hotels the guests had to cook and serve their own meals. It was a very effective and powerful warning of the resistance that could be offered on a large scale if necessary."[64] It also manifested the power of the trades unions and their identification with nationalist feeling.

Unity between nationalists was further strengthened by a concerted attack in the English press on nationalists and against the Irish clergy, bishops, and the Vatican. From 24 April 1918, what Curran called "a rabid anti-Catholic (no popery) campaign" began in the British press. "The campaign continued in fury for a fortnight and was helped by patriotic Roman Catholic Englishmen such as Lord Edmond Talbot, Lord Denbigh, James Hope, and the Catholic Union of Great Britain."[65]

In the United States, meanwhile, voices of protest were raised at the imposition of conscription, and in Australia Archbishop Mannix lobbied vigorously against it. On 2 May the Australian bishops cabled to de Valera and John Dillon a declaration in favour of Dominion Home Rule and against conscription. One English bishop spoke out in support of the Irish stance, namely, Peter E. Amigo, bishop of Southwark (1904-49). Familiar with Ireland's history, his empathy for the Irish, as he informed Lloyd George, began by his "working among the poor in the East End of London".[66] On 3 May he sent Walsh a copy of his response to Lord Denbigh's letter in the *Times*, in which he pointed out that "when nearly thirty bishops in Ireland with their clergy and people are all of one mind at present, there must be a great deal to be said for their point of view, even if we do not understand it".[67] Whether the letter had any impact on Denbeigh is not clear. Next day the Catholic Union passed a resolution appealing to the pope against the decision of the Irish bishops and dissociating itself "from a movement which cannot fail to hamper the full development of the military forces of the Allies, and thereby endanger the cause of humanity".[68]

The unity generated by the overall English attack was heralded in the *Nation* newspaper of 27 April with the observation – "Mr Lloyd George in a single fortnight has made a united Ireland – against himself." The unity in the Catholic population was perceptible in the national novena recommended by the bishops, which concluded on 11 May. The press reported the Dublin churches thronged to overflowing throughout the week. The confessional duty on the Saturday lasted up to midnight. Similar expressions of fervour were evident across the country.[69] The government's declared intention of conscripting the

Catholic clergy proved the climax of folly. It "inevitably drove the most conservative of conservative Irish bishops to share the leadership of opposition with Sinn Fein".[70]

The arrival of Field-Marshal Lord French, replacing Lord Wimborne, as lord lieutenant, had signalled both a change in personnel and the placing of the country under military command. The intention was to enforce conscription, but, according to Sir Henry Wilson, Lloyd George impressed on French "the necessity of putting the onus for first shooting on the rebels".[71] A suitable opportunity for action occurred fortuitously on 12 April when police arrested Joseph Dowling on an island off Galway. He had come ashore from a German submarine. In May the authorities used the occasion to proclaim a treasonable plot with Germany. No evidence was produced to substantiate the alleged plot, but it served as a pretext for sweeping arrests all over Ireland on the night of 17 March. Nearly all the senior officers of the Irish Volunteers and of the Sinn Fein organisers were detained. Seventy-three prisoners, including de Valera and Arthur Griffith, were deported to English prisons. The leaders of the opposition to conscription had been removed. The collapse of the opposition was expected. One key figure, however, escaped arrest, and the situation gave him a free hand to exercise his extraordinary gifts for organisation and motivation, and his capacity for ruthless action. He was Michael Collins.

During this critical period, the lord mayor, Laurence O'Neill, was "in continual communication with the Archbishop", Curran noted.[72] The government, following the arrest of nearly all the Sinn Fein leaders, took vigorous measures to prevent public meetings, drilling and the circulation of seditious literature. On 15 June the cities of Cork and Limerick and thirteen counties were declared "proclaimed districts"; and on 5 July Sir Frederick Shaw issued an order prohibiting the holding or taking part in any meetings, assemblies, or processions in public places, and the police were instructed that this applied to athletic meetings, feiseanna and so on.[73] The heavy-handed repression proved counter-productive. It was almost designed to be so, as the bishop of Southwark had tried to explain to Lloyd George even before the repression intensified.

In a letter to Lloyd George on 28 May he pointed to the need for an understanding of the Irish personality and temperament. "The appointment of Sir Edward Carson as Attorney-General in spite of his preparations for resistance to law in 1914 had", Amigo pointed out, "a disastrous effect on the Irish." Again, there had been "little or no sympathy with the Easter Rebellion, but the way in which the Sinn Feiners were dealt with aroused the sympathy of an emotional race." He then offered advice based on his own experience:

> The Irish can be won, but never driven. You would have all the soldiers you need without any conscription, if the Irish could be made to trust British politicians, but every man and every woman in Ireland will resist conscription. The deportations of the Sinn Fein leaders will not help your

cause ... You are going to have disaster and we shall lose the war unless the Irish question is settled once and for all ... The Irish character is altogether different from the English. Why not try to rule Ireland accordingly.

The Irish bishops had been able to contain matters up to now, Amigo added. "Their influence is very powerful, but if care is not taken by the government the young people will be beyond restraint soon. While we boast that we are out to protect small nations, we are alienating the splendid Irish race ..."[74]

To Lloyd George the bishop may have seemed naive. The letter, regretfully, received but the barest one line acknowledgement from the prime minister's secretary.[75] The prime minister was embarked on a policy of coercion, and he was to travel further and further along that road despite his own protestations of benign intent. When President Wilson in his Independence Day address, 4 July 1918, announced yet again, "What we seek is the reign of law, based upon the consent of the governed and sustained by the organised opinion of mankind ...", Lloyd George cynically assured American troops the following day – "President Wilson yesterday made it clear what we are fighting for".[76]

As might be expected, the attitude of the Irish Catholic bishops and priests was not favourably influenced by government complaints about them to Rome. The complaints against priests accused them of inciting to armed resistance against conscription. On the denunciations, Monsignor O'Riordan sent a remarkable letter to Walsh on 8 June 1818. Cardinal Vannutelli had shown him a report giving detailed references to priests, places, and dates. O'Riordan had suggested that these were likely to have been made by police-detectives or spies, and probably only referred to meetings held after mass at which the parish priest explained the declaration of the bishops and gave the anti-conscription pledge. He added that even if the reports were true there were "24 bishops, 4 archbishops, with a cardinal, in Ireland" and if they were "either *incapable* or *unwilling* to deal with these cases", they were "not fit to hold the responsible offices given to them". "I said", O'Riordan continued, that "they would be thought quite capable of dealing with such cases, or worse, in other countries", and that "this latest attempt by government to use the Holy See for the purpose of muzzling the Irish bishops, and of bending the Irish people to its will, would not have been made or thought of, if the *Curia Romana* had not been found so pliant in the past to favour its purposes." He went on to convey to the cardinal, from his own grasp of Irish ecclesiastical history, the frustration of Irish churchmen for over a hundred years in the face of Roman misunderstanding. "I said", he assured Walsh, "that the Irish people, whilst they have the deepest reverence for the Holy See have the deepest suspicion of the *Curia Romana*. They all have it: I have it myself. He appeared greatly struck by the revelation." "Tis well", O'Riordan concluded, "I have no vocation for the *plenitudo sacerdotii* "(to be a bishop).[77]

In the face of the concentrated opposition in Ireland, the Imperial War Cabinet decided towards the end of June to put off the imposition of conscription, and to try by various other means to entice recruits. A secret meeting was arranged at Lady Granard's residence, Scribblestown House, for Thursday, 27 June, between Lord French and Cardinal Logue. The intention was to inform the cardinal that conscription was being abandoned, and to encourage him to promote recruiting. Logue, seeing he was being used, left quite annoyed. Walsh obtained his first glimpse of the efficiency of Sinn Fein intelligence on this occasion. The day before the secret meeting he was informed that it was to take place, and what its purpose was. Subsequently, he was acquainted with the result of the meeting.[78] A further expedient was tried on 8 October, the date of the general meeting of the Catholic hierarchy. A telegram addressed to Cardinal Logue, from the British Foreign Office, announced that Cardinal Gibbons, archbishop of Baltimore, wished Cardinal Logue to attend his jubilee celebrations. The English hierarchy would be represented by the bishop of Nottingham (a strong supporter of the war effort). Logue did not mention the telegram to the body of bishops; but having shown it to Walsh, both judged it a propaganda lure to convey to the United States that the Irish church was in harmony with the British government.[79]

The fact that Logue discussed the matter personally and privately with Walsh points to a dimension of the relations between bishops that might be easily overlooked, especially if one focuses on political differences as, for example, Curran does. There was a spirit of camaraderie, and even badinage, that existed between them in spite of differences. This is not something to be found in minutes of meetings, and rarely in diaries. One letter in Walsh's extensive papers provides a brief glimpse of this lighter side to episcopal conferences. On 5 September 1918, Fr Downey, of Eccles Street, Dublin, related to Walsh an incident involving the Cardinal, which Canon Lyons of Ardee had encouraged him to forward, adding "no one will enjoy it more than the Archbishop" – in itself an acknowledgement of Walsh's reputation for raillery, laughter, and an eye for the incongruous.

> The Cardinal was taking his morning swim, or preparing to take it. He walked out along the spring-board looking at the water, before undressing. He lost his footing and fell in! He scrambled out as well as he could – drenched from head to foot. Nothing daunted, he pulled off his dripping garments – and plunged in as usual! Had his swim – landed safe, put on the wet clothes – all but his stockings. He could not pull them on. He put them in his pocket, walked back to his house, and felt nothing the worse of an adventure that would, assuredly, have prostrated the more robust of us for a week.

Fr Downey added: "Further deponent saith not, but knowing your Grace's forbearance, he ventures to say – that, perhaps, it is as well that this incident should be known before the meeting of the hierarchy in October."[80]

A further alleged effort to convert key churchmen to the war effort took place just two days after the sinking of the 'Leinster', when grief and shock were widespread. Manoel, the deposed king of Portugal, called on Archbishop Walsh on 12 October, accompanied by Lord Granard and the under-secretary, Sir James McMahon. The visit had an unexpected lighter side. "The king", Curran observed, "remained in private with the Archbishop for over half an hour" and tried hard to induce him "to attend his Red Cross meeting on Monday, or, failing that, to send a letter as Cardinal Logue was doing". Walsh, seeing this as another government initiative to involve him indirectly in showing support for the war and things British, refused the invitation, "although Manoel repeatedly pressed his request, almost beyond the limits of courtesy". Walsh was much taken by the king's "youthfulness and geniality", and recognised that he did not realise that "he was being made a tool" of British propaganda. On King Manoel asking the archbishop why he refused, he received the answer "that the Red Cross was a British society coming to get Irish money". As he seemed mystified at this distinction, Walsh endeavoured to explain. 'Suppose", he said, "a Spanish society came to Portugal for Portuguese money, would you support it?" "No", said Manoel. "Then", declared the archbishop, "why do you expect us?" "But Spain and Portugal are different nations!" "So are Ireland and England." "But Portugal has a history going back a thousand years!" "Ireland has a history going back two thousand years." "Spain and Portugal have different languages!" "So have Ireland and England, and much more different from one another than Spanish and Portuguese." And so the conversation continued, Curran concluded, "until King Manoel did not know where he was."[81]

The menacing prospect of conscription again loomed in mid-October. It was rumoured in Ireland that the government had decided to issue the order in council for conscription on the day of the re-assembling of parliament, 15 October. In Sinn Fein ranks, where a militant spirit had taken over, the government's projected decision was seen as a declaration of war, and there was serious talk of a precipitous strike by the Volunteers to forestall the British military. In the rumour filled atmosphere, British military were drafted into "strategic positions" and the guard on certain buildings was doubled and trebled.[82] The tension eased, however, as the German offensive ground to a halt, and the German army began to retreat in good order. On 28 October, Austria sued for peace. By 31 October, the Turkish forces had surrendered. It was clear that the war was all but over.[83]

The general election of 1918

On 2 November, Lloyd George circulated a letter postponing Home Rule "until the condition of Ireland makes it possible. As to this last point, the government will be chiefly guided by the advice it may receive from the Lord Lieutenant and the Irish government". It seemed an indefinite postponement of Home

Rule, and a commitment, also, to the non-coercion of Ulster.[84] The Irish Labour party, called on the lord mayor of Dublin to form "a national conference" which would "give expression to Ireland's demand for self-determination". Lawrence O'Neill, called a meeting of the Anti-Conscription Conference at the Mansion House on 9 November to consider the Labour party's proposal calling on the Conference to assume the responsibility "of having Ireland's claim for self-determination brought before the various governments of the world".[85] That day, 9 November, the Kaiser abdicated. Two days later, 11 November, the armistice was signed. A new world order was emerging. At 5.30 p.m. that evening, Lord Mayor Laurence O'Neill, called on Archbishop Walsh "and had a long conference with him on the Irish question".[86] It seems likely that the forthcoming general election featured in their discussion. On 14 November the election was called for 14 December. In October the franchise had been granted at last to women to vote and stand for parliament – if they were over thirty years of age. It was to mean an access of strength for Sinn Fein.[87]

Where the archbishop's support was likely to be was indicated on Sunday, 24 November, when Sean T. O'Ceallaigh brought Richard Mulcahy, the Sinn Fein candidate for the Drumcondra area, to visit him. Walsh received them courteously, and while he was too shrewd to promise Mulcahy his vote, "he assured him", according to Curran, "that he would not vote against him"![88] The campaign for the election became intense during the final week of November. The bishops in the northern counties were concerned lest divisions between the nationalist parties would result in a disproportionate number of seats falling to unionists. On 26 November the Ulster bishops met and pleaded for agreement between Sinn Fein and the Irish parliamentary party with regard to candidates for nationalist seats. On 28 November, Cardinal Logue wrote strongly against the indecision of the Irish party representatives "This letter, supported by a public letter of Archbishop Walsh, settled the question. It was agreed to divide the eight threatened nationalist seats equally."[89]

The previous day, 27 November, three of the four bishops in the ecclesiastical province of Dublin came out publicly in support of the Irish party. They were Dr Brownrigg of Ossory; Dr Codd, bishop of Ferns; and Dr Foley, the bishop of Kildare and Leighlin.[90] This public stance by his suffragan bishops, obliged Walsh to give public expression to his own views, which, he maintained, he had not intended to make public. His letter to the editors of the evening papers on 27 November had serious electoral consequences. He wrote, he declared, because the appearance of letters in the public press from three bishops of the Dublin ecclesiastic province might lead to "a grave misconception" if he maintained silence and did not declare, "in reference to the momentous issues now before the country", that his views were "altogether different from those expressed in the letters of those three venerated prelates". He concluded with a plea to the "two parties now claiming the support of nationalist Ireland" to come to a temporary "working arrangement" for the elections so that parliamentary seats might not be handed over to "the common enemy".[91] Walsh's expressed difference from the Bishops of Ossory, Kildare, and Ferns, was likely to have influenced the result: Ossory (the Kilkenny area) returned two Sinn Fein candidates, as did Kildare, and in Carlow the Sinn Fein candidate was returned unopposed.[92]

Wednesday, 4 December, was nomination day for the general election. It promised well for Sinn Fein. They were returned unopposed by the Irish party in 25 constituencies: 17 in Munster, 3 in Connacht, 2 in Ulster, and 3 in Leinster.[93] Walsh voted for the first time in a parliamentary election as the archbishop of Dublin. "In fact", as he was then entitled to do, "he voted twice", Curran recorded, "once for Dick Mulcahy here in Drumcondra, and then for Lawless, against John Clancy, at Finglas for (the) North Dublin" constituency.[94]

As the country waited on the results of the election, Walsh continued to be consulted on issues affecting Sinn Fein and the country. On 23 December, Curran received a telegram from Gloucester prison, signed "Arthur Griffith, Thomas Dillon, Robert Brennan", stating that no mass had been arranged for the prisoners for Christmas Day. Curran informed Walsh and, as he noted in his diary, "the Archbishop immediately telegraphed to Dr Burton, bishop of Clifton, asking his help. As a result, the bishop of Clifton took the matter up very earnestly and made all arrangements for mass for the internees on Christmas Day". "Not so helpful", Curran added, "was the attitude of a number of prison chaplains, some of whom showed their hostility by coldly intimating that their official arrangements did not contemplate the presence of political internees."[95]

From Rome, on 8 December, Monsignor Michael O'Riordan reported happily that a letter from the bishop of Canea (Dr Donnelly) stated "that your Grace is wonderfully well in health". O'Riordan then went on to tell of "an epidemic of bunting and boasting here in Rome ... since we beat the Germans and Austrians", and added that shortly there was likely to be bell-ringing at the coming of Wilson. "His apartments are being prepared at the Quirinal ... The name of Wilson is on the lips of every *ragazzino del Trastevere*."[96] Impossible expectations had been created by the American president. In Ireland, too, he was the focal point of hope during December 1918, as the appeal to the Peace Conference for recognition was being prepared. The lord mayor of Dublin "had more than one interview with the Archbishop" with regard to a proposal "that the Lord Mayor should approach President Wilson". In one of these interviews, on 19 December, the question was raised of inviting Wilson to Ireland to receive the freedom of the City of Dublin. "The Archbishop", Curran observed, "resolutely opposed any such proposal since Wilson refused to acknowledge the Mansion House appeal though he acknowledged the receipt of the Ulster counter appeal." Indeed, Curran added in his diary, "the Archbishop considers Wilson to be anti-Irish and anti-Catholic, and that it would be demeaning for us to invite a man who did not condescend to answer the Mansion House appeal."[97]

Christmas passed in an atmosphere of political excitement as people waited for the election results. They were announced on 28 December, and proclaimed a resounding victory for Sinn Fein. Out of the 105 candidates returned for Ireland, 73 were Sinn Fein, 6 were Irish parliamentary party, and 26 were unionist. In 24 of the 32 counties, Sinn Fein were victorious. Only in four counties – Derry, Armagh, Down, Antrim – did unionists poll a majority. The Irish party practically vanished. The British press was dismayed by the results. Some sought various explanations, other than a desire for independence. The *Times*, however, felt obliged to admit "the overwhelming nature of the victory of Sinn Fein", and that the general election in Ireland "was treated by all parties as a plebiscite and admittedly Sinn Fein swept the country".[98]

The year had been one of great historical significance and of elation. The unity and victory in the struggle over conscription gave a powerful boost to national morale, and William Walsh savoured it. For so long he had felt removed from politics, and now once again he was able to play a role, and his health, fortunately, was better than it had been for some years. His role had not been inconsiderable where Sinn Fein was concerned. The previous year his support of the party's candidate in the South Longford election had identified the organisation with the popular anti-partition cause and brought a narrow electoral success. In 1918 his meetings with de Valera and the lord mayor on the conscription issue, his ensuring of de Valera's presence, and that of the Mansion House representatives, at the bishops' conference at Maynooth, and his announcement of his support for Sinn Fein in the general election, all contributed to the standing and constitutional acceptability of that organisation. Walsh's own authority and reputation also ensured that there was no concerted criticism by the hierarchy on the grounds of Sinn Fein's flirtation with violence and secret societies. Such concerted action, of course, would not have been popular with the electorate, and Walsh had always been sensitive to popular feeling. By and large, the Irish Catholic hierarchy, as Dr John Bernard, the Irish Protestant primate, maintained, continued to have as their "dominant motive" the desire "to keep control over their people", and as their dominant fear the loss of that control. Bernard had observed perceptively that the Catholic hierarchy were primarily influenced by three factors: Nationalistic sentiments (they are "peasants bred in a Home Rule tradition"); a desire not to forfeit influence over their people (hence, he suggested, their approach to the Plan of Campaign and to conscription); and a genuine "desire to prevent bloodshed".[99]

How to combine the second and third factors was a problem which would expand to critical proportions in 1919. It was rendered more acute by the enthusiasm of many of the younger clergy for Sinn Fein, where they were made welcome and not kept at a distance as seemed to be more the practice in the Irish party after the Parnell split; and also by Sinn Fein's sensitivity to the church's requirements in the field of education.[100] As 1918 ended, however, Walsh, like many others, had a sense of being part of historic change in Ireland, and he faced the new year with a mixture of expectation and trepidation.

XVII

The great ordeal: compassion and enduring to the end, 1919-21

1. REPRESSION, SUPPRESSION, AND INTRANSIGENCE

Different faces of Sinn Fein

A significant part of the Sinn Fein political programme was its purpose not to attend the Westminster parliament, and to set up an Irish parliament. On 21 January 1919, the first meeting of the Irish parliament, or Dail Eireann, was held at the Mansion House, Dublin. Thirty seven of the elected members were absent, in gaol or overseas. Proceedings were conducted with conscious decorum, and in Irish. The government made no attempt to interfere.[1]

On the very day the Dáil met, however, a significant escalation in local violence occurred. The difficulty in restraining the younger population, which Bishop Amigo had warned Lloyd George about, had become manifest in outbreaks of violence in different parts of the country in an effort to secure arms. Now on 21 January 1919, Dan Breen and a small band of companions shot two policemen dead at Soloheadbeg, Co. Tipperary, and stole the cargo of explosives they were transporting. The two constables were popular men, and what Archbishop John Harty of Cashel denounced as "cold-blooded murder" was widely condemned. The local curate, a strong Sinn Fein supporter, having condemned "this frightful outrage", then added significantly that "Ireland's enemies would try and saddle this crime on the new popular movement striving for her independence, but in that they were wrong. The leaders of the movement were far too logical and god-fearing to countenance such crimes".[2] The words were significant in that they pointed to a perception of the Sinn Fein movement that had become widespread among Catholic churchmen. In March 1919, Thomas O'Dea, bishop of Galway, assured O'Riordan, at the Irish College Rome, that "the Sinn Feiners in my diocese are the very reverse of anti-clerical or anti-religious".[3] Even bishops who had opposed them at the general election, such as William Codd of Ferns, and the bishop of Kildare and Leighlin, Patrick Foley, had a similar story. "They are most exemplary in attending to their religious duties and living good Christian lives", Foley informed O'Riordan on 21 March 1919, adding that there had been "some raids for arms, and some incendiarism, in his diocese" but that "it is only the extreme wing of the Sinn Fein movement from whom any real danger is likely to arise".[4]

Such reports were good news to O'Riordan seeking to forestall any effort by the British government to secure a Roman condemnation of Sinn Fein; but they had a wider significance. They underlined that in Ireland the revolutionaries were not anti-clerical and irreligious as so often in Europe; and, indeed, even the most extreme of them saw no clash with their religious belief in being ardently republican in arms.

On 3 February a current of excitement went through the country with the news that de Valera, and two other prominent Sinn Fein prisoners, Sean McGarry and Sean Milroy, had escaped from Lincoln gaol. De Valera's return was welcomed by a number of the hierarchy, who thought he was the only one who could take charge of the whole movement and keep the extremists in check.[5] His escape gave a new impetus to the preparation for the Paris Peace Conference of drafts supporting Ireland's claim to independence.

Harbouring de Valera

On 18 February, the Archbishop's House and its environs became the focus of a strange political interlude. That day Curran received a telephone message that Harry Boland, of Sinn Fein, wished to see him next day at Gill's book-shop. He met with Boland on 19 and 20 February. To his "intense astonishment", Boland proposed that Curran should conceal de Valera at Archbishop's House as it would be "the last place suspected, and it was feared that all the usual places of refuge were known or under observation. A further attraction was the possibility of exercise in the grounds". Curran "thrashed out all the *pros* and *cons*" with Boland and Michael Collins. On Friday, 21 February, to his consternation, Boland and Collins called to Archbishop's House to inspect the place of hiding which he had proposed. "The first condition that I had laid down", Curran recounted, "was that every possible precaution was to be taken to safeguard the position of the *Archbishop. Accordingly, the first step was that he was not to be informed, or to know of it. Therefore, I ruled out the House, but I suggested either of the two lodges*, the garage lodge, which was towards the Tolka (river) end of the grounds, or the gate lodge, directly on the Drumcondra road. The garage lodge was ruled out because it was too much under observation from a neighbouring cottage. It was, therefore, decided to fall back on the gate lodge, which was occupied by the archbishop's valet, William Kelly, and his family. A drawback in this case was the fear that Kelly's two young boys might not be able to keep silent, even though unaware of the identity of the visitor. Having inspected the position, Harry Boland and Michael Collins agreed that it would be suitable, and it was finally settled that, as soon as possible after de Valera's arrival, which was expected in the course of the following week, he would stay in the gate lodge. Outside William Kelly's family, not a soul was informed of this except the *Archbishop's housekeeper*, Miss Corless, whom, from the very beginning, I had consulted, and whose cooperation was essential."[6]

"Sessions of the beatification of the Irish martyrs were being held at the House" during all this time, and many people passed in front of the lodge. Curran was informed on Monday, 24 February, to expect his guest the following night at 8.00 p.m. Punctually at 8.00 p.m. de Valera arrived at the postern gate, which gave access to the Clonliffe premises from the Distillery Stores. He was accompanied by Boland and the custodian of the distillery premises, Mr Denis Lynch (a brother of Diarmuid of Sinn Fein). As they walked through the deserted grounds, de Valera spoke to Curran of "his own personal associations with Clonliffe". He had taught mathematics, mathematical physics and experimental physics to the students at Holy Cross College Clonliffe for the first and second arts examinations in the Royal University in the years before 1909.[7] "In the lodge", Curran continued, "de Valera resided in the room to the right of the entrance, which was fitted up as a bed-sitting room. He spent most of his time revising 'Ireland's Claim to Independence', which was to be presented at the Paris Peace Conference. Each evening after dinner-time, we walked together in the grounds".

There was a kind of twilight atmosphere about the venture, a blending of light and shade, of openness and secrecy. Thus, Curran reported that "during these days, by the wish of de Valera, I arranged for Fr Tim Corcoran, SJ, to meet him. On 28 February, Fr Corcoran came at 7.30 p.m. to discuss the appeal to the Peace Conference, which he had been revising during the week. I think de Valera also saw Fr McErlean the previous day on the same matter. McErlean was attending the Archbishop's House in connection with the process of the Irish martyrs. Also when I informed him that Mr Tom Morrissey, of the Public Records Office, was visiting the Archbishop's House on the same business, de Valera asked to see him, as an old friend." On Friday, 28 February, or the Saturday, Curran was not sure, "a meeting of the ministry took place. It was held in the Dublin Whiskey Distillers premises." "I think it was on Monday, 3rd March," Curran added, "or else the last thing on Sunday night, that de Valera left us."

Thus, Curran concluded his account of a picaresque situation where an escaped revolutionary hid and held court secretly on the premises of an archbishop celebrated for his astuteness and legal acumen, and where those closest to the archbishop conspired to keep him in the dark. Whether Walsh came to suspect what was on foot is not clear, but, in any event, he probably did not wish "to know".

Curran had expected de Valera to stay for two or three weeks while arrangements were made for his transfer to Liverpool, and from there to New York by steamship, and he remained under that impression until the eve of de Valera's departure.

"Possibly as a result of the meeting of the ministry", he surmised, "the programme was changed".[8] It is not unlikely that Collins, concerned at the risks being taken by de Valera in meeting various people, arranged to have him travel earlier than planned to the United States.[9] In England, however, de Valera's departure was delayed following the release of Arthur Griffith and the other "German plot" prisoners. Their release raised the question whether the government now would call off the hunt for the Lincoln escapees.

MOUNTING TENSION AND A CRITICAL ILLNESS

The state of the country, meantime, exercised the bishops in their Lenten pastorals which appeared on 2 March. All protested at the misgovernment of the country and contrasted the way British ministers spoke about small nations during the war and the government's actual policy towards Ireland. Walsh warned in his pastoral: "Our people are now shut out by law from the employments of methods of seeking redress regarded as constitutional in the past. It would be unreasonable, and indeed impossible to expect that they can long rest content with such a state of things."[10]

The tension and dissatisfaction in the country was augmented by the treatment of Irish nationalist prisoners, especially in Belfast prison where sectarianism added a cruel edge to political disagreement. On 15 March, the lord mayor, Laurence O'Neill, called on the archbishop with a signed protest by the members of Dublin Corporation against the treatment of political prisoners in Belfast – pointing out that they had been in solitary confinement in their cells for eight weeks, had been handcuffed for six and a half weeks, been unable to attend their religious duties for eight weeks, and had been "obliged to perform all the functions of nature while handcuffed and without leaving their cells". As the Corporation were unable to protest in the usual manner in the newspapers because of censorship, they requested the opportunity of informing the public by "holding meetings at Catholic churches of your archdiocese on St Patrick's Day after last mass".[11] The document was sent also to Cardinal Logue and, perhaps, to the rest of the hierarchy. Walsh exchanged views with Cardinal Logue, who, on 14 March, announced that he had had the corporation's document amended on some points, and had informed the lord mayor that he did not object to they having "parish meetings" provided they used the amended document and that there were "no party political speeches".[12] There is no indication that Walsh differed from the cardinal in his response.

Later that month, he had had his first serious set-back in health for two years. On 27 March, Sir Joseph Redmond was called, and immediately despatched the patient to bed. In April, there seemed to be a recovery, and then on 17 April Walsh recorded in his diary: "10.30. Sir J. Redmond (kept in bed, afraid of eczema)". Thereafter, his condition deteriorated rapidly. By 22 April he had a day and night nurse, and his doctors visited in the afternoon and at night. He was so ill, Curran observed, that "he received the last sacraments and public prayers were asked for his recovery".[13] He appears to have suffered a mild stroke. On 25 April, Cardinal Logue, writing of the archbishop's illness to

Curran, referred to his "paralysis".[14] Two days later, 27 April, a telegram from Cardinal Gasparri, Rome, stated: "The Holy Father praying that Archbishop be spared for good of church and country, cordially imparts apostolic benediction". Two days later again, Walsh's resilient constitution had begun to recover. "Delighted to hear ... that his Grace was improving", Bishop Hackett of Waterford wrote to Curran on 29 April. By 5 May, Walsh was able to take some food and to walk across the room, and on 10 May he received the Irish-American delegates to the Peace Conference.

The American delegates

These delegates were the men appointed at a meeting of the Irish Race Convention at Philadelphia, on 22 and 23 February 1919, to go to Paris to obtain a hearing at the Peace Conference for de Valera, Griffith, and Count Plunkett, the selected Irish delegates. The three American delegates were: Frank P. Walsh, a prominent New York lawyer and the former joint chairman of the National War Labour Board; Michael J. Ryan, a former corporation counsel of Philadelphia; and Edward F. Dunne, of Chicago, an ex-governor of Illinois. They were to place Ireland's case before the Peace Conference, if a hearing was refused the Irish delegates. They arrived in Ireland on 3 May, stayed ten days, and were feted throughout the country, except Belfast, and were conferred with the freedom of Limerick city. Their arrival coincided with further heightened tension. A number of police had been shot, and the counties of Cork. Limerick, Roscommon and Tipperary were under direct military rule.[15] In Limerick, indeed, in the month before their arrival, a labour strike had taken place against the imposition of martial law and a Limerick soviet was temporarily established. On their arrival in Dublin, the lord mayor wrote to Archbishop's House requesting the archbishop to meet the delegates. It was an acknowledgement of Walsh's historical stature with Irish and Irish-American nationalists; and an indirect confirmation that he had largely succeeded in keeping the church in tune with national aspirations and hence preserved its influence.

In response to the request, Curran went to the Mansion House where a reception was being held for the delegates. The reception, he observed, was delayed by "some hundreds of soldiers and the Dublin metropolitan police" holding up the "approaches to the Mansion House from 5.00 p.m. until 8.00 p.m." Earlier in the day the delegates had attended a meeting of the dail and had witnesssed a raid by military and police seeking to capture Michael Collins. Their first hand experience of repression spoke more eloquently than any words from Sinn Fein representatives. At the reception Curran arranged with the lord mayor, de Valera, Richard Mulcahy, and the delegates for a short visit to the archbishop the following day.[16]

"About 11.30 a.m. the next day (10th May)", Curran recalled, "the delegates arrived. Mr de Valera turned up before them. The delegation was accompanied by the Lord Mayor who, earlier that morning, had accompanied them to

Mountjoy prison. On their arrival … the Archbishop thanked the delegation for their visit to Ireland and for their interest in the Irish cause, and asked them to convey to Cardinal Gibbons his appreciation of his help at the Philadelphia Convention. He expressed his regret that his serious illness had prevented his receiving them properly when they attended the pro-cathedral for mass on the preceding Sunday, and remarked that the delegates had an experience on the previous evening 'of the kind of government under which we are living in Ireland'."[17]

The delegation returned to Paris on 12 or 13 May, well prepared to press the Irish case. Curran rounded off his account of the American delegation with the comment that "they neither succeeded in obtaining an opportunity for Ireland's representatives to be heard, nor for they themselves to be heard in their place". He added, however, that on 6 June 1919, they "sent a copy of their report on conditions in Ireland to the US President with a demand for investigation at the Peace Conference, and also to Lloyd George, and on 8 June they sent copies of the report to the *Times*, and all leading English journals".[18] Not mentioned, however, was the delegates' meeting with President Wilson on 11 June, and their efforts to persuade him to apply to Ireland his celebrated war-time aim of self-determination for small nations.[19] Wilson's failure to respond helped to generate Irish-American opposition to his campaign on the Peace treaty. "He found himself", in Curran's summary conclusion, "preceded, dogged, and followed-up by Irish American associations through every step of his journey".[20]

On 1 June 1919, de Valera left Ireland for the United States. At their meeting that month, the Irish hierarchy protested against the military government of the country. They "asserted the right of Ireland to be mistress of her own destiny, and thanked the Senate, the House of Representatives, also the hierarchy, clergy, and people of every denomination in America for so nobly espousing the cause of the Irish people."[21]

Recovery, illness, recovery

Walsh attended that bishops' meeting. During May he had made a gradual recovery from his various ailments. On 17 June he was able to note, "Glendoo. 1st walk since illness", and on 1 July he set out for Knockabbey, Co. Meath, to recuperate. There on Sunday, 6 July, he entered in his diary, "1st mass since illness". But on 22 July, he was "ill at night", and thereafter he was attended by a local physician, Dr Steen, then was brought to Dublin under the care of Sir Joseph Redmond and a Dr Blayney, who appeared to be a kidney specialist in that a catheter is mentioned in relation to one of his visits. By 4 August, however, Walsh was back at Knockabbey after another remarkable recovery.

On 2 September he returned to Drumcondra and appeared to be in good health. His return coincided with the Dail's decision to sanction "the issue of a National Loan simultaneously in Ireland and the United States of America" in order "to develop and sustain the Irish nation in its island home". "The amount authorised for issue in Ireland" was "£250,000".[22] On 17 September Arthur Griffith and Mulcahy called on the archbishop in connection with the Loan. Mulcahy was to call on him again in its regard two months later, with far reaching effect as will be seen.. Meanwhile, Walsh gave further signs of recovery. He was present at ordinations on 20 and 21 September, and on 30 September his diary recorded a visit from "Chief Rabbi Herzog", the father of a future president of Israel. Bishop Robert Browne of Cloyne, who had corresponded with him with regard to the problem of burses for Irish colleges in Europe, and especially in Paris, wrote gratefully on 23 September: "I am deeply obliged and indebted to you for your long letter just now to hand. First it is an evident proof that you are restored to perfect health again. I am rejoiced to think so."[23] Also in September, Walsh gave further evidence of how his own frailty had deepened his empathy for the pain of others. The writer and scholar, Stephen MacKenna, wrote in some distress to complain of the rudeness and inhumanity of a religious sister deputed to nurse his gravely ill wife.[24] Walsh, in response, so entered into his hurt that MacKenna was greatly moved and expressed his appreciation to his friends and in a letter to the archbishop. His brief, undated communication, was written towards the end of September, 1919. "Excuse me if, in the midst of most distressing times", he began, "I can snatch only a moment to say that I am most deeply touched by the beautiful kindness of your most gracious letter and am very thankful for the effective information your Grace gives me." He added with respect to Walsh's recent illness:

> It was a great joy to all Ireland that your Lordship's illness took the good turn, giving us the hope that we shall have you for many years to bring light and strength to your admiring people.[25]

Walsh's return to health, however, was short-lived. He attended the convocation of the National University on 7 October, and two days later caught a cold. On 20 October, Sir Joseph Redmond refused to allow him attend the October meeting of the hierarchy at Maynooth the following day. Nevertheless, by 6 November he was sufficiently well to receive Richard (Dick) Mulcahy, with whom he had an important discussion regarding the National Loan. Following this visit, Walsh "arranged to write to Cardinal O'Connell (of Boston) in support of the Dail Loan."[26] He wrote the letter on 10 November, recommending the Dail Loan and subscribing £105.

Another significant letter

The letter was posted on 11 November, published in New York on 5 December, telegraphed the same day, and appeared in the *Westminster Gazette*.[27] It was a strong indictment of the British government in Ireland and created an immense impression. The *Westminster Gazette* published it under the following headings:

IRISH FERMENT
Dr Walsh's Letter to American Cardinal
Rampant Disaffection.[28]

"My Dear Lord Cardinal ", Walsh commenced, "I wish to contribute a hundred guineas (£105 sterling) to the Irish National Fund inaugurated under the auspices of the elected body known as the Dail Eireann, our Irish parliament. I cannot but think that, as far as our people of Irish race are concerned, their knowledge of the fact that I have subscribed to the Fund would be of at least as much help as any subscription of mine could be."

He went on to point out that none of the Irish newspapers dared to publish the fact that he had subscribed. Knowing his Eminence's deep interest in Ireland, he trusted that he would help to make known his (Walsh's) subscription to the Dail Eireann Fund. He then outlined some of the restrictions under which they lived. "Freedom of the press, the right to public meeting, the right of personal liberty, even the right of trial by jury, no longer exist in this country except so far as they can exist subject to the absolutely uncontrolled discretion of some military ruler technically designated the 'competent military authority'." "All this has had its natural effect", he continued, "– the driving of disaffection under ground, with no less natural result that disaffection, driven under ground, naturally finds an outlet in crime. "The 'competent military authority',", Walsh concluded, "do not seem to realise that there is no possible remedy for this lamentable state of things, so long as the source of all the evil, the present system of military rule in Ireland, is maintained."[29]

The reply from Cardinal O'Connell was even more forthright. "No one with a drop of true Celtic blood in his veins", he declared, "could be silent beholding how stupidly and how brutally England is governing Ireland today. One would think that for very shame the English would now at last get out of Ireland and leave the Irish to take care of their own affairs". He finished with the assurance: "I gave your Grace's letter to the press and it was published all over the country with good results."[30]

Walsh's letter to Cardinal O'Connell on 10 November was not published in England and Ireland until 4 December. It was first published by the *Morning Post*. Two days later, claiming that the author of the letter had to be Curran, as the archbishop was known to be frequently ill, the paper's "special correspondent" had a fateful interview with Curran.

Curran's blunder

That Curran allowed himself to be the focus of an interview was unwise. In the course of the interview his strong nationalist views usurped at times the caution and balance of a churchman, and, coming from the archbishop's secretary, proved embarrassing for Walsh. He represented the archbishop as seeing English rule as "the source of all evil", and conceded that Dr Walsh's subscription to the

Sinn Fein Fund indicated his support for "total separation" from England. Worse still, asked if Dr Walsh sanctioned "deliberate murder such as the killing of constables?" Curran was less than clear, differentiating between criminal murders by criminals, and political killings, which led the sub-editor, not surprisingly, to have as the sub-heading, "Murderers who are not Murderers".[31]

Curran, like the bishops and many others, found himself faced with a moral dilemma: killing was wrong, and must not be condoned; but to condemn the killing of soldiers and police was to appear to take sides with an unwanted and oppressive government and to have one's condemnation used by the government as a propaganda weapon against the popular movement and this, in turn, was likely to provoke anger against the church in the Irish Catholic community.

The *Morning Post* published Curran's interview on 9 December. Coincidentally or designedly, Cardinal Logue met with Walsh that afternoon, following a meeting of the episcopal standing committee. Walsh decided Curran would have to go. His diary for 16 December stated: "P. Dunne arrived, Curran left". Three days later there occurred an attempt to assassinate Lord French. Deeply annoyed, and knowing that, in the wake of Curran's interview, he had to speak out, Walsh drafted a circular letter to all the churches, and consulted two others[32] who assisted in the revision of it. It was a balanced, carefully-crafted letter.

A careful letter

"The attempted assassination of the Viceroy", he began, "which startled and shocked the city yesterday, calls for the melancholy protest of every Irishman who loves his country and hopes to see the present rule of coercive government in Ireland brought to a final close." "Surely", he went on, "there is no one in Ireland sunk in such ignorance of the moral law as not to know that murder, both in itself and in its consequences, is one of the most appalling crimes in the whole catalogue of guilt." Denunciations, in his experience, had never put a stop to crime, nor did they carry weight with those at whom they were aimed. So, turning again to the assassination attempt, he implied a distinction between the perpetrators and the good men seeking the best for the country, and put the rhetorical question:

> Is there any rational man capable of deluding himself into the belief that such a method of seeking redress of the misgovernment of this country is likely to help on the efforts of the righteous men who are working earnestly, with the single purpose of re-establishing in our country the reign of liberty and justice.[33]

It was an elusive letter. It sought to distance the official church from seeming to support murderers, while yet being careful to suggest that there were good and caring men, presumably the leaders of the movement, who were earnestly seeking what was best for the country. Again, while condemning murder, he wished to avoid giving any opening to government supporters to use the occasion of the attempted assassination for blanket denunciations of nationalists or of the Sinn Fein movement.

On the effect of the letter, and its reception by certain supporters of Sinn Fein, Walsh received a salutary, if somewhat autocratic response from the well known barrister A.M. Serjeant Sullivan. "Within the churches yesterday", he wrote on 22 December, "Your Grace's letter"; "outside the churches the other instructors of our Catholic people were 'explaining' the letter read inside and were distributing your 'real' sentiments in the shape of a leaflet." This presented "the official creed preached at the doors of your churches:

> Years ago ... according to the lights of the people potheen making was illegal, the killing of a policeman murder, but according to the lights of the people today and the circumstances now existing these acts are not illegal or wrong ... Today we have an Irish Republican government in existence ... We have an army to defend that government. This army cannot be expected to come out into the open and face alone the might of the British Empire. Its ... tactics are admirably suited to the circumstances, and duty is duty for the faithful soldier of the Irish Republic when he shoots down a policeman.

"The propaganda of anarchy and outrage is open and notorious", Sullivan continued, and "the silence of the pulpit is diligently represented as the approval of the church". He concluded portentously: "Before these 'Catholic' assassins have fulfilled their promise and have ended my life, I desire to put upon record both here and at Rome that I have called your Grace's attention to the state of affairs that is stealing away our people from the church;" and with regard to 'the silence of the pulpit', "I desire most solemnly to warn your Grace of this public scandal and to call upon you to end it."[34]

Walsh did not reply to the letter, which led Serjeant Sullivan to surmise that his letter never reached the archbishop. "In his household", he proclaimed, "and among his staff, were spies. Much was written and spoken in his name of which he knew nothing."[35] The archbishop's secretary and first biographer, Patrick J. Walsh, described the surmise and comment as without foundation. It was the archbishop's "invariable custom to open and read all letters addressed to him".[36]

The most unfortunate victims in the tensions and bitterness of these years were the returned ex-servicemen. The British army was seen as the enemy by nationalist Ireland, and Irish men who went generously to fight for small nations and to secure Home Rule for their country now found themselves scorned and discriminated against. It was a situation which could not but weigh on Walsh. One of the letters which he retained in his papers emphasised the injustice involved. The letter enclosed a newspaper cutting of his public letter to Cardinal O'Connell juxta positioned beside a newspaper reference to a one-legged ex-soldier from Dublin, who was remanded in England for not paying his fare from

Holyhead to London. "He came to London, he said, to look for work, because it was quite useless for any ex-soldier to ask for employment in Dublin; he would only be laughed at." The letter was just signed "A Canny Scot liberated from the effete and derogatory dogmas of Rome" who headed his correspondence – "Oh, for a Cromwell"![37]

Destination Rome

Michael Curran, meantime, had left Archbishop's House for work at Maynooth College. He and Dr Walsh remained on good terms. Wishing, perhaps, to put his indiscretion behind him, and encouraged by Walsh, he applied for the position of vice-rector of the Irish College Rome. It was a post and location in which, in Walsh's view, his strong nationalism and his ecclesial experience could play, in conjunction with the rector of the college, an important part in counteracting English influence at the Vatican. On 22 December, they came together again at Archbishop's House to discuss what Walsh termed "financial business".[38] The archbishop was clearly mindful of the dedicated service given by Curran over many years. The following day, Curran declared himself overwhelmed by his Grace's generosity in arranging an allowance for him on the lines of that received by the notorial staff in the canonisation process, as well as a retiring allowance in respect of his work as secretary and archivist.[39]

Before Curran could be appointed to Rome, a new rector had to be appointed to succeed Monsignor Michael O'Riordan who had died. Walsh pressed the case of the current vice-rector, a priest of his archdiocese, John Hagan, a man of strong nationalist views. He persuaded the other archbishops to appoint him, even though some of them were unhappy about Hagan's political outlook.[40] Having assured Hagan of his appointment on 29 December,[41] Walsh telegraphed him recommending Curran. Hagan replied by letter on 30 December 1919, that "of several who had written applying for the post" there was "no one so well qualified in every respect and certainly none whom I should welcome more."[42]

That Walsh's own health, meantime, was seen as currently restored and his mental faculties alert was signified by a letter from Joseph McGrath, registrar of the National University, on 23 December, notifying him that he had been appointed a member of the Finance Committee by the Senate for the year commencing the 16 December 1919.[43] His own lively curiosity and mental agility, moreover, had him corresponding once more with the scripture scholar, Fr Patrick Boylan, who, on 11 November, had forwarded to him "a copy of one of the most scientific elementary introductions to Hebrew grammar".[44]

Oppression and rumours

In the final months of the year the Dail was suppressed and many of its members arrested. The remainder, and the Volunteers, took this as a declaration of war against the express will of the nation manifested in general election. Lloyd George, meanwhile, was rumoured to be preparing a new Home Rule bill which would offer to Ireland, exclusive of the six north-eastern counties, full dominion status, free from imperial taxation, and with control of customs and excise. On 7 December two prominent Catholics, former attorney-general, Sir James O'Connor, and Sir James McMahon, under-secretary, came to visit the archbishop on the matter.[45] Walsh could not see the prime minister involving himself in a break with the Tories, the northern unionists, and the treasury, and said so.[46] In the event, Lloyd George, on 22 December, introduced a "Better Government for Ireland" Bill, which proposed separate restricted parliaments for the six counties of the north-east, and for the remainder of the country, with powers to create a council of representatives of both Irish parliaments. The Bill evoked no interest amongst the majority population. There was too much tension, suspicion, and bitterness to consider minor overtures. Ireland was being administered as the *Westminster Gazette* observed on 17 December, "like a country invaded in a time of war", and, on the other side, in the words of the *Times* special correspondent in Ireland – "The prospect of dying for Ireland haunts the dreams of thousands of youths today ... You can neither terrify nor bribe Sinn Fein."[47] In England, nevertheless, some still hoped there might be a set back for Sinn Fein in the forthcoming local elections in January 1920

2. ENDURING THE YEAR OF TERROR, 1920

During 1919, incidents of violence on the part of the Volunteers, or the army of the Irish Republic (IRA) as they were now known, had been numerous but mostly on a small scale. In the final month of the year the attempt to assassinate Lord French marked a new assertiveness. This heralded a second phase in the struggle, which reached a crescendo of terror and counter-terror, of ambush and reprisals, during the final months of 1920.

The new phase commenced on 1 January 1920, when three barracks were attacked in Cork. Similar attacks in other counties followed in succeeding days, and Wexford, Waterford and Kilkenny were placed under martial law. In this climate the municipal elections were held on 15 January. The public response across the country was emphatic. Of the 206 councils elected throughout Ireland, 172 were returned with a majority of Sinn Fein representatives. Of the twelve cities and boroughs of Ireland, eleven declared for Sinn Fein, the unionists holding only Belfast. Two of the six counties, Fermanagh and Tyrone, voted in a majority for Sinn Fein, and in Derry, the "maiden city" of the covenanters, a Catholic nationalist became mayor. Almost all the new councils, before long, severed their connection with the British administration and declared their allegiance to the Dail.

Walsh rejoiced at the overall result, and in at least two instances sent congratulations: to the bishop of Derry on 21 January on the "magnificent victory" and "splendid example of unity set to those elsewhere whose foolish obstinacy has led to the sacrifice of seats otherwise secure";[48] and to Alderman Kelly imprisoned in Britain at Wormwood Scrubs.[49] On 26 January, Walsh noted in his diary a visit by the lord mayor and William T. Cosgrave of Sinn Fein. The subject of the meeting is not clear, but the bishops were due to meet the next day at Maynooth. At that meeting on 27 January, the hierarchy "made a strong pronouncement against government by force and demanded that Ireland be granted 'the right of every civilised nation to choose her own government'."[50]

On the government's use of force in repression, and the fear it generated, W.B. Yeats wrote evocatively in a poem entitled "Nineteen Hundred and Nineteen":

> Now days are dragon-ridden, the nightmare
> Rides upon sleep: a drunken soldiery
> Can leave the mother, murdered at her door,
> To crawl in her own blood, and go scot-free.[51]

The extent and intensity of the repression was greatly magnified in March 1920, by the arrival of a hard-bitten body of ex-service men to bolster the police force. They were soon known as the Black and Tans because of their motley uniform of black police trousers and tan top. They first appeared in Limerick in March, making their debut in a manner which became almost a trade-mark – arriving in lorries, shooting up the city, and insisting on being supplied with free alchol. On 20 March, Thomas MacCurtain, Sinn Fein lord mayor of Cork, was shot dead in the presence of his wife by the forces of "law and order" in disguise. He was succeeded by the deputy mayor, another Sinn Fein supporter, Terence MacSwiney, whose courage and principled stand was to make him an international figure.

The prison problem

Sinn Fein used all its resources to emphasise and punish the excesses of the security forces. It carried the struggle into the prisons. The indiscriminate imprisonment of people on suspicion, without charge, had given rise to bitter resentment and a desire to fight back. Availing of that, Sinn Fein orchestrated the demand that such prisoners be treated as political prisoners rather than as common criminals, and resorted to one of the few resources available, the old Irish weapon, hunger strike. In those early days, death was expected more quickly than it actually occurred. Mountjoy prison in Dublin became a focus of public attention. Anxious crowds gathered outside praying for the strikers, and police and military stood guard at the prison. In the first half of April 1920, there were seventy-two Sinn Fein prisoners on hunger strike. A plea for their release was sent to the lord lieutenant on 12 April by the Catholic chaplains, Mountjoy prison. They had visited the prisoners, and found many of them "in a very weak state". They consulted Archbishop Walsh.[52] He, concerned about the general state of the country, and at what might occur if the 72 men were allowed to die, decided to make his concerns public. He used the format of an interview in the Dublin *Evening Herald*. It appeared on the same day as the chaplains' appeal to the lord lieutenant, and the following day was reported in the *Freeman's Journal*.

"As far as I can see", Walsh commenced, "we are face to face with the near prospect of an appalling catastrophe," and "I have the greatest possible apprehension of the consequence of the present obstinately rigid adherence to the maintenance of the present rules". "Lord French says he has no power to alter them", the press representative countered. His Grace replied that if his Excellency said it they were bound to believe him. "It only shows up", he asserted, "what is known in Dublin as Castle government. We all know its powers for evil. His Excellency's statement throws further light on its helplessness for good. The sooner it is got rid of in some rational way the better prospect there will be of the restoration of some sort of peace in this country."

It was not many days, he continued, since there was a similar state of things in Wormwood Scrubbs. Then it was formally stated "on the highest official authority" that the rules could not be relaxed, "and that any prisoner who 'might chose to commit suicide' – I think these were the words – should himself bear the responsibility". Next day, nevertheless, the government's obstinate resistance changed, "and Mr William O'Brien of this city ... was transferred to a place where he could be treated with some regard to the dictates of humanity". Walsh failed to see why something similar could not be done in Mountjoy.

'The Irish side of this protest will hardly be understood in England,' said the interviewer, and his Grace replied: "I have long since ceased to trouble myself about what they do or think or say in England. I cannot, however, conceive the possibility of many things that are at present being done by the Castle government in Ireland being tolerated by public opinion for one week in England – that is if the victims were not Irish but English." Giving further expression to his deep sense of justice and equality, Walsh commented that it was "appalling to think of what we may be on the verge of in Ireland". It was all the result "of the abominable obstinacy of the government here in treating men as criminals, who, so far from having been convicted of any crime, have never been put on their trial or have never even been told what they are charged with." "I trust", he concluded, "that Dublin Castle has by this time recognised the fearful responsibility that it seems to be incurring with, apparently, the lightest of hearts. I have nothing more to add."[53]

The following day, 13 April, the lord lieutenant replied to the prison chaplains. He denied any comparison between the situation of the prisoners in Mountjoy and that of Alderman William O'Brien to whom reference had been made, and stated that with regard to the prisoners at Mountjoy it was not proposed "to recede from the decision of his Majesty's government announced in the notice of 22 November 1919".[54]

There was some pleasant news for Walsh, however, during April and May. His former secretary, Fr Michael Curran, sent him on 15 April a long news-filled letter on his first weeks at the Irish College. He outlined various occurrences in Rome, and concluded with the news that all the preparations were "well in hand" for the beatification of Oliver Plunkett.[55]

A beatification and its side-effects

The occasion of the beatification on 23 May 1920, proved a marked success in ecclesial terms, but it also had another beneficial effect from Curran's political viewpoint. He recounted in his memoirs how the occasion "was availed of by Hagan to make a strong Irish assertion" and to win over members of the Irish hierarchy who were unfriendly to Sinn Fein.[56] This last was greatly aided by what Curran saw as "the providential" presence in Rome of Arthur Balfour, the ex-chief secretary of "notorious ill-fame", seeking a condemnation from the Holy See of the Irish national movement. Moreover, the address of Cardinal O'Connell of Boston in support of Irish self-determination had a powerful impact. Speaking on 23 May, he urged the Irish bishops to prevent "the decay of the church in Ireland, as had happened in France, by standing by their people". In allusion to the canonisation of Joan of Arc at the same time, he added that "he trusted that it would not be necessary for a peasant girl to arise and lead Ireland in driving out the invader". This frank, impassioned address, in Rome itself, Curran commented approvingly, "gave courage to all friends to speak as frankly, and closed the mouths of many of our celebrated critics". The address was widely circulated and created something of a sensation in British circles.[57]

Cardinal O'Connell's reference to Joan of Arc evoked the feeling of empathy with the French saint felt by many Irish people at the time. Her struggle against England was seen as similar to theirs. Thus, the Dublin Municipal Council adopted a resolution, which they sent to Archbishop Walsh on 13 May 1920, stating that they, "The Corporation of Dublin, Capital of the Ancient Kingdom of Ireland, hail with joy the approaching canonisation of Blessed Joan of Arc, who was burned to death at Rouen in 1431 by the English Army of Occupation, for the crime of trying to free her country ..." The resolution was in Irish and in French, and they asked his Grace to forward it "to the Cardinal Archbishop of Paris"; and they also forwarded copies "to George Gavan Duffy, Representative of Ireland, for transmission to the municipalities of Paris, Orleans, Rheims and Rouen".[58]

The need for a new auxiliary bishop, and diocesan matters

Given Walsh's poor health and advanced years, and the declining health of Bishop Donnelly, it had been evident for a considerable time that the diocese needed an active auxiliary bishop. Walsh, either because he wished to keep all the reins in his own hands or/and did not wish to embarrass Bishop Donnelly, made no attempt to seek a new auxiliary. Nicholas Donnelly's death towards the end of March, however, made an appointment necessary. After some time of grief at the loss of a friend as well as an assistant,[59] Walsh applied to Rome. He was requested to send on three suitable names. On 11 May, he wrote to the members of the diocesan chapter for their choice of candidates, asking them to offer mass for guidance and then in strictest confidence to send him "the names of three, or any lesser number, of priests of the diocese".[60] On 4 June, Patrick Foley, bishop of Kildare, expressed the hope that Father Edward J. Byrne would be appointed. He had been "greatly struck with the exordium of his panegyric on the late Auxiliary". Walsh's last great ecclesiastical ceremony was to be the consecration of Dr Byrne at the pro-cathedral on 28 October 1920.

Meanwhile, Walsh's continued clarity of mind, and his administrative strength, were very much in evidence in coping with difficulties within the diocese. In the parish of Rathmines, for example, he was faced with problems created by the elderly Archdeacon M.A. Fricker. It was left to him to negotiate with the Advisory Building Committee who had been involved in plans for the restoration of the parish church. He wrote to them on 11 April suggesting a meeting. The letter indicated once more an excessive outpouring of energy. "Time is somewhat pressing", he wrote, "and it is unfortunate that the coming week is an exceptionally busy one for me. Friday is practically my only available day for a meeting. By that day, I shall have the tenders for the seats, and also for the concrete flooring for the sanctuary". He would also have a report on the tenders from the architect. The venue for the meeting could be the Archbishop's House, or if more convenient, "some place in Rathmines. It is quite the same to me".[61]

In that same month a new dimension to the armed struggle came with the appointment as chief secretary of an unflincing and unrelenting figure determined to put an end to the IRA, Sir Hamar Greenwood. To sharpen and co-ordinate the pressure on nationalists generally, a new force known as the Auxiliaries was inaugurated on 27 July. They were hardened ex-officers of the British army. Their formation was an acknowledgement that by mid-summer 1920 the IRA had the police on the retreat. More than 300 police stations had been abandoned. The republican courts had virtually taken over from those of the crown

Terror unrestrained

In August, however, the tempo of pressure from the crown forces was raised considerably throughout the country. Areas which had not been associated with IRA violence were subjected to police and Black and Tan raids and vandalism. On 9 August the Restoration of Order in Ireland Act was introduced. This conferred emergency powers on the military command to arrest and imprison, without trial, even without charge, for an indefinite time, anyone suspected of dealing with Sinn Fein. Under this measure numerous people were arrested. Among them, on 12 August, was Terence MacSwiney, who was arrested at City Hall, Cork, presiding over an IRA meeting. Refusing to recognise the authority of his court-martial, he went on hunger-strike to secure his release. Fearful of the excitement likely to gather around his place of imprisonment, the administration moved him after a few days to Brixton prison in England.

The extent of the pressure, and the large number of imprisonments, weakened the IRA. Greenwood and General Macready felt the tide had turned, that they were winning the war. In Britain, however, there was growing unease at the atrocities being committed in the name of "law and order", and overtures towards peace were encouraged by Lloyd George.

Walsh and the first peace overture

One of the first to come forward with overtures was M.J. O'Connor, a solicitor from Wexford. He sent his proposals for settlement to the earl of Shaftesbury and a number of other prominent people, as well as to well-known clergy and, at least, two of the hierarchy. Walsh was a recipient. His reply on 12 September was "vintage Walsh", cutting through to the nub of the problem in the country and declining to deal with anything that distracted from it. O'Connor proposed that the Act of Union be repealed and the Kingdom of Ireland reconstructed.

Walsh considered that such proposals only gave the government an opportunity "of throwing dust in the eyes of the public". Three questions needed to be answered, he declared, before any negotiation could be considered. Were the government "prepared to give Ireland the independence in favour of which the electorate declared so clearly and so emphatically at the general election?" Were "they prepared to express their adoption of a policy, within the lines of that declaration, by embodying it in the form of a parliamentary bill?" Were "they prepared to make all this a reality by unequivocally pledging themselves to stand or fall by the reception given to that bill by the two houses of parliament?" He found it difficult, he stated, "to suppose that anyone in his senses" would regard it likely, "just now at least", that any one of the three questions would be answered in the affirmative by the prime minister, or anyone authorised to speak for the ministry. "For myself", Walsh concluded "I can only say that until all three questions are answered in the affirmative, I do not see my way to spending one minute of my time in what I regard as the unprofitable and even dangerous work of supplying the ministry with subjects for dissection."[62]

The month of October brought striking and contrasting statements. Lloyd George on 9 October sought to justify the policy of reprisals and terror, and rejected the idea of giving dominion status Home Rule to Ireland because it would give them their own army and possession of the ports.[63] The Irish Catholic bishops at their October meeting, however, issued a statement which the *Irish Independent* described as "possibly one of the weightiest ever made in the age-long struggle for Irish freedom".[64]

The bishops' statement

They had previously protested at the treatment accorded a "brother prelate", Daniel Mannix, archbishop of Melbourne, who had merely "used his right as a citizen of the Empire to criticise the conduct of the government",[65] and for that was refused permission to land in Ireland, but was allowed disembark in England, where he was kept under surveillance. Now, at their meeting on 19 October, the bishops spoke out vigorously not only against the treatment of Mannix but against

> countless indiscriminate raids and arrests in the darkness of night, prolonged imprisonments without trial, ... the burning of houses, town halls, factories, creameries and crops ... by men maddened with plundered drink and bent on loot, the flogging and massacre of civilians, all perpetrated by the forces of the Crown, who have established a reign of frightfulness which ... has a parallel only in the horrors of Turkish atrocities, or in the outrages of the Red Army of Bolshevist Russia.[66]

With reference to Ulster, they observed wryly that "all Ireland must be coerced for the sake of the north east, and even Tyrone and Fermanagh must be put under a British government against their wills". They demanded a full enquiry by tribunal into recent atrocities, and denounced both the exclusion from Ireland of Mannix, and the continued imprisonment of Lord Mayor MacSwiney and the other hunger strikers.

Cardinal Logue and twenty-eight bishops signed the declaration. Given Walsh's long hegemony amongst his fellow prelates, especially in relation to political and educational matters, it may be assumed that his contribution to the October declaration was considerable. In Rome, Hagan had the declaration translated into Italian and French, and circulated widely 5,000 copies in each language. The bishops' specific reference to Terence MacSwiney reflected the world-wide interest in his principled hunger-strike.

Terence MacSwiney. The will to endure

MacSwiney's combination of idealism and humanity, of courage and spirituality, made a deep impression. Prayers were offered for him in countless churches, though amongst a number of clergy and bishops there was concern that hunger-strike unto death was suicide. Curran observed that a section of the English Catholic press, some leading lay Catholics, and some prominent English-born ecclesiastics, notably Cardinal Bourne in Westminster, and Cardinal Gasquet in Rome, sought the condemnation of MacSwiney's hunger-strike by the Vatican.

As the days dragged on and MacSwiney and his fellow hunger-strikers continued to endure, the press of the world carried reports. On the 46th day of the ordeal, about 27 September, Mary MacSwiney, already known as a formidable uncompromising republican, informed Walsh that she had written to the cardinal suggesting that as her brother "and his comrades have lasted so long in the struggle they are making, ... it must be that God means to save them in spite of all". She wondered if a pronouncement from the hierarchy "condemning the actions of the government on the grounds of Christianity and civilisation, might prove effective at this stage". Copies might be sent to the Holy Father and to bishops throughout the world. In making this suggestion she was endeavouring, as she felt sure his Grace would understand, "to leave no stone unturned which may help to obtain my brother's release, without any compromise of principle". She concluded with the hope that Walsh would approve of her suggestion and come to their help.[67]

His reply is not known. The hierarchy as a body did not respond for another ten or eleven days. Then the appeal was signed and circulated in their name by MacSwiney's bishop, Daniel Cohalan of Cork. It pointed out that the men were "in their ninth week of hunger-strike, and must be on the verge of death. Their case", the appeal emphasised, "has evoked universal sympathy, even the sympathy of those who differ from them politically and in religion. All, with the exception of the Lord Mayor of Cork, are untried prisoners, and the sentence inflicted on the Lord Mayor was altogether disproportionate to the alleged charges." Calling on the government for the men's "immediate release", the bishops expressed their belief that to detain them in prison, "involving what would be virtually a sentence of death, would be harsh, imprudent, impolitic, and prejudicial to the hopes of peace and of a satisfactory settlement of the Irish difficulty".[68]

There was no release for Terence MacSwiney. He died on 25 October 1920, on the 74th day of his fast. During his long protracted dying, he was visited by numerous friends, and by many bishops and priests. All were impressed by the depth of his religious faith, by his calmness, lucidity, and the consciousness that his sacrifice was forwarding the cause of the Irish Republic.

Initially the authorities raised impediments to the body being buried outside of England, and then to the funeral passing through Dublin. Eventually the restrictions seemed to be lifted, and the body was allowed lie in state in Southwark cathedral with the permission of the bishop, Dr Amigo, provided nothing was done that could be regarded as a political demonstration.[69] Amigo, who had been supportive of Terence MacSwiney from the date of his arrival in Brixton jail, subsequently defended his actions against his critics by stating of MacSwiney: "He was an excellent Catholic and a Lord Mayor. He had every right to be treated with honour by the Church which, while respecting nationality, is the Church of all."[70] His efforts for MacSwiney did not stop at looking after his spiritual welfare, he pleaded with Lloyd George for his release, and pointed out to Bonar Law, with gentle directness, the inappropriateness of his standing in judgement – "Even at a time when we were already engaged in a 'life and death' struggle, you yourself with Sir Edward Carson at Belfast on 28

September 1914 were speaking words which produce their unfortunate result today in Ireland. Cannot the clemency shown to you then, be now shown to the Lord Mayor?"[71]

At 7.00 p.m. on 27 October MacSwiney's body arrived at the church and from then until eleven o'clock thousands filed past the coffin where the corpse lay under a glass panel. Next day the bishop of Portsmouth offered the solemn requiem in the presence of Bishop Amigo and Archbishops Mannix of Melbourne and Kennealy of Simla. The cathedral was packed to suffocation. Later in the afternoon, there was an impressive mile-and-a-half long procession as the cortege made its way to Euston station.

That day, 28 October, Archbishop Walsh received a telegram which stated briefly: "The Irish Executive have been informed this evening that the government have decided that the remains of the late Lord Mayor of Cork are not to be conveyed via Dublin. A special steamer will be available at Holyhead to carry the remains direct to Queenstown."[72] The ship, with a heavy contingent of troops and Auxiliaries aboard, ensured that the coffin was brought to Cork. The family and mourners, however, insisted on travelling independently by the mail boat to Dublin. There, they were met by a large representative party, and the procession to the pro-cathedral, as planned. "Next morning", as the biographer of Terence MacSwiney noted,

> a requiem mass was said by Archbishop Walsh, in spite of his great age, at which Dr Spence, Archbishop of Adelaide, Dr Clune, Archbishop of Perth, and Dr Foley, Bishop of Ballarat, were present. A general cessation of work had been arranged by the trade unions that day, and another great procession accompanied the empty hearse and the friends and relations of the Lord Mayor to Kingsbridge and the Cork train.[73]

At Cork there was a lying in state in the City Hall, attended by vast crowds, and Bishop Cohalan observed: "Periodically, the memory of the martyr's death will remind a young generation of the fundamental question of the freedom of Ireland".[74]

Talk of martyrdom in the cause of Ireland from a bishop, in the presence of numerous prelates also paying respect, signified the impact of MacSwiney's struggle and death, and the reverence and pride it evoked. For Walsh, himself a living symbol of a churchman in tune with the nationalist spirit of his people, the enduring strength of MacSwiney's principles and courage was deeply moving. His own struggle to act as celebrant of the solemn requiem mass on such an emotion-charged occasion was his tribute to a dead patriot, and his way of participating in the lord mayor's act of ultimate defiance.

But this was not the only emotion-charged event of those days. There was another patriot, a much younger figure, a Dublin boy, who had been sentenced to death, and whose situation greatly moved the archbishop. The youth's cause, indeed, evoked interest and concern not only in Ireland, America, and Britain, but also in Italy, Spain, and France.

Kevin Barry. Pleading for mercy

Kevin Barry, a university student of eighteen years, took part in a raid to take rifles from British soldiers. Shooting broke out. Three soldiers were killed. Barry was captured, ill treated, and sentenced to death. His age, personal character, and the maximum publicity engineered by Michael Collins, attracted enormous attention and gave rise to numerous pleas for mercy. Archbishop Walsh, as will be seen, was one of those who pleaded earnestly for the young man. In vain. A conference of government ministers, presided over by Lloyd George, decided on 28 October against any commutation of the penalty. He was executed on 1 November 1920. Young Barry, a deeply spiritual person, had made an altar in his cell at which he attended two masses on the morning of his execution. The religious fervour of MacSwiney, Barry, and some other prisoners, made a deep impression in Rome and helped foil British efforts to demonise Sinn Fein and the movement for independence. Kevin Barry's execution was the first since 1916.

The counter-effect of the 1916 executions had given Walsh hope that Barry would be spared. He committed himself to securing a commutation of the sentence. Despite the physical effort and psychological reluctance, he called on the commander-in-chief, General Nevil Macready, urging a reprieve, and emphasising Barry's extreme youth. Macready responded that the victims of the crime were also mere youths, one being younger than Barry, and they too left mothers to mourn their loss. Walsh also approached Sir John Anderson, joint under secretary with James MacMahon, who later wrote of the aged archbishop being carried up to his room to make his appeal. "I had to tell him to my sorrow", Anderson declared, "that to do what he asked would be to proclaim the helplessness of the law, and the law was very 'effective'."[75] Walsh, nevertheless, went to the viceroy, Lord French. Again without success.

The archbishop's efforts were deeply appreciated by the Barry family, the students of University College, and the public generally. The public's response was suggested by the manner in which, following his death some six months later, the press effusively recalled his "noble effort":

> A mighty man, in the true sense of the word, the great Archbishop of Dublin did not consider that it was beneath the dignity of his high office to call at the Castle, and was not offended at being sent from one high official to another, and even went to the length of going to the Viceregal Lodge ... in the effort to save young Barry's life, and when his Grace told Lord French what the execution of young Barry would lead to, *his judgement was borne out by after events.*
>
> The churchman, proud but simple, dignified but sorrowful; the soldier of many battles, puzzled and dismayed, with the look of *painful help-*

lessness in his face, who pleaded he could do nothing, but wished he could – that it was a matter entirely out of his hands, as *the Cabinet had decreed that young Barry should meet his fate.* However, the Archbishop had done his part.[76]

Curran, indeed, recorded in his memoirs that he had been informed by the archbishop's entourage "that, so deeply was he affected by the execution of Kevin Barry, he never again recovered his good spirits".[77]

Walsh's efforts, however, did not go without criticism. On the day before the execution he made a final effort. He had read in all the churches of the diocese a statement, presumably explaining Barry's views and pleading extenuating circumstances, but to at least one member of the congregation at University Church it was "a long, violent and prejudicial political treatise" identifying "Sinn Fein principles with Catholicity". "The hierarchy and the priesthood", he added, "should confine themselves to the word of God." Had they done so there might not have been "the cruel and cowardly murders of the police force ...by those of their own creed and country".[78]

The alleged warning of "what the execution of young Barry would lead to", which the newspaper stated was "borne out by events", referred, presumably, to a growth in the number of Volunteers and in violence. Tim Healy wrote to Lord Beaverbrook on 15 November 1920: "The Shins have got thousands of recruits by the hanging of young Barry ... Nobody has been frightened save those who have lost property and in no country do the propertied classes make or unmake revolutions." "Of course", he continued sardonically, "like the man who tried to make his donkey do without food and would have succeeded only the brute died, your military geniuses are assuring Lloyd George that they are on the eve of success".[79]

The policy of reprisals continued to be backed by the British cabinet. On 9 November at the Guildhall banquet Lloyd George made the celebrated speech in which he claimed – "We have murder by the throat ... we had to reorganise the police. When the government was ready we struck the terrorists and now the terrorists are complaining of terror."[80] Michael Collins, indeed, was conscious that a reorganisation of the government's intelligence network had brought about much of the recent government successes. On Sunday, 21 November, his special squad shot nineteen agents in cold blood. One or two of the victims were probably not agents. The action destroyed the Castle's intelligence system, but that afternoon the security forces surrounded Croke Park, where a football match between Dublin and Tipperary was in progress, and turned their rifles and machine-guns on the crowd. Fourteen people died and hundreds were injured. Greenwood reported to the cabinet that the police fired in self-defence. In succeeding days, Dublin lived in fear. There were widespread arrests.

Archbishop's household not immune

One of those arrested was the archbishop's valet, William Kelly. This obliged Walsh to make a second plea to General Macready in the space of a month. Immediately he heard of the arrest, he composed a suppliant letter aimed at restoring Kelly to his family, and veiling his own annoyance and anger:

> A most extraordinary thing has just now occurred in this house. My valet, William Kelly, who has been with me for at least twenty years, – a singularly steady middle-aged man, who, with his wife and young family, occupies the lodge, here, has been arrested by a military officer, acting, as he states, and, as I have no doubt, under orders … From what I know of my valet, I feel perfectly confident that a serious mistake has been made, possibly as a result of false information in some way conveyed to the authorities.

"I know how much occupied you must be at a time such as this", Walsh went on, "but is it too much to ask you to have the matter looked into by some one in whom you can have confidence to let you know how the matter really stands?" He concluded almost submissively, stating that if things were normal, he would have asked to call personally at the Royal Hospital to see Macready about this, but it was close to curfew time and he understood the road was closed to motor traffic. A reply from general headquarters informed him that Macready was absent, and apologised for inconvenience caused him,[81] but stated that the officer commanding the Dublin district reported that Kelly was "concerned in the revolutionary movement". He could, however, be given into his Grace's charge, if his Grace gave an undertaking "that he will surrender himself for trial if called upon".[82] Walsh expressed his distress and annoyance to the archbishop of Tuam, Dr Gilmartin. The latter sympathised with him on 29 November, but added pointedly that "the assassinations in Dublin were mad crimes. They are having their sequel all over the country in arrests, causing great dislocation to family business."[83]

The excesses and endless violence, including the burning of Cork city by government forces, were circulated in the United States of America, at Paris and Rome, by Sinn Fein propaganda, and this publicity and public pressure obliged Lloyd George to encourage overtures for peace, while not halting the security forces in their intimidation and deliberate policy of terror.

Positive reactions and peace proposals

In Britain, also, there was a reaction against the excesses, and the bitter divisions being caused in the United Kingdom. On 29 October, Henry Somerville sent a "statement" to Walsh signed by a number of British Catholics of all parties expressing their "grief and shame" at the present situation and seeking reconciliation between Great Britain and Ireland on the basis of acknowledged equality. The "statement" had been sent to the prime minister, Walsh was informed.[84] A further public declaration of support came from Cardinal Mercier and the Belgian bishops, and an assurance of their prayers and sympathy. The impact of their declaration evoked from the *Morning Post* the pronouncement that the cardinal would have been thought to be "the last man in the world to have associated himself with a movement ... inspired by anti-Christ."[85]

A further positive development in a dark month was the offer of financial aid from America for "devastated areas". Arthur Griffith informed Walsh on 18 November that he had received a message from the United States which signified that "an appeal from the Irish hierarchy to the American bishops" would secure "a wide movement here for material assistance". He offered to call on his Grace on the matter.[86] The body involved in collecting aid was the influential American Committee for Relief in Ireland. It worked through the reputable White Cross organisation, which was to disburse some five million dollars for relief in Ireland in the spring and summer of 1921.[87] Walsh encouraged and provided assistance to an Irish White Cross organisation, working at times through Count Plunkett.[88]

The first substantial move towards peace and a settlement came from Patrick Clune, the Redemptorist archbishop of Perth. He approached Lloyd George on 1 December 1920, and offered to promote peace. He had been a chaplain during the war to the Catholics in the Australian forces. Lloyd George was impressed. Clune came to Ireland on 3 December, and obtained a secret meeting with Collins the following day. They worked out a formula for a truce apparently consistent with Clune's conversation with Lloyd George. Under this formula both sides would cease all acts of violence "with the object of creating an atmosphere favourable to the meeting together of the representatives of the Irish people, with a view to bringing about a permanent peace".[89]

Lloyd George, faced by the reluctance of his military advisers, added to the terms of the truce the requirement that the IRA must first surrender their arms. This was unthinkable to the Irish leaders. Subsequently, it was suggested to Clune that direct intervention on the part of the Irish hierarchy might bring about a settlement. Clune consulted with Bishop Fogarty of Killaloe, and had a number of meetings with Walsh. Clune's reply regarding the bishops as intercessors might have been dictated by Walsh. It countered any government ploy to bypass the Dail and the elected representatives with the astute comment "that while the bishops would be willing to discuss matters with the representatives of Dail Eireann, they could not think of usurping the functions of the National Assembly".[90] Clune left Ireland with a high estimation of the Sinn Fein leadership. This was to prove important in later deliberations in Rome.[91]

As Christmas approached there was an easing of tension except in the northern counties where the Government of Ireland Act – establishing two subordinate parliaments, and thereby legalising partition – was due to become law. The Act became law on 23 December. The same day Eamon de Valera secretly arrived back in Ireland. Before long, both sides wondered what difference his return would make.

Archbishop Walsh's health, meanwhile, continued to fluctuate. On 14 November, Tim Healy observed – "We were delighted to see you in such vigour and spirits and trust God will preserve you to witness a day of triumph."[92] Three days later, Bishop Gilmartin wrote that he "was sorry to learn ... that your Grace is not as well as usual".[93] There was no expectation, however, that Walsh would not "witness a day of triumph" or that he had only a few months to live.

3. THE FINAL MONTHS, 1921

At the commencement of the new year, Walsh was in his eighty-first year and feeling well. He had much to concern him. To the continued government-authorised reprisals, was added a renewed danger of condemnation from Rome. A letter from Hagan, the rector of the Irish College, on 23 January, announced that, shortly after his arrival in Rome, Archbishop Clune was taken aback to learn that a papal pronouncement was about to be made which, while aimed at condemning violence on all sides, would be seen as a particular attack on Sinn Fein. Clune had protested strongly to Monsignor Ceretti, protector of the Irish College, and to the pope, both of whom recommended him to see Cardinal Merry del Val. Only after a third call, was Clune able to meet the cardinal. The latter frankly admitted that his purpose was "to remind the people of Ireland that there was such a thing as the fifth commandment". Clune was now convinced that the papal pronouncement was abandoned, but Hagan was not so sure. The words of Irishmen on happenings in Ireland were treated as partisan. He pointed to the scandal of a pronouncement having been prepared without "even the representatives of the Irish bishops" being "asked for as much as one word of information on the subject". The bishop of Southwark, however, was in Rome, and "doing yeoman service" to counteract the British propaganda. Unfortunately, he was going home shortly.[94]

On 2 February, Hagan observed that Merry del Val was "very unscrupulous" and had become "a sort of leader of the English forces". He was sheltering "behind the utterances" of the bishops of Cork, Tuam and Kilmore, who had been publicly critical of the IRA. Walsh responded with two letters in close succession, on 9 and 10 February, neither of which appear to be extant. The letter of the 9th seems to have been what Hagan needed. "A copy of your letter of the 9th", he reported on 14 February, "is being made at the present moment and shall be sent at once to Cerretti for immediate presentation to P. Max" (the pope).[95]

Also causing concern at this stage was the continuous intransigence of Cardinal Bourne and the organ of his archdiocese, the *Westminster Cathedral Chronicle*. That paper proclaimed in January that Ireland was "bound and gagged by the bloody hands of men who have been themselves bound and sworn to the immoral principles of Bolshevism, in the desecrated name of nationalism"! (p. 11) Walsh was disgusted, but not surprised, when the cardinal himself followed it on 13 February with a pastoral letter, which he caused to be read in all the churches of the diocese, and which enclosed for public reading Cardinal Manning's condemnation of Fenianism, which Bourne was now identifying with Sinn Fein. Thus, as Curran noted, he equated Sinn Fein, successful in general elections, with organisations which were "in opposition to the law of God and to the Catholic Church". The English press seized gladly on the pastoral. In Westminster diocese, however, Irish Catholics loudly interrupted the reading of the letter in the churches and were said to be planning organised meetings.[96]

Shortly afterwards, on 17 February, Cardinal Logue forwarded to Bishop Amigo of Southwark a detailed account of the atrocities committed by a camp of Black and Tans at Gormanstown, Co. Dublin, "a nest of bandits and homicides". Amigo sent a copy of the letter, on 21 February, to the king, the archbishop of Canterbury, and Sir Robert Cecil. The latter read the cardinal's letter in the House of Commons, and Randall Davidson, archbishop of Canterbury, condemned the Black and Tans in the Lords. King George V's secretary assured Amigo that His Majesty was "deeply concerned at the deplorable condition of affairs still existing in Ireland". In retrospect, the debate in the House of Commons at the end of February was a turning point. Public opinion was turning against Lloyd George on the Irish question.[97]

Heartened by the signs of change, the Irish Catholic residents in London assembled in mass meeting at the Kingsway Hall, on Friday, 18 March 1921, to enter their "emphatic protest" against the pastoral of Cardinal Bourne. They sent a copy of their protest to Benedict XV, to Cardinal Bourne, to all the members of the Catholic hierarchy in England, and to various organs of the British, Irish, and foreign press. A copy was also sent to Archbishop Walsh. Their statement, which they claimed represented the indignation of Irish people across the world, declared bluntly:

> We consider that that letter, which entered no protest against the continuous acts of unchristian brutality perpetrated by the English government in Ireland, was written at the dictates of a bigoted anti-Irish coterie, and was intended to assist the present coalition government of England in their efforts to thwart the will of the Irish nation.

They went on to "warn Cardinal Bourne that, whilst, as dutiful Catholics, we will respect and obey the Church in matters of faith and morals, we will not suffer any ecclesiastical dictation or interference in political matters, no matter how high or eminent the authority which seeks unlawfully to impose such dictation or interference".[98]

It was a salvo which could not but evoke sympathetic echoes in William Walsh, however much he might deplore that people had been driven to such a protest against church authorities. It was one of the last written communications he received before his final illness.

Meanwhile in Ireland, Walsh was distressed and angered as the litany of outrages expanded. On 28 February, six republican prisoners were executed by firing squad in Cork, and their remains refused to their relations. The bishop of Cork, Dr Cohalan, condemned the executions, warned that "the government would only succeed in driving everyone into the ranks of the Irish Republican Army, as they had driven the country into the arms of Sinn Fein in 1916".[99] Archbishop Walsh had received notice of the impending executions, and that some of the men were known to be innocent and that "even the secret court" had recommended "one of them for mercy".[100] He immediately "made the most strenuous efforts" to arrange a meeting with the lord lieutenant and the commander of the crown forces, but to no avail.[101] The next he knew was the announcement of the executions in the evening papers of 28 February.

That evening Walsh arranged for an interview with the *Independent*. He only knew what he read in the newspapers, he informed the interviewer, but what he had read he could "only characterise as barbarous". "Six victims of the tyranny now dominant in Ireland were to be put to death. The tyrants had a free hand. What justification can be pleaded for the method of execution that was chosen?

> The victims were shot two by two. Four of the six had to stand aside, and in their hearing the shots were fired by which the first two victims were done to death. Similarly, two more were kept in agonising suspense while the other two were disposed of.

"Could any greater refinement of cruelty be imagined?" Walsh continued. "If there is any justice left in Irish administration, whatever officers of so-called justice are responsible for what has been done in the name of justice, will surely be called to a strict account for it."[102]

The orgy of reprisals went on. Six British soldiers were killed in incidents in Cork. In Limerick on 7 March, the mayor, George Clancy, and two other leading citizens, were murdered in their homes by government forces. Seven days later, again in the face of appeals and condemnations, six more republican prisoners were killed. This time death was by hanging, and in Dublin. There were public demonstrations, and, at the request of the Irish Labour Party, there was a general stoppage of work in Dublin until 11.00 a.m. Cardinal Logue, Archbishop Walsh, and the lord mayor, "used their utmost influence in appeals for mercy, but in vain". There was very slender evidence in the case of two of those hanged, and in the case of one man, Patrick Moran, the injustice seemed blatant. Walsh wrote to Moran's solicitor, appealing once again to the legal authority of Chief Baron Palles:

> that, when the evidence, on which a charge is based, fails to sustain it, not merely in the case of a capital charge, but in the case of any charge, great or small, the only result consistent with justice is withdrawal of the

charge and acquittal. I apply this without hesitation in the case of your client.

"This", as Curran observed, "was the last public intervention of the Archbishop in political affairs."[103]

Meantime, almost as a relief, and reminiscent of earlier days, there was a flurry of correspondence in which his Grace assertively took a position which mystified his petitioners and created confusion and tension. This interchange occurred in relation to chaplaincy at the Royal Hibernian Military School, Phoenix Park.

Father J.P. McSwiggan, an elderly man, was chaplain. He seems to have been unable to fulfil the position adequately. The governors of the school, unwilling to dismiss him, encouraged him to resign, and on 21 January enquired whether a letter from him was to be taken as a formal resignation. McSwiggan passed the governors' letter to the archbishop, who seemed to feel that proper protocol and legal correctness was not being observed. He reacted accordingly. "How could the board conceive that Fr McSwiggan could do anything so sense-less as to write a letter resigning his office in the school?" Walsh demanded. He had no authority to resign without consulting him. He, moreover, did not see grounds for resignation. He had asked for information regarding Fr McSwiggan's discharge of his duties, but had not received an answer. He could not be expected, therefore, to co-operate in getting rid of an officer who had not failed to discharge his duties. The interchange of letters continued through February and into March, the governors seeking to have another chaplain appointed, the archbishop complaining of discourtesy in that his questions had not been answered, and the governors, it seems, not clear as to what exactly was his problem.

Eventually, Charles A. O'Connor, Master of the Rolls, a Catholic governor, wrote on 6 March that he was "exceedingly troubled" by his Grace's letter as he had never experienced anything from him but "the greatest kindness". But what was he to do? he asked. "Everytime the R.C. chaplaincy came up for consider-ation" he felt ashamed "that the spiritual department was the only one in the school in which slackness and inefficiency prevailed". Walsh was moved by O'Connor's letter. "I am dreadfully put about at your being distressed at any-thing done by me. It seems to be that there is a chain of misunderstanding in reference to the Hibernian school and its chaplaincy." He proceeded to explain once more the position from his point of view, only this time the explanation seemed far more straightforward than previously. Appointment was a matter for the board. They should let him know the chaplain they wished to appoint. On his learning that the man was willing to accept the office, and on his being sat-isfied of his suitability, he would give him the necessary "faculties" to discharge his duties; but he still required an answer from the governors to the question regarding Fr McSwiggan's discharge of his duties. He felt he was entitled to such an answer, as was Fr McSwiggan.[104] The correspondence ceased at this point. The matter was not fully resolved in the archbishop's remaining days, but a more relaxed and open atmosphere prevailed.

The last illness

During March, Walsh's health declined seriously, and on 20 March his physicians, Drs. Blaney and Ryan, decided that an operation was necessary. Next day, Walsh asked for the prayers of the children of the Sacred Heart Home, Drumcondra, and the prayers of his valet's children, met with the vicars of the diocese at 12.00 p.m., hosted dinner at 2.00 p.m., and at 4.00 p.m. was brought to a private nursing home in Eccles Street, attached to the Mater Misericordiae Hospital.[105] That day, 21 March, in a barely legible hand, he drafted a notice to be sent to the clergy and laity of the diocese announcing that the archbishop was seriously ill, and adding:

> His Grace earnestly requests the prayers of the faithful for his spiritual and temporal welfare. The Prayers for Peace ordered in the Archbishop's letter of 14th of last October, will, of course, be continued, whilst the present need for them lasts.[106]

On Tuesday, 22 March, a minor operation was successfully performed, which he bore remarkably well. Subsequently, however, it became clear that a more serious operation was required. This was arranged for Monday, 4 April, but by then his condition had so deteriorated as to make the operation impossible. He lingered until 2.23 a.m. on Saturday morning, 9 April. "Up to the very end", the *Freeman's Journal* of that date stated over-elaborately, "his keenness of intellect, his powers of memory, and his interest in affairs was unimpaired". That he was conscious until near the end, seems to have been the case. P.J. Walsh, writing of his "serene faith" and his final hours, observed: "Several times during his last illness he had the act of faith read for him; and when the end was near at hand, as his life ebbed slowly away, clasping the hand of the priest who was reading, he pressed it in token of assent after each article of the Creed. When about to receive the viaticum on Friday morning, he said it would be his last communion, and he tried to prepare with especial care ..." Also on the Friday, as his voice became faint and his eyes dim, he roused his determined will for the final time to write – "I wish to leave my grand piano to the convent, Merrion Blind Asylum, as an addition to the enjoyment of the all but hopeless affliction of the blindness of the young, and, with the piano, the pianola and the music rolls". "On the day of his death, as the litany of Our Lady was being recited, he asked that it should be said more slowly, so that he might join with greater deliberation in the responses." "Up to the last moments of consciousness", his secretary added, "he continued to make acts of faith, hope, contrition, resignation, and gratitude to God for granting him a comparatively painless death."[107]

Over the next few days, tributes from all sides conveyed a nation-wide appreciation of an exceptional man. The editorial in the *Freeman's Journal*, under the heading, "The Dead Archbishop", opened with sentences which summed up the feelings of many:

> A great Irishman and a great churchman has passed away in the death of the Archbishop of Dublin. Intellectually he was one of the foremost Irishmen of his generation. His capacities were as many as his mind was big. A scholar, a theologian, a born administrator, a citizen of statesman-like quality, there was scarcely in life a career in which, had he chosen it, he would not have reached that first rank.

The opening words were followed by a detailed account of Walsh's life, running to several pages. A somewhat similar format was followed in the other main Irish papers, and in the English papers there was also coverage.

Funeral arrangements and burial

Arrangements for the funeral were necessarily detailed and complicated. A variety of bodies and persons wished to be represented at mass at the Pro-Cathedral – the lord mayor of Dublin and corporation, the corporations of Cork, Waterford, Kilkenny, and Dun Laoghaire, various urban and county councils, representatives of the National University and of other educational bodies, representatives of different hospitals, and of many charitable and professional bodies, and of the Irish Labour party. In the funeral procession further provision had to be made for the carriages of representatives of Dail Eireann, and of the Protestant archbishops; for the representatives of the Jewish community, for the lord chief justice of Ireland, the Master of the Rolls, the provost of Trinity College Dublin, the College of Physicians, Cumann na mBan, the trades unions, and many other bodies. In front of the hearse in the extensive procession, the lead was taken, appropriately, by school children, girls, and boys of St Vincent de Paul's orphanage, followed by the Christian Brothers, Clonliffe students, priests, and carriages containing the metropolitan chapter, bishops and other prelates, and finally Cardinal Logue's carriage.[108]

Meantime, unexpected predicaments were presented by Viscount French, the viceroy, sending a telegram of sympathy and signifying his desire of being represented at the funeral, and by General Macready, commander-in-chief of the British forces in Ireland, sending condolences and stating that he, and the army, wished to be present also. Given the feeling in the country, their presence at the obsequies of Archbishop Walsh, who was so identified with nationalist Ireland and whose pleas for condemned prisoners had been rejected by them, would have been bizarre and offensive. Moreover, word was received on Wednesday, 13 April, "that the presence of any representative of the viceroy or of the commander-in-chief of the forces of the crown would lead to a vigorous demonstration of protest and to a withdrawal of the offer made by the stewards of their services in marshalling the funeral procession". After consultation with Dr Dunne, bishop of Spigaz, and Monsignor Fitzpatrick, Fr Patrick J. Walsh, the archbishop's secretary, was requested to arrange interviews with Lord French and General Macready.

Walsh was graciously received by both men, who expressed their understanding of the situation. Macready assured him that he "would see that all flags in government offices in Dublin would be flown at half-mast ... that no troops would appear on the streets, and that there would be no interference". Walsh amused Lord French by informing him that letters of condolence arrived by the same post from General Macready and the IRA commander-in-chief, Richard J. Mulcahy, which led French to remark "that Smuts, against whom he fought in South Africa, was described as a blood-thirsty murderer etc. etc. just as Mulcahy was today ..."[109]

Archbishop Walsh died on Saturday, 9 April, but was not buried until Thursday, 14 April. On the Sunday, mass was celebrated in the presence of the remains, and "Mr Leo Whelan sketched the body, and Mr Albert Power took a death-mask". The remains were visited privately, mostly by the clergy. From Monday to Wednesday the lying-in-state was open to the general public, and long queues formed to pay their respects. On Thursday, 14 April, following 11.00 a.m. office and requiem high mass, with music provided, appropriately, by the Dublin Priests' Choir and the Palestrina Choir, the cortege procession moved along crowd-lined streets to Glasnevin cemetery. There the most fitting final tribute was paid to the socially-minded archbishop, "the different funeral trades and the grave-diggers of Glasnevin, waived all strike difficulties" in order that he might be laid to rest "in all honour and reverence".[110]

William J. Walsh was a munificent prelate. He left little of his own. At his death his "personal assets amounted to between £700 or £800", apart from a figure of £1000 "for the carrying on of the household" and to pay to those who served him: £250 to his valet, William Kelly; to his chauffeur, £150; the housemaid, in his employment for 10 years, £100; to another servant £25; and to each of the other servants, the cook, two kitchen-maids, and two groundsmen, one year's wages.

XVIII

Epilogue – a retrospection and assessment

Walsh's friend, the ecclesiastical historian, Myles V. Ronan, observed that "he was welded to so many movements and undertakings, for such an extensive span of years," that "he seemed an institution rather than a man."[1] At Walsh's death, therefore, the national daily papers devoted many pages to a detailed summary of his long life, and in succeeding weeks articles on the archbishop appeared in reviews and magazines. Not surprisingly, in all these literary media of communication, much was made of Walsh's facility in writing: of his many books, his numerous articles, and a seemingly endless flow of letters to newspapers on a multitude of topics.

Walsh's books covered a range of subjects. A list of his main works is given in the Appendix. There was one projected book, however, which was never published. He planned a work of major proportions dealing with the canon law of the Catholic Church in its relation to the civil law of charity. He worked on this theme for some twenty years and accumulated a vast amount of manuscript material, which he left instructions was to be destroyed. The instructions were carried out. His secretary and biographer, P.J. Walsh, gave this as an instance of his Grace's severe criticism of his own work. "He was unwilling that an imperfect and possibly an inaccurate and misleading book of reference should be associated, even posthumously, with his name."[2] On the other hand, the archbishop's friend and regular legal consultant, James Murnaghan, who frequently discussed and assisted with the projected book, informed his wife of his Grace's crushing disappointment when another book appeared on the same subject before he had completed his work. Hence, the decision to destroy his accumulated manuscripts.[3]

Walsh's many articles appeared mainly in such periodicals as the *Contemporary Review*, the *Fortnightly Review*, the *Dublin Review*, and especially the *Irish Ecclesiastical Record*. In this last, the *Sources for the History of Irish Civilisation* records over fifty of his articles.[4] In addition to all of these, of course, there was the almost weekly stream of letters to various newspapers.

Although the range of subjects in Walsh's writings was unusually wide, the main emphasis was on education. In that field, as has been seen, much of his time and attention was focused. It will be recalled that he served on the Intermediate Education Board, 1892-1909, became a commissioner of Charitable Donations and Bequests in 1893, a role linked to educational establishments, and was a commissioner of National Education from 1895 to 1901. His influence on education boards, moreover, led to the establishment of a large number of additional primary schools throughout the diocese. He was, indeed, "a great school builder", and "school places multiplied under his stimulus, year after year, to provide education for the children of the people".5 His efforts, besides, facilitated the securing of grants for the Catholic teacher training colleges at Drumcondra and at Carysfort, Blckrock.6 He also gave active support to the new Technical Education Association, 1893.7 Most of all, perhaps, his influence was felt in the quest for a solution to the University Question. Not surprisingly, therefore, the *Westminster Gazette*, referring to his work for education, remarked, on 9 April 1921, that:

> In pamphlets and in speeches, in the councils of the bishops, and upon public platforms, he was never weary of advocating the cause he had at heart; and it was said of him that he had filled more newspaper columns than any other contemporary writer upon education questions with "Letters to the Editor".8

In their account of Walsh's career, most of the main Irish newspapers recalled the major events in his long life. In a book of this length a summary of their summary retrospection may be welcome to the reader. They recalled Walsh's enrolment as a child in the Repeal Association, his contribution to the *Nation* newspaper, his attendance at Newman's university, followed by a brilliant career at Maynooth as student and professor, and then as a successful president whose prompt action saved much of the college from fire, and whose suavity and warm welcome charmed the Empress Elizabeth of Austria. His work in founding the Catholic Headmasters' Association, and his writings on the Land Acts, were also noted, as was the strong opposition presented by the government to his appointment as archbishop. His capacity as an administrator, and the effective functioning of his large archdiocese received attention, but the main newspaper emphasis with respect to the early years of his episcopacy was on his impact on political and social issues: his support of the Land League and of Home Rule, the Persico mission, his part in the discrediting of Pigott, the Parnell split, and then the reunification of the Irish party. His work for education, especially with respect to the University Question, and his contribution in the area of arbitration and in respect of the unemployed and of orphans, were mentioned at some length, but, not surprisingly in 1921, even more attention was given to more recent years: his significant silence in 1916, his letter that influenced the Longford by-election, the part he played in opposing conscription, his support of Sinn Fein, his appeals for clemency for hunger-strikers and for Kevin Barry and other condemned prisoners, and his strong criticism of government repression and injustice.

From these accounts it is evident that considerable though Walsh's contribution was in the field of education, his more striking impact was seen to be in socio-political affairs. As Shane Leslie later observed, he "stepped into the arena, and dared do battle politically", and, as a consequence, he, like Mannix of

Melbourne, was disqualified for the red hat of cardinal.[9] The manner in which he stepped into the arena, however, kept the official church in tune with the popular struggle for justice in land and in trades union affairs, and for independence in political matters, and thereby helped preserve the loyalty of the people to the Catholic Church, which, in turn, gave the Church a dominant, even, at times, a domineering role in the life of the new Irish state; an eventuality which might not have been altogether pleasing to him, in that he hated the partition of the country, and was sensitive to the northern Protestant's distrust of episcopal influence in social and political affairs.

Discussion of might-have-beens is a fruitless exercise, yet one is almost lured into it by Walsh's historical presence. He was the great link figure. He had met O'Connell as a child. He corresponded with Gladstone, and corresponded and worked with Davitt and Parnell; supported the Irish language, refused to condemn 1916, subsequently gave support to Sinn Fein at a vital moment, and played a subtle diplomatic role in bringing about unity of church and state in the struggle against conscription. Walsh's very continued existence was a moral force, as Myles Ronan observed. It encouraged prelates and people to know he was at hand to give them "the benefit of his long and useful experience". Part of that experience, which seemed so very relevant in his last years, was "to distrust the word of an English cabinet minister" and to require from him "propositions in writing". Hence, Ronan ventured to say, that had he been spared to see the end of the fight for national freedom, "he would have found a formula which would have prevented the post-treaty troubles".[10] Shane Leslie, too, opined, "had he kept his health and lived a year longer into the fateful 1922, who can refuse to believe that Irish history would have been very different."[11] All, vain speculation and oversimplification? Perhaps, and yet possibly his was a voice that would have weighed decisively with de Valera, who had never known his own father and viewed Walsh in such a role, if his own words are to be taken as he uttered them:

> Although I had not met his Grace so very often, I felt for him something of the intimate personal affection of son for father. You can scarcely realise what confidence it gave me, a novice, during the 3 or 4 years I have been in public life, to feel that there was always one at hand on whom I could rely for wise counsel and wisdom in any hour of need.[12]

That such considerations could arise concerning any churchman, said something very significant about William J. Walsh's place in the minds and hearts of those who knew him, and of his reputation as a patriot and a wise arbitrator.

A FINAL ASSESSMENT

But, what of Walsh's more negative aspects? In his own life-time and for many years after his death he was frequently depicted as the vindictive evil genius who plotted Parnell's downfall. That part of the Parnellite myth, which was reflected vividly in the writings of Joyce and Yeats, has dissolved in the light of historical research, as has the other myth which presented him as the inhuman, uncaring clergyman who unreasonably prevented hungry children going for a holiday to England in 1913.

In this account of Walsh's life, however, many other criticisms have been noted. He was accused of identifying himself unduly with the nationalist cause. He could be prejudiced, persistent, and mordant, as in his attitude to the Royal University and its senate; and he was stubborn and manipulative in seeking his own favoured solution to the university question. He showed himself tetchy and domineering in the All Hallows controversy and in his treatment of the Carmelite, Fr Coghlan; and Lord Carnarvon and Countess Plunkett, on occasion, found him rude and dismissive. Walsh, undoubtedly, was very conscious of his own ability and could be impatient with those who disagreed with him. Moreover, as has been seen, he frequently sought publicity. His practice of writing to the newspapers on a seemingly endless range of issues reflected a wish to be centre-stage, and he persisted even though Archbishop Persico and many of his fellow bishops deplored the practice, and though, as he probably knew, he was wittily dubbed "William the Silent" by Dublin's journalists and literati![13]

In reviewing Walsh's failings, however, one notices that many of them are the reverse side of positive features. Thus, his identification with the nationalist majority was part of his abiding concern to preserve his people's loyalty to Catholicism and to Rome; and his attitudes on the university question, as on the land issue, were a reflection of his ardent desire for equality and justice. His *penchant* for writing letters to newspapers also takes on a different aspect when one accepts that the written word was his forte. He was a poor preacher. The press was his pulpit. The pen his medium. And his width and depth of knowledge enabled him to use this special strength to the full. As to the vanity, impulsiveness, occasional outbursts of impatience, dominance, and tetchiness, none of these were such as to render him in any way a petty or unpleasant person. His graciousness and largeness of mind and vision were characteristics frequently noted.

Ultimately, when one asks what was the driving force which made him such a sure and powerful voice at a critical period in his country's history, one is faced with his consciousness that he was inferior to no one and more talented than most, and that he had inherited a tradition moulded by O'Connell which filled him with the impelling desire that he and his countrymen be accorded justice, respect, and equality. This desire shines out in all his major ventures – in the land and university questions, in his arbitration on labour issues, in his empathy for the workers in 1913, and in his affinity with the ideals of Sinn Fein in his final years. And through it all of course, there ran the strong human and christian virtues of deep, practical concern and compassion for the poor, the vulnerable youth, the homeless, and the sick.

In the overall context, therefore, of his great ability, remarkable work-rate, compassionate spirit, practical achievements, and national stature, Walsh's failings add a human fallible dimension which, although they may partly ridicule the estimation of his admiring friend, Lord Mayor Laurence O'Neill, that he was "the greatest archbishop of Dublin since St Laurence O'Toole", still allow stand, even after eighty years, the editorial judgement of the *Freeman's Journal* of 21 April 1921, that William J. Walsh was "a great Irishman and a great churchman". He ranks among the other outstanding archbishops with which Dublin was graced in the nineteenth century, John Thomas Troy, Daniel Murray, and Paul Cullen.

APPENDIX

Dr Walsh's main writings

His first work arose out of the case of *O'Keeffe v. McDonald* at the Wicklow summer assizes in 1875 (published 1875). The following year he translated *Louise Lateau*: an essay, addressed to Jews and Christians, by Dr Augustus Rholing. In 1879 he published *A Harmony of the Gospel Narratives of the Passion* ...; and the next year *Tractatus de Actibus Humanis*, which had a second edition in 1891. His *Plain Exposition of the Irish Land Act of 1881* was published in 1881. As was his *Evidence Given before the Royal Commission on the Irish Land Act* in reference to the eviction of the Trustees of Maynooth College from the farm of Laragh. *The Queen's Colleges of theRoyal University* (No. 1) appeared in 1882, and *The Queen's Colleges of the Royal University* (No. 2) in 1884. Also in 1884, *Officium Defunctorum et Ordo Exsequarum* (2nd ed. 1890); and in 1885 *Grammar of Gregorian Music*. Two books of his Addresses followed. In 1886 *Addresses delivered by Most Rev. Archbishop Walsh, Archbishop of Dublin*, in reply to Addresses of Congratulation on his appointment to the archbishopric (2nd ed., 1890); and *Addesses on the Irish Education Question* in 1890. That year also there was *Statement of Chief Grievances of Irish Catholics on the matter of Education: Primary, Intermediate and University*. In 1893 he published his most widely read work in many respects, *Bimetallism and Monometallism: What they are and How they bear upon the Irish Land Question* (2nd ed., 1894; 3rd ed., 1894, German ed., 1893, French ed., 1894). He returned to *The Irish University Question* in 1897. Then, after a lapse of five years, he wrote *Trinity College and the University of Dublin* (1902); and later *Trinity College and Its Medical School* (1906). There was a lapse of six yers before *The Motu Proprio and Its Critics* (1912); and a further six years before the final work in 1918, *O'Connell, Bishop Murray, and the Board of Bequests*.

NOTES

I FROM BIRTH TO ORDINATION, 1841-66

1 Dublin Diocesan Archives (DDA). Walsh Papers. Box "Walsh Biographical".
2 Patrick J. Walsh, *William J. Walsh, Archbishop of Dublin* (Dublin, 1928), p. 1.
3 *Thom's Directory* has Ralph Walsh (watch & clock maker) at no. 11 Essex Quay from 1841 to 1852; and in 1853 at 19 Parliament Street; pp. 916, 930.
4 DDA. "Walsh Biographical". Undated letter from 3 Hardwick Place, Dublin. The woman mentions she had ten children, had been deserted by her husband, claims to speak Franch and German, would wish to give tuition and would welcome some commendation from the archbishop.
5 The only "Knockkelly" to be found in the Census of Ireland, 1851, or in the Griffith's Valuation of 1852, is situated in Co. Tipperary. Spelled, Knockkelly, it is in the parish of Peppardstown in Tipperary South Riding. A Richard Crane (not Creane) features as a lessor of a number of small holdings, but there is no mention in Griffith's "valuation of tenements" for Knockkelly of a Walsh or a Pierce. See *General Alphabetical Index to the Townlands and Towns, Parishes and Baronies of Ireland, 1851* (based on the census of 1851) (Dublin, 1861; repr. Genealogical Publishing Co., Baltimore, Maryland, 1989); p. 614. The archbishop's correspondent mentions a Kendrick family, and the valuation shows a Pierce Kendrick, which just may suggest a connection with Walsh's mother.
6 Ambrose Macauley, *Dr Russell of Maynooth* (London, 1983), pp. 58-60.
7 DDA. "Walsh Biographical". A printed indication of his correspondence with the bishops on the measure may be seen in the *Catholic Registry*, 1846, pp. 403-10.
8 DDA. Newspaper cuttings in "Walsh Biographical".
9 DDA. Walsh Papers 1880, no. 368/7.
10 P.J. Walsh, op. cit., p. 2.
11 Myles V. Ronan. *Most Rev. W.J. Walsh, D.D.* (pamphlet, Bray, 1927), p. 2.
12 Idem, pp. 11-12.
13 DDA. Walsh Papers. Box 357. I. f. 350/2.
14 P.J. Walsh, p. 5.
15 M.V. Ronan, p. 1.
16 Idem.
17 DDA. "Walsh Biographical".
18 DDA. Wm. J. Rigney, "Bartholomew Woodlock and the Catholic University of Ireland, 1861-79", vol. 2., PhD thesis, University College, Dublin (1995).
19 P.J. Walsh, op. cit., p. 14.
20 DDA. Walsh Papers, in unsorted miscelaneous papers.
21 P.J. Walsh, p. 15.
22 DDA. 19 Nov. 1864; f. 368/6.
23 P.J. Walsh, pp. 16-18.
24 Fr Dunne, Royal University: Walsh; DDA. 357. I. f. 350/2.
25 P.J. Walsh, pp. 16-18.

II FROM PROFESSOR TO COLLEGE PRESIDENT, 1867-80

1 P.J. Walsh. op. cit., p. 19.
2 *Dublin Evening Post*, 18 April 1867.
3 O'Hanlon–Walsh, 11 Aug. 1867; DDA. Walsh Papers, in unsorted miscel. papers.
4 P.J. Walsh, p. 24.
5 Idem, p. 23.
6 Idem, p. 25.
7 P.J. Corish. *Maynooth College, 1795-1995* (Dublin, 1995), p. 201.

8 Idem, p. 224.

9 Emmet Larkin, *The Roman Catholic Church and the Emergence of the Modern Irish Political System, 1874-1878* (Dublin, 1996), 25 Feb. 1875; p. 57.

10 Idem, p. 79. Walsh replied on 22 Dec. that Warren's reputation stood high with all who knew him at Maynooth.

11 DDA. Walsh Papers. f. 368/6

12 Corish. op. cit., p. 180.

13 Idem, p. 228.

14 Idem, p. 213.

15 Idem, p. 230.

16 Cit. Larkin. op. cit., p. 182.

17 DDA. Walsh–Cullen, 11 Oct. 1874; see Macauley below.

18 Idem, 1875.

19 DDA. 1876. These three letters are quoted by A. Macauley in *Dr Russell of Maynooth* (London, 1983), pp. 308-9.

20 Larkin, op. cit., p. 186.

21 Idem, pp. 187-8.

22 Walsh letter, 13 Jan. 1877; DDA. 1877. f. 368/7.

23 Cit. Larkin, op. cit., p. 192.

24 DDA. 1875. f. 368/6.

25 P.J. Walsh, op. cit., ch. 3; and Desmond Bowen, *Paul Cullen and the Shaping of Modern Irish Catholicism* (Dublin, 1983), pp. 233-44.

26 Fr O'Keefe withdrew from his parish, the interdict was lifted, and he faded from the scene. In his final years he received practical assistance from Drs Cullen and Walsh. He died in 1879. See. P.J. Walsh, op. cit., p. 71.

27 P.J. Walsh, p. 56.

28 Idem, p. 27

29 Larkin, op. cit., pp. 193-4.

30 Idem, p. 194.

31 Idem; and P.J. Walsh, p. 73.

32 Corish, op. cit., p. 182.

33 Larkin, p. 195.

34 Corish, p. 182.

35 DDA. Cullen Papers. cit. Larkin. p. 196.

36 Larkin, idem.

37 Idem, pp. 114-15.

38 Idem.

39 Idem, p. 115.

40 Corish, pp. 187-8.

41 Idem, p. 237. On the fire and visit of the empress, see P.J. Walsh, pp. 83-7.

42 Corish, pp. 210-11; P.J. Walsh, pp. 89-92.

43 Corish, p. 231.

44 Idem, p. 234.

45 Idem.

46 DDA. Moran–Walsh, 22 July 1881; Box. 357. I. f. 350/3.

47 Walsh–Fr Scannell, 8 Jan. 1883, and 11 Jan. to unnamed bishop; DDA. Walsh Papers, unsorted miscel. papers.

48 Irish Jesuit Archives (IJA). John V. Cassidy–Wm. Delany, 22 June 1878, enclosing a letter from Fitzgibbon. On Delany's role see T.J. Morrissey, *Towards a National University. William Delany, S.J. 1835-1924* (Dublin, 1983), ch. 2.

49 IJA. Delany–Walsh, 27 Sept. 1878. See Morrissey, op. cit., p. 35.

50 Moran–Cullen, 29 Sept.; Larkin, op. cit., pp. 312-13.

51 P.J. Walsh, pp. 77-80.

52 Larkin, p. 313.

53 Morrissey, op. cit., pp. 35-6.

54 P.J. Walsh, p. 80.

55 Morrissey. p. 36.

56 Moran–Propaganda. Archivio della Sacra Congregazione de Propaganda Fide. Scritture Referite nelle Congreg. Generali 1021, 107r-108v.; cit. Corish, p. 235.

57 Corish, p. 208.

58 DDA. 337/4/57: Gillooly–McCabe, 14 Sept. 1879; cit. Corish, p. 182.

59 Walsh–McCabe, 8 July 1881; f. 346/6; cit. Corish, p. 182.

60 Walsh–McCabe, 21 March 1884; DDA. f. 360/4; cit. Corish, p. 223

61 Corish, p. 208.

62 Idem, p. 219.

63 Idem, p. 220.

64 Idem, p. 228.

65 DDA. Walsh Papers. Miscel. unsorted papers; no date.

66 Corish, pp. 194-5.

67 Walter McDonald, *Reminiscences of a*

Maynooth Professor (London, 1925), pp. 85-6.

III   FIRST INVOLVEMENT IN LAND
       AND UNIVERSITY QUESTIONS

1 Much has been written on this development. See E. Larkin, *The Historical Dimension of Irish Catholicism* (Washington, 1984 ed.), ch. 2. "The Doctrinal Revolution, 1850-1875"; E. Larkin & H. Freudenberger, trans. & ed., *A Redemptorist Missionary in Ireland. 1851-54*, memoirs of Joseph Prost CSSR (Cork, 1998); S. Connolly, *Religion and Society in Nineteenth Century Ireland* (Dundalk, 1985); K.A. Laheen, SJ, *The Jesuits in Killaloe, 1850-80* (Newmarket-on-Fergus, 1998); K.A. Laheen, SJ (ed.), "Jesuit Parish Memoirs, 1863-76" in *Collectanea Hibernia*, nos 39-41 (Naas, 1997-99).
2 E. Larkin, *Historical Dimensions of Irish Catholicism*, pp. 109, 122.
3 J. Morley, *Life of Gladstone*, vol. 1, p. 695; and see P.J. Walsh, op. cit., p. 98.
4 *Report of the Royal Commission on the Irish Land Act* (D. 700), E. 2; cit. P.J. Walsh, p. 105.
5 P.J. Walsh, pp. 107-8.
6 Idem, p. 108.
7 Nulty–Walsh, 10 April 1881; DDA. Box 357. I. f. 350/3.
8 P.J. Walsh, p. 107.
9 Idem.
10 Idem.
11 Butler–Walsh, 12 April: DDA. 357. I. f. 350/3.
12 P.J. Walsh, p. 109.
13 Butler–Walsh, 16 May 1881; 357. I. f. 350/3.
14 Leinster–Walsh, 28 April; DDA. f. 350/2.
15 P.J. Walsh, p. 110.
16 Patrick Duggan–Walsh, 2 Aug. 1881; DDA. 357. I. f. 350/3.
17 P.J. Walsh, p. 111.
18 Idem, p. 115.

19 IJA. Walsh–Delany, 23 Jan. 1881; see Morrissey, p. 59.
20 Walsh–Reffé, March 1881; cit. Morrissey, p. 59.
21 IJA. Delany's "Notes on the University Question", p. 11; Morrissey, *Towards a National University* ..., p. 58.
22 Cit. Morrissey, p. 60.
23 Walsh–Bishops, 14 April 1882; DDA. 375. I. f. 350/5
24 Corish, *Maynooth College*, pp. 215-19.
25 Neville's memorandum for bishops, Oct. 1882; DDA. McCabe Papers. f. 215/9
26 IJA. Delany–Browne, Jesuit provincial, Oct. 1883; Morrissey, p. 73.
27 Morrissey, p. 74.
28 Walsh–Delany, 23 Jan. 1884; section on National University of Ireland, f. 16; see Morrissey, p. 79.
29 Morrissey, pp. 81-2.
30 IJA. Lambert McKenna Ms. on Delany and the University; cit. Morrissey, p. 83.
31 P.J. Walsh, p. 127.
32 IJA. cit. Morrissey, p. 83.
33 IJA. Croke–Delany, 19 Feb. 1882; cit. Morrissey, p. 84.
34 IJA. Delany–Fr Whitty, Assist. General, 26 Dec. 1885; Morrissey, p. 85.
35 DDA. f. 17; Morrissey, p. 85.
36 IJA. McKenna Ms.; cit. Morrissey, p. 85.
37 DDA. Incomplete letter, undated. Box. 357. I. f. 350/5.
38 Idem.
39 DDA. Box. 357. I. f. 350/5. Undated, but evidently end of June, or early July, following Walsh's resignation.
40 IJA. Walsh–Delany, 31 May; cit. Morrissey, p. 86.
41 In papers relating to Bishop Butler, Nov. 1884, Limerick Diocesan Archives (LDA). Higgins sent the letter to Delany, who, it seems, had sent it to Butler.
42 IJA. Butler–Delany, 24 Nov. 1884; Morrissey, p. 91.
43 IJA. Butler–Fr Browne, provincial, 1 Dec. 1884; cit. Morrissey, pp. 91-2. Italics in text.

44 Cruise's letter in IJA Delany Papers; see Morrissey, pp. 92-5

45 IJA. Walsh–Delany, 5 Dec. 1884, Delany Papers. Italics in text.

46 IJA. Delany's summary: "Memorandum on the Public Correspondence on the Fellowships which appeared in the *Tablet* and *Freeman's Journal* in Dec. 1884."

47 Fr John J. O'Carroll was noted for his ability as a linguist, claiming competence in eighteen European languages.

48 Delany–Walsh, 5 Dec. 1884; DDA. In unsorted miscel. documents in Walsh Papers.

49 Cruise–Walsh, 7 Dec.; cit. Morrissey, p. 97.

50 Delany–Lord Emly, 12 Dec. 1884; National Library of Ireland (NLI), Monsell Ms. 8318(14).

51 P.J. Walsh, p. 129.

52 Corish, p. 235.

53 P.J. Walsh, p. 127.

54 Cit. P.J. Walsh, p. 136.

55 Granville Papers, Public Record Office, 30/29/142, cit. E. Larkin in *The Roman Catholic Church and the Creation of the Modern Irish State, 1878-1886* (Philadelphia, 1975), p. 253.

56 Croke–Kirby, 19 Feb. 1885; cit. Larkin, idem, p. 256.

57 Barrington–Granville, 12 Feb. 1885. Papers of Arthur Balfour, British Museum, 49690, cit. Larkin, p. 254.

58 *Freeman's Journal*, 2 Oct. 1884, cit. Larkin, p. 244.

IV   FROM PRESIDENT TO ARCHBISHOP

1 Errington–Lord Granville, 5 March 1885; Gr. 30/29/149; cit. Larkin, *The Roman Catholic Church and the Creation* ..., p. 260.

2 DDA. Croke–Walsh, 13 Feb. 1885; DDA. 357. II. f. 350/8.

3 Walsh–Croke, 14 Feb.; DDA.; cit. P.J. Walsh, p. 137.

4 Spencer–Granville, 19 Feb. 1885; Granville Papers. 30/29/149; cit. Larkin, p. 255.

5 Cit. P.J. Walsh, p. 141.

6 DDA. Walsh Papers. Section on Letters of Bishop Donnelly; 14 Feb. 1885.

7 P.J. Walsh, pp. 160-1; Larkin, p. 263.

8 Walsh–Croke, 14 March 1885; DDA. Walsh Papers.

9 MacEvilly–Kirby, 22 July 1883; Kirby Papers, Irish College Rome; cit. Larkin, p. 201.

10 P.J. Walsh, pp. 158-9.

11 Croke–Kirby, 19 Feb. 1885; Kirby Papers; cit. Larkin, p. 256.

12 Walsh, p. 162.

13 Idem, p. 163.

14 Errington–Abbot Smith, 6 March; cit. Larkin, p. 260.

15 Errington–Cardinal Jacobini, 5 March 1885, in Granville Papers, 30/29/149; cit. Larkin, p. 260.

16 Lee–Kirby, 16 March 1885, Kirby Papers; cit. Larkin, p. 269.

17 Walsh, p. 164.

18 Walsh–Fr Murphy (presumably Michael Murphy, Kingstown), 14 March 1885; DDA. f. 350/8

19 Letter dated 31 March 1885; DDA. f. 350/4

20 Errington–Granville, 26 March; Balfour Papers, 49690; cit Larkin, p. 275.

21 Based on memo of Sir Charles Dilke, president of the Local Government Board, following a meeting with his friend Archbishop Manning, 23 April; Dilke Papers, British Museum, Ms. 43887; cit. Larkin, p. 275.

22 Manning–Pope Leo XIII, 17 Feb. 1885; cit. Larkin, pp. 278-9.

23 Idem.; cit. Larkin, pp. 280-1.

24 S. Gwynn, *Life of Sir Charles Dilke* (London, 1917), vol. II. p. 131.

25 Idem.

26 Croke–Walsh, 17 May; DDA. f. 350/8

27 On this see Larkin, pp. 288-9.

28 Croke–Manning, 7 June; Croke Papers; cit. Larkin, pp. 288-9.

29 Manning–Croke, 12 June, copy in DDA. Walsh Papers. f. 350/1.

30 Croke–Walsh, 13 June; DDA. Walsh Papers: and see Larkin, p. 290.

31 P.J. Walsh, p. 166.

32 Croke–Kelly, 30 June; Kirby Papers; in Larkin, p. 295

33 Mac Evilly–Manning, 7 July; Larkin, p. 295.

34 Errington–Abbot Smith, in Larkin, p. 294.

35 Croke–Walsh, 28 June 1885; DDA. Walsh Papers. 357. II. f. 350/8.

36 Walsh–Croke, 30 June: idem. Also in P.J. Walsh. p. 167.

37 Walsh–Croke, 7 July; idem; also P. J. Walsh, p. 168.

38 Croke–Walsh, 8 July 1885; DDA. Box. 357. II. f. 350/8

39 *Life of Dilke*, vol. II, p. 156.

40 Walsh–Donnelly, 24 June 1885; DDA. Section of Letters of Walsh to Bishop Donnelly.

41 Walsh–The Revd Mother, Convent of St Alphonsus, Clonliffe West, 2 July '85; DDA. Walsh Papers, in box marked "Politics".

42 Typed notes relating to Dublin appointment in DDA. Walsh Papers. f. 350/1.

43 Walsh–Kirby, 10 July; DDA, in Larkin, p. 308.

44 Carnarvon Papers, Great Britain, P.R.O. London, 30/6/ 56; in Larkin, pp. 308-9.

45 Walsh–Carnarvon, 21 July 1885; DDA. Walsh Papers, in unsorted miscel. docs. from Irish College Rome.

46 Carnarvon–Walsh; DDA. Box. 357. II. f. 350/4.

47 Walsh–Croke, 23 July: idem. f. 350/1; see also Walsh, pp. 171-3.

48 P.J. Walsh, p. 175, who does not give the precise date in Sept., of the letter,

49 Letters of Walsh to Donnelly, 24 July 1885; DDA. Walsh Papers.

50 Larkin, op. cit., p. 319

51 Walsh–Kirby, 24 Aug.; in Kirby Papers, in Larkin p. 320.

52 Carnarvon–Walsh, 25 Aug.; DDA. 357. II. f. 350/4.

53 Walsh–Carnarvon, 30 Aug.; DDA. Walsh Papers. Unsorted miscel. papers.

54 Carnarvon–Walsh, 4 Sept.; Carnarvon Papers 30/6/ 58; in Larkin, p. 322.

55 DDA. Walsh Papers, in unsorted miscel. material.

56 P.J. Walsh, p. 181.

57 DDA. Walsh Papers. 357. I. f. 350/4: A notebook with "Addresses on occasion of clergy and laity preparing and approving a joint address of welcome to the new archbishop, 26 Aug.'85". Wm. Delany is one of the speakers.

58 Walsh. op. cit., p. 183.

59 Idem, p. 187.

60 Idem, p. 193.

61 Idem, p. 195.

62 Dr Cahill was an influential Dublin priest celebrated for a weekly letter posted up in certain neighbourhoods when Wm. Walsh was a boy.

63 Walsh, p. 185.

64 Walsh–Kirby, 23 Sept. 1885; Kirby Papers; cit. Larkin, p. 324.

V   THE LEADING EPISCOPAL VOICE ON LAND AND HOME RULE, 1885-7

1 Healy–Walsh, 6 Sept. 1885; DDA. Walsh Papers, f. 350/1.

2 Carnarvon 30/6/67, in Larkin, p. 329.

3 Morrissey, *Towards a National University*, pp. 104-9.

4 IJA. Delany Papers. Walsh–Delany, 5 Oct. 1885.

5 IJA. Delany Papers. Delany Memo: "Correspondence re. Grant-in-aid".

6 Larkin, p. 325.

7 Walsh, p. 512.

8 Memo. Carnarvon 30/6/67, in Larkin, pp. 329-30.

9 DDA. Manning–Walsh, 25 Dec. 1885; 357. I. f. 350/4

10 Walsh–Kirby, 29 Nov., Kirby Papers, cit. Larkin, p. 342.

11 Bishop Browne–Kirby, 15 Dec. 1885; idem; Larkin, p. 345.

12 Idem.

13 DDA. Walsh Papers. Book of newspapers extracts & cuttings, 1886.

14 DDA. Box file: "Calendar of Roman Correspondence, 1885-1889".

15 *Irish Catholic Directory*, 1886.

16 W.S. Blunt, *The Land War in Ireland* (London, 1912), pp. 42-3

17 Carnarvon–Salisbury, 7 Dec. 1885; Carnarvon Papers 30/6/55; Larkin, p. 346.

18 John Dillon Papers, T.C.D., Ms. 6765/1-42.

19 Walsh–Canon Dillon, 25 Sept.'85; Dillon Papers, idem.

20 Walsh–Kirby, 30 Dec.; Kirby Papers; Larkin, p. 350.

21 Larkin, p. 350.

22 Cit. by Henry Du Pre Labouchere–Gladstone, 22 Dec.'85, in Gladstone Papers, B.M.. Add. Ms. 46016 f 103; in Frank Callanan, *T.M. Healy*, p. 672, f.n. 114.

23 Carnarvon–Salisbury, 7 Dec. 1885; Carnarvon Papers. 30/6/55; Larkin, pp. 345-8.

24 Cit. Callanan, *T.M. Healy*, p. 213, from R.B. O'Brien, "Federal Union with Ireland" in *Nineteenth Century*, Jan. 1886, p. 35.

25 P.J. Walsh, p. 202; Larkin, p. 363.

26 Walsh–Gladstone, 17 Feb.; Gladstone–Walsh, 20 Feb.; British Library. Add. Ms. 56447, pp. 35ff.

27 Walsh–Gladstone, 18 Oct. 1886; Br. Lib. Add. Ms. 44499. pp. 97-98v.

28 Walsh–Gladstone, 18 Oct. 1886, re. article by Walsh on the operation of the Land Commission, 1881-1889; Br. Lib. Add. Ms. 44505, pp. 21ff.; Walsh–Gladstone, 26 Oct. re. Land issues and rents, idem. pp. 61ff.; Walsh–Gladstone, 30 Oct. 1888, in response to a letter of Gladstone on Land Acts, idem, pp. 80ff.

29 Walsh–Gladstone, 28 June '87; idem. Add. Ms. 44501, pp. 111-2.

30 Walsh–Gladstone, 30 May '87; idem. Ms. 44501, pp. 44-45v.

31 Walsh–Gladstone, 18 Oct. 1889; idem. Ms. 44508, pp. 81-84v.

32 Walsh–Gladstone, 5 Nov. '88 re. Mr Balfour; Ms. 44499, pp. 97-98v

33 Walsh–Gladstone, 5 March 1890; Ms. 44509, pp. 227-28v. Walsh–Gladstone, 20 May 1890; Ms. 44510, pp. 29-32v.

34 Gladstone–Walsh, 1 June 1887; Ms. 44501, p. 47

35 Walsh–Gladstone, 17 Feb. 1886; Ms. 56447, pp. 35-40v.

36 P.J. Walsh, pp. 207-9.

37 John Morley, *Life of Gladstone*, vol. II, p. 417.

38 Walsh, p. 211.

39 Walsh–Manning, 26 March 1886; cit. Walsh, pp. 213-14.

40 Walsh, p. 219.

41 "Interviews" on 11 & 16 August; DDA. Walsh Papers. Book of Extracts, vol. 1, 1886. Italics mine.

42 Walsh, p. 227.

43 For 11 and 16 Aug. 1886 in Bk. of Extracts, vol. 1, Sept. 1885–June 1887; DDA.

44 Walsh, p. 230.

45 W.B. Faherty, SJ, *Rebels or Reformers* (Chicago, 1987), ch. v, pp. 48-9.

46 F.S.L. Lyons. *Ireland since the Famine* (London, 1974 ed.), p. 189.

47 Walsh, p. 236.

48 Bk. of Extracts, vol. 1.; DDA.

49 Walsh, pp. 239-40;

50 Idem, pp. 241-2.

51 Idem, p. 247.

52 P.J. Joyce, *John Healy, Archbishop of Tuam* (Dublin, 1931), pp. 138-9.

53 Idem, p. 139.

54 Walsh–Kirby, 12 Dec. 1886; Kirby Papers; in *Archivium Hibernicum*, vol. 32, p. 8, no. 529.

55 See Walsh–O'Dwyer, 1877, regretting he could not visit him in Limerick, no date but a few days after Dr Russell's "Terrible accident"; LDA.

56 O'Dwyer–Walsh, 18 Oct.1886; DDA. f. 402/4.

57 Walsh–O'Dwyer, 20 Oct. 1886; LDA.

58 Dr Healy–O'Dwyer, 25 Oct. 1886; LDA.

59 O'Dwyer–Walsh, 2/3 Nov.; DDA. f. 405/5.

60 Walsh–O'Dwyer, 6 Nov. 1886; LDA.

61 O'Dwyer–Walsh, 24 Nov.; DDA. f. 402/5; also LDA.

62 O'Dwyer Papers, LDA; also in *Irish Times* and *Cork Examiner*.

63 Walsh–O'Dwyer, 10 Dec. f. 402/5; 11 Dec. f. 347/7.

64 Logue–O'Dwyer, 13 Dec. 1886; LDA.

65 Idem, 21 Dec.; LDA.

66 Logue–O'Dwyer, 23 March 1897; LDA.

67 O'Dwyer–Walsh, 8 Jan. 1887; DDA. f. 402/6, gives interchange of letters.

68 O'Dwyer–editor, 9 Jan. 1887; LDA.

69 Walsh–Kirby, 19 Dec.1886; Kirby Papers in *Archiv. Hib.*, 32, p. 9, no. 538.

70 Idem, 22 Jan. 1887; p. 9, no. 33.

71 O'Dwyer–Kirby, 9 March 1887; Kirby Papers in *Archiv. Hib.*, vol. 32. pp. 10-11, no. 138.

72 Walsh–Kirby, 28 Feb.1887; idem, p. 10, no. 120

73 Walsh–Kirby, 23 March 1887; idem, p. 11, no. 168.

74 Idem, 30 May; idem, p. 12, no. 284.

75 Croke–Kirby, 19 Dec. 1880; Kirby Papers, *Archiv. Hib.*, p. 99, no. 524a.

76 Walsh, p. 270.

77 Cit. Walsh, p. 271.

78 Shane Leslie, *Henry Edward Manning. His Life and Labours* (London 1921), p. 419.

79 Idem, p. 418.

80 Walsh–Kirby, 9 March 1887; Kirby Papers; cit. Larkin in *The Roman Catholic Church and the Plan of Campaign, 1886-88* (Cork, 1978), p. 24.

81 Larkin, ibid., pp. 95-6.

82 Kirby–Walsh, 20 June 1887; in Walsh, p. 278.

83 Walsh–Kirby, 27 June 1887; cit. Larkin, p. 99.

84 Walsh, p. 280.

85 Walsh, p. 281.

86 Idem, p. 282.

87 Idem, p. 283.

88 Walsh–Kirby, 4 July 1887; in Larkin, p. 109.

VI   THE COMPLEXITIES OF THE PERSICO MISSION

1 *Freeman's Journal* in DDA. "Extracts" vol. II, from 6 June 1887-19 Aug. 1888, relating to 7 July 1887 & subsequent days.

2 Persico–Manning, 12 Feb. 1888; Letters published in *United Irishman*, 23 April 1904.

3 Persico–Rampolla, 8 July 1887, Archivo Segreto Vaticano (ASV), Segretario di Stato, 1888, Rubrica 278, fascicle 1, f. 53 r-v; in *Collectanea Hibernica*, nos. 34-5 (1992-3), pp. 164-5.

4 Walsh–Manning, 8 July; Manning Papers; cit. E. Larkin, *The Roman Catholic Church and the Plan of Campaign, 1886-88*, p. 111.

5 Walsh, p. 291.

6 Larkin, op. cit., pp. 113-14.

7 Idem, p. 114.

8 Persico-Rampolla, 11 July 1887; ASV, Segretario di Stato, 1888; Rubrica 278; fasc. 1, ff. 72r. 73r; and to Rampolla, 18 July ff. 79r – 89r; in *Collect. Hib.*, nos 34-5, pp. 166, 167-8.

9 W.S. Blunt, *The Land War in Ireland*, pp. 272-3. Gualdi was not a Jesuit. Sir Charles Gavan Duffy was a former Young Irelander and later prime minister of Australia; Thomas O'Hagan was Lord Chancellor of Ireland.

10 *Memories of Father Healy of Little Bray* (London, 1896), pp. 290-1.

11 Blunt, pp. 272-4.

12 Larkin, op. cit., pp. 136-8.

13 Idem, p. 114.

14 Walsh–Kirby, 12 July; Kirby Papers; in Larkin, p. 113.

15 DDA. Diary 1887 in box "Walsh Biographical"; also *Freeman's Journal* ref. In DDA. "Extracts", vol. II.

16 Larkin, pp. 115-16.

17 Persico–Rampolla, 24 July 1887; ASV, ff. 82r-83v; *Collect. Hib.* nos 24-5, pp. 168-70.

18 Persico–Rampolla, 18 July 1887; idem, ff. 79r-89v; *Collect. Hib.* Ibidem, pp. 167-8.

19 Idem, 26 Aug.; ASV, fasic. 2, ff. 7r-8v; *Collect. Hib.* nos 36-7, pp. 274-6.

20 Idem, 14 Sept. Ibid., ff. 13r-14v; *Collect. Hib.* pp. 278-9.

21 Idem., 29 Sept. 1887; Ibid., fasic. 2, ff. 15r-16v; *Collect. Hib.* part 2, pp. 280-1.
22 Errington–Gladstone, 10 Sept. 1887; Gladstone Papers, British Museum, Add. Ms. 44501; in Larkin, p. 124.
23 Croke–Walsh, 4 Aug. 1887; DDA. cit. Larkin, p. 118.
24 Errington–Abbot Smith, OSB, 6 Aug. 1887; Smith Papers, Archives St Paul's Basilica outside the walls; in Larkin, p. 118.
25 DDA. "Extracts", vol. II, for 26 July.
26 Turner–Sir Redvers Buller, under secretary to Ireland, 25 July, who forwarded it to Balfour. Balfour Papers 29807; in Larkin, p. 117.
27 Idem.
28 Persico–Rampolla, 30 July; Ibid., fasc. 1, ff. 85r-86r, *Collect. Hib.* nos 34-5; pp. 170-1.
29 Persico–Rampolla, 8 Aug.; idem., ff. 88r-89r; *Collect. Hib.* pp. 171-2.
30 DDA. Croke–Walsh, 27 Aug. 1887; in Larkin, p. 120.
31 Idem., 2 Aug. 1887; cit. Larkin, p. 120.
32 S. Leslie, *Henry Edward Manning*, p. 422.
33 Persico–Rampolla, 16 Sept.; ASV, ff. 100r-101r; *Collect. Hib.*, part I, pp. 176-7.
34 DDA. "Extracts". vol. II, Sept. 1887, no date.
35 Larkin, op. cit., pp. 128-9.
36 Butcher–Lord de Vesci, a friend and Irish landlord, on 13 Sept. 1887, who forwarded it to Balfour. Balfour Papers. 49821; cit. Larkin, p. 125.
37 Walsh, p. 299.
38 Persico–Rampolla, 15 Oct. 1887; ASV, ff. 105r-106r; *Collect. Hib*, Part I, pp. 179-80.
39 DDA. "Extracts", vol. 2, Oct. 1887, p. 66.
40 Persico–Rampolla, 2 Nov. 1887; ASV, f. 119 r.v; *Collect. Hib.*, ibid., pp. 180-1.
41 DDA. "Extracts", vol. 2. No date or name of newspaper.
42 Persico–Rampolla, 18 Nov. 1887; ASV, fasic. 2; ff. 19r-20v; *Collect. Hib.* nos 36-37, pp. 283-4.

43 Idem, ff. 21r-22v; *Collect. Hib.*, pp. 285-6.
44 Persico–Rampolla. This is catalogued as 2 November, Rochestown; but as he was not in Rochestown at that date, it had to be written later in the month. ASV, fasic 1, f. 117 r; *Collect. Hib.*, Part 1, p. 182.
45 Ibid., f. 25r; *Collect. Hib.* idem, pp. 288-9.
46 Walsh, pp. 300-1. Persico–Walsh. He had previously told Walsh that he had all he needed on Home Rule and the Land Question.
47 Persico-Rampolla, 5 Dec. f. 29r; *Collect. Hib.*, p. 289.
48 Walsh, p. 303.
49 Persico–Rampolla, 14 Dec.; ASV fascic. 2, ff. 33r; *Collect. Hib.*, nos 36-7, p. 291.
50 "Relazione Sulla Condizione Religiosa e Civile d'Irlanda" in Archivio Vaticano, Segreteria di Stato, Anno 1888, Rubrica 278, fasc. 2, ff. 83r-144v. The use of r in a reference means reverse side of page: e.g. f. 129; f. 129r. For convenience the 123 pages are numbered consecutively, beginning at f. 83, with number 1, and so on.
51 Relazione etc. 83r-95; first 25 pp. of report.
52 Ibid., ff. 95-96, pp. 25-7.
53 ff. 96r-97; pp. 28-9.
54 f. 98; p. 30.
55 ff. 98r-101; pp. 32-7.
56 ff. 101r-102r; pp. 38-40.
57 ff. 127r-128; pp. 90-1.
58 f. 115; p. 65.
59 f. 118; p. 71.
60 f. 113r; p. 62.
61 f. 129r; p. 94.
62 ff. 128r-129; p. 92
63 ff. 129-129r; pp. 93-4.
64 f. 130; p. 95.
65 ff. 112-112r; pp. 59-60.
66 f. 134; p. 102.
67 f. 140; p. 114.
68 Idem.
69 f. 138; p. 110.

70 ff. 144-144r; p. 123.

71 f. 131r.; p. 97.

72 f. 135; p. 104.

73 f. 135r; p. 105.

74 Persico–Rampolla, 15 Dec. 1887. ASV, fasc. 2. f. 29r; *Collectanea Hibernica*, nos 36-7, pp. 292-3.

75 Idem. 18 Dec. 1887 to Rampolla; f. 35r; *Collect. Hib.* p. 294.

76 Walsh, p. 303.

77 On Christmas Day and on 28 Dec.

78 Persico-Manning, 6 Jan. from Capuchin Convent Cork; in *United Irishman*, 23 April 1904.

79 Walsh, p. 311.

80 Walsh–Manning, 22 Jan. 1888; Walsh, p. 312.

81 Croke–Walsh, 12 Jan. 1888: Persico had stayed with Croke before setting out. Walsh, p. 310.

82 Persico–Manning, 12 Feb. 1888; *United Irishman*, 23 April 1904.

83 Idem, 29 Feb. 1888; idem.

84 Persico–Rampolla, 6 Feb. 1888; ASV, fasc. 1. ff 129r-130v; *Collect. Hib.* no. 35, Part I, pp. 185-6.

85 Idem, 21 Feb; Archiv. idem. rubr. 278, fasc. 2. ff. 51r-52v; *Collect. Hib.*, Part 3, pp. 167-8.

86 E. Larkin, *The Roman Cath. Church and the Plan of Campaign*, pp. 193-4.

87 Persico–Rampolla, 15 March 1888; ASV, rubr. 278, fasc. 2. ff. 55r-56v.; *Collect. Hib.*, nos. 37-8, Part 3, pp. 171-2.

88 Idem. f. 57r; *Collect. Hib.* idem, p. 173.

VII PAPAL CONDEMNATION OF THE PLAN, ITS MANNER AND EFFECT, 1888

1 Walsh–Croke, 12 Feb. 1888; in Larkin, *The R.C. Church and Plan of Campaign*, pp. 181-2.

2 Larkin, p. 189

3 Walsh–Manning, 2 April 1888; Larkin, p. 190

4 Walsh–Manning, 4 April, cit. S. Leslie, *Henry Edward Manning ...*, p. 425.

5 Larkin, p. 188.

6 Walsh, pp. 331-2.

7 Larkin, p. 203.

8 See Walsh, p. 334; Croke–Manning, 29 April; Larkin, p. 203.

9 *Irish Catholic* (Dublin), 5 May 1888; cit. Larkin, p. 204.

10 Walsh–Croke, 29 April 1888; Larkin, p. 204, & *Collect. Hib.*, 16, p. 108.

11 DDA. Walsh Papers. Section on letters Walsh–Donnelly, 29 April 1888.

12 Idem. Walsh–Donnelly, 8 May.

13 Manning–Walsh, 6 May 1888, in Walsh, p. 341.

14 Walsh, pp. 243-5.

15 Walsh, p. 350, & Larkin, p. 277.

16 O'Callaghan–Kirby, 2 June; Croke–Kirby, 6 June; Kirby Papers, Rome; in Larkin, pp. 255-6.

17 S. Leslie, *Henry Edward Manning ...*, pp. 428-9.

18 Blunt, p. 314.

19 Walsh, p. 351

20 Walsh–Logue, 26 May; in Walsh, pp. 352-3.

21 Walsh, p. 352.

22 DDA. Letter of Walsh–Donnelly, 15 May '88. ("H.O." = Holy Office)

23 Idem, Walsh-Donnelly, 17 May. Italics in text.

24 Idem, Walsh-Donnelly, 11 June.

25 Walsh, pp. 353-4.

26 Larkin, p. 236.

27 DDA. Letters Walsh to Donnelly, 11 June 1888.

28 Walsh, p. 359.

29 *Freeman's Journal*, 21 June; in DDA. "Extracts", vol. 2.

30 Some of the bishops' letters to Kirby indicate the state of the tenants and the reaction of many people to the papal condemnation. Walsh would have been immediately briefed by Croke who met him on his arrival on 22 June: see Larkin, pp. 234-6, and Walsh, pp. 361-2.

31 DDA. "Extracts", vol. 2.

32 Walsh–Kirby, 3 July '88; Kirby Papers; in *Archiv. Hib.*, vol. 32, p. 16; Larkin, p. 268; Italics in text.

33 Kirby Letters in *Archiv. Hib.*, 32, p. 16.

34 DDA. "Extracts", vol. 2.
35 Walsh, pp. 369-70, and Larkin, pp. 278-9.
36 *Freeman's Journal*, 18 July '88; Larkin, pp. 278-9.
37 Cit. F.S.L. Lyons, *Charles Stewart Parnell*, p. 620; P. O'Farrell. *Ireland's English Question* (London, 1971), p. 176.
38 Larkin, pp. 291-2.
39 Walsh–Croke, 15 Sept.; Croke Papers in *Collect. Hib.*, 16, p. 110.
40 Croke–Walsh, 22 Nov. 1888; Larkin, pp. 306-7.
41 Croke–Simeoni, 29 Nov. 1888; Croke Papers in *Collect. Hib.*, vol. 16, pp. 111-12; and in Larkin, pp. 307-8.
42 Walsh–Kirby, 7 Dec.; Kirby Papers; cit. Larkin, pp. 308-9.
43 Persico–Rampolla, 14 May, unfinished letter; ASV ff. 59r-70v. in *Collect. Hib*, Part 3, pp. 179-80.
44 Larkin, pp. 318-19.
45 Persico–Rampolla, 30 April; ASV f. 61r; *Collect. Hib.*, Part 3, p. 175.
46 Persico–Manning, 9 and 10 May 1888; *United Irishman*, 23 April 1904.
47 Walsh, p. 349 footnote.

VIII PIGOTT. THE PARNELL SPLIT
AND SEQUEL

1 M. Davitt, *The Fall of Feudalism in Ireland* (London, 1904), p. 566.
2 R. Pigott–Walsh, 6 Feb. 1885; DDA. Walsh Papers. f. 350/4, loose in box 357. II. Walsh had not yet been consecrated bishop.
3 Idem, 10 Feb..
4 Davitt, *Fall of Feudalism ...*, p. 574.
5 Walsh, pp. 393-4.
6 Walsh–Pigott, 9 March 1887; DDA. In box marked "Politics".
7 Walsh–Pigott, 7 May '87; Walsh, p. 398.
8 Davitt, p. 577.
9 Walsh, p. 404.
10 Davitt, p. 591.
11 Letters of Walsh–Donnelly, 4 May 1889; DDA.

12 DDA. Bk. of "Extracts", vol. 3, p. 132.
13 Idem, pp. 126-31..
14 Davitt, pp. 551-60; and see Walsh, p. 405.
15 Gladstone's diary entry, cit. Lyons, *Charles Stewart Parnell* (London, 1978 ed.), p. 450.
16 The *Times*, 20 Dec. 1889; cit. Lyons, p. 451.
17 DDA. "Extracts" vol. 5, 30 Dec. 1889, p. 84.
18 Lyons, pp. 455-66.
19 DDA. Bk. "Extracts", vol. 5, 30 Dec., p. 84.
20 Lyons, p. 463.
21 Davitt, p. 637
22 *Labour World*, 20 Nov. 1890; cit. Walsh, p. 406.
23 Davitt, p. 637.
24 Idem.
25 Walsh–Kirby, 21 Nov.; Kirby Papers, in *Archiv. Hib*, vol. 32, no. 405, p. 26.
26 See E. Larkin, *The Roman Catholic Church ... and the Fall of Parnell*, pp. 160-1, and text in *Manchester Guardian*, 23 June 1890; *Evening News & Post*, 20 June.
27 *The Moonshine*, 5 July, a London-based journal; DDA. in box "Biographical". *Glasgow Evening Citizen*, 21 June; DDA. idem.
28 Walsh in *Freeman's Journal*, 27 Aug.; DDA. "Extracts", vol. 6.
29 Press cutting, name of paper not given; idem.
30 O'Dwyer–Kirby, 28 Nov. 1890; Kirby Papers. *Archiv. Hib.*, 32, no. 415, p. 26.
31 Manning–Walsh, 19 Nov.; Walsh, p. 409.
32 S. Leslie, *Manning*, pp. 436-7.
33 Walsh, p. 407.
34 Cit. idem, pp. 407-8.
35 Walsh, p. 412.
36 Idem.
37 Idem, p. 413.
38 Walsh–Manning, 26 & 29 Nov. 1890; cit. Lyons, p. 513.
39 *Irish Catholic*, 29 Nov. 1890; DDA. in box "Walsh Biographical".

40 W.S. Churchill, *Life of Lord Randolph Churchill*, vol. II (London, 1906), pp. 437-8.

41 Cit. Lyons, p. 511.

42 S. Leslie, op. cit., p. 438.

43 Telegram Walsh–Murphy, 30 Nov. 1890; DDA. f. 404/4-6.

44 Newspaper cutting in "Walsh Biographical", DDA.

45 Walsh, p. 417.

46 Walsh, p. 418.

47 Cit. Leslie, p. 439. Italics mine.

48 Murphy–Walsh, 6 Dec.; DDA. f. 404/4-6.

49 O'Callaghan and O'Dwyer–Kirby, 6 Dec.; Kirby Papers, *Archiv. Hib.*, 32, no. 428, p. 26.

50 Walsh–Dr E.J. Byrne, 17 Dec. 1890; cit. Lyons, p. 541.

51 Parnell–Walsh, 18 Dec. 1890; in Lyons, p. 541.

52 Cit. Leslie, p. 441.

53 O'Callaghan–Kirby, 27 Dec. 1890; Kirby Papers, *Archiv. Hib.*, 32, no. 482, p. 27.

54 Healy–Walsh, 2 Jan. 1891; DDA. f. 405/3-6.

55 Croke–Walsh, 12 Jan. 1891; idem.

56 Italics mine.

57 Walsh, pp. 422-3.

58 Walsh–Jn. Dillon, 26 Jan. 1891; Dillon Papers, TCD., Ms. 6765

59 Donnelly–Bishop O'Dwyer, 30 Jan. 1891; Limerick Diocesan Archives (LDA).

60 Walsh–Kirby, 28 Jan.; Kirby Papers in *Archiv. Hib.*, 32, no. 54, p. 29.

61 On the Boulogne conference and Walsh see Emmet Larkin, *The Roman Catholic Church and the Fall of Parnell, 1888-1891* (Liverpool U. Press, 1979), pp. 249-53.

62 Walsh–Kirby, 11 Feb. 1891; Kirby Papers in *Archiv. Hib.*, 32, no. 76, p. 29.

63 Logue–Kirby, 21 Feb. 1891; idem, *Archiv. Hib.*, 32, no. 96, p. 30.

64 Walsh–Kirby, 22 Feb.; idem, no. 99.

65 Healy–Walsh, 4 April; cit. Lyons, p. 583.

66 Bishop O'Doherty (Derry)–Kirby, 20 April 1891; *Archiv. Hib.*, 32, no. 228, p. 32.

67 *Freeman's Journal*, 3 July 1891.

68 Walsh, pp. 427-8.

69 Donnelly–O'Dwyer, 9 and 24 Feb.; Letters of Dr Donnelly in Walsh Papers, DDA.

70 O'Dwyer–Donnelly, 25 Feb. 1891; idem.

71 O'Dwyer–Donnelly, 9 March; idem.

72 O'Dwyer–Donnelly, 20 March & 1 April; idem.

73 Coffey–Donnelly, 26 June; Donnelly Letters in Walsh Papers, DDA.

74 O'Dwyer–Donnelly, 30 June; idem.

75 O'Dwyer–Donnelly, 9 July, Donnelly–O'Dwyer, 11 July; idem.

76 O'Dwyer–Donnelly, 17 July, word illegible; idem.

77 Walsh–Kirby, 14 Aug.; in *Archiv. Hib.*, vol. 32, no. 477, p. 33.

78 DDA. Walsh diaries in box "Walsh Biographical".

79 Bk. of "Extracts", vol. 8, pp. 93ff..

80 Walsh, p. 429.

81 Bk. of "Extracts", idem..

82 Walsh-Dillon, 28 Oct. 1891; DDA. Walsh Papers, f. 405/3-6.

83 DDA. "Extracts", vol. 8, p. 113.

84 Walsh, p. 420.

85 Dillon–Walsh, 13 Nov.; DDA. f. 405/3-6.

86 Dillon–O'Hagan, 15 March, O'Hagan–Walsh, 31 March 1892; idem, f. 407/1-4.

87 W.B. Yeats, "Come Gather Round Me Parnellites" in *Last Poems*, 1936-'39.

88 E. Larkin. *The Roman Catholic Church in Ireland and the Fall of Parnell*, p. 288.

89 Walsh–Pope Leo XIII, 4 Nov. 1891; DDA. f. 405/3-6.

90 Croke–Walsh, 9 Nov. 1891; DDA. f. 405/ 3-6.

91 Croke–Walsh, 27 Dec.; idem.

92 Book of "Extracts", vol. 9, p. 101; excerpt from a unionist paper, but no name.

93 14 Jan. f. 407/1-4; "Extracts", 9, p. 58.

94 Kirby–Walsh, 19 Jan. 1892; DDA 1892, f. 407/1-4.

95 Idem. 27 Jan.

96 V.A. McClelland, *Cardinal Manning. His Public Life and Influence, 1865-92* (London, 1962), p. 198.

97 O'Dwyer–Donnelly, 28 Nov. 1892; Donnelly Letters. DDA. Walsh Papers.

98 P.J. Walsh, *William J. Walsh, Archbishop of Dublin*, pp. 430-1, 595. Salisbury in a speech at Birmingham on 24 Nov. 1891, accused Walsh and Croke of "defying not only their own country, but the Head of their own religion". (Extract, p. 595)

99 Walsh–Logue, 18 Dec. 1892; ADA. Toner Transcripts of Walsh–Logue Correspondence (pp. 129-99), p. 129.

100 O'Donnell–Walsh, 3 Jan. 1893; DDA. Walsh Papers 1893, Box 365. I. f. 356/2-7.

IX   THE BISHOP IN RETROSPECT, 1885-1900

1 P.J. Walsh, op. cit., p. 372.

2 D. Sheehy, "The 'Brick Palace' at Drumcondra ...", p. 7. DDA.

3 Walsh, p. 376.

4 Newspaper cutting, no name given; DDA. Bk. of "Extracts", 4, Sept. 1889, p. 91.

5 D. Sheehy, art. cit. The account of the house is based largely on this article.

6 Idem.

7 Idem.

8 Idem.

9 Idem.

10 Idem, cited Sheehy.

11 "Extracts", vol. 12. Title of paper not given.

12 Cit. Walsh, p. 374 f.n.

13 *Builder*, 5 Jan. 1917, mentions 24 new churches between 1860-1916, and mentions others without giving a date. The list is not exhaustive. DDA. In. vol. on "Church Building in Diocese of Dublin, 1860-1916".

14 In same volume. DDA.

15 *Irish Catholic Directory*, 1896.

16 Caitriona Clear, "The Homeless Young in 19th Century Ireland" in *Growing Up Poor* (Galway Labour History Group, 1993), p. 7.

17 Idem, pp. 16, 17.

18 *Irish Catholic Directory*, 1893.

19 Idem. 1900. Register of ecclesiastical events for 1895.

20 Walsh, p. 375.

21 See Walsh–Dr Tynan, 1 June 1897, re. move from church of St Michael's and John's, Dublin, to Blanchardstown. DDA. 369. I. f. 357/3.

22 DDA. 1894. 366. II. f. 356/8.

23 7 Nov. 1893; DDA. 1893, box 365. I. Clergy file.

24 6 Nov. 1893, DDA. 370/1, f. 357/8.

25 DDA. 1897. 369. I. f. 357/2.

26 DDA. 1896. 368. II. f. 370/2.

27 DDA. 1896. 368. I. f. 370/4

28 Walsh, p. 378.

29 *Irish Catholic Directory*, 1896, p. 357.

30 On catechism see Walsh, pp. 379-86.

31 Report 1912, p. 169 f.: DDA, Walsh Papers, 1912.

32 "Extracts", vol. 12, 15 May 1893.

33 *Irish Cath. Directory*, 1912. Register of eccles. events of 1911, p. 477.

34 Walsh–Donnelly, 14 Nov. 1895; DDA. Letters of Walsh–Donnelly, 1885-'95;

35 "Extracts", vol. 6, p. 6.

36 Speedy–Walsh, 7 Jan., Hayes–Walsh, 30 Jan. 1895; DDA. 1895. Box 367. II. f. 363/ 4-8.

37 F.H. O'Donnell, MP, *Political Priests and Irish Ruin*, pamphlet; cit. Elizabeth Malcolm in *Ireland Sober, Ireland Free* (Dublin 1986), p. 298.

38 Walsh, p. 373.

39 Cit. Malcolm, p. 301.

40 Idem, p. 302.

41 "Extracts", vol. 6, pp. 13-16.

42 L. McKenna, *Fr James Cullen, SJ* (London, 1924), p. 325.

43 "Extracts", 1893, vol. 6, pp. 83-5.

44 Idem, p. 298.

45 L. McKenna, op. cit., p. 352.

46 Docs. undated, in DDA. 1892, f. 405/3-6: ref. is either to Dermot O'Hurley, archbishop of Cashel, d. 1584, or Patrick O'Healy, OFM, bishop of Mayo, d. 1579, and Terence O'Brien, OP, bishop of Emly, d. 1651.

47 Morris–Walsh, 8 July 1891; f. 405/ 3-6.

48 Circular on Process from Denis Murphy, SJ, 20 Feb. 1892; DDA. "Walsh Biographical".

49 Irish Jesuit Archives (IJA), Hogan Papers, 26 June 1896.

50 Pollen–Walsh, 11 Jan. 1903; DDA. box. 375. II. File for Regulars (members of religious congregations), no number on file.

51 Walsh–Ed. Hogan, 11 Jan. 1905. Italics in text.: IJA. Hogan Papers.

52 *Freeman's Journal*, 9 April 1921, part of obituary tribute; see also MacInerney's articles mentioned, *Studies*, June and Dec. 1921.

53 Persico Report, ff. 135, p. 105.

54 Michael Curran, "The Late Archbishop of Dublin", *Dublin Review*, July-Sept. 1921, p. 105.

55 Cit. in *United Irishman*, 23 April 1904.

56 M. Curran. Art. cit.

57 St Charles Borromeo: sermon at his last synod in Milan.

58 Prof. Liam Ryan, Maynooth, *The Furrow*, Jan. 1983.

59 M.V. Ronan, *Most Rev. W.J. Walsh, DD*, pamphlet memoir (Bray, 1927), p. 10.

60 Malcolm, *Ireland Sober …*, pp. 301f.

61 "Extracts" vol. 13, pp. 90ff., 96.

62 Countess Plunkett–Walsh, 2 Aug. 1895, and other letters; DDA. 367. II. f. 363/4-8.

63 Diary, 18 Aug. 1895; in box "Walsh Biographical".

64 Donnelly–O'Dwyer, 25 March 1897; DDA. Donnelly Letters.

65 Walsh–Plunkett, 30 Oct. & 7 Nov. 1897; DDA.

66 P.J. Walsh, "Fide et Labore" in *Catholic Bulletin*, vol. xi, 1921, p. 286. An appreciation of Dr Walsh.

67 Walsh–O'Dwyer, 27 Jan. 1896; LDA.

68 Walsh–O'Dwyer, 29 Jan. 1896; LDA.

69 Walsh–O'Dwyer, 20 Feb. 1896; idem.

70 Idem, 24 Feb. Italics in text.

71 Donnelly-O'Dwyer, 14 May 1896; LDA.

72 Wm. Magennis–Logue, 13 March 1896; ADA. Toner Transcripts, pp. 284-6.

73 Walsh–Logue, 2 March; idem, p. 138. Walsh's strong public letter evoked from Dr O'Dwyer the unexpected comment that it was "one of the best you have ever written". It was "the policy of the Jesuit body everywhere", O'Dwyer continued, … "to postpone every interest of religion and duty of ecclesiastical propriety to their own ends and interests. Manning and Wiseman had that experience in Westminister, Vaughan in Salford, and here now you. Now the body that one would think would put their power and influence at the disposal of the Bishops systematically undermine us" (O'Dwyer–Walsh, 2 March 1896; DDA. 386. I. file 370/1-7 Bishops' file). Walsh did not need reminding that his mercurial headstrong colleague from Limerick, unlike his predecessor, Bishop Butler, had been at loggerheads with the local Jesuits from the start of his episcopacy, had challenged the order in connection with their Apostolic School at Mungret, and brought the matter to Rome only to have the decision go against him.

74 Calendar of correspondence of Cardinal Logue, 1887-1924, in section under Universities, pp. 298-9; ADA.

75 W. Magennis–Logue, 8 & 13 March 1896; ADA. idem, pp. 284-6.

76 Account in Provincial Archives, Discalced Carmelites, Clarendon St, Dublin 2, and in typed copy in DDA entitled: "A Painful Case/the 'Suspension' of Fr Aloysius Coghlan ODC, 1898".

77 *Freeman*, 3 Sept. 1885, in scrapbook in Blackrock College Archives.

78 In Reffé's file of documents, no. 209; BCA.

79 The account is taken largely from Kevin Condon, *The Missionary College of All Hallows, 1842-'91* (Dublin, 1986), pp. 154 ff.
80 Walsh–Simeoni, 30 March 1890; DDA. file 283/2. See Condon, p. 173.
81 Condon, p. 175.
82 Simeoni–Walsh, 20 May 1890; Letters and Decrees of the Cardinal Prefect, cit. Condon, p. 174.
83 Walsh–Simeoni, 6 May 1890; DDA. cit. Condon, p. 174.
84 Cit. Condon, p. 189.
85 Donnelly–O'Dwyer, 16 Dec. 1891; DDA. Donnelly Letters.
86 Fortune–Woodlock, 20 Oct. 1892; Ardagh Archives, cit. Condon, p. 190.
87 Walsh, p. 377.
88 M.V. Ronan. *The Most Rev. W.J. Walsh D.D.*, p. 12; in DDA. "Walsh Background" file.

X "TRUE MAN" – PATTERN OF A
LIFE, 1885-1912

1 Croke–Walsh, 4 May 1894; DDA. box 366. Bishops' file.
2 Walsh–Jn. Dillon, 17 April 1893; Dillon Papers, TCD, Ms. 6765.
3 Bishop Donnelly–O'Dwyer, 17 May 1893; DDA. Donnelly Letters.
4 Jn. D. Comrie. *Black's Medical Dictionary* (London, 1928 ed.), pp. 331-3.
5 Hayes–Walsh, 30 Jan.1895; DDA. 367. II. f. 363/ 4-8.
6 Woodlock–Walsh, 3 July 1895; DDA. 1895, Bishops' file.
7 Walsh–Hogan, 20 Aug. 1895; I JA. Hogan Papers.
8 Brownrigg–Walsh, 24 Aug. 1895; DDA. 366. Bishops' file.
9 Walsh—Donnelly, 11 May 1896; DDA. Letters of Donnelly.
10 Donnelly—O'Dwyer 27 May 1896; DDA. idem.
11 P.J. Walsh, "Fide et Labore" in *Catholic Bulletin*, vol. xi, 1921, pp. 277ff.
12 M. Curran, "The Late Archbishop of Dublin" in *Dublin Review*, July-Sept. 1921, p. 106.
13 M.V. Ronan, *The Most Rev. W.J. Walsh, D.D.*, pamphlet, pp. 13-14.
14 Walsh, "Fide et Labore", p. 277.
15 Walsh–J. Botrel, 26 Sept. 1896; BCA. Botrel Letters.
16 Diaries, 1896, in box "Walsh Biographical".
17 Walsh–Donnelly, 27 Sept. 1896; Donnelly Letters.
18 M.V. Ronan, op. cit., p. 14.
19 Walsh–Joseph McGrath, 14 Sept. 1900 (out of place in the file for 1909-10); NUI. Sir Joseph McGrath Papers.
20 Walsh–McGrath, 1 June 1905; NUI. idem.
21 Walsh–McGrath, 23 Sept. 1905; idem.
22 Walsh–McGrath, 12 Sept. 1908. Italics in text: idem.
23 McGrath–Walsh, 24 Sept. 1908; idem.
24 Walsh–McGrath, 11 April 1910; idem.
25 McGrath–Walsh, 16 April 1910: idem, Charles Doyle was, presumably, Judge Charles Doyle who as a boy, at a small school, the Crescent, Limerick, had gained first palce in the first Intermediate Examinations.
26 McGrath–Walsh, 10 Sept. 1913; idem.
27 Walsh–McGrath, 16 Sept. 1913; idem. Fergal did persevere and had a distinguished career. After a doctorate at Oxford, he was visiting lecturer at Fordham University, New York, and wrote the well-known work on Newman, *Newman's University: Idea and Reality* (Dublin 1951). Other works followed on aspects of Irish education.
28 Walsh–Donnelly, 1 March 1897; DDA. Donnelly Letters.
29 Walsh–Donnelly, 19 March 1897; idem.
30 Diary, 12 July 1897; DDA. "Walsh Biographical".
31 Diary, Oct. 1897; idem.
32 Walsh–Count Plunkett, 30 Oct. 1897; DDA. 1897, no file ref.
33 Walsh–Donnelly, 19 May 1899; DDA. Donnelly Letters.

34 *Black's Medical Dictionary*, p. 331.

35 Logue–Walsh, 22 July 1899; DDA. 371. I. f. 364/3.

36 Diary, 8 Oct. 1899; in "Walsh Biographical".

37 Walsh–Donnelly, 1 March 1897; Donnelly Letters.

38 Walsh–Donnelly, 2 Aug. 1898; idem.

39 Donnelly–O'Dwyer, 25 March 1897; idem

40 Croke–Walsh, 15 Jan. 1900; DDA. 372. I. f. 371/1

41 Healy–Walsh, 1 March 1900; DDA. 372. I. f. 371/1; Logue–Walsh, 8 April; idem.

42 Cadogan–Walsh, 26 Aug. 1900; Walsh–Cadogan, 29 Aug.; 372. II. f. 371/6

43 T.G. Gill–Walsh, 21 Jan. 1901; 373/2 f. 351/7.

44 Chief Baron C. Palles–Walsh, 7 July 1901; 373. II. f. 351/8 Laity.

45 Cadogan–Walsh, 1 July 1900; idem.

46 Logue–Walsh, 4 July 1901; ADA. Toner Transcr. of Logue Corresp. , p. 56.

47 *Irish Catholic Directory*, 1907, Register of ecclesiastical events, 1906.

48 Walsh–Countess Aberdeen, 30 May 1907; DDA. 379. II. f. 381/6 Laity.

49 Walsh's attitude to the Exhibition was also probably not uninfluenced by William Martin Murphy's prominent role in organising it. See T.J. Morrissey, *William Martin Murphy* (Dundalk, 1997), pp. 36-7.

50 Walsh–Lord Aberdeen, 29 Oct. 1909; Aberdeen–Walsh, 6 Nov. 1909; DDA. 381. II. f. 382/3. Laity.

51 Walsh–Aberdeen, 29 Oct. 1909; idem.

52 Logue–Walsh, 29 Aug. 1910; 382. I. f. 382/6.

53 Walsh–Logue, 9 Dec. 1910; ADA. Toner typescripts.

54 Walsh, p. 566.

55 Richard Kelly–Walsh, 14 Nov. 1911; DDA. 383. II. f. 383/3 Laity.

56 Logue–Walsh, 7 Jan. 1912; 384. I. f. 383/5.

57 Walsh, pp. 566-70.

58 Logue–Walsh, 27 March 1912; 384/1 f. 383/5

59 Redmond–Walsh, 7 March 1912; Walsh–Redmond, 20 March; DDA. 1912. Laity file.

60 E. de Marie–Walsh, 2 Feb. 1912; DDA. 384. II. f. 377/2.

61 O'Dwyer–Walsh, 24 June 1912; 384. I. f. 383/5

62 Palles–Walsh, 5 Aug. 1912; 384. II. f. 377/1

63 Jn. Healy–Walsh, 3 Sept. 1912; 384. I. f. 383/7.

64 J. Healy–Walsh, 24 Oct. 1912; 383/6. Priests' file.

65 *Black's Medical Dictionary*, pp. 637-9.

66 P.J. Walsh–Archbishop Walsh, 22 Aug. 1912; 384. I. f. 383/7.

67 Diary, 13 October 1912; DDA. "Walsh Biographical".

68 J.V. O'Brien, *'Dear Dirty Dublin'. A City in Distress, 1899-1916* (Berkley, L.A., 1982), p. 169.

69 Logue–Walsh, 15 Nov. 1912; DDA. 384. I. f. 383/5.

70 Logue–Walsh, 9 Dec. 1912; 384. I. f. 383/5.

71 Walsh, p. 581.

72 P.J. Walsh, "Fide et Labore", p. 282.

73 Idem, p. 277.

74 Idem, pp. 278-80.

75 Idem, p. 279.

76 M.V. Ronan, *The Most Rev. W.J. Walsh, D.D.*, pp. 12-13.

77 Idem, p. 15.

78 Walsh–Mrs Fitzgerald, 22 March 1901; 373. II. f. 351/8

79 Cadogan–Walsh, 13 Oct. 1901; 373. II. f. 351/8.

80 Henrietta Mac Donnell–Walsh, no date, but 1905; 377. II. f. 374/3. She reported further progress on 3 Dec. 1905.

81 Traill–Walsh, 31 Jan. 1903; 375. I. f. 365/4.

82 J. Lehane–Walsh, 3 Jan. 1902; 374. II. f. 358/8 Laity.

83 Aberdeen–Walsh, 6 Dec. 1907; 379. II. f. 381/6

84 Walsh, pp. 583-4.
85 M.V. Ronan, p. 13.
86 P.J. Walsh, "Fide et Labore", p. 286.

XI ARBITRATOR IN SOCIAL,
COMMERCIAL, AND POLITICAL
DISPUTES

1 James Meehan, *George O'Brien*, pp. ix, 5.
2 DDA. in box "Walsh Biographical".
3 Leslie, op. cit., p. 376
4 DDA. "Extracts", vol. 3, pp. 97, 100; 10 & 12 April.
5 Idem in *Times*, 11 May.
6 DDA. in box "Politics"
7 "Extracts", 4, p. 4; June 1889.
8 Idem, p. 8
9 *Echo* in box "Walsh Biographical", DDA.
10 Hedley–Walsh, 29 June 1898; DDA. Bishops' file.
11 "Extracts", 4. Italics in text.
12 Idem, and *Freeman*, 30 Dec. 1889.
13 *Freeman*, 18 March 1890; in "Extracts", vol. 6.
14 *Freeman*, 20 March 1890; idem.
15 *Freeman*, 24 March; idem, pp. 10, 11.
16 *Freeman*, 29 March; idem, p. 3.
17 Idem.
18 Idem.; "Extracts", pp. 23-4.
19 Idem.
20 *Freeman*, 24 March; "Extracts", 6, p. 12.
21 Idem.; "Extracts", 6, p. 21.
22 *Freeman*, 27 April; "Extracts", 6, p. 41.
23 Idem, 28 April; idem, p. 42.
24 Bk. of "Extracts", 6, pp. 42-3.
25 Idem, p. 45.
26 Idem, pp. 46-7.
27 Idem, p. 45.
28 Idem, pp. 46-7, *Evening Telegraph*, 29 April.
29 Idem, p. 46.
30 Idem, p. 47.
31 Idem, p. 51.
32 Idem, p. 52.
33 Idem, pp. 53-4.
34 Idem, p. 53.

35 Idem, pp. 61-2.
36 Idem, p. 63.
37 Idem, p. 67.
38 Idem, p. 70
39 Idem, p. 78.
40 *Freeman*, 15 May 1891; "Extracts", vol. 8.
41 Newspaper cutting, 5 June 1891, (*Freeman?*); "Extracts", vol. 8.
42 *Echo*, 8-8-1890.: DDA. in box "Walsh Biographical".
43 Croke–Walsh, 15 & 19 March 1892; DDA. f. 407/ 1-4.
44 Murphy–Walsh, 14 Jan. 1893; DDA. Laity file.
45 Dillon–Walsh, 17 Jan. 1893; idem.
46 Kernan–Walsh, 28 Jan. 1893; DDA. box 365. II. f. 356/ 2-7.
47 Walsh–Murphy, 6 March 1893; DDA. 1893, Laity file.
48 Walsh–Sexton, 7 March1893; idem.
49 Walsh–Dillon, 30 April 1893; Dillon Papers, TCD, Ms. 6765, no. 42.
50 Dillon–Walsh, no date but in 1893 file; DDA. Laity file.
51 Brownrigg–Walsh, 16, 20 March. DDA. 365 II, f. 356/2-7.
52 Fr John O'Hanlon–Walsh, 15 March 1893; DDA. 365. II. f. 356/2-7.
53 Brownrigg–Walsh, Easter Sunday, 1893; DDA. idem.
54 Walsh–Harrington, 20 Feb. 1895. Italics mine; DDA. 367. II. f. 363/4-8.
55 Walsh–Dillon, 24 Feb. 1895; Dillon Papers, TCD, Ms. 6765.
56 Dillon–Walsh, 1 March 1895; DDA. 367. II. f. 363/4-8.
57 Donnelly–O'Dwyer, 10 March 1895; Donnelly Letters. Walsh Papers. DDA.
58 Walsh–Dillon, 3 March 1895; Dillon Papers, TCD. Ms. 6765.
59 Walsh–Dillon, 5 July 1895; idem, no. 70.
60 Redmond–Walsh, 8 July 1895; 367. II. f. 363/4-8.
61 Walsh–Redmond, 12 July; idem.
62 Redmond–Walsh, 14 July 1895; idem.
63 Clarke family-Walsh, 16 Dec. 1895 (wrongly dated 1896); Walsh–Clarkes,

19 Dec. 1895; Clarkes–Walsh, 24 Dec. 1895; Walsh–Clarkes 31 Dec. 1895; Clarkes–Walsh, 4 Jan. 1896. DDA. Box. 367. II.

64 Walsh–Logue, 26 Jan. 1895; ADA. Toner typescripts of Logue Correspond., p. 131.

65 Idem, 23 Feb. 1895; idem, p. 133.

66 Healy–O'Dwyer, 24 Oct. 1896; LDA. Section H.

67 O'Dwyer–Walsh, 26 Oct. 1896; DDA. 1896. Bishops' file.

68 Walsh–Lord Mayor (copy), 30 Dec. 1896; ADA. Toner Typescripts, pp. 141-3.

69 Wm. O'Malley–Walsh, 30 Jan. 1897; DDA. 369. II. f. 357/4

70 Harrington–Walsh, 16 Jan. 1897; idem.

71 Idem. Resolution, 28 Feb. 1897.

72 Proposal of 24 August, from Cashel Branch of Irish National Federation, DDA. in 1898 folder, although no year given.

73 In printed doc. re. a national memorial, 1899 (should be in 1898); DDA. 371. II. f. 364/8

74 Walsh's diary, 1900, in "Walsh Biographical", DDA.

75 Harrington–Walsh, 22 Nov. 1900; DDA. 372. II. f. 371/5-6.

76 Dillon Papers, TCD, Ms. 6542: Memorandum book with various entries & newspaper cuttings, 1899-1903. The name of the paper is not given.

77 Redmond–Healy, 31 July 1900; in Healy, *Letters and Leaders* ..., vol. II, p. 449.

78 Printed notice signed by Wm. Patterson and D. Farrell of United Labourers of Ireland trade union, 5 June 1896; DDA. 1896.

79 Walsh–United Labourers, 7 June 1896; DDA. Laity file 1896.

80 Irish Industrial League–Walsh, 11 June 1896; idem.

81 Ennis–Walsh, 12 June 1896; idem.

82 Meade–Walsh, 22 Aug. 1896; DDA. 1896, Laity file.

83 Walsh–Secretary, 15 July 1897; idem, 1897.

84 Partridge–Walsh, 8 Dec. 1897; idem.

85 By Resolution, 15 April 1898; DDA. 1898, Laity file. And Terence Clarke, Central Secretary INTO–Walsh, 23 April 1898; idem.

86 "Never", well hardly ever! See his initiative re. railway dispute.

87 Walsh–Printers' Societies, 27 June 1899; DDA. 1899. 371. II. f. 364/8.

88 Jn. Simmons, Trades Council–Walsh, 24 March 1905; DDA. 377. II. f. 374/1

89 Slevin & Son–Walsh, 13 Dec. 1905; idem, f. 374/3.

90 M.J. O'Lehane–Walsh, 3 March 1905; idem, f. 374/1.

91 John Molony, *The Worker Question*, (Dublin, 1991), with translation of *Rerum Novarum*, pp. 184, 189.

XII THE UNIVERSITY QUESTION: REACHING A SOLUTION, AND CONSOLIDATION, 1897-1912

1 *The King* magazine, 8 Dec. 1900, p. 720.; DDA. Box of newspaper cuttings.

2 On the subsequent correspondence, see DDA. Laity file. 1 March 1901.

3 *Evening Herald*, 26 Oct. 1901; DDA. Cuttings.

4 Evelyn Bolster, *The Knights of St Columbanus* (Dublin, 1979) pp. 10-11.

5 Walsh–Ch. of Ireland, Archbishop of Armagh, 23 July 1903, DDA. Box 375/1; f. 365/4; and Armagh–Walsh, 27 July 1903; DDA idem.

6 Entry in Memorandum Book, 1893-1903, for Thus. 12 Feb. 1903. Dillon Papers, TCD. Ms. 6542.

7 *Irish Catholic Directory*, 1898, Register of ecclesiastical events, 1897, pp. 394-5.

8 P.J. Walsh, *Wm. J. Walsh. Archbishop of Dublin*, p. 553.

9 Logue–Walsh, 29 Nov. 1901; DDA. Box 373/1; f. 351/1

10 O'Dwyer–Donnelly, 9 May 1899; DDA. f. 373/4. Letters of O'Dwyer to Donnelly are in Walsh papers under 'Letters to Dr Donnelly'.

11 Thomas J. Morrissey, *Towards a National University. William Delany SJ (1835-1924)* (Dublin, 1983), pp. 175-7.
12 Irish Jesuit Archives. O'Dwyer–Delany, 13, 16, 18 Feb. 1901.
13 See Morrissey, op. cit., pp. 176-7
14 Cadogan–Walsh, 25 Feb. 1901; DDA. Box 373.II; f. 351/8
15 Walsh–Cadogan, 25 Feb.; idem.
16 Walsh–Fr David OFM, 13 April 1901; copy courtesy Justin McLoughlin OFM (1985), the Friary, 160 the Grove, Stratford, London. E 15 1NS.
17 Royal Commission on Univ. Educ. in Ireland; third report, p. xi.
18 David W. Miller, *Church, State and Nation in Ireland 1898-1921* (Dublin, 1973), pp. 65-6.
19 O'Dwyer–Dr Donnelly, 18 Nov. 1901; DDA. f. 373/4. Walsh papers. "Nixon" is Christopher Nixon, medical doctor, member of senate, later Sir Christopher Nixon; "Ross" is Sir John Ross of Bladensburg.
20 See Delany's controversy with 'Reviewer' in *Freeman's Journal*, letters on 17, 18, 20, 21 December 1901.;and letter to provincial to be shown to Cardinal Logue and Dr Walsh, 19 August, in Morrissey, op. cit., pp. 178-9.
21 Miller, op. cit., pp. 69, and 102.
22 Maisie Ward, *Insurrection versus Resurection* (London, 1937), p. 59.
23 Fathers of the Society of Jesus, *A Page of Irish History. Story of University College Dublin* (Dublin, 1930), pp. 520-21.
24 Mac Donnell–Alice Stopford Green, 30 Oct. 1902; NLI. Alice Stopford Green Papers, Mss. 15089(2). For this reference and much of the information on MacDonnell, I am indebted to Aiden O'Reilly's "Sir Anthony MacDonnell and University Reform, 1902-1908", NUI, MEd thesis, 1997, p. 26.
25 MacDonnell–His wife, 18 Nov. 1902; MacDonnell Papers, c 216, f. 20. Bodlein Library; O'Reilly thesis, p. 35.

26 MacDonnell papers, 21 Nov. 1906; c 367, ff. 1-6; O'Reilly, p. 35.
27 MacDonnell papers respectively: c 216, f. 23; c 216, f.26; c. 216, f. 34; O'Reilly, pp. 35-37.
28 Redmond–Dillon, 30 Sept. 1903; cit. Miller. p. 99.
29 Idem; in Miller, p. 101.
30 Walsh–Redmond, 16 Oct. 1903; DDA. Box 375. I.; f. 365/4 Laity.
31 *ICD*, 1904. Report of Eccles. Events. 1903.
32 J.W. Mac Kail & Guy Wyndham, *The Life and Letters of George Wyndham*, vol. II (London, undated), p. 467
33 Walsh–MacDonnell, 28 Oct. 1903; italics in text. MacDonnell papers, c 351, f. 146; O'Reilly p. 53.
34 P.J. Walsh, *William J. Walsh. Archbishop of Dublin*, p. 555.
35 *Ir. Cath. Dir.*, 1904, Report Eccl. Events 1903, 8 Dec., pp. 448-9.
36 MacDonnell papers. c. 367, ff. 15-20; O'Reilly, p. 62.
37 Idem. c. 367, f. 21; O'Reilly, pp. 63-4.
38 Walsh–Mac Donnell, 7 Jan. 1904; MacDonnell papers, c. 350, f. 149; italics as in text.
39 MacDonnell papers. c. 367, ff. 22-3; O'Reilly p. 66.
40 *Freeman's Journal*, 14 Jan. 1904, p. 5
41 Idem. 30 Jan. 1904, p. 5
42 Morrissey, *Towards a National Univ.*, p. 211.
43 Finbarr O'Driscoll, "Archbishop Walsh and St Mary's University College, 1893-1908" in *Irish Educational Studies*, vol. 5, no. 2 (Dublin, 1985), pp. 283-99.
44 Donal McCartney, *UCD. A National Idea* (Dublin, 1999), pp. 72-3.
45 Morrissey, op. cit., p. 215.
46 Idem, pp. 216-7
47 Walsh–Redmond, 13 Jan. 1904; in P.J. Walsh, op. cit., pp. 556-7.
48 Walsh, ibid., p. 557.
49 Morrissey, p. 221; *I.C.D.*, 1907, Register ... 1906, 9 March.
50 Miller, *Church, State and Nation ...*, p. 148.

51 Redmond–Bryce, 29 Jan. 1906; N.L.I. Bryce papers. Ms. 11, 012; in Miller, p. 148.

52. Barnett–Bryce, 14 Feb. 1906, Bryce papers. Ms. 11, 012; O'Reilly, p. 80.

53 MacDonnell–Bryce, 8 March 1906; idem. Ms. 11, 012 (3)

54 *ICD.*, 1907; Report ... 1906, pp. 459-60.

55 Idem, 31 July 1906, p. 465.

56 Ibid., p. 466.

57 MacDonnell papers c. 350, f. 29; O'Reilly, p. 85.

58 MacDonnell–Bryce, 18 Aug. 1906; Bryce papers. Ms. 11, 013; O'R. p. 85.

59 Royal Commission T.C.D. Appendix to Final Report, p. 421 (Cd 3312); H.C. 1907, xli.

60 Idem, pp. 421-2.; Miller, pp. 162-3.

61 Morrissey, op. cit., pp. 228-9.

62 Idem, and IJA. Delany–Healy, 21 Jan. 1907.

63 *A Page of Irish History*, pp. 535-6.

64 R.C. T.C.D. App. to Final Report, p. 271; cit. Miller. p. 163.

65 *F.J.*, 14 Nov. 1906; in Miller, p. 164.

66 MacDonnell papers. C. 354. f. 162; Miller, p. 117

67 Bryce–Camb. Bannerman, 23 Jan. 1907; Br. Mus. Camb. Bannerman papers. Add. Ms. 41, 211/ 364-5; Miller, p. 178.

68 Idem, 27 Jan., Add. Ms. 41, 211/ 366-7; Miller, p. 179

69 Morrissey. p. 233.

70 Healy–Delany, 24 Jan.; IJA. Delany papers.

71 Ross–O'Dwyer, 27 Jan. 1907; LDA. O'Dwyer papers.

72 O'Dwyer–Ross, 27 Jan. 1907; IJA. Delany papers. Letter passed on by Ross.

73 Morrissey, p. 235.

74 *Ir. Cath. Dir.*, 1908; Report on 1907, 8 Feb.

75 Idem, 5 Feb. 1907.

76 Walsh–MacDonnell, 4 Feb. 1907; MacDonnell papers. c. 351. ff. 154-7; Miller, p. 179. Italics mine.

77 Idem. Italics in text.

78 Miller, pp. 179-80.

79 *ICD*, 1908, Report ... 1907, p. 459.

80 *A Page of Irish History*, p. 533.

81 MacDonnell–to his wife, 19 Feb. 1907; MacDonnell papers. e217, f. 1; O'R. p. 89.

82 *ICD*, 1908, Report ... 1907. 26 Feb., p. 459.

83 Windle–Delany, 11 April 1907. IJA.

84 MacDonnell–Bryce, 12 March 1907. NLI. Bryce papers. Ms. 11, 015; O'Reilly, p. 89. Hamilton was president of Queen's College Belfast.

85 Delany–Birrell, 1907. n.d.; IJA. It could be argued that Gladstone's proposal was defeated as much by Cardinal Cullen and Catholic opposition as by "concerted Protestant opposition".

86 Morrissey, p. 288; L. O'Broin, *The Chief Secretary: Augustine Birrell in Ireland* (London, 1969), p. 136.

87 *Things Past Redress*, pp. 200-1.

88 Miller. pp. 189-90.

89 Birrell–Campbell Bannerman, 24 May 1907; B.M. The Campbell Bannerman papers, Add. Ms. 41,239/ 250-251; O'Broin, *Chief Secretary* ... pp. 15-16. & Miller, p. 188.

90 Redmond–Birrell, 25 May 1907. NLI. Ms. 15, 169; cit. Graine O'Flynn "Augustine Birrell and Archbishop William Walsh's influence on the founding of the National University of Ireland" in *Capuchin Annual*, 1976, pp. 148-9.

91 *ICD*, 1908, Report for 1907, 4 July 1907, p. 473.

92 L. O'Broin, *Chief Secretary* ..., p. 24.

93 G. O'Flynn, art. cit., *Capuchin Annual*, p. 150

94 Birrell–Walsh, 31 Dec. 1907. DDA. f. 14, (file on Nat. Univ. Ireland). Italics and exclamation in text.

95 Walsh–Birrell, 6 Jan. 1908; idem. Italics in text.

96 Cit. Prof. George O'Brien in "Fr Thomas Finlay, SJ, 1849-1940" in *Studies*, vol. xxix, March 1940, pp. 27ff.

97 Birrell-Delany, 4 Aug. 1908, in IJA; and see Morrissey. pp. 303-4.
98 O'Flynn, art. cit., p. 157.
99 *ICD*, 1909, Report of 1908, 31 March, p. 464.
100 Idem, pp. 480-1.
101 *ICD*, 1912 Report of events for 1911 (incl. end of 1910), pp. 472-3.
102 Account in IJA. See Morrissey, op. cit., pp. 321 ff.
103 IJA. Delany papers. See Morrissey, p. 332.
104 Miller, op. cit., pp. 238 ff.
105 Cit. Miller, p. 235.
106 Walsh–O'Dalaigh, 7 Dec. 1908. DDA. Box 380.II. f. 375/6 Laity.
107 Miller, p. 236.
108 Walsh–McGrath, 15 April 1910. NUI. McGrath papers.
109 O'Hanrahan (?)–Walsh, 16 Jan. 1912.; DDA. 1912. Laity file.
110 Louis McRedmond, "Christopher Palles" in *The Clongowes Union Centenary Chronicle* (Dublin, 1997), p. 67.
111 P.J. Walsh, op. cit., pp. 363-4.
112 Walsh–McGrath, 3 June 1912; NUI. McGrath papers.
113 Idem, 9 June 1912.
114 Walsh's draft amendment, 1913; NUI. McGrath papers.
115 P.J. Walsh, op cit., p. 364.
116 Dougherty–Walsh, 11 Dec. 1908; DDA. Box 380.II. f. 375/6 Laity.
117 Statement of Monsignor Michael Curran to Military Bureau, 1913-18, based on his diaries and memory, in NLI. Sean T. O'Ceallaigh papers. Special List A 9. Ms. 27, 728. vol. 1. Statement in 3 parts. This is part 1, p. 3.
118 Murphy in his address to the tramway workers on 19 July 1913, pointing to what happened in the rail strike as a warning against strike action. See T.J. Morrissey, *William Martin Murphy* (Dundalk, 1997), p. 48.

XIII   FROM RELATIVE QUIET TO A CITY IN TURMOIL, 1913

1 Walsh–Coffey, 10 Jan. 1913; DDA. Box 385. I. f. 384/3 Laity. The site became the location of University College Dublin.
2 *Irish Independent*, 10 Feb. 1913.
3 See 29 May 1913; DDA. Box 385. II. f. 384/2 Laity
4 Palles–Walsh, 30 Jan. 1913; DDA. Box 385. I. f. 384/3 Laity.
5 Walsh–Milner, 18 Feb. 1913; DDA. Box 385. I. f. 384/3 Laity.
6 See DDA. Sept. 1913. Box 385. I. f. 377/3 Laity.
7 Little–Walsh, 18 July 1913; DDA. Box 385. II. f. 384/1
8 Reports on proselytism. DDA. Box 385. I. f. 377/4 Priests.
9 DDA. Box 386. II. f. 378/1
10 *Ir. Cath. Dir.*, 1914. Record of Irish Eccles. Events 1913; pp. 516-17.
11 George Askwith, *Report on the Government Court of Enquiry into the 1913 Lock Out*, cit. Keogh, *The Rise of the Irish Working Class*, p. 98.
12 See Thomas Morrissey, *William Martin Murphy* (Dundalk, 1977).
13 *Daily Express*, 26 Aug. 1913.
14 Curran–Walsh, 26 Aug. 1913.; DDA. Box 385. I. f. 377/5. It is not clear who "Collins" was. There was no diocesan clergyman of that name at the time.
15 Curran–Walsh, 2 Sept. 1913; DDA. Box. 385. I. f. 377/ 5.
16 Idem. Italics in text. "Booth or Markievicz" refers to Constance Gore-Booth who married Count Casimir Markievicz, 1900, became an officer in the Irish Citizen Army and strongly supported the workers in 1913.
17 Vane de V.M. Vallance papers, N.L.I. Ms. 17883; cit. F.A. D'Arcy in "Larkin and the Dublin Lock-Out" in *James Larkin, Lion of the Fold*, ed. D. Nevin (Dublin, 1998), p. 38.
18 J. Healy–Walsh, 4 Sept. 1913; DDA. Box 385. I. f. 377/5.

19 *Irish Homestead,* 13 Sept.

20 Cit. Keogh. op. cit., p. 209.

21 Curran–Walsh, 22 Sept.; Box 385. I. f. 377/5

22 Curran refers to his Grace's account of his vacation, Curran–Walsh, 29 Sept.; Box 385. I. f. 377/5.

23 Diary of 7 Oct. & letter Marie Sherlock–Walsh, 9 Oct. thanking him. Box 385. I. f. 377/3 Laity.

24 Italics in text. Walsh–Aberdeen, 10 Oct. 1913; Box 385.I. f. 377/3.

25 G. Askwith, *Industrial Problems and Disputes* (London, 1920), p. 265, cit. Keogh, op. cit., p. 216.

26 "Employers Reply to Sir George Askwith's Findings", 14 Oct. 1913; DDA. Box 351. I. f. 377/3.

27 Askwith, op. cit., p. 267; cit. Keogh, p. 217.

28 Walsh–Aberdeen, 10 Oct. 1913; DDA. Box 385. I. f. 377/3

29 McGloughlin (of J & C McGloughlin Ltd. Art Workers in Iron, Copper and Brass)–Walsh, 23 Oct. 1913; Box 385. I. f. 377/3

30 D. Montefiore, from Edinburgh Hotel, Dublin–Walsh, 21 Oct.; Box 385. I. f. 377/3

31 M. Curran's statement to Irish Military Bureau; INL. S.T. O'Ceallaigh papers, Special List A9, Ms. 27, 728 (1), p. 5.

32 Walsh–Montefiore, 22 Oct.; Box 385. I. f. 377/3

33 F. McCormick–Walsh, 22 Oct.; Box 385. II. f. 384/1

34 P.L. O'Brien–Walsh, 22 Oct.; Box 385. I. f. 377/3

35 A. Connolly–Walsh, 24 Oct. from London; Box 385. I. f. 377/3

36 Wm. Pennington–Flavin, 23 Oct. 1913; Box 385. I. f. 377/3

37 Canon Spring Rice–Walsh, 23 Oct.; Box 385. I. f. 377/3; also in 385. II. f. 384/3

38 O'Connell–Flavin, 23 Oct.; Box 385. II. f. 384/3

39 *James Larkin Lion of the Fold,* ed. Nevin, p. 225.

40 See T.J. Morrissey, *A Man Called Hughes,* p. 41; *Irish Worker,* 8 Nov. 1913.

41 *Independent* 23 Oct.

42 Josephine M. Plunkett–Walsh, 24 Oct. 1913; Box 385. I. f. 384/ 3.

43 J.V. O'Brien, *'Dear Dirty Dublin',* p. 235.

44 Keogh, op. cit., p. 222; and see T.J. Morrissey, "The 1913 Lock-Out: Letters for the Archbishop" in *Studies,* Spring 1986, p. 99.

45 T.J. Morrissey, *A Man Called Hughes,* p. 41.

46 J. Connolly, "The Children, the ITGWU and the Archbishop" in *Forward,* 1 Nov.; given in *1913. Jim Larkin and the Dublin Lock Out* (Dublin, 1964 by Workers Union of Ireland), pp. 73-5.

47 Among his efforts repulsed were: The letter of McGloughlin on 23 October; letter of Chas. D. Coghlan, secretary of Employers–Walsh, 27 Oct.; Box 385. I. f. 377/3; and J. Oatis, 19 Dec.–Walsh, "don't interfere"; Box 385. II. f. 384/1. Also turned down was his proposal "to ask Lord MacDonnell and Sir A.M. Porter, former Master of the Rolls, to act as intermediaries" even though, according to the *Daily Express,* it had met "with a great deal of approval".

48 *ICD,* 1914, Report on Events 1913, under 24 Nov., p. 493

49 Josephine Plunkett–Walsh, 24 Oct.; Box 351. I. f. 384/ 3

50 M. Sherlock–Walsh, 27 Oct.; Box 385/1. f. 377/3

51 Dublin Children's Distress Fund, Report. Oct. 1913–Feb. 1914. Box 385. II. f. 384/3, Laity. The magnitude of the task of clothing the children may be gauged from the following: *boots and stockings* provided – boys, 3,461; girls 3,348. *Clothing* – Boys, suits, 1,434; jerseys, 1,416. Knickers, 1,424; shirts, 1,959. Girls, dresses, 2,840, other articles of clothing, 4,994.

52 S. Gwynn–Walsh, 29 Oct. 1913; Box 385/1. f. 377/3.

53 L.D.A. Excerpt of a letter from Donnelly to O'Dwyer, and evidently 1913.

54 *Freeman's Journal*, 27 Oct. 1913.

55 W.P. Partridge–Walsh, 21 Nov. 1913. Box. 385. I. f. 377/3

56 Logue–Walsh, 6 Nov. 1913; Box 385. I. f. 377/8 Bishops file.

57 Brownrigg–Walsh, 7 Nov.; Box 385/1. f. 377/8 Bishops.

58 *Freeman's Journal*, 29 Oct. 1913.

59 Maud Gonne MacBride–J.C. McQuaid, 2 Feb. 1942; DDA. in Archbishop McQuaid's papers, courtesy David Sheehy, archivist of Diocesan Archives.

60 Dougherty–Walsh, 25 Nov. 1913; Box 351. I. f. 373/3, also f. 384/2.

61 Leslie–Walsh, 25 Dec. 1913; Box 385. I. f. 377/3.

62 *Intelligence Notes, 1913-1916*, State Paper Office Dublin (1966), Police Reports; p. 52.

63 Undated, unfinished, well-written letter of a worker to Walsh; Box 385 II. f. 384/1

64 Keog,. op. cit., p. 238.

65 *ICD*, 1915, Record of Events 1914, Docs. 1914, pp. 546-7.

66 Idem.

67 Walsh had so abstained for years, and could be abrupt with people putting awkward or seemingly niggling questions. See reply to a letter from J.E. Lyon who declared that Fr Flavin had nominated Clr Shortall for election in opposition to a man called O'Neill whom Shortall allegedly termed the "nominee of socialism". Quoting this, Lyon asked the archbishop if Shortall was "justified in so slandering O'Neill". Walsh replied that he had "many things much more important to do than answering questions of that sort". Walsh–Lyon, 13 Jan. 1914; DDA. 1914. File 384/5. "Priests and drafts".

68 L. Sherlock–Walsh, 16 Jan. 1914; DDA. Box 386.II. f. 378/ 1

69 Cit. Keogh. p. 237; see *Irish Worker*, 14 Jan. 1914.

70 T. O'Guinety–Walsh, 18 Jan. 1914.; DDA. Laity file 1914.

71 J. Simmons–Walsh, 17 June 1914.; Box 386. II. f. 378/1.

72 Flavin–Dwyer, 18 June 1914; Box 386 .II. f. 378/1.

73 Walsh–Simmons, no date but c. 18 June 1914; Box 386.II. f. 378/1

74 See Resolutions of Dublin United Trades Council, 1910. DDA. Laity 383/2; and Partridge–Walsh, no date, but 1913; Laity 384/3.

75 S. Leslie–Walsh, 7 Nov. 1913; Box. 385. II. f. 384/3.

XIV   "AT THE TURN OF THE TIDE", 1914-15

1 'Manifesto of Irish Volunteers', 25 Nov. 1913, in *The Irish Volunteers 1913-15*, ed. F.X. Martin (Dublin, 1963), p. 100.

2 *Irish Volunteer*, 7 Feb. 1914.

3 Curran papers. NLI Ms. section. In Sean T. O'Ceallaigh papers, Special List A. 9. Ms. 27, 728 (1-3) – Statement of Monsignor Michael Curran to Bureau of Military History re. events 1913-21, in 3 vols. This ref. is to vol. 1, p. 7

4 Idem, p. 11.

5 Leslie–Walsh, 13 May 1914; Box 386. II. f. 378/1.

6 Walsh–Dom Nolan, 27 Sept. 1914; Box 386. I. f. 384/6

7 Vincent O'Brien–Walsh, 3 Jan. 1914; Box 386. II. f. 378/1

8 Walsh–Lord Mayor, 28 April 1914; Box 386. I. f. 384/6

9 Walsh–Dom P. Nolan, 27 Sept. 1914; 386. I. f. 384/6

10 *The Irish Worker*, 14 March 1914.

11 On these events in more detail see T.J. Morrissey, *A Man Called Hughes*, ch. 3.

12 *Weekly Freeman*, 1 Aug. 1914, letter written 29 July.

13 *Daily News*, 30 July 1914, under banner heading "Dublin's Day of Tears. Crowd of 50,000".

14 Morrissey, *A Man Called Hughes*, p. 58.

15 Idem.
16 D. Gwynn, *Life of John Redmond*, p. 382; ref. in L. O'Broin, *The Chief Secretary*, p. 109.
17 Cit. Bulmer Hobson, *Ireland, Yesterday and Tomorrow* (Tralee, 1968), p. 154.
18 Curran–Hagan, 30 Sept. 1914; Monsignor John Hagan papers (1914-1-20), Irish College Rome, Letter no. 110.
19 L. O'Broin, *Chief Secretary* ... , p. 110; F.X. Martin, *Irish History Studies*, March 1961, pp. 240-1.
20 Intelligence Notes 1914 on strength of Irish Volunteers in each province; from *Intelligence Notes, 1913-1916*. Sate Paper Office Dublin (1966). Police Reports.
21 Morrissey, op. cit., p. 59.
22 Curran. Statement to Bureau, Ms. 27, 728, vol. 1, pp. 8-10
23 Idem, p. 12.
24 Ward–Walsh, 24 Nov.; Box 386. II. f. 387/2. Idem, 7 Dec.; 386. II. f. 378/1
25 Curran. Ms. 27, 728. vol. 1, p. 12.
26 Ward–Walsh, 14 Dec. 1914; 386. II. f. 387/2
27 Curran. Ms. 27, 728. vol. 1, p. 13.
28 Walsh's Diary, 1915. Also, on the cathedral: letter to architect (from diary seems to be Byrne and Sons) thanks him for his interest in a project which "I have almost come to regard as impossible for realisation", then he goes on to discuss dimensions suggesting "the Catholic Cathedral of Westminster" for "a good general idea". Box 387. I. f. 378/4. No date, but in April 1915. On musical memories: Walsh–Dr Marchant, 15 Jan 1915.; 387. I. f. 378/4.
29 Logue–Walsh, 11 March 1915; 387. I. f. 378/5
30 Walsh–Bertram Wyndle, 22 March 1915, apologising for his delay in responding "to your important letter"; Box 387. I. f. 378/4
31 Curran. Ms. 27, 728, vol. 1, pp. 13-14.
32 Capt. Patrick J. Butler–Walsh, 7 April 1915; Box 387. II. file not numbered.
33 Card. Mercier–Walsh, 10 April 1915; Box 387. II. file not numbered. Mainly on war matters.
34 Walsh–Central Council of Recruiting, 12 May; 387. I. f. 378/4
35 Curran. Ms. idem. vol. 1, pp. 14-15.
36 Idem, p. 14.
37 Birrell to Royal Commission in *Sinn Fein Rebellion Handbook. Easter 1916*. Compiled by *Weekly Irish Times*, Dublin, 1917 edition, p. 157.
38 L. O'Broin, *The Chief Secretary*, p. 145.
39 Birrell. Idem, p. 159.
40 C. Currean & T. Mac Raghnall–Walsh, 16 July 1915; 387. II. f. 378/7
41 Walsh–to same, 17 July; idem.
42 The same–Walsh 18 July; idem.
43 Le Roux. *Tom Clarke*, p. 142, cit. Sean Farrell Moran, *Patrick Pearse and the Politics of Redemption* (Washington D.C., 1994), p. 146.
44 S. F. Moran, idem.
45 Curran. Ms., vol. 1. p. 18.
46 See Bulmer Hobson, *Ireland, Yesterday and Tomorrow*, pp. 78 ff.
47 Curran, Ms., vol. 1. p. 16.
48 Idem, p. 17.
49 Browne–Walsh, 19 Dec. 1915; 387. I. f. 378/5

XV THE ARCHBISHOP'S HOUSEHOLD AND 1916

1 Curran papers. Ms. 27, 728, vol. 1, p. 21; Statement to Bureau of Military History, Ms. In 3 vols. based mainly on Curran's diaries; in Sean T. O'Ceallaigh Papers, Special List A. 9., N.L.I. All references for 1916, are in vol. 1, written Ms. 27, 728 (1).
2 Curran–Logue, 3 Feb. 1916; A.D.A. Toner Typescripts of Logue Corresp. , p. 197.
3 Curran. Ms. 27, 728 (1), p. 22.
4 Doc. in DDA in box marked "Politics"; also Curran. loc. cit., pp. 22-7.
5 Mac Neill–O'Donnell, 18 April; A.D.A. Papers of His Eminence Cardinal O'Donnell, under "Political", folder 2, p. 128.
6 Curran. Ms. cit., pp. 22-7.
7 Idem, pp. 27-8.

8 Idem, p. 30.

9 Idem, p. 32.

10 Idem, pp. 32-3.

11 Curran. Idem, pp. 35-6.

12 Idem, pp. 37-9. Italics in text.

13 Idem, p. 40.

14 Idem, pp. 41-3.

15 Idem, p. 44.

16 Idem, p. 45.

17 Idem, p. 47.

18 Idem, p. 52.

19 Idem, p. 48.

20 Idem, p. 52.

21 Idem, p. 57.

22 Idem, p. 58.

23 Idem, p. 61.

24 Idem, p. 62.

25 Idem, p. 63.

26 Idem, p. 64.

27 Idem, pp. 66-8.

28 Idem, p. 69.

29 Archbishop's Diary, 2 May. DDA.

30 Curran. Ms. cit., p. 71.

31 Idem, p. 72.

32 Idem, p. 73. Italics mine.

33 D. Macardle, *The Irish Republic*, p. 129.

34 Curran, p. 74.

35 Idem, p. 78.

36 Idem, p. 79.

37 See esp. *Freeman's Journal*, *Irish Times*, 6 May and *Irish Catholic*. Summaries in *I.C.D*, 1917, pp. 509 ff. relating to 1916.

38 *ICD*, 1917, Record of 1916, p. 510.

39 Curran. p. 80.

40 P.J. Walsh, *William J. Walsh ...*, pp. 592-3.

41 Idem. Appendix. I. pp. 587 ff.

42 Curran, pp. 82-3.

43 Idem, pp. 86-7.

44 Idem, pp. 87-90.

45 Idem, p. 97.

46 Idem, p. 98.

47 From Irish National Assoc. Sydney–Walsh, 22 Nov.; DDA. but out of place in the Priests, Religious, and Colleges file. f. 385/4

48 T.M. Healy–Maurice Healy, May 1916, in T.M. Healy *Letters and Leaders of My Day*, vol. II. p. 562; cit. in T.J Morrissey, *William Martin Murphy*, p. 64.

49 Maxwell–Walsh, 6 May; DDA. 388. II. f. 385/7

50 Limerick Diocesan Archives. Cit. John Fleming and Sean O'Grady. *St Munchin's College, Limerick, 1796-1996*. p. 146 (Limerick 1996).

51 Mainchin Seoighe, *An tAthair Tomas de Bhal, 1879-1956* (An Sagart. Earrach 1967), cit. Fleming & O'Grady, op cit., p. 146.

52 Walsh-Hardinge, 26 May; DDA. 388. I. f. 385/1. Italics in text.

53 Curran, op. cit., pp. 99-100.

54 Idem, p. 101.

55 F.S.L. Lyons, *Ireland Since the Famine*, p. 375.

56 *ICD*, 1917, Report on 1916; at Maynooth, June.

57 Maxwell–Walsh, 19 June. 388. II. f. 385/5.

58 Walsh–Maxwell, 26 June; 388. II. f. 385/5

59 Sherlock–Walsh, 17 June; 388. II. f. 385/5.

60 Irish Relief Committee–Walsh, 8 July; 388. II. f. 385/5

61 Curran, pp. 102 and 162.

62 Idem.

63 Idem. under 18 July. p. 159.

64 Alice S. Green–Walsh, 22 July; 388. II. f. 385/7. Italics in text.

65 M. Moore–Walsh, 29 July; 388. II. f. 385/7.

66 Curran, pp. 166-8.

67 Curran–Walsh, 23 July; 388. II. f. 385/7

68 *Irish Independent*, Wed. 26 July.

69 Walsh–Dungannon Finance Committee, 4 Aug. 1916; DDA. "Draft Letters", 388.I. f. 385/1

70 Curran, p. 164.

71 Idem, p. 165.

72 Cit. Miller, *Church, State and Nation in Ireland 1898-1921*, pp. 345-6.

73 Curran, p. 166.

74 Blowick–Walsh, 30 Sept.; 388. II. f. 385/4

75 Curran, pp. 171-2.
76 Cardinal Archbishop N.Y.–Walsh, 16 Nov.; 388. I. f. 385 Bishops.
77 Macardle, *Ir. Republic*, pp. 190-1.
78 Stafford–Walsh, 23 Dec. 1916; 388. II. f. 385/7
79 Dillon–Walsh, 18 Dec., Logue–Walsh, 24 Dec. 1916; DDA. 388. I. f. 385/1
80 O'Riordan–Walsh, 9 Jan. 1917; 389. II. f. 379/3.

XVI   RENEWED ENERGY, AND SIGNIFICANT INTERVENTIONS, 1917-18

1 Brady–Walsh, 18 Jan. & 1 Feb. 1917; DDA. Box 385/8 f. 379/5
2 D. Macardle, *Irish Republic*, p. 195.
3 *A New Hist. of Ireland*, vol. III, p. 393.
4 Curran. Ms. 27, 728, vol. 2. pp. 192-3; NLI. Refs. to Curran Ms. in this chapter are from this source, vol. 2; also Walsh. Diary, 14 March.
5 Walsh–Attorney General, 12 April 1917; Bodleian Library. Special Collections and Western Manuscripts.
6 Macardle, op. cit., p. 199.
7 J.R. O'Connell–Walsh, 27 May 1917; DDA. f. 379/3. Lay.
8 Curran Ms., p. 278.
9 C. McHugh–Walsh, 1 May 1917; 389. I. f. 385/8 Bishops file.
10 *Irish Independent*, 8 May.
11 Walsh–O'Riordan, 16 June 1918: Irish Coll. Rome, Monsignor Michael O'Riordan Papers, no. 19 (May 1917-Aug. 1918) Letter no. 41.
12 Copy in DDA. In Box "Walsh Biographical".
13 Curran, idem, p. 199.
14 Walsh–O'Riordan, 16 June 1918.; Irish College Rome. Monsignor Ml. O'Riordan Papers, no. 19 (May 1917–Aug. 1918), Letter no. 41.
15 Press cutting, no name. DDA. In Box "Walsh Biographical".
16 Macardle, p. 204.
17 Largely a north-west Ulster organisation opposed to partition, of which Bishop McHugh of Derry was a prominent promoter.

18 Lord Dunraven, *Past Times and Pastimes* (2 vols, London, 1922), II, p. 60.
19 Walsh. Diary, 22 June.
20 *Birmingham Gazette*, date in June not clear, possibly 23 or 26 June; DDA. Cutting in Box "Walsh Biographical".
21 Curran, pp. 215-16.
22 Macardle, pp. 211-12.
23 L. O'Neill–Walsh, 20 April.; 389. II. f. 379/3
24 Brownrigg–Walsh, 25 July; 389. I. f. 385/5 Bishops.
25 Donnelly–Walsh, 20 Aug. 1917.; 389. I. f. 385/ 8.
26 Walsh, Diary 19-21 Sept.
27 Macardle, pp. 213-14.
28 Curran. Ms. p. 225.
29 F.S.L. Lyons, *Ireland since the Famine*, p. 387.
30 Dillon–Walsh, 25 April; DDA. 390. I. f. 379/7. Italics as in text. Walsh was trustee for the National Aid Organisation.
31 Macardle, p. 221.
32 *ICD*, 1918, Record of 1917, 25 Nov. p. 538k.
33 Curran, pp. 235-6.
34 *I. Independent*, Wed. 14 Nov. 1917.
35 DDA. Walsh Papers. From a typed document entitled: "Diocese of Dublin Cause for the Beatification and Canonisation of the Servants of God Dermot O'Hurley, Archbishop and Companions, who died in Ireland in defence of the Catholic faith 1579-1654", pp. 5-11, esp. 10-11; see also M.H. MacInerney in *I.E.R.* (Jan.-June 1918), esp. vol. xi., p. 414.
36 There are letters from L.J. Stafford, and also from one of the best known of the Irish chaplains, Francis A. Gleeson, on 25 April and 14 May 1918; DDA. 390. I. f. 386/2.
37 See for example, Walsh–Sir W. Byrne, 27 June 1918; NLI. Another Curran Ms, this time his typed memoirs, Ms. 27, 712 (1), pp. 392-4; in Sean T. O'Ceallaigh's Papers. Special List A. 9, N.L.I.

38 Notice from Dr Walsh. 390. I. f. 386/2.
39 Ld. Mayor, L. O'Neill–Walsh, 19 Oct. 1918; 390. I. f. 386/2.
40 O'Howard–Walsh, 30 Oct. 1918; 390. I. f. 386/2.
41 Walsh–Dear Sir, 3 Nov. 1918; 390. I. f. 386/2
42 Philomena Plunkett, C. na mBan–Walsh, 25 June: 390. II. f. 386/3.
43 Curran Ms. 27, 728 (2). Statement, pp. 248-7.
44 Harrison–Walsh, 11 March 1918; DDA. 390. II. f. 386/3.
45 Curran. Statement. Ms. 27, 728(2), (i.e. vol. 2), p. 247.
46 Idem, p. 249.
47 Idem, pp. 252-3.
48 Idem,
49 Idem, pp. 250, 252.
50 Idem, p. 254.
51 Idem, p. 256.
52 *Evening Telegraph*, Tues. 16 April 1918; DDA. Walsh papers.
53 *ICD*, 1919, Record of 1918, p. 509.
54 Curran, Idem. p. 261.
55 Idem, p. 261.
56 *ICD*, 1919, Record for 1918. 18 April. p. 511.
57 Idem, pp. 534-5.
58 Idem, p. 536.
59 Curran. Statement. vol. 2. pp. 262-3.
60 Idem, pp. 263-4.
61 Idem, p. 264; and Walsh's diary, 19 April.
62 Walsh's diary.
63 Curran, pp. 265-6.
64 Idem, pp. 266-67.
65 Curran, idem, p. 267.
66 M. Clifton, *Amigo: Friend of the Poor* (Westminister, 1987), p. 73.
67 In a letter from Amigo to Walsh, 3 May 1918; DDA. 390. I. f. 379/6.
68 Clifton, *Amigo* ..., p. 72.
69 Curran, idem, pp. 270-2.
70 Idem, p. 274.
71 Cit. D. Macardle, *Irish Republic*, p. 235.
72 Curran, p. 281.
73 Macardle, pp. 238-9.

74 Clifton, *Amigo* ..., p. 73.
75 Idem.
76 Macardle, p. 239.
77 O'Riordan–Walsh, 8 June 1918; DDA. 390. I. f. 386/1.
78 Curran, p. 395.
79 Curran memoirs. Ms. 27, 712 (1) (i.e. vol. 1), pp. 409-10.
80 Downey–Walsh, 5 Sept. 1918; DDA. 390. I. f. 379/7 (2)
81 Curran memoirs, idem, pp. 410-12.
82 Curran. memoirs, p. 415.
83 Idem, pp. 417-18.
84 Idem, pp. 419-20.
85 Curran Statement. Ms. 27, 728 (2), pp. 309-11.
86 Idem, pp. 310-11; and Walsh's diary.
87 Macardle, p. 243.
88 Idem.
89 Idem, pp. 432-5.
90 Idem, pp. 436-7.
91 Idem, pp. 438-41.
92 Idem.
93 Idem, p. 444.
94 Idem, p. 451.
95 Idem, p. 455.
96 O'Riordan–Walsh, 8 Dec. 1918; DDA. f. 386/1. Colleges.
97 Idem, p. 459.
98 *Times*, 9 and 17 Jan. 1919; in Macardle, p. 248.
99 J.H. Bernard–Dr Davidson, Archbishop of Canterbury, April 1918; cit. Miller, *Church, State and Nation in Ireland, 1898-21*, pp. 407-9.
100 See Miller, pp. 436-42.

XVII   THE GREAT ORDEAL:
COMPASSION AND ENDURING
TO THE END, 1919-21

1 Curran memoirs (1) (Ms. 27, 712, vol. 1.,) p. 461.
2 D. Keogh, *The Vatican, the Bishops and Irish Politics, 1919-1939*, p. 24.
3 O'Dea–O'Riordan, 9 March 1919, cit. Larkin, *The Historical Dimensions of Irish Catholicism* (Washington, DC, 1984), p. 118.

4 Foley–O'Riordan, 21 March 1919; idem, pp. 118-19.
5 Idem, p. 119.
6 Curran Memoirs (1), pp. 464ff.
7 Earl of Longford & Thomas P. O'Neill, *Eamon de Valera*, p. 14.
8 Curran memoirs, pp. 463-69.
9 T.P. Coogan, *De Valera*, p. 129, cites Mary Bromage's *De Valera and the March of a Nation* (London, 1956), p. 75, who stated that Collins was aghast at the hazards taken by de Valera to get to America. The coming and going to de Valera's lodge seems hazardous.
10 *ICD*, 1920, Record for 1919, pp. 501-2.
11 Town Clerk's Office–Dr Walsh, 11 March 1919; 391. II. f. 386/8. Walsh's diary has the Lord Mayor calling on 15 March re. political prisoners.
12 Logue–Walsh, 14 March 1919; 391. I. f. 386/4.
13 Curran Memoirs, vol. 2, p. 505 [i.e. Ms. 27, 712 (2)]; also Walsh's diary.
14 Logue–Curran, 25 April 1919; DDA. 391. f. 386/4.
15 Curran, pp. 475, 502.
16 Curran, pp. 505-6.
17 Curran, pp. 506-7.
18 Curran, pp. 518-19.
19 Coogan, *Michael Collins*, p. 112.
20 Curran, p. 536.
21 Idem. p. 537.
22 Printed Appeal in DDA. Box. 391. II. f. 386/8
23 Browne–Walsh, 23 Sept. 1919; 391. f. 386/4.
24 MacKenna–Walsh, Sept. 1919; Wm. Farrell-Walsh, 23 Sept.; DDA. 391 .II. f. 386/8.
25 MacKenna–Walsh, no date; DDA. 391. II. f. 386/8
26 Curran, Memoirs. vol. 2, p. 570.
27 Idem, p. 571.
28 Cit. idem, pp. 582-3.
29 Walsh–O'Connell, 10 Nov. 1919; DDA. 391. I. f. 386/4.
30 O'Connell–Walsh, 8 Dec. 1919; idem.
31 DDA. in box "Walsh Biographical" cutting from *Morning Post*, 9 Dec. 1919.
32 In brackets in his dairy. re. those he

consulted, Walsh has just "B & N".
33 DDA. Circular letter re. Assassination; 391. I. f. 386/4.
34 A.M. Sullivan–Walsh, 22-12-19; DDA. 391. II. f. 386/8
35 A.M. Sullivan, *Old Ireland* (London, 1927), p. 263.
36 P.J. Walsh, *William J. Walsh*, p. 377.
37 Letter to Walsh, 9 Dec. 1919; f. 386/ 8
38 Walsh's diary for 22 Dec.
39 Curran–Walsh, 23 Dec. 1919; 391. II. f. 386/8.
40 Keogh, *The Vatican, The Bishops*, p. 27.
41 Walsh diary, 29 Dec.
42 J. Hagan–Walsh, 30 Dec. 1919; 391. I. f. 386/5 (file "priests of Dublin diocese").
43 L. McGrath–Walsh, 23 Dec. 1919; 391.I. f. 386/7.
44 Boylan–Walsh, 11 Nov. 1919; 391. I. f. 386/5
45 Walsh's diary, 7 December.
46 T.M. Healy–Maurice Healy, 11 Dec. 1919, giving archbishop's response as identical to his own. T.M. Healy, *Letters and Leaders ...*, vol. II, p. 617.
47 *Times*, 13 Dec. 1919., cit Macardle, *Irish Republic*, pp. 293-4.
48 DDA. Telegram to Bishop Derry, 21 Jan.; 392. II. f. 380/1
49 Governor of prison–Walsh, 31 Jan. 1920, expressing Ald. Kelly's thanks; 392. II. f. 380/3 in file headed "Priests of the diocese".
50 Curran memoirs (3), p. 590 [Ms. 27, 712 (3). 1920-'21]
51 *Collected Poems of W.B. Yeats*, London, 1950 ed., p. 233.
52 Chaplains' plea sent to Walsh, c. 12 April; 392. II. f. 380/2.
53 *Freeman's Journal*, 13 April 1920.
54 Lord Lieutenant's reply attached to chaplains' letter; DDA. 392. II. f. 380/2.
55 Curran–Walsh, 15 April 1920; 392. II. f. 380/3.
56 Curran memoirs (3), p. 615.
57 Curran memoirs(3), p. 618.
58 John J. Flood, assistant to town clerk–Walsh, 13 May 1920; 392. I. f. 380/5.

59 See Logue–Walsh, 29 March 1920; letter of Walsh on 3 April ("Dear Sir"), to Governors of Hibernian School explaining his delay in replying; Box 392. I f. 380/ 4.

60 Walsh circular letter, 11 May; 392. II. f. 380/1.

61 Walsh–Building Committee, 11 April; 392. I. f. 380/4.

62 Walsh–M.J. O'Connor, 12 Sept.; 392. II. f. 380/1; & in *Independent*, 16 Sept.

63 Curran, Memoirs, idem, p. 670.

64 *Irish Independent*, 16 Sept. also cit., Curran, idem, pp. 671-2.

65 Hierarchy' statement; sent to Walsh for signature and approval by Bishop Robert Browne of Cloyne on 13 August; DDA. 392. II. f. 380/1.

66 Cit. Miller, op. cit., pp. 455-6.

67 Mary MacSwiney–Walsh, no date, but c. 27 Sept.; 392 .I. f. 380/4.

68 DDA. Undated doc. but probably c. 7 October; 392. II. f. 380/1.

69 M. Chavasse, *Terence MacSwiney* (Dublin, 1961), pp. 184-5. Omega requested that that there be no wearing of Irish Volunteer uniforms in the cathedral. On the first night the corpse lay in the glass-covered coffin wearing a Franciscan habit. That night, sadly, when the church was closed, IRA members dressed the corpse in a Volunteer uniform, and the thousands next day filed past a corpse in uniform. MacSwiney had asked to be buried in uniform. But the burial was a couple of days ahead. Bishop Amigo, naturally, felt let down and hurt at the violation of his conditions.

70 M. Clifton, *Amigo. Friend of the Poor*, p. 79.

71 Idem, pp. 74-5.

72 Telegram to Walsh, 28 Oct; 392. II. f. 380/3

73 Chavasse, p. 187.

74 Idem, p. 188.

75 J.W. Wheeler-Bennet. *John Anderson, Viscount Waverly* (London, 1962), pp. 390-1; cit. L. O Broin, *W.E. Wylie and the Irish Revoluton, 1916-1921* (Dublin, 1989), p. 107.

76 Newspaper cutting, no title, in Walsh papers, 1921. Italics as in text.

77 Curran memoirs, vol. 4.[Ms. 27, 712(4)], p. 755.

78 E. McDonnell–Walsh, 1 Nov. 1920; 392. I. f. 380/5

79 Healy–Beaverbrook, 15 Nov. 1920; NLI. Ms. 23266, cit. F. Callanan, *T.M. Healy*, p. 557.

80 T.P. Coogan, *Michael Collins*, p. 156.

81 Officer, name indistinct–Walsh, 23 Nov.; 392. II. f. 380/1

82 Idem. DDA. Walsh papers, in box marked "Politics".

83 Gilmartin–Walsh, 29 Nov.; 392. II. f. 380/1.

84 Somerville–Walsh, 29 Oct.; 392. I. f. 380/5. Italics mine.

85 Curran idem, pp. 684-5

86 Griffith–Walsh, 18 Nov.; DDA. Walsh papers in box marked "Politics".

87 Coogan, *Michael Collins*, p. 203.

88 Plunkett–Walsh, 17 Dec. 1920; 392. I. f. 380/ 4.

89 T.P. O'Neill. Introduction to Frank Gallagher's *The Anglo-Irish Treaty* (London, 1965), p. 22; cit. Miller, op. cit., p. 474.

90 P.J. Walsh, p. 576; T.P. O'Neill, Introduction to Gallagher *Anglo-Irish Treaty*, p. 25, cit. Miller, p. 476.

91 Coogan, p. 202.

92 Healy–Walsh, 14 Nov; 392. I. f. 380/4.

93 Gilmartin–Walsh, 17 Nov. 1920; 392. II. f. 380/1.

94 Hagan–Walsh, 23 Jan.; DDA. Box. 393. f. 380/6

95 Idem, 14 Feb.; idem.

96 On this whole episode see Curran, Memoirs (3), [Ms. 27, 712(3)], pp. 708-11.

97 Clifton, *Amigo: Friend of the Poor*, pp. 84-5.

98 DDA. 393. f. 380/7 Laity.

99 *Irish Independent*, 1 March 1921.

100 Author unknown, half of letter missing–Walsh, 25 Feb. 1921; 393. f. 380/7.

101 B.J. Canning, *Bishops of Ireland, 1870–1987* (Ballyshannon, 1987), p. 179; also *ICD*, 1922. Record of 1921, 28 Feb. p. 524.

102 *Irish Independent*, 1 March 1921.

103 Curran, Memoirs (4) [Ms. 27, 712, vol. 4], pp. 753-5.

104 O'Connor–Walsh, 6 March; Walsh–"Master of the Rolls", 9 March; all part of correspondence re. Hibernian Military School, 1920-21; DDA. 393. f. 380/7(2)

105 Final entries in Walsh's diary.

106 Walsh's draft and printed Notice 21 March; DDA. 393. f. 380/8

107 P.J. Walsh, "Fide et Labore" in *Catholic Bulletin*, vol. xi, 1921, pp. 282, 287.

108 Funeral arrangements. DDA. 393. f. 380/8 (2)

109 "Death of the Revd W.J. Walsh – Order of Events", Wed. 13 April. DDA. 393. f. 380/8

110 Fr Edward J. Burne, vicar capitular–Thomas Farren, 14 April 1921; NLI. Ms. 7341, Letters to Thomas Farren, ITGWU and secretary of Dublin Workers' Council.

XVIII   EPILOGUE – A RETROSPECTION AND ASSESSMENT

1 M. Ronan, *Most Rev. W.J. Walsh, DD*, p. 15

2 P.J. Walsh, "Fide et Labore" in *Catholic Bulletin*, idem, p. 287.

3 Interview with Mrs Alice Murnaghan, 1994.

4 *Sources for the History of Irish Civilisation*, ed. R.J. Hayes, vol. 5, ref. 941.5016.

5 *Freeman's Journal*, 9 April 1921, and Editorial, 9 April.

6 Idem.

7 DDA. Walsh papers. Books of Extracts, vol. xi, p. 87.

8 DDA. in Box "Walsh Biographical".

9 Shane Leslie, "Archbishop Walsh" in *The Shaping of Modern Ireland*, ed. C. Cruise O'Brien (London, 1960), p. 106.

10 M. Ronan, *Most Rev. W.J. Walsh, DD*, p. 15

11 S. Leslie, "Archbishop Walsh" in *The Shaping of Modern Ireland*, p. 103.

12 De Valera–Bishop (Byrne?), April 1921, cited in newspaper cutting, 14 April, in Walsh Papers, DDA. Name of paper not given, possibly *Freeman's Journal*.

13 Handwritten notes of P.J. Walsh for article or book on the archbishop, in box "Walsh Biographical"..

BIBLIOGRAPHY

PRIMARY SOURCES

Dublin Diocesan Archives
Archbishop William Walsh Papers
Bishop Nicholas Donnelly Papers, esp. correspondence with Bishop O'Dwyer of Limerick.
Archbishop Edward McCabe Papers
Bishop Bartholomew Woodlock Papers

Armagh Diocesan Archives
Cardinal Logue Papers, and Toner Transcripts

Limerick Diocesan Archives
Papers Limerick Diocesan Archives
Bishop George Butler
Bishop Edward Thomas O'Dwyer Papers

Irish Jesuit Archives
Dr William Delany Papers

Blackrock College Archives
Fr Edouard Reffé Papers and others

Courtesy Mr Gerald Murphy
William Martin Murphy Papers

Trinity College Dublin Archives
John Dillon Papers

Archivo Segreto Vaticano
The Persico Report

National Library of Ireland
Monsignor Michael Curran Papers, statement to the Irish Military Bureau for the years 1913-
    18, based on his diaries and recollections, in Sean T. O'Ceallaigh Papers
Wm. Monsell Papers (Ms. 8318)
Wm. O'Brien (Labour Leader) Papers
Wm. P. Partridge Ms (Ms. 2986)
John Redmond Papers

NLI and National Archives
Mins. and Reports of Dublin Chamber of Commerce

University College Dublin Archives
Prof. Eoin MacNeill Papers
General Richard Mulcahy Mss.

National University Ireland Archives
Minute Books of the Royal University Ireland
Joseph McGrath Papers

Bodleian Library Oxford and British Library, London
Archbishop Walsh's Corespondence with Gladstone

Archives Irish College Rome.
Monsignor Michael O'Riordan Papers
(Selection from, courtesy Jerome aan de Wiel, Glenstal Abbey School, Co. Limerick)

Bodleian Library, Oxford.
Sir Anthony MacDonnell Papers
[(Selection of, courtesy Dr Aidan O'Reilly, Maynooth College, MEd thesis "Sir Anthony MacDonnell and University Reform, 1902-1908" (NUI, 1977)]

PRINTED MANUSCRIPT MATERIAL

Monsignor Persico's Letters from Archivo Segreto Vaticano in *Collectanea Hibernica* (vols 24-5, 34-5.)
Papers of Archbishop Thomas William Croke, ed. M.Tierney, in *Collectanea Hibernica* (nos 11, 13, 16, 17).
Monsignor Tobias Kirby Papers, Irish College Rome, ed. P.J. Corish in *Archivium Hibernicum* (vol. 32).

PRINTED WORKS BASED ON DOCUMENTS, CONTEMPORARY REPORTS, OR
RECOLLECTIONS RELATING TO ARCHBISHOP WALSH

Patrick J. Walsh, *William J. Walsh, Archbishop of Dublin* (Dublin, 1928).
—, " 'Fide et Labore'. An appreciation of the late Archbishop Walsh", *Catholic Bulletin*, vol. xi, 1921.
Monsignor Michael Cronin, "The Late Archbishop of Dublin, 1841-1921" in *Dublin Review*, July-Sept. 1921.
Myles V. Ronan, *The Most Rev. W.J. Walsh, DD, Archbishop of Dublin* (Pamphlet, Bray, Co. Wicklow, 1927)
Shane Leslie, "Archbishop Walsh" in *The Shaping of Modern Ireland*, ed. C. Cruise O'Brien, (London, 1960)
—, *Henry Edward Manning. His Life and Labours* (London, 1921)
G. O'Flynn, "Augustine Birrell and Archbishop William Walsh's influence on the founding of the National University of Ireland", in *Capuchin Annual*, 1976.
F. O'Driscoll, "Archbishop Walsh and St Mary's University College, 1893-1908" in *Irish Educational Studies*, vol. 5, no. 2, 1985 (Dublin, 1986).
T.J. Morrissey, "The 1913 Lock-out: Letters for the Archbishop", *Studies*, Spring, 1986.
—, *Towards a National University. William Delany SJ [1835-1924]. An Era of Initiative in Irish Education* (Dublin, 1983).
The Irish Catholic Directory, esp. for years 1885-1921.
Wilfid Scawan Blunt, *The Land War in Ireland. A Personal Narrative of Events* (London, 1912).
D.W. Miller, *Church, State and Nation in Ireland, 1898-1921* (Dublin, 1973).
B.J. Canning, *Bishops of Ireland, 1870-1987* (Ballyshannon, 1987).
Emmet Larkin, *The Roman Catholic Church and the Creation of the Modern Irish State* (Philadelphia, 1975).

—, *The Roman Catholic Church and the Plan of Campaign, 1886-1888* (Cork, 1978).
—, *The Roman Catholic Church in Ireland and the Fall of Parnell, 1888-91* (Durham, NC, 1979),
—, *The Roman Catholic Church and the Emergence of the Modern Irish Political System, 1974-1978* (Dublin, 1996).
P.J. Corish, *Maynooth College, 1795-1995* (Dublin, 1995)

OFFICIAL PUBLICATIONS

Conference of Catholic Headmasters. Printed Report (Dublin, 1883).
Reports of the Intermediate Education Board for Ireland from 1895 down to 1907. [c-8034], 1896 xxvi etc.
Report of the Royal Commission on University Education in Ireland (Robertson Commission) [Cd-825-6], [Cd-899-900], [Cd. 1228-9], [Cd. 1483-4]; H.C. 1902, xxxi, xxxii; H.C. 1903, xxxii.
Report of Royal Commission on Trinity College Dublin and the University of Dublin (Fry Commission), [Cd. 3174], [Cd. 3176], [Cd. 3311-12]; H.C. 1906, lvi; H.C. 1907, xli.
Report of the Proceedings of the Irish Convention, (H.M.S. Dublin 1918).

NEWSPAPERS AND PERIODICALS

Daily Chronicle
Daily Express (Dublin)
Daily News
Dublin Review
Evening Mail (Dublin)
Freeman's Journal
Irish Independent
Irish Catholic
Irish Ecclesiastical Record
Irishman
Irish Times
Irish Worker

Irish Volunteer
Morning Post
Nation
Pall Mall Gazette
Saturday Review
Tablet
National Press
The Times,
United Ireland
United Irishman
Studies
The Leader

SELECT BIBLIOGRAPHY

N. Atkinson, *Irish Education. A History of Educational Institutions* (Dublin, 1969)
J. Biggs-Davison, *George Wyndham. A Study in Toryism* (London, 1951).
Augustine Birrell, *Things Past Redress* (London, 1936)
D. Bowen, *The Protestant Crusade in Ireland, 1800-1870* (Dublin, 1978).
N. Brennan, *Dr Mannix* (London, 1965).
F. Callanan, *T.M. Healy* (Cork, 1996).
M. Chavasse, *Terence MacSwiney* (London, 1961).
Randolph Churchill, *Intermediate Education in Ireland* (Dublin, 1878).
W.S. Churchill, *Lord Randolph Churchill* (London, 1952).

Ml. Clifton, *Amigo – Friend of the Poor. Bishop of Southwark 1904-1949* (Leominister, Herts., 1987).

K. Condon, *The Missionary College of All Hallows, 1842-1891* (Dublin, 1986).

T.P. Coogan, *The IRA* (New York, 1970).

—, *Michael Collins* (London, 1991).

—, *De Valera* (London, 1995).

P.J. Corish. (ed.), *A History of Irish Catholicism*, vol. 5 (Dublin, 1971).

—, *The Irish Catholic Experience* (Dublin, 1965).

M. Davitt, *The Fall of Feudalism in Ireland* (London, 1904).

W. Delany, *Irish University Education, facts and figures: a plea for fair play* (London, 1904. Pamphlet. N.L.I. 808 Education Ireland).

O. Dudley Edwards, and B. Ransom, *James Connolly. Selected Political Writings* (London, 1973).

'Educationist' (ed.), *The Irish Intermediate Education Act of 1878, with an Introduction* (Dublin, 1889).

W.B. Faherty, *Rebels or Reformers. Dissenting Priests in American Life* (Chicago, 1988).

S. Farragher, 'Blackrock and the Intermediate Act' in *Blackrock College Annual* (Dublin, 1958).

—, "Fr Joseph Edouard Reffé, dean of studies, 1864-1888" (Dublin, 1960).

R.F. Foster, *Lord Randolph Churchill: A Political Life* (Oxford, 1981).

—, *Modern Ireland, 1600-1972* (London, 1988).

J.A. Gaughan, *Alfred O'Rahilly*, vol. ii, *The Public Figure* (Dublin, 1989).

Henry George, *Progress and Poverty* (1870).

R. Gray, *Cardinal Manning* (London, 1985).

C.D. Greaves, *The Irish Transport and General Workers Union. The Formative Years, 1909-23* (Dublin, 1982).

D. Gwynn, *The Life of John Redmond* (London, 1932).

S. Gwynn, *John Redmond's Last Years* (London, 1919).

S. Gwynn & G.M. Tuckwell, *Life of Sir Charles W. Dilke*, vol. ii (London, 1917).

T.M. Healy, *Letters and Leaders of My Day*, 2 vols (London, 1928).

J. Joyce, *Stephen Hero* (London, 1940 ed.).

—, *Portrait of the Artist as a Young Man* (London, 1964 ed.).

P.J. Joyce, *John Healy, Archbishop of Tuam* (Dublin, 1931).

D. Keogh, *The Rise of the Irish Working Class.*(Belfast, 1982).

—, *The Vatican, the Bishops and Irish Politics, 1919-1939* (Cambridge, 1986).

M. Laffan, *The Partition of Ireland, 1911-1925* (Dublin, 1983).

E. Larkin, *James Larkin, Irish Labour Leader, 1876-1947* (London, 1989 ed.; original 1965)

—, *The Historical Dimensions of Irish Catholicism* (Washington, 1976)

J.J. Lee, *The Modernisation of Irish Society, 1848-1918* (Dublin, 1973).

—, *Ireland 1912-1985. Politics and Society* (Cambridge, 1989).

Shane Leslie, *Cardinal Gasquet* (London, 1953).

S. Levenson, *James Connolly. Socialist, Patriot, and Martyr* (London, 1977).

Longford, Earl of & T.P. O'Neill, *Eamon de Valera* (London, 1970).

F.S.L. Lyons, *The Irish Parliamentary Party, 1890-1910* (London, 1951).

—, *Ireland Since the Famine* (Glasgow, 1971).

—, *John Dillon* (London, 1968).

—,*Charles Stewart Parnell* (London, 1977).

D. Macardle, *The Irish Republic* (London, 1968 ed., original 1937).

A. Macauley, *Dr Russell of Maynooth* (London, 1983).

E. McCague, *Arthur Cox 1891-1965* (Dublin, 1994).

D. McCartney, *The Dawning of Democracy* (Dublin, 1987).

—, *UCD. A National Idea* (Dublin, 1999).

W. McDonald, *Reminiscences of a Maynooth Professor* (London, 1925).

V.A. McClelland, *Cardinal Manning. The Public Life and Influence, 1865-92* (London, 1962).

F. McGrath, "The University Question" in P.J. Corish (ed.), *A History of Irish Catholicism*, vol. 5 (Dublin, 1971).

R. McHugh (ed.), *Dublin 1916* (London, 1966).

L. McKenna, "The Catholic University of Ireland" in *Irish Ecclesiastical Record*, xxxi, 1928.

—, *Father James Cullen, S.J.* (London, 1924)

P. MacSuibhne, *Paul Cullen and his Contemporaries*, vol. ii (Kildare, 1962).

E. Malcolm, *"Ireland Sober, Ireland Free." Drink and Temperance in Nineteenth Century Ireland* (Dublin, 1986).

F.X. Martin (ed.), *The Irish Volunteers, 1913-15* (Dublin, 1963).

F.X. Martin & F.J. Byrne, *The Scholar Revolutionary, Eoin MacNeill, 1867-1945* (Shannon, 1973).

J. Moloney, *The Worker Question* (Dublin, 1991).

T.W. Moody, 'The Irish University Question in the Nineteenth Century' in *History*, xlii, 1958.

T.W. Moody, F.X. Martin, F.J. Byrne, *A New History of Ireland*, vol. viii (Oxford, 1982).

S.F. Moran, *Patrick Pearse and the Politics of Redemption* (Washington DC, 1994).

P.E. Moran, *The Writings of Cardinal Cullen*, 3 vols (Dublin, 1882).

J. Morley, *Life of William Ewart Gladstone*, 3 vols (London, 1903).

T.J. Morrissey, "The Paradox of James Connolly, Irish Marxist Socialist, 1868-1916, and the Papal Encyclicals, 1891-1991" in *Miltown Studies* (Dublin, Autumn 1991).

—, *A Man Called Hughes. The Life and Times of Seamus Hughes, 1881-1943* (Dublin, 1991).

—, *William Martin Murphy* (Dundalk 1997 for Hist. Assoc. Irl.).

D. Nevin (ed.), *Trade Union Century* (Cork, 1994).

—, *James Larkin. Lion of the Fold* (Dublin, 1998)

C. Cruise O'Brien, *Parnell and his Party, 1880-1890* (Oxford, 1957)

— (ed.), *The Shaping of Modern Ireland* (London, 1960)

—, *States of Ireland* (St Albans, Herts., 1974)

—, *Ancestral Voices* (Dublin, 1994).

Wm. O'Brien, *Forth the Banners Go* (Dublin, 1969).

L. O'Broin, *Dublin Castle and the 1916 Rising* (Dublin, 1966).

—, *The Chief Secretary. Augustine Birrell in Ireland* (London, 1969).

—, *Protestant Nationalists in Revolutionary Ireland. The Stopford Connection* (Dublin, 1985).

—, *W.E. Wylie and the Irish Revolution, 1916-1921* (Dublin, 1989).

P. O'Farrell, *England and Ireland since 1800* (Oxford, 1975).

F. Owen, *Tempestuous Journey. Lloyd George, His Life and Times* (London, 1954).

J.G. Snead-Cox, *Life of Cardinal Vaughan*, 2 vols (London, 1911).

W.B. Stanford & R.B. McDowell, *Mahaffy* (London, 1971).

J. Stephens, *The Insurrection in Dublin* (Dublin, 1954 ed.; orig. 1916)

Charles C. Tansill, *America and the Fight for Irish Freedom, 1866-1922* (New York, 1957)

Monica Taylor, *Sir Betram Windle* (London, 1932).

M. Tierney (ed.), *Struggle with Fortune: a centenary miscellany for Catholic University of Ireland, 1854, University College Dublin, 1954* (Dublin, 1954)

A. Wright, *Disturbed Dublin. The Story of the Great Strike, 1913-1914* (London, 1914).

INDEX

Abbey Theatre, 220
Aberdeen, Lady, 186
Aberdeen, Lord: *see* Gordon, G.H.
Adelaide Hospital, Dublin, 155
Alexandra College, Dublin, 219
All Hallows, 168, 169, 353
Aloysius OFMCap, Fr, 286
American League, 76
Amigo, Peter E., bp. of Southwark, 298,
   311, 312f, 319, 337, 338, 343, 344, 384n
Ancient Order of Hibernians, 236, 253,
   254f
Anderson, Sir John, joint under secretary,
   339
Archbishop's House, Drumcondra, 148f
Ashbourne Act 1885, 32
Ashe, Thomas 303f
Askwith, Sir George, president of the Board
   of Trade, 243f, 247f, 250
Asquith, H., prime minister, 269f, 289, 294,
   295, 297
Athy, Co. Kildare, 149, 172
Augustinians, 170

Balbriggan, 71
Balfour, Arthur, chief secretary, 92, 213,
   214, 226, 333
Ballymore-Eustace, 71
Barnett, P.A., 221
Barry, Kevin, 339f, 351
Beaverbrook, Lord, 340
Belfast gaol, 306
Belvedere College, Dublin, 92
Benedict XV, 282, 344
Bernard, John, C of I archbishop of
   Dublin, 288, 318
Bessborough Commission, 28ff, 114, 188
'Birds' Nests', 242f
Birrell, Augustine, chief secretary, 224,
   227ff, 261, 269, 275, 276, 287, 288
Black and Tans, 331, 334, 344
Blackrock College, Dublin, 21, 23, 35, 38,
   39, 41, 42, 46, 97, 168, 174
Blaney, Dr, 324, 347
Blowick, Revd John, 296
Blunt, Wilfred Scawen, 71, 90, 91, 112
Blythe, Ernest, 290
Boland, Harry, 320f
Borromeo, St Charles, 161
Botrel CSSp, Fr Jules, 174

Bourne, Francis, card. abp. of Westminister,
   272, 294f, 298, 336, 344
Bowden, Fr, adm. of Pro-Cathedral, Dublin,
   293
boycotting and intimidation, 95
Boylan, Revd Patrick, 329
Brady, P.J., MP, 299
Breen, Dan, 319
Brennan, Robert, 317
bricklayers' strike, 190
Brixton gaol, 337
Browne SJ, Thomas, provincial, 36
Browne, D.F., KC, 234
Browne, James, bp. of Ferns, 70
Browne, Robert, vice-president of
   Maynooth, bp. of Cloyne, 49; 278 , 325
Brownrigg, bp. of Ossory, 142, 173, 201,
   259, 279, 303, 316, 317
Bryce, James, chief secretary, 220, 222, 224,
   226, 228
Buckingham Palace Conference, 1914, 268
building labourers' strike, 190ff
Burke, Thomas Henry, under secretary, 122
Burton, Dr, bp. of Clifton, 224, 317
Butcher, Professor Samuel H., of Edinburgh
   University, 96, 215, 224
Butler Catechism, 154
Butler, Capt., friend of WJW, 273f
Butler, George, bp. of Limerick, 18, 30, 31,
   36, 37, 38, 39, 41, 68, 369n
Butler, Major-General Sir Redvers, under
   secretary, 96
Butler, Sir William, 273
Byrne, Dr E.J., editor of the *Freeman*, 132
Byrne, Fr, Edward J, later archbishop of
   Dublin, 24

Cadogan, Lord, 178, 185, 213
Cameron, Sir Charles, 156, 257
Campbell-Bannermann, Sir Henry, 220, 224,
   228
Canning, Hubert George de Burgh, earl of
   Clanricarde, 82
Canty, Maurice, of the Labourers'
   Association, 193
Capuchin friars, Church Street, Dublin, 94,
   170
Capuchins of Rochestown, Co. Cork, 97
Carlow by-election, 1890, 135, 137
Carlow College, 32, 38